A PEOPLE'S
HISTORY
OF THE
UNITED
STATES

ALSO BY HOWARD ZINN

Artists in Times of War

The Bomb

Disobedience and Democracy: Nine Fallacies on Law and Order

Emma: A Play

Failure to Quit: Reflections of an Optimistic Historian

The Future of History: Interviews with David Barsamian

Howard Zinn on Democratic Education (with Donaldo Macedo)

Howard Zinn on History

Howard Zinn on War

Justice in Everyday Life: The Way It Really Works

Just War (with Moises Saman and Gino Strada)

La Guardia in Congress

La Otra Historia de los Estados Unidos

Marx in Soho: A Play on History

New Deal Thought (editor)

Original Zinn: Conversations on History and Politics (with David Barsamian)

Passionate Declarations: Essays on War and Justice

A People's History of American Empire (written with Paul Buhle and illustrated by Mike Konopacki)

A People's History of the United States, Abridged Teaching Edition

The People Speak: American Voices, Some Famous, Some Little Known (editor)

The Politics of History

Postwar America: 1945–1971

A Power Governments Cannot Suppress

SNCC: The New Abolitionists

The Southern Mystique

Terrorism and War (with Anthony Arnove)

Three Plays: The Political Theater of Howard Zinn

Three Strikes (with Dana Frank and Robin D. G. Kelley)

The Twentieth Century: A People's History

Uncommon Sense from the Writings of Howard Zinn

Vietnam: The Logic of Withdrawal

Voices of a People's History of the United States (with Anthony Arnove)

You Can't Be Neutral on a Moving Train: A Personal History of Our Times

A Young People's History of the United States (adapted by Rebecca Stefoff)

The Zinn Reader: Writings on Disobedience and Democracy

A PEOPLE'S HISTORY OF THE UNITED STATES

HOWARD ZINN

Introduction by Anthony Arnove

HARPER

An Imprint of HarperCollinsPublishers

HarperCollins books may be purchased for educational, business, or sales promotional use. For information please e-mail the Special Markets Department at SPsales@harpercollins.com.

FIRST HARPER PERENNIAL MODERN CLASSICS DELUXE EDITION PUBLISHED 2010
REISSUED IN HARPER HARDCOVER EDITION 2017

Designed by Interrobang Design Studio

Library of Congress Cataloging-in-Publication Data is available upon request.

ISBN 978-0-06-269301-3

22 23 24 25 26 LBC 13 12 11 10 9

To Noah, Georgia, Serena, Naushon, Will—and their generation

ACKNOWLEDGMENTS

To my two editors, for their incalculable help: Cynthia Merman of Harper & Row, and Roslyn Zinn.

To Hugh Van Dusen, of HarperCollins, for wonderful help and support throughout the history of this book.

To Rick Balkin, my tirelessly attentive agent and friend.

To *Akwesasne Notes*, Mohawk Nation, for the passage from Ila Abernathy's poem.

To Dodd, Mead & Company, for the passage from "We Wear the Mask" from *The Complete Poems of Paul Laurence Dunbar.*

To Harper & Row, for "Incident" from *On These I Stand* by Countee Cullen. Copyright 1925 by Harper & Row Publishers, Inc.; renewed 1953 by Ida M. Cullen.

To Alfred A. Knopf, Inc., for the passage from "I, Too" from *Selected Poems of Langston Hughes*.

To *The New Trail*, 1953 School Yearbook of the Phoenix Indian School, Phoenix, Arizona, for the poem "It Is Not!"

To Random House, Inc., for the passage from "Lenox Avenue Mural" from *The Panther and the Lash: Poems of Our Time by Langston Hughes*.

To Esta Seaton, for her poem "Her Life," which first appeared in *The Ethnic American Woman* by Edith Blicksilver, Kendall/Hunt Publishing Company, 1978.

To Warner Bros., for the excerpt from "Brother Can You Spare a Dime?" Lyric by Jay Gomey, Music by E. Y. Harburg. © 1932 Warner Bros. Inc. Copyright Renewed. All Rights Reserved. Used By Permission.

CONTENTS

INTRODUCTION TO THE THIRTY-FIFTH ANNIVERSARY EDITION OF *A PEOPLE'S HISTORY OF THE UNITED STATES*

Howard Zinn fundamentally changed the way millions of people think about history with *A People's History of the United States*. He would be the first to say, however, that he didn't do so alone. The book grew out of his awareness of the importance of social movements throughout US history, some of which he played an active role in during the 1960s and 1970s and beyond, namely the Civil Rights Movement, mass mobilizations to end the Vietnam War, as well as other antiwar movements, and the many movements for higher wages and workers' rights and the rights of women, Latinos, Native Americans, gays and lesbians, and others. He was also quick to acknowledge the many people who informed his view of history: Woody Guthrie, whose songs about working people in the 1930s and 1940s opened up chapters of US history to him that his formal education had kept hidden; Philip S. Foner; Herbert Aptheker; Richard Hofstadter; Elizabeth Martínez; and other writers, editors, librarians, and historians who unearthed what he calls the "past's fugitive moments of compassion rather than . . . its solid centuries of warfare." But most of all, he acknowledged the people whose stories he weaves throughout this book: Eugene Debs, Fannie Lou Hamer, Frederick Douglass, Plough Jogger. Howard understood that he was writing to bring their voices and stories, their struggles and vision, to light, and inspire people to make change themselves. That is why he was so keen to publish a companion book to this volume, *Voices of a People's History of the United States*, which compiles the speeches, letters, manifestos, and other documents of people's history that he drew on to write *A People's History*—and to also remind people that this history continues in new forms today. And it is why he wanted to make the documentary film *The People Speak*, with artists such as Bob Dylan, Kerry Washington, Viggo Mortensen, and Danny Glover—to bring these voices vividly to life. He understood that his own words in this book, as meaningful as they are, were less vital to the success of *A People's History* than the words—and actions—of others he wove together into a narrative of US history told from below.

Howard was uniquely skilled as a writer, as this book reveals. Millions of people have read this book—a remarkable achievement for any work of popular history—and passed along their dog-eared copies to friends, family, fellow soldiers, and coworkers because it opened up new horizons for them. Of those readers, many went on to become teachers as a result. Many more felt the book had changed their lives and sent them down new paths. I'm one of them. Reading this book—and later having the great luck to meet and work with Howard—radically changed me. It made me care about history as no other teacher or experience had done. And it led me to see history as something that we are all part of making together and to realize that how we understand our past informs not only how we see the present, with all its complexity, but also how we might imagine a different future.

When *A People's History of the United States* came out in 1980, its first print run was a few thousand hardcover copies, considered modest for HarperCollins. But it soon found an audience excited to read a book that provided such a comprehensive and artful bottom-up view of US history, in contrast to the still-dominant tropes of Great White Men (and the occasional exceptional others) who "made history," an especially disempowering view. The civil rights leader Diane Nash, whom Howard knew through his work with the Student Nonviolent Coordinating Committee, recently commented on how hard it has been for our culture to embrace histories that feature the efforts of ordinary people whose names we may not even know or rarely learn from our textbooks. Discussing the critics of Ava DuVernay's 2014 film *Selma*, who said it unfairly diminished the role of President Lyndon Baines Johnson in bringing about civil rights legislation (an argument with which Howard was extremely familiar), she responded:

> Lyndon Johnson was president. It was his job to enforce the law. He should not have waited until Jimmie Lee Jackson's, James Reeb's, and Viola Liuzzo's lives were taken. He should not have waited until people were beaten and bloodied on Pettus Bridge before he enforced Negroes' right to vote in the South. I appreciate LBJ's enacting and signing the Voting Rights Act, but I wish he had been a self-starter when it came to our right to vote, so it would not have been necessary to go

to the lengths that we did—organizing a mass movement and risking our safety—in order to get the vote. It was the courage, work, thoughtfulness, sacrifice, discipline, and determination of citizens of the United States that obtained our right to vote.

Historically, inventions, musical innovations, and many more accomplishments and contributions developed by descendants of enslaved Africans in America have been misappropriated. We learn about presidents, battles, and dates. The impression too often perpetuated in history books and in popular culture is that you have to be a president, someone special, or White to have an important idea or to achieve major accomplishments. This is an idea that disempowers citizens and should not be propagated further.

Like Nash, Howard's experiences in the Civil Rights Movement gave him a different understanding of how history is made. It's an understanding that informs every page of this book.

When *A People's History of the United States* first came out, Ronald Reagan was on the path to becoming the president. Culturally, the country was moving noticeably rightward. Movements that sought to roll back the gains of the Civil Rights Movement, women's liberation movement, and other progressive changes of the 1960s and 1970s were gaining ground. Unions came under a sustained attack from which they have never recovered. In such an environment, this book could have been lost, published into obscurity. Why it wasn't is worth considering. First of all, as with any publishing effort, there was some luck involved. The *New York Times Book Review* could have decided the book didn't merit a review, as it so often does with books written from the standpoint of the left. Having decided to review it, the editors at the *Times* could have easily sent the book to be trashed by a figure of the newly aggressive right, as it so often does. Instead, they asked the highly regarded historian Eric Foner to review *A People's History of the United States*. And while not without criticisms of the book, Foner gave it an extremely positive notice. His words from the March 2, 1980, *New York Times Book Review* are worth considering:

[T]he 1970s witnessed an unprecedented redefinition of historical studies—a byproduct of the ferment of the 1960s—in which the distinctive experience of blacks, women, Indians, workers, and other neglected groups moved to the forefront of inquiry. . . .

Howard Zinn is the first historian to attempt to survey all of American history from the perspective of the new scholarship. A distinguished scholar and the author of nine previous books, Professor Zinn is also a veteran of the civil-rights and antiwar movements, and is currently an embattled defender of academic freedom at Boston University. He is refreshingly candid in announcing his purpose. Too much history, he contends, is written "from the point of view of governments, conquerors, diplomats, leaders." His *People's History*, by way of contrast, sides with the losers, the downtrodden, the underdog. It is a book "disrespectful of governments and respectful of people's movements of resistance." . . . .

Professor Zinn writes with an enthusiasm rarely encountered in the leaden prose of academic history. And his text is studded with telling quotations from labor leaders, war resisters, and fugitive slaves. There are vivid descriptions of events that are usually ignored.

However, Foner felt the book's "salutary emphasis on 'the enormous capacity of apparently helpless people to resist' is tempered by an underlying frustration at the meager results produced by this history of resistance." He continues:

The stirring protests, strikes, and rebellions never appear to accomplish anything. Uprisings are either crushed, deflected, or co-opted. Apparent victories, such as the emancipation of the slaves, simply serve the interests of businessmen; incremental gains, such as those of the 1930s, merely stabilize the system. Why such movements often fail to achieve their goals is never adequately explained.

Foner's view that the book "reflects a deeply pessimistic vision of the American experience" was, in the end, not shared by many other readers—who saw in the book a more affirmative—in fact, inspirational—story. Indeed, Howard is someone who consistently looked for the unrealized possibilities of history, one of the reasons this book has been considered so dangerous by so many figures of the establishment—whether in the academy or the halls of power. Howard was interested in historical potential—the what-might-have-been, the unrealized visions, the expanded horizons of protest—as much as he was in detailing forms of oppression. And a careful reading of this book will reveal, I believe, a deep appreciation of the human capacity to resist oppression, to collectively make history, to achieve ends those undertaking their protest perhaps never imagined possible and often did not live to see realized in their lifetime (even while recognizing that such gains can prove fragile and can never be taken for granted). For Howard, also, there was a joy in the effort itself. He had an appreciation of the bonds of solidarity, mutual affection, and creative expression that participation in social movements produced. The idea that *people* make history and can alter its course, that institutions have human origins and can be changed by humans, is truly subversive—and is a central reason this book has drawn the ire of so many censors and would-be censors. As Howard wrote at the end of his play *Marx in Soho*, "Remember, to be radical is simply to grasp the root of the problem. And the root is us."

Among the first champions of *A People's History of the United States* were the thousands of students who had been part of Howard's classes at Spelman College and Boston University, and many others who heard him speak on their college campuses and at antiwar rallies, and ordered it immediately for themselves and in some cases for courses they were teaching. The movements of the 1960s and early 1970s had also nurtured a new generation of receptive readers, many of whom were moving into roles as educators in high schools and on college campuses. Howard's classes were so popular that Boston University sought to limit participation in them. (Howard famously battled with the neoconservative president of the university, John Silber, coming close to losing his job on a few occasions, but in the end he came out on top.) Comically, one university administrator responded to his appeal for more teaching assistants for his huge introductory class by saying Howard could have more TAs if he would agree to *decrease* the class size. Instead, Howard enlisted student volunteers who would take his class one year for credit and then return the next year to lead sections.

In a matter of weeks after the release of *A People's History*, Harper-Collins found, unexpectedly, that it had sold out of the first hardcover edition. Then an interesting turn of history occurred. Howard's editor, Hugh Van Dusen, went to the hardcover division sales manager to push for a quick reprint and was rebuffed. The previous projections for the book were inauspicious. Perhaps there would be returns. A paperback would eventually come out in a future catalog. But Van Dusen fought for an accelerated paperback release, so, much earlier than planned, the book was available in an affordable popular edition. The book continued to catch on—and became, as no one predicted, a cultural touchstone and publishing phenomenon: a book that each year sold more copies than the year before (the opposite of the traditional trajectory). As of 2015, *A People's History of the United States* has sold more than 2.6 million copies in North America and been translated into more than twenty languages. Rarely does a month pass that I don't see someone engrossed in the book on the New York City subway system.

One of the readers of those early copies of *A People's History* was a young Matt Damon, whose mother, Nancy Carlsson-Paige, was a friend and movement ally of Howard's in Boston. Matt would famously go on to write, with Ben Affleck, a scene in the Oscar-winning film *Good Will Hunting* in which the self-educated working-class math genius he plays calls *A People's History* a book that will "knock you on your ass." That moment opened up new audiences for Howard and his work, and his ideas—and *A People's History*—entered into popular culture. Another reader was the cartoonist Matt Groening, who drew a copy of the book into an episode of his television series *The Simpsons*. Later, HBO's acclaimed series *The Sopranos* constructed a storyline around Howard's critical view of Christopher Columbus. The episode opens with a close-up of Anthony Soprano Jr. reading a hardcover edition of the book.

But it is really due to the many teachers heroically trying to encourage critical thinking among their students that this book continues to find new readers. This is not without its risks in this era of high-stakes testing and scapegoating teachers, while seeking to dismantle their unions and impose "patriotic" views of history. In 2014, in Colorado, students and teachers—some holding signs quoting Howard—walked out in protest when a local school board sought to ensure its Advanced Placement (AP) history courses "promote citizenship, patriotism, essentials and benefits of the free-market system, respect for authority, and respect for individual rights" and that they did not "encourage or condone civil disorder, social strife, or disregard of the law" (an interesting challenge if you want to teach, for example, the American Revolution or the history of abolitionism). In Oklahoma, in February 2015, members of the Common Education Committee voted to ban all AP US history courses because they focus on "what is bad about America."

In the state where I grew up, Indiana, then governor Mitch Daniels (now the president of Purdue University) sent e-mails just days after Howard's death in January 2010 openly celebrating his passing and seeking to ensure that no Indiana teachers were using *A People's History*. "This terrible anti-American academic finally passed away," Daniels wrote. "The obits and commentaries mentioned that his book *A People's History of the United States* is 'the textbook of choice in high schools and colleges around the country.' It is a truly execrable, antifactual piece of disinformation that misstates American history on every page. Can someone assure me that it is not in use anywhere in Indiana? If it is, how do we get rid of it before any more young people are force-fed a totally false version of our history?" It is clear why Daniels and his allies felt threatened by Howard's approach to history and his politics, and why someone who is seeking to dismantle present-day unions would not have wanted people studying the vital role they have played in protecting the rights of working people—or other examples of popular struggles challenging authority.

Despite these attacks, and even at the risk of losing one's job, people have continued to assign Howard's book alongside the assigned textbook, share their personal copies, photocopy sections for students, and read aloud passages of *A People's History*. In addition to drawing on the book, growing numbers of teachers across the United States use curricula and resources from organizations such as Voices of a People's History of the United States, the Zinn Education Project, Rethinking Schools, and Teaching for Change to bring a "people's history" to life in the classroom.

None of this is to say that Howard does not have his more serious critics, including those on the left. Howard had no issue with that. In encouraging critical thinking, he hoped people would apply the same independent mindset to his own views. That is why he opens *A People's History of the United States* by stating his point of view very directly:

> [I]n that inevitable taking of sides which comes from selection and emphasis in history, I prefer to try to tell the story of the discovery of America from the viewpoint of the Arawaks, of the Constitution from the standpoint of the slaves, of Andrew Jackson as seen by the Cherokees, of the Civil War as seen by the New York Irish, of the Mexican war as seen by the deserting soldiers of Scott's army, of the rise of industrialism as seen by the young women in the Lowell textile mills, of the Spanish-American War as seen by the Cubans, the conquest of the Philippines as seen by black soldiers on Luzon, the Gilded Age as seen by southern farmers, the First World War as seen by socialists, the Second World War as seen by pacifists, the

New Deal as seen by blacks in Harlem, the postwar American empire as seen by peons in Latin America. And so on, to the limited extent that any one person, however he or she strains, can "see" history from the standpoint of others.

Howard believed in laying his cards on the table. He did not hide behind the historian's easily available stance of distant, expert "objectivity." He had a point of view and was happy to be challenged and engage in dialogue about it.

There are some readers who wished he had included footnotes in this volume. Howard felt that missed the point of the book—which was to write an accessible and popular history. He wanted to welcome his readers, not intimidate them or scare them off, especially in a book that, at more than six hundred pages, is already daunting to embark on for the first time. Other historians found fault with Howard's departure from the narrow confines of academia. (Howard was more comfortable on a picket line than at a session of the Organization of American Historians, he'd be the first to admit.) More to the point, some readers have longed for more women's voices. Some have taken issue with his emphasis on spontaneity in history. My own feeling is that Howard's prediction in chapter twenty-four about "The Coming Revolt of the Guards"—"the intellectuals, the homeowners, the taxpayers, the skilled workers, the professionals, the servants of government" who make up "the middle classes"—was overly optimistic (as he himself later acknowledged)—yet at the same time he was remarkably prescient in writing about what he calls the "99 percent" versus the "1 percent" years before the Occupy movement popularized these terms. (Interestingly, others claimed credit for this slogan—or were given credit for it—ignoring Howard's much earlier use of the terms in this book.)

But such optimism was vital to Howard's politics and personality. It is what led him to undertake so ambitious a project as *A People's History of the United States* in the first place (an outcome that he frequently said would never have been possible without the encouragement of his wife, Roslyn Zinn). It is what brought him and his family to teach at Spelman College and become, unexpectedly, participants in the Civil Rights Movement. It is what led him to write three plays (*Emma, Daughter of Venus*, and *Marx in Soho*), in addition to his many other important works of history. Fundamentally, Howard had a confidence in people's ability to work together and change their circumstances. In a recent essay, the science-fiction writer Ursula K. Le Guin speaks of the "honest, uncompromising search for a realistic hope" and "a chance to transcend the paralyzing hierarchies of gender, race, class, nation, a chance to find a radical cure for the radical evil of our social system." Howard Zinn believed in taking that chance—and holding out that hope. But he did so because he was grounded in all the examples from our past—the abolitionist movement, the women's suffrage movement, the struggle for the right to organize unions and to work an eight-hour day—when people proved that causes that at one point seemed unrealistic and hopeless proved otherwise and in so doing provided what the Welsh socialist and cultural theorist Raymond Williams called "resources of hope."

In a way, the success of *A People's History of the United States* is an embodiment of Howard's wager on optimism. *A People's History* provided sustenance to a progressive countercurrent that developed from the early 1980s and grew as teachers, organizers, and the next generation of students developed new political initiatives and movements. (Howard dedicated our book *Voices of a People's History of the United States* to "the rebel voices of the coming generation.") At every step of that journey, Howard was there to fight alongside them. Throughout, in his many lectures, interviews, and speeches to antiwar protests, from the smallest gatherings to rallies of tens of thousands, he reminded us of the history of social change in this country, and kept coming back to his core ideas: that change comes from below; that progress comes only from people resisting and organizing—workers going on strike; consumers boycotting; soldiers refusing to fight, saying "no" to injustice and war; that we cannot rely on elected officials or leaders but instead have to rely on our individual and collective actions; that change never happens in a straight line but always has ups and downs, twists and turns; and that there are no guarantees in history.

But Howard added a distinctive element to these arguments by embodying the understanding that the shared experience of working alongside others for political change is the most rewarding, fulfilling, and meaningful life one can live. The sense of solidarity he had with people in struggle, the sense of joy he had in life, was infectious. He communicated to everyone around him that they mattered, that they were an active part of making history. In an article on the labor organizer and socialist Eugene Debs that Howard wrote in the 1990s, he said, "We are always in need of radicals who are also lovable," adding that we need to learn from Debs a "determination to hold up before a troubled public those ideas that are both bold and inviting—the more bold, the more inviting." When the actor David Strathairn read those lines at a celebration of Howard's life and work in California soon after his passing, it was clear to all of us in the audience that those words described Howard as much as they did Debs. Howard's ideas were bold, inviting, inspiring.

There are, from time to time, people who can crystallize the aims or goals of a movement in an especially compelling way, who can rally greater numbers of people to take a particular action and, in the case of Howard, make a lifelong commitment to activism. But such people cannot substitute for a movement. Debs, who understood this problem well, once put it this way: "I am no Moses to lead you out of the wilderness . . . because if I could lead you out, someone else could lead you in again." That was the spirit of Howard: think for yourself, act for yourself, challenge and question authority. But do it with others. As he wrote in *Marx in Soho*, "If you are going to break the law, do it with two thousand people . . . and Mozart."

In looking at Howard's lifetime of work, and his remarkable example, he has something else to teach us that is very important. As urgent as the present moment is, we need to build and strategize for the long-term, and have the patience to weather the setbacks and challenges that are coming. The kind of change we want, systemic change, will not happen overnight.

Howard achieved much in his lifetime. But as the continued impact of this book attests, his legacy continues. It continues in new scholarship, such as *An Indigenous People's History of the United States* by Roxanne Dunbar-Ortiz and *A People's History of Sports* by Dave Zirin, the album *Let England Shake* by P. J. Harvey, "people's libraries" and "Zinn lectures" at Occupy encampments, and in movements for labor rights, among so many other examples. It continues in classrooms where people are discussing and debating Howard's approach to history. It continues on the demonstrations where people hold placards with Howard's powerful words on war and social change. And it continues, now, with you.

Anthony Arnove wrote, directed, and produced *The People Speak* with Howard Zinn. He is the editor of several books, including *Voices of a People's History of the United States*, which Arnove coedited with Zinn and was released in an updated tenth-anniversary edition in 2014; *Howard Zinn Speaks*; *The Essential Chomsky*; a book of interviews with Zinn (*Terrorism and War*); and *Iraq Under Siege*; and is the author of *Iraq: The Logic of Withdrawal*. He was a producer of the Academy Award–nominated documentary *Dirty Wars* and is on the editorial board of Haymarket Books and *International Socialist Review*.

A PEOPLE'S
HISTORY
OF THE
UNITED
STATES

1

COLUMBUS, THE INDIANS, AND HUMAN PROGRESS

Arawak men and women, naked, tawny, and full of wonder, emerged from their villages onto the island's beaches and swam out to get a closer look at the strange big boat. When Columbus and his sailors came ashore, carrying swords, speaking oddly, the Arawaks ran to greet them, brought them food, water, gifts. He later wrote of this in his log:

> They . . . brought us parrots and balls of cotton and spears and many other things, which they exchanged for the glass beads and hawks' bells. They willingly traded everything they owned. . . . They were well-built, with good bodies and handsome features. . . . They do not bear arms, and do not know them, for I showed them a sword, they took it by the edge and cut themselves out of ignorance. They have no iron. Their spears are made of cane. . . . They would make fine servants. . . . With fifty men we could subjugate them all and make them do whatever we want.

These Arawaks of the Bahama Islands were much like Indians on the mainland, who were remarkable (European observers were to say again and again) for their hospitality, their belief in sharing. These traits did not stand out in the Europe of the Renaissance, dominated as it was by the religion of popes, the government of kings, the frenzy for money that marked Western civilization and its first messenger to the Americas, Christopher Columbus.

Columbus wrote:

> As soon as I arrived in the Indies, on the first Island which I found, I took some of the natives by force in order that they might learn and might give me information of whatever there is in these parts.

The information that Columbus wanted most was: Where is the gold? He had persuaded the king and queen of Spain to finance an expedition to the lands, the wealth, he expected would be on the other side of the Atlantic—the Indies and Asia, gold and spices. For, like other informed people of his time, he knew the world was round and he could sail west in order to get to the Far East.

Spain was recently unified, one of the new modern nation-states, like France, England, and Portugal. Its population, mostly poor peasants, worked for the nobility, who were 2 percent of the population and owned 95 percent of the land. Spain had tied itself to the Catholic Church, expelled all the Jews, driven out the Moors. Like other states of the modern world, Spain sought gold, which was becoming the new mark of wealth, more useful than land because it could buy anything.

There was gold in Asia, it was thought, and certainly silks and spices, for Marco Polo and others had brought back marvelous things from their overland expeditions centuries before. Now that the Turks had conquered Constantinople and the eastern Mediterranean, and controlled the land routes to Asia, a sea route was needed. Portuguese sailors were working their way around the southern tip of Africa. Spain decided to gamble on a long sail across an unknown ocean.

In return for bringing back gold and spices, they promised Columbus 10 percent of the profits, governorship over new-found lands, and the fame that would go with a new title: Admiral of the Ocean Sea. He was a merchant's clerk from the Italian city of Genoa, part-time weaver (the son of a skilled weaver), and expert sailor. He set out with three sailing ships, the largest of which was the *Santa Maria*, perhaps 100 feet long, and thirty-nine crew members.

Columbus would never have made it to Asia, which was thousands of miles farther away than he had calculated, imagining a smaller world. He would have been doomed by that great expanse of sea. But he was lucky. One-fourth of the way there he came upon an unknown, uncharted land that lay between Europe and Asia—the Americas. It was early October 1492, and thirty-three days since he and his crew had left the Canary Islands, off the Atlantic coast of Africa. Now they saw branches and sticks floating in the water. They saw flocks of birds.

These were signs of land. Then, on October 12, a sailor called Rodrigo saw the early morning moon shining on white sands, and cried out. It was an island in the Bahamas, the Caribbean sea. The first man to sight land was supposed to get a yearly pension of 10,000 maravedis for life, but Rodrigo never got it. Columbus claimed he had seen a light the evening before. He got the reward.

So, approaching land, they were met by the Arawak Indians, who swam out to greet them. The Arawaks lived in village communes, had a developed agriculture of corn, yams, cassava. They could spin and weave, but they had no horses or work animals. They had no iron, but they wore tiny gold ornaments in their ears.

This was to have enormous consequences: it led Columbus to take some of them aboard ship as prisoners because he insisted that they guide him to the source of the gold. He then sailed to what is now Cuba, then to Hispaniola (the island which today consists of Haiti and the Dominican Republic). There, bits of visible gold in the rivers, and a gold mask presented to Columbus by a local Indian chief, led to wild visions of gold fields.

On Hispaniola, out of timbers from the *Santa Maria*, which had run aground, Columbus built a fort, the first European military base in the Western Hemisphere. He called it Navidad (Christmas) and left thirty-nine crewmembers there, with instructions to find and store the gold. He took more Indian prisoners and put them aboard his two remaining ships. At one part of the island he got into a fight with Indians who refused to trade as many bows and arrows as he and his men wanted. Two were run through with swords and bled to death. Then the *Nina* and the *Pinta* set sail for the Azores and Spain. When the weather turned cold, the Indian prisoners began to die.

Columbus's report to the Court in Madrid was extravagant. He insisted he had reached Asia (it was Cuba) and an island off the coast of China (Hispaniola). His descriptions were part fact, part fiction:

> Hispaniola is a miracle. Mountains and hills, plains and pastures, are both fertile and beautiful ... the harbors are unbelievably good and there are many wide rivers of which the majority contain gold. .... There are many spices, and great mines of gold and other metals. ....

The Indians, Columbus reported, "are so naïve and so free with their possessions that no one who has not witnessed them would believe it. When you ask for something they have, they never say no. To the contrary, they offer to share with anyone. ...." He concluded his report by asking for a little help from their Majesties, and in return he would bring them from his next voyage "as much gold as they need . . . and as many slaves as they ask." He was full of religious talk: "Thus the eternal God, our Lord, gives victory to those who follow His way over apparent impossibilities."

Because of Columbus's exaggerated report and promises, his second expedition was given seventeen ships and more than twelve hundred men. The aim was clear: slaves and gold. They went from island to island in the Caribbean, taking Indians as captives. But as word spread of the Europeans' intent they found more and more empty villages. On Haiti, they found that the sailors left behind at Fort Navidad had been killed in a battle with the Indians, after they had roamed the island in gangs looking for gold, taking women and children as slaves for sex and labor.

Now, from his base on Haiti, Columbus sent expedition after expedition into the interior. They found no gold fields, but had to fill up the ships returning to Spain with some kind of dividend. In the year 1495, they went on a great slave raid, rounded up fifteen hundred Arawak men, women, and children, put them in pens guarded by Spaniards and dogs, then picked the five hundred best specimens to load onto ships. Of those five hundred, two hundred died en route. The rest arrived alive in Spain and were put up for sale by the archdeacon of the town, who reported that, although the slaves were "naked as the day they were born," they showed "no more embarrassment than animals." Columbus later wrote: "Let us in the name of the Holy Trinity go on sending all the slaves that can be sold."

But too many of the slaves died in captivity. And so Columbus, desperate to pay back dividends to those who had invested, had to make good his promise to fill the ships with gold. In the province of Cicao on Haiti, where he and his men imagined huge gold fields to exist, they ordered all persons fourteen years or older to collect a certain quantity of gold every three months. When they brought it, they were given copper tokens to hang around their necks. Indians found without a copper token had their hands cut off and bled to death.

The Indians had been given an impossible task. The only gold around was bits of dust garnered from the streams. So they fled, were hunted down with dogs, and were killed.

Trying to put together an army of resistance, the Arawaks faced Spaniards who had armor, muskets, swords, horses. When the Spaniards took prisoners they hanged them or burned them to death. Among the Arawaks, mass suicides began, with cassava poison. Infants were killed to save them from the Spaniards. In two years, through murder, mutilation, or suicide, half of the 250,000 Indians on Haiti were dead.

When it became clear that there was no gold left, the Indians were taken as slave labor on huge estates, known later as *encomiendas*. They were worked at a ferocious pace, and died by the thousands. By the year 1515, there were perhaps fifty thousand Indians left. By 1550, there were five hundred. A report of the year 1650 shows none of the original Arawaks or their descendants left on the island.

The chief source—and, on many matters the only source—of information about what happened on the islands after Columbus came is Bartolomé de las Casas, who, as a young priest, participated in the conquest of Cuba. For a time he owned a plantation on which Indian slaves worked, but he gave that up and became a vehement critic of Spanish cruelty. Las Casas transcribed Columbus's journal and, in his fifties, began a multivolume *History of the Indies*. In it, he describes the Indians. They are agile, he says, and can swim long distances, especially the women. They are not completely peaceful, because they do battle from time to time with other tribes, but their casualties seem small, and they fight when they are individually moved to do so because of some grievance, not on the orders of captains or kings.

Women in Indian society were treated so well as to startle the Spaniards. Las Casas describes sex relations:

> Marriage laws are non-existent: men and women alike choose their mates and leave them as they please, without offense, jealousy or anger. They multiply in great abundance; pregnant women work to the last minute and give birth almost painlessly; up the next day, they bathe in the river and are as clean and healthy as before giving birth. If they tire of their men, they give themselves abortions with herbs that force stillbirths, covering their shameful parts with leaves or cotton cloth; although on the whole, Indian men and women look upon total nakedness with as much casualness as we look upon a man's head or at his hands.

The Indians, Las Casas says, have no religion, at least no temples. They live in

> large communal bell-shaped buildings, housing up to 600 people at one time ... made of very strong wood and roofed with palm leaves. ... They prize bird feathers of various colors, beads made of fishbones, and green and white stones with which they adorn their ears and lips, but they put no value

on gold and other precious things. They lack all manner of commerce, neither buying nor selling, and rely exclusively on their natural environment for maintenance. They are extremely generous with their possessions and by the same token covet the possessions of their friends and expect the same degree of liberality. . . .

In Book Two of his *History of the Indies*, Las Casas (who at first urged replacing Indians by black slaves, thinking they were stronger and would survive, but later relented when he saw the effects on blacks) tells about the treatment of the Indians by the Spaniards. It is a unique account and deserves to be quoted at length:

> Endless testimonies . . . prove the mild and pacific temperament of the natives. . . . But our work was to exasperate, ravage, kill, mangle and destroy; small wonder, then, if they tried to kill one of us now and then. . . . The admiral, it is true, was blind as those who came after him, and he was so anxious to please the King that he committed irreparable crimes against the Indians. . . .

Las Casas tells how the Spaniards "grew more conceited every day" and after a while refused to walk any distance. They "rode the backs of Indians if they were in a hurry" or were carried on hammocks by Indians running in relays. "In this case they also had Indians carry large leaves to shade them from the sun and others to fan them with goose wings."

Total control led to total cruelty. The Spaniards "thought nothing of knifing Indians by tens and twenties and of cutting slices off them to test the sharpness of their blades." Las Casas tells how "two of these so-called Christians met two Indian boys one day, each carrying a parrot; they took the parrots and for fun beheaded the boys."

The Indians' attempts to defend themselves failed. And when they ran off into the hills they were found and killed. So, Las Casas reports, "they suffered and died in the mines and other labors in desperate silence, knowing not a soul in the world to whom they could turn for help." He describes their work in the mines:

> . . . mountains are stripped from top to bottom and bottom to top a thousand times; they dig, split rocks, move stones, and carry dirt on their backs to wash it in the rivers, while those who wash gold stay in the water all the time with their backs bent so constantly it breaks them; and when water invades the mines, the most arduous task of all is to dry the mines by scooping up pansful of water and throwing it up outside. . . .

After each six or eight months' work in the mines, which was the time required of each crew to dig enough gold for melting, up to a third of the men died.

While the men were sent many miles away to the mines, the wives remained to work the soil, forced into the excruciating job of digging and making thousands of hills for cassava plants.

> Thus husbands and wives were together only once every eight or ten months and when they met they were so exhausted and depressed on both sides . . . they ceased to procreate. As for the newly born, they died early because their mothers, overworked and famished, had no milk to nurse them, and for this reason, while I was in Cuba, 7000 children died in three months. Some mothers even drowned their babies from sheer desperation. . . . In this way, husbands died in the mines, wives died at work, and children died from lack of milk . . . and in a short time this land which was so great, so powerful and fertile . . . was depopulated. . . . My eyes have seen these acts so foreign to human nature, and now I tremble as I write. . . .

When he arrived on Hispaniola in 1508, Las Casas says, "there were 60,000 people living on this island, including the Indians; so that from 1494 to 1508, over three million people had perished from war, slavery, and the mines. Who in future generations will believe this? I myself writing it as a knowledgeable eyewitness can hardly believe it. . . ."

Thus began the history, five hundred years ago, of the European invasion of the Indian settlements in the Americas. That beginning, when you read Las Casas—even if his figures are exaggerations (were there 3 million Indians to begin with, as he says, or less than a million, as some historians have calculated, or 8 million as others now believe?)—is conquest, slavery, death. When we read the history books given to children in the United States, it all starts with heroic adventure—there is no bloodshed—and Columbus Day is a celebration.

Past the elementary and high schools, there are only occasional hints of something else. Samuel Eliot Morison, the Harvard historian, was the most distinguished writer on Columbus, the author of a multivolume biography, and was himself a sailor who retraced Columbus's route across the Atlantic. In his popular book *Christopher Columbus, Mariner,* written in 1954, he tells about the enslavement and the killing: "The cruel policy initiated by Columbus and pursued by his successors resulted in complete genocide."

That is on one page, buried halfway into the telling of a grand romance. In the book's last paragraph, Morison sums up his view of Columbus:

He had his faults and his defects, but they were largely the defects of the qualities that made him great—his indomitable will, his superb faith in God and in his own mission as the Christ-bearer to lands beyond the seas, his stubborn persistence despite neglect, poverty and discouragement. But there was no flaw, no dark side to the most outstanding and essential of all his qualities—his seamanship.

One can lie outright about the past. Or one can omit facts which might lead to unacceptable conclusions. Morison does neither. He refuses to lie about Columbus. He does not omit the story of mass murder; indeed he describes it with the harshest word one can use: genocide.

But he does something else—he mentions the truth quickly and goes on to other things more important to him. Outright lying or quiet omission takes the risk of discovery which, when made, might arouse the reader to rebel against the writer. To state the facts, however, and then to bury them in a mass of other information is to say to the reader with a certain infectious calm: yes, mass murder took place, but it's not that important—it should weigh very little in our final judgments; it should affect very little what we do in the world.

It is not that the historian can avoid emphasis of some facts and not of others. This is as natural to him as to the mapmaker, who, in order to produce a usable drawing for practical purposes, must first flatten and distort the shape of the earth, then choose out of the bewildering mass of geographic information those things needed for the purpose of this or that particular map.

My argument cannot be against selection, simplification, emphasis, which are inevitable for both cartographers and historians. But the mapmaker's distortion is a technical necessity for a common purpose shared by all people who need maps. The historian's distortion is more than technical, it is ideological; it is released into a world of contending interests, where any chosen emphasis supports (whether the historian means to or not) some kind of interest, whether economic or political or racial or national or sexual.

Furthermore, this ideological interest is not openly expressed in the way a mapmaker's technical interest is obvious ("This is a Mercator projection for long-range navigation—for short-range, you'd better use a different projection"). No, it is presented as if all readers of history had a common interest which historians serve to the best of their ability. This is not intentional deception; the historian has been trained in a society in which education and knowledge are put forward as technical problems of excellence and not as tools for contending social classes, races, nations.

To emphasize the heroism of Columbus and his successors as navigators and discoverers, and to deemphasize their genocide, is not a technical necessity but an ideological choice. It serves—unwittingly—to justify what was done.

My point is not that we must, in telling history, accuse, judge, condemn Columbus *in absentia*. It is too late for that; it would be a useless scholarly exercise in morality. But the easy acceptance of atrocities as a deplorable but necessary price to pay for progress (Hiroshima and Vietnam, to save Western civilization; Kronstadt and Hungary, to save socialism; nuclear proliferation, to save us all)—that is still with us. One reason these atrocities are still with us is that we have learned to bury them in a mass of other facts, as radioactive wastes are buried in containers in the earth. We have learned to give them exactly the same proportion of attention that teachers and writers often give them in the most respectable of classrooms and textbooks. This learned sense of moral proportion, coming from the apparent objectivity of the scholar, is accepted more easily than when it comes from politicians at press conferences. It is therefore more deadly.

The treatment of heroes (Columbus) and their victims (the Arawaks)—the quiet acceptance of conquest and murder in the name of progress—is only one aspect of a certain approach to history, in which the past is told from the point of view of governments, conquerors, diplomats, leaders. It is as if they, like Columbus, deserve universal acceptance, as if they—the Founding Fathers, Jackson, Lincoln, Wilson, Roosevelt, Kennedy, the leading members of Congress, the famous Justices of the Supreme Court—represent the nation as a whole. The pretense is that there really is such a thing as "the United States," subject to occasional conflicts and quarrels, but fundamentally a community of people with common interests. It is as if there really is a "national interest" represented in the Constitution, in territorial expansion, in the laws passed by Congress, the decisions of the courts, the development of capitalism, the culture of education and the mass media.

"History is the memory of states," wrote Henry Kissinger in his first book, *A World Restored*, in which he proceeded to tell the history of nineteenth-century Europe from the viewpoint of the leaders of Austria and England, ignoring the millions who suffered from those statesmen's policies. From his standpoint, the "peace" that Europe had before the French Revolution was "restored" by the diplomacy of a few national leaders. But for factory workers in England, farmers in France, colored people in Asia and Africa, women and children everywhere except in the upper classes, it was a world of conquest, violence, hunger, exploitation—a world not restored but disintegrated.

My viewpoint, in telling the history of the United States, is different: that we must not accept the memory of states as our own. Nations are not communities and never have been. The history of any country, presented as the history of a family, conceals fierce conflicts of interest (sometimes exploding, most often repressed) between conquerors and conquered, masters and slaves, capitalists and workers, dominators and dominated in race and sex. And in such a world of conflict, a world of victims and executioners, it is the job of thinking people, as Albert Camus suggested, not to be on the side of the executioners.

Thus, in that inevitable taking of sides which comes from selection and emphasis in history, I prefer to try to tell the story of the discovery of America from the viewpoint of the Arawaks, of the Constitution from the standpoint of the slaves, of Andrew Jackson as seen by the Cherokees, of the Civil War as seen by the New York Irish, of the Mexican war as seen by the deserting soldiers of Scott's army, of the rise of industrialism as seen by the young women in the Lowell textile mills, of the Spanish-American war as seen by the Cubans, the conquest of the Philippines as seen by black soldiers on Luzon, the Gilded Age as seen by southern farmers, the First World War as seen by socialists, the Second World War as seen by pacifists, the New Deal as seen by blacks in Harlem, the postwar American empire as seen by peons in Latin America. And so on, to the limited extent that any one person, however he or she strains, can "see" history from the standpoint of others.

My point is not to grieve for the victims and denounce the executioners. Those tears, that anger, cast into the past, deplete our moral energy for the present. And the lines are not always clear. In the long run, the oppressor is also a victim. In the short run (and so far, human history has consisted only of short runs), the victims, themselves desperate and tainted with the culture that oppresses them, turn on other victims.

Still, understanding the complexities, this book will be skeptical of governments and their attempts, through politics and culture, to ensnare ordinary people in a giant web of nationhood pretending to a common interest. I will try not to overlook the cruelties that victims inflict on one another as they are jammed together in the boxcars of the system. I don't want to romanticize them. But I do remember (in rough paraphrase) a statement I once read: "The cry of the poor is not always just, but if you don't listen to it, you will never know what justice is."

I don't want to invent victories for people's movements. But to think that history-writing must aim simply to recapitulate the failures that dominate the past is to make historians collaborators in an endless cycle of defeat. If history is to be creative, to anticipate a possible future without denying the past, it should, I believe, emphasize new possibilities by disclosing those hidden episodes of the past when, even if in brief flashes, people showed their ability to resist, to join together, occasionally to win. I am supposing, or perhaps only hoping, that our future may be found in the past's fugitive moments of compassion rather than in its solid centuries of warfare.

That, being as blunt as I can, is my approach to the history of the United States. The reader may as well know that before going on.

What Columbus did to the Arawaks of the Bahamas, Cortés did to the Aztecs of Mexico, Pizarro to the Incas of Peru, and the English settlers of Virginia and Massachusetts to the Powhatans and the Pequots.

The Aztec civilization of Mexico came out of the heritage of Mayan, Zapotec, and Toltec cultures. It built enormous constructions from stone tools and human labor, developed a writing system and a priesthood. It also engaged in (let us not overlook this) the ritual killing of thousands of people as sacrifices to the gods. The cruelty of the Aztecs, however, did not erase a certain innocence, and when a Spanish armada appeared at Vera Cruz, and a bearded white man came ashore, with strange beasts (horses), clad in iron, it was thought that he was the legendary Aztec man-god who had died three hundred years before, with the promise to return—the mysterious Quetzalcoatl. And so they welcomed him, with munificent hospitality.

That was Hernando Cortés, come from Spain with an expedition financed by merchants and landowners and blessed by the deputies of God, with one obsessive goal: to find gold. In the mind of Montezuma, the king of the Aztecs, there must have been a certain doubt about whether Cortés was indeed Quetzalcoatl, because he sent a hundred runners to Cortés, bearing enormous treasures, gold and silver wrought into objects of fantastic beauty, but at the same time begging him to go back. (The painter Dürer a few years later described what he saw just arrived in Spain from that expedition—a sun of gold, a moon of silver, worth a fortune.)

Cortés then began his march of death from town to town, using deception, turning Aztec against Aztec, killing with the kind of deliberateness that accompanies a strategy—to paralyze the will of the population by a sudden frightful deed. And so, in Cholulu, he invited the headmen of the Cholula nation to the square. And when they came, with thousands of unarmed retainers, Cortés's small army of Spaniards, posted around the square with cannon, armed with crossbows, mounted on horses, massacred them, down to the last man. Then they looted the city and moved on. When their cavalcade of murder was over they were in Mexico City, Montezuma was dead, and the Aztec civilization, shattered, was in the hands of the Spaniards.

All this is told in the Spaniards' own accounts.

In Peru, that other Spanish conquistador Pizarro, used the same tactics, and for the same reasons—the frenzy in the early capitalist states of Europe for gold, for slaves, for products of the soil, to pay the bondholders and stockholders of the expeditions, to finance the monarchical bureaucracies rising in Western Europe, to spur the growth of the new money economy rising out of feudalism, to participate in what Karl Marx would later call "the primitive accumulation of capital." These were the violent beginnings of an intricate system of technology, business, politics, and culture that would dominate the world for the next five centuries.

In the North American English colonies, the pattern was set early, as Columbus had set it in the islands of the Bahamas. In 1585, before there was any permanent English settlement in Virginia, Richard Grenville landed there with seven ships. The Indians he met were hospitable, but when one of them stole a small silver cup, Grenville sacked and burned the whole Indian village.

Jamestown itself was set up inside the territory of an Indian confederacy, led by the chief, Powhatan. Powhatan watched the English settle on his people's land, but did not attack, maintaining a posture of coolness. When the English were going through their "starving time" in the winter of 1610, some of them ran off to join the Indians, where they would at least be fed. When the summer came, the governor of the colony sent a messenger to ask Powhatan to return the runaways, whereupon Powhatan, according to the English account, replied with "noe other than prowde and disdaynefull Answers." Some soldiers were therefore sent out "to take Revendge." They fell upon an Indian settlement, killed fifteen or sixteen Indians, burned the houses, cut down the corn growing around the village, took the queen of the tribe and her children into boats, then ended up throwing the children overboard "and shoteinge owtt their Braynes in the water." The queen was later taken off and stabbed to death.

Twelve years later, the Indians, alarmed as the English settlements kept growing in numbers, apparently decided to try to wipe them out for good. They went on a rampage and massacred 347 men, women, and children. From then on it was total war.

Not able to enslave the Indians, and not able to live with them, the English decided to exterminate them. Edmund Morgan writes, in his history of early Virginia, *American Slavery, American Freedom:*

> Since the Indians were better woodsmen than the English and virtually impossible to track down, the method was to feign peaceful intentions, let them settle down and plant their corn wherever they chose, and then, just before harvest, fall upon them, killing as many as possible and burning the corn. . . . Within two or three years of the massacre the English had avenged the deaths of that day many times over.

In that first year of the white man in Virginia, 1607, Powhatan had addressed a plea to John Smith that turned out prophetic. How authentic it is may be in doubt, but it is so much like so many Indian statements that it may be taken as, if not the rough letter of that first plea, the exact spirit of it:

> I have seen two generations of my people die. . . . I know the difference between peace and war better than any man in my country. I am now grown old, and must die soon; my authority must descend to my brothers, Opitchapan, Opechancanough and Catatough—then to my two sisters, and then to my two daughters. I wish them to know as much as I do, and that your love to them may be like mine to you. Why will you take by force what you may have quietly by love? Why will you destroy us who supply you with food? What can you get by war? We can hide our provisions and run into the woods; then you will starve for wronging your friends. Why are you jealous of us? We are unarmed, and willing to give you what you ask, if you come in a friendly manner, and not so simple as not to know that it is much better to eat good meat, sleep comfortably, live quietly with my wives and children, laugh and be merry with the English, and trade for their copper and hatchets, than to run away from them, and to lie cold in the woods, feed on acorns, roots and such trash, and be so hunted that I can neither eat nor sleep. In these wars, my men must sit up watching, and if a twig break, they all cry out "Here comes Captain Smith!" So I must end my miserable life. Take away your guns and swords, the cause of all our jealousy, or you may all die in the same manner.

When the Pilgrims came to New England they too were coming not to vacant land but to territory inhabited by tribes of Indians. The governor of the Massachusetts Bay Colony, John Winthrop, created the excuse to take Indian land by declaring the area legally a "vacuum." The

Indians, he said, had not "subdued" the land, and therefore had only a "natural" right to it, but not a "civil right." A "natural right" did not have legal standing.

The Puritans also appealed to the Bible, Psalms 2:8: "Ask of me, and I shall give thee, the heathen for thine inheritance, and the uttermost parts of the earth for thy possession." And to justify their use of force to take the land, they cited Romans 13:2: "Whosoever therefore resisteth the power, resisteth the ordinance of God: and they that resist shall receive to themselves damnation."

The Puritans lived in uneasy truce with the Pequot Indians, who occupied what is now southern Connecticut and Rhode Island. But they wanted them out of the way; they wanted their land. And they seemed to want also to establish their rule firmly over Connecticut settlers in that area. The murder of a white trader, Indian-kidnaper, and troublemaker became an excuse to make war on the Pequots in 1636.

A punitive expedition left Boston to attack the Narragansett Indians on Block Island, who were lumped with the Pequots. As Governor Winthrop wrote:

> They had commission to put to death the men of Block Island, but to spare the women and children, and to bring them away, and to take possession of the island; and from thence to go to the Pequods to demand the murderers of Captain Stone and other English, and one thousand fathom of wampom for damages, etc. and some of their children as hostages, which if they should refuse, they were to obtain it by force.

The English landed and killed some Indians, but the rest hid in the thick forests of the island and the English went from one deserted village to the next, destroying crops. Then they sailed back to the mainland and raided Pequot villages along the coast, destroying crops again. One of the officers of that expedition, in his account, gives some insight into the Pequots they encountered: "The Indians spying of us came running in multitudes along the water side, crying, What cheer, Englishmen, what cheer, what do you come for? They not thinking we intended war, went on cheerfully. . . ."

So, the war with the Pequots began. Massacres took place on both sides. The English developed a tactic of warfare used earlier by Cortés and later, in the twentieth century, even more systematically: deliberate attacks on noncombatants for the purpose of terrorizing the enemy. This is ethnohistorian Francis Jennings's interpretation of Captain John Mason's attack on a Pequot village on the Mystic River near Long Island

Sound: "Mason proposed to avoid attacking Pequot warriors, which would have overtaxed his unseasoned, unreliable troops. Battle, as such, was not his purpose. Battle is only one of the ways to destroy an enemy's will to fight. Massacre can accomplish the same end with less risk, and Mason had determined that massacre would be his objective."

So the English set fire to the wigwams of the village. By their own account: "The Captain also said, We must Burn Them; and immediately stepping into the Wigwam . . . brought out a Fire Brand, and putting it into the Matts with which they were covered, set the Wigwams on Fire." William Bradford, in his *History of the Plymouth Plantation* written at the time, describes John Mason's raid on the Pequot village:

> Those that scaped the fire were slaine with the sword; some hewed to peeces, others rune throw with their rapiers, so as they were quickly dispatchte, and very few escaped. It was conceived they thus destroyed about 400 at this time. It was a fearful sight to see them thus frying in the fyer, and the streams of blood quenching the same, and horrible was the stincke and sente there of, but the victory seemed a sweete sacrifice, and they gave the prayers thereof to God, who had wrought so wonderfully for them, thus to inclose their enemise in their hands, and give them so speedy a victory over so proud and insulting an enimie.

As Dr. Cotton Mather, Puritan theologian, put it: "It was supposed that no less than 600 Pequot souls were brought down to hell that day."

The war continued. Indian tribes were used against one another, and never seemed able to join together in fighting the English. Jennings sums up:

> The terror was very real among the Indians, but in time they came to meditate upon its foundations. They drew three lessons from the Pequot War: (1) that the Englishmen's most solemn pledge would be broken whenever obligation conflicted with advantage; (2) that the English way of war had no limit of scruple or mercy; and (3) that weapons of Indian making were almost useless against weapons of European manufacture. These lessons the Indians took to heart.

A footnote in Virgil Vogel's book *This Land Was Ours* (1972) says: "The official figure on the number of Pequots now in Connecticut is twenty-one persons."

Forty years after the Pequot War, Puritans and Indians fought again. This time it was the Wampanoags, occupying the south shore of

Massachusetts Bay, who were in the way and also beginning to trade some of their land to people outside the Massachusetts Bay Colony. Their chief, Massasoit, was dead. His son Wamsutta had been killed by Englishmen, and Wamsutta's brother Metacom (later to be called King Philip by the English) became chief. The English found their excuse, a murder which they attributed to Metacom, and they began a war of conquest against the Wampanoags, a war to take their land. They were clearly the aggressors, but claimed they attacked for preventive purposes. As Roger Williams, more friendly to the Indians than most, put it: "All men of conscience or prudence ply to windward, to maintain their wars to be defensive."

Jennings says the elite of the Puritans wanted the war; the ordinary white Englishman did not want it and often refused to fight. The Indians certainly did not want war, but they matched atrocity with atrocity. When it was over, in 1676, the English had won, but their resources were drained; they had lost six hundred men. Three thousand Indians were dead, including Metacom himself. Yet the Indian raids did not stop.

For a while, the English tried softer tactics. But ultimately, it was back to annihilation. The Indian population of 10 million that lived north of Mexico when Columbus came would ultimately be reduced to less than a million. Huge numbers of Indians would die from diseases introduced by the whites. A Dutch traveler in New Netherland wrote in 1656 that "the Indians ... affirm, that before the arrival of the Christians, and before the smallpox broke out amongst them, they were ten times as numerous as they now are, and that their population had been melted down by this disease, whereof nine-tenths of them have died." When the English first settled Martha's Vineyard in 1642, the Wampanoags there numbered perhaps three thousand. There were no wars on that island, but by 1764, only 313 Indians were left there. Similarly, Block Island Indians numbered perhaps 1,200 to 1,500 in 1662, and by 1774 were reduced to fifty-one.

Behind the English invasion of North America, behind their massacre of Indians, their deception, their brutality, was that special powerful drive born in civilizations based on private property. It was a morally ambiguous drive; the need for space, for land, was a real human need. But in conditions of scarcity, in a barbarous epoch of history ruled by competition, this human need was transformed into the murder of whole peoples. Roger Williams said it was

a depraved appetite after the great vanities, dreams and shadows of this vanishing life, great portions of land, land in this wilderness, as if men were in as great necessity and danger for want of great portions of land, as poor, hungry, thirsty seamen have, after a sick and stormy, a long and starving passage. This is one of the gods of New England, which the living and most high Eternal will destroy and famish.

Was all this bloodshed and deceit—from Columbus to Cortés, Pizarro, the Puritans—a necessity for the human race to progress from savagery to civilization? Was Morison right in burying the story of genocide inside a more important story of human progress? Perhaps a persuasive argument can be made—as it was made by Stalin when he killed peasants for industrial progress in the Soviet Union, as it was made by Churchill explaining the bombings of Dresden and Hamburg, and Truman explaining Hiroshima. But how can the judgment be made if the benefits and losses cannot be balanced because the losses are either unmentioned or mentioned quickly?

That quick disposal might be acceptable ("Unfortunate, yes, but it had to be done") to the middle and upper classes of the conquering and "advanced" countries. But is it acceptable to the poor of Asia, Africa, Latin America, or to the prisoners in Soviet labor camps, or the blacks in urban ghettos, or the Indians on reservations—to the victims of that progress which benefits a privileged minority in the world? Was it acceptable (or just inescapable?) to the miners and railroaders of America, the factory hands, the men and women who died by the hundreds of thousands from accidents or sickness, where they worked or where they lived—casualties of progress? And even the privileged minority—must it not reconsider, with that practicality which even privilege cannot abolish, the value of its privileges, when they become threatened by the anger of the sacrificed, whether in organized rebellion, unorganized riot, or simply those brutal individual acts of desperation labeled crimes by law and the state?

If there *are* necessary sacrifices to be made for human progress, is it not essential to hold to the principle that those to be sacrificed must make the decision themselves? We can all decide to give up something of ours, but do we have the right to throw into the pyre the children of others, or even our own children, for a progress which is not nearly as clear or present as sickness or health, life or death?

What did people in Spain get out of all that death and brutality visited on the Indians of the Americas? For a brief period in history, there was the glory of a Spanish Empire in the Western Hemisphere. As Hans Koning sums it up in his book *Columbus: His Enterprise:*

For all the gold and silver stolen and shipped to Spain did not make the Spanish people richer. It gave their kings an edge in the balance of power for a time, a chance to hire more mercenary soldiers for their wars. They ended up losing those wars anyway, and all that was left was a deadly inflation, a starving population, the rich richer, the poor poorer, and a ruined peasant class.

Beyond all that, how certain are we that what was destroyed was inferior? Who were these people who came out on the beach and swam to bring presents to Columbus and his crew, who watched Cortés and Pizarro ride through their countryside, who peered out of the forests at the first white settlers of Virginia and Massachusetts?

Columbus called them Indians, because he miscalculated the size of the earth. In this book we too call them Indians, with some reluctance, because it happens too often that people are saddled with names given them by their conquerors.

And yet, there is some reason to call them Indians, because they did come, perhaps 25,000 years ago, from Asia, across the land bridge of the Bering Straits (later to disappear under water) to Alaska. Then they moved southward, seeking warmth and land, in a trek lasting thousands of years that took them into North America, then Central and South America. In Nicaragua, Brazil, and Ecuador their petrified footprints can still be seen, along with the print of bison, who disappeared about five thousand years ago, so they must have reached South America at least that far back.

Widely dispersed over the great land mass of the Americas, they numbered approximately 75 million people by the time Columbus came, perhaps 25 million in North America. Responding to the different environments of soil and climate, they developed hundreds of different tribal cultures, perhaps two thousand different languages. They perfected the art of agriculture, and figured out how to grow maize (corn), which cannot grow by itself and must be planted, cultivated, fertilized, harvested, husked, shelled. They ingeniously developed a variety of other vegetables and fruits, as well as peanuts and chocolate and tobacco and rubber.

On their own, the Indians were engaged in the great agricultural revolution that other peoples in Asia, Europe, Africa were going through about the same time.

While many of the tribes remained nomadic hunters and food gatherers in wandering, egalitarian communes, others began to live in more settled communities where there was more food, larger populations, more divisions of labor among men and women, more surplus to feed chiefs and priests, more leisure time for artistic and social work, for building houses. About a thousand years before Christ, while comparable constructions were going on in Egypt and Mesopotamia, the Zuñi and Hopi Indians of what is now New Mexico had begun to build villages consisting of large terraced buildings, nestled in among cliffs and mountains for protection from enemies, with hundreds of rooms in each village. Before the arrival of the European explorers, they were using irrigation canals, dams, were doing ceramics, weaving baskets, making cloth out of cotton.

By the time of Christ and Julius Caesar, there had developed in the Ohio River Valley a culture of so-called Moundbuilders, Indians who constructed thousands of enormous sculptures out of earth, sometimes in the shapes of huge humans, birds, or serpents, sometimes as burial sites, sometimes as fortifications. One of them was $3\frac{1}{2}$ miles long, enclosing 100 acres. These Moundbuilders seem to have been part of a complex trading system of ornaments and weapons from as far off as the Great Lakes, the Far West, and the Gulf of Mexico.

About A.D. 500, as this Moundbuilder culture of the Ohio Valley was beginning to decline, another culture was developing westward, in the valley of the Mississippi, centered on what is now St. Louis. It had an advanced agriculture, included thousands of villages, and also built huge earthen mounds as burial and ceremonial places near a vast Indian metropolis that may have had thirty thousand people. The largest mound was 100 feet high, with a rectangular base larger than that of the Great Pyramid of Egypt. In the city, known as Cahokia, were toolmakers, hide dressers, potters, jewelrymakers, weavers, saltmakers, copper engravers, and magnificent ceramists. One funeral blanket was made of twelve thousand shell beads.

From the Adirondacks to the Great Lakes, in what is now Pennsylvania and upper New York, lived the most powerful of the northeastern tribes, the League of the Iroquois, which included the Mohawks (People of the Flint), Oneidas (People of the Stone), Onondagas (People of the Mountain), Cayugas (People at the Landing), and Senecas (Great Hill People), thousands of people bound together by a common Iroquois language.

In the vision of the Mohawk chief Hiawatha, the legendary Dekaniwidah spoke to the Iroquois: "We bind ourselves together by taking hold of each other's hands so firmly and forming a circle so strong that if a tree should fall upon it, it could not shake nor break it, so that our people and grandchildren shall remain in the circle in security, peace and happiness."

In the villages of the Iroquois, land was owned in common and worked in common. Hunting was done together, and the catch was divided among the members of the village. Houses were considered common property and were shared by several families. The concept of private ownership of land and homes was foreign to the Iroquois. A French Jesuit priest who encountered them in the 1650s wrote: "No poorhouses are needed among them, because they are neither mendicants nor paupers. . . . Their kindness, humanity and courtesy not only makes them liberal with what they have, but causes them to possess hardly anything except in common."

Women were important and respected in Iroquois society. Families were matrilineal. That is, the family line went down through the female members, whose husbands joined the family, while sons who married then joined their wives' families. Each extended family lived in a "long house." When a woman wanted a divorce, she set her husband's things outside the door.

Families were grouped in clans, and a dozen or more clans might make up a village. The senior women in the village named the men who represented the clans at village and tribal councils. They also named the forty-nine chiefs who were the ruling council for the Five Nation confederacy of the Iroquois. The women attended clan meetings, stood behind the circle of men who spoke and voted, and removed the men from office if they strayed too far from the wishes of the women.

The women tended the crops and took general charge of village affairs while the men were always hunting or fishing. And since they supplied the moccasins and food for warring expeditions, they had some control over military matters. As Gary B. Nash notes in his fascinating study of early America, *Red, White, and Black:* "Thus power was shared between the sexes and the European idea of male dominancy and female subordination in all things was conspicuously absent in Iroquois society."

Children in Iroquois society, while taught the cultural heritage of their people and solidarity with the tribe, were also taught to be independent, not to submit to overbearing authority. They were taught equality in status and the sharing of possessions. The Iroquois did not use harsh punishment on children; they did not insist on early weaning or early toilet training, but gradually allowed the child to learn self-care.

All of this was in sharp contrast to European values as brought over by the first colonists, a society of rich and poor, controlled by priests, by governors, by male heads of families. For example, the pastor of the Pilgrim colony, John Robinson, thus advised his parishioners how to deal with their children: "And surely there is in all children . . . a stubbornness, and stoutness of mind arising from natural pride, which must, in the first place, be broken and beaten down; that so the foundation of their education being laid in humility and tractableness, other virtues may, in their time, be built thereon."

Gary Nash describes Iroquois culture:

> No laws and ordinances, sheriffs and constables, judges and juries, or courts or jails—the apparatus of authority in European societies—were to be found in the northeast woodlands prior to European arrival. Yet boundaries of acceptable behavior were firmly set. Though priding themselves on the autonomous individual, the Iroquois maintained a strict sense of right and wrong. . . . He who stole another's food or acted invalourously in war was "shamed" by his people and ostracized from their company until he had atoned for his actions and demonstrated to their satisfaction that he had morally purified himself.

Not only the Iroquois but other Indian tribes behaved the same way. In 1635, Maryland Indians responded to the governor's demand that if any of them killed an Englishman, the guilty one should be delivered up for punishment according to English law. The Indians said:

> It is the manner amongst us Indians, that if any such accident happen, wee doe redeeme the life of a man that is so slaine, with a 100 armes length of Beades and since that you are heere strangers, and come into our Countrey, you should rather conform yourselves to the Customes of our Countrey, than impose yours upon us. . . .

So, Columbus and his successors were not coming into an empty wilderness, but into a world which in some places was as densely populated as Europe itself, where the culture was complex, where human relations were more egalitarian than in Europe, and where the relations among men, women, children, and nature were more beautifully worked out than perhaps any place in the world.

They were people without a written language, but with their own laws, their poetry, their history kept in memory and passed on, in an oral vocabulary more complex than Europe's, accompanied by song, dance, and ceremonial drama. They paid careful attention to the development of personality, intensity of will, independence and flexibility, passion and potency, to their partnership with one another and with nature.

John Collier, an American scholar who lived among Indians in the 1920s and 1930s in the American Southwest, said of their spirit: "Could we make it our own, there would be an eternally inexhaustible earth and a forever lasting peace."

Perhaps there is some romantic mythology in that. But the evidence from European travelers in the sixteenth, seventeenth, and eighteenth centuries, put together recently by an American specialist on Indian life, William Brandon, is overwhelmingly supportive of much of that "myth." Even allowing for the imperfection of myths, it is enough to make us question, for that time and ours, the excuse of progress in the annihilation of races, and the telling of history from the standpoint of the conquerors and leaders of Western civilization.

2

DRAWING THE
COLOR LINE

A black American writer, J. Saunders Redding, describes the arrival of a
ship in North America in the year 1619:

> Sails furled, flag drooping at her rounded stern, she rode the tide in from
> the sea. She was a strange ship, indeed, by all accounts, a frightening ship, a
> ship of mystery. Whether she was trader, privateer, or man-of-war no one
> knows. Through her bulwarks black-mouthed cannon yawned. The flag she
> flew was Dutch; her crew a motley. Her port of call, an English settlement,
> Jamestown, in the colony of Virginia. She came, she traded, and shortly
> afterwards was gone. Probably no ship in modern history has carried a more
> portentous freight. Her cargo? Twenty slaves.

There is not a country in world history in which racism has been
more important, for so long a time, as the United States. And the problem of "the color line," as W. E. B. Du Bois put it, is still with us. So it is
more than a purely historical question to ask: How does it start?—and
an even more urgent question: How might it end? Or, to put it differently: Is it possible for whites and blacks to live together without hatred?

If history can help answer these questions, then the beginnings of
slavery in North America—a continent where we can trace the coming
of the first whites and the first blacks—might supply at least a few clues.

Some historians think those first blacks in Virginia were considered
as servants, like the white indentured servants brought from Europe.
But the strong probability is that, even if they were listed as "servants" (a
more familiar category to the English), they were viewed as being different from white servants, were treated differently, and in fact were slaves.

In any case, slavery developed quickly into a regular institution, into the normal labor relation of blacks to whites in the New World. With it developed that special racial feeling—whether hatred, or contempt, or pity, or patronization—that accompanied the inferior position of blacks in America for the next 350 years—that combination of inferior status and derogatory thought we call racism.

Everything in the experience of the first white settlers acted as a pressure for the enslavement of blacks.

The Virginians of 1619 were desperate for labor, to grow enough food to stay alive. Among them were survivors from the winter of 1609–1610, the "starving time," when, crazed for want of food, they roamed the woods for nuts and berries, dug up graves to eat the corpses, and died in batches until five hundred colonists were reduced to sixty.

In the *Journals* of the House of Burgesses of Virginia is a document of 1619 which tells of the first twelve years of the Jamestown colony. The first settlement had a hundred persons, who had one small ladle of barley per meal. When more people arrived, there was even less food. Many of the people lived in cavelike holes dug into the ground, and in the winter of 1609–1610, they were

> ... driven thru insufferable hunger to eat those things which nature most abhorred, the flesh and excrements of man as well of our own nation as of an Indian, digged by some out of his grave after he had lain buried three days and wholly devoured him; others, envying the better state of body of any whom hunger has not yet so much wasted as their own, lay wait and threatened to kill and eat them; one among them slew his wife as she slept in his bosom, cut her in pieces, salted her and fed upon her till he had clean devoured all parts saving her head. ...

A petition by thirty colonists to the House of Burgesses, complaining against the twelve-year governorship of Sir Thomas Smith, said:

> In those 12 years of Sir Thomas Smith, his government, we aver that the colony for the most part remained in great want and misery under most severe and cruel laws. . . . The allowance in those times for a man was only eight ounces of meale and half a pint of peas for a day . . . mouldy, rotten, full of cobwebs and maggots, loathsome to man and not fit for beasts, which forced many to flee for relief to the savage enemy, who being taken again were put to sundry deaths as by hanging, shooting and breaking upon the wheel . . . of whom one for stealing two or three pints of oatmeal had a bodkin thrust through his tongue and was tied with a chain to a tree until he starved. . . .

The Virginians needed labor, to grow corn for subsistence, to grow tobacco for export. They had just figured out how to grow tobacco, and in 1617 they sent off the first cargo to England. Finding that, like all pleasurable drugs tainted with moral disapproval, it brought a high price, the planters, despite their high religious talk, were not going to ask questions about something so profitable.

They couldn't force Indians to work for them, as Columbus had done. They were outnumbered, and while, with superior firearms, they could massacre Indians, they would face massacre in return. They could not capture them and keep them enslaved; the Indians were tough, resourceful, defiant, and at home in these woods, as the transplanted Englishmen were not.

White servants had not yet been brought over in sufficient quantity. Besides, they did not come out of slavery, and did not have to do more than contract their labor for a few years to get their passage and a start in the New World. As for the free white settlers, many of them were skilled craftsmen, or even men of leisure back in England, who were so little inclined to work the land that John Smith, in those early years, had to declare a kind of martial law, organize them into work gangs, and force them into the fields for survival.

There may have been a kind of frustrated rage at their own ineptitude, at the Indian superiority at taking care of themselves, that made the Virginians especially ready to become the masters of slaves. Edmund Morgan imagines their mood as he writes in his book *American Slavery, American Freedom:*

> If you were a colonist, you knew that your technology was superior to the Indians'. You knew that you were civilized, and they were savages. . . . But your superior technology had proved insufficient to extract anything. The Indians, keeping to themselves, laughed at your superior methods and lived from the land more abundantly and with less labor than you did. . . . And when your own people started deserting in order to live with them, it was too much. . . . So you killed the Indians, tortured them, burned their villages, burned their cornfields. It proved your superiority, in spite of your failures. And you gave similar treatment to any of your own people who succumbed to their savage ways of life. But you still did not grow much corn. . . .

Black slaves were the answer. And it was natural to consider imported blacks as slaves, even if the institution of slavery would not be regularized and legalized for several decades. Because, by 1619, a million blacks had already been brought from Africa to South America and the Caribbean, to the Portuguese and Spanish colonies, to work as slaves. Fifty years before Columbus, the Portuguese took ten African blacks to Lisbon—this was the start of a regular trade in slaves. African blacks had been stamped as slave labor for a hundred years. So it would have been strange if those twenty blacks, forcibly transported to Jamestown, and sold as objects to settlers anxious for a steadfast source of labor, were considered as anything but slaves.

Their helplessness made enslavement easier. The Indians were on their own land. The whites were in their own European culture. The blacks had been torn from their land and culture, forced into a situation where the heritage of language, dress, custom, family relations, was bit by bit obliterated except for the remnants that blacks could hold on to by sheer, extraordinary persistence.

Was their culture inferior—and so subject to easy destruction? Inferior in military capability, yes—vulnerable to whites with guns and ships. But in no other way—except that cultures that are different are often taken as inferior, especially when such a judgment is practical and profitable. Even militarily, while the Westerners could secure forts on the African coast, they were unable to subdue the interior and had to come to terms with its chiefs.

The African civilization was as advanced in its own way as that of Europe. In certain ways, it was more admirable; but it also included cruelties, hierarchical privilege, and the readiness to sacrifice human lives for religion or profit. It was a civilization of 100 million people, using iron implements and skilled in farming. It had large urban centers and remarkable achievements in weaving, ceramics, sculpture.

European travelers in the sixteenth century were impressed with the African kingdoms of Timbuktu and Mali, already stable and organized at a time when European states were just beginning to develop into the modern nation. In 1563, Ramusio, secretary to the rulers in Venice, wrote to the Italian merchants: "Let them go and do business with the King of Timbuktu and Mali and there is no doubt that they will be well-received there with their ships and their goods and treated well, and granted the favours that they ask. . . ."

A Dutch report, around 1602, on the West African kingdom of Benin, said: "The Towne seemeth to be very great, when you enter it. You go into a great broad street, not paved, which seemeth to be seven or eight times broader than the Warmoes Street in Amsterdam. . . . The Houses in this Towne stand in good order, one close and even with the other, as the Houses in Holland stand."

The inhabitants of the Guinea Coast were described by one traveler around 1680 as "very civil and good-natured people, easy to be dealt with, condescending to what Europeans require of them in a civil way, and very ready to return double the presents we make them."

Africa had a kind of feudalism, like Europe based on agriculture, and with hierarchies of lords and vassals. But African feudalism did not come, as did Europe's, out of the slave societies of Greece and Rome, which had destroyed ancient tribal life. In Africa, tribal life was still powerful, and some of its better features—a communal spirit, more kindness in law and punishment—still existed. And because the lords did not have the weapons that European lords had, they could not command obedience as easily.

In his book *The African Slave Trade*, Basil Davidson contrasts law in the Congo in the early sixteenth century with law in Portugal and England. In those European countries, where the idea of private property was becoming powerful, theft was punished brutally. In England, even as late as 1740, a child could be hanged for stealing a rag of cotton. But in the Congo, communal life persisted, the idea of private property was a strange one, and thefts were punished with fines or various degrees of servitude. A Congolese leader, told of the Portuguese legal codes, asked a Portuguese once, teasingly: "What is the penalty in Portugal for anyone who puts his feet on the ground?"

Slavery existed in the African states, and it was sometimes used by Europeans to justify their own slave trade. But, as Davidson points out, the "slaves" of Africa were more like the serfs of Europe—in other words, like most of the population of Europe. It was a harsh servitude, but they had rights which slaves brought to America did not have, and they were "altogether different from the human cattle of the slave ships and the American plantations." In the Ashanti Kingdom of West Africa, one observer noted that "a slave might marry; own property; himself own a slave; swear an oath; be a competent witness and ultimately become heir to his master. . . . An Ashanti slave, nine cases out of ten, possibly became an adopted member of the family, and in time his descendants so merged and intermarried with the owner's kinsmen that only a few would know their origin."

One slave trader, John Newton (who later became an antislavery leader), wrote about the people of what is now Sierra Leone:

The state of slavery, among these wild barbarous people, as we esteem them, is much milder than in our colonies. For as, on the one hand, they have no land in high cultivation, like our West India plantations, and therefore no call for that excessive, unintermitted labour, which exhausts our slaves: so, on the other hand, no man is permitted to draw blood even from a slave.

African slavery is hardly to be praised. But it was far different from plantation or mining slavery in the Americas, which was lifelong, morally crippling, destructive of family ties, without hope of any future. African slavery lacked two elements that made American slavery the most cruel form of slavery in history: the frenzy for limitless profit that comes from capitalistic agriculture; the reduction of the slave to less than human status by the use of racial hatred, with that relentless clarity based on color, where white was master, black was slave.

In fact, it was because they came from a settled culture, of tribal customs and family ties, of communal life and traditional ritual, that African blacks found themselves especially helpless when removed from this. They were captured in the interior (frequently by blacks caught up in the slave trade themselves), sold on the coast, then shoved into pens with blacks of other tribes, often speaking different languages.

The conditions of capture and sale were crushing affirmations to the black African of his helplessness in the face of superior force. The marches to the coast, sometimes for 1,000 miles, with people shackled around the neck, under whip and gun, were death marches, in which two of every five blacks died. On the coast, they were kept in cages until they were picked and sold. One John Barbot, at the end of the seventeenth century, described these cages on the Gold Coast:

> As the slaves come down to Fida from the inland country, they are put into a booth or prison . . . near the beach, and when the Europeans are to receive them, they are brought out onto a large plain, where the ship's surgeons examine every part of everyone of them, to the smallest member, men and women being stark naked. . . . Such as are allowed good and sound are set on one side . . . marked on the breast with a red-hot iron, imprinting the mark of the French, English, or Dutch companies. . . . The branded slaves after this are returned to their former booths where they await shipment, sometimes 10–15 days. . . .

Then they were packed aboard the slave ships, in spaces not much bigger than coffins, chained together in the dark, wet slime of the ship's bottom, choking in the stench of their own excrement. Documents of the time describe the conditions:

The height, sometimes, between decks, was only eighteen inches; so that the unfortunate human beings could not turn around, or even on their sides, the elevation being less than the breadth of their shoulders; and here they are usually chained to the decks by the neck and legs. In such a place the sense of misery and suffocation is so great, that the Negroes . . . are driven to frenzy.

On one occasion, hearing a great noise from belowdecks where the blacks were chained together, the sailors opened the hatches and found the slaves in different stages of suffocation, many dead, some having killed others in desperate attempts to breathe. Slaves often jumped overboard to drown rather than continue their suffering. To one observer a slave-deck was "so covered with blood and mucus that it resembled a slaughter house."

Under these conditions, perhaps one of every three blacks transported overseas died, but the huge profits (often double the investment on one trip) made it worthwhile for the slave trader, and so the blacks were packed into the holds like fish.

First the Dutch, then the English, dominated the slave trade. (By 1795 Liverpool had more than a hundred ships carrying slaves and accounted for half of all the European slave trade.) Some Americans in New England entered the business, and in 1637 the first American slave ship, the *Desire*, sailed from Marblehead. Its holds were partitioned into racks, 2 feet by 6 feet, with leg irons and bars.

By 1800, 10 to 15 million blacks had been transported as slaves to the Americas, representing perhaps one-third of those originally seized in Africa. It is roughly estimated that Africa lost 50 million human beings to death and slavery in those centuries we call the beginnings of modern Western civilization, at the hands of slave traders and plantation owners in Western Europe and America, the countries deemed the most advanced in the world.

In the year 1610, a Catholic priest in the Americas named Father Sandoval wrote back to a church functionary in Europe to ask if the capture, transport, and enslavement of African blacks was legal by church doctrine. A letter dated March 12, 1610, from Brother Luis Brandaon to Father Sandoval gives the answer:

Your Reverence writes me that you would like to know whether the Negroes who are sent to your parts have been legally captured. To this I reply that I think your Reverence should have no scruples on this point, because this is a matter which has been questioned by the Board of Conscience in Lisbon, and all its members are learned and conscientious men. Nor did the bishops who were in Sao Thome, Cape Verde, and here in Loando—all learned and virtuous men—find fault with it. We have been here ourselves for forty years and there have been among us very learned Fathers . . . never did they consider the trade as illicit. Therefore we and the Fathers of Brazil buy these slaves for our service without any scruple. . . .

With all of this—the desperation of the Jamestown settlers for labor, the impossibility of using Indians and the difficulty of using whites, the availability of blacks offered in greater and greater numbers by profit-seeking dealers in human flesh, and with such blacks possible to control because they had just gone through an ordeal which if it did not kill them must have left them in a state of psychic and physical helplessness—is it any wonder that such blacks were ripe for enslavement?

And under these conditions, even if some blacks might have been considered servants, would blacks be treated the same as white servants?

The evidence, from the court records of colonial Virginia, shows that in 1630 a white man named Hugh Davis was ordered "to be soundly whipt . . . for abusing himself . . . by defiling his body in lying with a Negro." Ten years later, six servants and "a negro of Mr. Reynolds" started to run away. While the whites received lighter sentences, "Emanuel the Negro to receive thirty stripes and to be burnt in the cheek with the letter R, and to work in shackle one year or more as his master shall see cause."

Although slavery was not yet regularized or legalized in those first years, the lists of servants show blacks listed separately. A law passed in 1639 decreed that "all persons except Negroes" were to get arms and ammunition—probably to fight off Indians. When in 1640 three servants tried to run away, the two whites were punished with a lengthening of their service. But, as the court put it, "the third being a negro named John Punch shall serve his master or his assigns for the time of his natural life." Also in 1640, we have the case of a Negro woman servant who begot a child by Robert Sweat, a white man. The court ruled "that the said negro woman shall be whipt at the whipping post and the said Sweat shall tomorrow in the forenoon do public penance for his offense at James citychurch. . . ."

This unequal treatment, this developing combination of contempt and oppression, feeling and action, which we call "racism"—was this the result of a "natural" antipathy of white against black? The question is important, not just as a matter of historical accuracy, but because any emphasis on "natural" racism lightens the responsibility of the social system. If racism can't be shown to be natural, then it is the result of certain conditions, and we are impelled to eliminate those conditions.

We have no way of testing the behavior of whites and blacks toward one another under favorable conditions—with no history of subordination, no money incentive for exploitation and enslavement, no desperation for survival requiring forced labor. All the conditions for black and white in seventeenth-century America were the opposite of that, all powerfully directed toward antagonism and mistreatment. Under such conditions even the slightest display of humanity between the races might be considered evidence of a basic human drive toward community.

Sometimes it is noted that, even before 1600, when the slave trade had just begun, before Africans were stamped by it—literally and symbolically—the color black was distasteful. In England, before 1600, it meant, according to the Oxford English Dictionary: "Deeply stained with dirt; soiled, dirty, foul. Having dark or deadly purposes, malignant; pertaining to or involving death, deadly; baneful, disastrous, sinister. Foul, iniquitous, atrocious, horribly wicked. Indicating disgrace, censure, liability to punishment, etc." And Elizabethan poetry often used the color white in connection with beauty.

It may be that, in the absence of any other overriding factor, darkness and blackness, associated with night and unknown, would take on those meanings. But the presence of another human being is a powerful fact, and the conditions of that presence are crucial in determining whether an initial prejudice, against a mere color, divorced from humankind, is turned into brutality and hatred.

In spite of such preconceptions about blackness, in spite of special subordination of blacks in the Americas in the seventeenth century, there is evidence that where whites and blacks found themselves with common problems, common work, common enemy in their master, they behaved toward one another as equals. As one scholar of slavery, Kenneth Stampp, has put it, Negro and white servants of the seventeenth century were "remarkably unconcerned about the visible physical differences."

Black and white worked together, fraternized together. The very fact that laws had to be passed after a while to forbid such relations indicates the strength of that tendency. In 1661 a law was passed in Virginia that "in case any English servant shall run away in company of any Negroes" he would have to give special service for extra years to the master of the runaway Negro. In 1691, Virginia provided for the banishment of any "white man or woman being free who shall intermarry with a negro, mulatoo, or Indian man or woman bond or free."

There is an enormous difference between a feeling of racial strangeness, perhaps fear, and the mass enslavement of millions of black people that took place in the Americas. The transition from one to the other cannot be explained easily by "natural" tendencies. It is not hard to understand as the outcome of historical conditions.

Slavery grew as the plantation system grew. The reason is easily traceable to something other than natural racial repugnance: the number of arriving whites, whether free or indentured servants (under four to seven years contract), was not enough to meet the need of the plantations. By 1700, in Virginia, there were 6,000 slaves, one-twelfth of the population. By 1763, there were 170,000 slaves, about half the population.

Blacks were easier to enslave than whites or Indians. But they were still not easy to enslave. From the beginning, the imported black men and women resisted their enslavement. Ultimately their resistance was controlled, and slavery was established for 3 million blacks in the South. Still, under the most difficult conditions, under pain of mutilation and death, throughout their two hundred years of enslavement in North America, these Afro-Americans continued to rebel. Only occasionally was there an organized insurrection. More often they showed their refusal to submit by running away. Even more often, they engaged in sabotage, slowdowns, and subtle forms of resistance which asserted, if only to themselves and their brothers and sisters, their dignity as human beings.

The refusal began in Africa. One slave trader reported that Negroes were "so wilful and loth to leave their own country, that they have often leap'd out of the canoes, boat and ship into the sea, and kept under water till they were drowned."

When the very first black slaves were brought into Hispaniola in 1503, the Spanish governor of Hispaniola complained to the Spanish court that fugitive Negro slaves were teaching disobedience to the Indians. In the 1520s and 1530s, there were slave revolts in Hispaniola, Puerto Rico, Santa Marta, and what is now Panama. Shortly after those rebellions, the Spanish established a special police for chasing fugitive slaves.

A Virginia statute of 1669 referred to "the obstinacy of many of them," and in 1680 the Assembly took note of slave meetings "under the pretense of feasts and brawls" which they considered of "dangerous consequence." In 1687, in the colony's Northern Neck, a plot was discovered in which slaves planned to kill all the whites in the area and escape during a mass funeral.

Gerald Mullin, who studied slave resistance in eighteenth-century Virginia in his work *Flight and Rebellion*, reports:

> The available sources on slavery in 18th-century Virginia—plantation and county records, the newspaper advertisements for runaways—describe rebellious slaves and few others. The slaves described were lazy and thieving; they feigned illnesses, destroyed crops, stores, tools, and sometimes attacked or killed overseers. They operated blackmarkets in stolen goods. Runaways were defined as various types, they were truants (who usually returned voluntarily), "outlaws". . . and slaves who were actually fugitives: men who visited relatives, went to town to pass as free, or tried to escape slavery completely, either by boarding ships and leaving the colony, or banding together in cooperative efforts to establish villages or hide-outs in the frontier. The commitment of another type of rebellious slave was total; these men became killers, arsonists, and insurrectionists.

Slaves recently from Africa, still holding on to the heritage of their communal society, would run away in groups and try to establish villages of runaways out in the wilderness, on the frontier. Slaves born in America, on the other hand, were more likely to run off alone, and, with the skills they had learned on the plantation, try to pass as free men.

In the colonial papers of England, a 1729 report from the lieutenant governor of Virginia to the British Board of Trade tells how "a number of Negroes, about fifteen . . . formed a design to withdraw from their Master and to fix themselves in the fastnesses of the neighboring Mountains. They had found means to get into their possession some Arms and Ammunition, and they took along with them some Provisions, their Cloths, bedding and working Tools. . . . Tho' this attempt has happily been defeated, it ought nevertheless to awaken us into some effectual measures. . . ."

Slavery was immensely profitable to some masters. James Madison told a British visitor shortly after the American Revolution that he could make $257 on every Negro in a year, and spend only $12 or $13 on his keep. Another viewpoint was of slaveowner Landon Carter, writing about fifty years earlier, complaining that his slaves so neglected their work and were so uncooperative ("either cannot or will not work") that he began to wonder if keeping them was worthwhile.

Some historians have painted a picture—based on the infrequency of organized rebellions and the ability of the South to maintain slavery for two hundred years—of a slave population made submissive by their condition; with their African heritage destroyed, they were, as Stanley

Elkins said, made into "Sambos," "a society of helpless dependents." Or as another historian, Ulrich Phillips, said, "by racial quality submissive." But looking at the totality of slave behavior, at the resistance of everyday life, from quiet noncooperation in work to running away, the picture becomes different.

In 1710, warning the Virginia Assembly, Governor Alexander Spotswood said:

> . . . freedom wears a cap which can without a tongue, call together all those who long to shake off the fetters of slavery and as such an Insurrection would surely be attended with most dreadful consequences so I think we cannot be too early in providing against it, both by putting our selves in a better posture of defence and by making a law to prevent the consultations of those Negroes.

Indeed, considering the harshness of punishment for running away, that so many blacks did run away must be a sign of a powerful rebelliousness. All through the 1700s, the Virginia slave code read:

> Whereas many times slaves run away and lie hid and lurking in swamps, woods, and other obscure places, killing hogs, and commiting other injuries to the inhabitants . . . if the slave does not immediately return, anyone whatsoever may kill or destroy such slaves by such ways and means as he . . . shall think fit. . . . If the slave is apprehended . . . it shall . . . be lawful for the county court, to order such punishment for the said slave, either by dismembering, or in any other way . . . as they in their discretion shall think fit, for the reclaiming any such incorrigible slave, and terrifying others from the like practices. . . .

Mullin found newspaper advertisements between 1736 and 1801 for 1,138 men runaways, and 141 women. One consistent reason for running away was to find members of one's family—showing that despite the attempts of the slave system to destroy family ties by not allowing marriages and by separating families, slaves would face death and mutilation to get together.

In Maryland, where slaves were about one-third of the population in 1750, slavery had been written into law since the 1660s, and statutes for controlling rebellious slaves were passed. There were cases where slave women killed their masters, sometimes by poisoning them, sometimes by burning tobacco houses and homes. Punishments ranged from whipping and branding to execution, but the trouble continued. In 1742, seven slaves were put to death for murdering their master.

Fear of slave revolt seems to have been a permanent fact of plantation life. William Byrd, a wealthy Virginia slaveowner, wrote in 1736:

> We have already at least 10,000 men of these descendants of Ham, fit to bear arms, and these numbers increase every day, as well by birth as by importation. And in case there should arise a man of desperate fortune, he might with more advantage than Cataline kindle a servile war . . . and tinge our rivers wide as they are with blood.

It was an intricate and powerful system of control that the slaveowners developed to maintain their labor supply and their way of life, a system both subtle and crude, involving every device that social orders employ for keeping power and wealth where it is. As Kenneth Stampp puts it:

> A wise master did not take seriously the belief that Negroes were natural-born slaves. He knew better. He knew that Negroes freshly imported from Africa had to be broken into bondage; that each succeeding generation had to be carefully trained. This was no easy task, for the bondsman rarely submitted willingly. Moreover, he rarely submitted completely. In most cases there was no end to the need for control—at least not until old age reduced the slave to a condition of helplessness.

The system was psychological and physical at the same time. The slaves were taught discipline, were impressed again and again with the idea of their own inferiority to "know their place," to see blackness as a sign of subordination, to be awed by the power of the master, to merge their interest with the master's, destroying their own individual needs. To accomplish this there was the discipline of hard labor, the breakup of the slave family, the lulling effects of religion (which sometimes led to "great mischief," as one slaveholder reported), the creation of disunity among slaves by separating them into field slaves and more privileged house slaves, and finally the power of law and the immediate power of the overseer to invoke whipping, burning, mutilation, and death. Dismemberment was provided for in the Virginia Code of 1705. Maryland passed a law in 1723 providing for cutting off the ears of blacks who struck whites, and that for certain serious crimes, slaves should be hanged and the body quartered and exposed.

Still, rebellions took place—not many, but enough to create constant fear among white planters. The first large-scale revolt in the North American colonies took place in New York in 1712. In New York, slaves were 10 percent of the population, the highest proportion in the northern states, where economic conditions usually did not require large numbers of field slaves. About twenty-five blacks and two Indians set fire to a building, then killed nine whites who came on the scene. They were captured by soldiers, put on trial, and twenty-one were executed. The governor's report to England said: "Some were burnt, others were hanged, one broke on the wheel, and one hung alive in chains in the town. . . ." One had been burned over a slow fire for eight to ten hours—all this to serve notice to other slaves.

A letter to London from South Carolina in 1720 reports:

> I am now to acquaint you that very lately we have had a very wicked and barbarous plot of the designe of the negroes rising with a designe to destroy all the white people in the country and then to take Charles Town in full body but it pleased God it was discovered and many of them taken prisoners and some burnt and some hang'd and some banish'd.

Around this time there were a number of fires in Boston and New Haven, suspected to be the work of Negro slaves. As a result, one Negro was executed in Boston, and the Boston Council ruled that any slaves who on their own gathered in groups of two or more were to be punished by whipping.

At Stono, South Carolina, in 1739, about twenty slaves rebelled, killed two warehouse guards, stole guns and gunpowder, and headed south, killing people in their way, and burning buildings. They were joined by others, until there were perhaps eighty slaves in all and, according to one account of the time, "they called out Liberty, marched on with Colours displayed, and two Drums beating." The militia found and attacked them. In the ensuing battle perhaps fifty slaves and twenty-five whites were killed before the uprising was crushed.

Herbert Aptheker, who did detailed research on slave resistance in North America for his book *American Negro Slave Revolts*, found about 250 instances where a minimum of ten slaves joined in a revolt or conspiracy.

From time to time, whites were involved in the slave resistance. As early as 1663, indentured white servants and black slaves in Gloucester County, Virginia, formed a conspiracy to rebel and gain their freedom. The plot was betrayed, and ended with executions. Mullin reports that the newspaper notices of runaways in Virginia often warned "ill-disposed" whites about harboring fugitives. Sometimes slaves and free men ran off together, or cooperated in crimes together. Sometimes, black male slaves ran off and joined white women. From time to time, white ship captains and watermen dealt with runaways, perhaps making the slave a part of the crew.

In New York in 1741, there were ten thousand whites in the city and two thousand black slaves. It had been a hard winter and the poor—slave and free—had suffered greatly. When mysterious fires broke out, blacks and whites were accused of conspiring together. Mass hysteria developed against the accused. After a trial full of lurid accusations by informers, and forced confessions, two white men and two white women were executed, eighteen slaves were hanged, and thirteen slaves were burned alive.

Only one fear was greater than the fear of black rebellion in the new American colonies. That was the fear that discontented whites would join black slaves to overthrow the existing order. In the early years of slavery, especially, before racism as a way of thinking was firmly ingrained, while white indentured servants were often treated as badly as black slaves, there was a possibility of cooperation. As Edmund Morgan sees it:

> There are hints that the two despised groups initially saw each other as sharing the same predicament. It was common, for example, for servants and slaves to run away together, steal hogs together, get drunk together. It was not uncommon for them to make love together. In Bacon's Rebellion, one of the last groups to surrender was a mixed band of eighty negroes and twenty English servants.

As Morgan says, masters, "initially at least, perceived slaves in much the same way they had always perceived servants . . . shiftless, irresponsible, unfaithful, ungrateful, dishonest. . . ." And "if freemen with disappointed hopes should make common cause with slaves of desperate hope, the results might be worse than anything Bacon had done."

And so, measures were taken. About the same time that slave codes, involving discipline and punishment, were passed by the Virginia Assembly,

> Virginia's ruling class, having proclaimed that all white men were superior to black, went on to offer their social (but white) inferiors a number of benefits previously denied them. In 1705 a law was passed requiring masters to provide white servants whose indenture time was up with ten bushels of corn, thirty shillings, and a gun, while women servants were to get 15 bushels of corn and forty shillings. Also, the newly freed servants were to get 50 acres of land.

Morgan concludes: "Once the small planter felt less exploited by taxation and began to prosper a little, he became less turbulent, less dangerous, more respectable. He could begin to see his big neighbor not as an extortionist but as a powerful protector of their common interests."

We see now a complex web of historical threads to ensnare blacks for slavery in America: the desperation of starving settlers, the special helplessness of the displaced African, the powerful incentive of profit for slave trader and planter, the temptation of superior status for poor whites, the elaborate controls against escape and rebellion, the legal and social punishment of black and white collaboration.

The point is that the elements of this web are historical, not "natural." This does not mean that they are easily disentangled, dismantled. It means only that there is a possibility for something else, under historical conditions not yet realized. And one of these conditions would be the elimination of that class exploitation which has made poor whites desperate for small gifts of status, and has prevented that unity of black and white necessary for joint rebellion and reconstruction.

Around 1700, the Virginia House of Burgesses declared:

The Christian Servants in this country for the most part consists of the Worser Sort of the people of Europe. And since . . . such numbers of Irish and other Nations have been brought in of which a great many have been soldiers in the late warrs that according to our present Circumstances we can hardly governe them and if they were fitted with Armes and had the Opertunity of meeting together by Musters we have just reason to fears they may rise upon us.

It was a kind of class consciousness, a class fear. There were things happening in early Virginia, and in the other colonies, to warrant it.

3

PERSONS OF MEAN AND VILE CONDITION

In 1676, seventy years after Virginia was founded, a hundred years before it supplied leadership for the American Revolution, that colony faced a rebellion of white frontiersmen, joined by slaves and servants, a rebellion so threatening that the governor had to flee the burning capital of Jamestown, and England decided to send a thousand soldiers across the Atlantic, hoping to maintain order among forty thousand colonists. This was Bacon's Rebellion. After the uprising was suppressed, its leader, Nathaniel Bacon, dead, and his associates hanged, Bacon was described in a Royal Commission report:

He was said to be about four or five and thirty years of age, indifferent tall but slender, black-hair'd and of an ominous, pensive, melancholly Aspect, of a pestilent and prevalent Logical discourse tending to atheisme. . . . He seduced the Vulgar and most ignorant people to believe (two thirds of each county being of that Sort) Soe that their whole hearts and hopes were set now upon Bacon. Next he charges the Governour as negligent and wicked, treacherous and incapable, the Lawes and Taxes as unjust and oppressive and cryes up absolute necessity of redress. Thus Bacon encouraged the Tumult and as the unquiet crowd follow and adhere to him, he listeth them as they come in upon a large paper, writing their name circular wise, that their Ringleaders might not be found out. Having connur'd them into this circle, given them Brandy to wind up the charme, and enjoyned them by an oath to stick fast together and to him and the oath being administered, he went and infected New Kent County ripe for Rebellion.

Bacon's Rebellion began with conflict over how to deal with the Indians, who were close by, on the western frontier, constantly threatening. Whites who had been ignored when huge land grants around Jamestown were given away had gone west to find land, and there they encountered Indians. Were those frontier Virginians resentful that the politicos and landed aristocrats who controlled the colony's government in Jamestown first pushed them westward into Indian territory, and then seemed indecisive in fighting the Indians? That might explain the character of their rebellion, not easily classifiable as either antiaristocrat or anti-Indian, because it was both.

And the governor, William Berkeley, and his Jamestown crowd—were they more conciliatory to the Indians (they wooed certain of them as spies and allies) now that they had monopolized the land in the East, could use frontier whites as a buffer, and needed peace? The desperation of the government in suppressing the rebellion seemed to have a double motive: developing an Indian policy which would divide Indians in order to control them (in New England at this very time, Massasoit's son Metacom was threatening to unite Indian tribes, and had done frightening damage to Puritan settlements in "King Philip's War"); and teaching the poor whites of Virginia that rebellion did not pay—by a show of superior force, by calling for troops from England itself, by mass hanging.

Violence had escalated on the frontier before the rebellion. Some Doeg Indians took a few hogs to redress a debt, and whites, retrieving the hogs, murdered two Indians. The Doegs then sent out a war party to kill a white herdsman, after which a white militia company killed twenty-four Indians. This led to a series of Indian raids, with the Indians, outnumbered, turning to guerrilla warfare. The House of Burgesses in Jamestown declared war on the Indians, but proposed to exempt those Indians who cooperated. This seemed to anger the frontierspeople, who wanted total war but also resented the high taxes assessed to pay for the war.

Times were hard in 1676. "There was genuine distress, genuine poverty. . . . All contemporary sources speak of the great mass of people as living in severe economic straits," writes Wilcomb Washburn, who, using British colonial records, has done an exhaustive study of Bacon's Rebellion. It was a dry summer, ruining the corn crop, which was needed for food, and the tobacco crop, needed for export. Governor Berkeley, in his seventies, tired of holding office, wrote wearily about his situation: "How miserable that man is that Governes a People where six parts of seaven at least are Poore Endebted Discontented and Armed."

His phrase "six parts of seaven" suggests the existence of an upper class not so impoverished. In fact, there was such a class already developed in Virginia. Bacon himself came from this class, had a good bit of land, and was probably more enthusiastic about killing Indians than about redressing the grievances of the poor. But he became a symbol of mass resentment against the Virginia establishment, and was elected in the spring of 1676 to the House of Burgesses. When he insisted on organizing armed detachments to fight the Indians, outside official control, Berkeley proclaimed him a rebel and had him captured, whereupon two thousand Virginians marched into Jamestown to support him. Berkeley let Bacon go, in return for an apology, but Bacon went off, gathered his militia, and began raiding the Indians.

Bacon's "Declaration of the People" of July 1676 shows a mixture of populist resentment against the rich and frontier hatred of the Indians. It indicted the Berkeley administration for unjust taxes, for putting favorites in high positions, for monopolizing the beaver trade, and for not protecting the western farmers from the Indians. Then Bacon went out to attack the friendly Pamunkey Indians, killing eight, taking others prisoner, plundering their possessions.

There is evidence that the rank and file of both Bacon's rebel army and Berkeley's official army were not as enthusiastic as their leaders. There were mass desertions on both sides, according to Washburn. In the fall, Bacon, aged twenty-nine, fell sick and died, because of, as a contemporary put it, "swarmes of Vermyn that bred in his body." A minister, apparently not a sympathizer, wrote this epitaph:

Bacon is Dead I am sorry at my heart
That lice and flux should take the hangmans part.

The rebellion didn't last long after that. A ship armed with thirty guns, cruising the York River, became the base for securing order, and its captain, Thomas Grantham, used force and deception to disarm the last rebel forces. Coming upon the chief garrison of the rebellion, he found four hundred armed Englishmen and Negroes, a mixture of free men, servants, and slaves. He promised to pardon everyone, to give freedom to slaves and servants, whereupon they surrendered their arms and dispersed, except for eighty Negroes and twenty English who insisted on keeping their arms. Grantham promised to take them to a garrison down the river, but when they got into the boat, he trained his big guns on them, disarmed them, and eventually delivered the slaves and servants to their masters. The remaining garrisons were overcome one by one. Twenty-three rebel leaders were hanged.

It was a complex chain of oppression in Virginia. The Indians were plundered by white frontiersmen, who were taxed and controlled by the Jamestown elite. And the whole colony was being exploited by England, which bought the colonists' tobacco at prices it dictated and made 100,000 pounds a year for the King. Berkeley himself, returning to England years earlier to protest the English Navigation Acts, which gave English merchants a monopoly of the colonial trade, had said:

> . . . we cannot but resent, that forty thousand people should be impoverish'd to enrich little more than forty Merchants, who being the only buyers of our Tobacco, give us what they please for it, and after it is here, sell it how they please; and indeed have forty thousand servants in us at cheaper rates, than any other men have slaves. . . .

From the testimony of the governor himself, the rebellion against him had the overwhelming support of the Virginia population. A member of his Council reported that the defection was "almost general" and laid it to "the Lewd dispositions of some Persons of desperate Fortunes" who had "the Vaine hopes of takeing the Countrey wholley out of his Majesty's handes into their owne." Another member of the Governor's Council, Richard Lee, noted that Bacon's Rebellion had started over Indian policy. But the "zealous inclination of the multitude" to support Bacon was due, he said, to "hopes of levelling."

"Levelling" meant equalizing the wealth. Levelling was to be behind countless actions of poor whites against the rich in all the English colonies, in the century and a half before the Revolution.

The servants who joined Bacon's Rebellion were part of a large underclass of miserably poor whites who came to the North American colonies from European cities whose governments were anxious to be rid of them. In England, the development of commerce and capitalism in the 1500s and 1600s, the enclosing of land for the production of wool, filled the cities with vagrant poor, and from the reign of Elizabeth on, laws were passed to punish them, imprison them in workhouses, or exile them. The Elizabethan definition of "rogues and vagabonds" included:

> . . . All persons calling themselves Schollers going about begging, all Seafaring men pretending losses of their Shippes or goods on the sea going about the Country begging, all idle persons going about in any Country either begging or using any subtile crafte or unlawful Games . . . comon Players of Interludes and Minstrells wandring abroad . . . all wandering

persons and comon Labourers being persons able in bodye using loytering and refusing to worke for such reasonable wages as is taxed or commonly given. . . .

Such persons found begging could be stripped to the waist and whipped bloody, could be sent out of the city, sent to workhouses, or transported out of the country.

In the 1600s and 1700s, by forced exile, by lures, promises, and lies, by kidnapping, by their urgent need to escape the living conditions of the home country, poor people wanting to go to America became commodities of profit for merchants, traders, ship captains, and eventually their masters in America. Abbot Smith, in his study of indentured servitude, *Colonists in Bondage,* writes: "From the complex pattern of forces producing emigration to the American colonies one stands out clearly as most powerful in causing the movement of servants. This was the pecuniary profit to be made by shipping them."

After signing the indenture, in which the immigrants agreed to pay their cost of passage by working for a master for five or seven years, they were often imprisoned until the ship sailed, to make sure they did not run away. In the year 1619, the Virginia House of Burgesses, born that year as the first representative assembly in America (it was also the year of the first importation of black slaves), provided for the recording and enforcing of contracts between servants and masters. As in any contract between unequal powers, the parties appeared on paper as equals, but enforcement was far easier for master than for servant.

The voyage to America lasted eight, tén, or twelve weeks, and the servants were packed into ships with the same fanatic concern for profits that marked the slave ships. If the weather was bad, and the trip took too long, they ran out of food. The sloop *Sea-Flower,* leaving Belfast in 1741, was at sea sixteen weeks, and when it arrived in Boston, forty-six of its 106 passengers were dead of starvation, six of them eaten by the survivors. On another trip, thirty-two children died of hunger and disease and were thrown into the ocean. Gottlieb Mittelberger, a musician, traveling from Germany to America around 1750, wrote about his voyage:

During the journey the ship is full of pitiful signs of distress—smells, fumes, horrors, vomiting, various kinds of sea sickness, fever, dysentery, headaches, heat, constipation, boils, scurvy, cancer, mouth-rot, and similar afflictions, all of them caused by the age and the high salted state of the food, especially of the meat, as well as by the very bad and filthy water. . . . Add to all that shortage of food, hunger, thirst, frost, heat, dampness, fear, misery, vexation, and lamentation as well as other troubles. . . . On board our ship, on a day on which we had a great storm, a woman about to give birth and unable to deliver under the circumstances, was pushed through one of the portholes into the sea. . . .

Indentured servants were bought and sold like slaves. An announcement in the *Virginia Gazette*, March 28, 1771, read:

Just arrived at Leedstown, the Ship Justitia, with about one Hundred Healthy Servants, Men Women & Boys. . . . The Sale will commence on Tuesday the 2nd of April.

Against the rosy accounts of better living standards in the Americas one must place many others, like one immigrant's letter from America: "Whoever is well off in Europe better remain there. Here is misery and distress, same as everywhere, and for certain persons and conditions incomparably more than in Europe."

Beatings and whippings were common. Servant women were raped. One observer testified: "I have seen an Overseer beat a Servant with a cane about the head till the blood has followed, for a fault that is not worth the speaking of. . . ." The Maryland court records showed many servant suicides. In 1671, Governor Berkeley of Virginia reported that in previous years four of five servants died of disease after their arrival. Many were poor children, gathered up by the hundreds on the streets of English cities and sent to Virginia to work.

The master tried to control completely the sexual lives of the servants. It was in his economic interest to keep women servants from marrying or from having sexual relations, because childbearing would interfere with work. Benjamin Franklin, writing as "Poor Richard" in 1736, gave advice to his readers: "Let thy maidservant be faithful, strong and homely."

Servants could not marry without permission, could be separated from their families, could be whipped for various offenses. Pennsylvania law in the seventeenth century said that marriage of servants "without the consent of the Masters . . . shall be proceeded against as for Adultery, or fornication, and Children to be reputed as Bastards."

Although colonial laws existed to stop excesses against servants, they were not very well enforced, we learn from Richard Morris's comprehensive study of early court records in *Government and Labor in Early America*. Servants did not participate in juries. Masters did. (And being propertyless, servants did not vote.) In 1666, a New England court accused a couple of the death of a servant after the mistress had cut off the servant's toes. The jury voted acquittal. In Virginia in the 1660s, a master was convicted of raping two women servants. He also was known to beat his own wife and children; he had whipped and chained another servant until he died. The master was berated by the court, but specifically cleared on the rape charge, despite overwhelming evidence.

Sometimes servants organized rebellions, but one did not find on the mainland the kind of large-scale conspiracies of servants that existed, for instance, on Barbados in the West Indies. (Abbot Smith suggests this was because there was more chance of success on a small island.)

However, in York County, Virginia, in 1661, a servant named Isaac Friend proposed to another, after much dissatisfaction with the food, that they "get a matter of Forty of them together, and get Gunnes & hee would be the first & lead them and cry as they went along, 'who would be for Liberty, and free from bondage', & that there would enough come to them and they would goe through the Countrey and kill those that made any opposition and that they would either be free or dye for it." The scheme was never carried out, but two years later, in Gloucester County, servants again planned a general uprising. One of them gave the plot away, and four were executed. The informer was given his freedom and 5,000 pounds of tobacco. Despite the rarity of servants' rebellions, the threat was always there, and masters were fearful.

Finding their situation intolerable, and rebellion impractical in an increasingly organized society, servants reacted in individual ways. The files of the county courts in New England show that one servant struck at his master with a pitchfork. An apprentice servant was accused of "laying violent hands upon his ... master, and throwing him downe twice and feching bloud of him, threatening to breake his necke, running at his face with a chayre. . . ." One maidservant was brought into court for being "bad, unruly, sulen, careles, destructive, and disobedient."

After the participation of servants in Bacon's Rebellion, the Virginia legislature passed laws to punish servants who rebelled. The preamble to the act said:

> Whereas many evil disposed servants in these late tymes of horrid rebellion taking advantage of the loosnes and liberty of the tyme, did depart from their service, and followed the rebells in rebellion, wholy neglecting their masters imployment whereby the said masters have suffered great damage and injury. . . .

Two companies of English soldiers remained in Virginia to guard against future trouble, and their presence was defended in a report to the Lords of Trade and Plantation saying: "Virginia is at present poor and more populous than ever. There is great apprehension of a rising among the servants, owing to their great necessities and want of clothes; they may plunder the storehouses and ships."

Escape was easier than rebellion. "Numerous instances of mass desertions by white servants took place in the Southern colonies," reports Richard Morris, on the basis of an inspection of colonial newspapers in the 1700s. "The atmosphere of seventeenth-century Virginia," he says, "was charged with plots and rumors of combinations of servants to run away." The Maryland court records show, in the 1650s, a conspiracy of a dozen servants to seize a boat and to resist with arms if intercepted. They were captured and whipped.

The mechanism of control was formidable. Strangers had to show passports or certificates to prove they were free men. Agreements among the colonies provided for the extradition of fugitive servants—these became the basis of the clause in the U.S. Constitution that persons "held to Service or Labor in one State . . . escaping into another . . . shall be delivered up. . . ."

Sometimes, servants went on strike. One Maryland master complained to the Provincial Court in 1663 that his servants did "peremptorily and positively refuse to goe and doe their ordinary labor." The servants responded that they were fed only "Beanes and Bread" and they were "soe weake, wee are not able to perform the imploym'ts hee puts us uppon." They were given thirty lashes by the court.

More than half the colonists who came to the North American shores in the colonial period came as servants. They were mostly English in the seventeenth century, Irish and German in the eighteenth century. More and more, slaves replaced them, as they ran away to freedom or finished their time, but as late as 1755, white servants made up 10 percent of the population of Maryland.

What happened to these servants after they became free? There are cheerful accounts in which they rise to prosperity, becoming landowners and important figures. But Abbot Smith, after a careful study, concludes that colonial society "was not democratic and certainly not equalitarian; it was dominated by men who had money enough to make others work for them." And: "Few of these men were descended from indentured servants, and practically none had themselves been of that class."

After we make our way through Abbot Smith's disdain for the servants, as "men and women who were dirty and lazy, rough, ignorant, lewd, and often criminal," who "thieved and wandered, had bastard children, and corrupted society with loathsome diseases," we find that "about one in ten was a sound and solid individual, who would if fortunate survive his 'seasoning,' work out his time, take up land, and wax decently prosperous." Perhaps another one in ten would become an artisan or an overseer. The rest, 80 percent, who were "certainly . . . shiftless, hopeless, ruined individuals," either "died during their servitude, returned to England after it was over, or became 'poor whites.'"

Smith's conclusion is supported by a more recent study of servants in seventeenth-century Maryland, where it was found that the first batches of servants became landowners and politically active in the colony, but by the second half of the century more than half the servants, even after ten years of freedom, remained landless. Servants became tenants, providing cheap labor for the large planters both during and after their servitude.

It seems quite clear that class lines hardened through the colonial period; the distinction between rich and poor became sharper. By 1700 there were fifty rich families in Virginia, with wealth equivalent to 50,000 pounds (a huge sum those days), who lived off the labor of black slaves and white servants, owned the plantations, sat on the governor's council, served as local magistrates. In Maryland, the settlers were ruled by a proprietor whose right of total control over the colony had been granted by the English King. Between 1650 and 1689 there were five revolts against the proprietor.

In the Carolinas, the Fundamental Constitutions were written in the 1660s by John Locke, who is often considered the philosophical father of the Founding Fathers and the American system. Locke's constitution set up a feudal-type aristocracy, in which eight barons would own 40 percent of the colony's land, and only a baron could be governor. When the crown took direct control of North Carolina, after a rebellion against the land arrangements, rich speculators seized half a million acres for themselves, monopolizing the good farming land near the coast. Poor people, desperate for land, squatted on bits of farmland and fought all through the pre-Revolutionary period against the landlords' attempts to collect rent.

Carl Bridenbaugh's study of colonial cities, *Cities in the Wilderness*, reveals a clear-cut class system. He finds:

The leaders of early Boston were gentlemen of considerable wealth who, in association with the clergy, eagerly sought to preserve in America the social arrangements of the Mother Country. By means of their control of trade and commerce, by their political domination of the inhabitants through church and Town Meeting, and by careful marriage alliances among themselves, members of this little oligarchy laid the foundations for an aristocratic class in seventeenth century Boston.

At the very start of the Massachusetts Bay Colony in 1630, the governor, John Winthrop, had declared the philosophy of the rulers: ". . . in all times some must be rich, some poore, some highe and eminent in power and dignitie; others meane and in subjection."

Rich merchants erected mansions; persons "of Qualitie" traveled in coaches or sedan chairs, had their portraits painted, wore periwigs, and filled themselves with rich food and Madeira. A petition came from the town of Deerfield in 1678 to the Massachusetts General Court: "You may be pleased to know that the very principle and best of the land; the best for soile; the best for situation; as laying in ye center and midle of the town: and as to quantity, nere half, belongs unto eight or nine proprietors. . . ."

In Newport, Rhode Island, Bridenbaugh found, as in Boston, that "the town meetings, while ostensibly democratic, were in reality controlled year after year by the same group of merchant aristocrats, who secured most of the important offices. . . ." A contemporary described the Newport merchants as ". . . men in flaming scarlet coats and waistcoats, laced and fringed with brightest glaring yellow. The Sly Quakers, not venturing on these charming coats and waistcoats, yet loving finery, figured away with plate on their sideboards."

The New York aristocracy was the most ostentatious of all. Bridenbaugh tells of "window hangings of camlet, japanned tables, gold-framed looking glasses, spinets and massive eight-day clocks . . . richly carved furniture, jewels and silverplate. . . . Black house servants."

New York in the colonial period was like a feudal kingdom. The Dutch had set up a patroonship system along the Hudson River, with enormous landed estates, where the barons controlled completely the lives of their tenants. In 1689, many of the grievances of the poor were mixed up in the farmers' revolt of Jacob Leisler and his group. Leisler was hanged, and the parceling out of huge estates continued. Under Governor Benjamin Fletcher, three-fourths of the land in New York was granted to about thirty people. He gave a friend a half million acres for a token annual payment of 30 shillings. Under Lord Cornbury in the early 1700s, one grant to a group of speculators was for 2 million acres.

In 1700, New York City church wardens had asked for funds from the common council because "the Crys of the poor and Impotent for want of Relief are Extreamly Grevious." In the 1730s, demand began to grow for institutions to contain the "many Beggarly people daily suffered to wander about the Streets." A city council resolution read:

> Whereas the Necessity, Number and Continual Increase of the Poor within this City is very Great and . . . frequently Commit divers misdemeanors within the Said City, who living Idly and unimployed, become debauched and Instructed in the Practice of Thievery and Debauchery. For Remedy Whereof . . . Resolved that there be forthwith built . . . A good, Strong and Convenient House and Tenement.

The two-story brick structure was called "Poor House, Work House, and House of Correction."

A letter to Peter Zenger's New York *Journal* in 1737 described the poor street urchin of New York as "an Object in Human Shape, half starv'd with Cold, with Cloathes out at the Elbows, Knees through the Breeches, Hair standing on end. . . . From the age about four to Fourteen they spend their Days in the Streets . . . then they are put out as Apprentices, perhaps four, five, or six years. . . ."

The colonies grew fast in the 1700s. English settlers were joined by Scotch-Irish and German immigrants. Black slaves were pouring in; they were 8 percent of the population in 1690; 21 percent in 1770. The population of the colonies was 250,000 in 1700; 1,600,000 by 1760. Agriculture was growing. Small manufacturing was developing. Shipping and trading were expanding. The big cities—Boston, New York, Philadelphia, Charleston—were doubling and tripling in size.

Through all that growth, the upper class was getting most of the benefits and monopolized political power. A historian who studied Boston tax lists in 1687 and 1771 found that in 1687 there were, out of a population of six thousand, about one thousand property owners, and that the top 5 percent—1 percent of the population—consisted of fifty rich individuals who had 25 percent of the wealth. By 1770, the top 1 percent of property owners owned 44 percent of the wealth.

As Boston grew, from 1687 to 1770, the percentage of adult males who were poor, perhaps rented a room, or slept in the back of a tavern, owned no property, doubled from 14 percent of the adult males to 29 percent. And loss of property meant loss of voting rights.

Everywhere the poor were struggling to stay alive, simply to keep from freezing in cold weather. All the cities built poorhouses in the 1730s, not just for old people, widows, crippled, and orphans, but for unemployed, war veterans, new immigrants. In New York, at midcentury, the city almshouse, built for one hundred poor, was housing over four hundred. A Philadelphia citizen wrote in 1748: "It is remarkable what an increase of the number of Beggars there is about this town this winter." In 1757, Boston officials spoke of "a great Number of Poor . . . who can scarcely procure from day to day daily Bread for themselves & Families."

Kenneth Lockridge, in a study of colonial New England, found that vagabonds and paupers kept increasing and "the wandering poor" were a distinct fact of New England life in the middle 1700s. James T. Lemon and Gary Nash found a similar concentration of wealth, a widening of the gap between rich and poor, in their study of Chester County, Pennsylvania, in the 1700s.

The colonies, it seems, were societies of contending classes—a fact obscured by the emphasis, in traditional histories, on the external struggle against England, the unity of colonists in the Revolution. The country therefore was not "born free" but born slave and free, servant and master, tenant and landlord, poor and rich. As a result, the political authorities were opposed "frequently, vociferously, and sometimes violently," according to Nash. "Outbreaks of disorder punctuated the last quarter of the seventeenth century, toppling established governments in Massachusetts, New York, Maryland, Virginia, and North Carolina."

Free white workers were better off than slaves or servants, but they still resented unfair treatment by the wealthier classes. As early as 1636, an employer off the coast of Maine reported that his workmen and fishermen "fell into a mutiny" because he had withheld their wages. They deserted en masse. Five years later, carpenters in Maine, protesting against inadequate food, engaged in a slowdown. At the Gloucester shipyards in the 1640s, what Richard Morris calls the "first lockout in American labor history" took place when the authorities told a group of troublesome shipwrights they could not "worke a stroke of worke more."

There were early strikes of coopers, butchers, bakers, protesting against government control of the fees they charged. Porters in the 1650s in New York refused to carry salt, and carters (truckers, teamsters, carriers) who went out on strike were prosecuted in New York City "for not obeying the Command and Doing their Dutyes as becomes them in their Places." In 1741, bakers combined to refuse to bake because they had to pay such high prices for wheat.

A severe food shortage in Boston in 1713 brought a warning from town selectmen to the General Assembly of Massachusetts saying the "threatening scarcity of provisions" had led to such "extravagant prices that the necessities of the poor in the approaching winter must needs be very pressing." Andrew Belcher, a wealthy merchant, was exporting grain to the Caribbean because the profit was greater there. On May 19, two hundred people rioted on the Boston Common. They attacked Belcher's ships, broke into his warehouses looking for corn, and shot the lieutenant governor when he tried to interfere.

Eight years after the bread riot on the Common, a pamphleteer protested against those who became rich "by grinding the poor," by studying "how to oppress, cheat, and overreach their neighbors." He denounced "The Rich, Great and Potent" who "with rapacious violence bear down all before them. . . ."

In the 1730s, in Boston, people protesting the high prices established by merchants demolished the public market in Dock Square while (as a conservative writer complained) "murmuring against the Government & the rich people." No one was arrested, after the demonstrators warned that arrests would bring "Five Hundred Men in Solemn League and Covenent" who would destroy other markets set up for the benefit of rich merchants.

Around the same time, in New York, an election pamphlet urged New York voters to join "Shuttle" the weaver, "Plane" the joiner, "Drive" the carter, "Mortar" the mason, "Tar" the mariner, "Snip" the tailor, "Smallrent" the fair-minded landlord, and "John Poor" the tenant, against "Gripe the Merchant, Squeeze the Shopkeeper, Spintext and Quible the Lawyer." The electorate was urged to vote out of office "people in Exalted Stations" who scorned "those they call the Vulgar, the Mob, the herd of Mechanicks."

In the 1730s, a committee of the Boston town meeting spoke out for Bostonians in debt, who wanted paper money issued to make it easier to pay off their debts to the merchant elite. They did not want, they declared, to "have our Bread and Water measured out to Us by those who Riot in Luxury & Wantonness on Our Sweat & Toil. . . ."

Bostonians rioted also against impressment, in which men were drafted for naval service. They surrounded the house of the governor, beat up the sheriff, locked up a deputy sheriff, and stormed the town house where the General Court sat. The militia did not respond when called to put them down, and the governor fled. The crowd was condemned by a merchants' group as a "Riotous Tumultuous Assembly of Foreign Seamen, Servants, Negroes, and Other Persons of Mean and Vile Condition."

In New Jersey in the 1740s and 1750s, poor farmers occupying land, over which they and the landowners had rival claims, rioted when rents were demanded of them. In 1745, Samuel Baldwin, who had long lived on his land and who held an Indian title to it, was arrested for nonpayment of rent to the proprietor and taken to the Newark jail. A contemporary described what happened then: "The People in general, supposing the Design of the Proprietors was to ruin them ... went to the Prison, opened the Door, took out Baldwin."

When two men who freed Baldwin were arrested, hundreds of New Jersey citizens gathered around the jail. A report sent by the New Jersey government to the Lords of Trade in London described the scene:

> Two of the new captains of the Newark Companies by the Sheriff's order went with their drumms, to the people, so met, and required all persons there, belong to their companies, to follow the drums and to defend the prison but none followed, tho many were there. . . . The multitude . . . between four and five of the clock in the afternoon lighted off their horses, and came towards the gaol, huzzaing and swinging their clubbs . . . till they came within reach of the guard, struck them with their clubbs, and the guard (having no orders to fire) returned the blows with their guns, and some were wounded on both sides, but none killed. The multitude broke the ranks of the soldiers, and pressed on the prison door, where the Sheriff stood with a sword, and kept them off, till they gave him several blows, and forced him out from thence. They then, with axes and other instruments, broke open the prison door, and took out the two prisoners. As also one other prisoner, that was confined for debt, and went away.

Through this period, England was fighting a series of wars (Queen Anne's War in the early 1700s, King George's War in the 1730s). Some merchants made fortunes from these wars, but for most people they meant higher taxes, unemployment, poverty. An anonymous pamphleteer in Massachusetts, writing angrily after King George's War, described the situation: "Poverty and Discontent appear in every Face (except the Countenances of the Rich) and dwell upon every Tongue." He spoke of a few men, fed by "Lust of Power, Lust of Fame, Lust of Money," who got rich during the war. "No Wonder such Men can build Ships, Houses, buy Farms, set up their Coaches, Chariots, live very splendidly, purchase Fame, Posts of Honour." He called them "Birds of prey . . . Enemies to all Communities—wherever they live."

The forced service of seamen led to a riot against impressment in Boston in 1747. Then crowds turned against Thomas Hutchinson, a rich merchant and colonial official who had backed the governor in putting down the riot, and who also designed a currency plan for

Massachusetts which seemed to discriminate against the poor. Hutchinson's house burned down, mysteriously, and a crowd gathered in the street, cursing Hutchinson and shouting, "Let it burn!"

By the years of the Revolutionary crisis, the 1760s, the wealthy elite that controlled the British colonies on the American mainland had 150 years of experience, had learned certain things about how to rule. They had various fears, but also had developed tactics to deal with what they feared.

The Indians, they had found, were too unruly to keep as a labor force, and remained an obstacle to expansion. Black slaves were easier to control, and their profitability for southern plantations was bringing an enormous increase in the importation of slaves, who were becoming a majority in some colonies and constituted one-fifth of the entire colonial population. But the blacks were not totally submissive, and as their numbers grew, the prospect of slave rebellion grew.

With the problem of Indian hostility, and the danger of slave revolts, the colonial elite had to consider the class anger of poor whites—servants, tenants, the city poor, the propertyless, the taxpayer, the soldier and sailor. As the colonies passed their hundredth year and went into the middle of the 1700s, as the gap between rich and poor widened, as violence and the threat of violence increased, the problem of control became more serious.

What if these different despised groups—the Indians, the slaves, the poor whites—should combine? Even before there were so many blacks, in the seventeenth century, there was, as Abbot Smith puts it, "a lively fear that servants would join with Negroes or Indians to overcome the small number of masters."

There was little chance that whites and Indians would combine in North America as they were doing in South and Central America, where the shortage of women, and the use of Indians on the plantations, led to daily contact. Only in Georgia and South Carolina, where white women were scarce, was there some sexual mixing of white men and Indian women. In general, the Indian had been pushed out of sight, out of touch. One fact disturbed: whites would run off to join Indian tribes, or would be captured in battle and brought up among the Indians, and when this happened the whites, given a chance to leave, chose to stay in the Indian culture. Indians, having the choice, almost never decided to join the whites.

Hector St. Jean Crevecoeur, the Frenchman who lived in America for almost twenty years, told, in *Letters from an American Farmer,* how children captured during the Seven Years' War and found by their parents, grown up and living with Indians, would refuse to leave their new families. "There must be in their social bond," he said, "something singularly captivating, and far superior to anything to be boasted among us; for thousands of Europeans are Indians, and we have no examples of even one of those Aborigines having from choice become Europeans."

But this affected few people. In general, the Indian was kept at a distance. And the colonial officialdom had found a way of alleviating the danger: by monopolizing the good land on the eastern seaboard, they forced landless whites to move westward to the frontier, there to encounter the Indians and to be a buffer for the seaboard rich against Indian troubles, while becoming more dependent on the government for protection. Bacon's Rebellion was instructive: to conciliate a diminishing Indian population at the expense of infuriating a coalition of white frontiersmen was very risky. Better to make war on the Indian, gain the support of the white, divert possible class conflict by turning poor whites against Indians for the security of the elite.

Might blacks and Indians combine against the white enemy? In the northern colonies (except on Cape Cod, Martha's Vineyard, and Rhode Island, where there was close contact and sexual mixing), there was not much opportunity for Africans and Indians to meet in large numbers. New York had the largest slave population in the North, and there was some contact between blacks and Indians, as in 1712 when Africans and Indians joined in an insurrection. But this was quickly suppressed.

In the Carolinas, however, whites were outnumbered by black slaves and nearby Indian tribes; in the 1750s, 25,000 whites faced 40,000 black slaves, with 60,000 Creek, Cherokee, Choctaw, and Chickasaw Indians in the area. Gary Nash writes: "Indian uprisings that punctuated the colonial period and a succession of slave uprisings and insurrectionary plots that were nipped in the bud kept South Carolinians sickeningly aware that only through the greatest vigilance and through policies designed to keep their enemies divided could they hope to remain in control of the situation."

The white rulers of the Carolinas seemed to be conscious of the need for a policy, as one of them put it, "to make Indians & Negros a checque upon each other lest by their Vastly Superior Numbers we should be crushed by one or the other." And so laws were passed prohibiting free blacks from traveling in Indian country. Treaties with Indian tribes contained clauses requiring the return of fugitive slaves. Governor Lyttletown of South Carolina wrote in 1738: "It has allways been the policy of this government to create an aversion in them [Indians] to Negroes."

Part of this policy involved using black slaves in the South Carolina militia to fight Indians. Still, the government was worried about black revolt, and during the Cherokee war in the 1760s, a motion to equip five hundred slaves to fight the Indians lost in the Carolina assembly by a single vote.

Blacks ran away to Indian villages, and the Creeks and Cherokees harbored runaway slaves by the hundreds. Many of these were amalgamated into the Indian tribes, married, produced children. But the combination of harsh slave codes and bribes to the Indians to help put down black rebels kept things under control.

It was the potential combination of poor whites and blacks that caused the most fear among the wealthy white planters. If there had been the natural racial repugnance that some theorists have assumed, control would have been easier. But sexual attraction was powerful, across racial lines. In 1743, a grand jury in Charleston, South Carolina, denounced "The Too Common Practice of Criminal Conversation with Negro and other Slave Wenches in this Province." Mixed offspring continued to be produced by white-black sex relations throughout the colonial period, in spite of laws prohibiting interracial marriage in Virginia, Massachusetts, Maryland, Delaware, Pennsylvania, the Carolinas, Georgia. By declaring the children illegitimate, they would keep them inside the black families, so that the white population could remain "pure" and in control.

What made Bacon's Rebellion especially fearsome for the rulers of Virginia was that black slaves and white servants joined forces. The final surrender was by "four hundred English and Negroes in Armes" at one garrison, and three hundred "freemen and African and English bond-servants" in another garrison. The naval commander who subdued the four hundred wrote: "Most of them I persuaded to goe to their Homes, which accordingly they did, except about eighty Negroes and twenty English which would not deliver their Armes."

All through those early years, black and white slaves and servants ran away together, as shown both by the laws passed to stop this and the records of the courts. In 1698, South Carolina passed a "deficiency law" requiring plantation owners to have at least one white servant for every six male adult Negroes. A letter from the southern colonies in 1682 complained of "no white men to superintend our negroes, or repress an insurrection of negroes. . . ." In 1691, the House of Commons received "a petition of divers merchants, masters of ships, planters and others, trading to foreign plantations . . . setting forth, that the plantations cannot be maintained without a considerable number of white servants, as well to keep the blacks in subjection, as to bear arms in case of invasion."

A report to the English government in 1721 said that in South Carolina "black slaves have lately attempted and were very near succeeding in a new revolution . . . and therefore, it may be necessary . . . to propose some new law for encouraging the entertainment of more white servants in the future. The militia of this province does not consist of above 2000 men." Apparently, two thousand were not considered sufficient to meet the threat.

This fear may help explain why Parliament, in 1717, made transportation to the New World a legal punishment for crime. After that, tens of thousands of convicts could be sent to Virginia, Maryland, and other colonies. It also makes understandable why the Virginia Assembly, after Bacon's Rebellion, gave amnesty to white servants who had rebelled, but not to blacks. Negroes were forbidden to carry any arms, while whites finishing their servitude would get muskets, along with corn and cash. The distinctions of status between white and black servants became more and more clear.

In the 1720s, with fear of slave rebellion growing, white servants were allowed in Virginia to join the militia as substitutes for white freemen. At the same time, slave patrols were established in Virginia to deal with the "great dangers that may . . . happen by the insurrections of negroes. . . ." Poor white men would make up the rank and file of these patrols, and get the monetary reward.

Racism was becoming more and more practical. Edmund Morgan, on the basis of his careful study of slavery in Virginia, sees racism not as "natural" to black-white difference, but something coming out of class scorn, a realistic device for control. "If freemen with disappointed hopes should make common cause with slaves of desperate hope, the results might be worse than anything Bacon had done. The answer to the problem, obvious if unspoken and only gradually recognized, was racism, to separate dangerous free whites from dangerous black slaves by a screen of racial contempt."

There was still another control which became handy as the colonies grew, and which had crucial consequences for the continued rule of the elite throughout American history. Along with the very rich and the very poor, there developed a white middle class of small planters, independent farmers, city artisans, who, given small rewards for joining forces with merchants and planters, would be a solid buffer against black slaves, frontier Indians, and very poor whites.

The growing cities generated more skilled workers, and the governments cultivated the support of white mechanics by protecting them from the competition of both slaves and free Negroes. As early as 1686, the council in New York ordered that "noe Negro or Slave be suffered to work on the bridge as a Porter about any goods either imported or Exported from or into this Citty." In the southern towns too, white craftsmen and traders were protected from Negro competition. In 1764 the South Carolina legislature prohibited Charleston masters from employing Negroes or other slaves as mechanics or in handicraft trades.

Middle-class Americans might be invited to join a new elite by attacks against the corruption of the established rich. The New Yorker Cadwallader Colden, in his *Address to the Freeholders* in 1747, attacked the wealthy as tax dodgers unconcerned with the welfare of others (although he himself was wealthy) and spoke for the honesty and dependability of "the midling rank of mankind" in whom citizens could best trust "our liberty & Property." This was to become a critically important rhetorical device for the rule of the few, who would speak to the many of "our" liberty, "our" property, "our" country.

Similarly, in Boston, the rich James Otis could appeal to the Boston middle class by attacking the Tory Thomas Hutchinson. James Henretta has shown that while it was the rich who ruled Boston, there were political jobs available for the moderately well-off, as "cullers of staves," "measurer of Coal Baskets," "Fence Viewer." Aubrey Land found in Maryland a class of small planters who were not "the beneficiary" of the planting society as the rich were, but who had the distinction of being called planters, and who were "respectable citizens with community obligations to act as overseers of roads, appraisers of estates and similar duties." It helped the alliance to accept the middle class socially in "a round of activities that included local politics . . . dances, horseracing, and cockfights, occasionally punctuated with drinking brawls. . . ."

The *Pennsylvania Journal* wrote in 1756: "The people of this province are generally of the middling sort, and at present pretty much upon a level. They are chiefly industrious farmers, artificers or men in trade; they enjoy and are fond of freedom, and the meanest among them thinks he has a right to civility from the greatest." Indeed, there was a substantial middle class fitting that description. To call them "the people" was to omit black slaves, white servants, displaced Indians. And the term "middle class" concealed a fact long true about this country, that, as Richard Hofstadter said: "It was . . . a middle-class society governed for the most part by its upper classes."

Those upper classes, to rule, needed to make concessions to the middle class, without damage to their own wealth or power, at the expense of slaves, Indians, and poor whites. This bought loyalty. And to bind that loyalty with something more powerful even than material advantage, the ruling group found, in the 1760s and 1770s, a wonderfully useful device. That device was the language of liberty and equality, which could unite just enough whites to fight a Revolution against England, without ending either slavery or inequality.

4

TYRANNY IS TYRANNY

Around 1776, certain important people in the English colonies made a discovery that would prove enormously useful for the next two hundred years. They found that by creating a nation, a symbol, a legal unity called the United States, they could take over land, profits, and political power from favorites of the British Empire. In the process, they could hold back a number of potential rebellions and create a consensus of popular support for the rule of a new, privileged leadership.

When we look at the American Revolution this way, it was a work of genius, and the Founding Fathers deserve the awed tribute they have received over the centuries. They created the most effective system of national control devised in modern times, and showed future generations of leaders the advantages of combining paternalism with command.

Starting with Bacon's Rebellion in Virginia, by 1760, there had been eighteen uprisings aimed at overthrowing colonial governments. There had also been six black rebellions, from South Carolina to New York, and forty riots of various origins.

By this time also, there emerged, according to Jack Greene, "stable, coherent, effective and acknowledged local political and social elites." And by the 1760s, this local leadership saw the possibility of directing much of the rebellious energy against England and her local officials. It was not a conscious conspiracy, but an accumulation of tactical responses.

After 1763, with England victorious over France in the Seven Years' War (known in America as the French and Indian War), expelling them from North America, ambitious colonial leaders were no longer threatened by the French. They now had only two rivals left: the English and the Indians. The British, wooing the Indians, had declared Indian lands beyond the Appalachians out of bounds to whites (the Proclamation of 1763). Perhaps once the British were out of the way, the Indians could be dealt with. Again, no conscious forethought strategy by the colonial elite, but a growing awareness as events developed.

With the French defeated, the British government could turn its attention to tightening control over the colonies. It needed revenues to pay for the war, and looked to the colonies for that. Also, the colonial trade had become more and more important to the British economy, and more profitable: it had amounted to about 500,000 pounds in 1700 but by 1770 was worth 2,800,000 pounds.

So, the American leadership was less in need of English rule, the English more in need of the colonists' wealth. The elements were there for conflict.

The war had brought glory for the generals, death to the privates, wealth for the merchants, unemployment for the poor. There were 25,000 people living in New York (there had been 7,000 in 1720) when the French and Indian War ended. A newspaper editor wrote about the growing "Number of Beggers and wandering Poor" in the streets of the city. Letters in the papers questioned the distribution of wealth: "How often have our Streets been covered with Thousands of Barrels of Flour for trade, while our near Neighbors can hardly procure enough to make a Dumplin to satisfy hunger?"

Gary Nash's study of city tax lists shows that by the early 1770s, the top 5 percent of Boston's taxpayers controlled 49% of the city's taxable assets. In Philadelphia and New York too, wealth was more and more concentrated. Court-recorded wills showed that by 1750 the wealthiest people in the cities were leaving 20,000 pounds (equivalent to about $5 million today).

In Boston, the lower classes began to use the town meeting to vent their grievances. The governor of Massachusetts had written that in these town meetings "the meanest Inhabitants . . . by their constant Attendance there generally are the majority and outvote the Gentlemen, Merchants, Substantial Traders and all the better part of the Inhabitants."

What seems to have happened in Boston is that certain lawyers, editors, and merchants of the upper classes, but excluded from the ruling circles close to England—men like James Otis and Samuel Adams—organized a "Boston Caucus" and through their oratory and their writing "molded laboring-class opinion, called the 'mob' into action, and shaped its behaviour." This is Gary Nash's description of Otis, who, he says, "keenly aware of the declining fortunes and the resentment of ordinary townspeople, was mirroring as well as molding popular opinion."

We have here a forecast of the long history of American politics, the mobilization of lower-class energy by upper-class politicians, for their own purposes. This was not purely deception; it involved, in part, a genuine recognition of lower-class grievances, which helps to account for its effectiveness as a tactic over the centuries. As Nash puts it:

> James Otis, Samuel Adams, Royall Tyler, Oxenbridge Thacher, and a host of other Bostonians, linked to the artisans and laborers through a network of neighborhood taverns, fire companies, and the Caucus, espoused a vision of politics that gave credence to laboring-class views and regarded as entirely legitimate the participation of artisans and even laborers in the political process.

In 1762, Otis, speaking against the conservative rulers of the Massachusetts colony represented by Thomas Hutchinson, gave an example of the kind of rhetoric that a lawyer could use in mobilizing city mechanics and artisans:

> I am forced to get my living by the labour of my hand; and the sweat of my brow, as most of you are and obliged to go thro' good report and evil report, for bitter bread, earned under the frowns of some who have no natural or divine right to be above me, and entirely owe their grandeur and honor to grinding the faces of the poor. . . .

Boston seems to have been full of class anger in those days. In 1763, in the Boston *Gazette*, someone wrote that "a few persons in power" were promoting political projects "for keeping the people poor in order to make them humble."

This accumulated sense of grievance against the rich in Boston may account for the explosiveness of mob action after the Stamp Act of 1765. Through this Act, the British were taxing the colonial population to pay for the French war, in which colonists had suffered to expand the British Empire. That summer, a shoemaker named Ebenezer MacIntosh led a mob in destroying the house of a rich Boston merchant named Andrew Oliver. Two weeks later, the crowd turned to the home of Thomas Hutchinson, symbol of the rich elite who ruled the colonies in the name of England. They smashed up his house with axes, drank the wine in his wine cellar, and looted the house of its furniture and other objects. A report by colony officials to England said that this was part of a larger scheme in which the houses of fifteen rich people were to be destroyed, as part of "a War of Plunder, of general levelling and taking away the Distinction of rich and poor."

It was one of those moments in which fury against the rich went further than leaders like Otis wanted. Could class hatred be focused against the pro-British elite, and deflected from the nationalist elite? In New York, that same year of the Boston house attacks, someone wrote to the New York *Gazette*, "Is it equitable that 99, rather 999, should suffer for the Extravagance or Grandeur of one, especially when it is considered that men frequently owe their Wealth to the impoverishment of their Neighbors?" The leaders of the Revolution would worry about keeping such sentiments within limits.

Mechanics were demanding political democracy in the colonial cities: open meetings of representative assemblies, public galleries in the legislative halls, and the publishing of roll-call votes, so that constituents could check on representatives. They wanted open-air meetings where the population could participate in making policy, more equitable taxes, price controls, and the election of mechanics and other ordinary people to government posts.

Especially in Philadelphia, according to Nash, the consciousness of the lower middle classes grew to the point where it must have caused some hard thinking, not just among the conservative Loyalists sympathetic to England, but even among leaders of the Revolution. "By mid-1776, laborers, artisans, and small tradesmen, employing extralegal measures when electoral politics failed, were in clear command in Philadelphia." Helped by some middle-class leaders (Thomas Paine, Thomas Young, and others), they "launched a full-scale attack on wealth and even on the right to acquire unlimited private property."

During elections for the 1776 convention to frame a constitution for Pennsylvania, a Privates Committee urged voters to oppose "great and overgrown rich men . . . they will be too apt to be framing distinctions in society." The Privates Committee drew up a bill of rights for the convention, including the statement that "an enormous proportion of property vested in a few individuals is dangerous to the rights, and destructive of the common happiness, of mankind; and therefore every free state hath a right by its laws to discourage the possession of such property."

In the countryside, where most people lived, there was a similar conflict of poor against rich, one which political leaders would use to mobilize the population against England, granting some benefits for the rebellious poor, and many more for themselves in the process. The tenant riots in New Jersey in the 1740s, the New York tenant uprisings of the 1750s and 1760s in the Hudson Valley, and the rebellion in northeastern New York that led to the carving of Vermont out of New York

State were all more than sporadic rioting. They were long-lasting social movements, highly organized, involving the creation of countergovernments. They were aimed at a handful of rich landlords, but with the landlords far away, they often had to direct their anger against farmers who had leased the disputed land from the owners. (See Edward Countryman's pioneering work on rural rebellion.)

Just as the Jersey rebels had broken into jails to free their friends, rioters in the Hudson Valley rescued prisoners from the sheriff and one time took the sheriff himself as prisoner. The tenants were seen as "chiefly the dregs of the People," and the posse that the sheriff of Albany County led to Bennington in 1771 included the privileged top of the local power structure.

The land rioters saw their battle as poor against rich. A witness at a rebel leader's trial in New York in 1766 said that the farmers evicted by the landlords "had an equitable Title but could not be defended in a Course of Law because they were poor and . . . poor men were always oppressed by the rich." Ethan Allen's Green Mountain rebels in Vermont described themselves as "a poor people . . . fatigued in settling a wilderness country," and their opponents as "a number of Attorneys and other gentlemen, with all their tackle of ornaments, and compliments, and French finesse."

Land-hungry farmers in the Hudson Valley turned to the British for support against the American landlords; the Green Mountain rebels did the same. But as the conflict with Britain intensified, the colonial leaders of the movement for independence, aware of the tendency of poor tenants to side with the British in their anger against the rich, adopted policies to win over people in the countryside.

In North Carolina, a powerful movement of white farmers was organized against wealthy and corrupt officials in the period from 1766 to 1771, exactly those years when, in the cities of the Northeast, agitation was growing against the British, crowding out class issues. The movement in North Carolina was called the Regulator movement, and it consisted, says Marvin L. Michael Kay, a specialist in the history of that movement, of "class-conscious white farmers in the west who attempted to democratize local government in their respective counties." The Regulators referred to themselves as "poor Industrious peasants," as "labourers," "the wretched poor," "oppressed" by "rich and powerful . . . designing Monsters."

The Regulators saw that a combination of wealth and political power ruled North Carolina, and denounced those officials "whose highest Study is the promotion of their wealth." They resented the tax system, which was especially burdensome on the poor, and the combination of merchants and lawyers who worked in the courts to collect debts from the harassed farmers. In the western counties where the movement developed, only a small percentage of the households had slaves, and 41 percent of these were concentrated, to take one sample western county, in less than 2 percent of the households. The Regulators did not represent servants or slaves, but they did speak for small owners, squatters, and tenants.

A contemporary account of the Regulator movement in Orange County describes the situation:

> Thus were the people of Orange insulted by The sheriff, robbed and plundered ... neglected and condemned by the Representatives and abused by the Magistracy; obliged to pay Fees regulated only by the Avarice of the officer; obliged to pay a Tax which they believed went to inrich and aggrandise a few, who lorded it over them continually; and from all these Evils they saw no way to escape; for the Men in Power, and Legislation, were the Men whose interest it was to oppress, and make gain of the Labourer.

In that county in the 1760s, the Regulators organized to prevent the collection of taxes, or the confiscation of the property of tax delinquents. Officials said "an absolute Insurrection of a dangerous tendency has broke out in Orange County," and made military plans to suppress it. At one point seven hundred armed farmers forced the release of two arrested Regulator leaders. The Regulators petitioned the government on their grievances in 1768, citing "the unequal chances the poor and the weak have in contentions with the rich and powerful."

In another county, Anson, a local militia colonel complained of "the unparalleled tumults, Insurrections, and Commotions which at present distract this County." At one point a hundred men broke up the proceedings at a county court. But they also tried to elect farmers to the assembly, asserting "that a majority of our assembly is composed of Lawyers, Clerks, and others in Connection with them. . . ." In 1770 there was a large-scale riot in Hillsborough, North Carolina, in which they disrupted a court, forced the judge to flee, beat three lawyers and two merchants, and looted stores.

The result of all this was that the assembly passed some mild reform legislation, but also an act "to prevent riots and tumults," and the governor prepared to crush them militarily. In May of 1771 there was a decisive battle in which several thousand Regulators were defeated by a disciplined army using cannon. Six Regulators were hanged. Kay says that in the three western counties of Orange, Anson, and Rowan, where the Regulator movement was concentrated, it had the support of six thousand to seven thousand men out of a total white taxable population of about eight thousand.

One consequence of this bitter conflict is that only a minority of the people in the Regulator counties seem to have participated as patriots in the Revolutionary War. Most of them probably remained neutral.

Fortunately for the Revolutionary movement, the key battles were being fought in the North, and here, in the cities, the colonial leaders had a divided white population; they could win over the mechanics, who were a kind of middle class, who had a stake in the fight against England, who faced competition from English manufacturers. The biggest problem was to keep the propertyless people, who were unemployed and hungry in the crisis following the French war, under control.

In Boston, the economic grievances of the lowest classes mingled with anger against the British and exploded in mob violence. The leaders of the Independence movement wanted to use that mob energy against England, but also to contain it so that it would not demand too much from them.

When riots against the Stamp Act swept Boston in 1767, they were analyzed by the commander of the British forces in North America, General Thomas Gage, as follows:

> The Boston Mob, raised first by the Instigation of Many of the Principal Inhabitants, Allured by Plunder, rose shortly after of their own Accord, attacked, robbed, and destroyed several Houses, and amongst others, that of the Lieutenant Governor. . . . People then began to be terrified at the Spirit they had raised, to perceive that popular Fury was not to be guided, and each individual feared he might be the next Victim to their Rapacity. The same Fears spread thro' the other Provinces, and there has been as much Pains taken since, to prevent Insurrections, of the People, as before to excite them.

Gage's comment suggests that leaders of the movement against the Stamp Act had instigated crowd action, but then became frightened by the thought that it might be directed against their wealth, too. At this time, the top 10 percent of Boston's taxpayers held about 66 percent of Boston's taxable wealth, while the lowest 30 percent of the taxpaying population had no taxable property at all. The propertyless could not vote and so (like blacks, women, Indians) could not participate in town meetings. This included sailors, journeymen, apprentices, servants.

Dirk Hoerder, a student of Boston mob actions in the Revolutionary period, calls the Revolutionary leadership "the Sons of Liberty type drawn from the middling interest and well-to-do merchants . . . a hesitant leadership," wanting to spur action against Great Britain, yet worrying about maintaining control over the crowds at home.

It took the Stamp Act crisis to make this leadership aware of its dilemma. A political group in Boston called the Loyal Nine—merchants, distillers, shipowners, and master craftsmen who opposed the Stamp Act—organized a procession in August 1765 to protest it. They put fifty master craftsmen at the head, but needed to mobilize shipworkers from the North End and mechanics and apprentices from the South End. Two or three thousand were in the procession (Negroes were excluded). They marched to the home of the stampmaster and burned his effigy. But after the "gentlemen" who organized the demonstration left, the crowd went further and destroyed some of the stampmaster's property. These were, as one of the Loyal Nine said, "amazingly inflamed people." The Loyal Nine seemed taken aback by the direct assault on the wealthy furnishings of the stampmaster.

The rich set up armed patrols. Now a town meeting was called and the same leaders who had planned the demonstration denounced the violence and disavowed the actions of the crowd. As more demonstrations were planned for November 1, 1765, when the Stamp Act was to go into effect, and for Pope's Day, November 5, steps were taken to keep things under control; a dinner was given for certain leaders of the rioters to win them over. And when the Stamp Act was repealed, due to overwhelming resistance, the conservative leaders severed their connections with the rioters. They held annual celebrations of the first anti-Stamp Act demonstration, to which they invited, according to Hoerder, not the rioters but "mainly upper and middle-class Bostonians, who traveled in coaches and carriages to Roxbury or Dorchester for opulent feasts."

When the British Parliament turned to its next attempt to tax the colonies, this time by a set of taxes which it hoped would not excite as much opposition, the colonial leaders organized boycotts. But, they stressed, "No Mobs or Tumults, let the Persons and Properties of your most inveterate Enemies be safe." Samuel Adams advised: "No Mobs— No Confusions—No Tumult." And James Otis said that "no possible circumstances, though ever so oppressive, could be supposed sufficient to justify private tumults and disorders. . . ."

Impressment and the quartering of troops by the British were directly hurtful to the sailors and other working people. After 1768, two thousand soldiers were quartered in Boston, and friction grew between the crowds and the soldiers. The soldiers began to take the jobs of working people when jobs were scarce. Mechanics and shopkeepers lost work or business because of the colonists' boycott of British goods. In 1769, Boston set up a committee "to Consider of some Suitable Methods of employing the Poor of the Town, whose Numbers and distresses are dayly increasing by the loss of its Trade and Commerce."

On March 5, 1770, grievances of ropemakers against British soldiers taking their jobs led to a fight. A crowd gathered in front of the customhouse and began provoking the soldiers, who fired and killed first Crispus Attucks, a mulatto worker, then others. This became known as the Boston Massacre. Feelings against the British mounted quickly. There was anger at the acquittal of six of the British soldiers (two were punished by having their thumbs branded and were discharged from the army). The crowd at the Massacre was described by John Adams, defense attorney for the British soldiers, as "a motley rabble of saucy boys, negroes, and molattoes, Irish teagues and outlandish jack tarrs." Perhaps ten thousand people marched in the funeral procession for the victims of the Massacre, out of a total Boston population of sixteen thousand. This led England to remove the troops from Boston and try to quiet the situation.

Impressment was the background of the Massacre. There had been impressment riots through the 1760s in New York and in Newport, Rhode Island, where five hundred seamen, boys, and Negroes rioted after five weeks of impressment by the British. Six weeks before the Boston Massacre, there was a battle in New York of seamen against British soldiers taking their jobs, and one seaman was killed.

In the Boston Tea Party of December 1773, the Boston Committee of Correspondence, formed a year before to organize anti-British actions, "controlled crowd action against the tea from the start," Dirk Hoerder says. The Tea Party led to the Coercive Acts by Parliament, virtually establishing martial law in Massachusetts, dissolving the colonial government, closing the port in Boston, and sending in troops. Still, town meetings and mass meetings rose in opposition. The seizure of a powder store by the British led four thousand men from all around Boston to assemble in Cambridge, where some of the wealthy officials had their sumptuous homes. The crowd forced the officials to resign. The Committees of Correspondence of Boston and other towns welcomed this gathering, but warned against destroying private property.

Pauline Maier, who studied the development of opposition to Britain in the decade before 1776 in her book *From Resistance to Revolution*, emphasizes the moderation of the leadership and, despite their desire for resistance, their "emphasis on order and restraint." She notes: "The officers and committee members of the Sons of Liberty were drawn almost entirely from the middle and upper classes of colonial society." In Newport, Rhode Island, for instance, the Sons of Liberty, according to a contemporary writer, "contained some Gentlemen of the First Figure in Town for Opulence, Sense and Politeness." In North Carolina "one of the wealthiest of the gentlemen and freeholders" led the Sons of Liberty. Similarly in Virginia and South Carolina. And "New York's leaders, too, were involved in small but respectable independent business ventures." Their aim, however, was to broaden their organization, to develop a mass base of wage earners.

Many of the Sons of Liberty groups declared, as in Milford, Connecticut, their "greatest abhorrence" of lawlessness, or as in Annapolis, opposed "all riots or unlawful assemblies tending to the disturbance of the public tranquility." John Adams expressed the same fears: "These tarrings and featherings, this breaking open Houses by rude and insolent Rabbles, in Resentment for private Wrongs or in pursuing of private Prejudices and Passions, must be discountenanced."

In Virginia, it seemed clear to the educated gentry that something needed to be done to persuade the lower orders to join the revolutionary cause, to deflect their anger against England. One Virginian wrote in his diary in the spring of 1774: "The lower Class of People here are in tumult on account of Reports from Boston, many of them expect to be press'd & compell'd to go and fight the Britains!" Around the time of the Stamp Act, a Virginia orator addressed the poor: "Are not the gentlemen made of the same materials as the lowest and poorest among you? . . . Listen to no doctrines which may tend to divide us, but let us go hand in hand, as brothers. . . ."

It was a problem for which the rhetorical talents of Patrick Henry were superbly fitted. He was, as Rhys Isaac puts it, "firmly attached to the world of the gentry," but he spoke in words that the poorer whites of Virginia could understand. Henry's fellow Virginian Edmund Randolph recalled his style as "simplicity and even carelessness. . . . His pauses, which for their length might sometimes be feared to dispell the attention, rivited it the more by raising the expectation."

Patrick Henry's oratory in Virginia pointed a way to relieve class tension between upper and lower classes and form a bond against the British. This was to find language inspiring to all classes, specific enough in its listing of grievances to charge people with anger against the British, vague enough to avoid class conflict among the rebels, and stirring enough to build patriotic feeling for the resistance movement.

Tom Paine's *Common Sense*, which appeared in early 1776 and became the most popular pamphlet in the American colonies, did this. It made the first bold argument for independence, in words that any fairly literate person could understand: "Society in every state is a blessing, but Government even in its best state is but a necessary evil. . . ."

Paine disposed of the idea of the divine right of kings by a pungent history of the British monarchy, going back to the Norman conquest of 1066, when William the Conqueror came over from France to set himself on the British throne: "A French bastard landing with an armed Banditti and establishing himself king of England against the consent of the natives, is in plain terms a very paltry rascally original. It certainly hath no divinity in it."

Paine dealt with the practical advantages of sticking to England or being separated; he knew the importance of economics:

I challenge the warmest advocate for reconciliation to show a single advantage that this continent can reap by being connected with Great Britain. I repeat the challenge; not a single advantage is derived. Our corn will fetch its price in any market in Europe, and our imported goods must be paid for by them where we will. . . .

As for the bad effects of the connection with England, Paine appealed to the colonists' memory of all the wars in which England had involved them, wars costly in lives and money:

But the injuries and disadvantages which we sustain by that connection are without number. . . . any submission to, or dependence on, Great Britain, tends directly to involve this Continent in European wars and quarrels, and set us at variance with nations who would otherwise seek our friendship. . . .

He built slowly to an emotional pitch:

Everything that is right or reasonable pleads for separation. The blood of the slain, the weeping voice of nature cries, 'TIS TIME TO PART.

Common Sense went through twenty-five editions in 1776 and sold hundreds of thousands of copies. It is probable that almost every literate colonist either read it or knew about its contents. Pamphleteering had become by this time the chief theater of debate about relations with England. From 1750 to 1776 four hundred pamphlets had appeared arguing one or another side of the Stamp Act or the Boston Massacre or the Tea Party or the general questions of disobedience to law, loyalty to government, rights and obligations.

Paine's pamphlet appealed to a wide range of colonial opinion angered by England. But it caused some tremors in aristocrats like John Adams, who were with the patriot cause but wanted to make sure it didn't go too far in the direction of democracy. Paine had denounced the so-called balanced government of Lords and Commons as a deception, and called for single-chamber representative bodies where the people could be represented. Adams denounced Paine's plan as "so democratical, without any restraint or even an attempt at any equilibrium or counter-poise, that it must produce confusion and every evil work." Popular assemblies needed to be checked, Adams thought, because they were "productive of hasty results and absurd judgements."

Paine himself came out of "the lower orders" of England—a staymaker, tax official, teacher, poor emigrant to America. He arrived in Philadelphia in 1774, when agitation against England was already strong in the colonies. The artisan mechanics of Philadelphia, along with journeymen, apprentices, and ordinary laborers, were forming into a politically conscious militia, "in general damn'd riff-raff—dirty, mutinous, and disaffected," as local aristocrats described them. By speaking plainly and strongly, he could represent those politically conscious lower-class people (he opposed property qualifications for voting in Pennsylvania). But his great concern seems to have been to speak for a middle group. "There is an extent of riches, as well as an extreme of poverty, which, by harrowing the circles of a man's acquaintance, lessens his opportunities of general knowledge."

Once the Revolution was under way, Paine more and more made it clear that he was not for the crowd action of lower-class people—like those militia who in 1779 attacked the house of James Wilson. Wilson was a Revolutionary leader who opposed price controls and wanted a more conservative government than was given by the Pennsylvania Constitution of 1776. Paine became an associate of one of the wealthiest men in Pennsylvania, Robert Morris, and a supporter of Morris's creation, the Bank of North America.

Later, during the controversy over adopting the Constitution, Paine would once again represent urban artisans, who favored a strong central government. He seemed to believe that such a government could represent some great common interest. In this sense, he lent himself perfectly to the myth of the Revolution—that it was on behalf of a united people.

The Declaration of Independence brought that myth to its peak of eloquence. Each harsher measure of British control—the Proclamation of 1763 not allowing colonists to settle beyond the Appalachians, the Stamp Tax, the Townshend taxes, including the one on tea, the stationing of troops and the Boston Massacre, the closing of the port of Boston and the dissolution of the Massachusetts legislature—escalated colonial rebellion to the point of revolution. The colonists had responded with the Stamp Act Congress, the Sons of Liberty, the Committees of Correspondence, the Boston Tea Party, and finally, in 1774, the setting up of a Continental Congress—an illegal body, forerunner of a future independent government. It was after the military clash at Lexington and Concord in April 1775, between colonial Minutemen and British troops, that the Continental Congress decided on separation. They organized a small committee to draw up the Declaration of Independence, which Thomas Jefferson wrote. It was adopted by the Congress on July 2, and officially proclaimed July 4, 1776.

By this time there was already a powerful sentiment for independence. Resolutions adopted in North Carolina in May of 1776, and sent to the Continental Congress, declared independence of England, asserted that all British law was null and void, and urged military preparations. About the same time, the town of Malden, Massachusetts, responding to a request from the Massachusetts House of Representatives that all towns in the state declare their views on independence, had met in town meeting and unanimously called for independence: ". . . we therefore renounce with disdain our connexion with a kingdom of slaves; we bid a final adieu to Britain."

"When in the Course of human events, it becomes necessary for one people to dissolve the political bands . . . they should declare the causes. . . ." This was the opening of the Declaration of Independence. Then, in its second paragraph, came the powerful philosophical statement:

> We hold these truths to be self-evident, that all men are created equal, that they are endowed by their Creator with certain unalienable Rights, that among these are Life, Liberty and the pursuit of Happiness. That to secure these rights, Governments are instituted among Men, deriving their just powers from the consent of the governed, that whenever any Form of Government becomes destructive of these ends, it is the Right of the People to alter or to abolish it, and to institute new Government. . . .

It then went on to list grievances against the king, "a history of repeated injuries and usurpations, all having in direct object the establishment of an absolute Tyranny over these States." The list accused the king of dissolving colonial governments, controlling judges, sending "swarms of Officers to harass our people," sending in armies of occupation, cutting off colonial trade with other parts of the world, taxing the colonists without their consent, and waging war against them, "transporting large Armies of foreign Mercenaries to compleat the works of death, desolation and tyranny."

All this, the language of popular control over governments, the right of rebellion and revolution, indignation at political tyranny, economic burdens, and military attacks, was language well suited to unite large numbers of colonists, and persuade even those who had grievances against one another to turn against England.

Some Americans were clearly omitted from this circle of united interest drawn by the Declaration of Independence: Indians, black slaves, women. Indeed, one paragraph of the Declaration charged the King with inciting slave rebellions and Indian attacks:

> He has excited domestic insurrections amongst us, and has endeavoured to bring on the inhabitants of our frontiers, the merciless Indian Savages, whose known rule of warfare is an undistinguished destruction of all ages, sexes and conditions.

Twenty years before the Declaration, a proclamation of the legislature of Massachusetts of November 3, 1755, declared the Penobscot Indians "rebels, enemies and traitors" and provided a bounty: "For every scalp of a male Indian brought in ... forty pounds. For every scalp of such female Indian or male Indian under the age of twelve years that shall be killed ... twenty pounds. ..."

Thomas Jefferson had written a paragraph of the Declaration accusing the King of transporting slaves from Africa to the colonies and "suppressing every legislative attempt to prohibit or to restrain this execrable commerce." This seemed to express moral indignation against slavery and the slave trade (Jefferson's personal distaste for slavery must be put alongside the fact that he owned hundreds of slaves to the day he died). Behind it was the growing fear among Virginians and some other southerners about the growing number of black slaves in the colonies (20 percent of the total population) and the threat of slave revolts as the number of slaves increased. Jefferson's paragraph was removed by the Continental Congress, because slaveholders themselves disagreed about the desirability of ending the slave trade. So even that gesture toward the black slave was omitted in the great manifesto of freedom of the American Revolution.

The use of the phrase "all men are created equal" was probably not a deliberate attempt to make a statement about women. It was just that women were beyond consideration as worthy of inclusion. They were politically invisible. Though practical needs gave women a certain authority in the home, on the farm, or in occupations like midwifery, they were simply overlooked in any consideration of political rights, any notions of civic equality.

To say that the Declaration of Independence, even by its own language, was limited to life, liberty, and happiness for white males is not to denounce the makers and signers of the Declaration for holding the ideas expected of privileged males of the eighteenth century. Reformers and radicals, looking discontentedly at history, are often accused of expecting too much from a past political epoch—and sometimes they do. But the point of noting those outside the arc of human rights in the Declaration is not, centuries late and pointlessly, to lay impossible moral burdens on that time. It is to try to understand the way in which the Declaration functioned to mobilize certain groups of Americans, ignoring others. Surely, inspirational language to create a secure consensus is still used, in our time, to cover up serious conflicts of interest in that consensus, and to cover up, also, the omission of large parts of the human race.

The philosophy of the Declaration, that government is set up by the people to secure their life, liberty, and happiness, and is to be overthrown when it no longer does that, is often traced to the ideas of John Locke, in his *Second Treatise on Government*. That was published in England in 1689, when the English were rebelling against tyrannical kings and setting up parliamentary government. The Declaration, like Locke's *Second Treatise*, talked about government and political rights, but ignored the existing inequalities in property. And how could people truly have equal rights, with stark differences in wealth?

Locke himself was a wealthy man, with investments in the silk trade and slave trade, income from loans and mortgages. He invested heavily in the first issue of the stock of the Bank of England, just a few years after he had written his *Second Treatise* as the classic statement of liberal democracy. As adviser to the Carolinas, he had suggested a government of slaveowners run by wealthy land barons.

Locke's statement of people's government was in support of a revolution in England for the free development of mercantile capitalism at home and abroad. Locke himself regretted that the labor of poor children "is generally lost to the public till they are twelve or fourteen years old" and suggested that all children over three, of families on relief, should attend "working schools" so they would be "from infancy ... inured to work."

The English revolutions of the seventeenth century brought representative government and opened up discussions of democracy. But, as the English historian Christopher Hill wrote in *The Puritan Revolution:* "The establishment of parliamentary supremacy, of the rule of law, no doubt mainly benefited the men of property." The kind of arbitrary taxation that threatened the security of property was overthrown, monopolies were ended to give more free reign to business, and sea power began to be used for an imperial policy abroad, including the conquest of Ireland. The Levellers and the Diggers, two political movements which wanted to carry equality into the economic sphere, were put down by the Revolution.

One can see the reality of Locke's nice phrases about representative government in the class divisions and conflicts in England that followed the Revolution that Locke supported. At the very time the American scene was becoming tense, in 1768, England was racked by riots and strikes—of coal heavers, saw mill workers, hatters, weavers, sailors—because of the high price of bread and the miserable wages. The *Annual Register* reviewed the events of the spring and summer of 1768:

> A general dissatisfaction unhappily prevailed among several of the lower orders of the people. This ill temper, which was partly occasioned by the high price of provisions, and partly proceeded from other causes, too frequently manifested itself in acts of tumult and riot, which were productive of the most melancholy consequences.

"The people" who were, supposedly, at the heart of Locke's theory of people's sovereignty were defined by a British member of Parliament: "I don't mean the mob. . . . I mean the middling people of England, the manufacturer, the yeoman, the merchant, the country gentleman. . . ."

In America, too, the reality behind the words of the Declaration of Independence (issued in the same year as Adam Smith's capitalist manifesto, *The Wealth of Nations*) was that a rising class of important people needed to enlist on their side enough Americans to defeat England, without disturbing too much the relations of wealth and power that had developed over 150 years of colonial history. Indeed, 69 percent of the signers of the Declaration of Independence had held colonial office under England.

When the Declaration of Independence was read, with all its flaming radical language, from the town hall balcony in Boston, it was read by

Thomas Crafts, a member of the Loyal Nine group, conservatives who had opposed militant action against the British. Four days after the reading, the Boston Committee of Correspondence ordered the townsmen to show up on the Common for a military draft. The rich, it turned out, could avoid the draft by paying for substitutes; the poor had to serve. This led to rioting, and shouting: "Tyranny is Tyranny let it come from whom it may."

5

A KIND OF REVOLUTION

The American victory over the British army was made possible by the existence of an already-armed people. Just about every white male had a gun, and could shoot. The Revolutionary leadership distrusted the mobs of poor. But they knew the Revolution had no appeal to slaves and Indians. They would have to woo the armed white population.

This was not easy. Yes, mechanics and sailors, some others, were incensed against the British. But general enthusiasm for the war was not strong. While much of the white male population went into military service at one time or another during the war, only a small fraction stayed. John Shy, in his study of the Revolutionary army (*A People Numerous and Armed*), says they "grew weary of being bullied by local committees of safety, by corrupt deputy assistant commissaries of supply, and by bands of ragged strangers with guns in their hands calling themselves soldiers of the Revolution." Shy estimates that perhaps a fifth of the population was actively treasonous. John Adams had estimated a third opposed, a third in support, a third neutral.

Alexander Hamilton, an aide of George Washington and an up-and-coming member of the new elite, wrote from his headquarters: ". . . our countrymen have all the folly of the ass and all the passiveness of the sheep. . . . They are determined not to be free. . . . If we are saved, France and Spain must save us."

Slavery got in the way in the South. South Carolina, insecure since the slave uprising in Stono in 1739, could hardly fight against the British; her militia had to be used to keep slaves under control.

The men who first joined the colonial militia were generally "hallmarks of respectability or at least of full citizenship" in their communities, Shy says. Excluded from the militia were friendly Indians, free Negroes, white servants, and free white men who had no stable home.

But desperation led to the recruiting of the less respectable whites. Massachusetts and Virginia provided for drafting "strollers" (vagrants) into the militia. In fact, the military became a place of promise for the poor, who might rise in rank, acquire some money, change their social status.

Here was the traditional device by which those in charge of any social order mobilize and discipline a recalcitrant population—offering the adventure and rewards of military service to get poor people to fight for a cause they may not see clearly as their own. A wounded American lieutenant at Bunker Hill, interviewed by Peter Oliver, a Tory (who admittedly might have been looking for such a response), told how he had joined the rebel forces:

> I was a Shoemaker, & got my living by my Labor. When this Rebellion came on, I saw some of my Neighbors got into Commission, who were no better than myself. I was very ambitious, & did not like to see those Men above me. I was asked to enlist, as a private Soldier . . . I offered to enlist upon having a Lieutenants Commission; which was granted. I imagined my self now in a way of Promotion: if I was killed in Battle, there would be an end of me, but if my Captain was killed, I should rise in Rank, & should still have a Chance to rise higher. These Sir! were the only Motives of my entering into the Service; for as to the Dispute between Great Britain & the Colonies, I know nothing of it. . . .

John Shy investigated the subsequent experience of that Bunker Hill lieutenant. He was William Scott, of Peterborough, New Hampshire, and after a year as prisoner of the British he escaped, made his way back to the American army, fought in battles in New York, was captured again by the British, and escaped again by swimming the Hudson River one night with his sword tied around his neck and his watch pinned to his hat. He returned to New Hampshire, recruited a company of his own, including his two eldest sons, and fought in various battles, until his health gave way. He watched his eldest son die of camp fever after six years of service. He had sold his farm in Peterborough for a note that, with inflation, became worthless. After the war, he came to public attention when he rescued eight people from drowning after their boat turned over in New York harbor. He then got a job surveying western lands with the army, but caught a fever and died in 1796.

Scott was one of many Revolutionary fighters, usually of lower military ranks, from poor and obscure backgrounds. Shy's study of the Peterborough contingent shows that the prominent and substantial citizens of the town had served only briefly in the war. Other American towns show the same pattern. As Shy puts it: "Revolutionary America may have been a middle-class society, happier and more prosperous than any other in its time, but it contained a large and growing number of fairly poor people, and many of them did much of the actual fighting and suffering between 1775 and 1783: A very old story."

The military conflict itself, by dominating everything in its time, diminished other issues, made people choose sides in the one contest that was publicly important, forced people onto the side of the Revolution whose interest in Independence was not at all obvious. Ruling elites seem to have learned through the generations—consciously or not—that war makes them more secure against internal trouble.

The force of military preparation had a way of pushing neutral people into line. In Connecticut, for instance, a law was passed requiring military service of all males between sixteen and sixty, omitting certain government officials, ministers, Yale students and faculty, Negroes, Indians, and mulattos. Someone called to duty could provide a substitute or get out of it by paying 5 pounds. When eighteen men failed to show up for military duty they were jailed and, in order to be released, had to pledge to fight in the war. Shy says: "The mechanism of their political conversion was the militia." What looks like the democratization of the military forces in modern times shows up as something different: a way of forcing large numbers of reluctant people to associate themselves with the national cause, and by the end of the process believe in it.

Here, in the war for liberty, was conscription, as usual, cognizant of wealth. With the impressment riots against the British still remembered, impressment of seamen by the American navy was taking place by 1779. A Pennsylvania official said: "We cannot help observing how similar this Conduct is to that of the British Officers during our Subjection to Great Britain and are persuaded it will have the same unhappy effects viz. an estrangement of the Affections of the People from ... Authority ... which by an easy Progression will proceed to open Opposition ... and bloodshed."

Watching the new, tight discipline of Washington's army, a chaplain in Concord, Massachusetts, wrote: "New lords, new laws. The strictest government is taking place and great distinction is made between officers & men. Everyone is made to know his place & keep it, or be immediately tied up, and receive not one but 30 or 40 lashes."

The Americans lost the first battles of the war: Bunker Hill, Brooklyn Heights, Harlem Heights, the Deep South; they won small battles at Trenton and Princeton, and then in a turning point, a big battle at

Saratoga, New York, in 1777. Washington's frozen army hung on at Valley Forge, Pennsylvania, while Benjamin Franklin negotiated an alliance with the French monarchy, which was anxious for revenge on England. The war turned to the South, where the British won victory after victory, until the Americans, aided by a large French army, with the French navy blocking off the British from supplies and reinforcements, won the final victory of the war at Yorktown, Virginia, in 1781.

Through all this, the suppressed conflicts between rich and poor among the Americans kept reappearing. In the midst of the war, in Philadelphia, which Eric Foner describes as "a time of immense profits for some colonists and terrible hardships for others," the inflation (prices rose in one month that year by 45 percent) led to agitation and calls for action. One Philadelphia newspaper carried a reminder that in Europe "the People have always done themselves justice when the scarcity of bread has arisen from the avarice of forestallers. They have broken open magazines—appropriated stores to their own use without paying for them—and in some instances have hung up the culprits who created their distress."

In May of 1779, the First Company of Philadelphia Artillery petitioned the Assembly about the troubles of "the midling and poor" and threatened violence against "those who are avariciously intent upon amassing wealth by the destruction of the more virtuous part of the community." That same month, there was a mass meeting, an extralegal gathering, which called for price reductions and initiated an investigation of Robert Morris, a rich Philadelphian who was accused of holding food from the market. In October came the "Fort Wilson riot," in which a militia group marched into the city and to the house of James Wilson, a wealthy lawyer and Revolutionary official who had opposed price controls and the democratic constitution adopted in Pennsylvania in 1776. The militia were driven away by a "silk stocking brigade" of well-off Philadelphia citizens.

It seemed that the majority of white colonists, who had a bit of land, or no property at all, were still better off than slaves or indentured servants or Indians, and could be wooed into the coalition of the Revolution. But when the sacrifices of war became more bitter, the privileges and safety of the rich became harder to accept. About 10 percent of the white population (an estimate of Jackson Main in *The Social Structure of Revolutionary America*), large landholders and merchants, held 1,000 pounds or more in personal property and 1,000 pounds in land, at the least, and these men owned nearly half the wealth of the country and held as slaves one-seventh of the country's people.

The Continental Congress, which governed the colonies through the war, was dominated by rich men, linked together in factions and compacts by business and family connections. These links connected North and South, East and West. For instance, Richard Henry Lee of Virginia was connected with the Adamses of Massachusetts and the Shippens of Pennsylvania. Delegates from middle and southern colonies were connected with Robert Morris of Pennsylvania through commerce and land speculation. Morris was superintendent of finance, and his assistant was Gouverneur Morris.

Morris's plan was to give more assurance to those who had loaned money to the Continental Congress, and gain the support of officers by voting half-pay for life for those who stuck to the end. This ignored the common soldier, who was not getting paid, who was suffering in the cold, dying of sickness, watching the civilian profiteers get rich. On New Year's Day, 1781, the Pennsylvania troops near Morristown, New Jersey, perhaps emboldened by rum, dispersed their officers, killed one captain, wounded others, and were marching, fully armed, with cannon, toward the Continental Congress at Philadelphia.

George Washington handled it cautiously. Informed of these developments by General Anthony Wayne, he told Wayne not to use force. He was worried that the rebellion might spread to his own troops. He suggested Wayne get a list of the soldiers' grievances, and said Congress should not flee Philadelphia, because then the way would be open for the soldiers to be joined by Philadelphia citizens. He sent Knox rushing to New England on his horse to get three months' pay for the soldiers, while he prepared a thousand men to march on the mutineers, as a last resort. A peace was negotiated, in which one-half the men were discharged; the other half got furloughs.

Shortly after this, a smaller mutiny took place in the New Jersey Line, involving two hundred men who defied their officers and started out for the state capital at Trenton. Now Washington was ready. Six hundred men, who themselves had been well fed and clothed, marched on the mutineers and surrounded and disarmed them. Three ringleaders were put on trial immediately, in the field. One was pardoned, and two were shot by firing squads made up of their friends, who wept as they pulled the triggers. It was "an example," Washington said.

Two years later, there was another mutiny in the Pennsylvania line. The war was over and the army had disbanded, but eighty soldiers, demanding their pay, invaded the Continental Congress headquarters in Philadelphia and forced the members to flee across the river to Princeton—"ignominiously turned out of doors," as one historian sorrowfully wrote (John Fiske, *The Critical Period*), "by a handful of drunken mutineers."

What soldiers in the Revolution could do only rarely, rebel against their authorities, civilians could do much more easily. Ronald Hoffman says: "The Revolution plunged the states of Delaware, Maryland, North Carolina, South Carolina, Georgia, and, to a much lesser degree, Virginia into divisive civil conflicts that persisted during the entire period of struggle." The southern lower classes resisted being mobilized for the revolution. They saw themselves under the rule of a political elite, win or lose against the British.

In Maryland, for instance, by the new constitution of 1776, to run for governor one had to own 5,000 pounds of property; to run for state senator, 1,000 pounds. Thus, 90 percent of the population were excluded from holding office. And so, as Hoffman says, "small slave holders, non-slaveholding planters, tenants, renters and casual day laborers posed a serious problem of social control for the Whig elite."

With black slaves 25 percent of the population (and in some counties 50 percent), fear of slave revolts grew. George Washington had turned down the requests of blacks, seeking freedom, to fight in the Revolutionary army. So when the British military commander in Virginia, Lord Dunmore, promised freedom to Virginia slaves who joined his forces, this created consternation. A report from one Maryland county worried about poor whites encouraging slave run-aways:

> The insolence of the Negroes in this county is come to such a height, that we are under a necessity of disarming them which we affected on Saturday last. We took about eighty guns, some bayonets, swords, etc. The malicious and imprudent speeches of some among the lower classes of whites have induced them to believe that their freedom depended on the success of the King's troops. We cannot therefore be too vigilant nor too rigourous with those who promote and encourage this disposition in our slaves.

Even more unsettling was white rioting in Maryland against leading families, supporting the Revolution, who were suspected of hoarding needed commodities. The class hatred of some of these disloyal people was expressed by one man who said "it was better for the people to lay down their arms and pay the duties and taxes laid upon them by King and Parliament than to be brought into slavery and to be commanded and ordered about as they were." A wealthy Maryland land-owner, Charles Carroll, took note of the surly mood all around him:

There is a mean low dirty envy which creeps thro all ranks and cannot suffer a man a superiority of fortune, of merit, or of understanding in fellow citizens—either of these are sure to entail a general ill will and dislike upon the owners.

Despite this, Maryland authorities retained control. They made concessions, taxing land and slaves more heavily, letting debtors pay in paper money. It was a sacrifice by the upper class to maintain power, and it worked.

In the lower South, however, in the Carolinas and Georgia, according to Hoffman, "vast regions were left without the slightest apparition of authority." The general mood was to take no part in a war that seemed to have nothing for them. "Authoritative personages on both sides demanded that common people supply material, reduce consumption, leave their families, and even risk their lives. Forced to make hard decisions, many flailed out in frustration or evaded and defied first one side, then the other. . . ."

Washington's military commander in the lower South, Nathanael Greene, dealt with disloyalty by a policy of concessions to some, brutality to others. In a letter to Thomas Jefferson he described a raid by his troops on Loyalists. "They made a dreadful carnage of them, upwards of one hundred were killed and most of the rest cut to pieces. It has had a very happy effect on those disaffected persons of which there were too many in this country." Greene told one of his generals "to strike terror into our enemies and give spirit to our friends." On the other hand, he advised the governor of Georgia "to open a door for the disaffected of your state to come in. . . ."

In general, throughout the states, concessions were kept to a minimum. The new constitutions that were drawn up in all states from 1776 to 1780 were not much different from the old ones. Although property qualifications for voting and holding office were lowered in some instances, in Massachusetts they were increased. Only Pennsylvania abolished them totally. The new bills of rights had modifying provisions. North Carolina, providing for religious freedom, added "that nothing herein contained shall be construed to exempt preachers of treasonable or seditious discourses, from legal trial and punishment." Maryland, New York, Georgia, and Massachusetts took similar cautions.

The American Revolution is sometimes said to have brought about the separation of church and state. The northern states made such declarations, but after 1776 they adopted taxes that forced everyone to support Christian teachings. William G. McLoughlin, quoting Supreme Court

Justice David Brewer in 1892 that "this is a Christian nation," says of the separation of church and state in the Revolution that it "was neither conceived of nor carried out. . . . Far from being left to itself, religion was imbedded into every aspect and institution of American life."

One would look, in examining the Revolution's effect on class relations, at what happened to land confiscated from fleeing Loyalists. It was distributed in such a way as to give a double opportunity to the Revolutionary leaders: to enrich themselves and their friends, and to parcel out some land to small farmers to create a broad base of support for the new government. Indeed, this became characteristic of the new nation: finding itself possessed of enormous wealth, it could create the richest ruling class in history, and still have enough for the middle classes to act as a buffer between the rich and the dispossessed.

The huge landholdings of the Loyalists had been one of the great incentives to Revolution. Lord Fairfax in Virginia had more than 5 million acres encompassing twenty-one counties. Lord Baltimore's income from his Maryland holdings exceeded 30,000 pounds a year. After the Revolution, Lord Fairfax was protected; he was a friend of George Washington. But other Loyalist holders of great estates, especially those who were absentees, had their land confiscated. In New York, the number of freeholding small farmers increased after the Revolution, and there were fewer tenant farmers, who had created so much trouble in the pre-Revolution years.

Although the numbers of independent farmers grew, according to Rowland Berthoff and John Murrin, "the class structure did not change radically." The ruling group went through personnel changes as "the rising merchant families of Boston, New York or Philadelphia . . . slipped quite credibly into the social status—and sometimes the very houses of those who failed in business or suffered confiscation and exile for loyalty to the crown."

Edmund Morgan sums up the class nature of the Revolution this way: "The fact that the lower ranks were involved in the contest should not obscure the fact that the contest itself was generally a struggle for office and power between members of an upper class: the new against the established." Looking at the situation after the Revolution, Richard Morris comments: "Everywhere one finds inequality." He finds "the people" of "We the people of the United States" (a phrase coined by the very rich Gouverneur Morris) did not mean Indians or blacks or women or white servants. In fact, there were more indentured servants than ever, and the Revolution "did nothing to end and little to ameliorate white bondage."

Carl Degler says *(Out of Our Past):* "No new social class came to power through the door of the American revolution. The men who engineered the revolt were largely members of the colonial ruling class." George Washington was the richest man in America. John Hancock was a prosperous Boston merchant. Benjamin Franklin was a wealthy printer. And so on.

On the other hand, town mechanics, laborers, and seamen, as well as small farmers, were swept into "the people" by the rhetoric of the Revolution, by the camaraderie of military service, by the distribution of some land. Thus was created a substantial body of support, a national consensus, something that, even with the exclusion of ignored and oppressed people, could be called "America."

Staughton Lynd's close study of Dutchess County, New York, in the Revolutionary period corroborates this. There were tenant risings in 1766 against the huge feudal estates in New York. The Rensselaerwyck holding was a million acres. Tenants, claiming some of this land for themselves, unable to get satisfaction in the courts, turned to violence. In Poughkeepsie, 1,700 armed tenants had closed the courts and broken open the jails. But the uprising was crushed.

During the Revolution, there was a struggle in Dutchess County over the disposition of confiscated Loyalist lands, but it was mainly between different elite groups. One of these, the Poughkeepsie anti-Federalists (opponents of the Constitution), included men on the make, newcomers in land and business. They made promises to the tenants to gain their support, exploiting their grievances to build their own political careers and maintain their own fortunes.

During the Revolution, to mobilize soldiers, the tenants were promised land. A prominent landowner of Dutchess County wrote in 1777 that a promise to make tenants freeholders "would instantly bring you at least six thousand able farmers into the field." But the farmers who enlisted in the Revolution and expected to get something out of it found that, as privates in the army, they received $6.66 a month, while a colonel received $75 a month. They watched local government contractors like Melancton Smith and Matthew Paterson become rich, while the pay they received in continental currency became worthless with inflation.

All this led tenants to become a threatening force in the midst of the war. Many stopped paying rent. The legislature, worried, passed a bill to confiscate Loyalist land and add four hundred new freeholders to the 1,800 already in the county. This meant a strong new voting bloc for the faction of the rich that would become anti-Federalists in 1788. Once the new landholders were brought into the privileged circle of the Revolution and seemed politically under control, their leaders, Melancton Smith and others, at first opposed to adoption of the Constitution, switched to support, and with New York ratifying, adoption was ensured. The new freeholders found that they had stopped being tenants, but were now mortgagees, paying back loans from banks instead of rent to landlords.

It seems that the rebellion against British rule allowed a certain group of the colonial elite to replace those loyal to England, give some benefits to small landholders, and leave poor white working people and tenant farmers in very much their old situation.

What did the Revolution mean to the Native Americans, the Indians? They had been ignored by the fine words of the Declaration, had not been considered equal, certainly not in choosing those who would govern the American territories in which they lived, nor in being able to pursue happiness as they had pursued it for centuries before the white Europeans arrived. Now, with the British out of the way, the Americans could begin the inexorable process of pushing the Indians off their lands, killing them if they resisted. In short, as Francis Jennings puts it, the white Americans were fighting against British imperial control in the East, and for their own imperialism in the West.

Before the Revolution, the Indians had been subdued by force in Virginia and in New England. Elsewhere, they had worked out modes of coexistence with the colonies. But around 1750, with the colonial population growing fast, the pressure to move westward onto new land set the stage for conflict with the Indians. Land agents from the East began appearing in the Ohio River valley, on the territory of a confederation of tribes called the Covenant Chain, for which the Iroquois were spokesmen. In New York, through intricate swindling, 800,000 acres of Mohawk land were taken, ending the period of Mohawk–New York friendship. Chief Hendrick of the Mohawks is recorded speaking his bitterness to Governor George Clinton and the provincial council of New York in 1753:

> Brother when we came here to relate our Grievances about our Lands, we expected to have something done for us, and we have told you that the Covenant Chain of our Forefathers was like to be broken, and brother you tell us that we shall be redressed at Albany, but we know them so well, we will not trust to them, for they [the Albany merchants] are no people but Devils so . . . as soon as we come home we will send up a Belt of Wampum to our Brothers the other 5 Nations to acquaint them the Covenant Chain is

broken between you and us. So brother you are not to expect to hear of me any more, and Brother we desire to hear no more of you.

When the British fought the French for North America in the Seven Years' War, the Indians fought on the side of the French. The French were traders but not occupiers of Indian lands, while the British clearly coveted their hunting grounds and living space. Someone reported the conversation of Shingas, chief of the Delaware Indians, with the British General Braddock, who sought his help against the French:

> Shingas asked General Braddock, whether the Indians that were friends to the English might not be permitted to Live and Trade among the English and have Hunting Ground sufficient to Support themselves and Familys. . . . On which General Braddock said that No Savage Should Inherit the Land. . . . On which Shingas and the other Chiefs answered That if they might not have Liberty to Live on the Land they would not Fight for it. . . .

When that war ended in 1763, the French, ignoring their old allies, ceded to the British lands west of the Appalachians. The Indians therefore united to make war on the British western forts; this is called "Pontiac's Conspiracy" by the British, but "a liberation war for independence" in the words used by Francis Jennings. Under orders from British General Jeffrey Amherst, the commander of Fort Pitts gave the attacking Indian chiefs, with whom he was negotiating, blankets from the smallpox hospital. It was a pioneering effort at what is now called biological warfare. An epidemic soon spread among the Indians.

Despite this, and the burning of villages, the British could not destroy the will of the Indians, who continued guerrilla war. A peace was made, with the British agreeing to establish a line at the Appalachians, beyond which settlements would not encroach on Indian territory. This was the Royal Proclamation of 1763, and it angered Americans (the original Virginia charter said its land went westward to the ocean). It helps to explain why most of the Indians fought for England during the Revolution. With their French allies, then their English allies, gone, the Indians faced a new land-coveting nation—alone.

The Americans assumed now that the Indian land was theirs. But the expeditions they sent westward to establish this were overcome—which they recognized in the names they gave these battles: Harmar's Humiliation and St. Clair's Shame. And even when General Anthony Wayne defeated the Indians' western confederation in 1798 at the Battle of Fallen Timbers, he had to recognize their power. In the Treaty of

Grenville, it was agreed that in return for certain cessions of land the United States would give up claims to the Indian lands north of the Ohio, east of the Mississippi, and south of the Great Lakes, but that if the Indians decided to sell these lands they would offer them first to the United States.

Jennings, putting the Indian into the center of the American Revolution—after all, it was Indian land that everyone was fighting over—sees the Revolution as a "multiplicity of variously oppressed and exploited peoples who preyed upon each other." With the eastern elite controlling the lands on the seaboard, the poor, seeking land, were forced to go West, there becoming a useful bulwark for the rich because, as Jennings says, "the first target of the Indian's hatchet was the frontiersman's skull."

The situation of black slaves as a result of the American Revolution was more complex. Thousands of blacks fought with the British. Five thousand were with the Revolutionaries, most of them from the North, but there were also free blacks from Virginia and Maryland. The lower South was reluctant to arm blacks. Amid the urgency and chaos of war, thousands took their freedom—leaving on British ships at the end of the war to settle in England, Nova Scotia, the West Indies, or Africa. Many others stayed in America as free blacks, evading their masters.

In the northern states, the combination of blacks in the military, the lack of powerful economic need for slaves, and the rhetoric of Revolution led to the end of slavery—but very slowly. As late as 1810, thirty thousand blacks, one-fourth of the black population of the North, remained slaves. In 1840 there were still a thousand slaves in the North. In the upper South, there were more free Negroes than before, leading to more control legislation. In the lower South, slavery expanded with the growth of rice and cotton plantations.

What the Revolution did was to create space and opportunity for blacks to begin making demands of white society. Sometimes these demands came from the new, small black elites in Baltimore, Philadelphia, Richmond, Savannah, sometimes from articulate and bold slaves. Pointing to the Declaration of Independence, blacks petitioned Congress and the state legislatures to abolish slavery, to give blacks equal rights. In Boston, blacks asked for city money, which whites were getting, to educate their children. In Norfolk, they asked to be allowed to testify in court. Nashville blacks asserted that free Negroes "ought to have the same opportunities of doing well that any Person . . . would have." Peter Mathews, a free Negro butcher in Charleston, joined other free black artisans and tradesmen in petitioning the legislature to repeal discriminatory laws against blacks. In 1780, seven blacks in Dartmouth, Massachusetts, petitioned the legislature for the right to vote, linking taxation to representation:

> . . . we apprehend ourselves to be Aggreeved, in that while we are not allowed the Privilage of freemen of the State having no vote or Influence in the Election of those that Tax us yet many of our Colour (as is well known) have cheerfully Entered the field of Battle in the defense of the Common Cause and that (as we conceive) against a similar Exertion of Power (in Regard to taxation) too well known to need a recital in this place. . . .

A black man, Benjamin Banneker, who taught himself mathematics and astronomy, predicted accurately a solar eclipse, and was appointed to plan the new city of Washington, wrote to Thomas Jefferson:

> I suppose it is a truth too well attested to you, to need a proof here, that we are a race of beings, who have long labored under the abuse and censure of the world; that we have long been looked upon with an eye of contempt; and that we have long been considered rather as brutish than human, and scarcely capable of mental endowments. . . . I apprehend you will embrace every opportunity to eradicate that train of absurd and false ideas and opinions, which so generally prevails with respect to us; and that your sentiments are concurrent with mine, which are, that one universal Father hath given being to us all; and that he hath not only made us all of one flesh, but that he hath also, without partiality, afforded us all the same sensations and endowed us all with the same facilities. . . .

Banneker asked Jefferson "to wean yourselves from those narrow prejudices which you have imbibed."

Jefferson tried his best, as an enlightened, thoughtful individual might. But the structure of American society, the power of the cotton plantation, the slave trade, the politics of unity between northern and southern elites, and the long culture of race prejudice in the colonies, as well as his own weaknesses—that combination of practical need and ideological fixation—kept Jefferson a slaveowner throughout his life.

The inferior position of blacks, the exclusion of Indians from the new society, the establishment of supremacy for the rich and powerful in the new nation—all this was already settled in the colonies by the time of the Revolution. With the English out of the way, it could now be put on paper, solidified, regularized, made legitimate, by the Constitution of the United States, drafted at a convention of Revolutionary leaders in Philadelphia.

To many Americans over the years, the Constitution drawn up in 1787 has seemed a work of genius put together by wise, humane men who created a legal framework for democracy and equality. This view is stated, a bit extravagantly, by the historian George Bancroft, writing in the early nineteenth century:

> The Constitution establishes nothing that interferes with equality and individuality. It knows nothing of differences by descent, or opinions, of favored classes, or legalized religion, or the political power of property. It leaves the individual alongside of the individual. . . . As the sea is made up of drops, American society is composed of separate, free, and constantly moving atoms, ever in reciprocal action . . . so that the institutions and laws of the country rise out of the masses of individual thought which, like the waters of the ocean, are rolling evermore.

Another view of the Constitution was put forward early in the twentieth century by the historian Charles Beard (arousing anger and indignation, including a denunciatory editorial in the *New York Times*). He wrote in his book *An Economic Interpretation of the Constitution:*

> Inasmuch as the primary object of a government, beyond the mere repression of physical violence, is the making of the rules which determine the property relations of members of society, the dominant classes whose rights are thus to be determined must perforce obtain from the government such rules as are consonant with the larger interests necessary to the continuance of their economic processes, or they must themselves control the organs of government.

In short, Beard said, the rich must, in their own interest, either control the government directly or control the laws by which government operates.

Beard applied this general idea to the Constitution, by studying the economic backgrounds and political ideas of the fifty-five men who gathered in Philadelphia in 1787 to draw up the Constitution. He found that a majority of them were lawyers by profession, that most of them were men of wealth, in land, slaves, manufacturing, or shipping, that half of them had money loaned out at interest, and that forty of the fifty-five held government bonds, according to the records of the Treasury Department.

Thus, Beard found that most of the makers of the Constitution had some direct economic interest in establishing a strong federal government: the manufacturers needed protective tariffs; the moneylenders wanted to stop the use of paper money to pay off debts; the land speculators wanted protection as they invaded Indian lands; slaveowners needed federal security against slave revolts and runaways; bondholders wanted a government able to raise money by nationwide taxation, to pay off those bonds.

Four groups, Beard noted, were not represented in the Constitutional Convention: slaves, indentured servants, women, men without property. And so the Constitution did not reflect the interests of those groups.

He wanted to make it clear that he did not think the Constitution was written merely to benefit the Founding Fathers personally, although one could not ignore the $150,000 fortune of Benjamin Franklin, the connections of Alexander Hamilton to wealthy interests through his father-in-law and brother-in-law, the great slave plantations of James Madison, the enormous landholdings of George Washington. Rather, it was to benefit the groups the Founders represented, the "economic interests they understood and felt in concrete, definite form through their own personal experience."

Not everyone at the Philadelphia Convention fitted Beard's scheme. Elbridge Gerry of Massachusetts was a holder of landed property, and yet he opposed the ratification of the Constitution. Similarly, Luther Martin of Maryland, whose ancestors had obtained large tracts of land in New Jersey, opposed ratification. But, with a few exceptions, Beard found a strong connection between wealth and support of the Constitution.

By 1787 there was not only a positive need for strong central government to protect the large economic interests, but also immediate fear of rebellion by discontented farmers. The chief event causing this fear was an uprising in the summer of 1786 in western Massachusetts, known as Shays' Rebellion.

In the western towns of Massachusetts there was resentment against the legislature in Boston. The new Constitution of 1780 had raised the property qualifications for voting. No one could hold state office without being quite wealthy. Furthermore, the legislature was refusing to issue paper money, as had been done in some other states, like Rhode Island, to make it easier for debt-ridden farmers to pay off their creditors.

Illegal conventions began to assemble in some of the western counties to organize opposition to the legislature. At one of these, a man named Plough Jogger spoke his mind:

I have been greatly abused, have been obliged to do more than my part in the war; been loaded with class rates, town rates, province rates, Continental rates and all rates . . . been pulled and hauled by sheriffs, constables and collectors, and had my cattle sold for less than they were worth. . . .

. . . The great men are going to get all we have and I think it is time for us to rise and put a stop to it, and have no more courts, nor sheriffs, nor collectors nor lawyers. . . .

The chairman of that meeting used his gavel to cut short the applause. He and others wanted to redress their grievances, but peacefully, by petition to the General Court (the legislature) in Boston.

However, before the scheduled meeting of the General Court, there were going to be court proceedings in Hampshire County, in the towns of Northampton and Springfield, to seize the cattle of farmers who hadn't paid their debts, to take away their land, now full of grain and ready for harvest. And so, veterans of the Continental army, also aggrieved because they had been treated poorly on discharge—given certificates for future redemption instead of immediate cash—began to organize the farmers into squads and companies. One of these veterans was Luke Day, who arrived the morning of court with a fife-and-drum corps, still angry with the memory of being locked up in debtors' prison in the heat of the previous summer.

The sheriff looked to the local militia to defend the court against these armed farmers. But most of the militia was with Luke Day. The sheriff did manage to gather five hundred men, and the judges put on their black silk robes, waiting for the sheriff to protect their trip to the courthouse. But there at the courthouse steps, Luke Day stood with a petition, asserting the people's constitutional right to protest the unconstitutional acts of the General Court, asking the judges to adjourn until the General Court could act on behalf of the farmers. Standing with Luke Day were fifteen hundred armed farmers. The judges adjourned.

Shortly after, at courthouses in Worcester and Athol, farmers with guns prevented the courts from meeting to take away their property, and the militia were too sympathetic to the farmers, or too outnumbered, to act. In Concord, a fifty-year-old veteran of two wars, Job Shattuck, led a caravan of carts, wagons, horses, and oxen onto the town green, while a message was sent to the judges:

The voice of the People of this county is such that the court shall not enter this courthouse until such time as the People shall have redress of the grievances they labor under at the present.

A county convention then suggested the judges adjourn, which they did.

At Great Barrington, a militia of a thousand faced a square crowded with armed men and boys. But the militia was split in its opinion. When the chief justice suggested the militia divide, those in favor of the court's sitting to go on the right side of the road, and those against on the left, two hundred of the militia went to the right, eight hundred to the left, and the judges adjourned. Then the crowd went to the home of the chief justice, who agreed to sign a pledge that the court would not sit until the Massachusetts General Court met. The crowd went back to the square, broke open the county jail, and set free the debtors. The chief justice, a country doctor, said: "I have never heard anybody point out a better way to have their grievances redressed than the people have taken."

The governor and the political leaders of Massachusetts became alarmed. Samuel Adams, once looked on as a radical leader in Boston, now insisted people act within the law. He said "British emissaries" were stirring up the farmers. People in the town of Greenwich responded: You in Boston have the money, and we don't. And didn't you act illegally yourselves in the Revolution? The insurgents were now being called Regulators. Their emblem was a sprig of hemlock.

The problem went beyond Massachusetts. In Rhode Island, the debtors had taken over the legislature and were issuing paper money. In New Hampshire, several hundred men, in September of 1786, surrounded the legislature in Exeter, asking that taxes be returned and paper money issued; they dispersed only when military action was threatened.

Daniel Shays entered the scene in western Massachusetts. A poor farm hand when the revolution broke out, he joined the Continental army, fought at Lexington, Bunker Hill, and Saratoga, and was wounded in action. In 1780, not being paid, he resigned from the army, went home, and soon found himself in court for nonpayment of debts. He also saw what was happening to others: a sick woman, unable to pay, had her bed taken from under her.

What brought Shays fully into the situation was that on September 19, the Supreme Judicial Court of Massachusetts met in Worcester and indicted eleven leaders of the rebellion, including three of his friends, as "disorderly, riotous and seditious persons" who "unlawfully and by force of arms" prevented "the execution of justice and the laws of the commonwealth." The Supreme Judicial Court planned to meet again in Springfield a week later, and there was talk of Luke Day's being indicted.

Shays organized seven hundred armed farmers, most of them veterans of the war, and led them to Springfield. There they found a general with nine hundred soldiers and a cannon. Shays asked the general for permission to parade, which the general granted, so Shays and his men moved through the square, drums banging and fifes blowing. As they marched, their ranks grew. Some of the militia joined, and reinforcements began coming in from the countryside. The judges postponed hearings for a day, then adjourned the court.

Now the General Court, meeting in Boston, was told by Governor James Bowdoin to "vindicate the insulted dignity of government." The recent rebels against England, secure in office, were calling for law and order. Sam Adams helped draw up a Riot Act, and a resolution suspending habeas corpus, to allow the authorities to keep people in jail without trial. At the same time, the legislature moved to make some concessions to the angry farmers, saying certain old taxes could now be paid in goods instead of money.

This didn't help. In Worcester, 160 insurgents appeared at the courthouse. The sheriff read the Riot Act. The insurgents said they would disperse only if the judges did. The sheriff shouted something about hanging. Someone came up behind him and put a sprig of hemlock in his hat. The judges left.

Confrontations between farmers and militia now multiplied. The winter snows began to interfere with the trips of farmers to the courthouses. When Shays began marching a thousand men into Boston, a blizzard forced them back, and one of his men froze to death.

An army came into the field, led by General Benjamin Lincoln, on money raised by Boston merchants. In an artillery duel, three rebels were killed. One soldier stepped in front of his own artillery piece and lost both arms. The winter grew worse. The rebels were outnumbered and on the run. Shays took refuge in Vermont, and his followers began to surrender. There were a few more deaths in battle, and then sporadic, disorganized, desperate acts of violence against authority: the burning of barns, the slaughter of a general's horses. One government soldier was killed in an eerie night-time collision of two sleighs.

Captured rebels were put on trial in Northampton and six were sentenced to death. A note was left at the door of the high sheriff of Pittsfield:

I understand that there is a number of my countrymen condemned to die because they fought for justice. I pray have a care that you assist not in the execution of so horrid a crime, for by all that is above, he that condemns and he that executes shall share alike. . . . Prepare for death with speed, for your life or mine is short. When the woods are covered with leaves, I shall return and pay you a short visit.

Thirty-three more rebels were put on trial and six more condemned to death. Arguments took place over whether the hangings should go forward. General Lincoln urged mercy and a Commission of Clemency, but Samuel Adams said: "In monarchy the crime of treason may admit of being pardoned or lightly punished, but the man who dares rebel against the laws of a republic ought to suffer death." Several hangings followed; some of the condemned were pardoned. Shays, in Vermont, was pardoned in 1788 and returned to Massachusetts, where he died, poor and obscure, in 1825.

It was Thomas Jefferson, in France as ambassador at the time of Shays' Rebellion, who spoke of such uprisings as healthy for society. In a letter to a friend he wrote: "I hold it that a little rebellion now and then is a good thing. . . . It is a medicine necessary for the sound health of government. . . . God forbid that we should ever be twenty years without such a rebellion. . . . The tree of liberty must be refreshed from time to time with the blood of patriots and tyrants. It is its natural manure."

But Jefferson was far from the scene. The political and economic elite of the country were not so tolerant. They worried that the example might spread. A veteran of Washington's army, General Henry Knox, founded an organization of army veterans, "The Order of the Cincinnati," presumably (as one historian put it) "for the purpose of cherishing the heroic memories of the struggle in which they had taken part," but also, it seemed, to watch out for radicalism in the new country. Knox wrote to Washington in late 1786 about Shays' Rebellion, and in doing so expressed the thoughts of many of the wealthy and powerful leaders of the country:

> The people who are the insurgents have never paid any, or but very little taxes. But they see the weakness of government; they feel at once their own poverty, compared with the opulent, and their own force, and they are determined to make use of the latter, in order to remedy the former. Their creed is "That the property of the United States has been protected from the confiscations of Britain by the joint exertions of all, and therefore ought to be the common property of all. And he that attempts opposition to this creed is an enemy to equity and justice and ought to be swept from off the face of the earth."

Alexander Hamilton, aide to Washington during the war, was one of the most forceful and astute leaders of the new aristocracy. He voiced his political philosophy:

All communities divide themselves into the few and the many. The first are the rich and well-born, the other the mass of the people. The voice of the people has been said to be the voice of God; and however generally this maxim has been quoted and believed, it is not true in fact. The people are turbulent and changing; they seldom judge or determine right. Give therefore to the first class a distinct permanent share in the government. . . . Can a democratic assembly who annually revolve in the mass of the people be supposed steadily to pursue the public good? Nothing but a permanent body can check the imprudence of democracy. . . .

At the Constitutional Convention, Hamilton suggested a President and Senate chosen for life.

The Convention did not take his suggestion. But neither did it provide for popular elections, except in the case of the House of Representatives, where the qualifications were set by the state legislatures (which required property-holding for voting in almost all the states), and excluded women, Indians, slaves. The Constitution provided for Senators to be elected by the state legislators, for the President to be elected by electors chosen by the state legislators, and for the Supreme Court to be appointed by the President.

The problem of democracy in the post-Revolutionary society was not, however, the Constitutional limitations on voting. It lay deeper, beyond the Constitution, in the division of society into rich and poor. For if some people had great wealth and great influence; if they had the land, the money, the newspapers, the church, the educational system—how could voting, however broad, cut into such power? There was still another problem: wasn't it the nature of representative government, even when most broadly based, to be conservative, to prevent tumultuous change?

It came time to ratify the Constitution, to submit to a vote in state conventions, with approval of nine of the thirteen required to ratify it. In New York, where debate over ratification was intense, a series of newspaper articles appeared, anonymously, and they tell us much about the nature of the Constitution. These articles, favoring adoption of the Constitution, were written by James Madison, Alexander Hamilton, and John Jay, and came to be known as the *Federalist Papers* (opponents of the Constitution became known as anti-Federalists).

In *Federalist Paper # 10*, James Madison argued that representative government was needed to maintain peace in a society ridden by factional disputes. These disputes came from "the various and unequal distribution of property. Those who hold and those who are without property have ever formed distinct interests in society." The problem, he said, was how to control the factional struggles that came from inequalities in wealth. Minority factions could be controlled, he said, by the principle that decisions would be by vote of the majority.

So the real problem, according to Madison, was a majority faction, and here the solution was offered by the Constitution, to have "an extensive republic," that is, a large nation ranging over thirteen states, for then "it will be more difficult for all who feel it to discover their own strength, and to act in unison with each other. . . . The influence of factious leaders may kindle a flame within their particular States, but will be unable to spread a general conflagration through the other States."

Madison's argument can be seen as a sensible argument for having a government which can maintain peace and avoid continuous disorder. But is it the aim of government simply to maintain order, as a referee, between two equally matched fighters? Or is it that government has some special interest in maintaining a certain kind of order, a certain distribution of power and wealth, a distribution in which government officials are not neutral referees but participants? In that case, the disorder they might worry about is the disorder of popular rebellion against those monopolizing the society's wealth. This interpretation makes sense when one looks at the economic interests, the social backgrounds, of the makers of the Constitution.

As part of his argument for a large republic to keep the peace, James Madison tells quite clearly, in *Federalist #10*, whose peace he wants to keep: "A rage for paper money, for an abolition of debts, for an equal division of property, or for any other improper or wicked project, will be less apt to pervade the whole body of the Union than a particular member of it."

When economic interest is seen behind the political clauses of the Constitution, then the document becomes not simply the work of wise men trying to establish a decent and orderly society, but the work of certain groups trying to maintain their privileges, while giving just enough rights and liberties to enough of the people to ensure popular support.

In the new government, Madison would belong to one party (the Democrat-Republicans) along with Jefferson and Monroe. Hamilton would belong to the rival party (the Federalists) along with Washington and Adams. But both agreed—one a slaveholder from Virginia, the other a merchant from New York—on the aims of this new government they were establishing. They were anticipating the long-fundamental agreement of the two political parties in the American system. Hamilton wrote elsewhere in the *Federalist Papers* that the new Union would be able "to repress domestic faction and insurrection." He referred directly to Shays' Rebellion: "The tempestuous situation from which Massachusetts has scarcely emerged evinces that dangers of this kind are not merely speculative."

It was either Madison or Hamilton (the authorship of the individual papers is not always known) who in *Federalist Paper #63* argued the necessity of a "well-constructed Senate" as "sometimes necessary as a defence to the people against their own temporary errors and delusions" because "there are particular moments in public affairs when the people, stimulated by some irregular passion, or some illicit advantage, or misled by the artful misrepresentations of interested men, may call for measures which they themselves will afterwards be the most ready to lament and condemn." And: "In these critical moments, how salutary will be the interference of some temperate and respectable body of citizens in order to check the misguided career, and to suspend the blow meditated by the people against themselves, until reason, justice, and truth can regain their authority over the public mind?"

The Constitution was a compromise between slaveholding interests of the South and moneyed interests of the North. For the purpose of uniting the thirteen states into one great market for commerce, the northern delegates wanted laws regulating interstate commerce, and urged that such laws require only a majority of Congress to pass. The South agreed to this, in return for allowing the trade in slaves to continue for twenty years before being outlawed.

Charles Beard warned us that governments—including the government of the United States—are not neutral, that they represent the dominant economic interests, and that their constitutions are intended to serve these interests. One of his critics (Robert E. Brown, *Charles Beard and the Constitution*) raises an interesting point. Granted that the Constitution omitted the phrase "life, liberty and the pursuit of happiness," which appeared in the Declaration of Independence, and substituted "life, liberty, or property"—well, why shouldn't the Constitution protect property? As Brown says about Revolutionary America, "practically everybody was interested in the protection of property" because so many Americans owned property.

However, this is misleading. True, there were many property owners. But some people had much more than others. A few people had great amounts of property; many people had small amounts; others had none. Jackson Main found that one-third of the population in the Revolutionary period were small farmers, while only 3 percent of the population had truly large holdings and could be considered wealthy.

Still, one-third was a considerable number of people who felt they had something at stake in the stability of a new government. This was a larger base of support for government than anywhere in the world at the end of the eighteenth century. In addition, the city mechanics had an important interest in a government which would protect their work from foreign competition. As Staughton Lynd puts it: "How is it that the city workingmen all over America overwhelmingly and enthusiastically supported the United States Constitution?"

This was especially true in New York. When the ninth and tenth states had ratified the Constitution, four thousand New York City mechanics marched with floats and banners to celebrate. Bakers, blacksmiths, brewers, ship joiners and shipwrights, coopers, cartmen and tailors, all marched. What Lynd found was that these mechanics, while opposing elite rule in the colonies, were nationalist. Mechanics comprised perhaps half the New York population. Some were wealthy, some were poor, but all were better off than the ordinary laborer, the apprentice, the journeyman, and their prosperity required a government that would protect them against the British hats and shoes and other goods that were pouring into the colonies after the Revolution. As a result, the mechanics often supported wealthy conservatives at the ballot box.

The Constitution, then, illustrates the complexity of the American system: that it serves the interests of a wealthy elite, but also does enough for small property owners, for middle-income mechanics and farmers, to build a broad base of support. The slightly prosperous people who make up this base of support are buffers against the blacks, the Indians, the very poor whites. They enable the elite to keep control with a minimum of coercion, a maximum of law—all made palatable by the fanfare of patriotism and unity.

The Constitution became even more acceptable to the public at large after the first Congress, responding to criticism, passed a series of amendments known as the Bill of Rights. These amendments seemed to make the new government a guardian of people's liberties: to speak, to publish, to worship, to petition, to assemble, to be tried fairly, to be secure at home against official intrusion. It was, therefore, perfectly designed to build popular backing for the new government. What was not made clear—it was a time when the language of freedom was new and its reality untested—was the shakiness of anyone's liberty when entrusted to a government of the rich and powerful.

Indeed, the same problem existed for the other provisions of the Constitution, like the clause forbidding states to "impair the obligation of contract," or that giving Congress the power to tax the people and to appropriate money. They all sound benign and neutral until one asks: Tax who, for what? Appropriate what, for whom? To protect everyone's contracts seems like an act of fairness, of equal treatment, until one considers that contracts made between rich and poor, between employer and employee, landlord and tenant, creditor and debtor, generally favor the more powerful of the two parties. Thus, to protect these contracts is to put the great power of the government, its laws, courts, sheriffs, police, on the side of the privileged—and to do it not, as in premodern times, as an exercise of brute force against the weak but as a matter of law.

The First Amendment of the Bill of Rights shows that quality of interest hiding behind innocence. Passed in 1791 by Congress, it provided that "Congress shall make no law . . . abridging the freedom of speech, or of the press. . . ." Yet, seven years after the First Amendment became part of the Constitution, Congress passed a law very clearly abridging the freedom of speech.

This was the Sedition Act of 1798, passed under John Adams's administration, at a time when Irishmen and Frenchmen in the United States were looked on as dangerous revolutionaries because of the recent French Revolution and the Irish rebellions. The Sedition Act made it a crime to say or write anything "false, scandalous and malicious" against the government, Congress, or the President, with intent to defame them, bring them into disrepute, or excite popular hatreds against them.

This act seemed to directly violate the First Amendment. Yet, it was enforced. Ten Americans were put in prison for utterances against the government, and every member of the Supreme Court in 1798–1800, sitting as an appellate judge, held it constitutional.

There was a legal basis for this, one known to legal experts, but not to the ordinary American, who would read the First Amendment and feel confident that he or she was protected in the exercise of free speech. That basis has been explained by historian Leonard Levy. Levy points out that it was generally understood (not in the population, but in higher circles) that, despite the First Amendment, the British common law of "seditious libel" still ruled in America. This meant that while the government could not exercise "prior restraint"—that is, prevent an utterance or publication in advance—it could legally punish the speaker or writer afterward. Thus, Congress has a convenient legal basis for the laws it has enacted since that time, making certain kinds of speech a crime. And, since punishment after the fact is an excellent deterrent to the exercise of free expression, the claim of "no prior restraint" itself is destroyed. This leaves the First Amendment much less than the stone wall of protection it seems at first glance.

Are the economic provisions in the Constitution enforced just as weakly? We have an instructive example almost immediately in Washington's first administration, when Congress's power to tax and appropriate money was immediately put to use by the Secretary of the Treasury, Alexander Hamilton.

Hamilton, believing that government must ally itself with the richest elements of society to make itself strong, proposed to Congress a series of laws, which it enacted, expressing this philosophy. A Bank of the United States was set up as a partnership between the government and certain banking interests. A tariff was passed to help the manufacturers. It was agreed to pay bondholders—most of the war bonds were now concentrated in a small group of wealthy people—the full value of their bonds. Tax laws were passed to raise money for this bond redemption.

One of these tax laws was the Whiskey Tax, which especially hurt small farmers who raised grain that they converted into whiskey and then sold. In 1794 the farmers of western Pennsylvania took up arms and rebelled against the collection of this tax. Secretary of the Treasury Hamilton led the troops to put them down. We see then, in the first years of the Constitution, that some of its provisions—even those paraded most flamboyantly (like the First Amendment)—might be treated lightly. Others (like the power to tax) would be powerfully enforced.

Still, the mythology around the Founding Fathers persists. To say, as one historian (Bernard Bailyn) has done recently, that "the destruction of privilege and the creation of a political system that demanded of its leaders the responsible and humane use of power were their highest aspirations" is to ignore what really happened in the America of these Founding Fathers.

Bailyn says:

> Everyone knew the basic prescription for a wise and just government. It was so to balance the contending powers in society that no one power could overwhelm the others and, unchecked, destroy the liberties that belonged to all. The problem was how to arrange the institutions of government so that this balance could be achieved.

Were the Founding Fathers wise and just men trying to achieve a good balance? In fact, they did not want a balance, except one which kept things as they were, a balance among the dominant forces at that time. They certainly did not want an equal balance between slaves and masters, propertyless and property holders, Indians and white.

As many as half the people were not even considered by the Founding Fathers as among Bailyn's "contending powers" in society. They were not mentioned in the Declaration of Independence, they were absent in the Constitution, they were invisible in the new political democracy. They were the women of early America.

6

THE INTIMATELY
OPPRESSED

It is possible, reading standard histories, to forget half the population of the country. The explorers were men, the landholders and merchants men, the political leaders men, the military figures men. The very invisibility of women, the overlooking of women, is a sign of their submerged status.

In this invisibility they were something like black slaves (and thus slave women faced a double oppression). The biological uniqueness of women, like skin color and facial characteristics for Negroes, became a basis for treating them as inferiors. True, with women, there was something more practically important in their biology than skin color—their position as childbearers—but this was not enough to account for the general push backward for all of them in society, even those who did not bear children, or those too young or too old for that. It seems that their physical characteristics became a convenience for men, who could use, exploit, and cherish someone who was at the same time servant, sex mate, companion, and bearer-teacher-warden of his children.

Societies based on private property and competition, in which monogamous families became practical units for work and socialization, found it especially useful to establish this special status of women, something akin to a house slave in the matter of intimacy and oppression, and yet requiring, because of that intimacy, and long-term connection with children, a special patronization, which on occasion, especially in the face of a show of strength, could slip over into treatment as an equal. An oppression so private would turn out hard to uproot.

Earlier societies—in America and elsewhere—in which property was held in common and families were extensive and complicated, with aunts and uncles and grandmothers and grandfathers all living together, seemed to treat women more as equals than did the white societies that later overran them, bringing "civilization" and private property.

In the Zuñi tribes of the Southwest, for instance, extended families—large clans—were based on the woman, whose husband came to live with her family. It was assumed that women owned the houses, and the fields belonged to the clans, and the women had equal rights to what was produced. A woman was more secure, because she was with her own family, and she could divorce the man when she wanted to, keeping their property.

Women in the Plains Indian tribes of the Midwest did not have farming duties but had a very important place in the tribe as healers, herbalists, and sometimes holy people who gave advice. When bands lost their male leaders, women would become chieftains. Women learned to shoot small bows, and they carried knives, because among the Sioux a woman was supposed to be able to defend herself against attack.

The puberty ceremony of the Sioux was such as to give pride to a young Sioux maiden:

> Walk the good road, my daughter, and the buffalo herds wide and dark as cloud shadows moving over the prairie will follow you. . . . Be dutiful, respectful, gentle and modest, my daughter. And proud walking. If the pride and the virtue of the women are lost, the spring will come but the buffalo trails will turn to grass. Be strong, with the warm, strong heart of the earth. No people goes down until their women are weak and dishonored. . . .

It would be an exaggeration to say that women were treated equally with men; but they were treated with respect, and the communal nature of the society gave them a more important place.

The conditions under which white settlers came to America created various situations for women. Where the first settlements consisted almost entirely of men, women were imported as sex slaves, childbearers, companions. In 1619, the year that the first black slaves came to Virginia, ninety women arrived at Jamestown on one ship: "Agreeable persons, young and incorrupt . . . sold with their own consent to settlers as wives, the price to be the cost of their own transportation."

Many women came in those early years as indentured servants—often teenaged girls—and lived lives not much different from slaves, except that the term of service had an end. They were to be obedient to masters and mistresses. The authors of *America's Working Women* (Baxandall, Gordon, and Reverby) describe the situation:

They were poorly paid and often treated rudely and harshly, deprived of good food and privacy. Of course these terrible conditions provoked resistance. Living in separate families without much contact with others in their position, indentured servants had one primary path of resistance open to them: passive resistance, trying to do as little work as possible and to create difficulties for their masters and mistresses. Of course the masters and mistresses did not interpret it that way, but saw the difficult behavior of their servants as sullenness, laziness, malevolence and stupidity.

For instance, the General Court of Connecticut in 1645 ordered that a certain "Susan C., for her rebellious carriage toward her mistress, to be sent to the house of correction and be kept to hard labor and coarse diet, to be brought forth the next lecture day to be publicly corrected, and so to be corrected weekly, until order be given to the contrary."

Sexual abuse of masters against servant girls became commonplace. The court records of Virginia and other colonies show masters brought into court for this, so we can assume that these were especially flagrant cases; there must have been many more instances never brought to public light.

In 1756, Elizabeth Sprigs wrote to her father about her servitude:

> What we unfortunate English People suffer here is beyond the probility of you in England to Conceive, let it suffice that I one of the unhappy Number, am toiling almost Day and Night, and very often in the Horses druggery, with only this comfort that you Bitch you do not halfe enough, and then tied up and whipp'd to that Degree that you'd not serve an Annimal, scarce any thing but Indian Corn and Salt to eat and that even begrudged nay many Negroes are better used, almost naked no shoes nor stockings to wear . . . what rest we can get is to rap ourselves up in a Blanket and ly upon the Ground. . . .

Whatever horrors can be imagined in the transport of black slaves to America must be multiplied for black women, who were often one-third of the cargo. Slave traders reported:

> I saw pregnant women give birth to babies while chained to corpses which our drunken overseers had not removed. . . . packed spoon-fashion they often gave birth to children in the scalding perspiration from the human cargo. . . . On board the ship was a young negro woman chained to the deck, who had lost her senses soon after she was purchased and taken on board.

A woman named Linda Brent who escaped from slavery told of another burden:

> But I now entered on my fifteenth year—a sad epoch in the life of a slave girl. My master began to whisper foul words in my ear. Young as I was, I could not remain ignorant of their import. . . . My master met me at every turn, reminding me that I belonged to him, and swearing by heaven and earth that he would compel me to submit to him. If I went out for a breath of fresh air, after a day of unwearied toil, his footsteps dogged me. If I knelt by my mother's grave, his dark shadow fell on me even there. The light heart which nature had given me became heavy with sad forebodings. . . .

Even free white women, not brought as servants or slaves but as wives of the early settlers, faced special hardships. Eighteen married women came over on the *Mayflower.* Three were pregnant, and one of them gave birth to a dead child before they landed. Childbirth and sickness plagued the women; by the spring, only four of those eighteen women were still alive.

Those who lived, sharing the work of building a life in the wilderness with their men, were often given a special respect because they were so badly needed. And when men died, women often took up the men's work as well. All through the first century and more, women on the American frontier seemed close to equality with their men.

But all women were burdened with ideas carried over from England with the colonists, influenced by Christian teachings. English law was summarized in a document of 1632 entitled "The Lawes Resolutions of Womens Rights":

> In this consolidation which we call wedlock is a locking together. It is true, that man and wife are one person, but understand in what manner. When a small brooke or little river incorporateth with Rhodanus, Humber, or the Thames, the poor rivulet looseth her name. . . . A woman as soon as she is married, is called *covert* . . . that is, "veiled"; as it were, clouded and overshadowed; she hath lost her streame. I may more truly, farre away, say to a married woman, Her new self is her superior; her companion, her master. . . .

Julia Spruill describes the woman's legal situation in the colonial period: "The husband's control over the wife's person extended to the right of giving her chastisement. . . . But he was not entitled to inflict permanent injury or death on his wife. . . ."

As for property: "Besides absolute possession of his wife's personal property and a life estate in her lands, the husband took any other income that might be hers. He collected wages earned by her labor. . . . Naturally it followed that the proceeds of the joint labor of husband and wife belonged to the husband."

For a woman to have a child out of wedlock was a crime, and colonial court records are full of cases of women being arraigned for "bastardy"—the father of the child untouched by the law and on the loose. A colonial periodical of 1747 reproduced a speech "of Miss Polly Baker before a Court of Judicature, at Connecticut near Boston in New England; where she was prosecuted the fifth time for having a Bastard Child." (The speech was Benjamin Franklin's ironic invention.)

May it please the honourable bench to indulge me in a few words: i am a poor, unhappy woman, who have no money to fee lawyers to plead for me. . . . This is the fifth time, gentlemen, that I have been dragg'd before your court on the same account; twice I have paid heavy fines, and twice have been brought to publick punishment, for want of money to pay those fines. This may have been agreeable to the laws, and I don't dispute it; but since laws are sometimes unreasonable in themselves, and therefore repealed; and others bear too hard on the subject in particular circumstances . . . I take the liberty to say, that I think this law, by which I am punished, both unreasonable in itself, and particularly severe with regard to me. . . . Abstracted from the law, I cannot conceive . . . what the nature of my offense is. I have brought five fine children into the world, at the risque of my life; I have maintained them well by my own industry, without burthening the township, and would have done it better, if it had not been for the heavy charges and fines I have paid. . . . nor has anyone the least cause of complaint against me, unless, perhaps, the ministers of justice, because I have had children without being married, by which they missed a wedding fee. But can this be a fault of mine? . . .

What must poor young women do, whom customs and nature forbid to solicit the men, and who cannot force themselves upon husbands, when the laws take no care to provide them any, and yet severely punish them if they do their duty without them; the duty of the first and great command of nature and nature's God, encrease and multiply; a duty from the steady performance of which nothing has been able to deter me, but for its sake I have hazarded the loss of the publick esteem, and have frequently endured publick disgrace and punishment; and therefore ought, in my humble opinion, instead of a whipping, to have a statue erected to my memory.

The father's position in the family was expressed in *The Spectator*, an influential periodical in America and England: "Nothing is more gratifying to the mind of man than power or dominion; and . . . as I am the father of a family . . . I am perpetually taken up in giving out orders, in prescribing duties, in hearing parties, in administering justice, and in distributing rewards and punishments. . . . In short, sir, I look upon my family as a patriarchal sovereignty in which I am myself both king and priest."

No wonder that Puritan New England carried over this subjection of women. At a trial of a woman for daring to complain about the work a carpenter had done for her, one of the powerful church fathers of Boston, the Reverend John Cotton, said: ". . . that the husband should obey his wife, and not the wife the husband, that is a false principle. For God hath put another law upon women: wives, be subject to your husbands in all things."

A best-selling "pocket book," published in London, was widely read in the American colonies in the 1700s. It was called *Advice to a Daughter*:

> You must first lay it down for a Foundation in general, That there is Inequality in Sexes, and that for the better Oeconomy of the World; the Men, who were to be the Law-givers, had the larger share of Reason bestow'd upon them; by which means your Sex is the better prepar'd for the Compliance that is necessary for the performance of those Duties which seem'd to be most properly assign'd to it. . . . Your Sex wanteth our Reason for your Conduct, and our Strength for your Protection: Ours wanteth your Gentleness to soften, and to entertain us. . . .

Against this powerful education, it is remarkable that women nevertheless rebelled. Women rebels have always faced special disabilities: they live under the daily eye of their master; and they are isolated one from the other in households, thus missing the daily camaraderie which has given heart to rebels of other oppressed groups.

Anne Hutchinson was a religious woman, mother of thirteen children, and knowledgeable about healing with herbs. She defied the church fathers in the early years of the Massachusetts Bay Colony by insisting that she, and other ordinary people, could interpret the Bible for themselves. A good speaker, she held meetings to which more and more women came (and even a few men), and soon groups of sixty or more were gathering at her home in Boston to listen to her criticisms of local ministers. John Winthrop, the governor, described her as "a woman of a haughty and fierce carriage, of a nimble wit and active spirit, and a very voluble tongue, more bold than a man, though in understanding and judgement, inferior to many women."

Anne Hutchinson was put on trial twice: by the church for heresy, and by the government for challenging their authority. At her civil trial she was pregnant and ill, but they did not allow her to sit down until she was close to collapse. At her religious trial she was interrogated for weeks, and again she was sick, but challenged her questioners with expert knowledge of the Bible and remarkable eloquence. When finally she repented in writing, they were not satisfied. They said: "Her repentance is not in her countenance."

She was banished from the colony, and when she left for Rhode Island in 1638, thirty-five families followed her. Then she went to the shores of Long Island, where Indians who had been defrauded of their land thought she was one of their enemies; they killed her and her family. Twenty years later, the one person back in Massachusetts Bay who had spoken up for her during her trial, Mary Dyer, was hanged by the government of the colony, along with two other Quakers, for "rebellion, sedition, and presumptuous obtruding themselves."

It remained rare for women to participate openly in public affairs, although on the southern and western frontiers conditions made this occasionally possible. Julia Spruill found in Georgia's early records the story of Mary Musgrove Matthews, daughter of an Indian mother and an English father, who could speak the Creek language and became an adviser on Indian affairs to Governor James Oglethorpe of Georgia. Spruill finds that as the communities became more settled, women were thrust back farther from public life and seemed to behave more timorously than before. One petition: "It is not the province of our sex to reason deeply upon the policy of the order."

During the Revolution, however, Spruill reports, the necessities of war brought women out into public affairs. Women formed patriotic groups, carried out anti-British actions, wrote articles for independence. They were active in the campaign against the British tea tax, which made tea prices intolerably high. They organized Daughters of Liberty groups, boycotting British goods, urging women to make their own clothes and buy only American-made things. In 1777 there was a women's counterpart to the Boston Tea Party—a "coffee party," described by Abigail Adams in a letter to her husband John:

> One eminent, wealthy, stingy merchant (who is a bachelor) had a hogshead of coffee in his store, which he refused to sell the committee under six shillings per pound. A number of females, some say a hundred, some say

more, assembled with a cart and trunks, marched down to the warehouse, and demanded the keys, which he refused to deliver. Upon which one of them seized him by his neck and tossed him into the cart. Upon his finding no quarter, he delivered the keys when they tipped up the cart and discharged him; then opened the warehouse, hoisted out the coffee themselves, put it into the trunks and drove off. . . . A large concourse of men stood amazed, silent spectators of the whole transaction.

It has been pointed out by women historians recently that the contributions of working-class women in the American Revolution have been mostly ignored, unlike the genteel wives of the leaders (Dolly Madison, Martha Washington, Abigail Adams). Margaret Corbin, called "Dirty Kate," Deborah Sampson Garnet, and "Molly Pitcher" were rough, lower-class women, prettified into ladies by historians. While poor women, in the last years of the fighting, went to army encampments, helped, and fought, they were represented later as prostitutes, whereas Martha Washington was given a special place in history books for visiting her husband at Valley Forge.

When feminist impulses are recorded, they are, almost always, the writings of privileged women who had some status from which to speak freely, more opportunity to write and have their writings recorded. Abigail Adams, even before the Declaration of Independence, in March of 1776, wrote to her husband:

> . . . in the new code of laws which I suppose it will be necessary for you to make, I desire you would remember the ladies, and be more generous to them than your ancestors. Do not put such unlimited power in the hands of husbands. Remember, all men would be tyrants if they could. If particular care and attention are not paid to the ladies, we are determined to foment a rebellion, and will not hold ourselves bound to obey the laws in which we have no voice of representation.

Nevertheless, Jefferson underscored his phrase "all men are created equal" by his statement that American women would be "too wise to wrinkle their foreheads with politics." And after the Revolution, none of the new state constitutions granted women the right to vote, except for New Jersey, and that state rescinded the right in 1807. New York's constitution specifically disfranchised women by using the word "male."

While perhaps 90 percent of the white male population were literate around 1750, only 40 percent of the women were. Working-class women had little means of communicating, and no means of recording

whatever sentiments of rebelliousness they may have felt at their subordination. Not only were they bearing children in great numbers, under
great hardships, but they were working in the home. Around the time of
the Declaration of Independence, four thousand women and children in
Philadelphia were spinning at home for local plants under the "putting
out" system. Women also were shopkeepers and innkeepers and
engaged in many trades. They were bakers, tinworkers, brewers, tan-
ners, ropemakers, lumberjacks, printers, morticians, woodworkers, stay-
makers, and more.

Ideas of female equality were in the air during and after the
Revolution. Tom Paine spoke out for the equal rights of women. And
the pioneering book of Mary Wollstonecraft in England, *A Vindication of
the Rights of Women,* was reprinted in the United States shortly after the
Revolutionary War. Wollstonecraft was responding to the English conservative and opponent of the French Revolution, Edmund Burke, who
had written in his *Reflections on the Revolution in France* that "a woman is
but an animal, and an animal not of the highest order." She wrote:

> I wish to persuade women to endeavor to acquire strength, both of mind
> and body, and to convince them that soft phrases, susceptibility of heart,
> delicacy of sentiment, and refinement of taste, are almost synonymous with
> epithets of weakness, and that those beings who are only the objects of pity
> and that kind of love . . . will soon become objects of contempt. . . .
>
> I wish to show that the first object of laudable ambition is to obtain a
> character as a human being, regardless of the distinction of sex.

Between the American Revolution and the Civil War, so many elements of American society were changing—the growth of population,
the movement westward, the development of the factory system, expansion of political rights for white men, educational growth to match the
new economic needs—that changes were bound to take place in the situation of women. In preindustrial America, the practical need for
women in a frontier society had produced some measure of equality;
women worked at important jobs—publishing newspapers, managing
tanneries, keeping taverns, engaging in skilled work. In certain professions, like midwifery, they had a monopoly. Nancy Cott tells of a grand-
mother, Martha Moore Ballard, on a farm in Maine in 1795, who "baked
and brewed, pickled and preserved, spun and sewed, made soap and
dipped candles" and who, in twenty-five years as a midwife, delivered
more than a thousand babies. Since education took place inside the family, women had a special role there.

There was complex movement in different directions. Now, women were being pulled out of the house and into industrial life, while at the same time there was pressure for women to stay home where they were more easily controlled. The outside world, breaking into the solid cubicle of the home, created fears and tensions in the dominant male world, and brought forth ideological controls to replace the loosening family controls: the idea of "the woman's place," promulgated by men, was accepted by many women.

As the economy developed, men dominated as mechanics and tradesmen, and aggressiveness became more and more defined as a male trait. Women, perhaps precisely because more of them were moving into the dangerous world outside, were told to be passive. Clothing styles developed—for the rich and middle class of course, but, as always, there was the intimidation of style even for the poor—in which the weight of women's clothes, corsets and petticoats, emphasized female separation from the world of activity.

It became important to develop a set of ideas, taught in church, in school, and in the family, to keep women in their place even as that place became more and more unsettled. Barbara Welter *(Dimity Convictions)* has shown how powerful was the "cult of true womanhood" in the years after 1820. The woman was expected to be pious. A man writing in *The Ladies' Repository:* "Religion is exactly what a woman needs, for it gives her that dignity that bests suits her dependence." Mrs. John Sandford, in her book *Woman, in Her Social and Domestic Character,* said: "Religion is just what woman needs. Without it she is ever restless or unhappy."

Sexual purity was to be the special virtue of a woman. It was assumed that men, as a matter of biological nature, would sin, but woman must not surrender. As one male author said: "If you do, you will be left in silent sadness to bewail your credulity, imbecility, duplicity, and premature prostitution." A woman wrote that females would get into trouble if they were "high spirited not prudent."

The role began early, with adolescence. Obedience prepared the girl for submission to the first proper mate. Barbara Welter describes this:

The assumption is twofold: the American female was supposed to be so infinitely lovable and provocative that a healthy male could barely control himself when in the same room with her, and the same girl, as she "comes out" of the cocoon of her family's protectiveness, is so palpitating with undirected affection, so filled to the brim with tender feelings, that she fixes her love on the first person she sees. She awakes from the midsummer night's dream of adolescence, and it is the responsibility of her family and society to see that her eyes fall on a suitable match and not some clown with the head of an ass. They do their part by such restrictive measures as segregated (by sex and/or class) schools, dancing classes, travel, and other external controls. She is required to exert the inner control of obedience. The combination forms a kind of societal chastity belt which is not unlocked until the marriage partner has arrived, and adolescence is formally over.

When Amelia Bloomer in 1851 suggested in her feminist publication that women wear a kind of short skirt and pants, to free themselves from the encumbrances of traditional dress, this was attacked in the popular women's literature. One story has a girl admiring the "bloomer" costume, but her professor admonishes her that they are "only one of the many manifestations of that wild spirit of socialism and agrarian radicalism which is at present so rife in our land."

In *The Young Lady's Book* of 1830: ". . . in whatever situation of life a woman is placed from her cradle to her grave, a spirit of obedience and submission, pliability of temper, and humility of mind, are required from her." And one woman wrote, in 1850, in the book *Greenwood Leaves:* "True feminine genius is ever timid, doubtful, and clingingly dependent; a perpetual childhood." Another book, *Recollections of a Southern Matron:* "If any habit of his annoyed me, I spoke of it once or twice, calmly, then bore it quietly." Giving women "Rules for Conjugal and Domestic Happiness," one book ended with: "Do not expect too much."

The woman's job was to keep the home cheerful, maintain religion, be nurse, cook, cleaner, seamstress, flower arranger. A woman shouldn't read too much, and certain books should be avoided. When Harriet Martineau, a reformer of the 1830s, wrote *Society in America*, one reviewer suggested it be kept away from women: "Such reading will unsettle them for their true station and pursuits, and they will throw the world back again into confusion."

A sermon preached in 1808 in New York:

How interesting and important are the duties devolved on females as wives . . . the counsellor and friend of the husband; who makes it her daily study to lighten his cares, to soothe his sorrows, and to augment his joys; who, like a guardian angel, watches over his interests, warns him against dangers, comforts him under trials; and by her pious, assiduous, and attractive deportment, constantly endeavors to render him more virtuous, more useful, more honourable, and more happy.

Women were also urged, especially since they had the job of educating children, to be patriotic. One women's magazine offered a prize to the woman who wrote the best essay on "How May an American Woman Best Show Her Patriotism."

It was in the 1820s and 1830s, Nancy Cott tells us (*The Bonds of Womanhood*), that there was an outpouring of novels, poems, essays, sermons, and manuals on the family, children, and women's role. The world outside was becoming harder, more commercial, more demanding. In a sense, the home carried a longing for some utopian past, some refuge from immediacy.

Perhaps it made acceptance of the new economy easier to be able to see it as only part of life, with the home a haven. In 1819, one pious wife wrote: ". . . the air of the world is poisonous. You must carry an antidote with you, or the infection will prove fatal." All this was not, as Cott points out, to challenge the world of commerce, industry, competition, capitalism, but to make it more palatable.

The cult of domesticity for the woman was a way of pacifying her with a doctrine of "separate but equal"—giving her work equally as important as the man's, but separate and different. Inside that "equality" there was the fact that the woman did not choose her mate, and once her marriage took place, her life was determined. One girl wrote in 1791: "The die is about to be cast which will probably determine the future happiness or misery of my life. . . . I have always anticipated the event with a degree of solemnity almost equal to that which will terminate my present existence."

Marriage enchained, and children doubled the chains. One woman, writing in 1813: "The idea of soon giving birth to my third child and the consequent duties I shall be called to discharge distresses me so I feel as if I should sink." This despondency was lightened by the thought that something important was given the woman to do: to impart to her children the moral values of self-restraint and advancement through individual excellence rather than common action.

The new ideology worked; it helped to produce the stability needed by a growing economy. But its very existence showed that other currents were at work, not easily contained. And giving the woman her sphere created the possibility that she might use that space, that time, to prepare for another kind of life.

The "cult of true womanhood" could not completely erase what was visible as evidence of woman's subordinate status: she could not vote, could not own property; when she did work, her wages were one-fourth to one-half what men earned in the same job. Women were excluded from the professions of law and medicine, from colleges, from the ministry.

Putting all women into the same category—giving them all the same domestic sphere to cultivate—created a classification (by sex) which blurred the lines of class, as Nancy Cott points out. However, forces were at work to keep raising the issue of class. Samuel Slater had introduced industrial spinning machinery in New England in 1789, and now there was a demand for young girls—literally, "spinsters"—to work the spinning machinery in factories. In 1814, the power loom was introduced in Waltham, Massachusetts, and now all the operations needed to turn cotton fiber into cloth were under one roof. The new textile factories swiftly multiplied, with women 80 to 90 percent of their operatives—most of these women between fifteen and thirty.

Some of the earliest industrial strikes took place in these textile mills in the 1830s. Eleanor Flexner *(A Century of Struggle)* gives figures that suggest why: women's daily average earnings in 1836 were less than $37\frac{1}{2}$ cents, and thousands earned 25 cents a day, working twelve to sixteen hours a day. In Pawtucket, Rhode Island, in 1824, came the first known strike of women factory workers; 202 women joined men in protesting a wage cut and longer hours, but they met separately. Four years later, women in Dover, New Hampshire, struck alone. And in Lowell, Massachusetts, in 1834, when a young woman was fired from her job, other girls left their looms, one of them then climbing the town pump and making, according to a newspaper report, "a flaming Mary Wollstonecraft speech on the rights of women and the iniquities of the 'moneyed aristocracy' which produced a powerful effect on her auditors and they determined to have their own way, if they died for it."

A journal kept by an unsympathetic resident of Chicopee, Massachusetts, recorded an event of May 2, 1843:

> Great turnout among the girls . . . after breakfast this morning a procession preceded by a painted window curtain for a banner went round the square, the number sixteen. They soon came past again . . . then numbered forty-four. They marched around a while and then dispersed. After dinner they sallied forth to the number of forty-two and marched around to Cabot. . . . They marched around the streets doing themselves no credit. . . .

There were strikes in various cities in the 1840s, more militant than those early New England "turnouts," but mostly unsuccessful. A succession of strikes in the Allegheny mills near Pittsburgh demanded a shorter workday. Several times in those strikes, women armed with sticks and stones broke through the wooden gates of a textile mill and stopped the looms.

Catharine Beecher, a woman reformer of the time, wrote about the factory system:

> Let me now present the facts I learned by observation or inquiry on the spot. I was there in mid-winter, and every morning I was awakened at five, by the bells calling to labor. The time allowed for dressing and breakfast was so short, as many told me, that both were performed hurriedly, and then the work at the mill was begun by lamplight, and prosecuted without remission till twelve, and chiefly in a standing position. Then half an hour only allowed for dinner, from which the time for going and returning was deducted. Then back to the mills, to work till seven o'clock. . . . it must be remembered that all the hours of labor are spent in rooms where oil lamps, together with from 40 to 80 persons, are exhausting the healthful principle of the air . . . and where the air is loaded with particles of cotton thrown from thousands of cards, spindles, and looms.

And the life of upper-class women? Frances Trollope, an Englishwoman, in her book *Domestic Manners of the Americans*, wrote:

> Let me be permitted to describe the day of a Philadelphian lady of the first class. . . .
>
> This lady shall be the wife of a senator and a lawyer in the highest repute and practice. . . . She rises, and her first hour is spent in the scrupulously nice arrangement of her dress; she descends to her parlor, neat, stiff, and silent; her breakfast is brought in by her free black footman; she eats her fried ham and her salt fish, and drinks her coffee in silence, while her husband reads one newspaper, and puts another under his elbow; and then perhaps, she washes the cups and saucers. Her carriage is ordered at eleven; till that hour she is employed in the pastry room, her snow-white apron protecting her mouse-colored silk. Twenty minutes before her carriage should appear, she retires to her chamber, as she calls it; shakes and folds up her still snowwhite apron, smooths her rich dress, and . . . sets on her elegant bonnet . . . then walks downstairs, just at the moment that her free black coachman announces to her free black footman that the carriage waits. She steps into it, and gives the word: "Drive to the Dorcas Society."

At Lowell, a Female Labor Reform Association put out a series of "Factory Tracts." The first was entitled "Factory Life as It Is By an

Operative" and spoke of the textile mill women as "nothing more nor less than slaves in every sense of the word! Slaves, to a system of labor which requires them to toil from five until seven o'clock, with one hour only to attend to the wants of nature—slaves to the will and requirements of the 'powers that be.' . . . "

In 1845, the New York *Sun* carried this item:

> "Mass Meeting of Young Women"—We are requested to call the attention of the young women of the city engaged in industrous pursuits to the call for a mass meeting in the Park this afternoon at 4 o'clock.
>
> We are also requested to appeal to the gallantry of the men of this city . . . and respectfully ask them not to be present at this meeting as those for whose benefit it is called prefer to deliberate by themselves.

Around that time, the New York *Herald* carried a story about "700 females, generally of the most interesting state and appearance," meeting "in their endeavor to remedy the wrongs and oppressions under which they labor." The *Herald* editorialized about such meetings: ". . . we very much doubt whether it will terminate in much good to female labor of any description. . . . All combinations end in nothing."

The title of Nancy Cott's book *The Bonds of Womanhood* reflects her double view of what was happening to women in the early nineteenth century. They were trapped in the bonds of the new ideology of "women's sphere" in the home, and, when forced out to work in factories, or even in middle-class professions, found another kind of bondage. On the other hand, these conditions created a common consciousness of their situation and forged bonds of solidarity among them.

Middle-class women, barred from higher education, began to monopolize the profession of primary-school teaching. As teachers, they read more, communicated more, and education itself became subversive of old ways of thinking. They began to write for magazines and newspapers, and started some ladies' publications. Literacy among women doubled between 1780 and 1840. Women became health reformers. They formed movements against double standards in sexual behavior and the victimization of prostitutes. They joined in religious organizations. Some of the most powerful of them joined the antislavery movement. So, by the time a clear feminist movement emerged in the 1840s, women had become practiced organizers, agitators, speakers.

When Emma Willard addressed the New York legislature in 1819 on the subject of education for women, she was contradicting the statement made just the year before by Thomas Jefferson (in a letter) in which he suggested women should not read novels "as a mass of trash" with few exceptions. "For a like reason, too, much poetry should not be indulged." Female education should concentrate, he said, on "ornaments too, and the amusements of life.... These, for a female, are dancing, drawing, and music."

Emma Willard told the legislature that the education of women "has been too exclusively directed to fit them for displaying to advantage the charms of youth and beauty." The problem, she said, was that "the taste of men, whatever it might happen to be, has been made into a standard for the formation of the female character." Reason and religion teach us, she said, that "we too are primary existences . . . not the satellites of men."

In 1821, Willard founded the Troy Female Seminary, the first recognized institution for the education of girls. She wrote later of how she upset people by teaching her students about the human body:

> Mothers visiting a class at the Seminary in the early thirties were so shocked at the sight of a pupil drawing a heart, arteries and veins on a blackboard to explain the circulation of the blood, that they left the room in shame and dismay. To preserve the modesty of the girls, and spare them too frequent agitation, heavy paper was pasted over the pages in their textbooks which depicted the human body.

Women struggled to enter the all-male professional schools. Dr. Harriot Hunt, a woman physician who began to practice in 1835, was twice refused admission to Harvard Medical School. But she carried on her practice, mostly among women and children. She believed strongly in diet, exercise, hygiene, and mental health. She organized a Ladies Physiological Society in 1843 where she gave monthly talks. She remained single, defying convention here too.

Elizabeth Blackwell got her medical degree in 1849, having overcome many rebuffs before being admitted to Geneva College. She then set up the New York Dispensary for Poor Women and Children "to give to poor women an opportunity of consulting physicians of their own sex." In her first *Annual Report*, she wrote:

> My first medical consultation was a curious experience. In a severe case of pneumonia in an elderly lady I called in consultation a kind-hearted physician of high standing.... This gentleman, after seeing the patient, went with me into the parlour. There he began to walk about the room in some agitation, exclaiming, "A most extraordinary case! Such a one never happened to me before; I really do not know what to do!" I listened in surprise

and much perplexity, as it was a clear case of pneumonia and of no unusual degree of danger, until at last I discovered that his perplexity related to *me*, not to the patient, and to the propriety of consulting with a lady physician!

Oberlin College pioneered in the admission of women. But the first girl admitted to the theology school there, Antoinette Brown, who graduated in 1850, found that her name was left off the class list. With Lucy Stone, Oberlin found a formidable resister. She was active in the peace society and in antislavery work, taught colored students, and organized a debating club for girls. She was chosen to write the commencement address, then was told it would have to be read by a man. She refused to write it.

Lucy Stone began lecturing on women's rights in 1847 in a church in Gardner, Massachusetts, where her brother was a minister. She was tiny, weighed about 100 pounds, was a marvelous speaker. As lecturer for the American Anti-Slavery Society, she was, at various times, deluged with cold water, sent reeling by a thrown book, attacked by mobs.

When she married Henry Blackwell, they joined hands at their wedding and read a statement:

> While we acknowledge our mutual affection by publicly assuming the relationship of husband and wife . . . we deem it a duty to declare that this act on our part implies no sanction of, nor promise of voluntary obedience to such of the present laws of marriage as refuse to recognize the wife as an independent, rational being, while they confer upon the husband an injurious and unnatural superiority. . . .

She was one of the first to refuse to give up her name after marriage. She was "Mrs. Stone." When she refused to pay taxes because she was not represented in the government, officials took all her household goods in payment, even her baby's cradle.

After Amelia Bloomer, a postmistress in a small town in New York State, developed the bloomer, women activists adopted it in place of the old whale-boned bodice, the corsets and petticoats. Elizabeth Cady Stanton, who was one of the leaders of the feminist movement in this period, told of how she first saw a cousin of hers wearing bloomers:

> To see my cousin with a lamp in one hand and a baby in the other, walk upstairs, with ease and grace while, with flowing robes, I pulled myself up with difficulty, lamp and baby out of the question, readily convinced me that there was sore need of a reform in woman's dress and I promptly donned a similar costume.

Women, after becoming involved in other movements of reform—antislavery, temperance, dress styles, prison conditions—turned, emboldened and experienced, to their own situation. Angelina Grimké, a southern white woman who became a fierce speaker and organizer against slavery, saw that movement leading further:

> Let us all first wake up the nation to lift millions of slaves of both sexes from the dust, and turn them into men and then . . . it will be an easy matter to take millions of females from their knees and set them on their feet, or in other words transform them from babies into women.

Margaret Fuller was perhaps the most formidable intellectual among the feminists. Her starting point, in *Woman in the Nineteenth Century*, was the understanding that "there exists in the minds of men a tone of feeling toward woman as toward slaves. . . ." She continued: "We would have every arbitrary barrier thrown down. We would have every path open to Woman as freely as to Man." And: "What woman needs is not as a woman to act or rule, but as a nature to grow, as an intellect to discern, as a soul to live freely and unimpeded. . . ."

There was much to overcome. One of the most popular writers of the mid-nineteenth century, the Reverend John Todd (one of his many best-selling books gave advice to young men on the results of masturbation—"the mind is greatly deteriorated"), commented on the new feminist mode of dress:

> Some have tried to become semi-men by putting on the Bloomer dress. Let me tell you in a word why it can never be done. It is this: woman, robed and folded in her long dress, is beautiful. She walks gracefully. . . . If she attempts to run, the charm is gone. . . . Take off the robes, and put on pants, and show the limbs, and grace and mystery are all gone.

In the 1830s, a pastoral letter from the General Association of Ministers of Massachusetts commanded ministers to forbid women to speak from pulpits: ". . . when she assumes the place and tone of man . . . we put ourselves in self-defense against her."

Sarah Grimké, Angelina's sister, wrote in response a series of articles, "Letters on the Condition of Women and the Equality of the Sexes":

> During the early part of my life, my lot was cast among the butterflies of the fashionable world; and of this class of women, I am constrained to say, both from experience and observation, that their education is miserably deficient;

that they are taught to regard marriage as the one thing needful, the only avenue to distinction. . . .

She said: "I ask no favors for my sex. I surrender not our claim to equality. All I ask of our brethren is that they will take their feet from off our necks, and permit us to stand upright on the ground which God has designed us to occupy. . . . To me it is perfectly clear that whatsoever it is morally right for a man to do, it is morally right for a woman to do."

Sarah could write with power; Angelina was the firebrand speaker. Once she spoke six nights in a row at the Boston Opera House. To the argument of some well-meaning fellow abolitionists that they should not advocate sexual equality because it was so outrageous to the common mind that it would hurt the campaign for the abolition of slavery, she responded:

> We cannot push Abolitionism forward with all our might until we take up the stumbling block out of the road. . . . If we surrender the right to speak in public this year, we must surrender the right to petition next year, and the right to write the year after, and so on. What then can woman do for the slave, when she herself is under the feet of man and shamed into silence?

Angelina was the first woman (in 1838) to address a committee of the Massachusetts state legislature on antislavery petitions. She later said: "I was so near fainting under the tremendous pressure of feeling. . . ." Her talk attracted a huge crowd, and a representative from Salem proposed that "a Committee be appointed to examine the foundations of the State House of Massachusetts to see whether it will bear another lecture from Miss Grimké!"

Speaking out on other issues prepared the way for speaking on the situation of women: Dorothea Dix, in 1843, addressed the legislature of Massachusetts on what she saw in the prisons and almshouses in the Boston area:

> I tell what I have seen, painful and shocking as the details often are. . . . I proceed, gentlemen, briefly to call your attention to the present state of insane persons confined within this Commonwealth in cages, closets, cellars, stalls, pens; chained, naked, beaten with rods, and lashed into obedience! . . .

Frances Wright was a writer, founder of a utopian community, immigrant from Scotland in 1824, a fighter for the emancipation of slaves, for birth control and sexual freedom. She wanted free public education for all children over two years of age in state-supported boarding schools. She expressed in America what the utopian socialist Charles Fourier had said in France, that the progress of civilization depended on the progress of women. In her words:

> I shall venture the assertion, that, until women assume the place in society which good sense and good feeling alike assign to them, human improvement must advance but feebly. . . . Men will ever rise or fall to the level of the other sex. . . . Let them not imagine that they know aught of the delights which intercourse with the other sex can give, until they have felt the sympathy of mind with mind, and heart with heart; until they bring into that intercourse every affection, every talent, every confidence, every refinement, every respect. Until power is annihilated on one side, fear and obedience on the other, and both restored to their birthright—equality.

Women put in enormous work in antislavery societies all over the country, gathering thousands of petitions to Congress. Eleanor Flexner writes in *A Century of Struggle:*

> Today, countless file boxes in the National Archives in Washington bear witness to that anonymous and heart-breaking labor. The petitions are yellowed and frail, glued together, page on page, covered with ink blots, signed with scratchy pens, with an occasional erasure by one who fearfully thought better of so bold an act. . . . They bear the names of women's anti-slavery societies from New England to Ohio. . . .

In the course of this work, events were set in motion that carried the movement of women for their own equality racing alongside the movement against slavery. In 1840, a World Anti-Slavery Society Convention met in London. After a fierce argument, it was voted to exclude women, but it was agreed they could attend meetings in a curtained enclosure. The women sat in silent protest in the gallery, and William Lloyd Garrison, one abolitionist who had fought for the rights of women, sat with them.

It was at that time that Elizabeth Cady Stanton met Lucretia Mott and others, and began to lay the plans that led to the first Women's Rights Convention in history. It was held at Seneca Falls, New York, where Elizabeth Cady Stanton lived as a mother, a housewife, full of resentment at her condition, declaring: "A woman is a nobody. A wife is everything." She wrote later:

I now fully understood the practical difficulties most women had to contend with in the isolated household, and the impossibility of woman's best development if, in contact, the chief part of her life, with servants and children. . . . The general discontent I felt with woman's portion as wife, mother, housekeeper, physician, and spiritual guide, the chaotic condition into which everything fell without her constant supervision, and the wearied, anxious look of the majority of women, impressed me with the strong feeling that some active measures should be taken to remedy the wrongs of society in general and of women in particular. My experiences at the World Anti-Slavery Convention, all I had read of the legal status of women, and the oppression I saw everywhere, together swept across my soul. . . . I could not see what to do or where to begin—my only thought was a public meeting for protest and discussion.

An announcement was put in the *Seneca County Courier* calling for a meeting to discuss the "rights of woman" the 19th and 20th of July. Three hundred women and some men came. A Declaration of Principles was signed at the end of the meeting by sixty-eight women and thirty-two men. It made use of the language and rhythm of the Declaration of Independence:

> When in the course of human events, it becomes necessary for one portion of the family of man to assume among the people of the earth a position different from that they have hitherto occupied . . .
>
> We hold these truths to be self-evident: that all men and women are created equal; that they are endowed by their Creator with certain inalienable rights; that among these are life, liberty and the pursuit of happiness. . . .
>
> The history of mankind is a history of repeated injuries and usurpations on the part of man toward woman, having in direct object the establishment of an absolute tyranny over her. To prove this, let facts be submitted to a candid world. . . .

Then came the list of grievances: no right to vote, no right to her wages or to property, no rights in divorce cases, no equal opportunity in employment, no entrance to colleges, ending with: "He had endeavored, in every way that he could, to destroy her confidence in her own powers, to lessen her self-respect and to make her willing to lead a dependent and abject life. . . ."

And then a series of resolutions, including: "That all laws which prevent woman from occupying such a station in society as her conscience shall dictate, or which place her in a position inferior to that of man, are contrary to the great precept of nature, and therefore of no force or authority."

A series of women's conventions in various parts of the country followed the one at Seneca Falls. At one of these, in 1851, an aged black woman, who had been born a slave in New York, tall, thin, wearing a gray dress and white turban, listened to some male ministers who had been dominating the discussion. This was Sojourner Truth. She rose to her feet and joined the indignation of her race to the indignation of her sex:

> That man over there says that woman needs to be helped into carriages and lifted over ditches. . . . Nobody ever helps me into carriages, or over mud-puddles or gives me any best place. And a'nt I a woman?
>
> Look at my arm! I have ploughed, and planted, and gathered into barns, and no man could head me! And a'nt I a woman?
>
> I would work as much and eat as much as a man, when I could get it, and bear the lash as well. And a'nt I a woman?
>
> I have borne thirteen children and seen em most all sold off to slavery, and when I cried out with my mother's grief, none but Jesus heard me! And a'nt I a woman?

Thus were women beginning to resist, in the 1830s and 1840s and 1850s, the attempt to keep them in their "woman's sphere." They were taking part in all sorts of movements, for prisoners, for the insane, for black slaves, and also for all women.

In the midst of these movements, there exploded, with the force of government and the authority of money, a quest for more land, an urge for national expansion.

7

AS LONG AS GRASS GROWS OR WATER RUNS

If women, of all the subordinate groups in a society dominated by rich white males, were closest to home (indeed, *in* the home), the most interior, then the Indians were the most foreign, the most exterior. Women, because they were so near and so needed, were dealt with more by patronization than by force. The Indian, not needed—indeed, an obstacle—could be dealt with by sheer force, except that sometimes the language of paternalism preceded the burning of villages.

And so, Indian Removal, as it has been politely called, cleared the land for white occupancy between the Appalachians and the Mississippi, cleared it for cotton in the South and grain in the North, for expansion, immigration, canals, railroads, new cities, and the building of a huge continental empire clear across to the Pacific Ocean. The cost in human life cannot be accurately measured, in suffering not even roughly measured. Most of the history books given to children pass quickly over it.

Statistics tell the story. We find these in Michael Rogin's *Fathers and Children:* In 1790, there were 3,900,000 Americans, and most of them lived within 50 miles of the Atlantic Ocean. By 1830, there were 13 million Americans, and by 1840, 4,500,000 had crossed the Appalachian Mountains into the Mississippi Valley—that huge expanse of land crisscrossed by rivers flowing into the Mississippi from east and west. In 1820, 120,000 Indians lived east of the Mississippi. By 1844, fewer than 30,000 were left. Most of them had been forced to migrate westward. But the word "force" cannot convey what happened.

In the Revolutionary War, almost every important Indian nation fought on the side of the British. The British signed for peace and went home; the Indians were already home, and so they continued fighting the Americans on the frontier, in a set of desperate holding operations. Washington's war-enfeebled militia could not drive them back. After scouting forces were demolished one after the other, he tried to follow a policy of conciliation. His Secretary of War, Henry Knox, said: "The Indians being the prior occupants, possess the right of the soil." His Secretary of State, Thomas Jefferson, said in 1791 that where Indians lived within state boundaries they should not be interfered with, and that the government should remove white settlers who tried to encroach on them.

But as whites continued to move westward, the pressure on the national government increased. By the time Jefferson became President, in 1800, there were 700,000 white settlers west of the mountains. They moved into Ohio, Indiana, Illinois, in the North; into Alabama and Mississippi in the South. These whites outnumbered the Indians about eight to one. Jefferson now committed the federal government to promote future removal of the Creek and the Cherokee from Georgia. Aggressive activity against the Indians mounted in the Indiana Territory under Governor William Henry Harrison.

When Jefferson doubled the size of the nation by purchasing the Louisiana Territory from France in 1803—thus extending the western frontier from the Appalachians across the Mississippi to the Rocky Mountains—he thought the Indians could move there. He proposed to Congress that Indians should be encouraged to settle down on smaller tracts and do farming; also, they should be encouraged to trade with whites, to incur debts, and then to pay off these debts with tracts of land. "... Two measures are deemed expedient. First to encourage them to abandon hunting.... Secondly, To Multiply trading houses among them ... leading them thus to agriculture, to manufactures, and civilization. ..."

Jefferson's talk of "agriculture ... manufactures ... civilization" is crucial. Indian removal was necessary for the opening of the vast American lands to agriculture, to commerce, to markets, to money, to the development of the modern capitalist economy. Land was indispensable for all this, and after the Revolution, huge sections of land were bought up by rich speculators, including George Washington and Patrick Henry. In North Carolina, rich tracts of land belonging to the Chickasaw Indians were put on sale, although the Chickasaws were among the few Indian tribes fighting on the side of the Revolution, and a treaty had been signed with them guaranteeing their land. John Donelson, a state surveyor, ended up with 20,000 acres of land near what is now Chattanooga. His son-in-law made twenty-two trips out of Nashville in 1795 for land deals. This was Andrew Jackson.

Jackson was a land speculator, merchant, slave trader, and the most aggressive enemy of the Indians in early American history. He became a hero of the War of 1812, which was not (as usually depicted in American textbooks) just a war against England for survival, but a war for the expansion of the new nation, into Florida, into Canada, into Indian territory.

Tecumseh, a Shawnee chief and noted orator, tried to unite the Indians against the white invasion:

> The way, and the only way, to check and to stop this evil, is for all the Redmen to unite in claiming a common and equal right in the land, as it was at first and should be yet; for it was never divided, but belongs to all for the use of each. That no part has a right to sell, even to each other, much less to strangers—those who want all and will not do with less.

Angered when fellow Indians were induced to cede a great tract of land to the United States government, Tecumseh organized in 1811 an Indian gathering of five thousand, on the bank of the Tallapoosa River in Alabama, and told them: "Let the white race perish. They seize your land; they corrupt your women, they trample on the ashes of your dead! Back whence they came, upon a trail of blood, they must be driven."

The Creeks, who occupied most of Georgia, Alabama, and Mississippi, were divided among themselves. Some were willing to adopt the civilization of the white man in order to live in peace. Others, insisting on their land and their culture, were called "Red Sticks." The Red Sticks in 1813 massacred 250 people at Fort Mims, whereupon Jackson's troops burned down a Creek village, killing men, women, children. Jackson established the tactic of promising rewards in land and plunder: ". . . if either party, cherokees, friendly creeks, or whites, takes property of the Red Sticks, the property belongs to those who take it."

Not all his enlisted men were enthusiastic for the fighting. There were mutinies; the men were hungry, their enlistment terms were up, they were tired of fighting and wanted to go home. Jackson wrote to his wife about "the once brave and patriotic volunteers . . . sunk . . . to mere whining, complaining, seditioners and mutineers. . . ." When a seventeen-year-old soldier who had refused to clean up his food, and threatened his officer with a gun, was sentenced to death by a court-martial, Jackson turned down a plea for commutation of sentence and ordered the execution to proceed. He then walked out of earshot of the firing squad.

Jackson became a national hero when in 1814 he fought the Battle of Horseshoe Bend against a thousand Creeks and killed eight hundred of them, with few casualties on his side. His white troops had failed in a frontal attack on the Creeks, but the Cherokees with him, promised governmental friendship if they joined the war, swam the river, came up behind the Creeks, and won the battle for Jackson.

When the war ended, Jackson and friends of his began buying up the seized Creek lands. He got himself appointed treaty commissioner and dictated a treaty which took away half the land of the Creek nation. Rogin says it was "the largest single Indian cession of southern American land." It took land from Creeks who had fought with Jackson as well as those who had fought against him, and when Big Warrior, a chief of the friendly Creeks, protested, Jackson said:

> Listen. . . . The United States would have been justified by the Great Spirit, had they taken all the land of the nation. . . . Listen—the truth is, the great body of the Creek chiefs and warriors did not respect the power of the United States—They thought we were an insignificant nation—that we would be overpowered by the British. . . . They were fat with eating beef— they wanted flogging. . . . We bleed our enemies in such cases to give them their senses.

As Rogin puts it: "Jackson had conquered 'the cream of the Creek country,' and it would guarantee southwestern prosperity. He had supplied the expanding cotton kingdom with a vast and valuable acreage."

Jackson's 1814 treaty with the Creeks started something new and important. It granted Indians individual ownership of land, thus splitting Indian from Indian, breaking up communal landholding, bribing some with land, leaving others out—introducing the competition and conniving that marked the spirit of Western capitalism. It fitted well the old Jeffersonian idea of how to handle the Indians, by bringing them into "civilization."

From 1814 to 1824, in a series of treaties with the southern Indians, whites took over three-fourths of Alabama and Florida, one-third of Tennessee, one-fifth of Georgia and Mississippi, and parts of Kentucky and North Carolina. Jackson played a key role in those treaties, and, according to Rogin, "His friends and relatives received many of the patronage appointments—as Indian agents, traders, treaty commissioners, surveyors and land agents. . . ."

Jackson himself described how the treaties were obtained: ". . . we addressed ourselves feelingly to the predominant and governing passion of all Indian tribes, i.e., their avarice or fear." He encouraged white squatters to move into Indian lands, then told the Indians the government could not remove the whites and so they had better cede the lands or be wiped out. He also, Rogin says, "practiced extensive bribery."

These treaties, these land grabs, laid the basis for the cotton kingdom, the slave plantations. Every time a treaty was signed, pushing the Creeks from one area to the next, promising them security there, whites would move into the new area and the Creeks would feel compelled to sign another treaty, giving up more land in return for security elsewhere.

Jackson's work had brought the white settlements to the border of Florida, owned by Spain. Here were the villages of the Seminole Indians, joined by some Red Stick refugees, and encouraged by British agents in their resistance to the Americans. Settlers moved into Indian lands. Indians attacked. Atrocities took place on both sides. When certain villages refused to surrender people accused of murdering whites, Jackson ordered the villages destroyed.

Another Seminole provocation: escaped black slaves took refuge in Seminole villages. Some Seminoles bought or captured black slaves, but their form of slavery was more like African slavery than cotton plantation slavery. The slaves often lived in their own villages, their children often became free, there was much intermarriage between Indians and blacks, and soon there were mixed Indian-black villages—all of which aroused southern slaveowners who saw this as a lure to their own slaves seeking freedom.

Jackson began raids into Florida, arguing it was a sanctuary for escaped slaves and for marauding Indians. Florida, he said, was essential to the defense of the United States. It was that classic modern preface to a war of conquest. Thus began the Seminole War of 1818, leading to the American acquisition of Florida. It appears on classroom maps politely as "Florida Purchase, 1819"—but it came from Andrew Jackson's military campaign across the Florida border, burning Seminole villages, seizing Spanish forts, until Spain was "persuaded" to sell. He acted, he said, by the "immutable laws of self-defense."

Jackson then became governor of the Florida Territory. He was able now to give good business advice to friends and relatives. To a nephew, he suggested holding on to property in Pensacola. To a friend, a surgeon-general in the army, he suggested buying as many slaves as possible, because the price would soon rise.

Leaving his military post, he also gave advice to officers on how to deal with the high rate of desertion. (Poor whites—even if willing to give their lives at first—may have discovered the rewards of battle going to the rich.) Jackson suggested whipping for the first two attempts, and the third time, execution.

The leading books on the Jacksonian period, written by respected historians (*The Age of Jackson* by Arthur Schlesinger; *The Jacksonian Persuasion* by Marvin Meyers), do not mention Jackson's Indian policy, but there is much talk in them of tariffs, banking, political parties, political rhetoric. If you look through high school textbooks and elementary school textbooks in American history you will find Jackson the frontiersman, soldier, democrat, man of the people—not Jackson the slaveholder, land speculator, executioner of dissident soldiers, exterminator of Indians.

This is not simply hindsight (the word used for thinking back *differently* on the past). After Jackson was elected President in 1828 (following John Quincy Adams, who had followed Monroe, who had followed Madison, who had followed Jefferson), the Indian Removal bill came before Congress and was called, at the time, "the leading measure" of the Jackson administration and "the greatest question that ever came before Congress" except for matters of peace and war. By this time the two political parties were the Democrats and Whigs, who disagreed on banks and tariffs, but not on issues crucial for the white poor, the blacks, the Indians—although some white working people saw Jackson as their hero, because he opposed the rich man's Bank.

Under Jackson, and the man he chose to succeed him, Martin Van Buren, seventy thousand Indians east of the Mississippi were forced westward. In the North, there weren't that many, and the Iroquois Confederation in New York stayed. But the Sac and Fox Indians of Illinois were removed, after the Black Hawk War (in which Abraham Lincoln was an officer, although he was not in combat). When Chief Black Hawk was defeated and captured in 1832, he made a surrender speech:

> I fought hard. But your guns were well aimed. The bullets flew like birds in the air, and whizzed by our ears like the wind through the trees in the winter. My warriors fell around me. . . . The sun rose dim on us in the morning, and at night it sunk in a dark cloud, and looked like a ball of fire. That was the last sun that shone on Black Hawk. . . . He is now a prisoner to the white men. . . . He has done nothing for which an Indian ought to be ashamed. He has fought for his countrymen, the squaws and papooses, against white men, who came year after year, to cheat them and take away their lands. You know the cause of our making war. It is known to all white men. They ought to be ashamed of it. Indians are not deceitful. The white men speak bad of the Indian and look at him spitefully. But the Indian does not tell lies. Indians do not steal.

An Indian who is as bad as the white men could not live in our nation; he would be put to death, and eaten up by the wolves. The white men are bad schoolmasters; they carry false books, and deal in false actions; they smile in the face of the poor Indian to cheat him; they shake them by the hand to gain their confidence, to make them drunk, to deceive them, and ruin our wives. We told them to leave us alone, and keep away from us; they followed on, and beset our paths, and they coiled themselves among us, like the snake. They poisoned us by their touch. We were not safe. We lived in danger. We were becoming like them, hypocrites and liars, adulterous lazy drones, all talkers and no workers. . . .

The white men do not scalp the head; but they do worse—they poison the heart. . . . Farewell, my nation! . . . Farewell to Black Hawk.

Black Hawk's bitterness may have come in part from the way he was captured. Without enough support to hold out against the white troops, with his men starving, hunted, pursued across the Mississippi, Black Hawk raised the white flag. The American commander later explained: "As we neared them they raised a white flag and endeavored to decoy us, but we were a little too old for them." The soldiers fired, killing women and children as well as warriors. Black Hawk fled; he was pursued and captured by Sioux in the hire of the army. A government agent told the Sac and Fox Indians: "Our Great Father . . . will forbear no longer. He has tried to reclaim them, and they grow worse. He is resolved to sweep them from the face of the earth. . . . If they cannot be made good they must be killed."

The removal of the Indians was explained by Lewis Cass—Secretary of War, governor of the Michigan territory, minister to France, presidential candidate:

A principle of progressive improvement seems almost inherent in human nature. . . . We are all striving in the career of life to acquire riches of honor, or power, or some other object, whose possession is to realize the day dreams of our imaginations; and the aggregate of these efforts constitutes the advance of society. But there is little of this in the constitution of our savages.

Cass—pompous, pretentious, honored (Harvard gave him an honorary doctor of laws degree in 1836, at the height of Indian removal)—claimed to be an expert on the Indians. But he demonstrated again and again, in Richard Drinnon's words *(Violence in the American Experience: Winning the West)*, a "quite marvelous ignorance of Indian life." As governor of the Michigan Territory, Cass took millions of acres from the Indians by treaty: "We must frequently promote their interest against their inclination."

His article in the *North American Review* in 1830 made the case for Indian Removal. We must not regret, he said, "the progress of civilization and improvement, the triumph of industry and art, by which these regions have been reclaimed, and over which freedom, religion, and science are extending their sway." He wished that all this could have been done with "a smaller sacrifice; that the aboriginal population had accommodated themselves to the inevitable change of their condition. . . . But such a wish is vain. A barbarous people, depending for subsistence upon the scanty and precarious supplies furnished by the chase, cannot live in contact with a civilized community."

Drinnon comments on this (writing in 1969): "Here were all the necessary grounds for burning villages and uprooting natives, Cherokee and Seminole, and later Cheyenne, Philippine, and Vietnamese."

If the Indians would only move to new lands across the Mississippi, Cass promised in 1825 at a treaty council with Shawnees and Cherokees, "The United States will never ask for your land there. This I promise you in the name of your great father, the President. That country he assigns to his red people, to be held by them and their children's children forever."

The editor of the *North American Review*, for whom Cass wrote this article, told him that his project "only defers the fate of the Indians. In half a century their condition beyond the Mississippi will be just what it is now on this side. Their extinction is inevitable." As Drinnon notes, Cass did not dispute this, yet published his article as it was.

Everything in the Indian heritage spoke out against leaving their land. A council of Creeks, offered money for their land, said: "We would not receive money for land in which our fathers and friends are buried." An old Choctaw chief said, responding, years before, to President Monroe's talk of removal: "I am sorry I cannot comply with the request of my father. . . . We wish to remain here, where we have grown up as the herbs of the woods; and do not wish to be transplanted into another soil." A Seminole chief had said to John Quincy Adams: "Here our navel strings were first cut and the blood from them sunk into the earth, and made the country dear to us."

Not all the Indians responded to the white officials' common designation of them as "children" and the President as "father." It was reported that when Tecumseh met with William Henry Harrison, Indian fighter and future President, the interpreter said: "Your father requests you to take a chair." Tecumseh replied: "My father! The sun is my father, and the earth is my mother; I will repose upon her bosom."

As soon as Jackson was elected President, Georgia, Alabama, and Mississippi began to pass laws to extend the states' rule over the Indians in their territory. These laws did away with the tribe as a legal unit, outlawed tribal meetings, took away the chiefs' powers, made the Indians subject to militia duty and state taxes, but denied them the right to vote, to bring suits, or to testify in court. Indian territory was divided up, to be distributed by state lottery. Whites were encouraged to settle on Indian land.

However, federal treaties and federal laws gave Congress, not the states, authority over the tribes. The Indian Trade and Intercourse Act, passed by Congress in 1802, said there could be no land cessions except by treaty with a tribe, and said federal law would operate in Indian territory. Jackson ignored this, and supported state action.

It was a neat illustration of the uses of the federal system: depending on the situation, blame could be put on the states, or on something even more elusive, the mysterious Law before which all men, sympathetic as they were to the Indian, must bow. As Secretary of War John Eaton explained to the Creeks of Alabama (Alabama itself was an Indian name, meaning "Here we may rest"): "It is not your Great Father who does this; but the laws of the Country, which he and every one of his people is bound to regard."

The proper tactic had now been found. The Indians would not be "forced" to go West. But if they chose to stay they would have to abide by state laws, which destroyed their tribal and personal rights and made them subject to endless harassment and invasion by white settlers coveting their land. If they left, however, the federal government would give them financial support and promise them lands beyond the Mississippi. Jackson's instructions to an army major sent to talk to the Choctaws and Cherokees put it this way:

> Say to my red Choctaw children, and my Chickasaw children to listen—my white children of Mississippi have extended their law over their country. . . . Where they now are, say to them, their father cannot prevent them from being subject to the laws of the state of Mississippi. . . . The general government will be obliged to sustain the States in the exercise of their right. Say to the chiefs and warriors that I am their friend, that I wish to act as their friend but they must, by removing from the limits of the States of Mississippi and Alabama and by being settled on the lands I offer them, put it in my power to be such—There, beyond the limits of any

State, in possession of land of their own, which they shall possess as long as Grass grows or water runs. I am and will protect them and be their friend and father.

That phrase "as long as Grass grows or water runs" was to be recalled with bitterness by generations of Indians. (An Indian GI, veteran of Vietnam, testifying publicly in 1970 not only about the horror of the war but about his own maltreatment as an Indian, repeated that phrase and began to weep.)

As Jackson took office in 1829, gold was discovered in Cherokee territory in Georgia. Thousands of whites invaded, destroyed Indian property, staked out claims. Jackson ordered federal troops to remove them, but also ordered Indians as well as whites to stop mining. Then he removed the troops, the whites returned, and Jackson said he could not interfere with Georgia's authority.

The white invaders seized land and stock, forced Indians to sign leases, beat up Indians who protested, sold alcohol to weaken resistance, killed game which Indians needed for food. But to put all the blame on white mobs, Rogin says, would be to ignore "the essential roles played by planter interests and government policy decisions." Food shortages, whiskey, and military attacks began a process of tribal disintegration. Violence by Indians upon other Indians increased.

Treaties made under pressure and by deception broke up Creek, Choctaw, and Chickasaw tribal lands into individual holdings, making each person a prey to contractors, speculators, and politicians. The Chickasaws sold their land individually at good prices and went west without much suffering. The Creeks and Choctaws remained on their individual plots, but great numbers of them were defrauded by land companies. According to one Georgia bank president, a stockholder in a land company, "Stealing is the order of the day."

Indians complained to Washington, and Lewis Cass replied:

Our citizens were disposed to buy and the Indians to sell. . . . The subsequent disposition which shall be made of these payments seems to be utterly beyond the reach of the Government. . . . The improvident habits of the Indian cannot be controlled by regulations. . . . If they waste it, as waste it they too often will, it is deeply to be regretted yet still it is only exercising a right conferred upon them by the treaty.

The Creeks, defrauded of their land, short of money and food, refused to go West. Starving Creeks began raiding white farms, while

Georgia militia and settlers attacked Indian settlements. Thus began the Second Creek War. One Alabama newspaper sympathetic to the Indians wrote: "The war with the Creeks is all humbug. It is a base and diabolical scheme, devised by interested men, to keep an ignorant race of people from maintaining their just rights, and to deprive them of the small remaining pittance placed under their control."

A Creek man more than a hundred years old, named Speckled Snake, reacted to Andrew Jackson's policy of removal:

> Brothers! I have listened to many talks from our great white father. When he first came over the wide waters, he was but a little man . . . very little. His legs were cramped by sitting long in his big boat, and he begged for a little land to light his fire on. . . . But when the white man had warmed himself before the Indians' fire and filled himself with their hominy, he became very large. With a step he bestrode the mountains, and his feet covered the plains and the valleys. His hand grasped the eastern and the western sea, and his head rested on the moon. Then he became our Great Father. He loved his red children, and he said, "Get a little further, lest I tread on thee."
>
> Brothers! I have listened to a great many talks from our great father. But they always began and ended in this—"Get a little further; you are too near me."

Dale Van Every, in his book *The Disinherited*, sums up what removal meant to the Indian:

> In the long record of man's inhumanity exile has wrung moans of anguish from many different peoples. Upon no people could it ever have fallen with a more shattering impact than upon the eastern Indians. The Indian was peculiarly susceptible to every sensory attribute of every natural feature of his surroundings. He lived in the open. He knew every marsh, glade, hill top, rock, spring, creek, as only the hunter can know them. He had never fully grasped the principle establishing private ownership of land as any more rational than private ownership of air but he loved the land with a deeper emotion than could any proprietor. He felt himself as much a part of it as the rocks and trees, the animals and birds. His homeland was holy ground, sanctified for him as the resting place of the bones of his ancestors and the natural shrine of his religion. He conceived its waterfalls and ridges, its clouds and mists, its glens and meadows, to be inhabited by the myriad of spirits with whom he held daily communion. It was from this rain-washed land of forests, streams and lakes, to which he was held by the traditions of his forebears and his own spiritual aspirations,

that he was to be driven to the arid, treeless plains of the far west, a desolate region then universally known as the Great American Desert.

According to Van Every, just before Jackson became President, in the 1820s, after the tumult of the War of 1812 and the Creek War, the southern Indians and the whites had settled down, often very close to one another, and were living in peace in a natural environment which seemed to have enough for all of them. They began to see common problems. Friendships developed. White men were allowed to visit the Indian communities and Indians often were guests in white homes. Frontier figures like Davy Crockett and Sam Houston came out of this setting, and both—unlike Jackson—became lifelong friends of the Indian.

The forces that led to removal did not come, Van Every insists, from the poor white frontiersmen who were neighbors of the Indians. They came from industrialization and commerce, the growth of populations, of railroads and cities, the rise in value of land, and the greed of businessmen. "Party managers and land speculators manipulated the growing excitement. . . . Press and pulpit whipped up the frenzy." Out of that frenzy the Indians were to end up dead or exiled, the land speculators richer, the politicians more powerful. As for the poor white frontiersman, he played the part of a pawn, pushed into the first violent encounters, but soon dispensable.

There had been three voluntary Cherokee migrations westward, into the beautiful wooded country of Arkansas, but there the Indians found themselves almost immediately surrounded and penetrated by white settlers, hunters, trappers. These West Cherokees now had to move farther west, this time to arid land, land too barren for white settlers. The federal government, signing a treaty with them in 1828, announced the new territory as "a permanent home . . . which shall under the most solemn guarantee of the United States be and remain theirs forever. . . ." It was still another lie, and the plight of the western Cherokees became known to the three-fourths of the Cherokees who were still in the East, being pressured by the white man to move on.

With 17,000 Cherokees surrounded by 900,000 whites in Georgia, Alabama, and Tennessee, the Cherokees decided that survival required adaptation to the white man's world. They became farmers, blacksmiths, carpenters, masons, owners of property. A census of 1826 showed 22,000 cattle, 7,600 horses, 46,000 swine, 726 looms, 2,488 spinning wheels, 172 wagons, 2,943 plows, 10 saw mills, 31 grist mills, 62 blacksmith shops, 8 cotton machines, 18 schools.

The Cherokees' language—heavily poetic, metaphorical, beautifully expressive, supplemented by dance, drama, and ritual—had always been a language of voice and gesture. Now their chief, Sequoyah, invented a written language, which thousands learned. The Cherokees' newly established Legislative Council voted money for a printing press, which on February 21, 1828, began publishing a newspaper, the *Cherokee Phoenix*, printed in both English and Sequoyah's Cherokee.

Before this, the Cherokees had, like Indian tribes in general, done without formal government. As Van Every puts it:

> The foundation principle of Indian government had always been the rejec-
> tion of government. The freedom of the individual was regarded by practi-
> cally all Indians north of Mexico as a canon infinitely more precious than
> the individual's duty to his community or nation. This anarchistic attitude
> ruled all behavior, beginning with the smallest social unit, the family. The
> Indian parent was constitutionally reluctant to discipline his children. Their
> every exhibition of self-will was accepted as a favorable indication of the
> development of maturing character. . . .

There was an occasional assembling of a council, with a very loose and changing membership, whose decisions were not enforced except by the influence of public opinion. A Moravian minister who lived among them described Indian society:

> Thus has been maintained for ages, without convulsions and without civil
> discords, this traditional government, of which the world, perhaps, does not
> offer another example; a government in which there are no positive laws, but
> only long established habits and customs, no code of jurisprudence, but the
> experience of former times, no magistrates, but advisers, to whom the people
> nevertheless, pay a willing and implicit obedience, in which age confers rank,
> wisdom gives power, and moral goodness secures title to universal respect.

Now, surrounded by white society, all this began to change. The Cherokees even started to emulate the slave society around them: they owned more than a thousand slaves. They were beginning to resemble that civilization the white men spoke about, making what Van Every calls "a stupendous effort" to win the good will of Americans. They even welcomed missionaries and Christianity. None of this made them more desirable than the land they lived on.

Jackson's 1829 message to Congress made his position clear: "I informed the Indians inhabiting parts of Georgia and Alabama that their attempt to establish an independent government would not be countenanced by the Executive of the United States, and advised them to emigrate beyond the Mississippi or submit to the laws of those States." Congress moved quickly to pass a removal bill.

There were defenders of the Indians. Perhaps the most eloquent was Senator Theodore Frelinghuysen of New Jersey, who told the Senate, debating removal:

> We have crowded the tribes upon a few miserable acres on our southern frontier; it is all that is left to them of their once boundless forest: and still, like the horse-leech, our insatiated cupidity cries, give! give! ... Sir ... Do the obligations of justice change with the color of the skin?

The North was in general against the removal bill. The South was for it. It passed the House 102 to 97. It passed the Senate narrowly. It did not mention force, but provided for helping the Indians to move. What it implied was that if they did not, they were without protection, without funds, and at the mercy of the states.

Now the pressures began on the tribes, one by one. The Choctaws did not want to leave, but fifty of their delegates were offered secret bribes of money and land, and the Treaty of Dancing Rabbit Creek was signed: Choctaw land east of the Mississippi was ceded to the United States in return for financial help in leaving, compensation for property left behind, food for the first year in their new homes, and a guarantee they would never again be required to move. For twenty thousand Choctaws in Mississippi, though most of them hated the treaty, the pressure now became irresistible. Whites, including liquor dealers and swindlers, came swarming onto their lands. The state passed a law making it a crime for Choctaws to try to persuade one another on the matter of removal.

In late 1831, thirteen thousand Choctaws began the long journey west to a land and climate totally different from what they knew. "Marshaled by guards, hustled by agents, harried by contractors, they were being herded on the way to an unknown and unwelcome destination like a flock of sick sheep." They went on ox wagons, on horses, on foot, then to be ferried across the Mississippi River. The army was supposed to organize their trek, but it turned over its job to private contractors who charged the government as much as possible, gave the Indians as little as possible. Everything was disorganized. Food disappeared. Hunger came. Van Every again:

The long somber columns of groaning ox wagons, driven herds and straggling crowds on foot inched on westward through swamps and forests, across rivers and over hills, in their crawling struggle from the lush lowlands of the Gulf to the arid plains of the west. In a kind of death spasm one of the last vestiges of the original Indian world was being dismembered and its collapsing remnants jammed bodily into an alien new world.

The first winter migration was one of the coldest on record, and people began to die of pneumonia. In the summer, a major cholera epidemic hit Mississippi, and Choctaws died by the hundreds. The seven thousand Choctaws left behind now refused to go, choosing subjugation over death. Many of their descendants still live in Mississippi.

As for the Cherokees, they faced a set of laws passed by Georgia: their lands were taken, their government abolished, all meetings prohibited. Cherokees advising others not to migrate were to be imprisoned. Cherokees could not testify in court against any white. Cherokees could not dig for the gold recently discovered on their land. A delegation of them, protesting to the federal government, received this reply from Jackson's new Secretary of War, Eaton: "If you will go to the setting sun there you will be happy; there you can remain in peace and quietness; so long as the waters run and the oaks grow that country shall be guaranteed to you and no white man shall be permitted to settle near you."

The Cherokee nation addressed a memorial to the nation, a public plea for justice. They reviewed their history:

> After the peace of 1783, the Cherokees were an independent people, absolutely so, as much as any people on earth. They had been allies to Great Britain. . . . The United States never subjugated the Cherokees; on the contrary, our fathers remained in possession of their country and with arms in their hands. . . . In 1791, the treaty of Holston was made. . . . The Cherokees acknowledged themselves to be under the protection of the United States, and of no other sovereign. . . . A cession of land was also made to the United States. On the other hand, the United States . . . stipulated that white men should not hunt on these lands, not even enter the country, without a passport; and gave a solemn guarantee of all Cherokee lands not ceded. . . .

They discussed removal:

> We are aware that some persons suppose it will be for our advantage to remove beyond the Mississippi. We think otherwise. Our people universally

think otherwise.... We wish to remain on the land of our fathers. We have a perfect and original right to remain without interruption or molestation. The treaties with us, and laws of the United States made in pursuance of treaties, guarantee our residence and our privileges, and secure us against intruders. Our only request is, that these treaties may be fulfilled, and these laws executed....

Now they went beyond history, beyond law:

We intreat those to whom the foregoing paragraphs are addressed, to remember the great law of love. "Do to others as ye would that others should do to you."... We pray them to remember that, for the sake of principle, their forefathers were compelled to leave, therefore driven from the old world, and that the winds of persecution wafted them over the great waters and landed them on the shores of the new world, when the Indian was the sole lord and proprietor of these extensive domains—Let them remember in what way they were received by the savage of America, when power was in his hand, and his ferocity could not be restrained by any human arm. We urge them to bear in mind, that those who would not ask of them a cup of cold water, and a spot of earth ... are the descendants of these, whose origin, as inhabitants of North America, history and tradition are alike insufficient to reveal. Let them bring to remembrance all these facts, and they cannot, and we are sure, they will not fail to remember, and sympathize with us in these our trials and sufferings.

Jackson's response to this, in his second Annual Message to Congress in December 1830, was to point to the fact that the Choctaws and Chickasaws had already agreed to removal, and that "a speedy removal" of the rest would offer many advantages to everyone. For whites it "will place a dense and civilized population in large tracts of country now occupied by a few savage hunters." For Indians, it will "perhaps cause them, gradually, under the protection of the Government and through the influence of good counsels, to cast off their savage habits and become an interesting, civilized, and Christian community."

He reiterated a familiar theme. "Toward the aborigines of the country no one can indulge a more friendly feeling than myself...." However: "The waves of population and civilization are rolling to the westward, and we now propose to acquire the countries occupied by the red men of the South and West by a fair exchange...."

Georgia passed a law making it a crime for a white person to stay in Indian territory without taking an oath to the state of Georgia. When the white missionaries in the Cherokee territory declared their sympathies openly for the Cherokees to stay, Georgia militia entered the territory in the spring of 1831 and arrested three of the missionaries, including Samuel Worcester. They were released when they claimed protection as federal employees (Worcester was a federal postmaster). Immediately the Jackson administration took away Worcester's job, and the militia moved in again that summer, arresting ten missionaries as well as the white printer of the *Cherokee Phoenix*. They were beaten, chained, and forced to march 35 miles a day to the county jail. A jury tried them, found them guilty. Nine were released when they agreed to swear allegiance to Georgia's laws, but Samuel Worcester and Elizur Butler, who refused to grant legitimacy to the laws repressing the Cherokees, were sentenced to four years at hard labor.

This was appealed to the Supreme Court, and in *Worcester* v. *Georgia*, John Marshall, for the majority, declared that the Georgia law on which Worcester was jailed violated the treaty with the Cherokees, which by the Constitution was binding on the states. He ordered Worcester freed. Georgia ignored him, and President Jackson refused to enforce the court order.

Georgia now put Cherokee land on sale and moved militia in to crush any sign of Cherokee resistance. The Cherokees followed a policy of nonviolence, though their property was being taken, their homes were being burned, their schools were closed, their women mistreated, and liquor was being sold in their churches to render them even more helpless.

The same year Jackson was declaring states' rights for Georgia on the Cherokee question in 1832, he was attacking South Carolina's right to nullify a federal tariff. His easy reelection in 1832 (687,000 to 530,000 for his opponent Henry Clay) suggested that his anti-Indian policies were in keeping with popular sentiment, at least among those white males who could vote (perhaps 2 million of the total population of 13 million). Jackson now moved to speed up Indian removal. Most of the Choctaws and some of the Cherokees were gone, but there were still 22,000 Creeks in Alabama, 18,000 Cherokees in Georgia, and 5,000 Seminoles in Florida.

The Creeks had been fighting for their land ever since the years of Columbus, against Spaniards, English, French, and Americans. But by 1832 they had been reduced to a small area in Alabama, while the population of Alabama, growing fast, was now over 300,000. On the basis of extravagant promises from the federal government, Creek delegates in Washington signed the Treaty of Washington, agreeing to removal beyond the Mississippi. They gave up 5 million acres, with the provision that 2 million of these would go to individual Creeks, who could either sell or remain in Alabama with federal protection.

Van Every writes of this treaty:

> The interminable history of diplomatic relations between Indians and white men had before 1832 recorded no single instance of a treaty which had not been presently broken by the white parties to it . . . however solemnly embellished with such terms as "permanent," "forever," "for all time," "so long as the sun shall rise." . . . But no agreement between white men and Indians had ever been so soon abrogated as the 1832 Treaty of Washington. Within days the promises made in it on behalf of the United States had been broken.

A white invasion of Creek lands began—looters, land seekers, defrauders, whiskey sellers, thugs—driving thousands of Creeks from their homes into the swamps and forests. The federal government did nothing. Instead it negotiated a new treaty providing for prompt emigration west, managed by the Creeks themselves, financed by the national government. An army colonel, dubious that this would work, wrote:

> They fear starvation on the route; and can it be otherwise, when many of them are nearly starving now, without the embarrassment of a long journey on their hands. . . . You cannot have an idea of the deterioration which these Indians have undergone during the last two or three years, from a general state of comparative plenty to that of unqualified wretchedness and want. The free egress into the nation by the whites; encroachments upon their lands, even upon their cultivated fields; abuses of their person; hosts of traders, who, like locusts, have devoured their substance and inundated their homes with whiskey, have destroyed what little disposition to cultivation the Indians may once have had. . . . They are brow beat, and cowed, and imposed upon, and depressed with the feeling that they have no adequate protection in the United States, and no capacity of self-protection in themselves.

Northern political sympathizers with the Indian seemed to be fading away, preoccupied with other issues. Daniel Webster was making a rousing speech in the Senate for the "authority of law . . . the power of the general government," but he was not referring to Alabama, Georgia, and the Indians—he was talking about South Carolina's nullification of the tariff.

Despite the hardships, the Creeks refused to budge, but by 1836, both state and federal officials decided they must go. Using as a pretext some attacks by desperate Creeks on white settlers, it was declared that the Creek nation, by making "war," had forfeited its treaty rights.

The army would now force it to migrate west. Fewer than a hundred Creeks had been involved in the "war," but a thousand had fled into the woods, afraid of white reprisals. An army of eleven thousand was sent after them. The Creeks did not resist, no shots were fired, they surrendered. Those Creeks presumed by the army to be rebels or sympathizers were assembled, the men manacled and chained together to march westward under military guard, their women and children trailing after them. Creek communities were invaded by military detachments, the inhabitants driven to assembly points and marched westward in batches of two or three thousand. No talk of compensating them for land or property left behind.

Private contracts were made for the march, the same kind that had failed for the Choctaws. Again, delays and lack of food, shelter, clothing, blankets, medical attention. Again, old, rotting steamboats and ferries, crowded beyond capacity, taking them across the Mississippi. "By midwinter the interminable, stumbling procession of more than 15,000 Creeks stretched from border to border across Arkansas." Starvation and sickness began to cause large numbers of deaths. "The passage of the exiles could be distinguished from afar by the howling of trailing wolf packs and the circling flocks of buzzards," Van Every writes.

Eight hundred Creek men had volunteered to help the United States army fight the Seminoles in Florida in return for a promise that their families could remain in Alabama, protected by the federal government until the men returned. The promise was not kept. The Creek families were attacked by land-hungry white marauders—robbed, driven from their homes, women raped. Then the army, claiming it was for their safety, removed them from Creek country to a concentration camp on Mobile Bay. Hundreds died there from lack of food and from sickness.

When the warriors returned from the Seminole War, they and their families were hustled west. Moving through New Orleans, they encountered a yellow fever plague. They crossed the Mississippi—611 Indians crowded onto the aged steamer *Monmouth*. It went down in the Mississippi River and 311 people died, four of them the children of the Indian commander of the Creek volunteers in Florida.

A New Orleans newspaper wrote:

The fearful responsibility for this vast sacrifice of human life rests on the contractors ... The avaricious disposition to increase the profits on the speculation first induced the chartering of rotten, old, and unseaworthy boats, because they were of a class to be procured cheaply; and then to make those increased profits still larger, the Indians were packed upon those crazy vessels in such crowds that not the slightest regard seems to have been paid to their safety, comfort, or even decency.

The Choctaws and Chickasaws had quickly agreed to migrate. The Creeks were stubborn and had to be forced. The Cherokees were practicing a nonviolent resistance. One tribe—the Seminoles—decided to fight.

With Florida now belonging to the United States, Seminole territory was open to American land-grabbers. They moved down into north Florida from St. Augustine to Pensacola, and down the fertile coastal strip. In 1823, the Treaty of Camp Moultrie was signed by a few Seminoles who got large personal landholdings in north Florida and agreed that all the Seminoles would leave northern Florida and every coastal area and move into the interior. This meant withdrawing into the swamps of central Florida, where they could not grow food, where even wild game could not survive.

The pressure to move west, out of Florida, mounted, and in 1834 Seminole leaders were assembled and the U.S. Indian agent told them they must move west. Here were some of the replies of the Seminoles at that meeting:

We were all made by the same Great Father, and are all alike His Children. We all came from the same Mother, and were suckled at the same breast. Therefore, we are brothers, and as brothers, should treat together in an amicable way.

Your talk is a good one, but my people cannot say they will go. We are not willing to do so. If their tongues say yes, their hearts cry no, and call them liars.

If suddenly we tear our hearts from the homes around which they are twined, our heart-strings will snap.

The Indian agent managed to get fifteen chiefs and subchiefs to sign a removal treaty, the U.S. Senate promptly ratified it, and the War Department began making preparations for the migration. Violence between whites and Seminoles now erupted.

A young Seminole chief, Osceola, who had been imprisoned and chained by the Indian agent Thompson, and whose wife had been delivered into slavery, became a leader of the growing resistance. When Thompson ordered the Seminoles, in December 1835, to assemble for the journey, no one came. Instead, the Seminoles began a series of guerrilla attacks on white coastal settlements, all along the Florida perimeter, striking in surprise and in succession from the interior. They murdered white families, captured slaves, destroyed property. Osceola himself, in a lightning stroke, shot down Thompson and an army lieutenant.

That same day, December 28, 1835, a column of 110 soldiers was attacked by Seminoles, and all but three soldiers were killed. One of the survivors later told the story:

> It was 8 o'clock. Suddenly I heard a rifle shot ... followed by a musket shot. . . . I had not time to think of the meaning of these shots, before a volley, as if from a thousand rifles, was poured in upon us from the front, and all along our left flank. . . . I could only see their heads and arms, peering out from the long grass, far and near, and from behind the pine trees. . . .

It was the classic Indian tactic against a foe with superior firearms. General George Washington had once given parting advice to one of his officers: "General St. Clair, in three words, beware of surprise. . . . again and again, General, beware of surprise."

Congress now appropriated money for a war against the Seminoles. In the Senate, Henry Clay of Kentucky opposed the war; he was an enemy of Jackson, a critic of Indian removal. But his Whig colleague Daniel Webster displayed that unity across party lines which became standard in American wars:

> The view taken by the gentleman from Kentucky was undoubtedly the true one. But the war rages, the enemy is in force, and the accounts of their ravages are disastrous. The executive government has asked for the means of suppressing these hostilities, and it was entirely proper that the bill should pass.

General Winfield Scott took charge, but his columns of troops, marching impressively into Seminole territory, found no one. They became tired of the mud, the swamps, the heat, the sickness, the hunger—the classic fatigue of a civilized army fighting people on their own land. No one wanted to face Seminoles in the Florida swamps. In

1836, 103 commissioned officers resigned from the regular army, leaving only forty-six. In the spring of 1837, Major General Jesup moved into the war with an army of ten thousand, but the Seminoles just faded into the swamps, coming out from time to time to strike at isolated forces.

The war went on for years. The army enlisted other Indians to fight the Seminoles. But that didn't work either. Van Every says: "The adaptation of the Seminole to his environment was to be matched only by the crane or the alligator." It was an eight-year war. It cost $20 million and 1,500 American lives. Finally, in the 1840s, the Seminoles began to get tired. They were a tiny group against a huge nation with great resources. They asked for truces. But when they went forward under truce flags, they were arrested, again and again. In 1837, Osceola, under a flag of truce, had been seized and put in irons, then died of illness in prison. The war petered out.

Meanwhile the Cherokees had not fought back with arms, but had resisted in their own way. And so the government began to play Cherokee against Cherokee, the old game. The pressures built up on the Cherokee community—their newspaper suppressed, their government dissolved, the missionaries in jail, their land parceled among whites by the land lottery. In 1834, seven hundred Cherokees, weary of the struggle, agreed to go west; eighty-one died en route, including forty-five children—mostly from measles and cholera. Those who lived arrived at their destination across the Mississippi in the midst of a cholera epidemic and half of them died within a year.

The Cherokees were summoned to sign the removal treaty in New Echota, Georgia, in 1836, but fewer than five hundred of the seventeen thousand Cherokees appeared. The treaty was signed anyway. The Senate, including northerners who had once spoken for the Indian, ratified it, yielding, as Senator Edward Everett of Massachusetts said, to "the force of circumstances . . . the hard necessity." Now the Georgia whites stepped up their attacks to speed the removal.

The government did not move immediately against the Cherokees. In April 1838, Ralph Waldo Emerson addressed an open letter to President Van Buren, referring with indignation to the removal treaty with the Cherokees (signed behind the backs of an overwhelming majority of them) and asked what had happened to the sense of justice in America:

The soul of man, the justice, the mercy that is the heart's heart in all men, from Maine to Georgia, does abhor this business . . . a crime is projected that confounds our understandings by its magnitude, a crime that really deprives us as well as the Cherokees of a country for how could we call the conspiracy that should crush these poor Indians our government, or the land that was cursed by their parting and dying imprecations our country any more? You, sir, will bring down that renowned chair in which you sit into infamy if your seal is set to this instrument of perfidy; and the name of this nation, hitherto the sweet omen of religion and liberty, will stink to the world.

Thirteen days before Emerson sent this letter, Martin Van Buren had ordered Major General Winfield Scott into Cherokee territory to use whatever military force was required to move the Cherokees west. Five regiments of regulars and four thousand militia and volunteers began pouring into Cherokee country. General Scott addressed the Indians:

Cherokees—the President of the United States has sent me with a powerful army, to cause you, in obedience to the treaty of 1834, to join that part of your people who are already established in prosperity on the other side of the Mississippi. . . . The full moon of May is already on the wane, and before another shall have passed every Cherokee man, woman, and child . . . must be in motion to join their brethren in the far West. . . . My troops already occupy many positions in the country that you are about to abandon, and thousands and thousands are approaching from every quarter, to tender resistance and escape alike hopeless. . . . Chiefs, head men, and warriors—Will you then, by resistance, compel us to resort to arms? God forbid. Or will you, by flight, seek to hide yourselves in mountains and forests, and thus oblige us to hunt you down?

Some Cherokees had apparently given up on nonviolence: three chiefs who signed the Removal Treaty were found dead. But the seventeen thousand Cherokees were soon rounded up and crowded into stockades. On October 1, 1838, the first detachment set out in what was to be known as the Trail of Tears. As they moved westward, they began to die—of sickness, of drought, of the heat, of exposure. There were 645 wagons, and people marching alongside. Survivors, years later, told of halting at the edge of the Mississippi in the middle of winter, the river running full of ice, "hundreds of sick and dying penned up in wagons or stretched upon the ground." Grant Foreman, the leading authority on Indian removal, estimates that during confinement in the stockade or on the march westward four thousand Cherokees died.

In December 1838, President Van Buren spoke to Congress:

It affords sincere pleasure to apprise the Congress of the entire removal of the Cherokee Nation of Indians to their new homes west of the Mississippi. The measures authorized by Congress at its last session have had the happiest effects.

8

WE TAKE NOTHING BY CONQUEST, THANK GOD

Colonel Ethan Allen Hitchcock, a professional soldier, graduate of the Military Academy, commander of the 3rd Infantry Regiment, a reader of Shakespeare, Chaucer, Hegel, Spinoza, wrote in his diary:

> Fort Jesup, La., June 30, 1845. Orders came last evening by express from Washington City directing General Taylor to move without any delay to some point on the coast near the Sabine or elsewhere, and as soon as he shall hear of the acceptance by the Texas convention of the annexation resolutions of our Congress he is immediately to proceed with his whole command to the extreme western border of Texas and take up a position on the banks of or near the Rio Grande, and he is to expel any armed force of Mexicans who may cross that river. Bliss read the orders to me last evening hastily at tattoo. I have scarcely slept a wink, thinking of the needful preparations. I am now noting at reveille by candlelight and waiting the signal for muster.... Violence leads to violence, and if this movement of ours does not lead to others and to bloodshed, I am much mistaken.

Hitchcock was not mistaken. Jefferson's Louisiana Purchase had doubled the territory of the United States, extending it to the Rocky Mountains. To the southwest was Mexico, which had won its independence in a revolutionary war against Spain in 1821—a large country which included Texas and what are now New Mexico, Utah, Nevada, Arizona, California, and part of Colorado. After agitation, and aid from the United States, Texas broke off from Mexico in 1836 and declared itself the "Lone Star Republic." In 1845, the U.S. Congress brought it into the Union as a state.

In the White House now was James Polk, a Democrat, an expansionist, who, on the night of his inauguration, confided to his Secretary of the Navy that one of his main objectives was the acquisition of California. His order to General Taylor to move troops to the Rio Grande was a challenge to the Mexicans. It was not at all clear that the Rio Grande was the southern boundary of Texas, although Texas had forced the defeated Mexican general Santa Anna to say so when he was a prisoner. The traditional border between Texas and Mexico had been the Nueces River, about 150 miles to the north, and both Mexico and the United States had recognized that as the border. However, Polk, encouraging the Texans to accept annexation, had assured them he would uphold their claims to the Rio Grande.

Ordering troops to the Rio Grande, into territory inhabited by Mexicans, was clearly a provocation. Taylor had once denounced the idea of the annexation of Texas. But now that he had his marching orders, his attitude seemed to change. His visit to the tent of his aide Hitchcock to discuss the move is described in Hitchcock's diary:

> He seems to have lost all respect for Mexican rights and is willing to be an instrument of Mr. Polk for pushing our boundary as far west as possible. When I told him that, if he suggested a movement (which he told me he intended), Mr. Polk would seize upon it and throw the responsibility on him, he at once said he would take it, and added that if the President instructed him to use his discretion, he would ask no orders, but would go upon the Rio Grande as soon as he could get transportation. I think the General wants an additional brevet, and would strain a point to get it.

Taylor moved his troops to Corpus Christi, Texas, just across the Nueces River, and waited further instructions. They came in February 1846—to go down the Gulf Coast to the Rio Grande. Taylor's army marched in parallel columns across the open prairie, scouts far ahead and on the flanks, a train of supplies following. Then, along a narrow road, through a belt of thick chaparral, they arrived, March 28, 1846, in cultivated fields and thatched-roof huts hurriedly abandoned by the Mexican occupants, who had fled across the river to the city of Matamoros. Taylor set up camp, began construction of a fort, and implanted his cannons facing the white houses of Matamoros, whose inhabitants stared curiously at the sight of an army on the banks of a quiet river.

The Washington *Union*, a newspaper expressing the position of President Polk and the Democratic party, had spoken early in 1845 on the meaning of Texas annexation:

Let the great measure of annexation be accomplished, and with it the questions of boundary and claims. For who can arrest the torrent that will pour onward to the West? The road to California will be open to us. Who will stay the march of our western people?

They could have meant a peaceful march westward, except for other words, in the same newspaper: "A corps of properly organized volunteers . . . would invade, overrun, and occupy Mexico. They would enable us not only to take California, but to keep it." It was shortly after that, in the summer of 1845, that John O'Sullivan, editor of the *Democratic Review*, used the phrase that became famous, saying it was "Our manifest destiny to overspread the continent allotted by Providence for the free development of our yearly multiplying millions." Yes, manifest destiny.

All that was needed in the spring of 1846 was a military incident to begin the war that Polk wanted. It came in April, when General Taylor's quartermaster, Colonel Cross, while riding up the Rio Grande, disappeared. His body was found eleven days later, his skull smashed by a heavy blow. It was assumed he had been killed by Mexican guerrillas crossing the river. In a solemn military ceremony visible to the Mexicans of Matamoros crowding onto the roofs of their houses across the Rio Grande, Cross was buried with a religious service and three volleys of rifle fire.

The next day (April 25), a patrol of Taylor's soldiers was surrounded and attacked by Mexicans, and wiped out: sixteen dead, others wounded, the rest captured. Taylor sent a message to the governors of Texas and Louisiana asking them to recruit five thousand volunteers; he had been authorized to do this by the White House before he left for Texas. And he sent a dispatch to Polk: "Hostilities may now be considered as commenced."

The Mexicans had fired the first shot. But they had done what the American government wanted, according to Colonel Hitchcock, who wrote in his diary, even before those first incidents:

I have said from the first that the United States are the aggressors. . . . We have not one particle of right to be here. . . . It looks as if the government sent a small force on purpose to bring on a war, so as to have a pretext for taking California and as much of this country as it chooses, for, whatever becomes of this army, there is no doubt of a war between the United States and Mexico. . . . My heart is not in this business . . . but, as a military man, I am bound to execute orders.

And before those first clashes, Taylor had sent dispatches to Polk which led the President to note that "the probabilities are that hostilities might take place soon." On May 9, before news of any battles, Polk was suggesting to his cabinet a declaration of war, based on certain money claims against Mexico, and on Mexico's recent rejection of an American negotiator named John Slidell. Polk recorded in his diary what he said to the cabinet meeting:

> I stated . . . that up to this time, as we knew, we had heard of no open act of aggression by the Mexican army, but that the danger was imminent that such acts would be committed. I said that in my opinion we had ample cause of war, and that it was impossible . . . that I could remain silent much longer . . . that the country was excited and impatient on the subject. . . .

The country was not "excited and impatient." But the President was. When the dispatches arrived from General Taylor telling of casualties from the Mexican attack, Polk summoned the cabinet to hear the news, and they unanimously agreed he should ask for a declaration of war. Polk's message to Congress was indignant:

> The cup of forbearance had been exhausted even before the recent information from the frontier of the Del Norte [the Rio Grande]. But now, after reiterated menaces, Mexico has passed the boundary of the United States, has invaded our territory and shed American blood upon the American soil. . . .
>
> As war exists, notwithstanding all our efforts to avoid it, exists by the act of Mexico herself, we are called upon by every consideration of duty and patriotism to vindicate with decision the honor, the rights, and the interests of our country.

Polk spoke of the dispatch of American troops to the Rio Grande as a necessary measure of defense. As John Schroeder says (Mr. Polk's War): "Indeed, the reverse was true; President Polk had incited war by sending American soldiers into what was disputed territory, historically controlled and inhabited by Mexicans."

Congress then rushed to approve the war message. Schroeder comments: "The disciplined Democratic majority in the House responded with alacrity and high-handed efficiency to Polk's May 11 war recommendations." The bundles of official documents accompanying the war message, supposed to be evidence for Polk's statement, were not examined, but were tabled immediately by the House. Debate on the bill providing volunteers and money for the war was limited to two hours, and most of this was used up reading selected portions of the tabled documents, so that barely a half-hour was left for discussion of the issues.

The Whig party was presumably against the war in Mexico, but it was not against expansion. The Whigs wanted California, but preferred to do it without war. As Schroeder puts it, "theirs was a commercially oriented expansionism designed to secure frontage on the Pacific without recourse to war." Also, they were not so powerfully against the military action that they would stop it by denying men and money for the operation. They did not want to risk the accusation that they were putting American soldiers in peril by depriving them of the materials necessary to fight. The result was that Whigs joined Democrats in voting overwhelmingly for the war resolution, 174 to 14. The opposition was a small group of strongly antislavery Whigs, or "a little knot of ultraists," as one Massachusetts Congressman who voted for the war measure put it.

In the Senate, there was debate, but it was limited to one day, and "the tactics of stampede were there repeated," according to historian Frederick Merk. The war measure passed, 40 to 2, Whigs joining Democrats. Throughout the war, as Schroeder says, "the politically sensitive Whig minority could only harry the administration with a barrage of verbiage while voting for every appropriation which the military campaigns required." The newspaper of the Whigs, the *National Intelligencer* of Washington, took this position. John Quincy Adams of Massachusetts, who originally voted with "the stubborn 14," later voted for war appropriations.

Abraham Lincoln of Illinois was not yet in Congress when the war began, but after his election in 1846 he had occasion to vote and speak on the war. His "spot resolutions" became famous—he challenged Polk to specify the exact spot where American blood was shed "on the American soil." But he would not try to end the war by stopping funds for men and supplies. Speaking in the House on July 27, 1848, in support of the candidacy of General Zachary Taylor for President, he said:

> But, as General Taylor is, par excellence, the hero of the Mexican War, and as you Democrats say we Whigs have always opposed the war, you think it must be very awkward and embarrassing for us to go for General Taylor. The declaration that we have always opposed the war is true or false, according as one may understand the term "oppose the war." If to say "the war was unnecessarily and unconstitutionally commenced by the President" be opposing the war, then the Whigs have very generally

opposed it. . . . The marching an army into the midst of a peaceful Mexican settlement, frightening the inhabitants away, leaving their growing crops and other property to destruction, to you may appear a perfectly amiable, peaceful, unprovoking procedure; but it does not appear so to us. . . . But if, when the war had begun, and had become the cause of the country, the giving of our money and our blood, in common with yours, was support of the war, then it is not true that we have always opposed the war. With few individual exceptions, you have constantly had our votes here for all the necessary supplies. . . .

A handful of antislavery Congressmen voted against all war measures, seeing the Mexican campaign as a means of extending the southern slave territory. One of these was Joshua Giddings of Ohio, a fiery speaker, physically powerful, who called it "an aggressive, unholy, and unjust war." He explained his vote against supplying arms and men: "In the murder of Mexicans upon their own soil, or in robbing them of their country, I can take no part either now or hereafter. The guilt of these crimes must rest on others—I will not participate in them. . . ." Giddings pointed to the British Whigs who, during the American Revolution, announced in Parliament in 1776 that they would not vote supplies for a war to oppress Americans.

After Congress acted in May of 1846, there were rallies and demonstrations for the war in New York, Baltimore, Indianapolis, Philadelphia, and many other places. Thousands rushed to volunteer for the army. The poet Walt Whitman wrote in the Brooklyn *Eagle* in the early days of the war: "Yes: Mexico must be thoroughly chastised! . . . Let our arms now be carried with a spirit which shall teach the world that, while we are not forward for a quarrel, America knows how to crush, as well as how to expand!"

Accompanying all this aggressiveness was the idea that the United States would be giving the blessings of liberty and democracy to more people. This was intermingled with ideas of racial superiority, longings for the beautiful lands of New Mexico and California, and thoughts of commercial enterprise across the Pacific.

Speaking of California, the *Illinois State Register* asked: "Shall this garden of beauty be suffered to lie dormant in its wild and useless luxuriance? . . . myriads of enterprising Americans would flock to its rich and inviting prairies; the hum of Anglo-American industry would be heard in its valleys; cities would rise upon its plains and sea-coast, and the resources and wealth of the nation be increased in an incalculable degree." The *American Review* talked of Mexicans yielding to "a superior population, insensibly oozing into her territories, changing her customs, and out-living, out-trading, exterminating her weaker blood. . . ." The New York *Herald* was saying, by 1847: "The universal Yankee nation can regenerate and disenthrall the people of Mexico in a few years; and we believe it is a part of our destiny to civilize that beautiful country."

A letter appeared in the *New York Journal of Commerce* introducing God into the situation: "The supreme Ruler of the universe seems to interpose, and aid the energy of man towards benefiting mankind. His interposition . . . seems to me to be identified with the success of our arms. . . . That the redemption of 7,000,000 of souls from all the vices that infest the human race, is the ostensible object . . . appears manifest."

Senator H. V. Johnson said:

I believe we should be recreant to our noble mission, if we refused acquiescence in the high purposes of a wise Providence. War has its evils. In all ages it has been the minister of wholesale death and appalling desolation; but however inscrutable to us, it has also been made, by the Allwise Dispenser of events, the instrumentality of accomplishing the great end of human elevation and human happiness. . . . It is in this view, that I subscribe to the doctrine of "manifest destiny."

The *Congressional Globe* of February 11, 1847, reported:

Mr. Giles, of Maryland—I take it for granted, that we shall gain territory, and must gain territory, before we shut the gates of the temple of Janus. . . . We must march from ocean to ocean. . . . We must march from Texas straight to the Pacific ocean, and be bounded only by its roaring wave. . . . It is the destiny of the white race, it is the destiny of the Anglo-Saxon race. . . .

The American Anti-Slavery Society, on the other hand, said the war was "waged solely for the detestable and horrible purpose of extending and perpetuating American slavery throughout the vast territory of Mexico." A twenty-seven-year-old Boston poet and abolitionist, James Russell Lowell, began writing satirical poems in the Boston *Courier* (they were later collected as the *Biglow Papers*). In them, a New England farmer, Hosea Biglow, spoke, in his own dialect, on the war:

Ez fer war, I call it murder,—
    There you hev it plain an' flat;
I don't want to go no furder
    Than my Testyment fer that. . . .

They may talk o' Freedom's airy
   Tell they'er pupple in the face,—
It's a grand gret cemetary
   Fer the barthrights of our race;
They jest want this Californy
   So's to lug new slave-states in
To abuse ye, an' to scorn ye,
   An' to plunder ye like sin.

The war had barely begun, the summer of 1846, when a writer, Henry David Thoreau, who lived in Concord, Massachusetts, refused to pay his Massachusetts poll tax, denouncing the Mexican war. He was put in jail and spent one night there. His friends, without his consent, paid his tax, and he was released. Two years later, he gave a lecture, "Resistance to Civil Government," which was then printed as an essay, "Civil Disobedience":

> It is not desirable to cultivate a respect for the law, so much as for the right. . . . Law never made men a whit more just; and, by means of their respect for it, even the well-disposed are daily made the agents of injustice. A common and natural result of an undue respect for law is, that you may see a file of soldiers . . . marching in admirable order over hill and dale to the wars, against their wills, ay, against their common sense and consciences, which makes it very steep marching indeed, and produces a palpitation of the heart.

His friend and fellow writer, Ralph Waldo Emerson, agreed, but thought it futile to protest. When Emerson visited Thoreau in jail and asked, "What are you doing in there?" it was reported that Thoreau replied, "What are you doing out there?"

The churches, for the most part, were either outspokenly for the war or timidly silent. Generally, no one but the Congregational, Quaker, and Unitarian churches spoke clearly against the war. However, one Baptist minister, the Reverend Francis Wayland, president of Brown University, gave three sermons in the university chapel in which he said that only wars of self-defense were just, and in case of unjust war, the individual was morally obligated to resist it and lend no money to the government to support it.

The Reverend Theodore Parker, Unitarian minister in Boston, combined eloquent criticism of the war with contempt for the Mexican people, whom he called "a wretched people; wretched in their origin, history, and character," who must eventually give way as the Indians did. Yes, the United States should expand, he said, but not by war, rather by the power of her ideas, the pressure of her commerce, by "the steady advance of a superior race, with superior ideas and a better civilization . . . by being better than Mexico, wiser, humaner, more free and manly." Parker urged active resistance to the war in 1847: "Let it be infamous for a New England man to enlist; for a New England merchant to loan his dollars, or to let his ships in aid of this wicked war; let it be infamous for a manufacturer to make a cannon, a sword, or a kernel of powder to kill our brothers. . . ."

The racism of Parker was widespread. Congressman Delano of Ohio, an antislavery Whig, opposed the war because he was afraid of Americans mingling with an inferior people who "embrace all shades of color. . . . a sad compound of Spanish, English, Indian, and negro bloods . . . and resulting, it is said, in the production of a slothful, ignorant race of beings."

As the war went on, opposition grew. The American Peace Society printed a newspaper, the *Advocate of Peace*, which published poems, speeches, petitions, sermons against the war, and eyewitness accounts of the degradation of army life and the horrors of battle. The abolitionists, speaking through William Lloyd Garrison's *Liberator*, denounced the war as one "of aggression, of invasion, of conquest, and rapine—marked by ruffianism, perfidy, and every other feature of national depravity . . . " Considering the strenuous efforts of the nation's leaders to build patriotic support, the amount of open dissent and criticism was remarkable. Antiwar meetings took place in spite of attacks by patriotic mobs.

As the army moved closer to Mexico City, *The Liberator* daringly declared its wishes for the defeat of the American forces: "Every lover of Freedom and humanity, throughout the world, must wish them [the Mexicans] the most triumphant success. . . . We only hope that, if blood has had to flow, that it has been that of the Americans, and that the next news we shall hear will be that General Scott and his army are in the hands of the Mexicans. . . . We wish him and his troops no bodily harm, but the most utter defeat and disgrace."

Frederick Douglass, former slave, extraordinary speaker and writer, wrote in his Rochester newspaper the *North Star*, January 21, 1848, of "the present disgraceful, cruel, and iniquitous war with our sister republic. Mexico seems a doomed victim to Anglo Saxon cupidity and love of dominion." Douglass was scornful of the unwillingness of opponents of the war to take real action (even the abolitionists kept paying their taxes):

The determination of our slaveholding President to prosecute the war, and the probability of his success in wringing from the people men and money to carry it on, is made evident, rather than doubtful, by the puny opposition arrayed against him. No politician of any considerable distinction or eminence seems willing to hazard his popularity with his party . . . by an open and unqualified disapprobation of the war. None seem willing to take their stand for peace at all risks; and all seem willing that the war should be carried on, in some form or other.

Where was popular opinion? It is hard to say. After the first rush, enlistments began to dwindle. The 1846 elections showed much anti-Polk sentiment, but who could tell how much of this was due to the war? In Massachusetts, Congressman Robert Winthrop, who had voted for the war, was elected overwhelmingly against an antiwar Whig. Schroeder concludes that although Polk's popularity fell, "general enthusiasm for the Mexican War remained high." But this is a guess. There were no surveys of public opinion at that time. As for voting, a majority of the people did not vote at all—and how did these nonvoters feel about the war?

Historians of the Mexican war have talked easily about "the people" and "public opinion"—like Justin H. Smith, whose two-volume work *The War with Mexico* has long been a standard account: "Of course, too, all the pressure of warlike sentiment among our people . . . had to be recognized, more or less, for such is the nature of popular government."

Smith's evidence, however, is not from "the people" but from the newspapers, claiming to be the voice of the people. The New York *Herald* wrote in August 1845: "The multitude cry aloud for war." And the New York *Journal of Commerce*, half-playfully, half-seriously, wrote: "Let us go to war. The world has become stale and insipid, the ships ought to be all captured, and the cities battered down, and the world burned up, so that we can start again. There would be fun in that. Some interest,—something to talk about." The New York *Morning News* said "young and ardent spirits that throng the cities . . . want but a direction to their restless energies, and their attention is already fixed on Mexico."

Were the newspapers reporting a feeling in the public, or creating a feeling in the public? Those reporting this feeling, like Justin Smith, themselves express strong views about the need for war. Smith (who dedicates his book to Henry Cabot Lodge, one of the ultraexpansionists of American history) makes a long list of Mexican sins against the United States, and ends by saying: "It rested with our government, therefore, as the agent of national dignity and interests, to apply a remedy." He comments on Polk's call for war. "In truth no other course would have been patriotic or even rational."

It is impossible to know the extent of popular support of the war. But there is evidence that many organized workingmen opposed the war. Earlier, when the annexation of Texas was being considered, workingmen meeting in New England protested the annexation. A newspaper in Manchester, New Hampshire, wrote:

> We have heretofore held our peace in regard to the annexation of Texas, for the purpose of seeing whether our Nation would attempt so base an action. We call it base, because it would be giving men that live upon the blood of others, an opportunity of dipping their hand still deeper in the sin of slavery. . . . Have we not slaves enough now?

There were demonstrations of Irish workers in New York, Boston, and Lowell against the annexation of Texas, Philip Foner reports. In May, when the war against Mexico began, New York workingmen called a meeting to oppose the war, and many Irish workers came. The meeting called the war a plot by slaveowners and asked for the withdrawal of American troops from disputed territory. That year, a convention of the New England Workingmen's Association condemned the war and announced they would "not take up arms to sustain the Southern slaveholder in robbing one-fifth of our countrymen of their labor."

Some newspapers, at the very start of the war, protested. Horace Greeley wrote in the New York *Tribune*, May 12, 1846:

> We can easily defeat the armies of Mexico, slaughter them by thousands, and pursue them perhaps to their capital; we can conquer and "annex" their territory; but what then? Have the histories of the ruin of Greek and Roman liberty consequent on such extensions of empire by the sword no lesson for us? Who believes that a score of victories over Mexico, the "annexation" of half her provinces, will give us more Liberty, a purer Morality, a more prosperous Industry, than we now have? . . . Is not Life miserable enough, comes not Death soon enough, without resort to the hideous enginery of War?

What of those who fought the war—the soldiers who marched, sweated, got sick, died? The Mexican soldiers. The American soldiers.

We know little of the reactions of Mexican soldiers. We do know that Mexico was a despotism, a land of Indians and mestizos (Indians mixed with Spanish) controlled by criollos—whites of Spanish blood.

There were a million criollos, 2 million mestizos, 3 million Indians. Was the natural disinclination of peasants to fight for a country owned by landlords overcome by the nationalist spirit roused against an invader?

We know much more about the American army—volunteers, not conscripts, lured by money and opportunity for social advancement via promotion in the armed forces. Half of General Taylor's army were recent immigrants—Irish and German mostly. Whereas in 1830, 1 percent of the population of the United States was foreign-born, by the Mexican war the number was reaching 10 percent. Their patriotism was not very strong. Their belief in all arguments for expansion paraded in the newspapers was probably not great. Indeed, many of them deserted to the Mexican side, enticed by money. Some enlisted in the Mexican army and formed their own battalion, the San Patricio (St. Patrick's) Battalion.

At first there seemed to be enthusiasm in the army, fired by pay and patriotism. Martial spirit was high in New York, where the legislature authorized the governor to call fifty thousand volunteers. Placards read "Mexico or Death." There was a mass meeting of twenty thousand people in Philadelphia. Three thousand volunteered in Ohio.

This initial spirit soon wore off. A woman in Greensboro, North Carolina, recorded in her diary:

> Tuesday, January 5, 1847 . . . today was a general muster and speeches by Mr. Gorrell and Mr. Henry. General Logan received them in this street and requested all the Volunteers to follow after; as he walked up and down the street, I saw some 6 or 7, bad looking persons following, with poor Jim Laine in front. How many poor creatures have been and are still to be sacrificed upon the altar of pride and ambition?

Posters appealed for volunteers in Massachusetts: "Men of old Essex! Men of Newburyport! Rally around the bold, gallant and lionhearted Cushing. He will lead you to victory and to glory!" They promised pay of $7 to $10 a month, and spoke of a federal bounty of $24 and 160 acres of land. But one young man wrote anonymously to the Cambridge *Chronicle:*

> Neither have I the least idea of "joining" you, or in any way assisting the unjust war waging against Mexico. I have no wish to participate in such "glorious" butcheries of women and children as were displayed in the capture of Monterey, etc. Neither have I any desire to place myself under the dictation of a petty military tyrant, to every caprice of whose will I must

yield implicit obedience. No sir-ee! As long as I can work, beg, or go to the poor house, I won't go to Mexico, to be lodged on the damp ground, half starved, half roasted, bitten by mosquitoes and centipedes, stung by scorpions and tarantulas—marched, drilled, and flogged, and then stuck up to be shot at, for eight dollars a month and putrid rations. Well, I won't. . . . Human butchery has had its day. . . . And the time is rapidly approaching when the professional soldier will be placed on the same level as a bandit, the Bedouin, and the Thug.

Reports grew of men forced to be volunteers, impressed for service. One James Miller of Norfolk, Virginia, protested that he had been persuaded "by the influence of an unusual quantity of ardent spirits" to sign a paper enrolling for military service. "Next morning, I was dragged aboard of a boat landed at Fort Monroe, and closely immured in the guard house for sixteen days."

There were extravagant promises and outright lies to build up the volunteer units. A man who wrote a history of the New York Volunteers declared:

If it is cruel to drag black men from their homes, how much more cruel it is to drag white men from their homes under false inducements, and compelling them to leave their wives and children, without leaving a cent or any protection, in the coldest season of the year, to die in a foreign and sickly climate! . . . Many enlisted for the sake of their families, having no employment, and having been offered "three months' advance", and were promised that they could leave part of their pay for their families to draw in their absence. . . . I boldly pronounce, that the whole Regiment was got up by fraud—a fraud on the soldier, a fraud on the City of New York, and a fraud on the Government of the United States. . . .

By late 1846, recruitment was falling off, so physical requirements were lowered, and anyone bringing in acceptable recruits would get $2 a head. Even this didn't work. Congress in early 1847 authorized ten new regiments of regulars, to serve for the duration of the war, promising them 100 acres of public land upon honorable discharge. But dissatisfaction continued. Volunteers complained that the regulars were given special treatment. Enlisted men complained that the officers treated them as inferiors.

And soon, the reality of battle came in upon the glory and the promises. On the Rio Grande before Matamoros, as a Mexican army of five thousand under General Arista faced Taylor's army of three thousand, the shells began to fly, and artilleryman Samuel French saw his first death in battle. John Weems describes it:

> He happened to be staring at a man on horseback nearby when he saw a shot rip off the pommel of the saddle, tear through the man's body, and burst out with a crimson gush on the other side. Pieces of bone or metal tore into the horse's hip, split the lip and tongue and knocked teeth out of a second horse, and broke the jaw of a third.

Lieutenant Grant, with the 4th Regiment, "saw a ball crash into ranks nearby, tear a musket from one soldier's grasp and rip off the man's head, then dissect the face of a captain he knew." When the battle was over, five hundred Mexicans were dead or wounded. There were perhaps fifty American casualties. Weems describes the aftermath: "Night blanketed weary men who fell asleep where they dropped on the trampled prairie grass, while around them other prostrate men from both armies screamed and groaned in agony from wounds. By the eerie light of torches 'the surgeon's saw was going the livelong night.'"

Away from the battlefield, in the army camps, the romance of the recruiting posters was quickly forgotten. A young artillery officer wrote about the men camped at Corpus Christi in the summer of 1845, even before the war began:

> It . . . becomes our painful task to allude to the sickness, suffering and death, from criminal negligence. Two-thirds of the tents furnished the army on taking the field were worn out and rotten . . . provided for campaigning in a country almost deluged three months in the year. . . . During the whole of November and December, either the rains were pouring down with violence, or the furious "northers" were showering the frail tentpoles, and rending the rotten canvas. For days and weeks every article in hundreds of tents was thoroughly soaked. During those terrible months, the sufferings of the sick in the crowded hospital tents were horrible beyond conception. . . .

The 2nd Regiment of Mississippi Rifles, moving into New Orleans, was stricken by cold and sickness. The regimental surgeon reported: "Six months after our regiment had entered the service we had sustained a loss of 167 by death, and 134 by discharges." The regiment was packed into the holds of transports, eight hundred men into three ships. The surgeon continued:

The dark cloud of disease still hovered over us. The holds of the ships . . . were soon crowded with the sick. The effluvia was intolerable. . . . The sea became rough. . . . Through the long dark night the rolling ship would dash the sick man from side to side bruising his flesh upon the rough corners of his berth. The wild screams of the delirious, the lamentations of the sick, and the melancholy groans of the dying, kept up one continual scene of confusion. . . . Four weeks we were confined to the loathsome ships and before we had landed at the Brasos, we consigned twenty-eight of our men to the dark waves.

Meanwhile, by land and by sea, Anglo-American forces were moving into California. A young naval officer, after the long voyage around the southern cape of South America, and up the coast to Monterey in California, wrote in his diary:

Asia . . . will be brought to our very doors. Population will flow into the fertile regions of California. The resources of the entire country . . . will be developed. . . . The public lands lying along the route [of railroads] will be changed from deserts into gardens, and a large population will be settled. . . .

It was a separate war that went on in California, where Anglo-Americans raided Spanish settlements, stole horses, and declared California separated from Mexico—the "Bear Flag Republic." Indians lived there, and naval officer Revere gathered the Indian chiefs and spoke to them (as he later recalled):

I have called you together to have a talk with you. The country you inhabit no longer belongs to Mexico, but to a mighty nation whose territory extends from the great ocean you have all seen or heard of, to another great ocean thousands of miles toward the rising sun. . . . I am an officer of that great country, and to get here, have traversed both of those great oceans in a ship of war which, with a terrible noise, spits forth flames and hurls forth instruments of destruction, dealing death to all our enemies. Our armies are now in Mexico, and will soon conquer the whole country. But you have nothing to fear from us, if you do what is right. . . . if you are faithful to your new rulers. . . . We come to prepare this magnificent region for the use of other men, for the population of the world demands more room, and here is room enough for many millions, who will hereafter occupy and till the soil. But, in admitting others, we shall not displace you, if you act properly. . . . You can easily learn, but you are indolent. I hope you will alter your habits, and be industrious and frugal, and give up all the low vices which you practice; but if you are lazy and dissipated, you must, before many years, become extinct. We shall watch over you, and give you true liberty; but beware of sedition, lawlessness, and all other crimes, for the army which shields can assuredly punish, and it will reach you in your most retired hiding places.

General Kearney moved easily into New Mexico, and Santa Fe was taken without battle. An American staff officer described the reaction of the Mexican population to the U.S. army's entrance into the capital city:

> Our march into the city . . . was extremely warlike, with drawn sabres, and daggers in every look. From around corners, men with surly countenances and downcast looks regarded us with watchfulness, if not terror, and black eyes looked through latticed windows at our column of cavaliers, some gleaming with pleasure, and others filled with tears. . . . As the American flag was raised, and the cannon boomed its glorious national salute from the hill, the pent-up emotions of many of the women could be suppressed no longer . . . as the wail of grief arose above the din of our horses' tread, and reached our ears from the depth of the gloomy-looking buildings on every hand.

That was in August. In December, Mexicans in Taos, New Mexico, rebelled against American rule. As a report to Washington put it, "many of the most influential persons in the northern part of this territory were engaged in the rebellion." The revolt was put down, and arrests were made. But many of the rebels fled, and carried on sporadic attacks, killing a number of Americans, then hiding in the mountains. The American army pursued, and in a final desperate battle, in which six to seven hundred rebels were engaged, 150 were killed, and it seemed the rebellion was now over.

In Los Angeles, too, there was a revolt. Mexicans forced the American garrison there to surrender in September 1846. The United States did not retake Los Angeles until January, after a bloody battle.

General Taylor had moved across the Rio Grande, occupied Matamoros, and now moved southward through Mexico. But his volunteers became more unruly on Mexican territory. Mexican villages were pillaged. One officer wrote in his diary in the summer of 1846: "We reached Burrita about 5 P.M., many of the Louisiana volunteers were there, a lawless drunken rabble. They had driven away the inhabitants, taken possession of their houses, and were emulating each other in making beasts of themselves." Cases of rape began to multiply.

As the soldiers moved up the Rio Grande to Camargo, the heat became unbearable, the water impure, and sickness grew—diarrhea, dysentery, and other maladies—until a thousand were dead. At first the dead were buried to the sounds of the "Dead March" played by a military band. Then the number of dead was too great, and formal military funerals ceased.

Southward to Monterey and another battle, where men and horses died in agony, and one officer described the ground as "slippery with . . . foam and blood."

After Taylor's army took Monterey he reported "some shameful atrocities" by the Texas Rangers, and he sent them home when their enlistment expired. But others continued robbing and killing Mexicans. A group of men from a Kentucky regiment broke into one Mexican dwelling, threw out the husband, and raped his wife. Mexican guerrillas retaliated with cruel vengeance.

As the American armies advanced, more battles were fought, more thousands died on both sides, more thousands were wounded, more thousands sick with diseases. At one battle north of Chihuahua, three hundred Mexicans were killed and five hundred wounded, according to the American accounts, with few Anglo-American casualties: "The surgeons are now busily engaged in administering relief to the wounded Mexicans, and it is a sight to see the pile of legs and arms that have been amputated."

An artillery captain named John Vinton, writing to his mother, told of sailing to Vera Cruz:

> The weather is delightful, our troops in good health and spirits, and all things look auspicious of success. I am only afraid the Mexicans will not meet us & give us battle,—for, to gain everything without controversy after our large & expensive preparations . . . would give us officers no chance for exploits and honors.

Vinton died during the siege of Vera Cruz. The U.S. bombardment of the city became an indiscriminate killing of civilians. One of the navy's shells hit the post office; others burst all over the city. A Mexican observer wrote:

> The surgical hospital, which was situated in the Convent of Santo Domingo, suffered from the fire, and several of the inmates were killed by fragments of bombs bursting at that point. While an operation was being performed on a wounded man, the explosion of a shell extinguished the

lights, and when other illumination was brought, the patient was found torn in pieces, and many others dead and wounded.

In two days, 1,300 shells were fired into the city, until it surrendered. A reporter for the New Orleans *Delta* wrote: "The Mexicans variously estimate their loss at from 500 to 1000 killed and wounded, but all agree that the loss among the soldiery is comparatively small and the destruction among the women and children is very great."

Colonel Hitchcock, coming into the city, wrote: "I shall never forget the horrible fire of our mortars . . . going with dreadful certainty and bursting with sepulchral tones often in the centre of private dwellings— it was awful. I shudder to think of it." Still, Hitchcock, the dutiful soldier, wrote for General Scott "a sort of address to the Mexican people" which was then printed in English and Spanish by the tens of thousands saying ". . . we have not a particle of ill-will towards you—we treat you with all civility—we are not in fact your enemies; we do not plunder your people or insult your women or your religion . . . we are here for no earthly purpose except the hope of obtaining a peace."

That was Hitchcock the soldier. Then we have Weems the historian:

> If Hitchcock, the old anti-war philosopher, thus seemed to fit Henry David Thoreau's description of "small movable forts and magazines, at the service of some unscrupulous man in power", it should be remembered that Hitchcock was first of all a soldier—and a good one, as conceded even by the superiors he had antagonized.

It was a war of the American elite against the Mexican elite, each side exhorting, using, killing its own population as well as the other. The Mexican commander Santa Anna had crushed rebellion after rebellion, his troops also raping and plundering after victory. When Colonel Hitchcock and General Winfield Scott moved into Santa Anna's estate, they found its walls full of ornate paintings. But half his army was dead or wounded.

General Winfield Scott moved toward the last battle—for Mexico City—with ten thousand soldiers. They were not anxious for battle. Three days' march from Mexico City, at Jalapa, seven of his eleven regiments evaporated, their enlistment times up. Justin Smith writes:

> It would have been quite agreeable to linger at Jalapa . . . but the soldiers had learned what campaigning really meant. They had been allowed to go unpaid and unprovided for. They had met with hardships and privations not

counted upon at the time of enlistment. Disease, battle, death, fearful toil and frightful marches had been found realities. . . . In spite of their strong desire to see the Halls of the Montezumas, out of about 3700 men only enough to make one company would reengage, and special inducements, offered by the General, to remain as teamsters proved wholly ineffective.

On the outskirts of Mexico City, at Churubusco, Mexican and American armies clashed for three hours. As Weems describes it:

Those fields around Churubusco were now covered with thousands of human casualties and with mangled bodies of horses and mules that blocked roads and filled ditches. Four thousand Mexicans lay dead or wounded; three thousand others had been captured (including sixty-nine U.S. Army deserters, who required the protection of Scott's officers to escape execution at the hands of their former comrades). . . . The Americans lost nearly one thousand men killed, wounded, or missing.

As often in war, battles were fought without point. After one such engagement near Mexico City, with terrible casualties, a marine lieutenant blamed General Scott: "He had originated it in error and caused it to be fought, with inadequate forces, for an object that had no existence."

In the final battle for Mexico City, Anglo-American troops took the height of Chapultepec and entered the city of 200,000 people, General Santa Anna having moved northward. This was September 1847. A Mexican merchant wrote to a friend about the bombardment of the city: "In some cases whole blocks were destroyed and a great number of men, women and children killed and wounded."

General Santa Anna fled to Huamantla, where another battle was fought, and he had to flee again. An infantry lieutenant wrote to his parents what happened after an officer named Walker was killed in battle:

General Lane . . . told us to "avenge the death of the gallant Walker, to . . . take all we could lay hands on". And well and fearfully was his mandate obeyed. Grog shops were broken open first, and then, maddened with liquor, every species of outrage was committed. Old women and girls were stripped of their clothing—and many suffered still greater outrages. Men were shot by dozens . . . their property, churches, stores and dwelling houses ransacked. . . . Dead horses and men lay about pretty thick, while drunken soldiers, yelling and screeching, were breaking open houses or chasing some poor Mexicans who had abandoned their houses and fled for life. Such a scene I never hope to see again. It gave me a lamentable view of human nature . . . and made me for the first time ashamed of my country.

The editors of *Chronicles of the Gringos* sum up the attitude of the American soldiers to the war:

> Although they had volunteered to go to war, and by far the greater number of them honored their commitments by creditably sustaining hardship and battle, and behaved as well as soldiers in a hostile country are apt to behave, they did not like the army, they did not like war, and generally speaking, they did not like Mexico or the Mexicans. This was the majority: disliking the job, resenting the discipline and caste system of the army, and wanting to get out and go home.

One Pennsylvania volunteer, stationed at Matamoros late in the war, wrote:

> We are under very strict discipline here. Some of our officers are very good men but the balance of them are very tyrannical and brutal toward the men. . . . tonight on drill an officer laid a soldier's skull open with his sword. . . . But the time may come and that soon when officers and men will stand on equal footing. . . . A soldier's life is very disgusting.

On the night of August 15, 1847, volunteer regiments from Virginia, Mississippi, and North Carolina rebelled in northern Mexico against Colonel Robert Treat Paine. Paine killed a mutineer, but two of his lieutenants refused to help him quell the mutiny. The rebels were ultimately exonerated in an attempt to keep the peace.

Desertion grew. In March 1847 the army reported over a thousand deserters. The total number of deserters during the war was 9,207: 5,331 regulars, 3,876 volunteers. Those who did not desert became harder and harder to manage. General Cushing referred to sixty-five such men in the 1st Regiment of the Massachusetts Infantry as "incorrigibly mutinous and insubordinate."

The glory of the victory was for the President and the generals, not the deserters, the dead, the wounded. Of the 2nd Regiment of Mississippi Rifles, 167 died of disease. Two regiments from Pennsylvania went out 1,800 strong and came home with six hundred. John Calhoun of South Carolina said in Congress that 20 percent of the troops had died of battle or sickness. The Massachusetts Volunteers had started with 630 men. They came home with three hundred dead, mostly from disease, and at the reception dinner on their return their commander, General Cushing, was hissed by his men. The Cambridge *Chronicle* wrote: "Charges of the most serious nature against one and all of these military officials drop daily from the lips of the volunteers."

As the veterans returned home, speculators immediately showed up to buy the land warrants given by the government. Many of the soldiers, desperate for money, sold their 160 acres for less than $50. The New York *Commercial Advertiser* said in June 1847: "It is a well-known fact that immense fortunes were made out of the poor soldiers who shed their blood in the revolutionary war by speculators who preyed upon their distresses. A similar system of depredation was practised upon the soldiers of the last war."

Mexico surrendered. There were calls among Americans to take all of Mexico. The Treaty of Guadalupe Hidalgo, signed February 1848, just took half. The Texas boundary was set at the Rio Grande; New Mexico and California were ceded. The United States paid Mexico $15 million, which led the *Whig Intelligencer* to conclude that "we take nothing by conquest. . . . Thank God."

9

SLAVERY WITHOUT SUBMISSION, EMANCIPATION WITHOUT FREEDOM

The United States government's support of slavery was based on an overpowering practicality. In 1790, a thousand tons of cotton were being produced every year in the South. By 1860, it was a million tons. In the same period, 500,000 slaves grew to 4 million. A system harried by slave rebellions and conspiracies (Gabriel Prosser, 1800; Denmark Vesey, 1822; Nat Turner, 1831) developed a network of controls in the southern states, backed by the laws, courts, armed forces, and race prejudice of the nation's political leaders.

It would take either a full-scale slave rebellion or a full-scale war to end such a deeply entrenched system. If a rebellion, it might get out of hand, and turn its ferocity beyond slavery to the most successful system of capitalist enrichment in the world. If a war, those who made the war would organize its consequences. Hence, it was Abraham Lincoln who freed the slaves, not John Brown. In 1859, John Brown was hanged, with federal complicity, for attempting to do by small-scale violence what Lincoln would do by large-scale violence several years later—end slavery.

With slavery abolished by order of the government—true, a government pushed hard to do so, by blacks, free and slave, and by white abolitionists—its end could be orchestrated so as to set limits to emancipation. Liberation from the top would go only so far as the interests of the dominant groups permitted. If carried further by the momentum of war, the rhetoric of a crusade, it could be pulled back to a safer position. Thus, while the ending of slavery led to a reconstruction of national politics and economics, it was not a radical reconstruction, but a safe one—in fact, a profitable one.

The plantation system, based on tobacco growing in Virginia, North Carolina, and Kentucky, and rice in South Carolina, expanded into lush new cotton lands in Georgia, Alabama, Mississippi—and needed more slaves. But slave importation became illegal in 1808. Therefore, "from the beginning, the law went unenforced," says John Hope Franklin *(From Slavery to Freedom)*. "The long, unprotected coast, the certain markets, and the prospects of huge profits were too much for the American merchants and they yielded to the temptation. . . ." He estimates that perhaps 250,000 slaves were imported illegally before the Civil War.

How can slavery be described? Perhaps not at all by those who have not experienced it. The 1932 edition of a best-selling textbook by two northern liberal historians saw slavery as perhaps the Negro's "necessary transition to civilization." Economists or cliometricians (statistical historians) have tried to assess slavery by estimating how much money was spent on slaves for food and medical care. But can this describe the reality of slavery as it was to a human being who lived inside it? Are the *conditions* of slavery as important as the *existence* of slavery?

John Little, a former slave, wrote:

> They say slaves are happy, because they laugh, and are merry. I myself and three or four others, have received two hundred lashes in the day, and had our feet in fetters; yet, at night, we would sing and dance, and make others laugh at the rattling of our chains. Happy men we must have been! We did it to keep down trouble, and to keep our hearts from being completely broken: that is as true as the gospel! Just look at it,—must not we have been very happy? Yet I have done it myself—I have cut capers in chains.

A record of deaths kept in a plantation journal (now in the University of North Carolina Archives) lists the ages and cause of death of all those who died on the plantation between 1850 and 1855. Of the thirty-two who died in that period, only four reached the age of sixty, four reached the age of fifty, seven died in their forties, seven died in their twenties or thirties, and nine died before they were five years old.

But can statistics record what it meant for families to be torn apart, when a master, for profit, sold a husband or a wife, a son or a daughter? In 1858, a slave named Abream Scriven was sold by his master, and wrote to his wife: "Give my love to my father and mother and tell them good Bye for me, and if we Shall not meet in this world I hope to meet in heaven."

One recent book on slavery (Robert Fogel and Stanley Engerman, *Time on the Cross*) looks at whippings in 1840–1842 on the Barrow plantation in Louisiana with two hundred slaves: "The records show that over the course of two years a total of 160 whippings were administered, an average of 0.7 whippings per hand per year. About half the hands were not whipped at all during the period." One could also say: "Half of all slaves were whipped." That has a different ring. That figure (0.7 per hand per year) shows whipping was infrequent for any individual. But looked at another way, once every four or five days, *some* slave was whipped.

Barrow as a plantation owner, according to his biographer, was no worse than the average. He spent money on clothing for his slaves, gave them holiday celebrations, built a dance hall for them. He also built a jail and "was constantly devising ingenious punishments, for he realized that uncertainty was an important aid in keeping his gangs well in hand."

The whippings, the punishments, were work disciplines. Still, Herbert Gutman *(Slavery and the Numbers Game)* finds, dissecting Fogel and Engerman's statistics, "Over all, four in five cotton pickers engaged in one or more disorderly acts in 1840–41. . . . As a group, a slightly higher percentage of women than men committed seven or more disorderly acts." Thus, Gutman disputes the argument of Fogel and Engerman that the Barrow plantation slaves became "devoted, hardworking responsible slaves who identified their fortunes with the fortunes of their masters."

Slave revolts in the United States were not as frequent or as large-scale as those in the Caribbean islands or in South America. Probably the largest slave revolt in the United States took place near New Orleans in 1811. Four to five hundred slaves gathered after a rising at the plantation of a Major Andry. Armed with cane knives, axes, and clubs, they wounded Andry, killed his son, and began marching from plantation to plantation, their numbers growing. They were attacked by U.S. army and militia forces; sixty-six were killed on the spot, and sixteen were tried and shot by a firing squad.

The conspiracy of Denmark Vesey, himself a free Negro, was thwarted before it could be carried out in 1822. The plan was to burn Charleston, South Carolina, then the sixth-largest city in the nation, and to initiate a general revolt of slaves in the area. Several witnesses said thousands of blacks were implicated in one way or another. Blacks had made about 250 pike heads and bayonets and over three hundred daggers, according to Herbert Aptheker's account. But the plan was betrayed, and thirty-five blacks, including Vesey, were hanged. The trial record itself, published in Charleston, was ordered destroyed soon after publication, as too dangerous for slaves to see.

Nat Turner's rebellion in Southampton County, Virginia, in the summer of 1831, threw the slaveholding South into a panic, and then into a determined effort to bolster the security of the slave system. Turner, claiming religious visions, gathered about seventy slaves, who went on a rampage from plantation to plantation, murdering at least fifty-five men, women, and children. They gathered supporters, but were captured as their ammunition ran out. Turner and perhaps eighteen others were hanged.

Did such rebellions set back the cause of emancipation, as some moderate abolitionists claimed at the time? An answer was given in 1845 by James Hammond, a supporter of slavery:

> But if your course was wholly different—If you distilled nectar from your lips and discoursed sweetest music. . . . do you imagine you could prevail on us to give up a thousand millions of dollars in the value of our slaves, and a thousand millions of dollars more in the depreciation of our lands . . . ?

The slaveowner understood this, and prepared. Henry Tragle *(The Southampton Slave Revolt of 1831)*, says:

> In 1831, Virginia was an armed and garrisoned state. . . . With a total population of 1,211,405, the State of Virginia was able to field a militia force of 101,488 men, including cavalry, artillery, grenadiers, riflemen, and light infantry! It is true that this was a "paper army" in some ways, in that the county regiments were not fully armed and equipped, but it is still an astonishing commentary on the state of the public mind of the time. During a period when neither the State nor the nation faced any sort of exterior threat, we find that Virginia felt the need to maintain a security force roughly ten percent of the total number of its inhabitants: black and white, male and female, slave and free!

Rebellion, though rare, was a constant fear among slaveowners. Ulrich Phillips, a southerner whose *American Negro Slavery* is a classic study, wrote:

> A great number of southerners at all times held the firm belief that the negro population was so docile, so little cohesive, and in the main so

friendly toward the whites and so contented that a disastrous insurrection by them would be impossible. But on the whole, there was much greater anxiety abroad in the land than historians have told of. . . .

Eugene Genovese, in his comprehensive study of slavery, *Roll, Jordan, Roll*, sees a record of "simultaneous accommodation and resistance to slavery." The resistance included stealing property, sabotage and slowness, killing overseers and masters, burning down plantation buildings, running away. Even the accommodation "breathed a critical spirit and disguised subversive actions." Most of this resistance, Genovese stresses, fell short of organized insurrection, but its significance for masters and slaves was enormous.

Running away was much more realistic than armed insurrection. During the 1850s about a thousand slaves a year escaped into the North, Canada, and Mexico. Thousands ran away for short periods. And this despite the terror facing the runaway. The dogs used in tracking fugitives "bit, tore, mutilated, and if not pulled off in time, killed their prey," Genovese says.

Harriet Tubman, born into slavery, her head injured by an overseer when she was fifteen, made her way to freedom alone as a young woman, then became the most famous conductor on the Underground Railroad. She made nineteen dangerous trips back and forth, often disguised, escorting more than three hundred slaves to freedom, always carrying a pistol, telling the fugitives, "You'll be free or die." She expressed her philosophy: "There was one of two things I had a right to, liberty or death; if I could not have one, I would have the other; for no man should take me alive. . . ."

One overseer told a visitor to his plantation that "some negroes are determined never to let a white man whip them and will resist you, when you attempt it; of course you must kill them in that case."

One form of resistance was not to work so hard. W. E. B. Du Bois wrote, in *The Gift of Black Folk*:

As a tropical product with a sensuous receptivity to the beauty of the world, he was not as easily reduced to be the mechanical draft-horse which the northern European laborer became. He . . . tended to work as the results pleased him and refused to work or sought to refuse when he did not find the spiritual returns adequate; thus he was easily accused of laziness and driven as a slave when in truth he brought to modern manual labor a renewed valuation of life.

Ulrich Phillips described "truancy," "absconding," "vacations with-out leave," and "resolute efforts to escape from bondage altogether." He also described collective actions:

> Occasionally, however, a squad would strike in a body as a protest against severities. An episode of this sort was recounted in a letter of a Georgia overseer to his absent employer: "Sir, I write you a few lines in order to let you know that six of your hands has left the plantation—every man but Jack. They displeased me with their work and I give some of them a few lashes, Tom with the rest. On Wednesday morning, they were missing."

The instances where poor whites helped slaves were not frequent, but sufficient to show the need for setting one group against the other. Genovese says:

> The slaveholders . . . suspected that non-slaveholders would encourage slave disobedience and even rebellion, not so much out of sympathy for the blacks as out of hatred for the rich planters and resentment of their own poverty. White men sometimes were linked to slave insurrectionary plots, and each such incident rekindled fears.

This helps explain the stern police measures against whites who frater-nized with blacks.

Herbert Aptheker quotes a report to the governor of Virginia on a slave conspiracy in 1802: "I have just received information that three white persons are concerned in the plot; and they have arms and ammu-nition concealed under their houses, and were to give aid when the negroes should begin." One of the conspiring slaves said that it was "the common run of poor white people" who were involved.

In return, blacks helped whites in need. One black runaway told of a slave woman who had received fifty lashes of the whip for giving food to a white neighbor who was poor and sick.

When the Brunswick canal was built in Georgia, the black slaves and white Irish workers were segregated, the excuse being that they would do violence against one another. That may well have been true, but Fanny Kemble, the famous actress and wife of a planter, wrote in her journal:

> But the Irish are not only quarrelers, and rioters, and fighters, and drinkers, and despisers of niggers—they are a passionate, impulsive, warm-hearted, generous people, much given to powerful indignations, which break out

suddenly when not compelled to smoulder sullenly—pestilent sympathizers too, and with a sufficient dose of American atmospheric air in their lungs, properly mixed with a right proportion of ardent spirits, there is no saying but what they might actually take to sympathy with the slaves, and I leave you to judge of the possible consequences. You perceive, I am sure, that they can by no means be allowed to work together on the Brunswick Canal.

The need for slave control led to an ingenious device, paying poor whites—themselves so troublesome for two hundred years of southern history—to be overseers of black labor and therefore buffers for black hatred.

Religion was used for control. A book consulted by many planters was the *Cotton Plantation Record and Account Book*, which gave these instructions to overseers: "You will find that an hour devoted every Sabbath morning to their moral and religious instruction would prove a great aid to you in bringing about a better state of things amongst the Negroes."

As for black preachers, as Genovese puts it, "they had to speak a language defiant enough to hold the high-spirited among their flock but neither so inflammatory as to rouse them to battles they could not win nor so ominous as to arouse the ire of ruling powers." Practicality decided: "The slave communities, embedded as they were among numerically preponderant and militarily powerful whites, counseled a strategy of patience, of acceptance of what could not be helped, of a dogged effort to keep the black community alive and healthy—a strategy of survival that, like its African prototype, above all said yes to life in this world."

It was once thought that slavery had destroyed the black family. And so the black condition was blamed on family frailty, rather than on poverty and prejudice. Blacks without families, helpless, lacking kinship and identity, would have no will to resist. But interviews with ex-slaves, done in the 1930s by the Federal Writers Project of the New Deal for the Library of Congress, showed a different story, which George Rawick summarizes *(From Sundown to Sunup)*:

> The slave community acted like a generalized extended kinship system in which all adults looked after all children and there was little division between "my children for whom I'm responsible" and "your children for whom you're responsible." . . . A kind of family relationship in which older children have great responsibility for caring for younger siblings is obviously more functionally integrative and useful for slaves than the pattern of

sibling rivalry and often dislike that frequently comes out of contemporary middle-class nuclear families composed of highly individuated persons. . . . Indeed, the activity of the slaves in creating patterns of family life that were functionally integrative did more than merely prevent the destruction of personality. . . . It was part and parcel, as we shall see, of the social process out of which came black pride, black identity, black culture, the black community, and black rebellion in America.

Old letters and records dug out by historian Herbert Gutman *(The Black Family in Slavery and Freedom)* show the stubborn resistance of the slave family to pressures of disintegration. A woman wrote to her son from whom she had been separated for twenty years: "I long to see you in my old age. . . . Now my dear son I pray you to come and see your dear old Mother. . . . I love you Cato you love your Mother—You are my only son. . . ."

And a man wrote to his wife, sold away from him with their children: "Send me some of the children's hair in a separate paper with their names on the paper. . . . I had rather anything to had happened to me most than ever to have been parted from you and the children. . . . Laura I do love you the same. . . ."

Going through records of slave marriages, Gutman found how high was the incidence of marriage among slave men and women, and how stable these marriages were. He studied the remarkably complete records kept on one South Carolina plantation. He found a birth register of two hundred slaves extending from the eighteenth century to just before the Civil War; it showed stable kin networks, steadfast marriages, unusual fidelity, and resistance to forced marriages.

Slaves hung on determinedly to their selves, to their love of family, their wholeness. A shoemaker on the South Carolina Sea Islands expressed this in his own way: "I'se lost an arm but it hasn't gone out of my brains."

This family solidarity carried into the twentieth century. The remarkable southern black farmer Nate Shaw recalled that when his sister died, leaving three children, his father proposed sharing their care, and he responded:

That suits me, Papa. . . . Let's handle em like this: don't get the two little boys, the youngest ones, off at your house and the oldest one be at my house and we hold these little boys apart and won't bring em to see one another. I'll bring the little boy that I keep, the oldest one, around to your home amongst the other two. And you forward the others to my house and let em grow up knowin that they are brothers. Don't keep em separated in a way that they'll forget about one another. Don't do that, Papa.

Also insisting on the strength of blacks even under slavery, Lawrence Levine *(Black Culture and Black Consciousness)* gives a picture of a rich culture among slaves, a complex mixture of adaptation and rebellion, through the creativity of stories and songs:

We raise de wheat,
Dey gib us de corn;
We bake de bread,
Dey gib us de crust,
We sif de meal,
Dey gib us de huss;
We peel de meat,
Dey gib us de skin;
And dat's de way
Dey take us in;
We skim de pot,
Dey gib us de liquor,
An say dat's good enough for nigger.

There was mockery. The poet William Cullen Bryant, after attending a corn shucking in 1843 in South Carolina, told of slave dances turned into a pretended military parade, "a sort of burlesque of our militia trainings. . . ."

Spirituals often had double meanings. The song "O Canaan, sweet Canaan, I am bound for the land of Canaan" often meant that slaves meant to get to the North, their Canaan. During the Civil War, slaves began to make up new spirituals with bolder messages: "Before I'd be a slave, I'd be buried in my grave, and go home to my Lord and be saved." And the spiritual "Many Thousand Go":

No more peck o' corn for me, no more, no more,
No more driver's lash for me, no more, no more. . . .

Levine refers to slave resistance as "pre-political," expressed in countless ways in daily life and culture. Music, magic, art, religion, were all ways, he says, for slaves to hold on to their humanity.

While southern slaves held on, free blacks in the North (there were about 130,000 in 1830, about 200,000 in 1850) agitated for the abolition of slavery. In 1829, David Walker, son of a slave, but born free in North Carolina, moved to Boston, where he sold old clothes. The pamphlet he wrote and printed, *Walker's Appeal,* became widely known. It infuriated southern slaveholders; Georgia offered a reward of $10,000 to anyone who would deliver Walker alive, and $1,000 to anyone who would kill him. It is not hard to understand why when you read his *Appeal.*

There was no slavery in history, even that of the Israelites in Egypt, worse than the slavery of the black man in America, Walker said. ". . . show me a page of history, either sacred or profane, on which a verse can be found, which maintains, that the Egyptians heaped the insupportable insult upon the children of Israel, by telling them that they were not of the human family."

Walker was scathing to his fellow blacks who would assimilate: "I would wish, candidly . . . to be understood, that I would not give a pinch of snuff to be married to any white person I ever saw in all the days of my life."

Blacks must fight for their freedom, he said:

> Let our enemies go on with their butcheries, and at once fill up their cup. Never make an attempt to gain our freedom or natural right from under our cruel oppressors and murderers, until you see your way clear—when that hour arrives and you move, be not afraid or dismayed. . . . God has been pleased to give us two eyes, two hands, two feet, and some sense in our heads as well as they. They have no more right to hold us in slavery than we have to hold them. . . . Our sufferings will come to an end, in spite of all the Americans this side of eternity. Then we will want all the learning and talents among ourselves, and perhaps more, to govern ourselves.—"Every dog must have its day," the American's is coming to an end.

One summer day in 1830, David Walker was found dead near the doorway of his shop in Boston.

Some born in slavery acted out the unfulfilled desire of millions. Frederick Douglass, a slave, sent to Baltimore to work as a servant and as a laborer in the shipyard, somehow learned to read and write, and at twenty-one, in the year 1838, escaped to the North, where he became the most famous black man of his time, as lecturer, newspaper editor, writer. In his autobiography, *Narrative of the Life of Frederick Douglass,* he recalled his first childhood thoughts about his condition:

> Why am I a slave? Why are some people slaves, and others masters? Was there ever a time when this was not so? How did the relation commence?

Once, however, engaged in the inquiry, I was not very long in finding out the true solution of the matter. It was not color, but crime, not God, but man, that afforded the true explanation of the existence of slavery; nor was I long in finding out another important truth, viz: what man can make, man can unmake. . . .

I distinctly remember being, even then, most strongly impressed with the idea of being a free man some day. This cheering assurance was an inborn dream of my human nature—a constant menace to slavery—and one which all the powers of slavery were unable to silence or extinguish.

The Fugitive Slave Act passed in 1850 was a concession to the southern states in return for the admission of the Mexican war territories (California, especially) into the Union as nonslave states. The Act made it easy for slaveowners to recapture ex-slaves or simply to pick up blacks they claimed had run away. Northern blacks organized resistance to the Fugitive Slave Act, denouncing President Fillmore, who signed it, and Senator Daniel Webster, who supported it. One of these was J. W. Loguen, son of a slave mother and her white owner. He had escaped to freedom on his master's horse, gone to college, and was now a minister in Syracuse, New York. He spoke to a meeting in that city in 1850:

The time has come to change the tones of submission into tones of defiance—and to tell Mr. Fillmore and Mr. Webster, if they propose to execute this measure upon us, to send on their blood-hounds. . . . I received my freedom from Heaven, and with it came the command to defend my title to it. . . . I don't respect this law—I don't fear it—I won't obey it! It outlaws me, and I outlaw it. . . . I will not live a slave, and if force is employed to re-enslave me, I shall make preparations to meet the crisis as becomes a man. . . . Your decision tonight in favor of resistance will give vent to the spirit of liberty, and it will break the bands of party, and shout for joy all over the North. . . . Heaven knows that this act of noble daring will break out somewhere—and may God grant that Syracuse be the honored spot, whence it shall send an earthquake voice through the land!

The following year, Syracuse had its chance. A runaway slave named Jerry was captured and put on trial. A crowd used crowbars and a battering ram to break into the courthouse, defying marshals with drawn guns, and set Jerry free.

Loguen made his home in Syracuse a major station on the Underground Railroad. It was said that he helped 1,500 slaves on their way to Canada. His memoir of slavery came to the attention of his former mistress, and she wrote to him, asking him either to return or to send her $1,000 in compensation. Loguen's reply to her was printed in the abolitionist newspaper, *The Liberator*:

> Mrs. Sarah Logue. . . . You say you have offers to buy me, and that you shall sell me if I do not send you $1000, and in the same breath and almost in the same sentence, you say, "You know we raised you as we did our own children." Woman, did you raise your own children for the market? Did you raise them for the whipping post? Did you raise them to be driven off, bound to a coffle in chains? . . . Shame on you!
>
> But you say I am a thief, because I took the old mare along with me. Have you got to learn that I had a better right to the old mare, as you call her, than Manasseth Logue had to me? Is it a greater sin for me to steal his horse, than it was for him to rob my mother's cradle, and steal me? . . . Have you got to learn that human rights are mutual and reciprocal, and if you take my liberty and life, you forfeit your own liberty and life? Before God and high heaven, is there a law for one man which is not a law for every other man?
>
> If you or any other speculator on my body and rights, wish to know how I regard my rights, they need but come here, and lay their hands on me to enslave me. . . .
>
> Yours, etc. J. W. Loguen

Frederick Douglass knew that the shame of slavery was not just the South's, that the whole nation was complicit in it. On the Fourth of July, 1852, he gave an Independence Day address:

> Fellow Citizens: Pardon me, and allow me to ask, why am I called upon to speak here today? What have I or those I represent to do with your national independence? Are the great principles of political freedom and of natural justice, embodied in that Declaration of Independence, extended to us? And am I, therefore, called upon to bring our humble offering to the national altar, and to confess the benefits, and express devout gratitude for the blessings resulting from your independence to us?. . .
>
> What to the American slave is your Fourth of July? I answer, a day that reveals to him more than all other days of the year, the gross injustice and cruelty to which he is the constant victim. To him your celebration is a sham; your boasted liberty an unholy license; your national greatness, swelling vanity; your sounds of rejoicing are empty and heartless; your denunciation of tyrants, brass-fronted impudence; your shouts of liberty and equality, hollow mockery; your prayers and hymns, your sermons and

thanksgivings, with all your religious parade and solemnity, are to him mere bombast, fraud, deception, impiety, and hypocrisy—a thin veil to cover up crimes which would disgrace a nation of savages. There is not a nation of the earth guilty of practices more shocking and bloody than are the people of these United States at this very hour.

Go where you may, search where you will, roam through all the monarchies and despotisms of the Old World, travel through South America, search out every abuse and when you have found the last, lay your facts by the side of the everyday practices of this nation, and you will say with me that, for revolting barbarity and shameless hypocrisy, America reigns without a rival. . . .

Ten years after Nat Turner's rebellion, there was no sign of black insurrection in the South. But that year, 1841, one incident took place which kept alive the idea of rebellion. Slaves being transported on a ship, the *Creole*, overpowered the crew, killed one of them, and sailed into the British West Indies (where slavery had been abolished in 1833). England refused to return the slaves (there was much agitation in England against American slavery), and this led to angry talk in Congress of war with England, encouraged by Secretary of State Daniel Webster. The *Colored Peoples Press* denounced Webster's "bullying position," and, recalling the Revolutionary War and the War of 1812, wrote:

If war be declared . . . Will we fight in defense of a government which denies us the most precious right of citizenship? . . . The States in which we dwell have twice availed themselves of our voluntary services, and have repaid us with chains and slavery. Shall we a third time kiss the foot that crushes us? If so, we deserve our chains.

As the tension grew, North and South, blacks became more militant. Frederick Douglass spoke in 1857:

Let me give you a word of the philosophy of reforms. The whole history of the progress of human liberty shows that all concessions yet made to her august claims have been born of struggle. . . . If there is no struggle there is no progress. Those who profess to favor freedom and yet deprecate agitation, are men who want crops without plowing up the ground. They want rain without thunder and lightning. They want the ocean without the awful roar of its many waters. The struggle may be a moral one; or it may be a physical one; or it may be both moral and physical, but it must be a struggle. Power concedes nothing without a demand. It never did and it never will. . . .

There were tactical differences between Douglass and William Lloyd Garrison, white abolitionist and editor of *The Liberator*—differences between black and white abolitionists in general. Blacks were more willing to engage in armed insurrection, but also more ready to use existing political devices—the ballot box, the Constitution—anything to further their cause. They were not as morally absolute in their tactics as the Garrisonians. Moral pressure would not do it alone, the blacks knew; it would take all sorts of tactics, from elections to rebellion.

How ever-present in the minds of northern Negroes was the question of slavery is shown by black children in a Cincinnati school, a private school financed by Negroes. The children were responding to the question "What do you think *most* about?" Only five answers remain in the records, and all refer to slavery. A seven-year-old child wrote:

> Dear schoolmates, we are going next summer to buy a farm and to work part of the day and to study the other part if we live to see it and come home part of the day to see our mothers and sisters and cousins if we are got any and see our kind folks and to be good boys and when we get a man to get the poor slaves from bondage. And I am sorrow to hear that the boat . . . went down with 200 poor slaves from up the river. Oh how sorrow I am to hear that, it grieves my heart so that I could faint in one minute.

White abolitionists did courageous and pioneering work, on the lecture platform, in newspapers, in the Underground Railroad. Black abolitionists, less publicized, were the backbone of the antislavery movement. Before Garrison published his famous *Liberator* in Boston in 1831, the first national convention of Negroes had been held, David Walker had already written his "Appeal," and a black abolitionist magazine named *Freedom's Journal* had appeared. Of *The Liberator's* first twenty-five subscribers, most were black.

Blacks had to struggle constantly with the unconscious racism of white abolitionists. They also had to insist on their own independent voice. Douglass wrote for *The Liberator*, but in 1847 started his own newspaper in Rochester, *North Star*, which led to a break with Garrison. In 1854, a conference of Negroes declared: ". . . it is emphatically our battle; no one else can fight it for us. . . . Our relations to the Anti-Slavery movement must be and are changed. Instead of depending upon it we must lead it."

Certain black women faced the triple hurdle—of being abolitionists in a slave society, of being black among white reformers, and of being women in a reform movement dominated by men. When Sojourner

Truth rose to speak in 1853 in New York City at the Fourth National Woman's Rights Convention, it all came together. There was a hostile mob in the hall shouting, jeering, threatening. She said:

> I know that it feels a kind o' hissin' and ticklin' like to see a colored woman get up and tell you about things, and Woman's Rights. We have all been thrown down so low that nobody thought we'd ever get up again; but . . . we will come up again, and now I'm here. . . . we'll have our rights; see if we don't; and you can't stop us from them; see if you can. You may hiss as much as you like, but it is comin'. . . . I am sittin' among you to watch; and every once and awhile I will come out and tell you what time of night it is. . . .

After Nat Turner's violent uprising and Virginia's bloody repression, the security system inside the South became tighter. Perhaps only an outsider could hope to launch a rebellion. It was such a person, a white man of ferocious courage and determination, John Brown, whose wild scheme it was to seize the federal arsenal at Harpers Ferry, Virginia, and then set off a revolt of slaves through the South.

Harriet Tubman, 5 feet tall, some of her teeth missing, a veteran of countless secret missions piloting blacks out of slavery, was involved with John Brown and his plans. But sickness prevented her from joining him. Frederick Douglass too had met with Brown. He argued against the plan from the standpoint of its chances of success, but he admired the ailing man of sixty, tall, gaunt, white-haired.

Douglass was right; the plan would not work. The local militia, joined by a hundred marines under the command of Robert E. Lee, surrounded the insurgents. Although his men were dead or captured, John Brown refused to surrender: he barricaded himself in a small brick building near the gate of the armory. The troops battered down a door; a marine lieutenant moved in and struck Brown with his sword. Wounded, sick, he was interrogated. W. E. B. Du Bois, in his book *John Brown*, writes:

> Picture the situation: An old and blood-bespattered man, half-dead from the wounds inflicted but a few hours before; a man lying in the cold and dirt, without sleep for fifty-five nerve-wrecking hours, without food for nearly as long, with the dead bodies of his two sons almost before his eyes, the piled corpses of his seven slain comrades near and afar, a wife and a bereaved family listening in vain, and a Lost Cause, the dream of a lifetime, lying dead in his heart. . . .

Lying there, interrogated by the governor of Virginia, Brown said: "You had better—all you people at the South—prepare yourselves for a settlement of this question. . . . You may dispose of me very easily—I am nearly disposed of now, but this question is still to be settled,—this Negro question, I mean; the end of that is not yet."

Du Bois appraises Brown's action:

> If his foray was the work of a handful of fanatics, led by a lunatic and repudi- ated by the slaves to a man, then the proper procedure would have been to ignore the incident, quietly punish the worst offenders and either pardon the misguided leader or send him to an asylum. . . . While insisting that the raid was too hopelessly and ridiculously small to accomplish anything . . . the state nevertheless spent $250,000 to punish the invaders, stationed from one to three thousand soldiers in the vicinity and threw the nation into tur- moil.

In John Brown's last written statement, in prison, before he was hanged, he said: "I, John Brown, am quite certain that the crimes of this guilty land will never be purged away but with blood."

Ralph Waldo Emerson, not an activist himself, said of the execution of John Brown: "He will make the gallows holy as the cross."

Of the twenty-two men in John Brown's striking force, five were black. Two of these were killed on the spot, one escaped, and two were hanged by the authorities. Before his execution, John Copeland wrote to his parents:

> Remember that if I must die I die in trying to liberate a few of my poor and oppressed people from my condition of servitude which God in his Holy Writ has hurled his most bitter denunciations against. . . .
>
> I am not terrified by the gallows. . . .
>
> I imagine that I hear you, and all of you, mother, father, sisters, and brothers, say—"No, there is not a cause for which we, with less sorrow, could see you die." Believe me when I tell you, that though shut up in prison and under sentence of death, I have spent more happy hours here, and . . . I would almost as lief die now as at any time, for I feel that I am prepared to meet my Maker. . . .

John Brown was executed by the state of Virginia with the approval of the national government. It was the national government which, while weakly enforcing the law ending the slave trade, sternly enforced the laws providing for the return of fugitives to slavery. It was the national government that, in Andrew Jackson's administration, collaborated with the South to keep abolitionist literature out of the mails in the southern states. It was the Supreme Court of the United States that declared in 1857 that the slave Dred Scott could not sue for his freedom because he was not a person, but property.

Such a national government would never accept an end to slavery by rebellion. It would end slavery only under conditions controlled by whites, and only when required by the political and economic needs of the business elite of the North. It was Abraham Lincoln who combined perfectly the needs of business, the political ambition of the new Republican party, and the rhetoric of humanitarianism. He would keep the abolition of slavery not at the top of his list of priorities, but close enough to the top so it could be pushed there temporarily by abolitionist pressures and by practical political advantage.

Lincoln could skillfully blend the interests of the very rich and the interests of the black at a moment in history when these interests met. And he could link these two with a growing section of Americans, the white, up-and-coming, economically ambitious, politically active middle class. As Richard Hofstadter puts it:

> Thoroughly middle class in his ideas, he spoke for those millions of Americans who had begun their lives as hired workers—as farm hands, clerks, teachers, mechanics, flatboat men, and rail-splitters—and had passed into the ranks of landed farmers, prosperous grocers, lawyers, merchants, physicians and politicians.

Lincoln could argue with lucidity and passion against slavery on moral grounds, while acting cautiously in practical politics. He believed "that the institution of slavery is founded on injustice and bad policy, but that the promulgation of abolition doctrines tends to increase rather than abate its evils." (Put against this Frederick Douglass's statement on struggle, or Garrison's "Sir, slavery will not be overthrown without excitement, a most tremendous excitement.") Lincoln read the Constitution strictly, to mean that Congress, because of the Tenth Amendment (reserving to the states powers not specifically given to the national government), could not constitutionally bar slavery in the states.

When it was proposed to abolish slavery in the District of Columbia, which did not have the rights of a state but was directly under the jurisdiction of Congress, Lincoln said this would be Constitutional, but it should not be done unless the people in the District wanted it. Since most there were white, this killed the idea. As Hofstadter said of Lincoln's statement, it "breathes the fire of an uncompromising insistence on moderation."

Lincoln refused to denounce the Fugitive Slave Law publicly. He wrote to a friend: "I confess I hate to see the poor creatures hunted down . . . but I bite my lips and keep quiet." And when he did propose, in 1849, as a Congressman, a resolution to abolish slavery in the District of Columbia, he accompanied this with a section requiring local authorities to arrest and return fugitive slaves coming into Washington. (This led Wendell Phillips, the Boston abolitionist, to refer to him years later as "that slavehound from Illinois.") He opposed slavery, but could not see blacks as equals, so a constant theme in his approach was to free the slaves and to send them back to Africa.

In his 1858 campaign in Illinois for the Senate against Stephen Douglas, Lincoln spoke differently depending on the views of his listeners (and also perhaps depending on how close it was to the election). Speaking in northern Illinois in July (in Chicago), he said:

> Let us discard all this quibbling about this man and the other man, this race and that race and the other race being inferior, and therefore they must be placed in an inferior position. Let us discard all these things, and unite as one people throughout this land, until we shall once more stand up declaring that all men are created equal.

Two months later in Charleston, in southern Illinois, Lincoln told his audience:

> I will say, then, that I am not, nor ever have been, in favor of bringing about in any way the social and political equality of the white and black races (applause); that I am not, nor ever have been, in favor of making voters or jurors of negroes, nor of qualifying them to hold office, nor to intermarry with white people. . . .
>
> And inasmuch as they cannot so live, while they do remain together there must be the position of superior and inferior, and I as much as any other man am in favor of having the superior position assigned to the white race.

Behind the secession of the South from the Union, after Lincoln was elected President in the fall of 1860 as candidate of the new Republican party, was a long series of policy clashes between South and North. The clash was not over slavery as a moral institution—most northerners did not care enough about slavery to make sacrifices for it, certainly not the sacrifice of war. It was not a clash of peoples (most northern whites were not economically favored, not politically powerful; most southern whites were poor farmers, not decisionmakers) but of elites. The northern elite wanted economic expansion—free land, free labor, a free market, a high protective tariff for manufacturers, a bank of the United States. The slave interests opposed all that; they saw Lincoln and the Republicans as making continuation of their pleasant and prosperous way of life impossible in the future.

So, when Lincoln was elected, seven southern states seceded from the Union. Lincoln initiated hostilities by trying to repossess the federal base at Fort Sumter, South Carolina, and four more states seceded. The Confederacy was formed; the Civil War was on.

Lincoln's first Inaugural Address, in March 1861, was conciliatory toward the South and the seceded states: "I have no purpose, directly or indirectly, to interfere with the institution of slavery in the States where it exists. I believe I have no lawful right to do so, and I have no inclination to do so." And with the war four months on, when General John C. Frémont in Missouri declared martial law and said slaves of owners resisting the United States were to be free, Lincoln countermanded this order. He was anxious to hold in the Union the slave states of Maryland, Kentucky, Missouri, and Delaware.

It was only as the war grew more bitter, the casualties mounted, desperation to win heightened, and the criticism of the abolitionists threatened to unravel the tattered coalition behind Lincoln that he began to act against slavery. Hofstadter puts it this way: "Like a delicate barometer, he recorded the trend of pressures, and as the Radical pressure increased he moved toward the left." Wendell Phillips said that if Lincoln was able to grow "it is because we have watered him."

Racism in the North was as entrenched as slavery in the South, and it would take the war to shake both. New York blacks could not vote unless they owned $250 in property (a qualification not applied to whites). A proposal to abolish this, put on the ballot in 1860, was defeated two to one (although Lincoln carried New York by 50,000 votes). Frederick Douglass commented: "The black baby of Negro suffrage was thought too ugly to exhibit on so grand an occasion. The Negro was stowed away like some people put out of sight their deformed children when company comes."

Wendell Phillips, with all his criticism of Lincoln, recognized the possibilities in his election. Speaking at the Tremont Temple in Boston the day after the election, Phillips said:

If the telegraph speaks truth, for the first time in our history the slave has chosen a President of the United States. . . . Not an Abolitionist, hardly an antislavery man, Mr. Lincoln consents to represent an antislavery idea. A pawn on the political chessboard, his value is in his position; with fair effort, we may soon change him for knight, bishop or queen, and sweep the board. (Applause)

Conservatives in the Boston upper classes wanted reconciliation with the South. At one point they stormed an abolitionist meeting at that same Tremont Temple, shortly after Lincoln's election, and asked that concessions be made to the South "in the interests of commerce, manufactures, agriculture."

The spirit of Congress, even after the war began, was shown in a resolution it passed in the summer of 1861, with only a few dissenting votes: ". . . this war is not waged . . . for any purpose of . . . overthrowing or interfering with the rights of established institutions of those states, but . . . to preserve the Union."

The abolitionists stepped up their campaign. Emancipation petitions poured into Congress in 1861 and 1862. In May of that year, Wendell Phillips said: "Abraham Lincoln may not wish it; he cannot prevent it; the nation may not will it, but the nation cannot prevent it. I do not care what men want or wish; the negro is the pebble in the cog-wheel, and the machine cannot go on until you get him out."

In July Congress passed a Confiscation Act, which enabled the freeing of slaves of those fighting the Union. But this was not enforced by the Union generals, and Lincoln ignored the nonenforcement. Garrison called Lincoln's policy "stumbling, halting, prevaricating, irresolute, weak, besotted," and Phillips said Lincoln was "a first-rate second-rate man."

An exchange of letters between Lincoln and Horace Greeley, editor of the New York *Tribune*, in August of 1862, gave Lincoln a chance to express his views. Greeley wrote:

Dear Sir. I do not intrude to tell you—for you must know already—that a great proportion of those who triumphed in your election . . . are sorely disappointed and deeply pained by the policy you seem to be pursuing with regard to the slaves of rebels. . . . We require of you, as the first servant of the Republic, charged especially and preeminently with this duty, that you EXECUTE THE LAWS. . . . We think you are strangely and disastrously remiss . . . with regard to the emancipating provisions of the new Confiscation Act. . . .

We think you are unduly influenced by the councils . . . of certain politicians hailing from the Border Slave States.

Greeley appealed to the practical need of winning the war. "We must
have scouts, guides, spies, cooks, teamsters, diggers and choppers from
the blacks of the South, whether we allow them to fight for us or
not. . . . I entreat you to render a hearty and unequivocal obedience to
the law of the land."

Lincoln had already shown his attitude by his failure to countermand
an order of one of his commanders, General Henry Halleck, who forbade fugitive Negroes to enter his army's lines. Now he replied to
Greeley:

Dear Sir: . . . I have not meant to leave any one in doubt. . . . My paramount
object in this struggle is to save the Union, and is not either to save or
destroy Slavery. If I could save the Union without freeing any slave, I would
do it; and if I could save it by freeing all the slaves, I would do it; and if I
could do it by freeing some and leaving others alone, I would also do that.
What I do about Slavery and the colored race, I do because it helps to save
this Union; and what I forbear, I forbear because I do not believe it would
help to save the Union. . . . I have here stated my purpose according to my
view of official duty, and I intend no modification of my oft-expressed personal wish that all men, everywhere, could be free. Yours. A. Lincoln.

So Lincoln distinguished between his "personal wish" and his "official
duty."

When in September 1862, Lincoln issued his preliminary
Emancipation Proclamation, it was a military move, giving the South
four months to stop rebelling, threatening to emancipate their slaves if
they continued to fight, promising to leave slavery untouched in states
that came over to the North:

That on the 1st day of January, AD 1863, all persons held as slaves within
any State or designated part of a State the people whereof shall then be in
rebellion against the United States shall be then, thenceforward and forever
free. . . .

Thus, when the Emancipation Proclamation was issued January 1,
1863, it declared slaves free in those areas still fighting against the
Union (which it listed very carefully), and said nothing about slaves
behind Union lines. As Hofstadter put it, the Emancipation

Proclamation "had all the moral grandeur of a bill of lading." The *London Spectator* wrote concisely: "The principle is not that a human being cannot justly own another, but that he cannot own him unless he is loyal to the United States."

Limited as it was, the Emancipation Proclamation spurred antislavery forces. By the summer of 1864, 400,000 signatures asking legislation to end slavery had been gathered and sent to Congress, something unprecedented in the history of the country. That April, the Senate had adopted the Thirteenth Amendment, declaring an end to slavery, and in January 1865, the House of Representatives followed.

With the Proclamation, the Union army was open to blacks. And the more blacks entered the war, the more it appeared a war for their liberation. The more whites had to sacrifice, the more resentment there was, particularly among poor whites in the North, who were drafted by a law that allowed the rich to buy their way out of the draft for $300. And so the draft riots of 1863 took place, uprisings of angry whites in northern cities, their targets not the rich, far away, but the blacks, near at hand. It was an orgy of death and violence. A black man in Detroit described what he saw: a mob, with kegs of beer on wagons, armed with clubs and bricks, marching through the city, attacking black men, women, children. He heard one man say: "If we are got to be killed up for Negroes then we will kill every one in this town."

The Civil War was one of the bloodiest in human history up to that time: 600,000 dead on both sides, in a population of 30 million—the equivalent, in the United States of 1978, with a population of 250 million, of 5 million dead. As the battles became more intense, as the bodies piled up, as war fatigue grew, the existence of blacks in the South, 4 million of them, became more and more a hindrance to the South, and more and more an opportunity for the North. Du Bois, in *Black Reconstruction*, pointed this out:

> ... these slaves had enormous power in their hands. Simply by stopping work, they could threaten the Confederacy with starvation. By walking into the Federal camps, they showed to doubting Northerners the easy possibility of using them thus, but by the same gesture, depriving their enemies of their use in just these fields. . . .
>
> It was this plain alternative that brought Lee's sudden surrender. Either the South must make terms with its slaves, free them, use them to fight the North, and thereafter no longer treat them as bondsmen; or they could surrender to the North with the assumption that the North after the war must help them to defend slavery, as it had before.

George Rawick, a sociologist and anthropologist, describes the development of blacks up to and into the Civil War:

The slaves went from being frightened human beings, thrown among strange men, including fellow slaves who were not their kinsmen and who did not speak their language or understand their customs and habits, to what W. E. B. DuBois once described as the general strike whereby hundreds of thousands of slaves deserted the plantations, destroying the South's ability to supply its army.

Black women played an important part in the war, especially toward the end. Sojourner Truth, the legendary ex-slave who had been active in the women's rights movement, became recruiter of black troops for the Union army, as did Josephine St. Pierre Ruffin of Boston. Harriet Tubman raided plantations, leading black and white troops, and in one expedition freed 750 slaves. Women moved with the colored regiments that grew as the Union army marched through the South, helping their husbands, enduring terrible hardships on the long military treks, in which many children died. They suffered the fate of soldiers, as in April 1864, when Confederate troops at Fort Pillow, Tennessee, massacred Union soldiers who had surrendered—black and white, along with women and children in an adjoining camp.

It has been said that black acceptance of slavery is proved by the fact that during the Civil War, when there were opportunities for escape, most slaves stayed on the plantation. In fact, half a million ran away—about one in five, a high proportion when one considers that there was great difficulty in knowing where to go and how to live.

The owner of a large plantation in South Carolina and Georgia wrote in 1862: "This war has taught us the perfect impossibility of placing the least confidence in the negro. In too numerous instances those we esteemed the most have been the first to desert us." That same year, a lieutenant in the Confederate army and once mayor of Savannah, Georgia, wrote: "I deeply regret to learn that the Negroes still continue to desert to the enemy."

A minister in Mississippi wrote in the fall of 1862: "On my arrival was surprised to hear that our negroes stampeded to the Yankees last night or rather a portion of them. . . . I think every one, but with one or two exceptions will go to the Yankees. Eliza and her family are certain to go. She does not conceal her thoughts but plainly manifests her opinions by her conduct—insolent and insulting." And a woman's plantation journal of January 1865:

The people are all idle on the plantations, most of them seeking their own pleasure. Many servants have proven faithful, others false and rebellious against all authority and restraint. . . . Their condition is one of perfect anarchy and rebellion. They have placed themselves in perfect antagonism to their owners and to all government and control. . . . Nearly all the house servants have left their homes; and from most of the plantations they have gone in a body.

Also in 1865, a South Carolina planter wrote to the New York *Tribune* that

the conduct of the Negro in the late crisis of our affairs has convinced me that we were all laboring under a delusion. . . . I believed that these people were content, happy, and attached to their masters. But events and reflection have caused me to change these positions. . . . If they were content, happy and attached to their masters, why did they desert him in the moment of his need and flock to an enemy, whom they did not know; and thus left their perhaps really good masters whom they did know from infancy?

Genovese notes that the war produced no general rising of slaves, but: "In Lafayette County, Mississippi, slaves responded to the Emancipation Proclamation by driving off their overseers and dividing the land and implements among themselves." Aptheker reports a conspiracy of Negroes in Arkansas in 1861 to kill their enslavers. In Kentucky that year, houses and barns were burned by Negroes, and in the city of New Castle slaves paraded through the city "singing political songs, and shouting for Lincoln," according to newspaper accounts. After the Emancipation Proclamation, a Negro waiter in Richmond, Virginia, was arrested for leading "a servile plot," while in Yazoo City, Mississippi, slaves burned the courthouse and fourteen homes.

There were special moments: Robert Smalls (later a South Carolina Congressman) and other blacks took over a steamship, *The Planter*, and sailed it past the Confederate guns to deliver it to the Union navy.

Most slaves neither submitted nor rebelled. They continued to work, waiting to see what happened. When opportunity came, they left, often joining the Union army. Two hundred thousand blacks were in the army and navy, and 38,000 were killed. Historian James McPherson says: "Without their help, the North could not have won the war as soon as it did, and perhaps it could not have won at all."

What happened to blacks in the Union army and in the northern cities during the war gave some hint of how limited the emancipation would be, even with full victory over the Confederacy. Off-duty black soldiers were attacked in northern cities, as in Zanesville, Ohio, in February 1864, where cries were heard to "kill the nigger." Black soldiers were used for the heaviest and dirtiest work, digging trenches, hauling logs and cannon, loading ammunition, digging wells for white regiments. White privates received $13 a month; Negro privates received $10 a month.

Late in the war, a black sergeant of the Third South Carolina Volunteers, William Walker, marched his company to his captain's tent and ordered them to stack arms and resign from the army as a protest against what he considered a breach of contract, because of unequal pay. He was court-martialed and shot for mutiny. Finally, in June 1864, Congress passed a law granting equal pay to Negro soldiers.

The Confederacy was desperate in the latter part of the war, and some of its leaders suggested the slaves, more and more an obstacle to their cause, be enlisted, used, and freed. After a number of military defeats, the Confederate secretary of war, Judah Benjamin, wrote in late 1864 to a newspaper editor in Charleston: ". . . It is well known that General Lee, who commands so largely the confidence of the people, is strongly in favor of our using the negroes for defense, and emancipating them, if necessary, for that purpose. . . ." One general, indignant, wrote: "If slaves will make good soldiers, our whole theory of slavery is wrong."

By early 1865, the pressure had mounted, and in March President Davis of the Confederacy signed a "Negro Soldier Law" authorizing the enlistment of slaves as soldiers, to be freed by consent of their owners and their state governments. But before it had any significant effect, the war was over.

Former slaves, interviewed by the Federal Writers' Project in the thirties, recalled the war's end. Susie Melton:

> I was a young gal, about ten years old, and we done heard that Lincoln gonna turn the niggers free. Ol' missus say there wasn't nothin' to it. Then a Yankee soldier told someone in Williamsburg that Lincoln done signed the 'mancipation. Was wintertime and mighty cold that night, but everybody commenced getting ready to leave. Didn't care nothin' about missus—was going to the Union lines. And all that night the niggers danced and sang right out in the cold. Next morning at day break we all started out with blankets and clothes and pots and pans and chickens piled on our backs, 'cause missus said we couldn't take no horses or carts. And as the sun come up over the trees, the niggers started to singing:

Sun, you be here and I'll be gone
Sun, you be here and I'll be gone
Sun, you be here and I'll be gone
Bye, bye, don't grieve after me
Won't give you my place, not for yours
Bye, bye, don't grieve after me
Cause you be here and I'll be gone.

Anna Woods:

We wasn't there in Texas long when the soldiers marched in to tell us that we were free. . . . I remembers one woman. She jumped on a barrel and she shouted. She jumped off and she shouted. She jumped back on again and shouted some more. She kept that up for a long time, just jumping on a barrel and back off again.

Annie Mae Weathers said:

I remember hearing my pa say that when somebody came and hollered, "You niggers is free at last," say he just dropped his hoe and said in a queer voice, "Thank God for that."

The Federal Writers' Project recorded an ex-slave named Fannie Berry:

Niggers shoutin' and clappin' hands and singin'! Chillun runnin' all over the place beatin' time and yellin'! Everybody happy. Sho' did some celebratin'. Run to the kitchen and shout in the window:
   "Mammy, don't you cook no more.
   You's free! You's free!"

Many Negroes understood that their status after the war, whatever their situation legally, would depend on whether they owned the land they worked on or would be forced to be semislaves for others. In 1863, a North Carolina Negro wrote that "if the strict law of right and justice is to be observed, the country around me is the entailed inheritance of the Americans of African descent, purchased by the invaluable labor of our ancestors, through a life of tears and groans, under the lash and yoke of tyranny."

Abandoned plantations, however, were leased to former planters, and to white men of the North. As one colored newspaper said: "The slaves were made serfs and chained to the soil. . . . Such was the boasted freedom acquired by the colored man at the hands of the Yankee."

Under congressional policy approved by Lincoln, the property confiscated during the war under the Confiscation Act of July 1862 would revert to the heirs of the Confederate owners. Dr. John Rock, a black physician in Boston, spoke at a meeting: "Why talk about compensating masters? Compensate them for what? What do you owe them? What does the slave owe them? What does society owe them? Compensate the master? . . . It is the slave who ought to be compensated. The property of the South is by right the property of the slave. . . ."

Some land was expropriated on grounds the taxes were delinquent, and sold at auction. But only a few blacks could afford to buy this. In the South Carolina Sea Islands, out of 16,000 acres up for sale in March of 1863, freedmen who pooled their money were able to buy 2,000 acres, the rest being bought by northern investors and speculators. A freedman on the Islands dictated a letter to a former teacher now in Philadelphia:

> My Dear Young Missus: Do, my missus, tell Linkum dat we wants land—dis bery land dat is rich wid de sweat ob de face and de blood ob we back. . . . We could a bin buy all we want, but dey make de lots too big, and cut we out.
>
> De word cum from Mass Linkum's self, dat we take out claims and hold on ter um, an' plant um, and he will see dat we get um, every man ten or twenty acre. We too glad. We stake out an' list, but fore de time for plant, dese commissionaries sells to white folks all de best land. Where Linkum?

In early 1865, General William T. Sherman held a conference in Savannah, Georgia, with twenty Negro ministers and church officials, mostly former slaves, at which one of them expressed their need: "The way we can best take care of ourselves is to have land, and till it by our labor. . . ." Four days later Sherman issued "Special Field Order No. 15," designating the entire southern coastline 30 miles inland for exclusive Negro settlement. Freedmen could settle there, taking no more than 40 acres per family. By June 1865, forty thousand freedmen had moved onto new farms in this area. But President Andrew Johnson, in August of 1865, restored this land to the Confederate owners, and the freedmen were forced off, some at bayonet point.

Ex-slave Thomas Hall told the Federal Writers' Project:

> Lincoln got the praise for freeing us, but did he do it? He gave us freedom without giving us any chance to live to ourselve and we still had to depend

on the southern white man for work, food, and clothing, and he held us out of necessity and want in a state of servitude but little better than slavery.

The American government had set out to fight the slave states in 1861, not to end slavery, but to retain the enormous national territory and market and resources. Yet, victory required a crusade, and the momentum of that crusade brought new forces into national politics: more blacks determined to make their freedom mean something; more whites—whether Freedman's Bureau officials, or teachers in the Sea Islands, or "carpetbaggers" with various mixtures of humanitarianism and personal ambition—concerned with racial equality. There was also the powerful interest of the Republican party in maintaining control over the national government, with the prospect of southern black votes to accomplish this. Northern businessmen, seeing Republican policies as beneficial to them, went along for a while.

The result was that brief period after the Civil War in which southern Negroes voted, elected blacks to state legislatures and to Congress, introduced free and racially mixed public education to the South. A legal framework was constructed. The Thirteenth Amendment outlawed slavery: "Neither slavery nor involuntary servitude, except as a punishment for crime whereof the party shall have been duly convicted, shall exist within the United States, or any place subject to their jurisdiction." The Fourteenth Amendment repudiated the prewar Dred Scott decision by declaring that "all persons born or naturalized in the United States" were citizens. It also seemed to make a powerful statement for racial equality, severely limiting "states' rights":

> No State shall make or enforce any law which shall abridge the privileges or immunities of citizens of the United States; nor shall any State deprive any person of life, liberty, or property, without due process of law; nor deny to any person within its jurisdiction the equal protection of the laws.

The Fifteenth Amendment said: "The right of citizens of the United States to vote shall not be denied or abridged by the United States or by any State on account of race, color, or previous condition of servitude."

Congress passed a number of laws in the late 1860s and early 1870s in the same spirit—laws making it a crime to deprive Negroes of their rights, requiring federal officials to enforce those rights, giving Negroes the right to enter contracts and buy property without discrimination. And in 1875, a Civil Rights Act outlawed the exclusion of Negroes from hotels, theaters, railroads, and other public accommodations.

With these laws, with the Union army in the South as protection, and a civilian army of officials in the Freedman's Bureau to help them, southern Negroes came forward, voted, formed political organizations, and expressed themselves forcefully on issues important to them. They were hampered in this for several years by Andrew Johnson, Vice-President under Lincoln, who became President when Lincoln was assassinated at the close of the war. Johnson vetoed bills to help Negroes; he made it easy for Confederate states to come back into the Union without guaranteeing equal rights to blacks. During his presidency, these returned southern states enacted "black codes," which made the freed slaves like serfs, still working the plantations. For instance, Mississippi in 1865 made it illegal for freedmen to rent or lease farmland, and provided for them to work under labor contracts which they could not break under penalty of prison. It also provided that the courts could assign black children under eighteen who had no parents, or whose parents were poor, to forced labor, called apprenticeships— with punishment for runaways.

Andrew Johnson clashed with Senators and Congressmen who, in some cases for reasons of justice, in others out of political calculation, supported equal rights and voting for the freedman. These members of Congress succeeded in impeaching Johnson in 1868, using as an excuse that he had violated some minor statute, but the Senate fell one vote short of the two-thirds required to remove him from office. In the presidential election of that year, Republican Ulysses Grant was elected, winning by 300,000 votes, with 700,000 Negroes voting, and so Johnson was out as an obstacle. Now the southern states could come back into the Union only by approving the new Constitutional amendments.

Whatever northern politicians were doing to help their cause, southern blacks were determined to make the most of their freedom, in spite of their lack of land and resources. A study of blacks in Alabama in the first years after the war by historian Peter Kolchin finds that they began immediately asserting their independence of whites, forming their own churches, becoming politically active, strengthening their family ties, trying to educate their children. Kolchin disagrees with the contention of some historians that slavery had created a "Sambo" mentality of submission among blacks. "As soon as they were free, these supposedly dependent, childlike Negroes began acting like independent men and women."

Negroes were now elected to southern state legislatures, although in all these they were a minority except in the lower house of the South Carolina legislature. A great propaganda campaign was undertaken North and South (one which lasted well into the twentieth century, in the history textbooks of American schools) to show that blacks were inept, lazy, corrupt, and ruinous to the governments of the South when they were in office. Undoubtedly there was corruption, but one could hardly claim that blacks had invented political conniving, especially in the bizarre climate of financial finagling North and South after the Civil War.

It was true that the public debt of South Carolina, $7 million in 1865, went up to $29 million in 1873, but the new legislature introduced free public schools for the first time into the state. Not only were seventy thousand Negro children going to school by 1876 where none had gone before, but fifty thousand white children were going to school where only twenty thousand had attended in 1860.

Black voting in the period after 1869 resulted in two Negro members of the U.S. Senate (Hiram Revels and Blanche Bruce, both from Mississippi), and twenty Congressmen, including eight from South Carolina, four from North Carolina, three from Alabama, and one each from the other former Confederate states. (This list would dwindle rapidly after 1876; the last black left Congress in 1901.)

A Columbia University scholar of the twentieth century, John Burgess, referred to Black Reconstruction as follows:

> In place of government by the most intelligent and virtuous part of the people for the benefit of the governed, here was government by the most ignorant and vicious part of the population. . . . A black skin means membership in a race of men which has never of itself succeeded in subjecting passion to reason; has never, therefore, created civilization of any kind.

One has to measure against those words the black leaders in the postwar South. For instance, Henry MacNeal Turner, who had escaped from peonage on a South Carolina plantation at the age of fifteen, taught himself to read and write, read law books while a messenger in a lawyer's office in Baltimore, and medical books while a handyman in a Baltimore medical school, served as chaplain to a Negro regiment, and then was elected to the first postwar legislature of Georgia. In 1868, the Georgia legislature voted to expel all its Negro members—two senators, twenty-five representatives—and Turner spoke to the Georgia House of Representatives (a black woman graduate student at Atlanta University later brought his speech to light):

> Mr. Speaker. . . . I wish the members of this House to understand the position that I take. I hold that I am a member of this body. Therefore, sir, I

shall neither fawn or cringe before any party, nor stoop to beg them for my rights. . . . I am here to demand my rights, and to hurl thunderbolts at the men who would dare to cross the threshold of my manhood. . . .

The scene presented in this House, today, is one unparalleled in the history of the world. . . . Never, in the history of the world, has a man been arraigned before a body clothed with legislative, judicial or executive functions, charged with the offense of being of a darker hue than his fellowmen. . . . it has remained for the State of Georgia, in the very heart of the nineteenth century, to call a man before the bar, and there charge him with an act for which he is no more responsible than for the head which he carries upon his shoulders. The Anglo-Saxon race, sir, is a most surprising one. . . . I was not aware that there was in the character of that race so much cowardice, or so much pusillanimity. . . . I tell you, sir, that this is a question which will not die today. This event shall be remembered by posterity for ages yet to come, and while the sun shall continue to climb the hills of heaven. . . .

. . . we are told that if black men want to speak, they must speak through white trumpets; if black men want their sentiments expressed, they must be adulterated and sent through white messengers, who will quibble, and equivocate, and evade, as rapidly as the pendulum of a clock. . . .

The great question, sir is this: Am I a man? If I am such, I claim the rights of a man. . . .

Why, sir, though we are not white, we have accomplished much. We have pioneered civilization here; we have built up your country; we have worked in your fields, and garnered your harvests, for two hundred and fifty years! And what do we ask of you in return? Do we ask you for compensation for the sweat our fathers bore for you—for the tears you have caused, and the hearts you have broken, and the lives you have curtailed, and the blood you have spilled? Do we ask retaliation? We ask it not. We are willing to let the dead past bury its dead; but we ask you now for our RIGHTS. . . .

As black children went to school, they were encouraged by teachers, black and white, to express themselves freely, sometimes in catechism style. The records of a school in Louisville, Kentucky:

TEACHER: Now children, you don't think white people are any better than you because they have straight hair and white faces?

STUDENTS: No, sir.

TEACHER: No, they are no better, but they are different, they possess great power, they formed this great government, they control this vast country. . . . Now what makes them different from you?

STUDENTS: Money!

TEACHER: Yes, but what enabled them to obtain it? How did they get money?
STUDENTS: Got it off us, stole it off we all!

Black women helped rebuild the postwar South. Frances Ellen Watkins Harper, born free in Baltimore, self-supporting from the age of thirteen, working as a nursemaid, later as an abolitionist lecturer, reader of her own poetry, spoke all through the southern states after the war. She was a feminist, participant in the 1866 Woman's Rights Convention, and founder of the National Association of Colored Women. In the 1890s she wrote the first novel published by a black woman: *Iola Leroy or Shadows Uplifted.* In 1878 she described what she had seen and heard recently in the South:

> An acquaintance of mine, who lives in South Carolina, and has been engaged in mission work, reports that, in supporting the family, women are the mainstay; that two-thirds of the truck gardening is done by them in South Carolina; that in the city they are more industrious than the men. . . . When the men lose their work through their political affiliations, the women stand by them, and say, "stand by your principles."

Through all the struggles to gain equal rights for blacks, certain black women spoke out on their special situation. Sojourner Truth, at a meeting of the American Equal Rights Association, said:

> There is a great stir about colored men getting their rights, but not a word about the colored women; and if colored men get their rights, and not colored women theirs, you see the colored men will be masters over the women, and it will be just as bad as it was before. So I am for keeping the thing going while things are stirring; because if we wait till it is still, it will take a great while to get it going again. . . .
>
> I am above eighty years old; it is about time for me to be going. I have been forty years a slave and forty years free, and would be here forty years more to have equal rights for all. I suppose I am kept here because something remains for me to do; I suppose I am yet to help break the chain. I have done a great deal of work; as much as a man, but did not get so much pay. I used to work in the field and bind grain, keeping with the cradler; but men doing no more, got twice as much pay. . . . I suppose I am about the only colored woman that goes about to speak for the rights of the colored women. I want to keep the thing stirring, now that the ice is cracked. . . .

The Constitutional amendments were passed, the laws for racial equality were passed, and the black man began to vote and to hold office. But so long as the Negro remained dependent on privileged whites for work, for the necessities of life, his vote could be bought or taken away by threat of force. Thus, laws calling for equal treatment became meaningless. While Union troops—including colored troops— remained in the South, this process was delayed. But the balance of military powers began to change.

The southern white oligarchy used its economic power to organize the Ku Klux Klan and other terrorist groups. Northern politicians began to weigh the advantage of the political support of impoverished blacks—maintained in voting and office only by force—against the more stable situation of a South returned to white supremacy, accepting Republican dominance and business legislation. It was only a matter of time before blacks would be reduced once again to conditions not far from slavery.

Violence began almost immediately with the end of the war. In Memphis, Tennessee, in May of 1866, whites on a rampage of murder killed forty-six Negroes, most of them veterans of the Union army, as well as two white sympathizers. Five Negro women were raped. Ninety homes, twelve schools, and four churches were burned. In New Orleans, in the summer of 1866, another riot against blacks killed thirty-five Negroes and three whites.

Mrs. Sarah Song testified before a congressional investigating committee:

Have you been a slave?

I have been a slave.

What did you see of the rioting?

I saw them kill my husband; it was on Tuesday night, between ten and eleven o'clock; he was shot in the head while he was in bed sick. . . . There were between twenty and thirty men. . . . They came into the room. . . . Then one stepped back and shot him . . . he was not a yard from him; he put the pistol to his head and shot him three times. . . . Then one of them kicked him, and another shot him again when he was down. . . . He never spoke after he fell. They then went running right off and did not come back again. . . .

The violence mounted through the late 1860s and early 1870s as the Ku Klux Klan organized raids, lynchings, beatings, burnings. For Kentucky alone, between 1867 and 1871, the National Archives lists 116 acts of violence. A sampling:

1. A mob visited Harrodsburg in Mercer County to take from jail a man name Robertson Nov. 14, 1867. . . .
5. Sam Davis hung by a mob in Harrodsburg, May 28, 1868.
6. Wm. Pierce hung by a mob in Christian July 12, 1868.
7. Geo. Roger hung by a mob in Bradsfordville Martin County July 11, 1868. . . .
10. Silas Woodford age sixty badly beaten by disguised mob. . . .
109. Negro killed by Ku Klux Klan in Hay county January 14, 1871.

A Negro blacksmith named Charles Caldwell, born a slave, later elected to the Mississippi Senate, and known as "a notorious and turbulent Negro" by whites, was shot at by the son of a white Mississippi judge in 1868. Caldwell fired back and killed the man. Tried by an all-white jury, he argued self-defense and was acquitted, the first Negro to kill a white in Mississippi and go free after a trial. But on Christmas Day 1875, Caldwell was shot to death by a white gang. It was a sign. The old white rulers were taking back political power in Mississippi, and everywhere else in the South.

As white violence rose in the 1870s, the national government, even under President Grant, became less enthusiastic about defending blacks, and certainly not prepared to arm them. The Supreme Court played its gyroscopic role of pulling the other branches of government back to more conservative directions when they went too far. It began interpreting the Fourteenth Amendment—passed presumably for racial equality—in a way that made it impotent for this purpose. In 1883, the Civil Rights Act of 1875, outlawing discrimination against Negroes using public facilities, was nullified by the Supreme Court, which said: "Individual invasion of individual rights is not the subject-matter of the amendment." The Fourteenth Amendment, it said, was aimed at state action only. "No state shall . . . "

A remarkable dissent was written by Supreme Court Justice John Harlan, himself a former slaveowner in Kentucky, who said there was Constitutional justification for banning private discrimination. He noted that the Thirteenth Amendment, which banned slavery, applied to individual plantation owners, not just the state. He then argued that discrimination was a badge of slavery and similarly outlawable. He pointed also to the first clause of the Fourteenth Amendment, saying that anyone born in the United States was a citizen, and to the clause in Article 4, Section 2, saying "the citizens of each State shall be entitled to all privileges and immunities of citizens in the several States."

Harlan was fighting a force greater than logic or justice; the mood of the Court reflected a new coalition of northern industrialists and southern businessmen-planters. The culmination of this mood came in the decision of 1896, *Plessy* v. *Ferguson*, when the Court ruled that a railroad could segregate black and white if the segregated facilities were equal:

> The object of the amendment was undoubtedly to enforce the absolute equality of the two races before the law, but in the nature of things it could not have been intended to abolish distinctions based upon color, or to enforce social, as distinguished from political equality, or a commingling of the two races upon terms unsatisfactory to either.

Harlan again dissented: "Our Constitution is color-blind. . . ."

It was the year 1877 that spelled out clearly and dramatically what was happening. When the year opened, the presidential election of the past November was in bitter dispute. The Democratic candidate, Samuel Tilden, had 184 votes and needed one more to be elected: his popular vote was greater by 250,000. The Republican candidate, Rutherford Hayes, had 166 electoral votes. Three states not yet counted had a total of 19 electoral votes; if Hayes could get all of those, he would have 185 and be President. This is what his managers proceeded to arrange. They made concessions to the Democratic party and the white South, including an agreement to remove Union troops from the South, the last military obstacle to the reestablishment of white supremacy there.

Northern political and economic interests needed powerful allies and stability in the face of national crisis. The country had been in economic depression since 1873, and by 1877 farmers and workers were beginning to rebel. As C. Vann Woodward puts it in his history of the 1877 Compromise, *Reunion and Reaction*:

> It was a depression year, the worst year of the severest depression yet experienced. In the East labor and the unemployed were in a bitter and violent temper. . . . Out West a tide of agrarian radicalism was rising. . . . From both East and West came threats against the elaborate structure of protective tariffs, national banks, railroad subsidies and monetary arrangements upon which the new economic order was founded.

It was a time for reconciliation between southern and northern elites. Woodward asks: ". . . could the South be induced to combine with the Northern conservatives and become a prop instead of a menace to the new capitalist order?"

With billions of dollars' worth of slaves gone, the wealth of the old South was wiped out. They now looked to the national government for help: credit, subsidies, flood control projects. The United States in 1865 had spent $103,294,501 on public works, but the South received only $9,469,363. For instance, while Ohio got over a million dollars, Kentucky, her neighbor south of the river, got $25,000. While Maine got $3 million, Mississippi got $136,000. While $83 million had been given to subsidize the Union Pacific and Central Pacific railroads, thus creating a transcontinental railroad through the North, there was no such subsidy for the South. So one of the things the South looked for was federal aid to the Texas and Pacific Railroad.

Woodward says: "By means of appropriations, subsidies, grants, and bonds such as Congress had so lavishly showered upon capitalist enterprise in the North, the South might yet mend its fortunes—or at any rate the fortunes of a privileged elite." These privileges were sought with the backing of poor white farmers, brought into the new alliance against blacks. The farmers wanted railroads, harbor improvements, flood control, and, of course, land—not knowing yet how these would be used not to help them but to exploit them.

For example, as the first act of the new North-South capitalist cooperation, the Southern Homestead Act, which had reserved all federal lands—one-third of the area of Alabama, Arkansas, Florida, Louisiana, Mississippi—for farmers who would work the land, was repealed. This enabled absentee speculators and lumbermen to move in and buy up much of this land.

And so the deal was made. The proper committee was set up by both houses of Congress to decide where the electoral votes would go. The decision was: they belonged to Hayes, and he was now President.

As Woodward sums it up:

> The Compromise of 1877 did not restore the old order in the South. . . . It did assure the dominant whites political autonomy and non-intervention in matters of race policy and promised them a share in the blessings of the new economic order. In return, the South became, in effect, a satellite of the dominant region. . . .

The importance of the new capitalism in overturning what black power existed in the postwar South is affirmed by Horace Mann Bond's study of Alabama Reconstruction, which shows, after 1868, "a struggle between different financiers." Yes, racism was a factor but "accumulations of capital, and the men who controlled them, were as unaffected by attitudinal prejudices as it is possible to be. Without sentiment, without emotion, those who sought profit from an exploitation of Alabama's natural resources turned other men's prejudices and attitudes to their own account, and did so with skill and a ruthless acumen."

It was an age of coal and power, and northern Alabama had both. "The bankers in Philadelphia and New York, and even in London and Paris, had known this for almost two decades. The only thing lacking was transportation." And so, in the mid-1870s, Bond notes, northern bankers began appearing in the directories of southern railroad lines. J. P. Morgan appears by 1875 as director for several lines in Alabama and Georgia.

In the year 1886, Henry Grady, an editor of the Atlanta *Constitution*, spoke at a dinner in New York. In the audience were J. P. Morgan, H. M. Flagler (an associate of Rockefeller), Russell Sage, and Charles Tiffany. His talk was called "The New South" and his theme was: Let bygones be bygones; let us have a new era of peace and prosperity; the Negro was a prosperous laboring class; he had the fullest protection of the laws and the friendship of the southern people. Grady joked about the northerners who sold slaves to the South and said the South could now handle its own race problem. He received a rising ovation, and the band played "Dixie."

That same month, an article in the New York *Daily Tribune:*

> The leading coal and iron men of the South, who have been in this city during the last ten days, will go home to spend the Christmas holidays, thoroughly satisfied with the business of the year, and more than hopeful for the future. And they have good reason to be. The time for which they have been waiting for nearly twenty years, when Northern capitalists would be convinced not only of the safety but of the immense profits to be gained from the investment of their money in developing the fabulously rich coal and iron resources of Alabama, Tennessee, and Georgia, has come at last.

The North, it must be recalled, did not have to undergo a revolution in its thinking to accept the subordination of the Negro. When the Civil War ended, nineteen of the twenty-four northern states did not allow blacks to vote. By 1900, all the southern states, in new constitutions and new statutes, had written into law the disfranchisement and segregation of Negroes, and a *New York Times* editorial said: "Northern men . . . no longer denounce the suppression of the Negro vote. . . . The necessity of it under the supreme law of self-preservation is candidly recognized."

While not written into law in the North, the counterpart in racist thought and practice was there. An item in the Boston *Transcript*, September 25, 1895:

> A colored man who gives his name as Henry W. Turner was arrested last night on suspicion of being a highway robber. He was taken this morning to Black's studio, where he had his picture taken for the "Rogue's Gallery". That angered him, and he made himself as disagreeable as he possibly could. Several times along the way to the photographer's he resisted the police with all his might, and had to be clubbed.

In the postwar literature, images of the Negro came mostly from southern white writers like Thomas Nelson Page, who in his novel *Red Rock* referred to a Negro character as "a hyena in a cage," "a reptile," "a species of worm," "a wild beast." And, interspersed with paternalistic urgings of friendship for the Negro, Joel Chandler Harris, in his Uncle Remus stories, would have Uncle Remus say: "Put a spellin-book in a nigger's han's, en right den en dar' you loozes a plowhand. I kin take a bar'l stave an fling mo' sense inter a nigger in one minnit dan all de schoolhouses betwixt dis en de state er Midgigin."

In this atmosphere it was no wonder that those Negro leaders most accepted in white society, like the educator Booker T. Washington, a one-time White House guest of Theodore Roosevelt, urged Negro political passivity. Invited by the white organizers of the Cotton States and International Exposition in Atlanta in 1895 to speak, Washington urged the southern Negro to "cast down your bucket where you are"—that is, to stay in the South, to be farmers, mechanics, domestics, perhaps even to attain to the professions. He urged white employers to hire Negroes rather than immigrants of "strange tongue and habits." Negroes, "without strikes and labor wars," were the "most patient, faithful, law-abiding and unresentful people that the world has seen." He said: "The wisest among my race understand that the agitation of questions of social equality is the extremest folly."

Perhaps Washington saw this as a necessary tactic of survival in a time of hangings and burnings of Negroes throughout the South. It was a low point for black people in America. Thomas Fortune, a young black editor of the New York *Globe*, testified before a Senate committee in 1883 about the situation of the Negro in the United States. He spoke of "widespread poverty," of government betrayal, of desperate Negro attempts to educate themselves.

The average wage of Negro farm laborers in the South was about fifty cents a day, Fortune said. He was usually paid in "orders," not money, which he could use only at a store controlled by the planter, "a system of fraud." The Negro farmer, to get the wherewithal to plant his crop, had to promise it to the store, and when everything was added up at the end of the year he was in debt, so his crop was constantly owed to someone, and he was tied to the land, with the records kept by the planter and storekeeper so that the Negroes "are swindled and kept forever in debt." As for supposed laziness, "I am surprised that a larger number of them do not go to fishing, hunting, and loafing."

Fortune spoke of "the penitentiary system of the South, with its infamous chain-gang. . . . the object being to terrorize the blacks and furnish victims for contractors, who purchase the labor of these wretches from the State for a song. . . . The white man who shoots a negro always goes free, while the negro who steals a hog is sent to the chaingang for ten years."

Many Negroes fled. About six thousand black people left Texas, Louisiana, and Mississippi and migrated to Kansas to escape violence and poverty. Frederick Douglass and some other leaders thought this was a wrong tactic, but migrants rejected such advice. "We have found no leader to trust but God overhead of us," one said. Henry Adams, another black migrant, illiterate, a veteran of the Union army, told a Senate committee in 1880 why he left Shreveport, Louisiana: "We seed that the whole South—every state in the South—had got into the hands of the very men that held us slaves."

Even in the worst periods, southern Negroes continued to meet, to organize in self-defense. Herbert Aptheker reprints thirteen documents of meetings, petitions, and appeals of Negroes in the 1880s—in Baltimore, Louisiana, the Carolinas, Virginia, Georgia, Florida, Texas, Kansas—showing the spirit of defiance and resistance of blacks all over the South. This, in the face of over a hundred lynchings a year by this time.

Despite the apparent hopelessness of this situation, there were black leaders who thought Booker T. Washington wrong in advocating caution and moderation. John Hope, a young black man in Georgia, who heard Washington's Cotton Exposition speech, told students at a Negro college in Nashville, Tennessee:

> If we are not striving for equality, in heaven's name for what are we living? I regard it as cowardly and dishonest for any of our colored men to tell white people or colored people that we are not struggling for equality. . . . Yes, my

friends, I want equality. Nothing less. . . . Now catch your breath, for I am going to use an adjective: I am going to say we demand social equality. . . . I am no wild beast, nor am I an unclean thing.

Rise, Brothers! Come let us possess this land. . . . Be discontented. Be dissatisfied. . . . Be as restless as the tempestuous billows on the boundless sea. Let your discontent break mountain-high against the wall of prejudice, and swamp it to the very foundation. . . .

Another black man, who came to teach at Atlanta University, W. E. B. Du Bois, saw the late-nineteenth-century betrayal of the Negro as part of a larger happening in the United States, something happening not only to poor blacks but to poor whites. In his book *Black Reconstruction*, written in 1935, he said:

God wept; but that mattered little to an unbelieving age; what mattered most was that the world wept and still is weeping and blind with tears and blood. For there began to rise in America in 1876 a new capitalism and a new enslavement of labor.

Du Bois saw this new capitalism as part of a process of exploitation and bribery taking place in all the "civilized" countries of the world:

Home labor in cultured lands, appeased and misled by a ballot whose power the dictatorship of vast capital strictly curtailed, was bribed by high wage and political office to unite in an exploitation of white, yellow, brown and black labor, in lesser lands. . . .

Was Du Bois right—that in that growth of American capitalism, before and after the Civil War, whites as well as blacks were in some sense becoming slaves?

10

THE OTHER CIVIL WAR

A sheriff in the Hudson River Valley near Albany, New York, about to go into the hills in the fall of 1839 to collect back rents from tenants on the enormous Rensselaer estate, was handed a letter:

> . . . the tenants have organized themselves into a body, and resolved not to pay any more rent until they can be redressed of their grievances. . . . The tenants now assume the right of doing to their landlord as he has for a long time done with them, viz: as they please.
>
> You need not think this to be children's play. . . . if you come out in your official capacity . . . I would not pledge for your safe return. . . . A Tenant.

When a deputy arrived in the farming area with writs demanding the rent, farmers suddenly appeared, assembled by the blowing of tin horns. They seized his writs and burned them.

That December, a sheriff and a mounted posse of five hundred rode into the farm country, but found themselves in the midst of shrieking tin horns, eighteen hundred farmers blocking their path, six hundred more blocking their rear, all mounted, armed with pitchforks and clubs. The sheriff and his posse turned back, the rear guard parting to let them through.

This was the start of the Anti-Renter movement in the Hudson Valley, described by Henry Christman in *Tin Horns and Calico*. It was a protest against the patroonship system, which went back to the 1600s when the Dutch ruled New York, a system where (as Christman describes it) "a few families, intricately intermarried, controlled the destinies of three hundred thousand people and ruled in almost kingly splendor near two million acres of land."

The tenants paid taxes and rents. The largest manor was owned by the Rensselaer family, which ruled over about eighty thousand tenants and had accumulated a fortune of $41 million. The landowner, as one sympathizer of the tenants put it, could "swill his wine, loll on his cushions, fill his life with society, food, and culture, and ride his barouche and five saddle horses along the beautiful river valley and up to the backdrop of the mountain."

By the summer of 1839, the tenants were holding their first mass meeting. The economic crisis of 1837 had filled the area with unemployed seeking land, on top of the layoffs accompanying the completion of the Erie Canal, after the first wave of railroad building ended. That summer the tenants resolved: "We will take up the ball of the Revolution where our fathers stopped it and roll it to the final consummation of freedom and independence of the masses."

Certain men in the farm country became leaders and organizers: Smith Boughton, a country doctor on horseback; Ainge Devyr, a revolutionary Irishman. Devyr had seen monopoly of land and industry bring misery to the slumdwellers of London, Liverpool, and Glasgow, had agitated for change, had been arrested for sedition, and fled to America. He was invited to address a Fourth of July rally of farmers in Rensselaerville, where he warned his listeners: "If you permit unprincipled and ambitious men to monopolize the soil, they will become masters of the country in the certain order of cause and effect. . . ."

Thousands of farmers in Rensselaer country were organized into Anti-Rent associations to prevent the landlords from evicting. They agreed on calico Indian costumes, symbol of the Boston Tea Party and recalling original ownership of the soil. The tin horn represented an Indian call to arms. Soon ten thousand men were trained and ready.

Organizing went on in county after county, in dozens of towns along the Hudson. Handbills appeared:

ATTENTION
ANTI-RENTERS! AWAKE! AROUSE! . . .
Strike till the last armed foe expires,
Strike for your altars and your fires—
Strike for the green graves of your sires,
God and your happy homes!

Sheriffs and deputy sheriffs trying to serve writs on farmers were surrounded by calico-clad riders who had been summoned by tin horns sounding in the countryside—then tarred and feathered. The New York

Herald, once sympathetic, now deplored "the insurrectionary spirit of the mountaineers."

One of the most hated elements of the lease gave the landlord the right to the timber on all the farms. A man sent onto a tenant's land to gather wood for the landlord was killed. Tension rose. A farm boy was killed mysteriously, no one knew by whom, but Dr. Boughton was jailed. The governor ordered artillerymen into action, and a company of cavalry came up from New York City.

Petitions for an antirent bill, signed by 25,000 tenants, were put before the legislature in 1845. The bill was defeated. A kind of guerrilla war resumed in the country, between bands of "Indians" and sheriffs' posses. Boughton was kept in jail seven months, four and a half months of that in heavy irons, before being released on bail. Fourth of July meetings in 1845 attended by thousands of farmers pledged continued resistance.

When a deputy sheriff tried to sell the livestock of a farmer named Moses Earle, who owed $60 rent on 160 stony acres, there was a fight, and the deputy was killed. Similar attempts to sell livestock for rent payments were thwarted, again and again. The governor sent three hundred troops in, declaring a state of rebellion existed, and soon almost a hundred Anti-Renters were in jail. Smith Boughton was brought to trial. He was charged with taking papers from a sheriff but declared by the judge to have in fact committed "high treason, rebellion against your government, and armed insurrection" and sentenced to life imprisonment.

Those "Indians" found to be armed and disguised at Moses Earle's farm, where the deputy had been killed, were declared by the judge to be guilty of murder, and the jury was so instructed. All were found guilty, and the judge sentenced four to life imprisonment and two to be hanged. Two of the leaders were told to write letters urging the Anti-Renters to disband, as their only chance to escape heavy sentences. They wrote the letters.

The power of the law thus crushed the Anti-Rent movement. It was intended to make clear that farmers could not win by fighting—that they must confine their efforts to voting, to acceptable methods of reform. In 1845, the Anti-Renters elected fourteen members to the state legislature. Governor Silas Wright now commuted to life imprisonment the two death sentences and asked the legislature to give relief to the tenants, to end the feudal system in the Hudson Valley. Proposals to break up the huge estates on the death of the owners were defeated, but the legislature voted to make illegal the selling of tenant property for nonpayment of rent. A constitutional convention that year outlawed new feudal leases.

The next governor, elected in 1846 with Anti-Rent support, had promised to pardon the Anti-Rent prisoners, and he did. Throngs of farmers greeted them on their release. Court decisions in the 1850s began to limit the worst features of the manorial system, without changing the fundamentals of landlord-tenant relations.

Sporadic farmer resistance to the collection of back rents continued into the 1860s. As late as 1869, bands of "Indians" were still assembling to thwart sheriffs acting for a rich valley landowner named Walter Church. In the early 1880s a deputy sheriff trying to dispossess a farmer on behalf of Church was killed by shotgun fire. By this time most leases had passed into the hands of the farmers. In three of the main Anti-Rent counties, of twelve thousand farmers, only two thousand remained under lease.

The farmers had fought, been crushed by the law, their struggle diverted into voting, and the system stabilized by enlarging the class of small landowners, leaving the basic structure of rich and poor intact. It was a common sequence in American history.

Around the time of the Anti-Renter movement in New York, there was excitement in Rhode Island over Dorr's Rebellion. As Marvin Gettleman points out in *The Dorr Rebellion*, it was both a movement for electoral reform and an example of radical insurgency. It was prompted by the Rhode Island charter's rule that only owners of land could vote.

As more people left the farm for the city, as immigrants came to work in the mills, the disfranchised grew. Seth Luther, self-educated carpenter in Providence and spokesman for working people, wrote in 1833 the "Address on the Right of Free Suffrage," denouncing the monopoly of political power by "the mushroom lordlings, sprigs of nobility . . . small potato aristocrats" of Rhode Island. He urged non-cooperation with the government, refusing to pay taxes or to serve in the militia. Why, he asked, should twelve thousand working people in Rhode Island without the vote submit to five thousand who had land and could vote?

Thomas Dorr, a lawyer from a well-to-do family, became a leader of the suffrage movement. Working people formed the Rhode Island Suffrage Association, and in the spring of 1841 thousands paraded in Providence carrying banners and signs for electoral reform. Going outside the legal system, they organized their own "People's Convention" and drafted a new constitution without property qualifications for voting.

In early 1842, they invited votes on the constitution; fourteen thousand voted for it, including about five thousand with property—therefore a majority even of those legally entitled to vote by the charter. In

April they held an unofficial election, in which Dorr ran unopposed for governor, and six thousand people voted for him. The governor of Rhode Island in the meantime got the promise of President John Tyler that in the case of rebellion federal troops would be sent. There was a clause in the U.S. Constitution to meet just that kind of situation, providing for federal intervention to quell local insurrections on request of a state government.

Ignoring this, on May 3, 1842, the Dorr forces held an inauguration with a great parade of artisans, shopkeepers, mechanics, and militia marching through Providence. The newly elected People's Legislature was convened. Dorr led a fiasco of an attack on the state arsenal, his cannon misfiring. Dorr's arrest was ordered by the regular governor, and he went into hiding outside the state, trying to raise military support.

Despite the protests of Dorr and a few others, the "People's Constitution" kept the word "white" in its clause designating voters. Angry Rhode Island blacks now joined the militia units of the Law and Order coalition, which promised that a new constitutional convention would give them the right to vote.

When Dorr returned to Rhode Island, he found several hundred of his followers, mostly working people, willing to fight for the People's Constitution, but there were thousands in the regular militia on the side of the state. The rebellion disintegrated and Dorr again fled Rhode Island.

Martial law was declared. One rebel soldier, captured, was blindfolded and put before a firing squad, which fired with blank bullets. A hundred other militia were taken prisoner. One of them described their being bound by ropes into platoons of eight, marched on foot 16 miles to Providence, "threatened and pricked by the bayonet if we lagged from fatigue, the rope severely chafing our arms; the skin off mine.... no water till we reached Greenville ... no food until the next day.... and, after being exhibited, were put into the State prison."

A new constitution offered some reform. It still gave overrepresentation to the rural areas, limited the vote to property owners or those who paid a one-dollar poll tax, and would let naturalized citizens vote only if they had $134 in real estate. In the elections of early 1843, the Law and Order group, opposed by former Dorrites, used intimidation of state militia, of employees by employers, of tenants by landlords, to get out their vote. It lost in the industrial towns, but got the vote of the agrarian areas, and won all major offices.

Dorr returned to Rhode Island in the fall of 1843. He was arrested on the streets of Providence and tried for treason. The jury, instructed by the judge to ignore all political arguments and consider only whether Dorr had committed certain overt acts (which he never denied committing), found him guilty, whereupon the judge sentenced him to life imprisonment at hard labor. He spent twenty months in jail, and then a newly elected Law and Order governor, anxious to end Dorr's martyrdom, pardoned him.

Armed force had failed, the ballot had failed, the courts had taken the side of the conservatives. The Dorr movement now went to the U.S. Supreme Court, via a trespass suit by Martin Luther against Law and Order militiamen, charging that the People's Government was the legitimate government in Rhode Island in 1842. Daniel Webster argued against the Dorrites. If people could claim a constitutional right to overthrow an existing government, Webster said, there would be no more law and no more government; there would be anarchy.

In its decision, the Supreme Court established (*Luther* v. *Borden*, 1849) a long-lasting doctrine: it would not interfere in certain "political" questions, to be left to executive and legislature. The decision reinforced the essentially conservative nature of the Supreme Court: that on critical issues— war and revolution—it would defer to the President and Congress.

The stories of the Anti-Renter movement and Dorr's Rebellion are not usually found in textbooks on United States history. In these books, given to millions of young Americans, there is little on class struggle in the nineteenth century. The period before and after the Civil War is filled with politics, elections, slavery, and the race question. Even where specialized books on the Jacksonian period deal with labor and economic issues they center on the presidency, and thus perpetuate the traditional dependency on heroic leaders rather than people's struggles.

Andrew Jackson said he spoke for "the humble members of society— the farmer, mechanics and laborers. . . ." He certainly did not speak for the Indians being pushed off their lands, or slaves. But the tensions aroused by the developing factory system, the growing immigration, required that the government develop a mass base of support among whites. "Jacksonian Democracy" did just that.

Politics in this period of the 1830s and 1840s, according to Douglas Miller, a specialist in the Jacksonian period *(The Birth of Modern America)*, "had become increasingly centered around creating a popular image and flattering the common man." Miller is dubious, however, about the accuracy of that phrase "Jacksonian Democracy":

Parades, picnics, and campaigns of personal slander characterized Jacksonian politicking. But, although both parties aimed their rhetoric at the people and mouthed the sacred shibboleths of democracy, this did not mean that the common man ruled America. The professional politicians coming to the fore in the twenties and thirties, though sometimes self-made, were seldom ordinary. Both major parties were controlled largely by men of wealth and ambition. Lawyers, newspaper editors, merchants, industrialists, large landowners, and speculators dominated the Democrats as well as the Whigs.

Jackson was the first President to master the liberal rhetoric—to speak for the common man. This was a necessity for political victory when the vote was being demanded—as in Rhode Island—by more and more people, and state legislatures were loosening voting restrictions. As another Jacksonian scholar, Robert Remini (*The Age of Jackson*), says, after studying electoral figures for 1828 and 1832:

> Jackson himself enjoyed widespread support that ranged across all classes and sections of the country. He attracted farmers, mechanics, laborers, professionals and even businessmen. And all this without Jackson being clearly pro- or antilabor, pro- or antibusiness, pro- or antilower, middle or upper class. It has been demonstrated that he was a strikebreaker [Jackson sent troops to control rebellious workers on the Chesapeake and Ohio Canal], yet at different times . . . he and the Democrats received the backing of organized labor.

It was the new politics of ambiguity—speaking for the lower and middle classes to get their support in times of rapid growth and potential turmoil. The two-party system came into its own in this time. To give people a choice between two different parties and allow them, in a period of rebellion, to choose the slightly more democratic one was an ingenious mode of control. Like so much in the American system, it was not devilishly contrived by some master plotters; it developed naturally out of the needs of the situation. Remini compares the Jacksonian Democrat Martin Van Buren, who succeeded Jackson as President, with the Austrian conservative statesman Metternich: "Like Metternich, who was seeking to thwart revolutionary discontent in Europe, Van Buren and similar politicians were attempting to banish political disorder from the United States by a balance of power achieved through two well-organized and active parties."

The Jacksonian idea was to achieve stability and control by winning to the Democratic party "the middling interest, and especially . . . the substantial yeomanry of the country" by "prudent, judicious, well-considered reform." That is, reform that would not yield too much. These were the words of Robert Rantoul, a reformer, corporation lawyer, and Jacksonian Democrat. It was a forecast of the successful appeal of the Democratic party—and at times the Republican party—in the twentieth century.

Such new forms of political control were needed in the turbulence of growth, the possibility of rebellion. Now there were canals, railroads, the telegraph. In 1790, fewer than a million Americans lived in cities; in 1840 the figure was 11 million. New York had 130,000 people in 1820, a million by 1860. And while the traveler Alexis de Tocqueville had expressed astonishment at "the general equality of condition among the people," he was not very good at numbers, his friend Beaumont said. And his observation was not in accord with the facts, according to Edward Pessen, a historian of Jacksonian society (*Jacksonian America*).

In Philadelphia, working-class families lived fifty-five to a tenement, usually one room per family, with no garbage removal, no toilets, no fresh air or water. There was fresh water newly pumped from the Schuylkill River, but it was going to the homes of the rich.

In New York you could see the poor lying in the streets with the garbage. There were no sewers in the slums, and filthy water drained into yards and alleys, into the cellars where the poorest of the poor lived, bringing with it a typhoid epidemic in 1837, typhus in 1842. In the cholera epidemic of 1832, the rich fled the city; the poor stayed and died.

These poor could not be counted on as political allies of the government. But they were there—like slaves, or Indians—invisible ordinarily, a menace if they rose. There were more solid citizens, however, who might give steady support to the system—better-paid workers, landowning farmers. Also, there was the new urban white-collar worker, born in the rising commerce of the time, described by Thomas Cochran and William Miller (*The Age of Enterprise*):

> Dressed in drab alpaca, hunched over a high desk, this new worker credited and debited, indexed and filed, wrote and stamped invoices, acceptances, bills of lading, receipts. Adequately paid, he had some extra money and leisure time. He patronized sporting events and theaters, savings banks and insurance companies. He read Day's *New York Sun* or Bennett's *Herald*—the "penny press" supported by advertising, filled with police reports, crime stories, etiquette advice for the rising bourgeoisie. . . .

This was the advance guard of a growing class of white-collar workers and professionals in America who would be wooed enough and paid enough to consider themselves members of the bourgeois class, and to give support to that class in times of crisis.

The opening of the West was being helped by mechanization of the farm. Iron plows cut plowing time in half; by the 1850s John Deere Company was turning out ten thousand plows a year. Cyrus McCormick was making a thousand mechanical reapers a year in his factory in Chicago. A man with a sickle could cut half an acre of wheat in a day; with a reaper he could cut 10 acres.

Turnpikes, canals, and railroads were bringing more people west, more products east, and it became important to keep that new West, tumultuous and unpredictable, under control. When colleges were established out West, eastern businessmen, as Cochran and Miller say, were "determined from the start to control western education." Edward Everett, the Massachusetts politician and orator, spoke in 1833 on behalf of giving financial aid to western colleges:

> Let no Boston capitalist, then, let no man, who has a large stake in New England . . . think that he is called upon to exercise his liberality at a distance, toward those in whom he has no concern. . . . They ask you to give security to your own property, by diffusing the means of light and truth throughout the region, where so much of the power to preserve or to shake it resides. . . .

The capitalists of the East were conscious of the need for this "security to your own property." As technology developed, more capital was needed, more risks had to be taken, and a big investment needed stability. In an economic system not rationally planned for human need, but developing fitfully, chaotically out of the profit motive, there seemed to be no way to avoid recurrent booms and slumps. There was a slump in 1837, another in 1853. One way to achieve stability was to decrease competition, organize the businesses, move toward monopoly. In the mid-1850s, price agreements and mergers became frequent: the New York Central Railroad was a merger of many railroads. The American Brass Association was formed "to meet ruinous competition," it said. The Hampton County Cotton Spinners Association was organized to control prices, and so was the American Iron Association.

Another way to minimize risks was to make sure the government played its traditional role, going back to Alexander Hamilton and the first Congress, of helping the business interests. State legislatures gave charters to corporations giving them legal rights to conduct business, raise money—at first special charters, then general charters, so that any business meeting certain requirements could incorporate. Between 1790 and 1860, 2,300 corporations were chartered.

Railroad men traveled to Washington and to state capitals armed with money, shares of stock, free railroad passes. Between 1850 and 1857 they got 25 million acres of public land, free of charge, and millions of dollars in bonds—loans—from the state legislatures. In Wisconsin in 1856, the LaCrosse and Milwaukee Railroad got a million acres free by distributing about $900,000 in stocks and bonds to fifty-nine assemblymen, thirteen senators, the governor. Two years later the railroad was bankrupt and the bonds were worthless.

In the East, mill owners had become powerful, and organized. By 1850, fifteen Boston families called the "Associates" controlled 20 percent of the cotton spindleage in the United States, 39 percent of insurance capital in Massachusetts, 40 percent of banking resources in Boston.

In the schoolbooks, those years are filled with the controversy over slavery, but on the eve of the Civil War it was money and profit, not the movement against slavery, that was uppermost in the priorities of the men who ran the country. As Cochran and Miller put it:

> Webster was the hero of the North—not Emerson, Parker, Garrison, or Phillips; Webster the tariff man, the land speculator, the corporation lawyer, politician for the Boston Associates, inheritor of Hamilton's coronet. "The great object of government" said he "is the protection of property at home, and respect and renown abroad." For these he preached union; for these he surrendered the fugitive slave.

They describe the Boston rich:

> Living sumptuously on Beacon Hill, admired by their neighbors for their philanthropy and their patronage of art and culture, these men traded in State Street while overseers ran their factories, managers directed their railroads, agents sold their water power and real estate. They were absentee landlords in the most complete sense. Uncontaminated by the diseases of the factory town, they were also protected from hearing the complaints of their workers or suffering mental depression from dismal and squalid surroundings. In the metropolis, art, literature, education, science, flowered in the Golden Day; in the industrial towns children went to work with their fathers and mothers, schools and doctors were only promises, a bed of one's own was a rare luxury.

Ralph Waldo Emerson described Boston in those years: "There is a certain poor-smell in all the streets, in Beacon Street and Mount Vernon, as well as in the lawyers' offices, and the wharves, and the same meanness and sterility, and leave-all-hope-behind, as one finds in a boot manufacturer's premises." The preacher Theodore Parker told his congregation: "Money is this day the strongest power of the nation."

The attempts at political stability, at economic control, did not quite work. The new industrialism, the crowded cities, the long hours in the factories, the sudden economic crises leading to high prices and lost jobs, the lack of food and water, the freezing winters, the hot tenements in the summer, the epidemics of disease, the deaths of children—these led to sporadic reactions from the poor. Sometimes there were spontaneous, unorganized uprisings against the rich. Sometimes the anger was deflected into racial hatred for blacks, religious warfare against Catholics, nativist fury against immigrants. Sometimes it was organized into demonstrations and strikes.

"Jacksonian Democracy" had tried to create a consensus of support for the system to make it secure. Blacks, Indians, women, and foreigners were clearly outside the consensus. But also, white working people, in large numbers, declared themselves outside.

The full extent of the working-class consciousness of those years—as of any years—is lost in history, but fragments remain and make us wonder how much of this always existed underneath the very practical silence of working people. In 1827 an "Address ... before the Mechanics and Working Classes ... of Philadelphia" was recorded, written by an "Unlettered Mechanic," probably a young shoemaker, who said:

> We find ourselves oppressed on every hand—we labor hard in producing all the comforts of life for the enjoyment of others, while we ourselves obtain but a scanty portion, and even that in the present state of society depends on the will of employers.

Frances Wright of Scotland, an early feminist and utopian socialist, was invited by Philadelphia workingmen to speak on the Fourth of July 1829 to one of the first city-wide associations of labor unions in the United States. She asked if the Revolution had been fought "to crush down the sons and daughters of your country's industry under ... neglect, poverty, vice, starvation, and disease. . . ." She wondered if the new technology was not lowering the value of human labor, making people appendages to machines, crippling the minds and bodies of child laborers.

Later that year, George Henry Evans, a printer, editor of the *Workingman's Advocate*, wrote "The Working Men's Declaration of Independence." Among its list of "facts" submitted to "candid and impartial" fellow citizens:

1. The laws for levying taxes are . . . operating most oppressively on one class of society. . . .
3. The laws for private incorporation are all partial . . . favoring one class of society to the expense of the other. . . .
6. The laws . . . have deprived nine tenths of the members of the body politics, who are not wealthy, of the equal means to enjoy "life, liberty, and the pursuit of happiness." . . . The lien law in favor of the landlords against tenants . . . is one illustration among innumerable others.

Evans believed that "all on arriving at adult age are entitled to equal property."

A city-wide "Trades' Union" in Boston in 1834, including mechanics from Charlestown and women shoe binders from Lynn, referred to the Declaration of Independence:

We hold . . . that laws which have a tendency to raise any peculiar class above their fellow citizens, by granting special privileges, are contrary to and in defiance of those primary principles. . . .

Our public system of Education, which so liberally endows those seminaries of learning, which . . . are only accessible to the wealthy, while our common schools . . . are so illy provided for . . . Thus even in childhood the poor are apt to think themselves inferior. . . .

In his book *Most Uncommon Jacksonians*, Edward Pessen says: "The leaders of the Jacksonian labor movement were radicals. . . . How else describe men who believed American society to be torn with social conflict, disfigured by the misery of the masses, and dominated by a greedy elite whose power over every aspect of American life was based on private property?"

Episodes of insurrection of that time have gone unrecorded in traditional histories. Such was the riot in Baltimore in the summer of 1835, when the Bank of Maryland collapsed and its depositors lost their savings. Convinced that a great fraud had taken place, a crowd gathered and began breaking the windows of officials associated with the bank. When the rioters destroyed a house, the militia attacked, killing some twenty people, wounding a hundred. The next evening, other houses were attacked. The events were reported in *Niles' Weekly Register*, an important newspaper of that time:

> Last night (Sunday) at dark, the attack was renewed upon Reverdy Johnson's house. There was now no opposition. It was supposed that several thousand people were spectators of the scene. The house was soon entered, and its furniture, a very extensive law library, and all its contents, were cast forth, a bonfire made of them in front of the house. The whole interior of the house was torn out and cast upon the burning pile. The marble portico in front, and a great portion of the front wall were torn down by about 11 o'clock. . . . They proceeded to that of the mayor of the city, Jesse Hunt, esq. broke it open, took out the furniture, and burnt it before the door. . . .

During those years, trade unions were forming. (Philip Foner's *History of the Labor Movement in the U.S.* tells the story in rich detail.) The courts called them conspiracies to restrain trade and therefore illegal, as when in New York twenty-five members of the Union Society of Journeymen Tailors were found guilty of "conspiracy to injure trade, riot, assault, battery." The judge, levying fines, said: "In this favored land of law and liberty, the road to advancement is open to all. . . . Every American knows that or ought to know that he has no better friend than the laws and that he needs no artificial combination for his protection. They are of foreign origin and I am led to believe mainly upheld by foreigners."

A handbill was then circulated throughout the city:

The Rich Against the Poor!

Judge Edwards, the tool of the aristocracy, against the people! Mechanics and working men! A deadly blow has been struck at your liberty! . . . They have established the precedent that workingmen have no right to regulate the price of labor, or, in other words, the rich are the only judges of the wants of the poor man.

At City Hall Park, 27,000 people gathered to denounce the court decision, and elected a Committee of Correspondence which organized, three months later, a convention of Mechanics, Farmers, and Working Men, elected by farmers and working people in various towns in New York State. The convention met in Utica, drew up a Declaration of Independence from existing political parties, and established an Equal Rights party.

Although they ran their own candidates for office, there was no great confidence in the ballot as a way of achieving change. One of the great orators of the movement, Seth Luther, told a Fourth of July rally: "We will try the ballot box first. If that will not effect our righteous purpose, the next and last resort is the cartridge box." And one sympathetic local newspaper, the Albany *Microscope*, warned:

> Remember the regretted fate of the working-men—they were soon destroyed by hitching teams and rolling with parties. They admitted into their ranks, broken down lawyers and politicians. . . . They became perverted, and were unconsciously drawn into a vortex, from which they never escaped.

The crisis of 1837 led to rallies and meetings in many cities. The banks had suspended specie payments—refusing to pay hard money for the bank notes they had issued. Prices rose, and working people, already hard-pressed to buy food, found that flour that had sold at $5.62 a barrel was now $12 a barrel. Pork went up. Coal went up. In Philadelphia, twenty thousand people assembled, and someone wrote to President Van Buren describing it:

> This afternoon, the largest public meeting I ever saw assembled in Independence Square. It was called by placards posted through the city yesterday and last night. It was projected and carried on entirely by the working classes; without consultation or cooperation with any of those who usually take the lead in such matters. The officers and speakers were of those classes. . . . It was directed against the banks.

In New York, members of the Equal Rights party (often called the Locofocos) announced a meeting: "Bread, Meat, Rent, and Fuel! Their prices must come down! The people will meet in the Park, rain or shine, at 4 o'clock, P.M. on Monday afternoon. . . . All friends of humanity determined to resist monopolists and extortioners are invited to attend." The *Commercial Register*, a New York newspaper, reported on the meeting and what followed:

> At 4 o'clock, a concourse of several thousands had convened in front of the City Hall. . . . One of these orators . . . is reported to have expressly directed the popular vengeance against Mr. Eli Hart, who is one of our most extensive flour dealers on commission. "Fellow citizens!" he exclaimed, "Mr. Hart has now 53,000 barrels of flour in his store; let us go and offer him eight dollars a barrel, and if he does not take it . . . "

A large body of the meeting moved off in the direction of Mr. Hart's store . . . the middle door had been forced, and some twenty or thirty barrels of flour or more, rolled into the streets, and the heads staved in. At this point of time, Mr. Hart himself arrived on the ground, with a posse of officers from the police. The officers were assailed by a portion of the mob in Dey Street, their staves wrested from them, and shivered to pieces. . . .

Barrels of flour, by dozens, fifties and hundreds were tumbled into the street from the doors, and thrown in rapid succession from the windows. . . . About one thousand bushels of wheat, and four or five hundred barrels of flour, were thus wantonly and foolishly as well as wickedly destroyed. The most active of the destructionists were foreigners—indeed the greater part of the assemblage was of exotic origin, but there were probably five hundred or a thousand others, standing by and abetting their incendiary labors.

Amidst the falling and bursting of the barrels and sacks of wheat, numbers of women were engaged, like the crones who strip the dead in battle, filling the boxes and baskets with which they were provided, and their aprons, with flour, and making off with it. . . .

Night had now closed upon the scene, but the work of destruction did not cease until strong bodies of police arrived, followed, soon afterward, by detachments of troops. . . .

This was the Flour Riot of 1837. During the crisis of that year, 50,000 persons (one-third of the working class) were without work in New York City alone, and 200,000 (of a population of 500,000) were living, as one observer put it, "in utter and hopeless distress."

There is no complete record of the meetings, riots, actions, organized and disorganized, violent and nonviolent, which took place in the mid-nineteenth century, as the country grew, as the cities became crowded, with working conditions bad, living conditions intolerable, with the economy in the hands of bankers, speculators, landlords, merchants.

In 1835, fifty different trades organized unions in Philadelphia, and there was a successful general strike of laborers, factory workers, bookbinders, jewelers, coal heavers, butchers, cabinet workers—for the ten-hour day. Soon there were ten-hour laws in Pennsylvania and other states, but they provided that employers could have employees sign contracts for longer hours. The law at this time was developing a strong defense of contracts; it was pretended that work contracts were voluntary agreements between equals.

Weavers in Philadelphia in the early 1840s—mostly Irish immigrants working at home for employers—struck for higher wages, attacked the homes of those refusing to strike, and destroyed their work. A sheriff's posse tried to arrest some strikers, but it was broken up by four hundred weavers armed with muskets and sticks.

Soon, however, antagonism developed between these Irish Catholic weavers and native-born Protestant skilled workers over issues of religion. In May 1844 there were Protestant-Catholic riots in Kensington, a suburb of Philadelphia; nativist (anti-immigrant) rioters destroyed the weavers' neighborhoods and attacked a Catholic church. Middle-class politicians soon led each group into a different political party (the nativists into the American Republican party, the Irish into the Democratic party), party politics and religion now substituting for class conflict.

The result of all this, says David Montgomery, historian of the Kensington Riots, was the fragmentation of the Philadelphia working class. It "thereby created for historians the illusion of a society lacking in class conflict," while in reality the class conflicts of nineteenth-century America "were as fierce as any known to the industrial world."

The immigrants from Ireland, fleeing starvation there when the potato crop failed, were coming to America now, packed into old sailing ships. The stories of these ships differ only in detail from the accounts of the ships that earlier brought black slaves and later German, Italian, Russian immigrants. This is a contemporary account of one ship arriving from Ireland, detained at Grosse Isle on the Canadian border:

> On the 18th of May, 1847, the "Urania", from Cork, with several hundred immigrants on board, a large proportion of them sick and dying of the ship-fever, was put into quarantine at Grosse Isle. This was the first of the plague-smitten ships from Ireland which that year sailed up the St. Lawrence. But before the first week of June as many as eighty-four ships of various tonnage were driven in by an easterly wind; and of that enormous number of vessels there was not one free from the taint of malignant typhus, the offspring of famine and of the foul ship-hold. . . . a tolerably quick passage occupied from six to eight weeks. . . .
>
> Who can imagine the horrors of even the shortest passage in an emigrant ship crowded beyond its utmost capacity of stowage with unhappy beings of all ages, with fever raging in their midst . . . the crew sullen or brutal from very desperation, or paralyzed with terror of the plague—the miserable passengers unable to help themselves, or afford the least relief to each other; one-fourth, or one-third, or one-half of the entire number in different stages of the disease; many dying, some dead; the fatal poison intensified by the indescribable foulness of the air breathed and rebreathed

by the gasping sufferers—the wails of children, the ravings of the delirious, the cries and groans of those in mortal agony!

... there was no accommodation of any kind on the island ... sheds were rapidly filled with the miserable people.... Hundreds were literally flung on the beach, left amid the mud and stones to crawl on the dry land how they could.... Many of these ... gasped out their last breath on that fatal shore, not able to drag themselves from the slime in which they lay....

It was not until the 1st of November that the quarantine of Grosse Isle was closed. Upon that barren isle as many as 10,000 of the Irish race were consigned to the grave-pit....

How could these new Irish immigrants, themselves poor and despised, become sympathizers with the black slave, who was becoming more and more the center of attention, the subject of agitation in the country? Indeed, most working-class activists at this time ignored the plight of blacks. Ely Moore, a New York trade union leader elected to Congress, argued in the House of Representatives against receiving abolitionist petitions. Racist hostility became an easy substitute for class frustration.

On the other hand, a white shoemaker wrote in 1848 in the *Awl*, the newspaper of Lynn shoe factory workers:

... we are nothing but a standing army that keeps three million of our brethren in bondage.... Living under the shade of Bunker Hill monument, demanding in the name of humanity, our right, and withholding those rights from others because their skin is black! Is it any wonder that God in his righteous anger has punished us by forcing us to drink the bitter cup of degradation.

The anger of the city poor often expressed itself in futile violence over nationality or religion. In New York in 1849 a mob, largely Irish; stormed the fashionable Astor Place Opera House, where an English actor, William Charles Macready, was playing Macbeth, in competition with an American actor, Edwin Forrest, who was acting the same role in another production. The crowd, shouting "Burn the damn den of aristocracy," charged, throwing bricks. The militia were called out, and in the violence that followed about two hundred people were killed or wounded.

Another economic crisis came in 1857. The boom in railroads and manufacturing, the surge of immigration, the increased speculation in stocks and bonds, the stealing, corruption, manipulation, led to wild expansion and then crash. By October of that year, 200,000 were unemployed, and thousands of recent immigrants crowded into the eastern ports, hoping to work their way back to Europe. The *New York Times* reported: "Every ship for Liverpool now has all the passengers she can carry, and multitudes are applying to work their passage if they have no money to pay for it."

In Newark, New Jersey, a rally of several thousand demanded the city give work to the unemployed. And in New York, fifteen thousand people met at Tompkins Square in downtown Manhattan. From there they marched to Wall Street and paraded around the Stock Exchange shouting: "We want work!" That summer, riots occurred in the slum areas of New York. A mob of five hundred attacked the police one day with pistols and bricks. There were parades of the unemployed, demanding bread and work, looting shops. In November, a crowd occupied City Hall, and the U.S. marines were brought in to drive them out.

Of the country's work force of 6 million in 1850, half a million were women: 330,000 worked as domestics; 55,000 were teachers. Of the 181,000 women in factories, half worked in textile mills.

They organized. Women struck by themselves for the first time in 1825. They were the United Tailoresses of New York, demanding higher wages. In 1828, the first strike of mill women on their own took place in Dover, New Hampshire, when several hundred women paraded with banners and flags. They shot off gunpowder, in protest against new factory rules, which charged fines for coming late, forbade talking on the job, and required church attendance. They were forced to return to the mill, their demands unmet, and their leaders were fired and blacklisted.

In Exeter, New Hampshire, women mill workers went on strike ("turned out," in the language of that day) because the overseer was setting the clocks back to get more time from them. Their strike succeeded in exacting a promise from the company that the overseers would set their watches right.

The "Lowell system," in which young girls would go to work in the mills and live in dormitories supervised by matrons, at first seemed beneficent, sociable, a welcome escape from household drudgery or domestic service. Lowell, Massachusetts, was the first town created for the textile mill industry; it was named after the wealthy and influential Lowell family. But the dormitories became prisonlike, controlled by rules and regulations. The supper (served after the women had risen at four in the morning and worked until seven thirty in the evening) often consisted merely of bread and gravy.

So the Lowell girls organized. They started their own newspapers. They protested against the weaving rooms, which were poorly lit, badly ventilated, impossibly hot in the summer, damp and cold in the winter. In 1834, a cut in wages led the Lowell women to strike, proclaiming: "Union is power. Our present object is to have union and exertion, and we remain in possession of our own unquestionable rights. . . ." But the threat of hiring others to replace them brought them back to work at reduced wages (the leaders were fired).

The young women, determined to do better next time, organized a Factory Girls' Association, and 1,500 went on strike in 1836 against a raise in boardinghouse charges. Harriet Hanson was an eleven-year-old girl working in the mill. She later recalled:

> I worked in a lower room where I had heard the proposed strike fully, if not vehemently, discussed. I had been an ardent listener to what was said against this attempt at "oppression" on the part of the corporation, and naturally I took sides with the strikers. When the day came on which the girls were to turn out, those in the upper rooms started first, and so many of them left that our mill was at once shut down. Then, when the girls in my room stood irresolute, uncertain what to do . . . I, who began to think they would not go out, after all their talk, became impatient, and started on ahead, saying, with childish bravado, "I don't care what you do, *I* am going to turn out, whether anyone else does or not," and I marched out, and was followed by the others.
>
> As I looked back at the long line that followed me, I was more proud than I have ever been since. . . .

The strikers marched through the streets of Lowell, singing. They held out a month, but then their money ran out, they were evicted from the boardinghouses, and many of them went back to work. The leaders were fired, including Harriet Hanson's widowed mother, a matron in the boardinghouse, who was blamed for her child's going out on strike.

Resistance continued. One mill in Lowell, Herbert Gutman reports, discharged twenty-eight women for such reasons as "misconduct," "disobedience," "impudence," "levity," and "mutiny." Meanwhile, the girls tried to hold on to thoughts about fresh air, the country, a less harried way of life. One of them recalled: "I never cared much for machinery. I could not see into their complications or feel interested in them. . . . In sweet June weather I would lean far out of the window, and try not to hear the unceasing clash of sound inside."

In New Hampshire, five hundred men and women petitioned the Amoskeag Manufacturing Company not to cut down an elm tree to make space for another mill. They said it was "a beautiful and goodly tree," representing a time "when the yell of the red man and the scream of the eagle were alone heard on the banks of the Merrimack, instead of two giant edifices filled with the buzz of busy and well-remunerated industry."

In 1835, twenty mills went on strike to reduce the workday from thirteen and a half hours to eleven hours, to get cash wages instead of company scrip, and to end fines for lateness. Fifteen hundred children and parents went out on strike, and it lasted six weeks. Strikebreakers were brought in, and some workers went back to work, but the strikers did win a twelve-hour day and nine hours on Saturday. That year and the next, there were 140 strikes in the eastern part of the United States.

The crisis that followed the 1837 panic stimulated the formation in 1845 of the Female Labor Reform Association in Lowell, which sent thousands of petitions to the Massachusetts legislature asking for a ten-hour day. Finally, the legislature decided to hold public hearings, the first investigation of labor conditions by any governmental body in the country. Eliza Hemingway told the committee of the air thick with smoke from oil lamps burning before sunup and after sundown. Judith Payne told of her sickness due to the work in the mills. But after the committee visited the mills—for which the company prepared by a cleanup job—it reported: "Your committee returned fully satisfied that the order, decorum, and general appearance of things in and around the mills could not be improved by any suggestion of theirs or by any act of the legislature."

The report was denounced by the Female Labor Reform Association, and they worked successfully for the committee chairman's defeat at the next election, though they could not vote. But not much was done to change conditions in the mills. In the late 1840s, the New England farm women who worked in the mills began to leave them, as more and more Irish immigrants took their place.

Company towns now grew up around mills in Rhode Island, Connecticut, New Jersey, Pennsylvania, using immigrant workers who signed contracts pledging everyone in the family to work for a year. They lived in slum tenements owned by the company, were paid in scrip, which they could use only at company stores, and were evicted if their work was unsatisfactory.

In Paterson, New Jersey, the first of a series of mill strikes was started by children. When the company suddenly put off their dinner hour from noon to 1:00 P.M., the children marched off the job, their parents cheering them on. They were joined by other working people in the town—carpenters, masons, machinists—who turned the strike into a ten-hour-day struggle. After a week, however, with the threat of bringing in militia, the children returned to work, and their leaders were fired. Soon after, trying to prevent more trouble, the company restored the noon dinner hour.

It was the shoemakers of Lynn, Massachusetts, a factory town northeast of Boston, who started the largest strike to take place in the United States before the Civil War. Lynn had pioneered in the use of sewing machines in factories, replacing shoemaker artisans. The factory workers in Lynn, who began to organize in the 1830s, later started a militant newspaper, the *Awl*. In 1844, four years before Marx and Engels's *Communist Manifesto* appeared, the *Awl* wrote:

> The division of society into the producing and the non-producing classes, and the fact of the unequal distribution of value between the two, introduces us at once to another distinction—that of capital and labor. . . . labor now becomes a commodity. . . . Antagonism and opposition of interest is introduced in the community; capital and labor stand opposed.

The economic crisis of 1857 brought the shoe business to a halt, and the workers of Lynn lost their jobs. There was already anger at machine-stitching replacing shoemakers. Prices were up, wages were repeatedly cut, and by the fall of 1859 men were earning $3 a week and women were earning $1 a week, working sixteen hours a day.

In early 1860, a mass meeting of the newly formed Mechanics Association demanded higher wages. When the manufacturers refused to meet with their committees, the workers called a strike for Washington's Birthday. That morning three thousand shoemakers met in the Lyceum Hall in Lynn and set up committees of 100 to post the names of scabs, to guard against violence, to make sure shoes would not be sent out to be finished elsewhere.

In a few days, shoeworkers throughout New England joined the strike—in Natick, Newburyport, Haverhill, Marblehead, and other Massachusetts towns, as well as towns in New Hampshire and Maine. In a week, strikes had begun in all the shoe towns of New England, with Mechanics Associations in twenty-five towns and twenty thousand shoeworkers on strike. Newspapers called it "The Revolution at the North," "The Rebellion Among the Workmen of New England," "Beginning of the Conflict Between Capital and Labor."

One thousand women and five thousand men marched through the streets of Lynn in a blizzard, carrying banners and American flags.

Women shoebinders and stitchers joined the strike and held their own mass meeting. A New York *Herald* reporter wrote of them: "They assail the bosses in a style which reminds one of the amiable females who participated in the first French Revolution." A huge Ladies' Procession was organized, the women marching through streets high with snowdrifts, carrying signs: "American Ladies Will Not Be Slaves . . . Weak in Physical Strength but Strong in Moral Courage, We Dare Battle for the Right, Shoulder to Shoulder with our Fathers, Husbands, and Brothers." Ten days after that, a procession of ten thousand striking workers, including delegations from Salem, Marblehead, and other towns, men and women, marched through Lynn, in what was the greatest demonstration of labor to take place in New England up to that time.

Police from Boston and militia were sent in to make sure strikers did not interfere with shipments of shoes to be finished out of the state. The strike processions went on, while city grocers and provisions dealers provided food for the strikers. The strike continued through March with morale high, but by April it was losing force. The manufacturers offered higher wages to bring the strikers back into the factories, but without recognizing the unions, so that workers still had to face the employer as individuals.

Most of the shoeworkers were native-born Americans, Alan Dawley says in his study of the Lynn strike *(Class and Community)*. They did not accept the social and political order that kept them in poverty, however much it was praised in American schools, churches, newspapers. In Lynn, he says, "articulate, activist Irish shoe and leather workers joined Yankees in flatly rejecting the myth of success. Irish and Yankee workers jointly . . . looked for labor candidates when they went to the polls, and resisted strikebreaking by local police." Trying to understand why this fierce class spirit did not lead to independent revolutionary political action, Dawley concludes that the main reason is that electoral politics drained the energies of the resisters into the channels of the system.

Dawley disputes some historians who have said the high rate of mobility of workers prevented them from organizing in revolutionary ways. He says that while there was a high turnover in Lynn too, this "masked the existence of a virtually permanent minority who played the key role in organizing discontent." He also suggests that mobility helps people see that others are in similar conditions. He thinks the struggle of European workers for political democracy, even while they sought economic equality, made them class-conscious. American workers, however, had already gained political democracy by the 1830s, and so their economic battles could be taken over by political parties that blurred class lines.

Even this might not have stopped labor militancy and the rise of class consciousness, Dawley says, if not for the fact that "an entire generation was sidetracked in the 1860's because of the Civil War." Northern wage earners who rallied to the Union cause became allied with their employers. National issues took over from class issues: "At a time when scores of industrial communities like Lynn were seething with resistance to industrialism, national politics were preoccupied with the issues of war and reconstruction." And on these issues the political parties took positions, offered choices, obscured the fact that the political system itself and the wealthy classes it represented were responsible for the problems they now offered to solve.

Class-consciousness was overwhelmed during the Civil War, both North and South, by military and political unity in the crisis of war. That unity was weaned by rhetoric and enforced by arms. It was a war proclaimed as a war for liberty, but working people would be attacked by soldiers if they dared to strike, Indians would be massacred in Colorado by the U.S. army, and those daring to criticize Lincoln's policies would be put in jail without trial—perhaps thirty thousand political prisoners.

Still, there were signs in both sections of dissent from that unity— anger of poor against rich, rebellion against the dominant political and economic forces.

In the North, the war brought high prices for food and the necessities of life. Prices of milk, eggs, cheese were up 60 to 100 percent for families that had not been able to pay the old prices. One historian (Emerson Fite, *Social and Industrial Conditions in the North During the Civil War*) described the war situation: "Employers were wont to appropriate to themselves all or nearly all of the profits accruing from the higher prices, without being willing to grant to the employees a fair share of these profits through the medium of higher wages."

There were strikes all over the country during the war. The Springfield *Republican* in 1863 said that "the workmen of almost every branch of trade have had their strikes within the last few months," and the San Francisco *Evening Bulletin* said "striking for higher wages is now the rage among the working people of San Francisco." Unions were being formed as a result of these strikes. Philadelphia shoemakers in 1863 announced that high prices made organization imperative.

The headline in *Fincher's Trades' Review* of November 21, 1863, "THE REVOLUTION IN NEW YORK," was an exaggeration, but its list of labor activities was impressive evidence of the hidden resentments of the poor during the war:

The upheaval of the laboring masses in New York has startled the capitalists of that city and vicinity. . . .

The machinists are making a bold stand. . . . We publish their appeal in another column.

The City Railroad employees struck for higher wages, and made the whole population, for a few days, "ride on Shank's mare.". . .

The house painters of Brooklyn have taken steps to counteract the attempt of the bosses to reduce their wages.

The house carpenters, we are informed, are pretty well "out of the woods" and their demands are generally complied with.

The safe-makers have obtained an increase of wages, and are now at work.

The lithographic printers are making efforts to secure better pay for their labor.

The workmen on the iron clads are yet holding out against the contractors. . . .

The window shade painters have obtained an advance of 25 percent.

The horse shoers are fortifying themselves against the evils of money and trade fluctuations.

The sash and blind-makers are organized and ask their employers for 25 percent additional.

The sugar packers are remodelling their list of prices.

The glass cutters demand 15 percent to present wages.

Imperfect as we confess our list to be, there is enough to convince the reader that the social revolution now working its way through the land must succeed, if workingmen are only true to each other.

The stage drivers, to the number of 800, are on a strike. . . .

The workingmen of Boston are not behind. . . . In addition to the strike at the Charlestown Navy Yard. . . .

The riggers are on a strike. . . .

At this writing it is rumored, says the Boston *Post*, that a general strike is contemplated among the workmen in the iron establishments at South Boston, and other parts of the city.

The war brought many women into shops and factories, often over the objections of men who saw them driving wage scales down. In New York City, girls sewed umbrellas from six in the morning to midnight, earning $3 a week, from which employers deducted the cost of needles and thread. Girls who made cotton shirts received twenty-four cents for a twelve-hour day. In late 1863, New York working women held a mass meeting to find a solution to their problems. A Working Women's

Protective Union was formed, and there was a strike of women umbrella workers in New York and Brooklyn. In Providence, Rhode Island, a Ladies Cigar Makers Union was organized.

All together, by 1864, about 200,000 workers, men and women, were in trade unions, forming national unions in some of the trades, putting out labor newspapers.

Union troops were used to break strikes. Federal soldiers were sent to Cold Springs, New York, to end a strike at a gun works where workers wanted a wage increase. Striking machinists and tailors in St. Louis were forced back to work by the army. In Tennessee, a Union general arrested and sent out of the state two hundred striking mechanics. When engineers on the Reading Railroad struck, troops broke that strike, as they did with miners in Tioga County, Pennsylvania.

White workers of the North were not enthusiastic about a war which seemed to be fought for the black slave, or for the capitalist, for anyone but them. They worked in semislave conditions themselves. They thought the war was profiting the new class of millionaires. They saw defective guns sold to the army by contractors, sand sold as sugar, rye sold as coffee, shop sweepings made into clothing and blankets, paper-soled shoes produced for soldiers at the front, navy ships made of rotting timbers, soldiers' uniforms that fell apart in the rain.

The Irish working people of New York, recent immigrants, poor, looked upon with contempt by native Americans, could hardly find sympathy for the black population of the city who competed with them for jobs as longshoremen, barbers, waiters, domestic servants. Blacks, pushed out of these jobs, often were used to break strikes. Then came the war, the draft, the chance of death. And the Conscription Act of 1863 provided that the rich could avoid military service: they could pay $300 or buy a substitute. In the summer of 1863, a "Song of the Conscripts" was circulated by the thousands in New York and other cities. One stanza:

> *We're coming, Father Abraham, three hundred thousand more*
> *We leave our homes and firesides with bleeding hearts and sore*
> *Since poverty has been our crime, we bow to thy decree;*
> *We are the poor and have no wealth to purchase liberty.*

When recruiting for the army began in July 1863, a mob in New York wrecked the main recruiting station. Then, for three days, crowds of white workers marched through the city, destroying buildings, factories, streetcar lines, homes. The draft riots were complex—antiblack, antirich, anti-Republican. From an assault on draft headquarters, the rioters went on to attacks on wealthy homes, then to the murder of blacks. They marched through the streets, forcing factories to close, recruiting more members of the mob. They set the city's colored orphan asylum on fire. They shot, burned, and hanged blacks they found in the streets. Many people were thrown into the rivers to drown.

On the fourth day, Union troops returning from the Battle of Gettysburg came into the city and stopped the rioting. Perhaps four hundred people were killed. No exact figures have ever been given, but the number of lives lost was greater than in any other incident of domestic violence in American history.

Joel Tyler Headley (*The Great Riots of New York*) gave a graphic day-by-day description of what happened:

> Second Day. . . . the fire-bells continually ringing increased the terror that every hour became more widespread. Especially was this true of the negro population. . . . At one time there lay at the corner of Twenty-seventh Street and Seventh Avenue the dead body of a negro, stripped nearly naked, and around it a collection of Irishmen, absolutely dancing or shouting like wild Indians. . . . A negro barber's shop was next attacked, and the torch applied to it. A negro lodging house in the same street next received the visit of these furies, and was soon a mass of ruins. Old men, seventy years of age, and young children, too young to comprehend what it all meant, were cruelly beaten and killed. . . .

There were antidraft riots—not so prolonged or bloody—in other northern cities: Newark, Troy, Boston, Toledo, Evansville. In Boston the dead were Irish workers attacking an armory, who were fired on by soldiers.

In the South, beneath the apparent unity of the white Confederacy, there was also conflict. Most whites—two-thirds of them—did not own slaves. A few thousand families made up the plantation elite. The Federal Census of 1850 showed that a thousand southern families at the top of the economy received about $50 million a year income, while all the other families, about 660,000, received about $60 million a year.

Millions of southern whites were poor farmers, living in shacks or abandoned outhouses, cultivating land so bad the plantation owners had abandoned it. Just before the Civil War, in Jackson, Mississippi, slaves working in a cotton factory received twenty cents a day for board, and white workers at the same factory received thirty cents. A newspaper in North Carolina in August 1855 spoke of "hundreds of thousands of working class families existing upon half-starvation from year to year."

Behind the rebel battle yells and the legendary spirit of the Confederate army, there was much reluctance to fight. A sympathetic historian of the South, E. Merton Coulter, asked: "Why did the Confederacy fail? The forces leading to defeat were many but they may be summed up in this one fact: The people did not will hard enough and long enough to win." Not money or soldiers, but will power and morale were decisive.

The conscription law of the Confederacy too provided that the rich could avoid service. Did Confederate soldiers begin to suspect they were fighting for the privileges of an elite they could never belong to? In April 1863, there was a bread riot in Richmond. That summer, draft riots occurred in various southern cities. In September, a bread riot in Mobile, Alabama. Georgia Lee Tatum, in her study *Disloyalty in the Confederacy*, writes: "Before the end of the war, there was much disaffection in every state, and many of the disloyal had formed into bands—in some states into well-organized, active societies."

The Civil War was one of the first instances in the world of modern warfare: deadly artillery shells, Gatling guns, bayonet charges—combining the indiscriminate killing of mechanized war with hand-to-hand combat. The nightmare scenes could not adequately be described except in a novel like Stephen Crane's *The Red Badge of Courage*. In one charge before Petersburg, Virginia, a regiment of 850 Maine soldiers lost 632 men in half an hour. It was a vast butchery, 623,000 dead on both sides, and 471,000 wounded, over a million dead and wounded in a country whose population was 30 million.

No wonder that desertions grew among southern soldiers as the war went on. As for the Union army, by the end of the war, 200,000 had deserted.

Still, 600,000 had volunteered for the Confederacy in 1861, and many in the Union army were volunteers. The psychology of patriotism, the lure of adventure, the aura of moral crusade created by political leaders, worked effectively to dim class resentments against the rich and powerful, and turn much of the anger against "the enemy." As Edmund Wilson put it in *Patriotic Gore* (written after World War II):

We have seen, in our most recent wars, how a divided and arguing public opinion may be converted overnight into a national near-unanimity, an obedient flood of energy which will carry the young to destruction and overpower any effort to stem it. The unanimity of men at war is like that of a school of fish, which will swerve, simultaneously and apparently without leadership, when the shadow of an enemy appears, or like a sky-darkening flight of grass-hoppers, which, also all compelled by one impulse, will descend to consume the crops.

Under the deafening noise of the war, Congress was passing and Lincoln was signing into law a whole series of acts to give business interests what they wanted, and what the agrarian South had blocked before secession. The Republican platform of 1860 had been a clear appeal to businessmen. Now Congress in 1861 passed the Morrill Tariff. This made foreign goods more expensive, allowed American manufacturers to raise their prices, and forced American consumers to pay more.

The following year a Homestead Act was passed. It gave 160 acres of western land, unoccupied and publicly owned, to anyone who would cultivate it for five years. Anyone willing to pay $1.25 an acre could buy a homestead. Few ordinary people had the $200 necessary to do this; speculators moved in and bought up much of the land. Homestead land added up to 50 million acres. But during the Civil War, over 100 million acres were given by Congress and the President to various railroads, free of charge. Congress also set up a national bank, putting the government into partnership with the banking interests, guaranteeing their profits.

With strikes spreading, employers pressed Congress for help. The Contract Labor Law of 1864 made it possible for companies to sign contracts with foreign workers whenever the workers pledged to give twelve months of their wages to pay the cost of emigration. This gave the employers during the Civil war not only very cheap labor, but strikebreakers.

More important, perhaps, than the federal laws passed by Congress for the benefit of the rich were the day-to-day operations of local and state laws for the benefit of landlords and merchants. Gustavus Myers, in his *History of the Great American Fortunes*, comments on this in discussing the growth of the Astor family's fortune, much of it out of the rents of New York tenements:

> Is it not murder when, compelled by want, people are forced to fester in squalid, germ-filled tenements, where the sunlight never enters and where disease finds a prolific breeding-place? Untold thousands went to their deaths in these unspeakable places. Yet, so far as the Law was concerned, the rents collected by the Astors, as well as by other landlords, were honestly made. The whole institution of Law saw nothing out of the way in these conditions, and very significantly so, because, to repeat over and over again, Law did not represent the ethics or ideals of advanced humanity; it exactly reflected, as a pool reflects the sky, the demands and self-interest of the growing propertied classes. . . .

In the thirty years leading up to the Civil War, the law was increasingly interpreted in the courts to suit the capitalist development of the country. Studying this, Morton Horwitz *(The Transformation of American Law)* points out that the English commonlaw was no longer holy when it stood in the way of business growth. Mill owners were given the legal right to destroy other people's property by flood to carry on their business. The law of "eminent domain" was used to take farmers' land and give it to canal companies or railroad companies as subsidies. Judgments for damages against businessmen were taken out of the hands of juries, which were unpredictable, and given to judges. Private settlement of disputes by arbitration was replaced by court settlements, creating more dependence on lawyers, and the legal profession gained in importance. The ancient idea of a fair price for goods gave way in the courts to the idea of caveat emptor (let the buyer beware), thus throwing generations of consumers from that time on to the mercy of businessmen.

That contract law was intended to discriminate against working people and for business is shown by Horwitz in the following example of the early nineteenth century: the courts said that if a worker signed a contract to work for a year, and left before the year was up, he was not entitled to any wages, even for the time he had worked. But the courts at the same time said that if a building business broke a contract, it was entitled to be paid for whatever had been done up to that point.

The pretense of the law was that a worker and a railroad made a contract with equal bargaining power. Thus, a Massachusetts judge decided an injured worker did not deserve compensation, because, by signing the contract, he was agreeing to take certain risks. "The circle was completed; the law had come simply to ratify those forms of inequality that the market system produced."

It was a time when the law did not even pretend to protect working people—as it would in the next century. Health and safety laws were either nonexistent or unenforced. In Lawrence, Massachusetts, in 1860, on a winter day, the Pemberton Mill collapsed, with nine hundred workers inside, mostly women. Eighty-eight died, and although there was evidence that the structure had never been adequate to support the heavy machinery inside, and that this was known to the construction engineer, a jury found "no evidence of criminal intent."

Horwitz sums up what happened in the courts of law by the time of the Civil War:

By the middle of the nineteenth century the legal system had been reshaped to the advantage of men of commerce and industry at the expense of farmers, workers, consumers, and other less powerful groups within the society. . . . it actively promoted a legal redistribution of wealth against the weakest groups in the society.

In premodern times, the maldistribution of wealth was accomplished by simple force. In modern times, exploitation is disguised—it is accomplished by law, which has the look of neutrality and fairness. By the time of the Civil War, modernization was well under way in the United States.

With the war over, the urgency of national unity slackened, and ordinary people could turn more to their daily lives, their problems of survival. The disbanded armies now were in the streets, looking for work. In June 1865, *Fincher's Trades' Review* reported: "As was to be expected, the returned soldiers are flooding the streets already, unable to find employment."

The cities to which the soldiers returned were death traps of typhus, tuberculosis, hunger, and fire. In New York, 100,000 people lived in the cellars of the slums; 12,000 women worked in houses of prostitution to keep from starving; the garbage, lying 2 feet deep in the streets, was alive with rats. In Philadelphia, while the rich got fresh water from the Schuylkill River, everyone else drank from the Delaware, into which 13 million gallons of sewage were dumped every day. In the Great Chicago Fire in 1871, the tenements fell so fast, one after another, that people said it sounded like an earthquake.

A movement for the eight-hour day began among working people after the war, helped by the formation of the first national federation of unions, the National Labor Union. A three-month strike of 100,000 workers in New York won the eight-hour day, and at a victory celebration in June 1872, 150,000 workers paraded through the city. The *New York Times* wondered what proportion of the strikers were "thoroughly American."

Women, brought into industry during the war, organized unions: cigarmakers, tailoresses, umbrella sewers, capmakers, printers, laundresses, shoeworkers. They formed the Daughters of St. Crispin, and succeeded in getting the Cigarmakers Union and the National Typographical Union to admit women for the first time. A woman named Gussie Lewis of New York became corresponding secretary of the Typographers' Union. But the cigarmakers and typographers were only two of the thirty-odd national unions, and the general attitude toward women was one of exclusion.

In 1869, the collar laundresses of Troy, New York, whose work involved standing "over the wash tub and over the ironing table with furnaces on either side, the thermometer averaging 100 degrees, for wages averaging $2.00 and $3.00 a week" (according to a contemporary account), went on strike. Their leader was Kate Mullaney, second vice-president of the National Labor Union. Seven thousand people came to a rally to support them, and the women organized a cooperative collar and cuff factory to provide work and keep the strike going. But as time went on, outside support dwindled. The employers began making a paper collar, requiring fewer laundresses. The strike failed.

The dangers of mill work intensified efforts to organize. Work often went on around the clock. At a mill in Providence, Rhode Island, fire broke out one night in 1866. There was panic among the six hundred workers, mostly women, and many jumped to their deaths from upper-story windows.

In Fall River, Massachusetts, women weavers formed a union independent of the men weavers. They refused to take a 10 percent wage cut that the men had accepted, struck against three mills, won the men's support, and brought to a halt 3,500 looms and 156,000 spindles, with 3,200 workers on strike. But their children needed food; they had to return to work, signing an "iron-clad oath" (later called a "yellow-dog contract") not to join a union.

Black workers at this time found the National Labor Union reluctant to organize them. So they formed their own unions and carried on their own strikes—like the levee workers in Mobile, Alabama, in 1867, Negro longshoremen in Charleston, dockworkers in Savannah. This probably stimulated the National Labor Union, at its 1869 convention, to resolve to organize women and Negroes, declaring that it recognized "neither color nor sex on the question of the rights of labor." A journalist wrote about the remarkable signs of racial unity at this convention:

> When a native Mississippian and an ex-confederate officer, in addressing a convention, refers to a colored delegate who has preceded him as "the gentleman from Georgia" . . . when an ardent and Democratic partisan (from New York at that) declares with a rich Irish brogue that he asks for himself no privilege as a mechanic or as a citizen that he is not willing to concede to every other man, white or black . . . then one may indeed be warranted in asserting that time works curious changes. . . .

Most unions, however, still kept Negroes out, or asked them to form their own locals.

The National Labor Union began to expend more and more of its energy on political issues, especially currency reform, a demand for the issuance of paper money: Greenbacks. As it became less an organizer of labor struggles, and more a lobbyist with Congress, concerned with voting, it lost vitality. An observer of the labor scene, F. A. Sorge, wrote in 1870 to Karl Marx in England: "The National Labor Union, which had such brilliant prospects in the beginning of its career, was poisoned by Greenbackism and is slowly but surely dying."

Perhaps unions could not easily see the limits to legislative reform in an age where such reform laws were being passed for the first time, and hopes were high. The Pennsylvania legislature in 1869 passed a mine safety act providing for the "regulation and ventilation of mines, and for the protection of the lives of the miners." Only after a hundred years of continuing accidents in those mines would it be understood how insufficient those words were—except as a device to calm anger among miners.

In 1873, another economic crisis devastated the nation. It was the closing of the banking house of Jay Cooke—the banker who during the war had made $3 million a year in commissions alone for selling government bonds—that started the wave of panic. While President Grant slept in Cooke's Philadelphia mansion on September 18, 1873, the banker rode downtown to lock the door on his bank. Now people could not pay loans on mortgages: five thousand businesses closed and put their workers on the street.

It was more than Jay Cooke. The crisis was built into a system which was chaotic in its nature, in which only the very rich were secure. It was a system of periodic crisis—1837, 1857, 1873 (and later: 1893, 1907, 1919, 1929)—that wiped out small businesses and brought cold, hunger, and death to working people while the fortunes of the Astors, Vanderbilts, Rockefellers, Morgans, kept growing through war and peace, crisis and recovery. During the 1873 crisis, Carnegie was capturing the steel market, Rockefeller was wiping out his competitors in oil.

"LABOR DEPRESSION IN BROOKLYN" was the headline in the New York *Herald* in November 1873. It listed closings and layoffs: a felt-skirt factory, a picture-frame factory, a glass-cutting establishment, a steelworks factory. And women's trades: milliners, dressmakers, shoe-binders.

The depression continued through the 1870s. During the first three months of 1874, ninety thousand workers, almost half of them women, had to sleep in police stations in New York. They were known as "revolvers" because they were limited to one or two days a month in any one police station, and so had to keep moving. All over the country, people were evicted from their homes. Many roamed the cities looking for food.

Desperate workers tried to get to Europe or to South America. In 1878, the SS *Metropolis*, filled with laborers, left the United States for South America and sank with all aboard. The New York *Tribune* reported: "One hour after the news that the ship had gone down arrived in Philadelphia, the office of Messrs. Collins was besieged by hundreds of hunger-bitten, decent men, begging for the places of the drowned laborers."

Mass meeting and demonstrations of the unemployed took place all over the country. Unemployed councils were set up. A meeting in New York at Cooper Institute in late 1873, organized by trade unions and the American section of the First International (founded in 1864 in Europe by Marx and others), drew a huge crowd, overflowing into the streets. The meeting asked that before bills became law they should be approved by a public vote, that no individual should own more than $30,000; they asked for an eight-hour day. Also:

> Whereas, we are industrious, law-abiding citizens, who had paid all taxes and given support and allegiance to the government,
> Resolved, that we will in this time of need supply ourselves and our families with proper food and shelter and we will send our bills to the City Treasury, to be liquidated, until we shall obtain work. . . .

In Chicago, twenty thousand unemployed marched through the streets to City Hall asking "bread for the needy, clothing for the naked, and houses for the homeless." Actions like this resulted in some relief for about ten thousand families.

In January 1874, in New York City, a huge parade of workers, kept by the police from approaching City Hall, went to Tompkins Square, and there were told by the police they couldn't have the meeting. They stayed, and the police attacked. One newspaper reported:

> Police clubs rose and fell. Women and children ran screaming in all directions. Many of them were trampled underfoot in the stampede for the gates. In the street bystanders were ridden down and mercilessly clubbed by mounted officers.

Strikes were called in the textile mills of Fall River, Massachusetts. In the anthracite coal district of Pennsylvania, there was the "long strike," where Irish members of a society called the Ancient Order of Hibernians were accused of acts of violence, mostly on the testimony of a detective planted among the miners. These were the "Molly Maguires." They were tried and found guilty. Philip Foner believes, after a study of the evidence, that they were framed because they were labor organizers. He quotes the sympathetic *Irish World*, which called them "intelligent men whose direction gave strength to the resistance of the miners to the inhuman reduction of their wages." And he points to the *Miners' Journal*, put out by the coal mine owners, which referred to the executed men this way: "What did they do? Whenever prices of labor did not suit them they organized and proclaimed a strike."

All together, nineteen were executed, according to Anthony Bimba *(The Molly Maguires)*. There were scattered protests from workingmen's organizations, but no mass movement that could stop the executions.

It was a time when employers brought in recent immigrants—desperate for work, different from the strikers in language and culture—to break strikes. Italians were imported into the bituminous coal area around Pittsburgh in 1874 to replace striking miners. This led to the killing of three Italians, to trials in which jurors of the community exonerated the strikers, and bitter feelings between Italians and other organized workers.

The centennial year of 1876—one hundred years after the Declaration of Independence—brought forth a number of new declarations (reproduced by Philip Foner in *We the Other People*). Whites and blacks, separately, expressed their disillusionment. A "Negro Declaration of Independence" denounced the Republican party on which they had once depended to gain full freedom, and proposed independent political action by colored voters. And the Workingmen's party of Illinois, at a July 4 celebration organized by German socialists in Chicago, said in its Declaration of Independence:

> The present system has enabled capitalists to make laws in their own interests to the injury and oppression of the workers.
>
> It has made the name Democracy, for which our forefathers fought and died, a mockery and a shadow, by giving to property an unproportionate amount of representation and control over Legislation.
>
> It has enabled capitalists . . . to secure government aid, inland grants and money loans, to selfish railroad corporations, who, by monopolizing the means of transportation are enabled to swindle both the producer and the consumer. . . .
>
> It has presented to the world the absurd spectacle of a deadly civil war for the abolition of negro slavery while the majority of the white population, those who have created all the wealth of the nation, are compelled to suffer under a bondage infinitely more galling and humiliating. . . .

It has allowed the capitalists, as a class, to appropriate annually 5/6 of the entire production of the country. . . .

It has therefore prevented mankind from fulfilling their natural destinies on earth—crushed out ambition, prevented marriages or caused false and unnatural ones—has shortened human life, destroyed morals and fostered crime, corrupted judges, ministers, and statesmen, shattered confidence, love and honor among men, and made life a selfish, merciless struggle for existence instead of a noble and generous struggle for perfection, in which equal advantages should be given to all, and human lives relieved from an unnatural and degrading competition for bread. . . .

We, therefore, the representatives of the workers of Chicago, in mass meeting assembled, do solemnly publish and declare . . .

That we are absolved from all allegiance to the existing political parties of this country, and that as free and independent producers we shall endeavor to acquire the full power to make our own laws, manage our own production, and govern ourselves, acknowledging no rights without duties, no duties without rights. And for the support of this declaration, with a firm reliance on the assistance and cooperation of all workingmen, we mutually pledge to each other our lives, our means, and our sacred honor.

In the year 1877, the country was in the depths of the Depression. That summer, in the hot cities where poor families lived in cellars and drank infested water, the children became sick in large numbers. The *New York Times* wrote: ". . . already the cry of the dying children begins to be heard. . . . Soon, to judge from the past, there will be a thousand deaths of infants per week in the city." That first week in July, in Baltimore, where all liquid sewage ran through the streets, 139 babies died.

That year there came a series of tumultuous strikes by railroad workers in a dozen cities; they shook the nation as no labor conflict in its history had done.

It began with wage cuts on railroad after railroad, in tense situations of already low wages ($1.75 a day for brakemen working twelve hours), scheming and profiteering by the railroad companies, deaths and injuries among the workers—loss of hands, feet, fingers, the crushing of men between cars.

At the Baltimore & Ohio station in Martinsburg, West Virginia, workers determined to fight the wage cut went on strike, uncoupled the engines, ran them into the roundhouse, and announced no more trains would leave Martinsburg until the 10 percent cut was canceled. A crowd of support gathered, too many for the local police to disperse. B. & O.

officials asked the governor for military protection, and he sent in militia. A train tried to get through, protected by the militia, and a striker, trying to derail it, exchanged gunfire with a militiaman attempting to stop him. The striker was shot in his thigh and his arm. His arm was amputated later that day, and nine days later he died.

Six hundred freight trains now jammed the yards at Martinsburg. The West Virginia governor applied to newly elected President Rutherford Hayes for federal troops, saying the state militia was insufficient. In fact, the militia was not totally reliable, being composed of many railroad workers. Much of the U.S. army was tied up in Indian battles in the West. Congress had not appropriated money for the army yet, but J. P. Morgan, August Belmont, and other bankers now offered to lend money to pay army officers (but no enlisted men). Federal troops arrived in Martinsburg, and the freight cars began to move.

In Baltimore, a crowd of thousands sympathetic to the railroad strikers surrounded the armory of the National Guard, which had been called out by the governor at the request of the B. & O. Railroad. The crowd hurled rocks, and the soldiers came out, firing. The streets now became the scene of a moving, bloody battle. When the evening was over, ten men or boys were dead, more badly wounded, one soldier wounded. Half of the 120 troops quit and the rest went on to the train depot, where a crowd of two hundred smashed the engine of a passenger train, tore up tracks, and engaged the militia again in a running battle.

By now, fifteen thousand people surrounded the depot. Soon, three passenger cars, the station platform, and a locomotive were on fire. The governor asked for federal troops, and Hayes responded. Five hundred soldiers arrived and Baltimore quieted down.

The rebellion of the railroad workers now spread. Joseph Dacus, then editor of the St. Louis *Republican*, reported:

> Strikes were occurring almost every hour. The great State of Pennsylvania was in an uproar; New Jersey was afflicted by a paralyzing dread; New York was mustering an army of militia; Ohio was shaken from Lake Erie to the Ohio River; Indiana rested in a dreadful suspense. Illinois, and especially its great metropolis, Chicago, apparently hung on the verge of a vortex of confusion and tumult. St. Louis had already felt the effect of the premonitory shocks of the uprising. . . .

The strike spread to Pittsburgh and the Pennsylvania Railroad. Again, it happened outside the regular union, pent-up anger exploding without plan. Robert Bruce, historian of the 1877 strikes, writes (*1877:*

Year of Violence) about a flagman named Gus Harris. Harris refused to go out on a "double-header," a train with two locomotives carrying a double length of cars, to which railroaders had objected because it required fewer workers and made the brakemen's work more dangerous:

> The decision was his own, not part of a concerted plan or a general understanding. Had he lain awake that past night, listening to the rain, asking himself if he dared quit, wondering if anyone would join him, weighing the chances? Or had he simply risen to a breakfast that did not fill him, seen his children go off shabby and half-fed, walked brooding through the damp morning and then yielded impulsively to stored-up rage?

When Harris said he would not go, the rest of the crew refused too. The strikers now multiplied, joined by young boys and men from the mills and factories (Pittsburgh had 33 iron mills, 73 glass factories, 29 oil refineries, 158 coal mines). The freight trains stopped moving out of the city. The Trainman's Union had not organized this, but it moved to take hold, called a meeting, invited "all workingmen to make common cause with their brethren on the railroad."

Railroad and local officials decided that the Pittsburgh militia would not kill their fellow townsmen, and urged that Philadelphia troops be called in. By now two thousand cars were idle in Pittsburgh. The Philadelphia troops came and began to clear the track. Rocks flew. Gunfire was exchanged between crowd and troops. At least ten people were killed, all workingmen, most of them not railroaders.

Now the whole city rose in anger. A crowd surrounded the troops, who moved into a roundhouse. Railroad cars were set afire, buildings began to burn, and finally the roundhouse itself, the troops marching out of it to safety. There was more gunfire, the Union Depot was set afire, thousands looted the freight cars. A huge grain elevator and a small section of the city went up in flames. In a few days, twenty-four people had been killed (including four soldiers). Seventy-nine buildings had been burned to the ground. Something like a general strike was developing in Pittsburgh: mill workers, car workers, miners, laborers, and the employees at the Carnegie steel plant.

The entire National Guard of Pennsylvania, nine thousand men, was called out. But many of the companies couldn't move as strikers in other towns held up traffic. In Lebanon, Pennsylvania, one National Guard company mutinied and marched through an excited town. In Altoona, troops surrounded by rioters, immobilized by sabotaged engines, surrendered, stacked arms, fraternized with the crowd, and then were allowed to go home, to the accompaniment of singing by a quartet in an all-Negro militia company.

In Harrisburg, the state capital, as at so many places, teenagers made up a large part of the crowd, which included some Negroes. Philadelphia militia, on their way home from Altoona, shook hands with the crowd, gave up their guns, marched like captives through the streets, were fed at a hotel and sent home. The crowd agreed to the mayor's request to deposit the surrendered guns at the city hall. Factories and shops were idle. After some looting, citizens' patrols kept order in the streets through the night.

Where strikers did not manage to take control, as in Pottsville, Pennsylvania, it may well have been because of disunity. The spokesman of the Philadelphia & Reading Coal & Iron Company in that town wrote: "The men have no organization, and there is too much race jealousy existing among them to permit them to form one."

In Reading, Pennsylvania, there was no such problem—90 percent were native-born, the rest mostly German. There, the railroad was two months behind in paying wages, and a branch of the Trainman's Union was organized. Two thousand people gathered, while men who had blackened their faces with coal dust set about methodically tearing up tracks, jamming switches, derailing cars, setting fire to cabooses and also to a railroad bridge.

A National Guard company arrived, fresh from duty at the execution of the Molly Maguires. The crowd threw stones, fired pistols. The soldiers fired into the crowd. "Six men lay dead in the twilight," Bruce reports, "a fireman and an engineer formerly employed in the Reading, a carpenter, a huckster, a rolling-mill worker, a laborer. . . . A policeman and another man lay at the point of death." Five of the wounded died. The crowd grew angrier, more menacing. A contingent of soldiers announced it would not fire, one soldier saying he would rather put a bullet through the president of Philadelphia & Reading Coal & Iron. The 16th Regiment of the Morristown volunteers stacked its arms. Some militia threw their guns away and gave their ammunition to the crowd. When the Guardsmen left for home, federal troops arrived and took control, and local police began making arrests.

Meanwhile the leaders of the big railway brotherhoods, the Order of Railway Conductors, the Brotherhood of Locomotive Firemen, the Brotherhood of Engineers, disavowed the strike. There was talk in the press of "communistic ideas . . . widely entertained . . . by the workmen employed in mines and factories and by the railroads."

In fact, there was a very active Workingmen's party in Chicago, with several thousand members, most of them immigrants from Germany and Bohemia. It was connected with the First International in Europe. In the midst of the railroad strikes, that summer of 1877, it called a rally. Six thousand people came and demanded nationalization of the railroads. Albert Parsons gave a fiery speech. He was from Alabama, had fought in the Confederacy during the Civil War, married a brown-skinned woman of Spanish and Indian blood, worked as a typesetter, and was one of the best English-speaking orators the Workingmen's party had.

The next day, a crowd of young people, not especially connected with the rally of the evening before, began moving through the railroad yards, closed down the freights, went to the factories, called out the mill workers, the stockyard workers, the crewmen on the Lake Michigan ships, closed down the brickyards and lumberyards. That day also, Albert Parsons was fired from his job with the Chicago *Times* and declared blacklisted.

The police attacked the crowds. The press reported: "The sound of clubs falling on skulls was sickening for the first minute, until one grew accustomed to it. A rioter dropped at every whack, it seemed, for the ground was covered with them." Two companies of U.S. infantry arrived, joining National Guardsmen and Civil War veterans. Police fired into a surging crowd, and three men were killed.

The next day, an armed crowd of five thousand fought the police. The police fired again and again, and when it was over, and the dead were counted, they were, as usual, workingmen and boys, eighteen of them, their skulls smashed by clubs, their vital organs pierced by gunfire.

The one city where the Workingmen's party clearly led the rebellion was St. Louis, a city of flour mills, foundries, packing houses, machine shops, breweries, and railroads. Here, as elsewhere, there were wage cuts on the railroads. And here there were perhaps a thousand members of the Workingmen's party, many of them bakers, coopers, cabinetmakers, cigarmakers, brewery workers. The party was organized in four sections, by nationality: German, English, French, Bohemian.

All four sections took a ferry across the Mississippi to join a mass meeting of railroad men in East St. Louis. One of their speakers told the meeting: "All you have to do, gentlemen, for you have the numbers, is to unite on one idea—that the workingmen shall rule the country. What man makes, belongs to him, and the workingmen made this country." Railroaders in East St. Louis declared themselves on strike. The mayor of East St. Louis was a European immigrant, himself an active revolutionist as a youth, and railroad men's votes dominated the city.

In St. Louis, itself, the Workingmen's party called an open-air mass meeting to which five thousand people came. The party was clearly in the leadership of the strike. Speakers, excited by the crowd, became more militant: ". . . capital has changed liberty into serfdom, and we must fight or die." They called for nationalization of the railroads, mines, and all industry.

At another huge meeting of the Workingmen's party a black man spoke for those who worked on the steamboats and levees. He asked: "Will you stand to us regardless of color?" The crowd shouted back: "We will!" An executive committee was set up, and it called for a general strike of all branches of industry in St. Louis.

Handbills for the general strike were soon all over the city. There was a march of four hundred Negro steamboat men and roustabouts along the river, six hundred factory workers carrying a banner: "No Monopoly— Workingmen's Rights." A great procession moved through the city, ending with a rally of ten thousand people listening to Communist speakers: "The people are rising up in their might and declaring they will no longer submit to being oppressed by unproductive capital."

David Burbank, in his book on the St. Louis events, *Reign of the Rabble*, writes:

> Only around St. Louis did the original strike on the railroads expand into such a systematically organized and complete shut-down of all industry that the term general strike is fully justified. And only there did the socialists assume undisputed leadership. . . . no American city has come so close to being ruled by a workers' soviet, as we would now call it, as St. Louis, Missouri, in the year 1877.

The railroad strikes were making news in Europe. Marx wrote Engels: "What do you think of the workers of the United States? This first explosion against the associated oligarchy of capital which has occurred since the Civil War will naturally again be suppressed, but can very well form the point of origin of an earnest workers' party. . . ."

In New York, several thousand gathered at Tompkins Square. The tone of the meeting was moderate, speaking of "a political revolution through the ballot box." And: "If you will unite, we may have here within five years a socialistic republic. . . . Then will a lovely morning break over this darkened land." It was a peaceful meeting. It adjourned. The last words heard from the platform were: "Whatever we poor men may not have, we have free speech, and no one can take it from us." Then the police charged, using their clubs.

In St. Louis, as elsewhere, the momentum of the crowds, the meetings, the enthusiasm, could not be sustained. As they diminished, the police, militia, and federal troops moved in and the authorities took over. The police raided the headquarters of the Workingmen's party and arrested seventy people; the executive committee that had been for a while virtually in charge of the city was now in prison. The strikers surrendered; the wage cuts remained; 131 strike leaders were fired by the Burlington Railroad.

When the great railroad strikes of 1877 were over, a hundred people were dead, a thousand people had gone to jail, 100,000 workers had gone on strike, and the strikes had roused into action countless unemployed in the cities. More than half the freight on the nation's 75,000 miles of track had stopped running at the height of the strikes.

The railroads made some concessions, withdrew some wage cuts, but also strengthened their "Coal and Iron Police." In a number of large cities, National Guard armories were built, with loopholes for guns. Robert Bruce believes the strikes taught many people of the hardships of others, and that they led to congressional railroad regulation. They may have stimulated the business unionism of the American Federation of Labor as well as the national unity of labor proposed by the Knights of Labor, and the independent labor-farmer parties of the next two decades.

In 1877, the same year blacks learned they did not have enough strength to make real the promise of equality in the Civil War, working people learned they were not united enough, not powerful enough, to defeat the combination of private capital and government power. But there was more to come.

11

ROBBER BARONS
AND REBELS

In the year 1877, the signals were given for the rest of the century: the black would be put back; the strikes of white workers would not be tolerated; the industrial and political elites of North and South would take hold of the country and organize the greatest march of economic growth in human history. They would do it with the aid of, and at the expense of, black labor, white labor, Chinese labor, European immigrant labor, female labor, rewarding them differently by race, sex, national origin, and social class, in such a way as to create separate levels of oppression—a skillful terracing to stabilize the pyramid of wealth.

Between the Civil War and 1900, steam and electricity replaced human muscle, iron replaced wood, and steel replaced iron (before the Bessemer process, iron was hardened into steel at the rate of 3 to 5 tons a day; now the same amount could be processed in 15 minutes). Machines could now drive steel tools. Oil could lubricate machines and light homes, streets, factories. People and goods could move by railroad, propelled by steam along steel rails; by 1900 there were 193,000 miles of railroad. The telephone, the typewriter, and the adding machine speeded up the work of business.

Machines changed farming. Before the Civil War it took 61 hours of labor to produce an acre of wheat. By 1900, it took 3 hours, 19 minutes. Manufactured ice enabled the transport of food over long distances, and the industry of meatpacking was born.

Steam drove textile mill spindles; it drove sewing machines. It came from coal. Pneumatic drills now drilled deeper into the earth for coal. In 1860, 14 million tons of coal were mined; by 1884 it was 100 million tons. More coal meant more steel, because coal furnaces converted iron into steel; by 1880 a million tons of steel were being produced; by 1910, 25 million tons. By now electricity was beginning to replace steam. Electrical wire needed copper, of which 30,000 tons were produced in 1880; 500,000 tons by 1910.

To accomplish all this required ingenious inventors of new processes and new machines, clever organizers and administrators of the new corporations, a country rich with land and minerals, and a huge supply of human beings to do the back-breaking, unhealthful, and dangerous work. Immigrants would come from Europe and China, to make the new labor force. Farmers unable to buy the new machinery or pay the new railroad rates would move to the cities. Between 1860 and 1914, New York grew from 850,000 to 4 million, Chicago from 110,000 to 2 million, Philadelphia from 650,000 to 1½ million.

In some cases the inventor himself became the organizer of businesses—like Thomas Edison, inventor of electrical devices. In other cases, the businessman compiled other people's inventions, like Gustavus Swift, a Chicago butcher who put together the ice-cooled railway car with the ice-cooled warehouse to make the first national meat-packing company in 1885. James Duke used a new cigarette-rolling machine that could roll, paste, and cut tubes of tobacco into 100,000 cigarettes a day; in 1890 he combined the four biggest cigarette producers to form the American Tobacco Company.

While some multimillionaires started in poverty, most did not. A study of the origins of 303 textile, railroad, and steel executives of the 1870s showed that 90 percent came from middle- or upper-class families. The Horatio Alger stories of "rags to riches" were true for a few men, but mostly a myth, and a useful myth for control.

Most of the fortune building was done legally, with the collaboration of the government and the courts. Sometimes the collaboration had to be paid for. Thomas Edison promised New Jersey politicians $1,000 each in return for favorable legislation. Daniel Drew and Jay Gould spent $1 million to bribe the New York legislature to legalize their issue of $8 million in "watered stock" (stock not representing real value) on the Erie Railroad.

The first transcontinental railroad was built with blood, sweat, politics and thievery, out of the meeting of the Union Pacific and Central Pacific railroads. The Central Pacific started on the West Coast going east; it spent $200,000 in Washington on bribes to get 9 million acres of free land and $24 million in bonds, and paid $79 million, an overpayment of $36 million, to a construction company which really was its own. The construction was done by three thousand Irish and ten thousand Chinese, over a period of four years, working for one or two dollars a day.

The Union Pacific started in Nebraska going west. It had been given 12 million acres of free land and $27 million in government bonds. It created the Credit Mobilier company and gave them $94 million for construction when the actual cost was $44 million. Shares were sold cheaply to Congressmen to prevent investigation. This was at the suggestion of Massachusetts Congressman Oakes Ames, a shovel manufacturer and director of Credit Mobilier, who said: "There is no difficulty in getting men to look after their own property." The Union Pacific used twenty thousand workers—war veterans and Irish immigrants, who laid 5 miles of track a day and died by the hundreds in the heat, the cold, and the battles with Indians opposing the invasion of their territory.

Both railroads used longer, twisting routes to get subsidies from towns they went through. In 1869, amid music and speeches, the two crooked lines met in Utah.

The wild fraud on the railroads led to more control of railroad finances by bankers, who wanted more stability—profit by law rather than by theft. By the 1890s, most of the country's railway mileage was concentrated in six huge systems. Four of these were completely or partially controlled by the House of Morgan, and two others by the bankers Kuhn, Loeb, and Company.

J. P. Morgan had started before the war, as the son of a banker who began selling stocks for the railroads for good commissions. During the Civil War he bought five thousand rifles for $3.50 each from an army arsenal, and sold them to a general in the field for $22 each. The rifles were defective and would shoot off the thumbs of the soldiers using them. A congressional committee noted this in the small print of an obscure report, but a federal judge upheld the deal as the fulfillment of a valid legal contract.

Morgan had escaped military service in the Civil War by paying $300 to a substitute. So did John D. Rockefeller, Andrew Carnegie, Philip Armour, Jay Gould, and James Mellon. Mellon's father had written to him that "a man may be a patriot without risking his own life or sacrificing his health. There are plenty of lives less valuable."

It was the firm of Drexel, Morgan and Company that was given a U.S. government contract to float a bond issue of $260 million. The government could have sold the bonds directly; it chose to pay the bankers $5 million in commission.

On January 2, 1889, as Gustavus Myers reports:

> ... a circular marked "Private and Confidential" was issued by the three banking houses of Drexel, Morgan & Company, Brown Brothers &

Company, and Kidder, Peabody & Company. The most painstaking care was exercised that this document should not find its way into the press or otherwise become public. . . . Why this fear? Because the circular was an invitation . . . to the great railroad magnates to assemble at Morgan's house, No. 219 Madison Avenue, there to form, in the phrase of the day, an iron-clad combination. . . . a compact which would efface competition among certain railroads, and unite those interests in an agreement by which the people of the United States would be bled even more effectively than before.

There was a human cost to this exciting story of financial ingenuity. That year, 1889, records of the Interstate Commerce Commission showed that 22,000 railroad workers were killed or injured.

In 1895 the gold reserve of the United States was depleted, while twenty-six New York City banks had $129 million in gold in their vaults. A syndicate of bankers headed by J. P. Morgan & Company, August Belmont & Company, the National City Bank, and others offered to give the government gold in exchange for bonds. President Grover Cleveland agreed. The bankers immediately resold the bonds at higher prices, making $18 million profit.

A journalist wrote: "If a man wants to buy beef, he must go to the butcher. . . . If Mr. Cleveland wants much gold, he must go to the big banker."

While making his fortune, Morgan brought rationality and organization to the national economy. He kept the system stable. He said: "We do not want financial convulsions and have one thing one day and another thing another day." He linked railroads to one another, all of them to banks, banks to insurance companies. By 1900, he controlled 100,000 miles of railroad, half the country's mileage.

Three insurance companies dominated by the Morgan group had a billion dollars in assets. They had $50 million a year to invest—money given by ordinary people for their insurance policies. Louis Brandeis, describing this in his book *Other People's Money* (before he became a Supreme Court justice), wrote: "They control the people through the people's own money."

John D. Rockefeller started as a bookkeeper in Cleveland, became a merchant, accumulated money, and decided that, in the new industry of oil, who controlled the oil refineries controlled the industry. He bought his first oil refinery in 1862, and by 1870 set up Standard Oil Company of Ohio, made secret agreements with railroads to ship his oil with them if they gave him rebates—discounts—on their prices, and thus drove competitors out of business.

One independent refiner said: "If we did not sell out. . . . we would be crushed out. . . . There was only one buyer on the market and we had to sell at their terms." Memos like this one passed among Standard Oil officials: "Wilkerson & Co. received car of oil Monday 13th. . . . Please turn another screw." A rival refinery in Buffalo was rocked by a small explosion arranged by Standard Oil officials with the refinery's chief mechanic.

The Standard Oil Company, by 1899, was a holding company which controlled the stock of many other companies. The capital was $110 million, the profit was $45 million a year, and John D. Rockefeller's fortune was estimated at $200 million. Before long he would move into iron, copper, coal, shipping, and banking (Chase Manhattan Bank). Profits would be $81 million a year, and the Rockefeller fortune would total two billion dollars.

Andrew Carnegie was a telegraph clerk at seventeen, then secretary to the head of the Pennsylvania Railroad, then broker in Wall Street selling railroad bonds for huge commissions, and was soon a millionaire. He went to London in 1872, saw the new Bessemer method of producing steel, and returned to the United States to build a million-dollar steel plant. Foreign competition was kept out by a high tariff conveniently set by Congress, and by 1880 Carnegie was producing 10,000 tons of steel a month, making $1½ million a year in profit. By 1900 he was making $40 million a year, and that year, at a dinner party, he agreed to sell his steel company to J. P. Morgan. He scribbled the price on a note: $492,000,000.

Morgan then formed the U.S. Steel Corporation, combining Carnegie's corporation with others. He sold stocks and bonds for $1,300,000,000 (about 400 million more than the combined worth of the companies) and took a fee of 150 million for arranging the consolidation. How could dividends be paid to all those stockholders and bondholders? By making sure Congress passed tariffs keeping out foreign steel; by closing off competition and maintaining the price at $28 a ton; and by working 200,000 men twelve hours a day for wages that barely kept their families alive.

And so it went, in industry after industry—shrewd, efficient businessmen building empires, choking out competition, maintaining high prices, keeping wages low, using government subsidies. These industries were the first beneficiaries of the "welfare state." By the turn of the century, American Telephone and Telegraph had a monopoly of the nation's telephone system, International Harvester made 85 percent of all farm machinery, and in every other industry resources became concentrated, controlled. The banks had interests in so many of these monopolies as to create an interlocking network of powerful corporation directors, each of whom sat on the boards of many other corporations. According to a Senate report of the early twentieth century, Morgan at his peak sat on the board of forty-eight corporations; Rockefeller, thirty-seven corporations.

Meanwhile, the government of the United States was behaving almost exactly as Karl Marx described a capitalist state: pretending neutrality to maintain order, but serving the interests of the rich. Not that the rich agreed among themselves; they had disputes over policies. But the purpose of the state was to settle upper-class disputes peacefully, control lower-class rebellion, and adopt policies that would further the long-range stability of the system. The arrangement between Democrats and Republicans to elect Rutherford Hayes in 1877 set the tone. Whether Democrats or Republicans won, national policy would not change in any important way.

When Grover Cleveland, a Democrat, ran for President in 1884, the general impression in the country was that he opposed the power of monopolies and corporations, and that the Republican party, whose candidate was James Blaine, stood for the wealthy. But when Cleveland defeated Blaine, Jay Gould wired him: "I feel . . . that the vast business interests of the country will be entirely safe in your hands." And he was right.

One of Cleveland's chief advisers was William Whitney, a millionaire and corporation lawyer, who married into the Standard Oil fortune and was appointed Secretary of the Navy by Cleveland. He immediately set about to create a "steel navy," buying the steel at artificially high prices from Carnegie's plants. Cleveland himself assured industrialists that his election should not frighten them: "No harm shall come to any business interest as the result of administrative policy so long as I am President . . . a transfer of executive control from one party to another does not mean any serious disturbance of existing conditions."

The presidential election itself had avoided real issues; there was no clear understanding of which interests would gain and which would lose if certain policies were adopted. It took the usual form of election campaigns, concealing the basic similarity of the parties by dwelling on personalities, gossip, trivialities. Henry Adams, an astute literary commentator on that era, wrote to a friend about the election:

> We are here plunged in politics funnier than words can express. Very great
> issues are involved. . . . But the amusing thing is that no one talks about real

interests. By common consent they agree to let these alone. We are afraid to discuss them. Instead of this the press is engaged in a most amusing dispute whether Mr. Cleveland had an illegitimate child and did or did not live with more than one mistress.

In 1887, with a huge surplus in the treasury, Cleveland vetoed a bill appropriating $100,000 to give relief to Texas farmers to help them buy seed grain during a drought. He said: "Federal aid in such cases ... encourages the expectation of paternal care on the part of the government and weakens the sturdiness of our national character." But that same year, Cleveland used his gold surplus to pay off wealthy bondholders at $28 above the $100 value of each bond—a gift of $45 million.

The chief reform of the Cleveland administration gives away the secret of reform legislation in America. The Interstate Commerce Act of 1887 was supposed to regulate the railroads on behalf of the consumers. But Richard Olney, a lawyer for the Boston & Maine and other railroads, and soon to be Cleveland's Attorney General, told railroad officials who complained about the Interstate Commerce Commission that it would not be wise to abolish the Commission "from a railroad point of view." He explained:

> The Commission ... is or can be made, of great use to the railroads. It satisfies the popular clamor for a government supervision of railroads, at the same time that that supervision is almost entirely nominal.... The part of wisdom is not to destroy the Commission, but to utilize it.

Cleveland himself, in his 1887 State of the Union message, had made a similar point, adding a warning: "Opportunity for safe, careful, and deliberate reform is now offered; and none of us should be unmindful of a time when an abused and irritated people ... may insist upon a radical and sweeping rectification of their wrongs."

Republican Benjamin Harrison, who succeeded Cleveland as President from 1889 to 1893, was described by Matthew Josephson, in his colorful study of the post-Civil War years, *The Politicos:* "Benjamin Harrison had the exclusive distinction of having served the railway corporations in the dual capacity of lawyer and soldier. He prosecuted the strikers [of 1877] in the federal courts ... and he also organized and commanded a company of soldiers during the strike...."

Harrison's term also saw a gesture toward reform. The Sherman Anti-Trust Act, passed in 1890, called itself "An Act to protect trade and commerce against unlawful restraints" and made it illegal to form a "combination or conspiracy" to restrain trade in interstate or foreign commerce. Senator John Sherman, author of the Act, explained the need to conciliate the critics of monopoly: "They had monopolies . . . of old, but never before such giants as in our day. You must heed their appeal or be ready for the socialist, the communist, the nihilist. Society is now disturbed by forces never felt before. . . ."

When Cleveland was elected President again in 1892, Andrew Carnegie, in Europe, received a letter from the manager of his steel plants, Henry Clay Frick: "I am very sorry for President Harrison, but I cannot see that our interests are going to be affected one way or the other by the change in administration." Cleveland, facing the agitation in the country caused by the panic and depression of 1893, used troops to break up "Coxey's Army," a demonstration of unemployed men who had come to Washington, and again to break up the national strike on the railroads the following year.

Meanwhile, the Supreme Court, despite its look of somber, black-robed fairness, was doing its bit for the ruling elite. How could it be independent, with its members chosen by the President and ratified by the Senate? How could it be neutral between rich and poor when its members were often former wealthy lawyers, and almost always came from the upper class? Early in the nineteenth century the Court laid the legal basis for a nationally regulated economy by establishing federal control over interstate commerce, and the legal basis for corporate capitalism by making the contract sacred.

In 1895 the Court interpreted the Sherman Act so as to make it harmless. It said a monopoly of sugar refining was a monopoly in manufacturing, not commerce, and so could not be regulated by Congress through the Sherman Act (*U.S.* v. *E. C. Knight Co.*). The Court also said the Sherman Act could be used against interstate strikes (the railway strike of 1894) because they were in restraint of trade. It also declared unconstitutional a small attempt by Congress to tax high incomes at a higher rate (*Pollock* v. *Farmers' Loan & Trust Company*). In later years it would refuse to break up the Standard Oil and American Tobacco monopolies, saying the Sherman Act barred only "unreasonable" combinations in restraint of trade.

A New York banker toasted the Supreme Court in 1895: "I give you, gentlemen, the Supreme Court of the United States—guardian of the dollar, defender of private property, enemy of spoliation, sheet anchor of the Republic."

Very soon after the Fourteenth Amendment became law, the Supreme Court began to demolish it as a protection for blacks, and to develop it as a protection for corporations. However, in 1877, a Supreme Court decision *(Munn v. Illinois)* approved state laws regulating the prices charged to farmers for the use of grain elevators. The grain elevator company argued it was a person being deprived of property, thus violating the Fourteenth Amendment's declaration "nor shall any State deprive any person of life, liberty, or property without due process of law." The Supreme Court disagreed, saying that grain elevators were not simply private property but were invested with "a public interest" and so could be regulated.

One year after that decision, the American Bar Association, organized by lawyers accustomed to serving the wealthy, began a national campaign of education to reverse the Court decision. Its presidents said, at different times: "If trusts are a defensive weapon of property interests against the communistic trend, they are desirable." And: "Monopoly is often a necessity and an advantage."

By 1886, they succeeded. State legislatures, under the pressure of aroused farmers, had passed laws to regulate the rates charged farmers by the railroads. The Supreme Court that year *(Wabash v. Illinois)* said states could not do this, that this was an intrusion on federal power. That year alone, the Court did away with 230 state laws that had been passed to regulate corporations.

By this time the Supreme Court had accepted the argument that corporations were "persons" and their money was property protected by the due process clause of the Fourteenth Amendment. Supposedly, the Amendment had been passed to protect Negro rights, but of the Fourteenth Amendment cases brought before the Supreme Court between 1890 and 1910, nineteen dealt with the Negro, 288 dealt with corporations.

The justices of the Supreme Court were not simply interpreters of the Constitution. They were men of certain backgrounds, of certain interests. One of them (Justice Samuel Miller) had said in 1875: "It is vain to contend with Judges who have been at the bar the advocates for forty years of railroad companies, and all forms of associated capital. . . ." In 1893, Supreme Court Justice David J. Brewer, addressing the New York State Bar Association, said:

> It is the unvarying law that the wealth of the community will be in the hands of the few. . . . The great majority of men are unwilling to endure that long self-denial and saving which makes accumulations possible . . . and hence it always has been, and until human nature is remodeled always will be true, that the wealth of a nation is in the hands of a few, while the many subsist upon the proceeds of their daily toil.

This was not just a whim of the 1880s and 1890s—it went back to the Founding Fathers, who had learned their law in the era of *Blackstone's Commentaries,* which said: "So great is the regard of the law for private property, that it will not authorize the least violation of it; no, not even for the common good of the whole community."

Control in modern times requires more than force, more than law. It requires that a population dangerously concentrated in cities and factories, whose lives are filled with cause for rebellion, be taught that all is right as it is. And so, the schools, the churches, the popular literature taught that to be rich was a sign of superiority, to be poor a sign of personal failure, and that the only way upward for a poor person was to climb into the ranks of the rich by extraordinary effort and extraordinary luck.

In those years after the Civil War, a man named Russell Conwell, a graduate of Yale Law School, a minister, and author of best-selling books, gave the same lecture, "Acres of Diamonds," more than five thousand times to audiences across the country, reaching several million people in all. His message was that anyone could get rich if he tried hard enough, that everywhere, if people looked closely enough, were "acres of diamonds." A sampling:

> I say that you ought to get rich, and it is your duty to get rich. . . . The men who get rich may be the most honest men you find in the community. Let me say here clearly . . . ninety-eight out of one hundred of the rich men of America are honest. That is why they are rich. That is why they are trusted with money. That is why they carry on great enterprises and find plenty of people to work with them. It is because they are honest men. . . .
>
> . . . I sympathize with the poor, but the number of poor who are to be sympathized with is very small. To sympathize with a man whom God has punished for his sins . . . is to do wrong. . . . let us remember there is not a poor person in the United States who was not made poor by his own shortcomings. . . .

Conwell was a founder of Temple University. Rockefeller was a donor to colleges all over the country and helped found the University of Chicago. Huntington, of the Central Pacific, gave money to two Negro colleges, Hampton Institute and Tuskegee Institute. Carnegie gave money to colleges and to libraries. Johns Hopkins was founded by a millionaire merchant, and millionaires Cornelius Vanderbilt, Ezra Cornell, James Duke, and Leland Stanford created universities in their own names.

The rich, giving part of their enormous earnings in this way, became known as philanthropists. These educational institutions did not encourage dissent; they trained the middlemen in the American system—the teachers, doctors, lawyers, administrators, engineers, technicians, politicians—those who would be paid to keep the system going, to be loyal buffers against trouble.

In the meantime, the spread of public school education enabled the learning of writing, reading, and arithmetic for a whole generation of workers, skilled and semiskilled, who would be the literate labor force of the new industrial age. It was important that these people learn obedience to authority. A journalist observer of the schools in the 1890s wrote: "The unkindly spirit of the teacher is strikingly apparent; the pupils, being completely subjugated to her will, are silent and motionless, the spiritual atmosphere of the classroom is damp and chilly."

Back in 1859, the desire of mill owners in the town of Lowell that their workers be educated was explained by the secretary of the Massachusetts Board of Education:

> The owners of factories are more concerned than other classes and interests in the intelligence of their laborers. When the latter are well-educated and the former are disposed to deal justly, controversies and strikes can never occur, nor can the minds of the masses be prejudiced by demagogues and controlled by temporary and factious considerations.

Joel Spring, in his book *Education and the Rise of the Corporate State*, says: "The development of a factory-like system in the nineteenth-century schoolroom was not accidental."

This continued into the twentieth century, when William Bagley's *Classroom Management* became a standard teacher training text, reprinted thirty times. Bagley said: "One who studies educational theory aright can see in the mechanical routine of the classroom the educative forces that are slowly transforming the child from a little savage into a creature of law and order, fit for the life of civilized society."

It was in the middle and late nineteenth century that high schools developed as aids to the industrial system, that history was widely required in the curriculum to foster patriotism. Loyalty oaths, teacher certification, and the requirement of citizenship were introduced to control both the educational and the political quality of teachers. Also, in the latter part of the century, school officials—not teachers—were given control over textbooks. Laws passed by the states barred certain kinds of textbooks. Idaho and Montana, for instance, forbade textbooks propagating "political" doctrines, and the Dakota territory ruled that school libraries could not have "partisan political pamphlets or books."

Against this gigantic organization of knowledge and education for orthodoxy and obedience, there arose a literature of dissent and protest, which had to make its way from reader to reader against great obstacles. Henry George, a self-educated workingman from a poor Philadelphia family, who became a newspaperman and an economist, wrote a book that was published in 1879 and sold millions of copies, not only in the United States, but all over the world. His book *Progress and Poverty* argued that the basis of wealth was land, that this was becoming monopolized, and that a single tax on land, abolishing all others, would bring enough revenue to solve the problem of poverty and equalize wealth in the nation. Readers may not have been persuaded of his solutions, but they could see in their own lives the accuracy of his observations:

> It is true that wealth has been greatly increased, and that the average of comfort, leisure and refinement has been raised; but these gains are not general. In them the lowest class do not share. . . . This association of poverty with progress is the great enigma of our times. . . . There is a vague but general feeling of disappointment; an increased bitterness among the working classes; a widespread feeling of unrest and brooding revolution. . . . The civilized world is trembling on the verge of a great movement. Either it must be a leap upward, which will open the way to advances yet undreamed of, or it must be a plunge downward which will carry us back toward barbarism. . . .

A different kind of challenge to the economic and social system was given by Edward Bellamy, a lawyer and writer from western Massachusetts, who wrote, in simple, intriguing language, a novel called *Looking Backward*, in which the author falls asleep and wakes up in the year 2000, to find a socialistic society in which people work and live cooperatively. *Looking Backward*, which described socialism vividly, lovingly, sold a million copies in a few years, and over a hundred groups were organized around the country to try to make the dream come true.

It seemed that despite the strenuous efforts of government, business, the church, the schools, to control their thinking, millions of Americans were ready to consider harsh criticism of the existing system, to contemplate other possible ways of living. They were helped in this by the great movements of workers and farmers that swept the country in the 1880s and 1890s. These movements went beyond the scattered strikes and tenants' struggles of the period 1830–1877. They were nationwide movements, more threatening than before to the ruling elite, more danger-ously suggestive. It was a time when revolutionary organizations existed in major American cities, and revolutionary talk was in the air.

In the 1880s and 1890s, immigrants were pouring in from Europe at a faster rate than before. They all went through the harrowing ocean voyage of the poor. Now there were not so many Irish and German immigrants as Italians, Russians, Jews, Greeks—people from Southern and Eastern Europe, even more alien to native-born Anglo-Saxons than the earlier newcomers.

How the immigration of different ethnic groups contributed to the fragmentation of the working class, how conflicts developed among groups facing the same difficult conditions, is shown in an article in a Bohemian newspaper, *Svornost*, of February 27, 1880. A petition of 258 parents and guardians at the Throop School in New York, signed by over half the taxpayers of the school district, said "the petitioners have just as much right to request the teaching of Bohemian as have the German citizens to have German taught in the public schools. . . . In opposition to this, Mr. Vocke claims that there is a great deal of differ-ence between Germans and Bohemians, or in other words, they are superior."

The Irish, still recalling the hatred against them when they arrived, began to get jobs with the new political machines that wanted their vote. Those who became policemen encountered the new Jewish immigrants. On July 30, 1902, New York's Jewish community held a mass funeral for an important rabbi, and a riot took place, led by Irish who resented Jews coming into their neighborhood. The police force was dominantly Irish, and the official investigation of the riot indicated the police helped the rioters: ". . . it appears that charges of unprovoked and most brutal club-bing have been made against policemen, with the result that they were reprimanded or fined a day's pay and were yet retained upon the force."

There was desperate economic competition among the newcomers. By 1880, Chinese immigrants, brought in by the railroads to do the backbreaking labor at pitiful wages, numbered 75,000 in California, almost one-tenth of the population. They became the objects of contin-uous violence. The novelist Bret Harte wrote an obituary for a Chinese man named Wan Lee:

Dead, my revered friends, dead. Stoned to death in the streets of San Francisco, in the year of grace 1869 by a mob of halfgrown boys and Christian school children.

In Rock Springs, Wyoming, in the summer of 1885, whites attacked five hundred Chinese miners, massacring twenty-eight of them in cold blood.

The new immigrants became laborers, housepainters, stonecutters, ditchdiggers. They were often imported en masse by contractors. One Italian man, told he was going to Connecticut to work on the railroad, was taken instead to sulfate mines in the South, where he and his fellows were watched over by armed guards in their barracks and in the mines, given only enough money to pay for their railroad fare and tools, and very little to eat. He and others decided to escape. They were captured at gunpoint, ordered to work or die; they still refused and were brought before a judge, put in manacles, and, five months after their arrival, finally dismissed. "My comrades took the train for New York. I had only one dollar, and with this, not knowing either the country or the language, I had to walk to New York. After forty-two days I arrived in the city utterly exhausted."

Their conditions led sometimes to rebellion. A contemporary observer told how "some Italians who worked in a locality near Deal Lake, New Jersey, failing to receive their wages, captured the contractor and shut him up in the shanty, where he remained a prisoner until the county sheriff came with a posse to his rescue."

A traffic in immigrant child laborers developed, either by contract with desperate parents in the home country or by kidnapping. The children were then supervised by "padrones" in a form of slavery, sometimes sent out as beggar musicians. Droves of them roamed the streets of New York and Philadelphia.

As the immigrants became naturalized citizens, they were brought into the American two-party system, invited to be loyal to one party or the other, their political energy thus siphoned into elections. An article in *L'Italia*, in November 1894, called for Italians to support the Republican party:

> When American citizens of foreign birth refuse to ally themselves with the Republican Party, they make war upon their own welfare. The Republican Party stands for all that the people fight for in the Old World. It is the champion of freedom, progress, order, and law. It is the steadfast foe of monarchial class rule.

There were 5½ million immigrants in the 1880s, 4 million in the 1890s, creating a labor surplus that kept wages down. The immigrants were more controllable, more helpless than native workers; they were culturally displaced, at odds with one another, therefore useful as strike-breakers. Often their children worked, intensifying the problem of an oversized labor force and joblessness; in 1880 there were 1,118,000 children under sixteen (one out of six) at work in the United States. With everyone working long hours, families often became strangers to one another. A pants presser named Morris Rosenfeld wrote a poem, "My Boy," which became widely reprinted and recited:

> I have a little boy at home,
> A pretty little son;
> I think sometimes the world is mine
> In him, my only one. . . .
>
> 'Ere dawn my labor drives me forth;
> Tis night when I am free;
> A stranger am I to my child;
> And stranger my child to me. . . .

Women immigrants became servants, prostitutes, housewives, factory workers, and sometimes rebels. Leonora Barry was born in Ireland and brought to the United States. She got married, and when her husband died she went to work in a hosiery mill in upstate New York to support three young children, earning 65 cents her first week. She joined the Knights of Labor, which had fifty thousand women members in 192 women's assemblies by 1886. She became "master workman" of her assembly of 927 women, and was appointed to work for the Knights as a general investigator, to "go forth and educate her sister working-women and the public generally as to their needs and necessities." She described the biggest problem of women workers: "Through long years of endurance they have acquired, as a sort of second nature, the habit of submission and acceptance without question of any terms offered them, with the pessimistic view of life in which they see no hope." Her report for the year 1888 showed: 537 requests to help women organize, 100 cities and towns visited, 1,900 leaflets distributed.

In 1884, women's assemblies of textile workers and hatmakers went on strike. The following year in New York, cloak and shirt makers, men and women (holding separate meetings but acting together), went on strike. The New York *World* called it "a revolt for bread and butter." They won higher wages and shorter hours.

That winter in Yonkers, a few women carpet weavers were fired for joining the Knights, and in the cold of February, 2,500 women walked out and picketed the mill. Only seven hundred of them were members of the Knights, but all the strikers soon joined. The police attacked the picket line and arrested them, but a jury found them not guilty. A great dinner was held by working people in New York to honor them, with two thousand delegates from unions all over the city. The strike lasted six months, and the women won some of their demands, getting back their jobs, but without recognition of their union.

What was astonishing in so many of these struggles was not that the strikers did not win all that they wanted, but that, against such great odds, they dared to resist, and were not destroyed.

Perhaps it was the recognition that day-to-day combat was not enough, that fundamental change was needed, which stimulated the growth of revolutionary movements at this time. The Socialist Labor party, formed in 1877, was tiny, and torn by internal arguments, but it had some influence in organizing unions among foreign workers. In New York, Jewish socialists organized and put out a newspaper. In Chicago, German revolutionaries, along with native-born radicals like Albert Parsons, formed Social Revolutionary clubs. In 1883, an anarchist congress took place in Pittsburgh. It drew up a manifesto:

> ...All laws are directed against the working people.... Even the school serves only the purpose of furnishing the offspring of the wealthy with those qualities necessary to uphold their class domination. The children of the poor get scarcely a formal elementary training, and this, too, is mainly directed to such branches as tend to producing prejudices, arrogance, and servility; in short, want of sense. The Church finally seeks to make complete idiots out of the mass and to make them forego the paradise on earth by promising a fictitious heaven. The capitalist press, on the other hand, takes care of the confusion of spirits in public life.... The workers can therefore expect no help from any capitalistic party in their struggle against the existing system. They must achieve their liberation by their own efforts. As in former times, a privileged class never surrenders its tyranny, neither can it be expected that the capitalists of this age will give up their rulership without being forced to do it. ...

The manifesto asked "equal rights for all without distinction to sex or race." It quoted the *Communist Manifesto:* "Workmen of all lands, unite! You have nothing to lose but your chains; you have a world to win!"

In Chicago, the new International Working People's Association had five thousand members, published newspapers in five languages, organized mass demonstrations and parades, and through its leadership in strikes was a powerful influence in the twenty-two unions that made up the Central Labor Union of Chicago. There were differences in theory among all these revolutionary groups, but the theorists were often brought together by the practical needs of labor struggles, and there were many in the mid-1880s.

In early 1886, the Texas & Pacific Railroad fired a leader of the district assembly of the Knights of Labor, and this led to a strike which spread throughout the Southwest, tying up traffic as far as St. Louis and Kansas City. Nine young men recruited in New Orleans as marshals, brought to Texas to protect company property, learned about the strike and quit their jobs, saying, "as man to man we could not justifiably go to work and take the bread out of our fellow-workmen's mouths, no matter how much we needed it ourselves." They were then arrested for defrauding the company by refusing to work, and sentenced to three months in the Galveston county jail.

The strikers engaged in sabotage. A news dispatch from Atchison, Kansas:

> At 12:45 this morning the men on guard at the Missouri Pacific roundhouse were surprised by the appearance of 35 or 40 masked men. The guards were corralled in the oil room by a detachment of the visitors who stood guard with pistols . . . while the rest of them thoroughly disabled 12 locomotives which stood in the stalls.

In April, in East St. Louis, there was a battle between strikers and police. Seven workingmen were killed, whereupon workers burned the freight depot of the Louisville & Nashville. The governor declared martial law and sent in seven hundred National Guardsmen. With mass arrests, violent attacks by sheriffs and deputies, no support from the skilled, better-paid workers of the Railway Brotherhoods, the strikers could not hold out. After several months they surrendered, and many of them were blacklisted.

By the spring of 1886, the movement for an eight-hour day had grown. On May 1, the American Federation of Labor, now five years old, called for nationwide strikes wherever the eight-hour day was refused. Terence Powderly, head of the Knights of Labor, opposed the strike, saying that employers and employees must first be educated on the eight-hour day, but assemblies of the Knights made plans to strike. The grand chief of the Brotherhood of Locomotive Engineers opposed the eight-hour day, saying "two hours less work means two hours more loafing about the corners and two hours more for drink," but railroad workers did not agree and supported the eight-hour movement.

So, 350,000 workers in 11,562 establishments all over the country went out on strike. In Detroit, 11,000 workers marched in an eight-hour parade. In New York, 25,000 formed a torchlight procession along Broadway, headed by 3,400 members of the Bakers' Union. In Chicago, 40,000 struck, and 45,000 were granted a shorter working day to prevent them from striking. Every railroad in Chicago stopped running, and most of the industries in Chicago were paralyzed. The stockyards were closed down.

A "Citizens' Committee" of businessmen met daily to map strategy in Chicago. The state militia had been called out, the police were ready, and the Chicago *Mail* on May 1 asked that Albert Parsons and August Spies, the anarchist leaders of the International Working People's Association, be watched. "Keep them in view. Hold them personally responsible for any trouble that occurs. Make an example of them if trouble occurs."

Under the leadership of Parsons and Spies, the Central Labor Union, with twenty-two unions, had adopted a fiery resolution in the fall of 1885:

> Be it Resolved, That we urgently call upon the wage-earning class to arm itself in order to be able to put forth against their exploiters such an argument which alone can be effective: Violence, and further be it Resolved, that notwithstanding that we expect very little from the introduction of the eight-hour day, we firmly promise to assist our more backward brethren in this class struggle with all means and power at our disposal, so long as they will continue to show an open and resolute front to our common oppressors, the aristocratic vagabonds and exploiters. Our war-cry is "Death to the foes of the human race."

On May 3, a series of events took place which were to put Parsons and Spies in exactly the position that the Chicago *Mail* had suggested ("Make an example of them if trouble occurs"). That day, in front of the McCormick Harvester Works, where strikers and sympathizers fought scabs, the police fired into a crowd of strikers running from the scene, wounded many of them, and killed four. Spies, enraged, went to the printing shop of the *Arbeiter-Zeitung* and printed a circular in both English and German:

> Revenge!
>   Workingmen, to Arms!!!
>   . . . You have for years endured the most abject humiliations; . . . you

have worked yourself to death . . . your Children you have sacrificed to the factory lord—in short: you have been miserable and obedient slaves all these years: Why? To satisfy the insatiable greed, to fill the coffers of your lazy thieving master? When you ask them now to lessen your burdens, he sends his bloodhounds out to shoot you, kill you!

. . . To arms we call you, to arms!

A meeting was called for Haymarket Square on the evening of May 4, and about three thousand persons assembled. It was a quiet meeting, and as storm clouds gathered and the hour grew late, the crowd dwindled to a few hundred. A detachment of 180 policemen showed up, advanced on the speakers' platform, ordered the crowd to disperse. The speaker said the meeting was almost over. A bomb then exploded in the midst of the police, wounding sixty-six policemen, of whom seven later died. The police fired into the crowd, killing several people, wounding two hundred.

With no evidence on who threw the bomb, the police arrested eight anarchist leaders in Chicago. The Chicago *Journal* said: "Justice should be prompt in dealing with the arrested anarchists. The law regarding accessories to crime in this State is so plain that their trials will be short." Illinois law said that anyone inciting a murder was guilty of that murder. The evidence against the eight anarchists was their ideas, their literature; none had been at Haymarket that day except Fielden, who was speaking when the bomb exploded. A jury found them guilty, and they were sentenced to death. Their appeals were denied; the Supreme Court said it had no jurisdiction.

The event aroused international excitement. Meetings took place in France, Holland, Russia, Italy, Spain. In London a meeting of protest was sponsored by George Bernard Shaw, William Morris, and Peter Kropotkin, among others. Shaw had responded in his characteristic way to the turning down of an appeal by the eight members of the Illinois Supreme Court: "If the world must lose eight of its people, it can better afford to lose the eight members of the Illinois Supreme Court."

A year after the trial, four of the convicted anarchists—Albert Parsons, a printer, August Spies, an upholsterer, Adolph Fischer, and George Engel—were hanged. Louis Lingg, a twenty-one-year-old carpenter, blew himself up in his cell by exploding a dynamite tube in his mouth. Three remained in prison.

The executions aroused people all over the country. There was a funeral march of 25,000 in Chicago. Some evidence came out that a man named Rudolph Schnaubelt, supposedly an anarchist, was actually an agent of the police, an *agent provocateur,* hired to throw the bomb and thus enable the arrest of hundreds, the destruction of the revolutionary leadership in Chicago. But to this day it has not been discovered who threw the bomb.

While the immediate result was a suppression of the radical movement, the long-term effect was to keep alive the class anger of many, to inspire others—especially young people of that generation—to action in revolutionary causes. Sixty thousand signed petitions to the new governor of Illinois, John Peter Altgeld, who investigated the facts, denounced what had happened, and pardoned the three remaining prisoners. Year after year, all over the country, memorial meetings for the Haymarket martyrs were held; it is impossible to know the number of individuals whose political awakening—as with Emma Goldman and Alexander Berkman, long-time revolutionary stalwarts of the next generation—came from the Haymarket Affair.

(As late as 1968, the Haymarket events were alive; in that year a group of young radicals in Chicago blew up the monument that had been erected to the memory of the police who died in the explosion. And the trial of eight leaders of the antiwar movement in Chicago around that time evoked, in the press, in meetings, and in literature, the memory of the first "Chicago Eight," on trial for their ideas.)

After Haymarket, class conflict and violence continued, with strikes, lockouts, blacklisting, the use of Pinkerton detectives and police to break strikes with force, and courts to break them by law. During a strike of streetcar conductors on the Third Avenue Line in New York a month after the Haymarket Affair, police charged a crowd of thousands, using their clubs indiscriminately: "The New York *Sun* reported: "Men with broken scalps were crawling off in all directions. . . ."

Some of the energy of resentment in late 1886 was poured into the electoral campaign for mayor of New York that fall. Trade unions formed an Independent Labor party and nominated for mayor Henry George, the radical economist, whose *Progress and Poverty* had been read by tens of thousands of workers. George's platform tells something about the conditions of life for workers in New York in the 1880s. It demanded:

1. that property qualifications be abolished for members of juries.
2. that Grand Jurors be chosen from the lower-class as well as from the upperclass, which dominated Grand Juries.
3. that the police not interfere with peaceful meetings.
4. that the sanitary inspection of buildings be enforced.

5. that contract labor be abolished in public works.
6. that there be equal pay for equal work for women.
7. that the streetcars be owned by the municipal government.

The Democrats nominated an iron manufacturer, Abram Hewitt, and the Republicans nominated Theodore Roosevelt, at a convention presided over by Elihu Root, a corporation lawyer, with the nominating speech given by Chauncey Depew, a railroad director. In a campaign of coercion and bribery, Hewitt was elected with 41 percent of the vote, George came second with 31 percent of the vote, and Roosevelt third with 27 percent of the vote. The New York *World* saw this as a signal:

> The deep-voiced protest conveyed in the 67,000 votes for Henry George against the combined power of both political parties, of Wall Street and the business interests, and of the public press should be a warning to the community to heed the demands of Labor so far as they are just and reasonable. . . .

In other cities in the country too, labor candidates ran, polling 25,000 out of 92,000 votes in Chicago, electing a mayor in Milwaukee, and various local officials in Fort Worth, Texas, Eaton, Ohio, and Leadville, Colorado.

It seemed that the weight of Haymarket had not crushed the labor movement. The year 1886 became known to contemporaries as "the year of the great uprising of labor." From 1881 to 1885, strikes had averaged about 500 each year, involving perhaps 150,000 workers each year. In 1886 there were over 1,400 strikes, involving 500,000 workers. John Commons, in his *History of the Labor Movement in the United States*, saw in that:

> . . . the signs of a great movement by the class of the unskilled, which had finally risen in rebellion. . . . The movement bore in every way the aspect of a social war. A frenzied hatred of labour for capital was shown in every important strike. . . . Extreme bitterness toward capital manifested itself in all the actions of the Knights of Labor, and wherever the leaders undertook to hold it within bounds, they were generally discarded by their followers. . . .

Even among southern blacks, where all the military, political, and economic force of the southern states, with the acquiescence of the national government, was concentrated on keeping them docile and working, there were sporadic rebellions. In the cotton fields, blacks were dispersed in their work, but in the sugar fields, work was done in gangs, so there was opportunity for organized action. In 1880, they had struck to get a dollar a day instead of 75 cents, threatening to leave the state. Strikers were arrested and jailed, but they walked the roads along the sugar fields, carrying banners: "A DOLLAR A DAY OR KANSAS." They were arrested again and again for trespassing, and the strike was broken.

By 1886, however, the Knights of Labor was organizing in the sugar fields, in the peak year of the Knights' influence. The black workers, unable to feed and clothe their families on their wages, often paid in store scrip, asked a dollar a day once more. The following year, in the fall, close to ten thousand sugar laborers went on strike, 90 percent of them Negroes and members of the Knights. The militia arrived and gun battles began.

Violence erupted in the town of Thibodaux, which had become a kind of refugee village where hundreds of strikers, evicted from their plantation shacks, gathered, penniless and ragged, carrying their bed clothing and babies. Their refusal to work threatened the entire sugar crop, and martial law was declared in Thibodaux. Henry and George Cox, two Negro brothers, leaders in the Knights of Labor, were arrested, locked up, then taken from their cells, and never heard from again. On the night of November 22, shooting broke out, each side claiming the other was at fault; by noon the next day, thirty Negroes were dead or dying, and hundreds wounded. Two whites were wounded. A Negro newspaper in New Orleans wrote:

> . . . Lame men and blind women shot; children and hoary-headed grandsires ruthlessly swept down! The Negroes offered no resistance; they could not, as the killing was unexpected. Those of them not killed took to the woods, a majority of them finding refuge in this city. . . .
>
> Citizens of the United States killed by a mob directed by a State judge. . . . Laboring men seeking an advance in wages, treated as if they were dogs! . . .
>
> At such times and upon such occasions, words of condemnation fall like snow-flakes upon molten lead. The blacks should defend their lives, and if needs must die, die with their faces toward their persecutors fighting for their homes, their children and their lawful rights.

Native-born poor whites were not doing well either. In the South, they were tenant farmers rather than landowners. In the southern cities, they were tenants, not homeowners. C. Vann Woodward notes (*Origins of the New South)* that the city with the highest rate of tenancy in the United States was Birmingham, with 90 percent. And the slums of the southern cities were among the worst, poor whites living like the blacks, on unpaved dirt streets "choked up with garbage, filth and mud," according to a report of one state board of health.

There were eruptions against the convict labor system in the South, in which prisoners were leased in slave labor to corporations, used thus to depress the general level of wages and also to break strikes. In the year 1891, miners of the Tennessee Coal Mine Company were asked to sign an "iron-clad contract": pledging no strikes, agreeing to get paid in scrip, and giving up the right to check the weight of the coal they mined (they were paid by the weight). They refused to sign and were evicted from their houses. Convicts were brought in to replace them.

On the night of October 31, 1891, a thousand armed miners took control of the mine area, set five hundred convicts free, and burned down the stockades in which the convicts were kept. The companies surrendered, agreeing not to use convicts, not to require the "ironclad contract," and to let the miners check on the weight of the coal they mined.

The following year, there were more such incidents in Tennessee. C. Vann Woodward calls them "insurrections." Miners overpowered guards of the Tennessee Coal and Iron Company, burned the stockades, shipped the convicts to Nashville. Other unions in Tennessee came to their aid. An observer reported back to the Chattanooga Federation of Trades:

> I should like to impress upon people the extent of this movement. I have seen the written assurance of reinforcements to the miners of fully 7500 men, who will be on the field in ten hours after the first shot is fired.... The entire district is as one over the main proposition, "the convicts must go". I counted 840 rifles on Monday as the miners passed, while the vast multitude following them carried revolvers. The captains of the different companies are all Grand Army men. Whites and Negroes are standing shoulder to shoulder.

That same year, in New Orleans, forty-two union locals, with over twenty thousand members, mostly white but including some blacks (there was one black on the strike committee), called a general strike, involving half the population of the city. Work in New Orleans came to a stop. After three days—with strikebreakers brought in, martial law, and the threat of militia—the strike ended with a compromise, gaining hours and wages but without recognition of the unions as bargaining agents.

The year 1892 saw strike struggles all over the country: besides the general strike in New Orleans and the coal miners' strike in Tennessee, there was a railroad switchmen's strike in Buffalo, New York, and a copper miners' strike in Coeur d'Alene, Idaho. The Coeur d'Alene strike was marked by gun battles between strikers and strikebreakers, and many deaths. A newspaper account of July 11, 1892, reported:

> ... The long-dreaded conflict between the forces of the strikers and the nonunion men who have taken their places has come at last. As a result five men are known to be dead and 16 are already in the hospital; the Frisco mill on Canyon Creek is in ruins; the Gem mine has surrendered to the strikers, the arms of its employees have been captured, and the employees themselves have been ordered out of the country. Flushed with the success of these victories the turbulent element among the strikers are preparing to move upon other strongholds of the non-union men. . . .

The National Guard, brought in by the governor, was reinforced by federal troops: six hundred miners were rounded up and imprisoned in bullpens, scabs brought back, union leaders fired, the strike broken.

In early 1892, the Carnegie Steel plant at Homestead, Pennsylvania, just outside of Pittsburgh, was being managed by Henry Clay Frick while Carnegie was in Europe. Frick decided to reduce the workers' wages and break their union. He built a fence 3 miles long and 12 feet high around the steelworks and topped it with barbed wire, adding peepholes for rifles. When the workers did not accept the pay cut, Frick laid off the entire work force. The Pinkerton detective agency was hired to protect strikebreakers.

Although only 750 of the 3,800 workers at Homestead belonged to the union, three thousand workers met in the Opera House and voted overwhelmingly to strike. The plant was on the Monongahela River, and a thousand pickets began patrolling a 10-mile stretch of the river. A committee of strikers took over the town, and the sheriff was unable to raise a posse among local people against them.

On the night of July 5, 1892, hundreds of Pinkerton guards boarded barges 5 miles down the river from Homestead and moved toward the plant, where ten thousand strikers and sympathizers waited. The crowd warned the Pinkertons not to step off the barge. A striker lay down on the gangplank, and when a Pinkerton man tried to shove him aside, he fired, wounding the detective in the thigh. In the gunfire that followed on both sides, seven workers were killed.

The Pinkertons had to retreat onto the barges. They were attacked from all sides, voted to surrender, and then were beaten by the enraged crowd. There were dead on both sides. For the next several days the strikers were in command of the area. Now the state went into action: the governor brought in the militia, armed with the latest rifles and Gatling guns, to protect the import of strikebreakers.

Strike leaders were charged with murder; 160 other strikers were tried for other crimes. All were acquitted by friendly juries. The entire Strike Committee was then arrested for treason against the state, but no jury would convict them. The strike held for four months, but the plant was producing steel with strikebreakers who were brought in, often in locked trains, not knowing their destination, not knowing a strike was on. The strikers, with no resources left, agreed to return to work, their leaders blacklisted.

One reason for the defeat was that the strike was confined to Homestead, and other plants of Carnegie kept working. Some blast furnace workers did strike, but they were quickly defeated, and the pig iron from those furnaces was then used at Homestead. The defeat kept unionization from the Carnegie plants well into the twentieth century, and the workers took wage cuts and increases in hours without organized resistance.

In the midst of the Homestead strike, a young anarchist from New York named Alexander Berkman, in a plan prepared by anarchist friends in New York, including his lover Emma Goldman, came to Pittsburgh and entered the office of Henry Clay Frick, determined to kill him. Berkman's aim was poor; he wounded Frick and was overwhelmed, then was tried and found guilty of attempted murder. He served fourteen years in the state penitentiary. His *Prison Memoirs of an Anarchist* gave a graphic description of the assassination attempt and of his years in prison, when he changed his mind about the usefulness of assassinations but remained a dedicated revolutionary. Emma Goldman's autobiography, *Living My Life*, conveys the anger, the sense of injustice, the desire for a new kind of life, that grew among the young radicals of that day.

The year 1893 saw the biggest economic crisis in the country's history. After several decades of wild industrial growth, financial manipulation, uncontrolled speculation and profiteering, it all collapsed: 642 banks failed and 16,000 businesses closed down. Out of the labor force of 15 million, 3 million were unemployed. No state government voted relief, but mass demonstrations all over the country forced city governments to set up soup kitchens and give people work on streets or parks.

In New York City, in Union Square, Emma Goldman addressed a huge meeting of the unemployed and urged those whose children needed food to go into the stores and take it. She was arrested for "inciting to riot" and sentenced to two years in prison. In Chicago, it was estimated that 200,000 people were without work, the floors and stairways of City Hall and the police stations packed every night with homeless men trying to sleep.

The Depression lasted for years and brought a wave of strikes throughout the country. The largest of these was the nationwide strike of railroad workers in 1894 that began at the Pullman Company in Illinois, just outside of Chicago.

Annual wages of railroad workers, according to the report of the commissioner of labor in 1890, were $957 for engineers, the aristocrats of the railroad—but $575 for conductors, $212 for brakemen, and $124 for laborers. Railroad work was one of the most dangerous jobs in America; over two thousand railroad workers were being killed each year, and thirty thousand injured. The railroad companies called these "acts of God" or the result of "carelessness" on the part of the workers, but the *Locomotive Firemen's Magazine* said: "It comes to this: while railroad managers reduce their force and require men to do double duty, involving loss of rest and sleep . . . the accidents are chargeable to the greed of the corporation."

It was the Depression of 1893 that propelled Eugene Debs into a lifetime of action for unionism and socialism. Debs was from Terre Haute, Indiana, where his father and mother ran a store. He had worked on the railroads for four years until he was nineteen, but left when a friend was killed after falling under a locomotive. He came back to join a Railroad Brotherhood as a billing clerk. At the time of the great strikes of 1877, Debs opposed them and argued there was no "necessary conflict between capital and labor." But when he read Edward Bellamy's *Looking Backward*, it deeply affected him. He followed the events at Homestead, Coeur d'Alene, the Buffalo switchmen's strike, and wrote:

> If the year 1892 taught the workingmen any lesson worthy of heed, it was that the capitalist class, like a devilfish, had grasped them with its tentacles and was dragging them down to fathomless depths of degradation. To escape the prehensile clutch of these monsters, constitutes a standing challenge to organized labor for 1893.

In the midst of the economic crisis of 1893, a small group of railroad workers, including Debs, formed the American Railway Union, to unite all railway workers. Debs said:

A life purpose of mine has been the federation of railroad employees. To unify them into one great body is my object.... Class enrollment fosters class prejudices and class selfishness.... It has been my life's desire to unify railroad employees and to eliminate the aristocracy of labor ... and organize them so all will be on an equality....

Knights of Labor people came in, virtually merging the old Knights with the American Railway Union, according to labor historian David Montgomery.

Debs wanted to include everyone, but blacks were kept out: at a convention in 1894, the provision in the constitution barring blacks was affirmed by a vote of 112 to 100. Later, Debs thought this might have had a crucial effect on the outcome of the Pullman strike, for black workers were in no mood to cooperate with the strikers.

In June 1894, workers at the Pullman Palace Car Company went on strike. One can get an idea of the kind of support they got, mostly from the immediate vicinity of Chicago, in the first months of the strike, from a list of contributions put together by the Reverend William H. Carwardine, a Methodist pastor in the company town of Pullman for three years (he was sent away after he supported the strikers):

Typographical Union #16
Painters and Decorators Union #147
Carpenters' Union No. 23
Thirty-fourth Ward Republican Club
Grand Crossing Police
Hyde Park Water Department
Picnic at Gardener's Park
Milk Dealer's Union
Hyde Park Liquor Dealers
Fourteenth Precinct Police Station
Swedish Concert
Chicago Fire Department
German Singing Society
Cheque from Anaconda, Montana

The Pullman strikers appealed to a convention of the American Railway Union for support:

Mr. President and Brothers of the American Railway Union. We struck at Pullman because we were without hope. We joined the American Railway

Union because it gave us a glimmer of hope. Twenty thousand souls, men, women and little ones, have their eyes turned toward this convention today, straining eagerly through dark despondency for a glimmer of the heaven-sent message you alone can give us on this earth. . . .

You all must know that the proximate cause of our strike was the discharge of two members of our grievance committee. . . . Five reductions in wages. . . . The last was the most severe, amounting to nearly thirty per cent, and rents had not fallen. . . .

Water which Pullman buys from the city at 8 cents a thousand gallons he retails to us at 500 percent advance. . . . Gas which sells at 75 cents per thousand feet in Hyde Park, just north of us, he sells for $2.25. When we went to tell him our grievances he said we were all his "children.". . .

Pullman, both the man and the town, is an ulcer on the body politic. He owns the houses, the schoolhouses, and churches of God in the town he gave his once humble name. . . .

And thus the merry war—the dance of skeletons bathed in human tears—goes on, and it will go on, brothers, forever, unless you, the American Railway Union, stop it; end it; crush it out.

The American Railway Union responded. It asked its members all over the country not to handle Pullman cars. Since virtually all passenger trains had Pullman cars, this amounted to a boycott of all trains—a nationwide strike. Soon all traffic on the twenty-four railroad lines leading out of Chicago had come to a halt. Workers derailed freight cars, blocked tracks, pulled engineers off trains if they refused to cooperate.

The General Managers Association, representing the railroad owners, agreed to pay two thousand deputies, sent in to break the strike. But the strike went on. The Attorney General of the United States, Richard Olney, a former railroad lawyer, now got a court injunction against blocking trains, on the legal ground that the federal mails were being interfered with. When the strikers ignored the injunction, President Cleveland ordered federal troops to Chicago. On July 6, hundreds of cars were burned by strikers.

The following day, the state militia moved in, and the Chicago *Times* reported on what followed:

Company C. Second Regiment . . . disciplined a mob of rioters yesterday afternoon at Forty-ninth and Loomis Streets. The police assisted and . . . finished the job. There is no means of knowing how many rioters were killed or wounded. The mob carried off many of its dying and injured.

A crowd of five thousand gathered. Rocks were thrown at the militia, and the command was given to fire.

> ... To say that the mob went wild is but a weak expression. ... The command to charge was given. ... From that moment only bayonets were used. ... A dozen men in the front line of rioters received bayonet wounds. ...
>
> Tearing up cobble stones, the mob made a determined charge. ... the word was passed along the line for each officer to take care of himself. One by one, as occasion demanded, they fired point blank into the crowd. ... The police followed with their clubs. A wire fence inclosed the track. The rioters had forgotten it; when they turned to fly they were caught in a trap.
>
> The police were not inclined to be merciful, and driving the mob against the barbed wires clubbed it unmercifully. ... The crowd outside the fence rallied to the assistance of the rioters. ... The shower of stones was incessant. ...
>
> The ground over which the fight had occurred was like a battlefield. The men shot by the troops and police lay about like logs. ...

In Chicago that day, thirteen people were killed, fifty-three seriously wounded, seven hundred arrested. Before the strike was over, perhaps thirty-four were dead. With fourteen thousand police, militia, troops in Chicago, the strike was crushed. Debs was arrested for contempt of court, for violating the injunction that said he could not do or say anything to carry on the strike. He told the court: "It seems to me that if it were not for resistance to degrading conditions, the tendency of our whole civilization would be downward; after a while we would reach the point where there would be no resistance, and slavery would come."

Debs, in court, denied he was a socialist. But during his six months in prison, he studied socialism and talked to fellow prisoners who were socialists. Later he wrote: "I was to be baptized in Socialism in the roar of conflict ... in the gleam of every bayonet and the flash of every rifle the class struggle was revealed. ... This was my first practical struggle in Socialism."

Two years after he came out of prison, Debs wrote in the *Railway Times:*

> The issue is Socialism versus Capitalism. I am for Socialism because I am for humanity. We have been cursed with the reign of gold long enough. Money constitutes no proper basis of civilization. The time has come to regenerate society—we are on the eve of a universal change.

Thus, the eighties and nineties saw bursts of labor insurrection, more organized than the spontaneous strikes of 1877. There were now revolutionary movements influencing labor struggles, the ideas of socialism affecting labor leaders. Radical literature was appearing, speaking of fundamental changes, of new possibilities for living.

In this same period, those who worked on the land—farmers, North and South, black and white—were going far beyond the scattered tenant protests of the pre-Civil War years and creating the greatest movement of agrarian rebellion the country had ever seen.

When the Homestead Act was being discussed in Congress in 1860, a Senator from Wisconsin said he supported it:

> . . . because its benign operation will postpone for centuries, if it will not forever, all serious conflict between capital and labor in the older free States, withdrawing their surplus population to create in greater abundance the means of subsistence.

The Homestead Act did not have that effect. It did not bring tranquillity to the East by moving Americans to the West. It was not a safety valve for discontent, which was too great to be contained that way. As Henry Nash Smith says (*Virgin Land*), and as we have seen: "On the contrary, the three decades following its passage were marked by the most bitter and widespread labor trouble that had yet been seen in the United States."

It also failed to bring peace to the farm country of the West. Hamlin Garland, who made so many Americans aware of the life of the farmer, wrote in the preface to his novel *Jason Edwards*: "Free land is gone. The last acre of available farmland has now passed into private or corporate hands." In *Jason Edwards* a Boston mechanic takes his family West, drawn by advertising circulars. But he finds that all land within 30 miles of a railroad has been taken up by speculators. He struggles for five years to pay off a loan and get title to his farm, and then a storm destroys his wheat just before harvest.

Behind the despair so often registered in the farm country literature of that day, there must have been visions, from time to time, of a different way to live. In another Garland novel, *A Spoil of Office*, the heroine speaks at a farmers' picnic:

> I see a time when the farmer will not need to live in a cabin on a lonely farm. I see the farmers coming together in groups. I see them with time to read, and time to visit with their fellows. I see them enjoying lectures in beautiful

halls, erected in every village. I see them gather like the Saxons of old upon the green at evening to sing and dance. I see cities rising near them with schools, and churches, and concert halls and theaters. I see a day when the farmer will no longer be a drudge and his wife a bond slave, but happy men and women who will go singing to their pleasant tasks upon their fruitful farms. When the boys and girls will not go west nor to the city; when life will be worth living. In that day the moon will be brighter and the stars more glad, and pleasure and poetry and love of life come back to the man who tills the soil.

Hamlin Garland dedicated *Jason Edwards*, written in 1891, to the Farmers Alliance. It was the Farmers Alliance that was the core of the great movement of the 1880s and 1890s later known as the Populist Movement.

Between 1860 and 1910, the U.S. army, wiping out the Indian villages on the Great Plains, paved the way for the railroads to move in and take the best land. Then the farmers came for what was left. From 1860 to 1900 the population of the United States grew from 31 million to 75 million; now 20 million people lived west of the Mississippi, and the number of farms grew from 2 million to 6 million. With the crowded cities of the East needing food, the internal market for food was more than doubled; 82 percent of the farm produce was sold inside the United States.

Farming became mechanized—steel plows, mowing machines, reapers, harvesters, improved cotton gins for pulling the fibers away from the seed, and, by the turn of the century, giant combines that cut the grain, threshed it, and put it in bags. In 1830 a bushel of wheat had taken three hours to produce. By 1900, it took ten minutes. Specialization developed by region: cotton and tobacco in the South, wheat and corn in the Midwest.

Land cost money, and machines cost money—so farmers had to borrow, hoping that the prices of their harvests would stay high, so they could pay the bank for the loan, the railroad for transportation, the grain merchant for handling their grain, the storage elevator for storing it. But they found the prices for their produce going down, and the prices of transportation and loans going up, because the individual farmer could not control the price of his grain, while the monopolist railroad and the monopolist banker could charge what they liked.

William Faulkner, in his novel *The Hamlet*, described the man on whom southern farmers depended:

He was the largest landholder . . . in one county, and Justice of the Peace in the next, and election commissioner in both. . . . He was a farmer, a usurer, a veterinarian. . . . He owned most of the good land in the county and held mortgages on most of the rest. He owned the store and the cotton gin and the combined grist mill and blacksmith shop. . . .

The farmers who could not pay saw their homes and land taken away. They became tenants. By 1880, 25 percent of all farms were rented by tenants, and the number kept rising. Many did not even have money to rent and became farm laborers; by 1900 there were 4½ million farm laborers in the country. It was the fate that awaited every farmer who couldn't pay his debts.

Could the squeezed and desperate farmer turn to the government for help? Lawrence Goodwyn, in his study of the Populist movement *(The Democratic Promise)*, says that after the Civil War both parties now were controlled by capitalists. They were divided along North-South lines, still hung over with the animosities of the Civil War. This made it very hard to create a party of reform cutting across both parties to unite working people South and North—to say nothing of black and white, foreign-born and native-born.

The government played its part in helping the bankers and hurting the farmers; it kept the amount of money—based on the gold supply—steady, while the population rose, so there was less and less money in circulation. The farmer had to pay off his debts in dollars that were harder to get. The bankers, getting the loans back, were getting dollars worth more than when they loaned them out—a kind of interest on top of interest. That is why so much of the talk of farmers' movements in those days had to do with putting more money in circulation—by printing greenbacks (paper money for which there was no gold in the treasury) or by making silver a basis for issuing money.

It was in Texas that the Farmers Alliance movement began. It was in the South that the crop-lien system was most brutal. By this system the farmer would get the things he needed from the merchant: the use of the cotton gin at harvest time, whatever supplies were necessary. He didn't have money to pay, so the merchant would get a lien—a mortgage on his crop—on which the farmer might pay 25 percent interest. Goodwyn says "the crop lien system became for millions of Southerners, white and black, little more than a modified form of slavery." The man with the ledger became to the farmer "the furnishing man," to black farmers simply "the Man." The farmer would owe more money every year until finally his farm was taken away and he became a tenant.

Goodwyn gives two personal histories to illustrate this. A white farmer in South Carolina, between 1887 and 1895, bought goods and services from the furnishing merchant for $2,681.02 but was able to pay only $687.31, and finally he had to give his land to the merchant. A black farmer named Matt Brown, in Black Hawk, Mississippi, between 1884 and 1901, bought his supplies from the Jones store, kept falling further and further behind, and in 1905 the last entry in the merchant's ledger is for a coffin and burial supplies.

How many rebellions took place against this system we don't know. In Delhi, Louisiana, in 1889, a gathering of small farmers rode into town and demolished the stores of merchants "to cancel their indebtedness," they said.

In the height of the 1877 Depression, a group of white farmers gathered together on a farm in Texas and formed the first "Farmers Alliance." In a few years, it was across the state. By 1882, there were 120 suballiances in twelve counties. By 1886, 100,000 farmers had joined in two thousand suballiances. They began to offer alternatives to the old system: join the Alliance and form cooperatives; buy things together and get lower prices. They began putting their cotton together and selling it cooperatively—they called it "bulking."

In some states a Grange movement developed; it managed to get laws passed to help farmers. But the Grange, as one of its newspapers put it, "is essentially conservative and furnishes a stable, well-organized, rational and orderly opposition to encroachments upon the liberties of the people, in contrast to the lawless, desperate attempts of communism." It was a time of crisis, and the Grange was doing too little. It lost members, while the Farmers Alliance kept growing.

From the beginning, the Farmers Alliance showed sympathy with the growing labor movement. When Knights of Labor men went on strike against a steamship line in Galveston, Texas, one of the radical leaders of the Texas Alliance, William Lamb, spoke for many (but not all) Alliance members when he said in an open letter to Alliance people: "Knowing that the day is not far distant when the Farmers Alliance will have to use Boycott on manufacturers in order to get goods direct, we think it is a good time to help the Knights of Labor. . . ." Goodwyn says: "Alliance radicalism—Populism—began with this letter."

The Texas Alliance president opposed joining the boycott, but a group of Alliance people in Texas passed a resolution:

Whereas we see the unjust encroachments that the capitalists are making upon all the different departments of labor . . . we extend to the Knights of

Labor our hearty sympathy in their manly struggle against monopolistic oppression and . . . we propose to stand by the Knights.

In the summer of 1886, in the town of Cleburne, near Dallas, the Alliance gathered and drew up what came to be known as the "Cleburne Demands"—the first document of the Populist movement, asking "such legislation as shall secure to our people freedom from the onerous and shameful abuses that the industrial classes are now suffering at the hands of arrogant capitalists and powerful corporations." They called for a national conference of all labor organizations "to discuss such measures as may be of interest to the laboring classes," and proposed regulation of railroad rates, heavy taxation of land held only for speculative purposes, and an increase in the money supply.

The Alliance kept growing. By early 1887, it had 200,000 members in three thousand suballiances. By 1892 farmer lecturers had gone into forty-three states and reached 2 million farm families in what Goodwyn calls "the most massive organizing drive by any citizen institution of nineteenth century America." It was a drive based on the idea of cooperation, of farmers creating their own culture, their own political parties, gaining a respect not given them by the nation's powerful industrial and political leaders.

Organizers from Texas came to Georgia to form alliances, and in three years Georgia had 100,000 members in 134 of the 137 counties. In Tennessee, there were soon 125,000 members and 3,600 suballiances in ninety-two of the state's ninety-six counties. The Alliance moved into Mississippi "like a cyclone," someone said, and into Louisiana and North Carolina. Then northward into Kansas and the Dakotas, where thirty-five cooperative warehouses were set up.

One of the leading figures in Kansas was Henry Vincent, who started a journal in 1886 called *The American Nonconformist and Kansas Industrial Liberator,* saying in the first issue:

> This journal will aim to publish such matter as will tend to the education of the laboring classes, the farmers and the producer, and in every struggle it will endeavor to take the side of the oppressed as against the oppressor. . . .

By 1889, the Kansas Alliance had fifty thousand members and was electing local candidates to office.

Now there were 400,000 members in the National Farmers Alliance. And the conditions spurring the Alliance onward got worse. Corn which had brought 45 cents a bushel in 1870 brought 10 cents a bushel in

1889. Harvesting wheat required a machine to bind the wheat before it became too dry, and this cost several hundred dollars, which the farmer had to buy on credit, knowing the $200 would be twice as hard to get in a few years. Then he had pay a bushel of corn in freight costs for every bushel he shipped. He had to pay the high prices demanded by the grain elevators at the terminals. In the South the situation was worse than anywhere—90 percent of the farmers lived on credit.

To meet this situation, the Texas Alliance formed a statewide cooperative, a great Texas Exchange, which handled the selling of the farmers' cotton in one great transaction. But the Exchange itself needed loans to advance credit to its members; the banks refused. A call was issued to farmers to scrape together the needed capital for the Exchange to operate. Thousands came on June 9, 1888, to two hundred Texas courthouses and made their contributions, pledging $200,000. Ultimately, $80,000 was actually collected. It was not enough. The farmers' poverty prevented them from helping themselves. The banks won, and this persuaded the Alliances that monetary reform was crucial.

There was one victory along the way. Farmers were being charged too much for jute bags (to put cotton in), which were controlled by a trust. The Alliance farmers organized a boycott of jute, made their own bags out of cotton, and forced the jute manufacturers to start selling their bags at 5 cents a yard instead of 14 cents.

The complexity of Populist belief was shown in one of its important leaders in Texas, Charles Macune. He was a radical in economics (antitrust, anticapitalist), a conservative in politics (against a new party independent of the Democrats), and a racist. Macune came forward with a plan that was to become central to the Populist platform—the sub-Treasury plan. The government would have its own warehouses where farmers would store produce and get certificates from this sub-Treasury. These would be greenbacks, and thus much more currency would be made available, not dependent on gold or silver, but based on the amount of farm produce.

There were more Alliance experiments. In the Dakotas, a great cooperative insurance plan for farmers insured them against loss of their crops. Where the big insurance companies had asked 50 cents an acre, the cooperative asked 25 cents or less. It issued thirty thousand policies, covering 2 million acres.

Macune's sub-Treasury plan depended on the government. And since it would not be taken up by the two major parties, it meant (against Macune's own beliefs) organizing a third party. The Alliances went to work. In 1890 thirty-eight Alliance people were elected to Congress. In the South, the Alliance elected governors in Georgia and Texas. It took over the Democratic party in Georgia and won three-fourths of the seats in the Georgia legislature, six of Georgia's ten congressmen.

This was, however, Goodwyn says, "an elusive revolution, because the party machinery remained in the hands of the old crowd, and the crucial chairmanships of important committees, in Congress, in the state legislatures, remained in the hands of the conservatives, and corporate power, in the states, in the nation, could use its money to still get what it wanted."

The Alliances were not getting real power, but they were spreading new ideas and a new spirit. Now, as a political party, they became the People's party (or Populist party), and met in convention in 1890 in Topeka, Kansas. The great Populist orator from that state, Mary Ellen Lease, told an enthusiastic crowd:

> Wall Street owns the country. It is no longer a government of the people, by the people, and for the people, but a government of Wall Street, by Wall Street and for Wall Street. . . . Our laws are the output of a system which clothes rascals in robes and honesty in rags. . . . the politicians said we suffered from overproduction. Overproduction, when 10,000 little children . . . starve to death every year in the U.S. and over 100,000 shop girls in New York are forced to sell their virtue for bread. . . .
>
> There are thirty men in the United States whose aggregate wealth is over one and one-half billion dollars. There are half a million looking for work. . . . We want money, land and transportation. We want the abolition of the National Banks, and we want the power to make loans direct from the government. We want the accursed foreclosure system wiped out. . . . We will stand by our homes and stay by our firesides by force if necessary, and we will not pay our debts to the loan-shark companies until the Government pays its debts to us.
>
> The people are at bay, let the bloodhounds of money who have dogged us thus far beware.

At the People's party national convention in 1892 in St. Louis, a platform was drawn up. The preamble was written by, and read to the assemblage by, another of the great orators of the movement, Ignatius Donnelly:

> We meet in the midst of a nation brought to the verge of moral, political and material ruin. Corruption dominates the ballot box, the legislatures, the Congress, and touches even the ermine of the bench. The people are

demoralized. . . . The newspapers are subsidized or muzzled; public opinion silenced; business prostrate, our homes covered with mortgages, labor impoverished, and the land concentrating in the hands of capitalists.

The urban workmen are denied the right of organization for self-protection; imported pauperized labor beats down their wages; a hireling standing army . . . established to shoot them down. . . . The fruits of the toil of millions are boldly stolen to build up colossal fortunes. . . . From the same prolific womb of governmental injustice we breed two classes—paupers and millionaires. . . .

A People's party nominating convention in Omaha in July of 1892 nominated James Weaver, an Iowa Populist and former general in the Union army, for President. The Populist movement was now tied to the voting system. Their spokesman Polk had said they could "link their hands and hearts together and march to the ballot box and take possession of the government, restore it to the principles of our fathers, and run it in the interest of the people." Weaver got over a million votes, but lost.

A new political party had the job of uniting diverse groups—northern Republicans and southern Democrats, urban workers and country farmers, black and white. A Colored Farmers National Alliance grew in the South and had perhaps a million members, but it was organized and led by whites. There were also black organizers, but it was not easy for them to persuade black farmers that, even if economic reforms were won, blacks would have equal access to them. Blacks had tied themselves to the Republican party, the party of Lincoln and civil rights laws. The Democrats were the party of slavery and segregation. As Goodwyn puts it, "in an era of transcendent white prejudice, the curbing of 'vicious corporate monopoly' did not carry for black farmers the ring of salvation it had for white agrarians."

There were whites who saw the need for racial unity. One Alabama newspaper wrote:

> The white and colored Alliance are united in their war against trusts, and in the promotion of the doctrine that farmers should establish cooperative stores, and manufactures, and publish their own newspapers, conduct their own schools, and have a hand in everything else that concerns them as citizens or affects them personally or collectively.

The official newspaper of the Alabama Knights of Labor, the Alabama *Sentinel*, wrote: "The Bourbon Democracy are trying to down the Alliance with the old cry 'nigger'. It won't work though."

Some Alliance blacks made similar calls for unity. A leader of the Florida Colored Alliance said: "We are aware of the fact that the laboring colored man's interests and the laboring white man's interest are one and the same."

When the Texas People's party was founded in Dallas in the summer of 1891, it was interracial, and radical. There was blunt and vigorous debate among whites and blacks. A black delegate, active in the Knights of Labor, dissatisfied with vague statements about "equality," said:

> If we are equal, why does not the sheriff summon Negroes on juries? And why hang up the sign "Negro", in passenger cars. I want to tell my people what the People's Party is going to do. I want to tell them if it is going to work a black and white horse in the same field.

A white leader responded by urging there be a black delegate from every district in the state. "They are in the ditch just like we are." When someone suggested there be separate white and black Populist clubs which would "confer together," R. M. Humphrey, the white leader of the Colored Alliance, objected: "This will not do. The colored people are part of the people and they must be recognized as such." Two blacks were then elected to the state executive committee of the party.

Blacks and whites were in different situations. The blacks were mostly field hands, hired laborers; most white Alliance people were farm owners. When the Colored Alliance declared a strike in the cotton fields in 1891 for a dollar a day wages for cotton pickers, Leonidas Polk, head of the white Alliance, denounced it as hurting the Alliance farmer who would have to pay that wage. In Arkansas, a thirty-year-old black cotton picker named Ben Patterson led the strike, traveling from plantation to plantation to get support, his band growing, engaging in gun battles with a white posse. A plantation manager was killed, a cotton gin burned. Patterson and his band were caught, and fifteen of them were shot to death.

There was some black-white unity at the ballot box in the South—resulting in a few blacks elected in North Carolina local elections. An Alabama white farmer wrote to a newspaper in 1892: "I wish to God that Uncle Sam could put bayonets around the ballot box in the black belt on the first Monday in August so that the Negro could get a fair vote." There were black delegates to third-party conventions in Georgia: two in 1892, twenty-four in 1894. The Arkansas People's party platform spoke for the "downtrodden, regardless of race."

There were moments of racial unity. Lawrence Goodwyn found in east Texas an unusual coalition of black and white public officials: it had begun during Reconstruction and continued into the Populist period. The state government was in the control of white Democrats, but in Grimes County, blacks won local offices and sent legislators to the state capital. The district clerk was a black man; there were black deputy sheriffs and a black school principal. A night-riding White Man's Union used intimidation and murder to split the coalition, but Goodwyn points to "the long years of interracial cooperation in Grimes County" and wonders about missed opportunities.

Racism was strong, and the Democratic party played on this, winning many farmers from the Populist party. When white tenants, failing in the crop-lien system, were evicted from their land and replaced by blacks, race hatred intensified. Southern states were drawing up new constitutions, starting with Mississippi in 1890, to prevent blacks from voting by various devices, and to maintain ironclad segregation in every aspect of life.

The laws that took the vote away from blacks—poll taxes, literacy tests, property qualifications—also often ensured that poor whites would not vote. And the political leaders of the South knew this. At the constitutional convention in Alabama, one of the leaders said he wanted to take away the vote from "all those who are unfit and unqualified, and if the rule strikes a white man as well as a negro let him go." In North Carolina, the Charlotte *Observer* saw disfranchisement as "the struggle of the white people of North Carolina to rid themselves of the dangers of the rule of negroes and the lower class of whites."

Tom Watson, the Populist leader of Georgia, pleaded for racial unity:

> You are kept apart that you may be separately fleeced of your earnings. You are made to hate each other because upon that hatred is rested the keystone of the arch of financial despotism which enslaves you both. You are deceived and blinded that you may not see how this race antagonism perpetuates a monetary system which beggars both.

According to the black scholar Robert Allen, taking a look at Populism (*Reluctant Reformers*), Watson wanted black support for a white man's party. No doubt, when Watson found this support embarrassing and no longer useful, he became as eloquent in affirming racism as he had been in opposing it.

Still, Watson must have addressed some genuine feelings in poor whites whose class oppression gave them some common interest with blacks. When H. S. Doyle, a young black preacher who supported Watson for Congress, was threatened by a lynch mob, he came to Watson for protection, and two thousand white farmers helped Doyle escape.

It was a time that illustrated the complexities of class and race conflict. Fifteen blacks were lynched during Watson's election campaign. And in Georgia after 1891 the Alliance-controlled legislature, Allen points out, "passed the largest number of anti-black bills ever enacted in a single year in Georgia history." And yet, in 1896, the Georgia state platform of the People's party denounced lynch law and terrorism, and asked the abolition of the convict lease system.

C. Vann Woodward points to the unique quality of the Populist experience in the South: "Never before or since have the two races in the South come so close together as they did during the Populist struggles."

The Populist movement also made a remarkable attempt to create a new and independent culture for the country's farmers. The Alliance Lecture Bureau reached all over the country; it had 35,000 lecturers. The Populists poured out books and pamphlets from their printing presses. Woodward says:

> One gathers from yellowed pamphlets that the agrarian ideologists undertook to re-educate their countrymen from the ground up. Dismissing "history as taught in our schools" as "practically valueless", they undertook to write it over—formidable columns of it, from the Greek down. With no more compunction they turned all hands to the revision of economics, political theory, law, and government.

The *National Economist*, a Populist magazine, had 100,000 readers. Goodwyn counts over a thousand Populist journals in the 1890s. There were newspapers like the *Comrade*, published in the cotton country of Louisiana, and the *Toiler's Friend*, in rural Georgia. Also, *Revolution* was published in Georgia. In North Carolina, the Populist printing plant was burned. In Alabama, there was the *Living Truth*. It was broken into in 1892, its type scattered, and the next year the shop was set afire, but the press survived and the editor never missed an issue.

Hundreds of poems and songs came out of the Populist movement, like "The Farmer Is the Man":

> . . . the farmer is the man
> The Farmer is the man

Lives on credit till the fall
With the interest rates so high
It's a wonder he don't die
And the mortgage man's the one
     that gets it all.

The farmer is the man
The farmer is the man
Lives on credit till the fall
And his pants are wearing thin
His condition it's a sin
He's forgot that he's the man
     that feeds them all.

Books written by Populist leaders, such as Henry Demarest Lloyd's *Wealth Against Commonwealth*, and William Harvey Coin's *Financial School*, were widely read. An Alabama historian of that time, William Garrott Brown, said about the Populist movement that "no other political movement—not that of 1776, nor that of 1860–1861—ever altered Southern life so profoundly."

According to Lawrence Goodwyn, if the labor movement had been able to do in the cities what the Populists did in the rural areas, "to create among urban workers a culture of cooperation, self-respect, and economic analysis," there might have been a great movement for change in the United States. There were only fitful, occasional connections between the farmer and labor movements. Neither spoke eloquently enough to the other's needs. And yet, there were signs of a common consciousness that might, under different circumstances, lead to a unified, ongoing movement.

Norman Pollack says, on the basis of a close study of midwestern Populist newspapers, that "Populism regarded itself as a class movement, reasoning that farmers and workers were assuming the same material position in society." An editorial in the *Farmers' Alliance* spoke of a man working fourteen to sixteen hours a day: "He is brutalized both morally and physically. He has no ideas, only propensities, he has no beliefs, only instincts." Pollack sees that as a homespun version of Marx's idea of workers' alienation from his human self under capitalism, and finds many other parallels between Populist and Marxist ideas.

Undoubtedly, Populists, along with most white Americans, had racism and nativism in their thinking. But part of it was that they simply did not think race as important as the economic system. Thus, the

Farmers' Alliance said: "The people's party has sprung into existence not to make the black man free, but to emancipate all men . . . to gain for all industrial freedom, without which there can be no political freedom. . . ."

More important than theoretical connections were the Populist expressions of support for workers in actual struggles. The *Alliance-Independent* of Nebraska, during the great strike at the Carnegie steel plant, wrote: "All who look beneath the surface will see that the bloody battle fought at Homestead was a mere incident in the great conflict between capital and labor." Coxey's march of the unemployed drew sympathy in the farm areas; in Osceola, Nebraska, perhaps five thousand people attended a picnic in Coxey's honor. During the Pullman strike, a farmer wrote to the governor of Kansas: "Unquestionably, nearly, if not quite all Alliance people are in fullest sympathy with these striking men."

On top of the serious failures to unite blacks and whites, city workers and country farmers, there was the lure of electoral politics—all of that combining to destroy the Populist movement. Once allied with the Democratic party in supporting William Jennings Bryan for President in 1896, Populism would drown in a sea of Democratic politics. The pressure for electoral victory led Populism to make deals with the major parties in city after city. If the Democrats won, it would be absorbed. If the Democrats lost, it would disintegrate. Electoral politics brought into the top leadership the political brokers instead of the agrarian radicals.

There were those radical Populists who saw this. They said fusion with the Democrats to try to "win" would lose what they needed, an independent political movement. They said the much-ballyhooed free silver would not change anything fundamental in the capitalist system. One Texas radical said silver coinage would "leave undisturbed all the conditions which give rise to the undue concentration of wealth."

Henry Demarest Lloyd noted that the Bryan nomination was subsidized in part by Marcus Daly (of Anaconda Copper) and William Randolph Hearst (of the silver interests in the West). He saw through the rhetoric of Bryan that stirred the crowd of twenty thousand at the Democratic Convention ("we have petitioned, and our petitions have been scorned; we have entreated, and our entreaties have been disregarded; we have begged, and they have mocked when our calamity came. We beg no longer; we entreat no more, we petition no more. We defy them!"). Lloyd wrote bitterly:

> The poor people are throwing up their hats in the air for those who promise to lead them out of the wilderness by way of the currency route. . . . The

people are to be kept wandering forty years in the currency labyrinth, as they have for the last forty years been led up and down the tariff bill.

In the election of 1896, with the Populist movement enticed into the Democratic party, Bryan, the Democratic candidate, was defeated by William McKinley, for whom the corporations and the press mobilized, in the first massive use of money in an election campaign. Even the hint of Populism in the Democratic party, it seemed, could not be tolerated, and the big guns of the Establishment pulled out all their ammunition, to make sure.

It was a time, as election times have often been in the United States, to consolidate the system after years of protest and rebellion. The black was being kept under control in the South. The Indian was being driven off the western plains for good; on a cold winter day in 1890, U.S. army soldiers attacked Indians camped at Wounded Knee, South Dakota, and killed three hundred men, women, and children. It was the climax to four hundred years of violence that began with Columbus, establishing that this continent belonged to white men. But only to certain white men, because it was clear by 1896 that the state stood ready to crush labor strikes, by the law if possible, by force if necessary. And where a threatening mass movement developed, the two-party system stood ready to send out one of its columns to surround that movement and drain it of vitality.

And always, as a way of drowning class resentment in a flood of slogans for national unity, there was patriotism. McKinley had said, in a rare rhetorical connection between money and flag:

> . . . this year is going to be a year of patriotism and devotion to country. I am glad to know that the people in every part of the country mean to be devoted to one flag, the glorious Stars and Stripes; that the people of this country mean to maintain the financial honor of the country as sacredly as they maintain the honor of the flag.

The supreme act of patriotism was war. Two years after McKinley became President, the United States declared war on Spain.

12

THE EMPIRE AND
THE PEOPLE

Theodore Roosevelt wrote to a friend in the year 1897: "In strict confidence . . . I should welcome almost any war, for I think this country needs one."

The year of the massacre at Wounded Knee, 1890, it was officially declared by the Bureau of the Census that the internal frontier was closed. The profit system, with its natural tendency for expansion, had already begun to look overseas. The severe depression that began in 1893 strengthened an idea developing within the political and financial elite of the country: that overseas markets for American goods might relieve the problem of underconsumption at home and prevent the economic crises that in the 1890s brought class war.

And would not a foreign adventure deflect some of the rebellious energy that went into strikes and protest movements toward an external enemy? Would it not unite people with government, with the armed forces, instead of against them? This was probably not a conscious plan among most of the elite—but a natural development from the twin drives of capitalism and nationalism.

Expansion overseas was not a new idea. Even before the war against Mexico carried the United States to the Pacific, the Monroe Doctrine looked southward into and beyond the Caribbean. Issued in 1823 when the countries of Latin America were winning independence from Spanish control, it made plain to European nations that the United States considered Latin America its sphere of influence. Not long after, some Americans began thinking into the Pacific: of Hawaii, Japan, and the great markets of China.

There was more than thinking; the American armed forces had made forays overseas. A State Department list, "Instances of the Use of United States Armed Forces Abroad 1798–1945" (presented by Secretary of State Dean Rusk to a Senate committee in 1962 to cite precedents for the use of armed force against Cuba), shows 103 interventions in the affairs of other countries between 1798 and 1895. A sampling from the list, with the exact description given by the State Department:

1852–53—Argentina. Marines were landed and maintained in Buenos Aires to protect American interests during a revolution.

1853—Nicaragua—to protect American lives and interests during political disturbances.

1853–54—Japan—The "Opening of Japan" and the Perry Expedition. [The State Department does not give more details, but this involved the use of warships to force Japan to open its ports to the United States.]

1853–54—Ryukyu and Bonin Islands—Commodore Perry on three visits before going to Japan and while waiting for a reply from Japan made a naval demonstration, landing marines twice, and secured a coaling concession from the ruler of Naha on Okinawa. He also demonstrated in the Bonin Islands. All to secure facilities for commerce.

1854—Nicaragua—San Juan del Norte [Greytown was destroyed to avenge an insult to the American Minister to Nicaragua.]

1855—Uruguay—U.S. and European naval forces landed to protect American interests during an attempted revolution in Montevideo.

1859—China—For the protection of American interests in Shanghai.

1860—Angola, Portuguese West Africa—To protect American lives and property at Kissembo when the natives became troublesome.

1893—Hawaii—Ostensibly to protect American lives and property; actually to promote a provisional government under Sanford B. Dole. This action was disavowed by the United States.

1894—Nicaragua—To protect American interests at Bluefields following a revolution.

Thus, by the 1890s, there had been much experience in overseas probes and interventions. The ideology of expansion was widespread in the upper circles of military men, politicians, businessmen—and even among some of the leaders of farmers' movements who thought foreign markets would help them.

Captain A. T. Mahan of the U.S. navy, a popular propagandist for expansion, greatly influenced Theodore Roosevelt and other American leaders. The countries with the biggest navies would inherit the earth, he said. "Americans must now begin to look outward." Senator Henry Cabot Lodge of Massachusetts wrote in a magazine article:

> In the interests of our commerce . . . we should build the Nicaragua canal, and for the protection of that canal and for the sake of our commercial supremacy in the Pacific we should control the Hawaiian islands and maintain our influence in Samoa. . . . and when the Nicaraguan canal is built, the island of Cuba . . . will become a necessity. . . . The great nations are rapidly absorbing for their future expansion and their present defense all the waste places of the earth. It is a movement which makes for civilization and the advancement of the race. As one of the great nations of the world the United States must not fall out of the line of march.

A Washington *Post* editorial on the eve of the Spanish-American war:

> A new consciousness seems to have come upon us—the consciousness of strength—and with it a new appetite, the yearning to show our strength. . . . Ambition, interest, land hunger, pride, the mere joy of fighting, whatever it may be, we are animated by a new sensation. We are face to face with a strange destiny. The taste of Empire is in the mouth of the people even as the taste of blood in the jungle. . . .

Was that taste in the mouth of the people through some instinctive lust for aggression or some urgent self-interest? Or was it a taste (if indeed it existed) created, encouraged, advertised, and exaggerated by the millionaire press, the military, the government, the eager-to-please scholars of the time? Political scientist John Burgess of Columbia University said the Teutonic and Anglo-Saxon races were "particularly endowed with the capacity for establishing national states . . . they are entrusted . . . with the mission of conducting the political civilization of the modern world."

Several years before his election to the presidency, William McKinley said: "We want a foreign market for our surplus products." Senator Albert Beveridge of Indiana in early 1897 declared: "American factories are making more than the American people can use; American soil is producing more than they can consume. Fate has written our policy for us; the trade of the world must and shall be ours." The Department of State explained in 1898:

> It seems to be conceded that every year we shall be confronted with an increasing surplus of manufactured goods for sale in foreign markets if American operatives and artisans are to be kept employed the year around.

The enlargement of foreign consumption of the products of our mills and workshops has, therefore, become a serious problem of statesmanship as well as of commerce.

These expansionist military men and politicians were in touch with one another. One of Theodore Roosevelt's biographers tells us: "By 1890, Lodge, Roosevelt, and Mahan had begun exchanging views," and that they tried to get Mahan off sea duty "so that he could continue full-time his propaganda for expansion." Roosevelt once sent Henry Cabot Lodge a copy of a poem by Rudyard Kipling, saying it was "poor poetry, but good sense from the expansionist standpoint."

When the United States did not annex Hawaii in 1893 after some Americans (the combined missionary and pineapple interests of the Dole family) set up their own government, Roosevelt called this hesitancy "a crime against white civilization." And he told the Naval War College: "All the great masterful races have been fighting races. . . . No triumph of peace is quite so great as the supreme triumph of war."

Roosevelt was contemptuous of races and nations he considered inferior. When a mob in New Orleans lynched a number of Italian immigrants, Roosevelt thought the United States should offer the Italian government some remuneration, but privately he wrote his sister that he thought the lynching was "rather a good thing" and told her he had said as much at a dinner with "various dago diplomats . . . all wrought up by the lynching."

William James, the philosopher, who became one of the leading anti-imperialists of his time, wrote about Roosevelt that he "gushes over war as the ideal condition of human society, for the manly strenuousness which it involves, and treats peace as a condition of blubberlike and swollen ignobility, fit only for huckstering weaklings, dwelling in gray twilight and heedless of the higher life. . . ."

Roosevelt's talk of expansionism was not just a matter of manliness and heroism; he was conscious of "our trade relations with China." Lodge was aware of the textile interests in Massachusetts that looked to Asian markets. Historian Marilyn Young has written of the work of the American China Development Company to expand American influence in China for commercial reasons, and of State Department instructions to the American emissary in China to "employ all proper methods for the extension of American interests in China." She says (*The Rhetoric of Empire*) that the talk about markets in China was far greater than the actual amount of dollars involved at the time, but this talk was important in shaping American policy toward Hawaii, the Philippines, and all of Asia.

While it was true that in 1898, 90 percent of American products were sold at home, the 10 percent sold abroad amounted to a billion dollars. Walter Lafeber writes *(The New Empire)*: "By 1893, American trade exceeded that of every country in the world except England. Farm products, of course, especially in the key tobacco, cotton, and wheat areas, had long depended heavily on international markets for their prosperity." And in the twenty years up to 1895, new investments by American capitalists overseas reached a billion dollars. In 1885, the steel industry's publication *Age of Steel* wrote that the internal markets were insufficient and the overproduction of industrial products "should be relieved and prevented in the future by increased foreign trade."

Oil became a big export in the 1880s and 1890s: by 1891, the Rockefeller family's Standard Oil Company accounted for 90 percent of American exports of kerosene and controlled 70 percent of the world market. Oil was now second to cotton as the leading product sent overseas.

There were demands for expansion by large commercial farmers, including some of the Populist leaders, as William Appleman Williams has shown in *The Roots of the Modern American Empire*. Populist Congressman Jerry Simpson of Kansas told Congress in 1892 that with a huge agricultural surplus, farmers "must of necessity seek a foreign market." True, he was not calling for aggression or conquest—but once foreign markets were seen as important to prosperity, expansionist policies, even war, might have wide appeal.

Such an appeal would be especially strong if the expansion looked like an act of generosity—helping a rebellious group overthrow foreign rule—as in Cuba. By 1898, Cuban rebels had been fighting their Spanish conquerors for three years in an attempt to win independence. By that time, it was possible to create a national mood for intervention.

It seems that the business interests of the nation did not at first want military intervention in Cuba. American merchants did not need colonies or wars of conquest if they could just have free access to markets. This idea of an "open door" became the dominant theme of American foreign policy in the twentieth century. It was a more sophisticated approach to imperialism than the traditional empire-building of Europe. William Appleman Williams, in *The Tragedy of American Diplomacy*, says:

> This national argument is usually interpreted as a battle between imperialists led by Roosevelt and Lodge and anti-imperialists led by William Jennings Bryan and Carl Schurz. It is far more accurate and illuminating,

however, to view it as a three-cornered fight. The third group was a coalition of businessmen, intellectuals, and politicians who opposed traditional colonialism and advocated instead a policy of an open door through which America's preponderant economic strength would enter and dominate all underdeveloped areas of the world.

However, this preference on the part of some business groups and politicians for what Williams calls the idea of "informal empire," without war, was always subject to change. If peaceful imperialism turned out to be impossible, military action might be needed.

For instance, in late 1897 and early 1898, with China weakened by a recent war with Japan, German military forces occupied the Chinese port of Tsingtao at the mouth of Kiaochow Bay and demanded a naval station there, with rights to railways and coal mines on the nearby peninsula of Shantung. Within the next few months, other European powers moved in on China, and the partition of China by the major imperialist powers was under way, with the United States left behind.

At this point, the New York *Journal of Commerce*, which had advocated peaceful development of free trade, now urged old-fashioned military colonialism. Julius Pratt, a historian of U.S. expansionism, describes the turnabout:

> This paper, which has been heretofore characterized as pacifist, anti-imperialist, and devoted to the development of commerce in a free-trade world, saw the foundation of its faith crumbling as a result of the threatened partition of China. Declaring that free access to the markets of China, with its 400,000,000 people, would largely solve the problem of the disposal of our surplus manufactures, the *Journal* came out not only for a stern insistence upon complete equality of rights in China but unreservedly also for an isthmian canal, the acquisition of Hawaii, and a material increase in the navy—three measures which it had hitherto strenuously opposed. Nothing could be more significant than the manner in which this paper was converted in a few weeks. . . .

There was a similar turnabout in U.S. business attitudes on Cuba in 1898. Businessmen had been interested, from the start of the Cuban revolt against Spain, in the effect on commercial possibilities there. There already was a substantial economic interest in the island, which President Grover Cleveland summarized in 1896:

> It is reasonably estimated that at least from $30,000,000 to $50,000,000 of American capital are invested in the plantations and in railroad, mining, and

other business enterprises on the island. The volume of trade between the United States and Cuba, which in 1889 amounted to about $64,000,000, rose in 1893 to about $103,000,000.

Popular support of the Cuban revolution was based on the thought that they, like the Americans of 1776, were fighting a war for their own liberation. The United States government, however, the conservative product of another revolutionary war, had power and profit in mind as it observed the events in Cuba. Neither Cleveland, President during the first years of the Cuban revolt, nor McKinley, who followed, recognized the insurgents officially as belligerents; such legal recognition would have enabled the United States to give aid to the rebels without sending an army. But there may have been fear that the rebels would win on their own and keep the United States out.

There seems also to have been another kind of fear. The Cleveland administration said a Cuban victory might lead to "the establishment of a white and a black republic," since Cuba had a mixture of the two races. And the black republic might be dominant. This idea was expressed in 1896 in an article in *The Saturday Review* by a young and eloquent imperialist, whose mother was American and whose father was English—Winston Churchill. He wrote that while Spanish rule was bad and the rebels had the support of the people, it would be better for Spain to keep control:

> A grave danger represents itself. Two-fifths of the insurgents in the field are negroes. These men . . . would, in the event of success, demand a predominant share in the government of the country . . . the result being, after years of fighting, another black republic.

The reference to "another" black republic meant Haiti, whose revolution against France in 1803 had led to the first nation run by blacks in the New World. The Spanish minister to the United States wrote to the U.S. Secretary of State:

> In this revolution, the negro element has the most important part. Not only the principal leaders are colored men, but at least eight-tenths of their supporters. . . . and the result of the war, if the Island can be declared independent, will be a secession of the black element and a black Republic.

As Philip Foner says in his two-volume study *The Spanish-Cuban-American War*, "The McKinley Administration had plans for dealing with the Cuban situation, but these did not include independence for the island." He points to the administration's instructions to its minister to Spain, Stewart Woodford, asking him to try to settle the war because it "injuriously affects the normal function of business, and tends to delay the condition of prosperity," but not mentioning freedom and justice for the Cubans. Foner explains the rush of the McKinley administration into war (its ultimatum gave Spain little time to negotiate) by the fact that "if the United States waited too long, the Cuban revolutionary forces would emerge victorious, replacing the collapsing Spanish regime."

In February 1898, the U.S. battleship *Maine*, in Havana harbor as a symbol of American interest in the Cuban events, was destroyed by a mysterious explosion and sank, with the loss of 268 men. There was no evidence ever produced on the cause of the explosion, but excitement grew swiftly in the United States, and McKinley began to move in the direction of war. Walter Lafeber says:

> The President did not want war; he had been sincere and tireless in his efforts to maintain the peace. By mid-March, however, he was beginning to discover that, although he did not want war, he did want what only a war could provide: the disappearance of the terrible uncertainty in American political and economic life, and a solid basis from which to resume the building of the new American commercial empire.

At a certain point in that spring, both McKinley and the business community began to see that their object, to get Spain out of Cuba, could not be accomplished without war, and that their accompanying object, the securing of American military and economic influence in Cuba, could not be left to the Cuban rebels, but could be ensured only by U.S. intervention. The New York *Commercial Advertiser*, at first against war, by March 10 asked intervention in Cuba for "humanity and love of freedom, and above all, the desire that the commerce and industry of every part of the world shall have full freedom of development in the whole world's interest."

Before this, Congress had passed the Teller Amendment, pledging the United States not to annex Cuba. It was initiated and supported by those people who were interested in Cuban independence and opposed to American imperialism, and also by business people who saw the "open door" as sufficient and military intervention unnecessary. But by the spring of 1898, the business community had developed a hunger for action. The *Journal of Commerce* said: "The Teller amendment . . . must be interpreted in a sense somewhat different from that which its author intended it to bear."

There were special interests who would benefit directly from war. In Pittsburgh, center of the iron industry, the Chamber of Commerce advocated force, and the *Chattanooga Tradesman* said that the possibility of war "has decidedly stimulated the iron trade." It also noted that "actual war would very decidedly enlarge the business of transportation." In Washington, it was reported that a "belligerent spirit" had infected the Navy Department, encouraged "by the contractors for projectiles, ordnance, ammunition and other supplies, who have thronged the department since the destruction of the Maine."

Russell Sage, the banker, said that if war came, "There is no question as to where the rich men stand." A survey of businessmen said that John Jacob Astor, William Rockefeller, and Thomas Fortune Ryan were "feeling militant." And J. P. Morgan believed further talk with Spain would accomplish nothing.

On March 21, 1898, Henry Cabot Lodge wrote McKinley a long letter, saying he had talked with "bankers, brokers, businessmen, editors, clergymen and others" in Boston, Lynn, and Nahant, and "everybody," including "the most conservative classes," wanted the Cuban question "solved." Lodge reported: "They said for business one shock and then an end was better than a succession of spasms such as we must have if this war in Cuba went on." On March 25, a telegram arrived at the White House from an adviser to McKinley, saying: "Big corporations here now believe we will have war. Believe all would welcome it as relief to suspense."

Two days after getting this telegram, McKinley presented an ultimatum to Spain, demanding an armistice. He said nothing about independence for Cuba. A spokesman for the Cuban rebels, part of a group of Cubans in New York, interpreted this to mean the U.S. simply wanted to replace Spain. He responded:

In the face of the present proposal of intervention without previous recognition of independence, it is necessary for us to go a step farther and say that we must and will regard such intervention as nothing less than a declaration of war by the United States against the Cuban revolutionists. . . .

Indeed, when McKinley asked Congress for war on April 11, he did not recognize the rebels as belligerents or ask for Cuban independence. Nine days later, Congress, by joint resolution, gave McKinley the power to intervene. When American forces moved into Cuba, the rebels welcomed them, hoping the Teller Amendment would guarantee Cuban independence.

Many histories of the Spanish-American war have said that "public opinion" in the United States led McKinley to declare war on Spain and send forces to Cuba. True, certain influential newspapers had been pushing hard, even hysterically. And many Americans, seeing the aim of intervention as Cuban independence—and with the Teller Amendment as guarantee of this intention—supported the idea. But would McKinley have gone to war because of the press and some portion of the public (we had no public opinion surveys at that time) without the urging of the business community? Several years after the Cuban war, the chief of the Bureau of Foreign Commerce of the Department of Commerce wrote about that period:

> Underlying the popular sentiment, which might have evaporated in time, which forced the United States to take up arms against Spanish rule in Cuba, were our economic relations with the West Indies and the South American republics. . . . The Spanish-American War was but an incident of a general movement of expansion which had its roots in the changed environment of an industrial capacity far beyond our domestic powers of consumption. It was seen to be necessary for us not only to find foreign purchasers for our goods, but to provide the means of making access to foreign markets easy, economical and safe.

American labor unions had sympathy for the Cuban rebels as soon as the insurrection against Spain began in 1895. But they opposed American expansionism. Both the Knights of Labor and the American Federation of Labor spoke against the idea of annexing Hawaii, which McKinley proposed in 1897. Despite the feeling for the Cuban rebels, a resolution calling for U.S. intervention was defeated at the 1897 convention of the AFL. Samuel Gompers of the AFL wrote to a friend: "The sympathy of our movement with Cuba is genuine, earnest, and sincere, but this does not for a moment imply that we are committed to certain adventurers who are apparently suffering from Hysteria. . . ."

When the explosion of the *Maine* in February led to excited calls for war in the press, the monthly journal of the International Association of Machinists agreed it was a terrible disaster, but it noted that the deaths of workers in industrial accidents drew no such national clamor. It pointed to the Lattimer Massacre of September 10, 1897, during a coal strike in Pennsylvania. Miners marching on a highway to the Lattimer mine—Austrians, Hungarians, Italians, Germans—who had originally been imported as strikebreakers but then organized themselves, refused to disperse, whereupon the sheriff and his deputies opened fire, killing nineteen of them, most shot in the back, with no outcry in the press. The labor journal said that the

> ... carnival of carnage that takes place every day, month and year in the realm of industry, the thousands of useful lives that are annually sacrificed to the Moloch of greed, the blood tribute paid by labor to capitalism, brings forth no shout for vengeance and reparation. . . . Death comes in thousands of instances in mill and mine, claims his victims, and no popular uproar is heard.

The official organ of the Connecticut AFL, *The Craftsman*, also warned about the hysteria worked up by the sinking of the *Maine*:

> A gigantic . . . and cunningly-devised scheme is being worked ostensibly to place the United States in the front rank as a naval and military power. The real reason is that the capitalists will have the whole thing and, when any workingmen dare to ask for the living wage . . . they will be shot down like dogs in the streets.

Some unions, like the United Mine Workers, called for U.S. intervention after the sinking of the *Maine*. But most were against war. The treasurer of the American Longshoremen's Union, Bolton Hall, wrote "A Peace Appeal to Labor," which was widely circulated:

> If there is a war, you will furnish the corpses and the taxes, and others will get the glory. Speculators will make money out of it—that is, out of you. Men will get high prices for inferior supplies, leaky boats, for shoddy clothes and pasteboard shoes, and you will have to pay the bill, and the only satisfaction you will get is the privilege of hating your Spanish fellow-workmen, who are really your brothers and who have had as little to do with the wrongs of Cuba as you have.

Socialists opposed the war. One exception was the Jewish *Daily Forward*. *The People*, newspaper of the Socialist Labor party, called the issue of Cuban freedom "a pretext" and said the government wanted war to "distract the attention of the workers from their real interests." The *Appeal to Reason*, another Socialist newspaper, said the movement for war was "a favorite method of rulers for keeping the people from redressing domestic wrongs." In the San Francisco *Voice of Labor* a Socialist wrote: "It is a terrible thing to think that the poor workers of this country should be sent to kill and wound the poor workers of Spain merely because a few leaders may incite them to do so."

But after war was declared, Foner says, "the majority of the trade unions succumbed to the war fever." Samuel Gompers called the war "glorious and righteous" and claimed that 250,000 trade unionists had volunteered for military service. The United Mine Workers pointed to higher coal prices as a result of the war and said: "The coal and iron trades have not been so healthy for some years past as at present."

The war brought more employment and higher wages, but also higher prices. Foner says: "Not only was there a startling increase in the cost of living, but, in the absence of an income tax, the poor found themselves paying almost entirely for the staggering costs of the war through increased levies on sugar, molasses, tobacco, and other taxes. . . ." Gompers, publicly for the war, privately pointed out that the war had led to a 20 percent reduction of the purchasing power of workers' wages.

On May Day, 1898, the Socialist Labor party organized an antiwar parade in New York City, but the authorities would not allow it to take place, while a May Day parade called by the Jewish *Daily Forward*, urging Jewish workers to support the war, was permitted. The Chicago *Labor World* said: "This has been a poor man's war—paid for by the poor man. The rich have profited by it, as they always do. . . ."

The Western Labor Union was founded at Salt Lake City on May 10, 1898, because the AFL had not organized unskilled workers. It wanted to bring together all workers "irrespective of occupation, nationality, creed or color" and "sound the death knell of every corporation and trust that has robbed the American laborer of the fruits of his toil. . . ." The union's publication, noting the annexation of Hawaii during the war, said this proved that "the war which started as one of relief for the starving Cubans has suddenly changed to one of conquest."

The prediction made by longshoreman Bolton Hall, of wartime corruption and profiteering, turned out to be remarkably accurate. Richard Morris's *Encyclopedia of American History* gives startling figures:

> Of the more than 274,000 officers and men who served in the army during the Spanish-American War and the period of demobilization, 5,462 died in the various theaters of operation and in camps in the U.S. Only 379 of the deaths were battle casualties, the remainder being attributed to disease and other causes.

The same figures are given by Walter Millis in his book *The Martial Spirit*. In the *Encyclopedia* they are given tersely, and without mention of the "embalmed beef" (an army general's term) sold to the army by the meatpackers—meat preserved with boric acid, nitrate of potash, and artificial coloring matter.

In May of 1898, Armour and Company, the big meatpacking company of Chicago, sold the army 500,000 pounds of beef which had been sent to Liverpool a year earlier and had been returned. Two months later, an army inspector tested the Armour meat, which had been stamped and approved by an inspector of the Bureau of Animal Industry, and found 751 cases containing rotten meat. In the first sixty cases he opened, he found fourteen tins already burst, "the effervescent putrid contents of which were distributed all over the cases." (The description comes from the *Report of the Commission to Investigate the Conduct of the War Department in the War with Spain*, made to the Senate in 1900.) Thousands of soldiers got food poisoning. There are no figures on how many of the five thousand noncombat deaths were caused by that.

The Spanish forces were defeated in three months, in what John Hay, the American Secretary of State, later called a "splendid little war." The American military pretended that the Cuban rebel army did not exist. When the Spanish surrendered, no Cuban was allowed to confer on the surrender, or to sign it. General William Shafter said no armed rebels could enter the city of Santiago, and told the Cuban rebel leader, General Calixto García, that not Cubans, but the old Spanish civil authorities, would remain in charge of the municipal offices in Santiago.

American historians have generally ignored the role of the Cuban rebels in the war; Philip Foner, in his history, was the first to print García's letter of protest to General Shafter:

> I have not been honored with a single word from yourself informing me about the negotiations for peace or the terms of the capitulation by the Spaniards.
>
> . . . when the question arises of appointing authorities in Santiago de Cuba . . . I cannot see but with the deepest regret that such authorities are not elected by the Cuban people, but are the same ones selected by the Queen of Spain. . . .
>
> A rumor too absurd to be believed, General, describes the reason of your measures and of the orders forbidding my army to enter Santiago for fear of massacres and revenge against the Spaniards. Allow me, sir, to protest against even the shadow of such an idea. We are not savages ignoring the

rules of civilized warfare. We are a poor, ragged army, as ragged and poor as was the army of your forefathers in their noble war for independence. . . .

Along with the American army in Cuba came American capital. Foner writes:

> Even before the Spanish flag was down in Cuba, U.S. business interests set out to make their influence felt. Merchants, real estate agents, stock speculators, reckless adventurers, and promoters of all kinds of get-rich schemes flocked to Cuba by the thousands. Seven syndicates battled each other for control of the franchises for the Havana Street Railway, which were finally won by Percival Farquhar, representing the Wall Street interests of New York. Thus, simultaneously with the military occupation began . . . commercial occupation.

The *Lumbermen's Review,* spokesman for the lumber industry, said in the midst of the war: "The moment Spain drops the reigns of government in Cuba . . . the moment will arrive for American lumber interests to move into the island for the products of Cuban forests. Cuba still possesses 10,000,000 acres of virgin forest abounding in valuable timber . . . nearly every foot of which would be saleable in the United States and bring high prices."

Americans began taking over railroad, mine, and sugar properties when the war ended. In a few years, $30 million of American capital was invested. United Fruit moved into the Cuban sugar industry. It bought 1,900,000 acres of land for about twenty cents an acre. The American Tobacco Company arrived. By the end of the occupation, in 1901, Foner estimates that at least 80 percent of the export of Cuba's minerals were in American hands, mostly Bethlehem Steel.

During the military occupation a series of strikes took place. In September 1899, a gathering of thousands of workers in Havana launched a general strike for the eight-hour day, saying, ". . . we have determined to promote the struggle between the worker and the capitalist. For the workers of Cuba will no longer tolerate remaining in total subjection." The American General William Ludlow ordered the mayor of Havana to arrest eleven strike leaders, and U.S. troops occupied railroad stations and docks. Police moved through the city breaking up meetings. But the economic activity of the city had come to a halt. Tobacco workers struck. Printers struck. Bakers went on strike. Hundreds of strikers were arrested, and some of the imprisoned leaders were intimidated into calling for an end to the strike.

The United States did not annex Cuba. But a Cuban Constitutional Convention was told that the United States army would not leave Cuba until the Platt Amendment, passed by Congress in February 1901, was incorporated into the new Cuban Constitution. This Amendment gave the United States "the right to intervene for the preservation of Cuban independence, the maintenance of a government adequate for the protection of life, property, and individual liberty. . . ." It also provided for the United States to get coaling or naval stations at certain specified points.

The Teller Amendment and the talk of Cuban freedom before and during the war had led many Americans—and Cubans—to expect genuine independence. The Platt Amendment was now seen, not only by the radical and labor press, but by newspapers and groups all over the United States, as a betrayal. A mass meeting of the American Anti-Imperialist League at Faneuil Hall in Boston denounced it, ex-governor George Boutwell saying: "In disregard of our pledge of freedom and sovereignty to Cuba we are imposing on that island conditions of colonial vassalage."

In Havana, a torchlight procession of fifteen thousand Cubans marched on the Constitutional Convention, urging them to reject the Amendment. But General Leonard Wood, head of the occupation forces, assured McKinley: "The people of Cuba lend themselves readily to all sorts of demonstrations and parades, and little significance should be attached to them."

A committee was delegated by the Constitutional Convention to reply to the United States' insistence that the Platt Amendment be included in the Constitution. The committee report, *Penencia a la Convención*, was written by a black delegate from Santiago. It said:

> For the United States to reserve to itself the power to determine when this independence was threatened, and when, therefore, it should intervene to preserve it, is equivalent to handing over the keys to our house so that they can enter it at any time, whenever the desire seizes them, day or night, whether with good or evil design.

And:

> The only Cuban governments that would live would be those which count on the support and benevolence of the United States, and the clearest result of this situation would be that we would only have feeble and miserable governments . . . condemned to live more attentive to obtaining the blessings of the United States than to serving and defending the interests of Cuba. . . .

The report termed the request for coaling or naval stations "a mutilation of the fatherland." It concluded:

> A people occupied militarily is being told that before consulting their own government, before being free in their own territory, they should grant the military occupants who came as friends and allies, rights and powers which would annul the sovereignty of these very people. That is the situation created for us by the method which the United States has just adopted. It could not be more obnoxious and inadmissible.

With this report, the Convention overwhelmingly rejected the Platt Amendment.

Within the next three months, however, the pressure from the United States, the military occupation, the refusal to allow the Cubans to set up their own government until they acquiesced, had its effect; the Convention, after several refusals, adopted the Platt Amendment. General Leonard Wood wrote in 1901 to Theodore Roosevelt: "There is, of course, little or no independence left Cuba under the Platt Amendment."

Cuba was thus brought into the American sphere, but not as an outright colony. However, the Spanish-American war did lead to a number of direct annexations by the United States. Puerto Rico, a neighbor of Cuba in the Caribbean, belonging to Spain, was taken over by U.S. military forces. The Hawaiian Islands, one-third of the way across the Pacific, which had already been penetrated by American missionaries and pineapple plantation owners, and had been described by American officials as "a ripe pear ready to be plucked," was annexed by joint resolution of Congress in July of 1898. Around the same time, Wake Island, 2,300 miles west of Hawaii, on the route to Japan, was occupied. And Guam, the Spanish possession in the Pacific, almost all the way to the Philippines, was taken. In December of 1898, the peace treaty was signed with Spain, officially turning over to the United States Guam, Puerto Rico, and the Philippines, for a payment of $20 million.

There was heated argument in the United States about whether or not to take the Philippines. As one story has it, President McKinley told a group of ministers visiting the White House how he came to his decision:

> Before you go I would like to say just a word about the Philippine business. . . . The truth is I didn't want the Philippines, and when they came to us as a gift from the gods, I did not know what to do with them. . . . I sought counsel from all sides—Democrats as well as Republicans—but got little help.

I thought first we would only take Manila; then Luzon, then other islands, perhaps, also.

I walked the floor of the White House night after night until midnight; and I am not ashamed to tell you, gentlemen, that I went down on my knees and prayed Almighty God for light and guidance more than one night. And one night late it came to me this way—I don't know how it was, but it came:

1. That we could not give them back to Spain—that would be cowardly and dishonorable.

2. That we could not turn them over to France or Germany, our commercial rivals in the Orient—that would be bad business and discreditable.

3. That we could not leave them to themselves—they were unfit for self-government—and they would soon have anarchy and misrule over there worse than Spain's was; and

4. That there was nothing left for us to do but to take them all and to educate the Filipinos, and uplift and civilize and Christianize them, and by God's grace do the very best we could by them, as our fellow men for whom Christ also died. And then I went to bed and went to sleep and slept soundly.

The Filipinos did not get the same message from God. In February 1899, they rose in revolt against American rule, as they had rebelled several times against the Spanish. Emilio Aguinaldo, a Filipino leader, who had earlier been brought back from China by U.S. warships to lead soldiers against Spain, now became leader of the *insurrectos* fighting the United States. He proposed Filipino independence within a U.S. protectorate, but this was rejected.

It took the United States three years to crush the rebellion, using seventy thousand troops—four times as many as were landed in Cuba—and thousands of battle casualties, many times more than in Cuba. It was a harsh war. For the Filipinos the death rate was enormous from battle casualties and from disease.

The taste of empire was on the lips of politicians and business interests throughout the country now. Racism, paternalism, and talk of money mingled with talk of destiny and civilization. In the Senate, Albert Beveridge spoke, January 9, 1900, for the dominant economic and political interests of the country:

Mr. President, the times call for candor. The Philippines are ours forever. . . . And just beyond the Philippines are China's illimitable markets. We will not retreat from either. . . . We will not renounce our part in the mission of our race, trustee, under God, of the civilization of the world. . . .

The Pacific is our ocean. . . . Where shall we turn for consumers of our surplus? Geography answers the question. China is our natural customer. . . . The Philippines give us a base at the door of all the East. . . .

No land in America surpasses in fertility the plains and valleys of Luzon. Rice and coffee, sugar and cocoanuts, hemp and tobacco. . . . The wood of the Philippines can supply the furniture of the world for a century to come. At Cebu the best informed man on the island told me that 40 miles of Cebu's mountain chain are practically mountains of coal. . . .

I have a nugget of pure gold picked up in its present form on the banks of a Philippine creek. . . .

My own belief is that there are not 100 men among them who comprehend what Anglo-Saxon self-government even means, and there are over 5,000,000 people to be governed.

It has been charged that our conduct of the war has been cruel. Senators, it has been the reverse. . . . Senators must remember that we are not dealing with Americans or Europeans. We are dealing with Orientals.

The fighting with the rebels began, McKinley said, when the insurgents attacked American forces. But later, American soldiers testified that the United States had fired the first shot. After the war, an army officer speaking in Boston's Faneuil Hall said his colonel had given him orders to provoke a conflict with the insurgents.

In February 1899, a banquet took place in Boston to celebrate the Senate's ratification of the peace treaty with Spain. President McKinley himself had been invited by the wealthy textile manufacturer W. B. Plunkett to speak. It was the biggest banquet in the nation's history: two thousand diners, four hundred waiters. McKinley said that "no imperial designs lurk in the American mind," and at the same banquet, to the same diners, his Postmaster General, Charles Emory Smith, said that "what we want is a market for our surplus."

William James, the Harvard philosopher, wrote a letter to the Boston *Transcript* about "the cold pot grease of McKinley's cant at the recent Boston banquet" and said the Philippine operation "reeked of the infernal adroitness of the great department store, which has reached perfect expertness in the art of killing silently, and with no public squalling or commotion, the neighboring small concerns."

James was part of a movement of prominent American businessmen, politicians, and intellectuals who formed the Anti-Imperialist League in 1898 and carried on a long campaign to educate the American public about the horrors of the Philippine war and the evils of imperialism. It was an odd group (Andrew Carnegie belonged), including antilabor aristocrats and scholars, united in a common moral outrage at what was being done to the Filipinos in the name of freedom. Whatever their differences on other matters, they would all agree with William James's angry statement: "God damn the U.S. for its vile conduct in the Philippine Isles."

The Anti-Imperialist League published the letters of soldiers doing duty in the Philippines. A captain from Kansas wrote: "Caloocan was supposed to contain 17,000 inhabitants. The Twentieth Kansas swept through it, and now Caloocan contains not one living native." A private from the same outfit said he had "with my own hand set fire to over fifty houses of Filipinos after the victory at Caloocan. Women and children were wounded by our fire."

A volunteer from the state of Washington wrote: "Our fighting blood was up, and we all wanted to kill 'niggers.' . . . This shooting human beings beats rabbit hunting all to pieces."

It was a time of intense racism in the United States. In the years between 1889 and 1903, on the average, every week, two Negroes were lynched by mobs—hanged, burned, mutilated. The Filipinos were brown-skinned, physically identifiable, strange-speaking and strange-looking to Americans. To the usual indiscriminate brutality of war was thus added the factor of racial hostility.

In November 1901, the Manila correspondent of the Philadelphia *Ledger* reported:

> The present war is no bloodless, opera bouffe engagement; our men have been relentless, have killed to exterminate men, women, children, prisoners and captives, active insurgents and suspected people from lads of ten up, the idea prevailing that the Filipino as such was little better than a dog. . . . Our soldiers have pumped salt water into men to make them talk, and have taken prisoners people who held up their hands and peacefully surrendered, and an hour later, without an atom of evidence to show that they were even *insurrectos*, stood them on a bridge and shot them down one by one, to drop into the water below and float down, as examples to those who found their bullet-loaded corpses.

Early in 1901 an American general returning to the United States from southern Luzon said:

> One-sixth of the natives of Luzon have either been killed or have died of the dengue fever in the last few years. The loss of life by killing alone has been very great, but I think not one man has been slain except where his death has

served the legitimate purposes of war. It has been necessary to adopt what in other countries would probably be thought harsh measures.

Secretary of War Elihu Root responded to the charges of brutality: "The war in the Philippines has been conducted by the American army with scrupulous regard for the rules of civilized warfare. . . . with self-restraint and with humanity never surpassed."

In Manila, a Marine named Littletown Waller, a major, was accused of shooting eleven defenseless Filipinos, without trial, on the island of Samar. Other marine officers described his testimony:

> The major said that General Smith instructed him to kill and burn, and said that the more he killed and burned the better pleased he would be; that it was no time to take prisoners, and that he was to make Samar a howling wilderness. Major Waller asked General Smith to define the age limit for killing, and he replied "Everything over ten."

In the province of Batangas, the secretary of the province estimated that of the population of 300,000, one-third had been killed by combat, famine, or disease.

Mark Twain commented on the Philippine war:

> We have pacified some thousands of the islanders and buried them; destroyed their fields; burned their villages, and turned their widows and orphans out-of-doors; furnished heartbreak by exile to some dozens of disagreeable patriots; subjugated the remaining ten millions by Benevolent Assimilation, which is the pious new name of the musket; we have acquired property in the three hundred concubines and other slaves of our business partner, the Sultan of Sulu, and hoisted our protecting flag over that swag.
>
> And so, by these Providences of God—and the phrase is the government's, not mine—we are a World Power.

American firepower was overwhelmingly superior to anything the Filipino rebels could put together. In the very first battle, Admiral Dewey steamed up the Pasig River and fired 500-pound shells into the Filipino trenches. Dead Filipinos were piled so high that the Americans used their bodies for breastworks. A British witness said: "This is not war; it is simply massacre and murderous butchery." He was wrong; it was war.

For the rebels to hold out against such odds for years meant that they had the support of the population. General Arthur MacArthur, commander of the Filipino war, said: ". . . I believed that Aguinaldo's troops represented only a faction. I did not like to believe that the whole population of Luzon—the native population, that is—was opposed to us." But he said he was "reluctantly compelled" to believe this because the guerrilla tactics of the Filipino army "depended upon almost complete unity of action of the entire native population."

Despite the growing evidence of brutality and the work of the Anti-Imperialist League, some of the trade unions in the United States supported the action in the Philippines. The Typographical Union said it liked the idea of annexing more territory because English-language schools in those areas would help the printing trade. The publication of the glassmakers saw value in new territories that would buy glass. The railroad brotherhoods saw shipment of U.S. goods to the new territories meaning more work for railroad workers. Some unions repeated what big business was saying, that territorial expansion, by creating a market for surplus goods, would prevent another depression.

On the other hand, when the *Leather Workers' Journal* wrote that an increase in wages at home would solve the problem of surplus by creating more purchasing power inside the country, the *Carpenters' Journal* asked: "How much better off are the workingmen of England through all its colonial possessions?" The *National Labor Tribune*, publication of the Iron, Steel, and Tin Workers, agreed that the Philippines were rich with resources, but added:

> The same can be said of this country, but if anybody were to ask you if you owned a coal mine, a sugar plantation, or railroad you would have to say no . . . all those things are in the hands of the trusts controlled by a few. . . .

When the treaty for annexation of the Philippines was up for debate in Congress in early 1899, the Central Labor Unions of Boston and New York opposed it. There was a mass meeting in New York against annexation. The Anti-Imperialist League circulated more than a million pieces of literature against taking the Philippines. (Foner says that while the League was organized and dominated by intellectuals and business people, a large part of its half-million members were working-class people, including women and blacks.) Locals of the League held meetings all over the country. The campaign against the Treaty was a powerful one, and when the Senate did ratify it, it was by one vote.

The mixed reactions of labor to the war—lured by economic advantage, yet repelled by capitalist expansion and violence—ensured that labor could not unite either to stop the war or to conduct class war against the system at home. The reactions of black soldiers to the war were also mixed: there was the simple need to get ahead in a society where opportunities for success were denied the black man, and the military life gave such possibilities. There was race pride, the need to show that blacks were as courageous, as patriotic, as anyone else. And yet, there was with all this the consciousness of a brutal war, fought against colored people, a counterpart of the violence committed against black people in the United States.

Willard Gatewood, in his book *Smoked Yankees and the Struggle for Empire*, reproduces and analyzes 114 letters to Negro newspapers written by black soldiers in the period 1898–1902. The letters show all those conflicting emotions. Black soldiers encamped in Tampa, Florida, ran into bitter race hatred by white inhabitants there. And then, after they fought with distinction in Cuba, Negroes were not rewarded with officers' commissions; white officers commanded black regiments.

Negro soldiers in Lakeland, Florida, pistol-whipped a drugstore owner when he refused to serve one of them, and then, in a confrontation with a white crowd, killed a civilian. In Tampa, a race riot began when drunken white soldiers used a Negro child as a target to show their marksmanship; Negro soldiers retaliated, and then the streets "ran red with negro blood," according to press dispatches. Twenty-seven Negro soldiers and three whites were severely wounded. The chaplain of a black regiment in Tampa wrote to the Cleveland *Gazette:*

> Is America any better than Spain? Has she not subjects in her very midst who are murdered daily without a trial of judge or jury? Has she not subjects in her own borders whose children are half-fed and half-clothed, because their father's skin is black. . . . Yet the Negro is loyal to his country's flag.

The same chaplain, George Prioleau, talks of black veterans of the Cuban war "unkindly and sneeringly received" in Kansas City, Missouri. He says that "these black boys, heroes of our country, were not allowed to stand at the counters of restaurants and eat a sandwich and drink a cup of coffee, while the white soldiers were welcomed and invited to sit down at the tables and eat free of cost."

But it was the Filipino situation that aroused many blacks in the United States to militant opposition to the war. The senior bishop of the African Methodist Episcopal Church, Henry M. Turner, called the campaign in the Philippines "an unholy war of conquest" and referred to the Filipinos as "sable patriots."

There were four black regiments on duty in the Philippines. Many of the black soldiers established rapport with the brown-skinned natives on the islands, and were angered by the term "nigger" used by white troops to describe the Filipinos. An "unusually large number" of black troops deserted during the Philippines campaign, Gatewood says. The Filipino rebels often addressed themselves to "The Colored American Soldier" in posters, reminding them of lynchings back home, asking them not to serve the white imperialist against other colored people.

Some deserters joined the Filipino rebels. The most famous of these was David Fagan of the 24th Infantry. According to Gatewood: "He accepted a commission in the insurgent army and for two years wreaked havoc upon the American forces."

From the Philippines, William Simms wrote:

I was struck by a question a little Filipino boy asked me, which ran about this way: "Why does the American Negro come . . . to fight us where we are much a friend to him and have not done anything to him. He is all the same as me and me all the same as you. Why don't you fight those people in America who burn Negroes, that make a beast of you . . . ?"

Another soldier's letter of 1899:

Our racial sympathies would naturally be with the Filipinos. They are fighting manfully for what they conceive to be their best interests. But we cannot for the sake of sentiment turn our back upon our own country.

Patrick Mason, a sergeant in the 24th Infantry, wrote to the Cleveland *Gazette*, which had taken a strong stand against annexation of the Philippines:

Dear Sir: I have not had any fighting to do since I have been here and don't care to do any. I feel sorry for these people and all that have come under the control of the United States. I don't believe they will be justly dealt by. The first thing in the morning is the "Nigger" and the last thing at night is the "Nigger." . . . You are right in your opinions. I must not say much as I am a soldier. . . .

A black infantryman named William Fulbright wrote from Manila in June 1901 to the editor of a paper in Indianapolis: "This struggle on the islands has been naught but a gigantic scheme of robbery and oppression."

Back home, while the war against the Filipinos was going on, a group of Massachusetts Negroes addressed a message to President McKinley:

We the colored people of Massachusetts in mass meeting assembled . . . have resolved to address ourselves to you in an open letter, notwithstanding your extraordinary, your incomprehensible silence on the subject of our wrongs. . . .

. . . you have seen our sufferings, witnessed from your high place our awful wrongs and miseries, and yet you have at no time and on no occasion opened your lips on our behalf. . . .

With one accord, with an anxiety that wrenched our hearts with cruel hopes and fears, the Colored people of the United States turned to you when Wilmington, North Carolina was held for two dreadful days and nights in the clutch of a bloody revolution; when Negroes, guilty of no crime except the color of their skin and a desire to exercise the rights of their American citizenship, were butchered like dogs in the streets of that ill-fated town . . . for want of federal aid, which you would not and did not furnish. . . .

It was the same thing with that terrible ebullition of mob spirit at Phoenix, South Carolina, when black men were hunted and murdered, and white men [these were white radicals in Phoenix] shot and driven out of that place by a set of white savages. . . . We looked in vain for some word or some act from you. . . .

And when you made your Southern tour a little later, and we saw how cunningly you catered to Southern race prejudice. . . . How you preached patience, industry, moderation to your long-suffering black fellow citizens, and patriotism, jingoism and imperialism to your white ones. . . .

The "patience, industry, and moderation" preached to blacks, the "patriotism" preached to whites, did not fully sink in. In the first years of the twentieth century, despite all the demonstrated power of the state, large numbers of blacks, whites, men, women became impatient, immoderate, unpatriotic.

13

THE SOCIALIST CHALLENGE

War and jingoism might postpone, but could not fully suppress, the class anger that came from the realities of ordinary life. As the twentieth century opened, that anger reemerged. Emma Goldman, the anarchist and feminist, whose political consciousness was shaped by factory work, the Haymarket executions, the Homestead strike, the long prison term of her lover and comrade, Alexander Berkman, the depression of the 1890s, the strike struggles of New York, her own imprisonment on Blackwell's Island, spoke at a meeting some years after the Spanish-American war:

> How our hearts burned with indignation against the atrocious Spaniards! . . . But when the smoke was over, the dead buried, and the cost of the war came back to the people in an increase in the price of commodities and rent—that is, when we sobered up from our patriotic spree—it suddenly dawned on us that the cause of the Spanish-American war was the price of sugar. . . . that the lives, blood, and money of the American people were used to protect the interests of the American capitalists.

Mark Twain was neither an anarchist nor a radical. By 1900, at sixty-five, he was a world-acclaimed writer of funny-serious-American-to-the-bone stories. He watched the United States and other Western countries go about the world and wrote in the New York *Herald* as the century began: "I bring you the stately matron named Christendom, returning bedraggled, besmirched, and dishonored from pirate raids in Kiao-Chou, Manchuria, South Africa, and the Philippines, with her soul full of meanness, her pocket full of boodle, and her mouth full of pious hypocrisies."

There were writers of the early twentieth century who spoke for socialism or criticized the capitalist system harshly—not obscure pamphleteers, but among the most famous of American literary figures, whose books were read by millions: Upton Sinclair, Jack London, Theodore Dreiser, Frank Norris.

Upton Sinclair's novel *The Jungle*, published in 1906, brought the conditions in the meatpacking plants of Chicago to the shocked attention of the whole country, and stimulated demand for laws regulating the meat industry. But also, through the story of an immigrant laborer, Jurgis Rudkus, it spoke of socialism, of how beautiful life might be if people cooperatively owned and worked and shared the riches of the earth. *The Jungle* was first published in the Socialist newspaper *Appeal to Reason*; it was then read by millions as a book, and was translated into seventeen languages.

One of the influences on Upton Sinclair's thinking was a book, *People of the Abyss*, by Jack London. London was a member of the Socialist party. He had come out of the slums of San Francisco, the child of an unwed mother. He had been a newsboy, a cannery worker, a sailor, a fisherman, had worked in a jute mill and a laundry, hoboed the railroads to the East Coast, been clubbed by a policeman on the streets of New York and arrested for vagrancy in Niagara Falls, watched men beaten and tortured in jail, pirated oysters in San Francisco Bay, read Flaubert, Tolstoy, Melville, and the *Communist Manifesto*, preached socialism in the Alaskan gold camps in the winter of 1896, sailed 2,000 miles back through the Bering Sea, and became a world-famous writer of adventure books. In 1906, he wrote his novel *The Iron Heel*, with its warning of a fascist America, its ideal of a socialist brotherhood of man. In the course of it, through his characters, he indicts the system.

> In the face of the facts that modern man lives more wretchedly than the cave-man, and that his producing power is a thousand times greater than that of the cave-man, no other conclusion is possible than that the capitalist class has mismanaged . . . criminally and selfishly mismanaged.

And with this attack, the vision:

> Let us not destroy those wonderful machines that produce efficiently and cheaply. Let us control them. Let us profit by their efficiency and cheapness. Let us run them for ourselves. That, gentlemen, is socialism. . . .

It was a time when even a self-exiled literary figure living in Europe and not prone to political statements—the novelist Henry James—could tour the United States in 1904 and see the country as a "huge Rappacini garden, rank with each variety of the poison-plant of the money passion."

"Muckrakers," who raked up the mud and the muck, contributed to the atmosphere of dissent by simply telling what they saw. Some of the new mass-circulation magazines, ironically enough in the interest of profit, printed their articles: Ida Tarbell's exposure of the Standard Oil Company; Lincoln Steffens's stories of corruption in the major American cities.

By 1900, neither the patriotism of the war nor the absorption of energy in elections could disguise the troubles of the system. The process of business concentration had gone forward; the control by bankers had become more clear. As technology developed and corporations became larger, they needed more capital, and it was the bankers who had this capital. By 1904, more than a thousand railroad lines had been consolidated into six great combinations, each allied with either Morgan or Rockefeller interests. As Cochran and Miller say:

> The imperial leader of the new oligarchy was the House of Morgan. In its operations it was ably assisted by the First National Bank of New York (directed by George F. Baker) and the National City Bank of New York (presided over by James Stillman, agent of the Rockefeller interests). Among them, these three men and their financial associates occupied 341 directorships in 112 great corporations. The total resources of these corporations in 1912 was $22,245,000,000, more than the assessed value of all property in the twenty-two states and territories west of the Mississippi River. . . .

Morgan had always wanted regularity, stability, predictability. An associate of his said in 1901:

> With a man like Mr. Morgan at the head of a great industry, as against the old plan of many diverse interests in it, production would become more regular, labor would be more steadily employed at better wages, and panics caused by over-production would become a thing of the past.

But even Morgan and his associates were not in complete control of such a system. In 1907, there was a panic, financial collapse, and crisis. True, the very big businesses were not hurt, but profits after 1907 were not as high as capitalists wanted, industry was not expanding as fast as it might, and industrialists began to look for ways to cut costs.

One way was Taylorism. Frederick W. Taylor had been a steel company foreman who closely analyzed every job in the mill, and worked out a system of finely detailed division of labor, increased mechanization, and piecework wage systems, to increase production and profits. In 1911, he published a book on "scientific management" that became powerfully influential in the business world. Now management could control every detail of the worker's energy and time in the factory. As Harry Braverman said (*Labor and Monopoly Capital*), the purpose of Taylorism was to make workers interchangeable, able to do the simple tasks that the new division of labor required—like standard parts divested of individuality and humanity, bought and sold as commodities.

It was a system well fitted for the new auto industry. In 1909, Ford sold 10,607 autos; in 1913, 168,000; in 1914, 248,000 (45 percent of all autos produced). The profit: $30 million.

With immigrants a larger proportion of the labor force (in the Carnegie plants of Allegheny County in 1907, of the 14,359 common laborers, 11,694 were Eastern Europeans), Taylorism, with its simplified unskilled jobs, became more feasible.

In New York City, the new immigrants went to work in the sweatshops. The poet Edwin Markham wrote in *Cosmopolitan* magazine, January 1907:

> In unaired rooms, mothers and fathers sew by day and by night. Those in the home sweatshop must work cheaper than those in the factory sweatshops. . . . And the children are called in from play to drive and drudge beside their elders. . . .
>
> All the year in New York and in other cities you may watch children radiating to and from such pitiful homes. Nearly any hour on the East Side of New York City you can see them—pallid boy or spindling girl—their faces dulled, their backs bent under a heavy load of garments piled on head and shoulders, the muscles of the whole frame in a long strain. . . .
>
> Is it not a cruel civilization that allows little hearts and little shoulders to strain under these grown-up responsibilities, while in the same city, a pet cur is jeweled and pampered and aired on a fine lady's velvet lap on the beautiful boulevards?

The city became a battlefield. On August 10, 1905, the New York *Tribune* reported that a strike at Federman's bakery on the Lower East Side led to violence when Federman used scab labor to continue producing:

Strikers or their sympathizers wrecked the bake shop of Philip Federman at No. 183 Orchard Street early last night amid scenes of the most tumultuous excitement. Policemen smashed heads right and left with their nightsticks after two of their number had been roughly dealt with by the mob. . . .

There were five hundred garment factories in New York. A woman later recalled the conditions of work:

. . . dangerously broken stairways . . . windows few and so dirty. . . . The wooden floors that were swept once a year. . . . Hardly any other light but the gas jets burning by day and by night . . . the filthy, malodorous lavatory in the dark hall. No fresh drinking water. . . . mice and roaches. . . .

During the winter months . . . how we suffered from the cold. In the summer we suffered from the heat. . . .

In these disease-breeding holes we, the youngsters together with the men and women toiled from seventy and eighty hours a week! Saturdays and Sundays included! . . . A sign would go up on Saturday afternoon: "If you don't come in on Sunday, you need not come in on Monday." . . . Children's dreams of a day off shattered. We wept, for after all, we were only children. . . .

At the Triangle Shirtwaist Company, in the winter of 1909, women organized and decided to strike. Soon they were walking the picket line in the cold, knowing they could not win while the other factories were operating. A mass meeting was called of workers in the other shops, and Clara Lemlich, in her teens, an eloquent speaker, still bearing the signs of her recent beating on the picket line, stood up: "I offer a resolution that a general strike be declared now!" The meeting went wild; they voted to strike.

Pauline Newman, one of the strikers, recalled years later the beginning of the general strike:

Thousands upon thousands left the factories from every side, all of them walking down toward Union Square. It was November, the cold winter was just around the corner, we had no fur coats to keep warm, and yet there was the spirit that led us on and on until we got to some hall. . . .

I can see the young people, mostly women, walking down and not caring what might happen . . . the hunger, cold, loneliness. . . . They just didn't care on that particular day; that was their day.

The union had hoped three thousand would join the strike. Twenty thousand walked out. Every day a thousand new members joined the union, the International Ladies Garment Workers Union, which before this had few women. Colored women were active in the strike, which went on through the winter, against police, against scabs, against arrests and prison. In more than three hundred shops, workers won their demands. Women now became officials in the union. Pauline Newman again:

> We tried to educate ourselves. I would invite the girls to my rooms, and we took turns reading poetry in English to improve our understanding of the language. One of our favorites was Thomas Hood's "Song of the Shirt," and another . . . Percy Bysshe Shelley's "Mask of Anarchy." . . .
> "Rise like lions after slumber
> In unvanquishable number!
> Shake your chains to earth, like dew
> Which in sleep had fallen on you—
> Ye are many, they are few!"

The conditions in the factories did not change much. On the afternoon of March 25, 1911, a fire at the Triangle Shirtwaist Company that began in a rag bin swept through the eighth, ninth, and tenth floors, too high for fire ladders to reach. The fire chief of New York had said that his ladders could reach only to the seventh floor. But half of New York's 500,000 workers spent all day, perhaps twelve hours, above the seventh floor. The laws said factory doors had to open outward. But at the Triangle Company the doors opened in. The law said the doors could not be locked during working hours, but at the Triangle Company doors were usually locked so the company could keep track of the employees. And so, trapped, the young women were burned to death at their worktables, or jammed against the locked exit door, or leaped to their deaths down the elevator shafts. The New York *World* reported:

> . . . screaming men and women and boys and girls crowded out on the many window ledges and threw themselves into the streets far below. They jumped with their clothing ablaze. The hair of some of the girls streamed up aflame as they leaped. Thud after thud sounded on the pavements. It is a ghastly fact that on both the Greene Street and Washington Place sides of the building there grew mounds of the dead and dying. . . .
>
> From opposite windows spectators saw again and again pitiable companionships formed in the instant of death—girls who placed their arms around each other as they leaped.

When it was over, 146 Triangle workers, mostly women, were burned or crushed to death. There was a memorial parade down Broadway, and 100,000 marched.

There were more fires. And accidents. And sickness. In the year 1904, 27,000 workers were killed on the job, in manufacturing, transport, and agriculture. In one year, 50,000 accidents took place in New York factories alone. Hat and cap makers were getting respiratory diseases, quarrymen were inhaling deadly chemicals, lithographic printers were getting arsenic poisoning. A New York State Factory Investigation Commission reported in 1912:

> Sadie is an intelligent, neat, clean girl, who has worked from the time she got her working papers in embroidery factories. . . . In her work she was accustomed to use a white powder (chalk or talcum was usual) which was brushed over the perforated designs and thus transferred to the cloth. The design was easily brushed off when made of chalk or of talcum. . . . Her last employer therefore commenced using white lead powder, mixed with rosin, which cheapened the work as the powder could not be rubbed off and necessitate restamping.
>
> None of the girls knew of the change in powder, nor of the danger in its use. . . .
>
> Sadie had been a very strong, healthy girl, good appetite and color; she began to be unable to eat. . . . Her hands and feet swelled, she lost the use of one hand, her teeth and gums were blue. When she finally had to stop work, after being treated for months for stomach trouble, her physician advised her to go to a hospital. There the examination revealed the fact that she had lead poisoning. . . .

According to a report of the Commission on Industrial Relations, in 1914, 35,000 workers were killed in industrial accidents and 700,000 injured. That year the income of forty-four families making $1 million or more equaled the total income of 100,000 families earning $500 a year. The record shows an exchange between Commissioner Harris Weinstock of the Commission on Industrial Relations and President John Osgood, head of a Colorado coal company controlled by the Rockefellers:

WEINSTOCK: If a worker loses his life, are his dependents compensated in any way?

OSGOOD: Not necessarily. In some cases they are and in some cases not.

WEINSTOCK: If he is crippled for life is there any compensation?

OSGOOD: No sir, there is none. . . .

WEINSTOCK: Then the whole burden is thrown directly upon their shoulders.
   OSGOOD: Yes, sir.
WEINSTOCK: The industry bears none of it?
   OSGOOD: No, the industry bears none of it.

Unionization was growing. Shortly after the turn of the century there were 2 million members of labor unions (one in fourteen workers), 80 percent of them in the American Federation of Labor. The AFL was an exclusive union—almost all male, almost all white, almost all skilled workers. Although the number of women workers kept growing—it doubled from 4 million in 1890 to 8 million in 1910, and women were one-fifth of the labor force—only one in a hundred belonged to a union.

Black workers in 1910 made one-third of the earnings of white workers. Although Samuel Gompers, head of the AFL, would make speeches about its belief in equal opportunity, the Negro was excluded from most AFL unions. Gompers kept saying he did not want to interfere with the "internal affairs" of the South: "I regard the race problem as one with which you people of the Southland will have to deal; without the interference, too, of meddlers from the outside."

In the reality of struggle, rank-and-file workers overcame these separations from time to time. Foner quotes Mary McDowell's account of the formation of a women's union in the Chicago stockyards:

> It was a dramatic occasion on that evening, when an Irish girl at the door called out—"A Colored sister asks admission. What shall I do with her?" And the answer came from the Irish young woman in the chair—"Admit her, of course, and let all of you give her a hearty welcome!"

In New Orleans in 1907 a general strike on the levees, involving ten thousand workers (longshoremen, teamsters, freight handlers), black and white, lasted twenty days. The head of the Negro longshoremen, E. S. Swan, said:

> The whites and Negroes were never before so strongly cemented in a common bond and in my 39 years of experience of the levee, I never saw such solidarity. In all the previous strikes the Negro was used against the white man but that condition is now past and both races are standing together for their common interests. . . .

These were exceptions. In general, the Negro was kept out of the trade union movement. W. E. B. Du Bois wrote in 1913: "The net result of all this has been to convince the American Negro that his greatest enemy is not the employer who robs him, but his fellow white working-man."

Racism was practical for the AFL. The exclusion of women and foreigners was also practical. These were mostly unskilled workers, and the AFL, confined mostly to skilled workers, was based on the philosophy of "business unionism" (in fact, the chief official of each AFL union was called the "business agent"), trying to match the monopoly of production by the employer with a monopoly of workers by the union. In this way it won better conditions for some workers, and left most workers out.

AFL officials drew large salaries, hobnobbed with employers, even moved in high society. A press dispatch from Atlantic City, New Jersey, the fashionable seaside resort, in the summer of 1910:

> Engaged in a game of bathing suit baseball with President Sam Gompers, Secretary Frank Morrison and other leaders of the A.F. of L. on the beach this morning, John Mitchell, former head of the mine workers' union, lost a $1000 diamond ring presented to him by his admirers after the settlement of the big Pennsylvania coal strike. Capt. George Berke, a veteran life guard, found the ring, whereupon Mitchell peeled a hundred dollar bill from a roll he carried in his pocket and handed it to the captain as a reward for his find.

The well-paid leaders of the AFL were protected from criticism by tightly controlled meetings and by "goon" squads—hired toughs originally used against strikebreakers but after a while used to intimidate and beat up opponents inside the union.

In this situation—terrible conditions of labor, exclusivity in union organization—working people wanting radical change, seeing the root of misery in the capitalist system, moved toward a new kind of labor union. One morning in June 1905, there met in a hall in Chicago a convention of two hundred socialists, anarchists, and radical trade unionists from all over the United States. They were forming the I. W. W.—the Industrial Workers of the World. Big Bill Haywood, a leader of the Western Federation of Miners, recalled in his autobiography that he picked up a piece of board that lay on the platform and used it for a gavel to open the convention:

> Fellow workers. . . . This is the Continental Congress of the working-class. We are here to confederate the workers of this country into a working-class movement that shall have for its purpose the emancipation of the working-

class from the slave bondage of capitalism. . . . The aims and objects of this organization shall be to put the working-class in possession of the economic power, the means of life, in control of the machinery of production and distribution, without regard to the capitalist masters.

On the speakers' platform with Haywood were Eugene Debs, leader of the Socialist party, and Mother Mary Jones, a seventy-five-year-old white-haired woman who was an organizer for the United Mine Workers of America. The convention drew up a constitution, whose preamble said:

> The working class and the employing class have nothing in common. There can be no peace so long as hunger and want are found among millions of working people and the few, who make up the employing class, have all the good things of life.
> Between these two classes a struggle must go on until all the toilers come together on the political as well as on the industrial field, and take and hold that which they produce by their labor, through an economic organization of the working class without affiliation with any political party. . . .

One of the IWW pamphlets explained why it broke with the AFL idea of craft unions:

> The directory of unions of Chicago shows in 1903 a total of 56 different unions in the packing houses, divided up still more in 14 different national trades unions of the American Federation of Labor.
> What a horrible example of an army divided against itself in the face of a strong combination of employers. . . .

The IWW (or "Wobblies," as they came to be called, for reasons not really clear) aimed at organizing all workers in any industry into "One Big Union," undivided by sex, race, or skills. They argued against making contracts with the employer, because this had so often prevented workers from striking on their own, or in sympathy with other strikers, and thus turned union people into strikebreakers. Negotiations by leaders for contracts replaced continuous struggle by the rank and file, the Wobblies believed.

They spoke of "direct action":

> Direct action means industrial action directly by, for, and of the workers themselves, without the treacherous aid of labor misleaders or scheming

politicians. A strike that is initiated, controlled, and settled by the workers directly affected is direct action. . . . Direct action is industrial democracy.

One IWW pamphlet said: "Shall I tell you what direct action means? The worker on the job shall tell the boss when and where he shall work, how long and for what wages and under what conditions."

The IWW people were militant, courageous. Despite a reputation given them by the press, they did not believe in initiating violence, but did fight back when attacked. In McKees Rocks, Pennsylvania, they led a strike of six thousand workers in 1909 against an affiliate of the U.S. Steel Company, defied the state troopers, and battled with them. They promised to take a trooper's life for every worker killed (in one gun battle four strikers and three troopers were killed), and managed to keep picketing the factories until the strike was won.

The IWW saw beyond strikes:

Strikes are mere incidents in the class war; they are tests of strength, periodical drills in the course of which the workers train themselves for concerted action. This training is most necessary to prepare the masses for the final "catastrophe," the general strike which will complete the expropriation of the employers.

The idea of anarcho-syndicalism was developing strongly in Spain and Italy and France at this time—that the workers would take power, not by seizing the state machinery in an armed rebellion, but by bringing the economic system to a halt in a general strike, then taking it over to use for the good of all. IWW organizer Joseph Ettor said:

If the workers of the world want to win, all they have to do is recognize their own solidarity. They have nothing to do but fold their arms and the world will stop. The workers are more powerful with their hands in their pockets than all the property of the capitalists. . . .

It was an immensely powerful idea. In the ten exciting years after its birth, the IWW became a threat to the capitalist class, exactly when capitalist growth was enormous and profits huge. The IWW never had more than five to ten thousand enrolled members at any one time; people came and went, and perhaps a hundred thousand were members at one time or another. But their energy, their persistence, their inspiration to others, their ability to mobilize thousands at one place, one time, made them an influence on the country far beyond their numbers. They traveled everywhere (many were unemployed or migrant workers); they organized, wrote, spoke, sang, spread their message and their spirit.

They were attacked with all the weapons the system could put together: the newspapers, the courts, the police, the army, mob violence. Local authorities passed laws to stop them from speaking; the IWW defied these laws. In Missoula, Montana, a lumber and mining area, hundreds of Wobblies arrived by boxcar after some had been prevented from speaking. They were arrested one after another until they clogged the jails and the courts, and finally forced the town to repeal its antispeech ordinance.

In Spokane, Washington, in 1909, an ordinance was passed to stop street meetings, and an IWW organizer who insisted on speaking was arrested. Thousands of Wobblies marched into the center of town to speak. One by one they spoke and were arrested, until six hundred were in jail. Jail conditions were brutal, and several men died in their cells, but the IWW won the right to speak.

In Fresno, California, in 1911, there was another free speech fight. The San Francisco *Call* commented:

> It is one of those strange situations which crop up suddenly and are hard to understand. Some thousands of men, whose business it is to work with their hands, tramping and stealing rides, suffering hardships and facing dangers— to get into jail. . . .

In jail they sang, they shouted, they made speeches through the bars to groups that gathered outside the prison. As Joyce Kornbluh reports in her remarkable collection of IWW documents, *Rebel Voices*:

> They took turns lecturing about the class struggle and leading the singing of Wobbly songs. When they refused to stop, the jailor sent for fire department trucks and ordered the fire hoses turned full force on the prisoners. The men used their mattresses as shields, and quiet was only restored when the icy water reached knee-high in the cells.

When city officials heard that thousands more were planning to come into town, they lifted the ban on street speaking and released the prisoners in small groups.

That same year in Aberdeen, Washington, once again laws against free speech, arrests, prison, and, unexpectedly, victory. One of the men arrested, "Stumpy" Payne, a carpenter, farm hand, editor of an IWW newspaper, wrote about the experience:

Here they were, eighteen men in the vigor of life, most of whom came long distances through snow and hostile towns by beating their way, penniless and hungry, into a place where a jail sentence was the gentlest treatment that could be expected, and where many had already been driven into the swamps and beaten nearly to death. . . . Yet here they were, laughing with boyish glee at tragic things that to them were jokes. . . .

But what was the motive behind the actions of these men? . . . Why were they here? Is the call of Brotherhood in the human race greater than any fear or discomfort, despite the efforts of the masters of life for six thousand years to root out that call of Brotherhood from our minds?

In San Diego, Jack White, a Wobbly arrested in a free-speech fight in 1912, sentenced to six months in the county jail on a bread and water diet, was asked if he had anything to say to the court. A stenographer recorded what he said:

The prosecuting attorney, in his plea to the jury, accused me of saying on a public platform at a public meeting, "To hell with the courts, we know what justice is." He told a great truth when he lied, for if he had searched the innermost recesses of my mind he could have found that thought, never expressed by me before, but which I express now, "To hell with your courts, I know what justice is," for I have sat in your court room day after day and have seen members of my class pass before this, the so-called bar of justice. I have seen you, Judge Sloane, and others of your kind, send them to prison because they dared to infringe upon the sacred rights of property. You have become blind and deaf to the rights of man to pursue life and happiness, and you have crushed those rights so that the sacred right of property shall be preserved. Then you tell me to respect the law. I do not. I did violate the law, as I will violate every one of your laws and still come before you and say "To hell with the courts." . . .

The prosecutor lied, but I will accept his lie as a truth and say again so that you, Judge Sloane, may not be mistaken as to my attitude, "To hell with your courts, I know what justice is."

There were also beatings, tarrings and featherings, defeats. One IWW member, John Stone, tells of being released from the jail at San Diego at midnight with another IWW man and forced into an automobile:

We were taken out of the city, about twenty miles, where the machine stopped. . . . a man in the rear struck me with a blackjack several times on the head and shoulders; the other man then struck me on the mouth with his fist. The men in the rear then sprang around and kicked me in the stomach. I then started to run away; and heard a bullet go past me. I stopped. . . . In the morning I examined Joe Marko's condition and found that the back of his head had been split open.

In 1916, in Everett, Washington, a boatload of Wobblies was fired on by two hundred armed vigilantes gathered by the sheriff, and five Wobblies were shot to death, thirty-one wounded. Two of the vigilantes were killed, nineteen wounded. The following year—the year the United States entered World War I—vigilantes in Montana seized IWW organizer Frank Little, tortured him, and hanged him, leaving his body dangling from a railroad trestle.

Joe Hill, an IWW organizer, wrote dozens of songs—biting, funny, class-conscious, inspiring—that appeared in IWW publications and in its *Little Red Song Book*. He became a legend in his time and after. His song "The Preacher and the Slave" had a favorite IWW target, the church:

> *Long-haired preachers come out every night,*
> *Try to tell you what's wrong and what's right;*
> *But when asked how 'bout something to eat*
> *They will answer with voices so sweet:*
>
> *You will eat, bye and bye,*
> *In that glorious land above the sky;*
> *Work and pray, live on hay,*
> *You'll get pie in the sky when you die.*

His song "Rebel Girl" was inspired by the strike of women at the textile mills in Lawrence, Massachusetts, and especially by the IWW leader of that strike, Elizabeth Gurley Flynn:

> *There are women of many descriptions*
> *In this queer world, as everyone knows,*
> *Some are living in beautiful mansions,*
> *And are wearing the finest of clothes.*
> *There are blue-blooded queens and princesses,*
> *Who have charms made of diamonds and pearl,*
> *But the only and Thoroughbred Lady*
> *Is the Rebel Girl.*

In November 1915, Joe Hill was accused of killing a grocer in Salt Lake City, Utah, in a robbery. There was no direct evidence presented to the court that he had committed the murder, but there were enough pieces of evidence to persuade a jury to find him guilty. The case became known throughout the world, and ten thousand letters went to the governor in protest, but with machine guns guarding the entrance to the prison, Joe Hill was executed by a firing squad. He had written Bill Haywood just before this: "Don't waste any time in mourning. Organize."

The IWW became involved in a set of dramatic events in Lawrence, Massachusetts, in the year 1912, where the American Woolen Company owned four mills. The work force were immigrant families— Portuguese, French-Canadian, English, Irish, Russian, Italian, Syrian, Lithuanian, German, Polish, Belgian—who lived in crowded, flammable wooden tenements. The average wage was $8.76 a week. A woman physician in Lawrence, Dr. Elizabeth Shapleigh, wrote:

> A considerable number of the boys and girls die within the first two or three years after beginning work . . . thirty-six out of every 100 of all the men and women who work in the mill die before or by the time they are twenty-five years of age.

It was in January, midwinter, when pay envelopes distributed to weavers at one of the mills—Polish women—showed that their wages, already too low to feed their families, had been reduced. They stopped their looms and walked out of the mill. The next day, five thousand workers at another mill quit work, marched to still another mill, rushed the gates, shut off the power to the looms, and called on the other workers to leave. Soon ten thousand workers were on strike.

A telegram went to Joseph Ettor, a twenty-six-year-old Italian, an IWW leader in New York, to come to Lawrence to help conduct the strike. He came. A committee of fifty was set up, representing every nationality among the workers, to make the important decisions. Less than a thousand millworkers belonged to the IWW, but the AFL had ignored the unskilled workers, and so they turned to the IWW leadership in the strike.

The IWW organized mass meetings and parades. The strikers had to supply food and fuel for 50,000 people (the entire population of Lawrence was 86,000); soup kitchens were set up, and money began arriving from all over the country—from trade unions, IWW locals, socialist groups, individuals.

The mayor called out the local militia; the governor ordered out the state police. A parade of strikers was attacked by police a few weeks after the strike began. This led to rioting all that day. In the evening, a striker, Anna LoPizzo, was shot and killed. Witnesses said a policeman did it, but the authorities arrested Joseph Ettor and another IWW organizer who had come to Lawrence, a poet named Arturo Giovanitti. Neither was at the scene of the shooting, but the charge was that "Joseph Ettor and Arturo Giovanitti did incite, procure, and counsel or command the said person whose name is not known to commit the said murder. . . ."

With Ettor, head of the strike committee, in jail, Big Bill Haywood was called in to replace him; other IWW organizers, including Elizabeth Gurley Flynn, came into Lawrence. Now there were twenty-two companies of militia and two troops of cavalry in the city. Martial law was declared, and citizens were forbidden to talk on the street. Thirty-six strikers were arrested, many sentenced to a year in prison. On Tuesday, January 30, a young Syrian striker, John Ramy, was bayoneted to death. But the strikers were still out, and the mills were not working. Ettor said: "Bayonets cannot weave cloth."

In February, the strikers began mass picketing, seven thousand to ten thousand pickets in an endless chain, marching through the mill districts, with white armbands: "Don't be a scab." But their food was running out and the children were hungry. It was proposed by the New York *Call*, a Socialist newspaper, that the children of strikers be sent to sympathetic families in other cities to take care of them while the strike lasted. This had been done by strikers in Europe, never in the United States—but in three days, the *Call* got four hundred letters offering to take children. The IWW and the Socialist party began to organize the children's exodus, taking applications from families who wanted them, arranging medical exams for the youngsters.

On February 10, over a hundred children, aged four to fourteen, left Lawrence for New York City. They were greeted at Grand Central Station by five thousand Italian Socialists singing the "Marseillaise" and the "Internationale." The following week, another hundred children came to New York, and thirty-five to Barre, Vermont. It was becoming clear: if the children were taken care of, the strikers could stay out, for their spirit was high. The city officials in Lawrence, citing a statute on child neglect, said no more children would be permitted to leave Lawrence.

Despite the city edict, a group of forty children assembled on February 24 to go to Philadelphia. The railroad station was filled with police, and the scene that followed was described to Congressmen by a member of the Women's Committee of Philadelphia:

When the time approached to depart, the children arranged in a long line, two by two, in orderly procession, with their parents near at hand, were about to make their way to the train when the police closed in on us with their clubs, beating right and left, with no thought of children, who were in the most desperate danger of being trampled to death. The mothers and children were thus hurled in a mass and bodily dragged to a military truck, and even then clubbed, irrespective of the cries of the panic-stricken women and children. . . .

A week after that, women returning from a meeting were surrounded by police and clubbed; one pregnant woman was carried unconscious to a hospital and gave birth to a dead child.

Still, the strikers held out. "They are always marching and singing," reporter Mary Heaton Vorse wrote. "The tired, gray crowds ebbing and flowing perpetually into the mills had waked and opened their mouths to sing."

The American Woolen Company decided to give in. It offered raises of 5 to 11 percent (the strikers insisted that the largest increases go to the lowest-paid), time and a quarter for overtime, and no discrimination against those who had struck. On March 14, 1912, ten thousand strikers gathered on the Lawrence Common and, with Bill Haywood presiding, voted to end the strike.

Ettor and Giovanitti went on trial. Support for them had been mounting all over the country. There were parades in New York and Boston; on September 30, fifteen thousand Lawrence workers struck for twenty-four hours to show their support for the two men. After that, two thousand of the most active strikers were fired, but the IWW threatened to call another strike, and they were put back. A jury found Ettor and Giovanitti not guilty, and that afternoon, ten thousand people assembled in Lawrence to celebrate.

The IWW took its slogan "One Big Union" seriously. Women, foreigners, black workers, the lowliest and most unskilled of workers, were included when a factory or mine was organized. When the Brotherhood of Timber Workers organized in Louisiana and invited Bill Haywood to speak to them in 1912 (shortly after the Lawrence victory), he expressed surprise that no Negroes were at the meeting. He was told it was against the law to have interracial meetings in Louisiana. Haywood told the convention:

You work in the same mills together. Sometimes a black man and a white man chop down the same tree together. You are meeting in convention now to discuss the conditions under which you labor. . . . Why not be sensible about this and call the Negroes into the Convention? If it is against the law, this is one time when the law should be broken.

Negroes were invited into the convention, which then voted to affiliate with the IWW.

In 1900 there were 500,000 women office workers—in 1870 there had been 19,000. Women were switchboard operators, store workers, nurses. Half a million were teachers. The teachers formed a Teachers League that fought against the automatic firing of women who became pregnant. The following "Rules for Female Teachers" were posted by the school board of one town in Massachusetts:

1. Do not get married.
2. Do not leave town at any time without permission of the school board.
3. Do not keep company with men.
4. Be home between the hours of 8 P.M. and 6 A.M.
5. Do not loiter downtown in ice cream stores.
6. Do not smoke.
7. Do not get into a carriage with any man except your father or brother.
8. Do not dress in bright colors.
9. Do not dye your hair.
10. Do not wear any dress more than two inches above the ankle.

The conditions of women working in a Milwaukee brewery were described by Mother Mary Jones, who worked there briefly in 1910 (she was close to eighty at this time):

> Condemned to slave daily in the wash-room in wet shoes and wet clothes, surrounded with foul-mouthed, brutal foremen . . . the poor girls work in the vile smell of sour beer, lifting cases of empty and full bottles weighing from 100 to 150 pounds. . . . Rheumatism is one of the chronic ailments and is closely followed by consumption. . . . The foreman even regulates the time the girls may stay in the toilet room. . . . Many of the girls have no home nor parents and are forced to feed and clothe and shelter themselves . . . on $3.00 a week. . . .

In the laundries, women organized. In 1909, the *Handbook* of the Women's Trade Union Industrial League wrote about women in steam laundries:

How would you like to iron a shirt a minute? Think of standing at a mangle just above the washroom with the hot steam pouring up through the floor for 10, 12, 14 and sometimes 17 hours a day! Sometimes the floors are made of cement and then it seems as though one were standing on hot coals, and the workers are dripping with perspiration. . . . They are . . . breathing air laden with particles of soda, ammonia, and other chemicals! The Laundry Workers Union . . . in one city reduced this long day to 9 hours, and has increased the wages 50 percent. . . .

Labor struggles could make things better, but the country's resources remained in the hands of powerful corporations whose motive was profit, whose power commanded the government of the United States. There was an idea in the air, becoming clearer and stronger, an idea not just in the theories of Karl Marx but in the dreams of writers and artists through the ages: that people might cooperatively use the treasures of the earth to make life better for everyone, not just a few.

Around the turn of the century, strike struggles were multiplying—in the 1890s there had been about a thousand strikes a year; by 1904 there were four thousand strikes a year. Law and military force again and again took the side of the rich. It was a time when hundreds of thousands of Americans began to think of socialism.

Debs wrote in 1904, three years after the formation of the Socialist party:

The "pure and simple" trades union of the past does not answer the requirements of today. . . .

The attempt of each trade to maintain its own independence separately and apart from others results in increasing jurisdictional entanglements, fruitful of dissension, strife and ultimate disruption. . . .

The members of a trades union should be taught . . . that the labor movement means more, infinitely more, than a paltry increase in wages and the strike necessary to secure it; that while it engages to do all that possibly can be done to better the working conditions of its members, its higher object is to overthrow the capitalist system of private ownership of the tools of labor, abolish wage-slavery and achieve the freedom of the whole working class and, in fact, of all mankind. . . .

What Debs accomplished was not in theory, or analysis, but in expressing eloquently, passionately, what people were feeling. The writer Heywood Broun once quoted a fellow Socialist speaking of Debs: "That old man with the burning eyes actually believes that there can be such a thing as the brotherhood of man. And that's not the funniest part of it. As long as he's around I believe it myself."

Eugene Debs had become a Socialist while in jail in the Pullman strike. Now he was the spokesman of a party that made him its presidential candidate five times. The party at one time had 100,000 members, and 1,200 office holders in 340 municipalities. Its main newspaper, *Appeal to Reason*, for which Debs wrote, had half a million subscribers, and there were many other Socialist newspapers around the country, so that, all together, perhaps a million people read the Socialist press.

Socialism moved out of the small circles of city immigrants—Jewish and German socialists speaking their own languages—and became American. The strongest Socialist state organization was in Oklahoma, which in 1914 had twelve thousand dues-paying members (more than New York State), and elected over a hundred Socialists to local office, including six to the Oklahoma state legislature. There were fifty-five weekly Socialist newspapers in Oklahoma, Texas, Louisiana, Arkansas, and summer encampments that drew thousands of people.

James Green describes these Southwest radicals, in his book *Grass-Roots Socialism*, as "indebted homesteaders, migratory tenant farmers, coal miners and railroad workers, 'redbone' lumberjacks from the piney woods, preachers and schoolteachers from the sunbaked prairies . . . village artisans and atheists . . . the unknown people who created the strongest regional Socialist movement in United States history." Green continues:

> The Socialist movement . . . was painstakingly organized by scores of former Populists, militant miners, and blacklisted railroad workers, who were assisted by a remarkable cadre of professional agitators and educators and inspired by occasional visits from national figures like Eugene V. Debs and Mother Jones. . . . This core of organizers grew to include indigenous dissenters. . . . a much larger group of amateur agitators who canvassed the region selling newspapers, forming reading groups, organizing locals, and making soapbox speeches.

There was almost a religious fervor to the movement, as in the eloquence of Debs. In 1906, after the imprisonment in Idaho of Bill Haywood and two other officers of the Western Federation of Miners on an apparently faked murder charge, Debs wrote a flaming article in the *Appeal to Reason*:

> Murder has been plotted and is about to be executed in the name and under the forms of law. . . .

It is a foul plot; a damnable conspiracy; a hellish outrage. . . .

If they attempt to murder Moyer, Haywood and their brothers, a million revolutionists, at least, will meet them with guns. . . .

Capitalist courts never have done, and never will do, anything for the working class. . . .

A special revolutionary convention of the proletariat . . . would be in order, and, if extreme measures are required, a general strike could be ordered and industry paralyzed as a preliminary to a general uprising.

If the plutocrats begin the program, we will end it.

Theodore Roosevelt, after reading this, sent a copy to his Attorney General, W. H. Moody, with a note: "Is it possible to proceed against Debs and the proprietor of this paper criminally?"

As the Socialists became more successful at the polls (Debs got 900,000 votes in 1912, double what he had in 1908), and more concerned with increasing that appeal, they became more critical of IWW tactics of "sabotage" and "violence," and in 1913 removed Bill Haywood from the Socialist Party Executive Committee, claiming he advocated violence (although some of Debs's writings were far more inflammatory).

Women were active in the socialist movement, more as rank-and-file workers than as leaders—and, sometimes, as sharp critics of socialist policy. Helen Keller, for instance, the gifted blind-mute-deaf woman with her extraordinary social vision, commented on the expulsion of Bill Haywood in a letter to the New York *Call*:

It is with the deepest regret that I have read the attacks upon Comrade Haywood . . . such an ignoble strife between two factions which should be one, and that, too, at a most critical period in the struggle of the proletariat. . . .

What? Are we to put difference of party tactics before the desperate needs of the workers? . . . While countless women and children are breaking their hearts and ruining their bodies in long days of toil, we are fighting one another. Shame upon us!

Only 3 percent of the Socialist party's members were women in 1904. At the national convention that year, there were only eight women delegates. But in a few years, local socialist women's organizations, and a national magazine, *Socialist Woman*, began bringing more women into the party, so that by 1913, 15 percent of the membership was women. The editor of *Socialist Woman*, Josephine Conger-Kaneko, insisted on the importance of separate groups for women:

In the separate organization the most unsophisticated little woman may soon learn to preside over a meeting, to make motions, and to defend her stand with a little "speech". After a year or two of this sort of practice she is ready to work with the men. And there is a mighty difference between working *with* the men, and simply sitting in obedient reverence under the shadow of their aggressive power.

Socialist women were active in the feminist movement of the early 1900s. According to Kate Richards O'Hare, the Socialist leader from Oklahoma, New York women socialists were superbly organized. During the 1915 campaign in New York for a referendum on women's suffrage, in one day at the climax of the campaign, they distributed 60,000 English leaflets, 50,000 Yiddish leaflets, sold 2,500 one-cent books and 1,500 five-cent books, put up 40,000 stickers, and held 100 meetings.

But were there problems of women that went beyond politics and economics, that would not be solved automatically by a socialist system? Once the economic base of sexual oppression was corrected, would equality follow? Battling for the vote, or for anything less than revolutionary change—was that pointless? The argument became sharper as the women's movement of the early twentieth century grew, as women spoke out more, organized, protested, paraded—for the vote, and for recognition as equals in every sphere, including sexual relations and marriage.

Charlotte Perkins Gilman, whose writing emphasized the crucial question of economic equality between the sexes, wrote a poem called "The Socialist and the Suffragist," ending with:

"A lifted world lifts women up,"
The Socialist explained.
"You cannot lift the world at all
While half of it is kept so small,"
the Suffragist maintained.
The world awoke, and tartly spoke:
"Your work is all the same;
Work together or work apart,
Work, each of you, with all your heart—
Just get into the game!"

When Susan Anthony, at eighty, went to hear Eugene Debs speak (twenty-five years before, he had gone to hear her speak, and they had not met since then), they clasped hands warmly, then had a brief exchange. She said, laughing: "Give us suffrage, and we'll give you socialism." Debs replied: "Give us socialism and we'll give you suffrage."

There were women who insisted on uniting the two aims of socialism and feminism, like Crystal Eastman, who imagined new ways of men and women living together and retaining their independence, different from traditional marriage. She was a socialist, but wrote once that a woman "knows that the whole of woman's slavery is not summed up in the profit system, nor her complete emancipation assured by the downfall of capitalism."

In the first fifteen years of the twentieth century, there were more women in the labor force, more with experience in labor struggles. Some middle-class women, conscious of women's oppression and wanting to do something, were going to college and becoming aware of themselves as not just housewives. The historian William Chafe writes *(Women and Equality)*:

> Female college students were infused with a self-conscious sense of mission and a passionate commitment to improve the world. They became doctors, college professors, settlement house workers, business women, lawyers, and architects. Spirited by an intense sense of purpose as well as camaraderie, they set a remarkable record of accomplishment in the face of overwhelming odds. Jane Addams, Grace and Edith Abbott, Alice Hamilton, Julia Lathrop, Florence Kelley—all came out of this pioneering generation and set the agenda of social reform for the first two decades of the 20th century.

They were defying the culture of mass magazines, which were spreading the message of woman as companion, wife, homemaker. Some of these feminists married; some did not. All struggled with the problem of relations with men, like Margaret Sanger, pioneer of birth control education, who suffered a nervous breakdown inside an apparently happy but confining marriage; she had to leave husband and children to make a career for herself and feel whole again. Sanger had written in *Woman and the New Race*: "No woman can call herself free who does not own and control her own body. No woman can call herself free until she can choose conscientiously whether she will or will not be a mother."

It was a complicated problem. Kate Richards O'Hare, for example, believed in the home, but thought socialism would make that better. When she ran for Congress in 1910 in Kansas City she said: "I long for domestic life, home and children with every fiber of my being. . . . Socialism is needed to restore the home."

On the other hand, Elizabeth Gurley Flynn wrote in her autobiography, *Rebel Girl*:

> A domestic life and possibly a large family had no attraction for me. . . . I wanted to speak and write, to travel, to meet people, to see places, to organize for the I.W.W. I saw no reason why I, as a woman, should give up my work for this. . . .

While many women in this time were radicals, socialists, anarchists, an even larger number were involved in the campaign for suffrage, and the mass support for feminism came from them. Veterans of trade union struggles joined the suffrage movement, like Rose Schneiderman of the Garment Workers. At a Cooper Union meeting in New York, she replied to a politician who said that women, given the vote, would lose their femininity:

> Women in the laundries . . . stand for thirteen or fourteen hours in the terrible steam and heat with their hands in hot starch. Surely these women won't lose any more of their beauty and charm by putting a ballot in a ballot box once a year than they are likely to lose standing in foundries or laundries all year round.

Every spring in New York, the parades for women's suffrage kept growing. In 1912, a news report:

> All along Fifth Avenue from Washington Square, where the parade formed, to 57th Street, where it disbanded, were gathered thousands of men and women of New York. They blocked every cross street on the line of march. Many were inclined to laugh and jeer, but none did. The sight of the impressive column of women striding five abreast up the middle of the street stifled all thought of ridicule. . . . women doctors, women lawyers . . . women architects, women artists, actresses and sculptors; women waitresses, domestics; a huge division of industrial workers . . . all marched with an intensity and purpose that astonished the crowds that lined the streets.

From Washington, in the spring of 1913, came a *New York Times* report:

> In a woman's suffrage demonstration to-day the capital saw the greatest parade of women in its history. . . . In the parade over 5000 women passed down Pennsylvania Avenue. . . . It was an astonishing demonstration. It was estimated . . . that 500,000 persons watched the women march for their cause.

Some women radicals were skeptical. Emma Goldman, the anarchist and feminist, spoke her mind forcefully, as always, on the subject of women's suffrage:

Our modern fetish is universal suffrage. . . . The women of Australia and New Zealand can vote, and help make the laws. Are the labor conditions better there? . . .

The history of the political activities of man proves that they have given him absolutely nothing that he could not have achieved in a more direct, less costly, and more lasting manner. As a matter of fact, every inch of ground he has gained has been through a constant fight, a ceaseless struggle for self-assertion, and not through suffrage. There is no reason whatever to assume that woman, in her climb to emancipation, has been, or will be, helped by the ballot. . . .

Her development, her freedom, her independence, must come from and through herself. First, by asserting herself as a personality. Second, by refusing the right to anyone over her body; by refusing to bear children, unless she wants them; by refusing to be a servant to God, the State, society, the husband, the family, etc. by making her life simpler, but deeper and richer. . . . Only that, and not the ballot, will set woman free. . . .

And Helen Keller, writing in 1911 to a suffragist in England:

Our democracy is but a name. We vote? What does that mean? It means that we choose between two bodies of real, though not avowed, autocrats. We choose between Tweedledum and Tweedledee. . . .

You ask for votes for women. What good can votes do when ten-elevenths of the land of Great Britain belongs to 200,000 and only one-eleventh to the rest of the 40,000,000? Have your men with their millions of votes freed themselves from this injustice?

Emma Goldman was not postponing the changing of woman's condition to some future socialist era—she wanted action more direct, more immediate, than the vote. Helen Keller, while not an anarchist, also believed in continuous struggle outside the ballot box. Blind, deaf, she fought with her spirit, her pen. When she became active and openly socialist, the Brooklyn *Eagle*, which had previously treated her as a heroine, wrote that "her mistakes spring out of the manifest limitations of her development." Her response was not accepted by the *Eagle*, but printed in the New York *Call*. She wrote that when once she met the editor of the Brooklyn *Eagle* he complimented her lavishly. "But now that I have come out for socialism he reminds me and the public that I am blind and deaf and especially liable to error. . . ." She added:

> Oh, ridiculous Brooklyn *Eagle*! What an ungallant bird it is! Socially blind and deaf, it defends an intolerable system, a system that is the cause of much of the physical blindness and deafness which we are trying to prevent. . . . The *Eagle* and I are at war. I hate the system which it represents. . . . When it fights back, let it fight fair. . . . It is not fair fighting or good argument to remind me and others that I cannot see or hear. I can read. I can read all the socialist books I have time for in English, German and French. If the editor of the Brooklyn *Eagle* should read some of them, he might be a wiser man, and make a better newspaper. If I ever contribute to the Socialist movement the book that I sometimes dream of, I know what I shall name it: Industrial Blindness and Social Deafness.

Mother Jones did not seem especially interested in the feminist movement. She was busy organizing textile workers and miners, and organizing their wives and children. One of her many feats was the organization of a children's march to Washington to demand the end of child labor (as the twentieth century opened, 284,000 children between the ages of ten and fifteen worked in mines, mills, factories). She described this:

> In the spring of 1903, I went to Kensington, Pennsylvania, where seventy-five thousand textile workers were on strike. Of this number at least ten thousand were little children. The workers were striking for more pay and shorter hours. Every day little children came into Union Headquarters, some with their hands off, some with the thumb missing, some with their fingers off at the knuckle. They were stooped little things, round shouldered and skinny. . . .
>
> I asked some of the parents if they would let me have their little boys and girls for a week or ten days, promising to bring them back safe and sound. . . . A man named Sweeny was marshall. . . . A few men and women went with me. . . . The children carried knapsacks on their backs in which was a knife and fork, a tin cup and plate. . . . One little fellow had a drum and another had a fife. . . . We carried banners that said: . . . "We want time to play. . . .

The children marched through New Jersey and New York and down to Oyster Bay to try to see President Theodore Roosevelt, but he refused to see them. "But our march had done its work. We had drawn the attention of the nation to the crime of child labor."

That same year, children working sixty hours a week in textile mills in Philadelphia went on strike, carrying signs: "WE WANT TO GO TO SCHOOL!" "55 HOURS OR NOTHING!"

One gets a sense of the energy and fire of some of those turn-of-the-century radicals by looking at the police record of Elizabeth Gurley Flynn:

> 1906–16, Organizer, lecturer for I.W.W.
>
> 1918–24, Organizer, Workers Defense Union
>
> Arrested in New York, 1906, free-speech case, dismissed; active in Spokane, Washington, free-speech fight, 1909; arrested, Missoula, Montana, 1909, in free-speech fight of I.W.W., Spokane, Washington, free-speech fight of I.W.W., hundreds arrested; in Philadelphia arrested three times, 1911, at strike meetings of Baldwin Locomotive Works; active in Lawrence textile strike, 1912; hotel-workers strike, 1912, New York; Paterson textile strike, 1913; defense work for Ettor-Giovanitti case, 1912; Mesaba Range strike, Minnesota, 1916; Everett IWW case, Spokane, Washington, 1916; Joe Hill defense, 1914. Arrested Duluth, Minnesota, 1917, charged with vagrancy under law passed to stop I.W.W. and pacifist speakers, case dismissed. Indicted in Chicago IWW case, 1917. . . .

Black women faced double oppression. A Negro nurse wrote to a newspaper in 1912:

> We poor colored women wage-earners in the South are fighting a terrible battle. . . . On the one hand, we are assailed by black men, who should be our natural protectors; and, whether in the cook kitchen, at the washtub, over the sewing machine, behind the baby carriage, or at the ironing board, we are but little more than pack horses, beasts of burden, slaves! . . .

In this early part of the twentieth century, labeled by generations of white scholars as "the Progressive period," lynchings were reported every week; it was the low point for Negroes, North and South, "the nadir," as Rayford Logan, a black historian, put it. In 1910 there were 10 million Negroes in the United States, and 9 million of them were in the South.

The government of the United States (between 1901 and 1921, the Presidents were Theodore Roosevelt, William Howard Taft, Woodrow Wilson)—whether Republican or Democrat—watched Negroes being lynched, observed murderous riots against blacks in Statesboro, Georgia, Brownsville, Texas, and Atlanta, Georgia, and did nothing.

There were Negroes in the Socialist party, but the Socialist party did not go much out of its way to act on the race question. As Ray Ginger writes of Debs: "When race prejudice was thrust at Debs, he always publicly repudiated it. He always insisted on absolute equality. But he failed to accept the view that special measures were sometimes needed to achieve this equality."

Blacks began to organize: a National Afro-American Council formed in 1903 to protest against lynching, peonage, discrimination, disfranchisement; the National Association of Colored Women, formed around the same time, condemned segregation and lynchings. In Georgia in 1906 there was an Equal Rights Convention, which pointed to 260 Georgia Negroes lynched since 1885. It asked the right to vote, the right to enter the militia, to be on juries. It agreed blacks should work hard. "And at the same time we must agitate, complain, protest and keep protesting against the invasion of our manhood rights. . . ."

W. E. B. Du Bois, teaching in Atlanta, Georgia, in 1905, sent out a letter to Negro leaders throughout the country, calling them to a conference just across the Canadian border from Buffalo, near Niagara Falls. It was the start of the "Niagara Movement."

Du Bois, born in Massachusetts, the first black to receive a Ph.D. degree from Harvard University (1895), had just written and published his poetic, powerful book *The Souls of Black Folk*. Du Bois was a Socialist sympathizer, although only briefly a party member.

One of his associates in calling the Niagara meeting was William Monroe Trotter, a young black man in Boston, of militant views, who edited a weekly newspaper, the *Guardian*. In it he attacked the moderate ideas of Booker T. Washington. When, in the summer of 1903, Washington spoke to an audience of two thousand at a Boston church, Trotter and his supporters prepared nine provocative questions, which caused a commotion and led to fistfights. Trotter and a friend were arrested. This may have added to the spirit of indignation which led Du Bois to spearhead the Niagara meeting. The tone of the Niagara group was strong:

> We refuse to allow the impression to remain that the Negro-American assents to inferiority, is submissive under oppression and apologetic before insults. Through helplessness we may submit, but the voice of protest of ten million Americans must never cease to assail the ears of their fellows so long as America is unjust.

A race riot in Springfield, Illinois, prompted the formation of the National Association for the Advancement of Colored People in 1910. Whites dominated the leadership of the new organization; Du Bois was the only black officer. He was also the first editor of the NAACP periodical *The Crisis*. The NAACP concentrated on legal action and education, but Du Bois represented in it that spirit which was embodied in the Niagara movement's declaration: "Persistent manly agitation is the way to liberty."

What was clear in this period to blacks, to feminists, to labor organizers and socialists, was that they could not count on the national government. True, this was the "Progressive Period," the start of the Age of Reform; but it was a reluctant reform, aimed at quieting the popular risings, not making fundamental changes.

What gave it the name "Progressive" was that new laws were passed. Under Theodore Roosevelt, there was the Meat Inspection Act, the Hepburn Act to regulate railroads and pipelines, a Pure Food and Drug Act. Under Taft, the Mann-Elkins Act put telephone and telegraph systems under the regulation of the Interstate Commerce Commission. In Woodrow Wilson's presidency, the Federal Trade Commission was introduced to control the growth of monopolies, and the Federal Reserve Act to regulate the country's money and banking system. Under Taft were proposed the Sixteenth Amendment to the Constitution, allowing a graduated income tax, and the Seventeenth Amendment, providing for the election of Senators directly by popular vote instead of by the state legislatures, as the original Constitution provided. Also at this time, a number of states passed laws regulating wages and hours, providing for safety inspection of factories and compensation for injured workmen.

It was a time of public investigations aimed at soothing protest. In 1913 the Pujo Committee of Congress studied the concentration of power in the banking industry, and the Commission on Industrial Relations of the Senate held hearings on labor-management conflict.

Undoubtedly, ordinary people benefited to some extent from these changes. The system was rich, productive, complex; it could give enough of a share of its riches to enough of the working class to create a protective shield between the bottom and the top of the society. A study of immigrants in New York between 1905 and 1915 finds that 32 percent of Italians and Jews rose out of the manual class to higher levels (although not to *much* higher levels). But it was also true that many Italian immigrants did not find the opportunities inviting enough for them to stay. In one four-year period, seventy-three Italians left New York for every one hundred that arrived. Still, enough Italians became construction workers, enough Jews became businessmen and professionals, to create a middle-class cushion for class conflict.

Fundamental conditions did not change, however, for the vast majority of tenant farmers, factory workers, slum dwellers, miners, farm laborers, working men and women, black and white. Robert Wiebe sees in the Progressive movement an attempt by the system to adjust to changing conditions in order to achieve more stability. "Through rules with impersonal sanctions, it sought continuity and predictability in a world of endless change. It assigned far greater power to government . . . and it encouraged the centralization of authority." Harold Faulkner concluded that this new emphasis on strong government was for the benefit of "the most powerful economic groups."

Gabriel Kolko calls it the emergence of "political capitalism," where the businessmen took firmer control of the political system because the private economy was not efficient enough to forestall protest from below. The businessmen, Kolko says, were not opposed to the new reforms; they initiated them, pushed them, to stabilize the capitalist system in a time of uncertainty and trouble.

For instance, Theodore Roosevelt made a reputation for himself as a "trust-buster" (although his successor, Taft, a "conservative," while Roosevelt was a "Progressive," launched more antitrust suits than did Roosevelt). In fact, as Wiebe points out, two of J. P. Morgan's men—Elbert Gary, chairman of U.S. Steel, and George Perkins, who would later become a campaigner for Roosevelt—"arranged a general understanding with Roosevelt by which . . . they would cooperate in any investigation by the Bureau of Corporations in return for a guarantee of their companies' legality." They would do this through private negotiations with the President. "A gentleman's agreement between reasonable people," Wiebe says, with a bit of sarcasm.

The panic of 1907, as well as the growing strength of the Socialists, Wobblies, and trade unions, speeded the process of reform. According to Wiebe: "Around 1908 a qualitative shift in outlook occurred among large numbers of these men of authority. . . ." The emphasis was now on "enticements and compromises." It continued with Wilson, and "a great many reform-minded citizens indulged the illusion of a progressive fulfillment."

What radical critics now say of those reforms was said at the time (1901) by the *Bankers' Magazine*: "As the business of the country has learned the secret of combination, it is gradually subverting the power of the politician and rendering him subservient to its purposes. . . ."

There was much to stabilize, much to protect. By 1904, 318 trusts, with capital of more than seven billion dollars, controlled 40% of the U.S. manufacturing.

In 1909, a manifesto of the new Progressivism appeared—a book called *The Promise of American Life* by Herbert Croly, editor of the *New*

Republic and an admirer of Theodore Roosevelt. He saw the need for discipline and regulation if the American system were to continue. Government should do more, he said, and he hoped to see the "sincere and enthusiastic imitation of heroes and saints"—by whom he may have meant Theodore Roosevelt.

Richard Hofstadter, in his biting chapter on the man the public saw as the great lover of nature and physical fitness, the war hero, the Boy Scout in the White House, says: "The advisers to whom Roosevelt listened were almost exclusively representatives of industrial and finance capital—men like Hanna, Robert Bacon, and George W. Perkins of the House of Morgan, Elihu Root, Senator Nelson W. Aldrich ... and James Stillman of the Rockefeller interests." Responding to his worried brother-in-law writing from Wall Street, Roosevelt replied: "I intend to be most conservative, but in the interests of the corporations themselves and above all in the interests of the country."

Roosevelt supported the regulatory Hepburn Act because he feared something worse. He wrote to Henry Cabot Lodge that the railroad lobbyists who opposed the bill were wrong: "I think they are very short-sighted not to understand that to beat it means to increase the movement for government ownership of the railroads." His action against the trusts was to induce them to accept government regulation, in order to prevent destruction. He prosecuted the Morgan railroad monopoly in the Northern Securities Case, considering it an antitrust victory, but it hardly changed anything, and, although the Sherman Act provided for criminal penalties, there was no prosecution of the men who had planned the monopoly—Morgan, Harriman, Hill.

As for Woodrow Wilson, Hofstadter points out he was a conservative from the start. As a historian and political scientist, Wilson wrote *(The State)*: "In politics nothing radically novel may safely be attempted." He urged "slow and gradual" change. His attitude toward labor, Hofstadter says, was "generally hostile," and he spoke of the "crude and ignorant minds" of the Populists.

James Weinstein *(The Corporate Ideal in the Liberal State)* has studied the reforms of the Progressive period, especially the process by which business and government, sometimes with the aid of labor leaders, worked out the legislative changes they thought necessary. Weinstein sees "a conscious and successful effort to guide and control the economic and social policies of federal, state, and municipal governments by various business groupings in their own long-range interest. . . ." While the "original impetus" for reform came from protesters and radicals, "in the current century, particularly on the federal level, few reforms were enacted without the tacit approval, if not the guidance, of the large corporate interests." These interests assembled liberal reformers and intellectuals to aid them in such matters.

Weinstein's definition of liberalism—as a means of stabilizing the system in the interests of big business—is different from that of the liberals themselves. Arthur Schlesinger writes: "Liberalism in America has been ordinarily the movement on the part of the other sections of society to restrain the power of the business community." If Schlesinger is describing the hope or intent of these other sections, he may be right. If he is describing the actual effect of these liberal reforms, that restraint has not happened.

The controls were constructed skillfully. In 1900, a man named Ralph Easley, a Republican and conservative, a schoolteacher and journalist, organized the National Civic Federation. Its aim was to get better relations between capital and labor. Its officers were mostly big businessmen, and important national politicians, but its first vice-president, for a long time, was Samuel Gompers of the AFL. Not all big businesses liked what the National Civic Federation was doing. Easley called these critics anarchists, opposed to the rational organization of the system. "In fact," Easley wrote, "our enemies are the Socialists among the labor people and the anarchists among the capitalists."

The NCF wanted a more sophisticated approach to trade unions, seeing them as an inevitable reality, therefore wanting to come to agreements with them rather than fight with them: better to deal with a conservative union than face a militant one. After the Lawrence textile strike of 1912, John Golden, head of the conservative AFL Textile Union Workers, wrote Easley that the strike had given manufacturers "a very rapid education" and "some of them are falling all over themselves now to do business with our organization."

The National Civic Federation did not represent all opinions in the business world; the National Association of Manufacturers didn't want to recognize organized labor in any way. Many businessmen did not want even the puny reforms proposed by the Civic Federation—but the Federation's approach represented the sophistication and authority of the modern state, determined to do what was best for the capitalist class as a whole, even if this irritated some capitalists. The new approach was concerned with the long-range stability of the system, even at the cost, sometimes, of short-term profits.

Thus, the Federation drew up a model workmen's compensation bill in 1910, and the following year twelve states passed laws for compensation or accident insurance. When the Supreme Court said that year that

New York's workmen's compensation law was unconstitutional because it deprived corporations of property without due process of law, Theodore Roosevelt was angry. Such decisions, he said, added "immensely to the strength of the Socialist Party." By 1920, forty-two states had workmen's compensation laws. As Weinstein says: "It represented a growing maturity and sophistication on the part of many large corporation leaders who had come to understand, as Theodore Roosevelt often told them, that social reform was truly conservative."

As for the Federal Trade Commission, established by Congress in 1914 presumably to regulate trusts, a leader of the Civic Federation reported after several years of experience with it that it "has apparently been carrying on its work with the purpose of securing the confidence of well-intentioned business men, members of the great corporations as well as others."

In this period, cities also put through reforms, many of them giving power to city councils instead of mayors, or hiring city managers. The idea was more efficiency, more stability. "The end result of the movements was to place city government firmly in the hands of the business class," Weinstein says. What reformers saw as more democracy in city government, urban historian Samuel Hays sees as the centralization of power in fewer hands, giving business and professional men more direct control over city government.

The Progressive movement, whether led by honest reformers like Senator Robert La Follette of Wisconsin or disguised conservatives like Roosevelt (who was the Progressive party candidate for President in 1912), seemed to understand it was fending off socialism. The Milwaukee *Journal*, a Progressive organ, said the conservatives "fight socialism blindly . . . while the Progressives fight it intelligently and seek to remedy the abuses and conditions upon which it thrives."

Frank Munsey, a director of U.S. Steel, writing to Roosevelt, seeing him as the best candidate for 1912, confided in him that the United States must move toward a more "parental guardianship of the people" who needed "the sustaining and guiding hand of the State." It was "the work of the state to think for the people and plan for the people," the steel executive said.

It seems quite clear that much of this intense activity for Progressive reform was intended to head off socialism. Easley talked of "the menace of Socialism as evidenced by its growth in the colleges, churches, newspapers." In 1910, Victor Berger became the first member of the Socialist party elected to Congress; in 1911, seventy-three Socialist mayors were elected, and twelve hundred lesser officials in 340 cities and towns. The press spoke of "The Rising Tide of Socialism."

A privately circulated memorandum suggested to one of the departments of the National Civic Federation: "In view of the rapid spread in the United States of socialistic doctrines," what was needed was "a carefully planned and wisely directed effort to instruct public opinion as to the real meaning of socialism." The memorandum suggested that the campaign "must be very skillfully and tactfully carried out," that it "should not violently attack socialism and anarchism as such" but should be "patient and persuasive" and defend three ideas: "individual liberty; private property; and inviolability of contract."

It is hard to say how many Socialists saw clearly how useful reform was to capitalism, but in 1912, a left-wing Socialist from Connecticut, Robert LaMonte, wrote: "Old age pensions and insurance against sickness, accident and unemployment are cheaper, are better business than jails, poor houses, asylums, hospitals." He suggested that progressives would work for reforms, but Socialists must make only "impossible demands," which would reveal the limitations of the reformers.

Did the Progressive reforms succeed in doing what they intended— stabilize the capitalist system by repairing its worst defects, blunt the edge of the Socialist movement, restore some measure of class peace in a time of increasingly bitter clashes between capital and labor? To some extent, perhaps. But the Socialist party continued to grow. The IWW continued to agitate. And shortly after Woodrow Wilson took office there began in Colorado one of the most bitter and violent struggles between workers and corporate capital in the history of the country.

This was the Colorado coal strike that began in September 1913 and culminated in the "Ludlow Massacre" of April 1914. Eleven thousand miners in southern Colorado, mostly foreign-born—Greeks, Italians, Serbs—worked for the Colorado Fuel & Iron Corporation, which was owned by the Rockefeller family. Aroused by the murder of one of their organizers, they went on strike against low pay, dangerous conditions, and feudal domination of their lives in towns completely controlled by the mining companies. Mother Jones, at this time an organizer for the United Mine Workers, came into the area, fired up the miners with her oratory, and helped them in those critical first months of the strike, until she was arrested, kept in a dungeonlike cell, and then forcibly expelled from the state.

When the strike began, the miners were immediately evicted from their shacks in the mining towns. Aided by the United Mine Workers Union, they set up tents in the nearby hills and carried on the strike, the picketing, from these tent colonies. The gunmen hired by the Rockefeller interests—the Baldwin-Felts Detective Agency—using

Gatling guns and rifles, raided the tent colonies. The death list of miners grew, but they hung on, drove back an armored train in a gun battle, fought to keep out strikebreakers. With the miners resisting, refusing to give in, the mines not able to operate, the Colorado governor (referred to by a Rockefeller mine manager as "our little cowboy governor") called out the National Guard, with the Rockefellers supplying the Guard's wages.

The miners at first thought the Guard was sent to protect them, and greeted its arrivals with flags and cheers. They soon found out the Guard was there to destroy the strike. The Guard brought strike-breakers in under cover of night, not telling them there was a strike. Guardsmen beat miners, arrested them by the hundreds, rode down with their horses parades of women in the streets of Trinidad, the central town in the area. And still the miners refused to give in. When they lasted through the cold winter of 1913–1914, it became clear that extraordinary measures would be needed to break the strike.

In April 1914, two National Guard companies were stationed in the hills overlooking the largest tent colony of strikers, the one at Ludlow, housing a thousand men, women, children. On the morning of April 20, a machine gun attack began on the tents. The miners fired back. Their leader, a Greek named Lou Tikas, was lured up into the hills to discuss a truce, then shot to death by a company of National Guardsmen. The women and children dug pits beneath the tents to escape the gunfire. At dusk, the Guard moved down from the hills with torches, set fire to the tents, and the families fled into the hills; thirteen people were killed by gunfire.

The following day, a telephone linesman going through the ruins of the Ludlow tent colony lifted an iron cot covering a pit in one of the tents and found the charred, twisted bodies of eleven children and two women. This became known as the Ludlow Massacre.

The news spread quickly over the country. In Denver, the United Mine Workers issued a "Call to Arms"—"Gather together for defensive purposes all arms and ammunition legally available." Three hundred armed strikers marched from other tent colonies into the Ludlow area, cut telephone and telegraph wires, and prepared for battle. Railroad workers refused to take soldiers from Trinidad to Ludlow. At Colorado Springs, three hundred union miners walked off their jobs and headed for the Trinidad district, carrying revolvers, rifles, shotguns.

In Trinidad itself, miners attended a funeral service for the twenty-six dead at Ludlow, then walked from the funeral to a nearby building, where arms were stacked for them. They picked up rifles and moved into the hills, destroying mines, killing mine guards, exploding mine shafts. The press reported that "the hills in every direction seem suddenly to be alive with men."

In Denver, eighty-two soldiers in a company on a troop train headed for Trinidad refused to go. The press reported: "The men declared they would not engage in the shooting of women and children. They hissed the 350 men who did start and shouted imprecations at them."

Five thousand people demonstrated in the rain on the lawn in front of the state capital at Denver asking that the National Guard officers at Ludlow be tried for murder, denouncing the governor as an accessory. The Denver Cigar Makers Union voted to send five hundred armed men to Ludlow and Trinidad. Women in the United Garment Workers Union in Denver announced four hundred of their members had volunteered as nurses to help the strikers.

All over the country there were meetings, demonstrations. Pickets marched in front of the Rockefeller office at 26 Broadway, New York City. A minister protested in front of the church where Rockefeller sometimes gave sermons, and was clubbed by the police.

The *New York Times* carried an editorial on the events in Colorado, which were now attracting international attention. The *Times* emphasis was not on the atrocity that had occurred, but on the mistake in tactics that had been made. Its editorial on the Ludlow Massacre began: "Somebody blundered. . . ." Two days later, with the miners armed and in the hills of the mine district, the *Times* wrote: "With the deadliest weapons of civilization in the hands of savage-minded men, there can be no telling to what lengths the war in Colorado will go unless it is quelled by force. . . . The President should turn his attention from Mexico long enough to take stern measures in Colorado."

The governor of Colorado asked for federal troops to restore order, and Woodrow Wilson complied. This accomplished, the strike petered out. Congressional committees came in and took thousands of pages of testimony. The union had not won recognition. Sixty-six men, women, and children had been killed. Not one militiaman or mine guard had been indicted for crime.

Still, Colorado had been a scene of ferocious class conflict, whose emotional repercussions had rolled through the entire country. The threat of class rebellion was clearly still there in the industrial conditions of the United States, in the undeterred spirit of rebellion among working people—whatever legislation had been passed, whatever liberal reforms were on the books, whatever investigations were undertaken and words of regret and conciliation uttered.

The *Times* had referred to Mexico. On the morning that the bodies were discovered in the tent pit at Ludlow, American warships were attacking Vera Cruz, a city on the coast of Mexico—bombarding it, occupying it, leaving a hundred Mexicans dead—because Mexico had arrested American sailors and refused to apologize to the United States with a twenty-one-gun salute. Could patriotic fervor and the military spirit cover up class struggle? Unemployment, hard times, were growing in 1914. Could guns divert attention and create some national consensus against an external enemy? It surely was a coincidence—the bombardment of Vera Cruz, the attack on the Ludlow colony. Or perhaps it was, as someone once described human history, "the natural selection of accidents." Perhaps the affair in Mexico was an instinctual response of the system for its own survival, to create a unity of fighting purpose among a people torn by internal conflict.

The bombardment of Vera Cruz was a small incident. But in four months the First World War would begin in Europe.

14

WAR IS THE HEALTH
OF THE STATE

"War is the health of the state," the radical writer Randolph Bourne said, in the midst of the First World War. Indeed, as the nations of Europe went to war in 1914, the governments flourished, patriotism bloomed, class struggle was stilled, and young men died in frightful numbers on the battlefields—often for a hundred yards of land, a line of trenches.

In the United States, not yet in the war, there was worry about the health of the state. Socialism was growing. The IWW seemed to be everywhere. Class conflict was intense. In the summer of 1916, during a Preparedness Day parade in San Francisco, a bomb exploded, killing nine people; two local radicals, Tom Mooney and Warren Billings, were arrested and would spend twenty years in prison. Shortly after that Senator James Wadsworth of New York suggested compulsory military training for all males to avert the danger that "these people of ours shall be divided into classes." Rather: "We must let our young men know that they owe some responsibility to this country."

The supreme fulfillment of that responsibility was taking place in Europe. Ten million were to die on the battlefield; 20 million were to die of hunger and disease related to the war. And no one since that day has been able to show that the war brought any gain for humanity that would be worth one human life. The rhetoric of the socialists, that it was an "imperialist war," now seems moderate and hardly arguable. The advanced capitalist countries of Europe were fighting over boundaries, colonies, spheres of influence; they were competing for Alsace-Lorraine, the Balkans, Africa, the Middle East.

The war came shortly after the opening of the twentieth century, in the midst of exultation (perhaps only among the elite in the Western world) about progress and modernization. One day after the English declared war, Henry James wrote to a friend: "The plunge of civilization into this abyss of blood and darkness . . . is a thing that so gives away the whole long age during which we have supposed the world to be . . . gradually bettering." In the first Battle of the Marne, the British and French succeeded in blocking the German advance on Paris. Each side had 500,000 casualties.

The killing started very fast, and on a large scale. In August 1914, a volunteer for the British army had to be 5 feet 8 inches to enlist. By October, the requirement was lowered to 5 feet 5 inches. That month there were thirty thousand casualties, and then one could be 5 feet 3. In the first three months of war, almost the entire original British army was wiped out.

For three years the battle lines remained virtually stationary in France. Each side would push forward, then back, then forward again—for a few yards, a few miles, while the corpses piled up. In 1916 the Germans tried to break through at Verdun; the British and French counterattacked along the Seine, moved forward a few miles, and lost 600,000 men. One day, the 9th Battalion of the King's Own Yorkshire Light Infantry launched an attack with eight hundred men. Twenty-four hours later, there were eighty-four left.

Back home, the British were not told of the slaughter. One English writer recalled: "The most bloody defeat in the history of Britain . . . might occur . . . and our Press come out bland and copious and graphic with nothing to show that we had not had quite a good day—a victory really. . . ." The same thing was happening on the German side; as Erich Maria Remarque wrote in his great novel, on days when men by the thousands were being blown apart by machine guns and shells, the official dispatches announced "All Quiet on the Western Front."

In July 1916, British General Douglas Haig ordered eleven divisions of English soldiers to climb out of their trenches and move toward the German lines. The six German divisions opened up with their machine guns. Of the 110,000 who attacked, 20,000 were killed, 40,000 more wounded—all those bodies strewn on no man's land, the ghostly territory between the contending trenches. On January 1, 1917, Haig was promoted to field marshal. What happened that summer is described tersely in William Langer's *An Encyclopedia of World History*:

Despite the opposition of Lloyd George and the skepticism of some of his subordinates, Haig proceeded hopefully to the main offensive. The third battle of Ypres was a series of 8 heavy attacks, carried through in driving rain and fought over ground water-logged and muddy. No break-through was effected, and the total gain was about 5 miles of territory, which made the Ypres salient more inconvenient than ever and cost the British about 400,000 men.

The people of France and Britain were not told the extent of the casualties. When, in the last year of the war, the Germans attacked ferociously on the Somme, and left 300,000 British soldiers dead or wounded, London newspapers printed the following, we learn from Paul Fussell's *The Great War and Modern Memory*:

> WHAT CAN I DO?
> How the Civilian May Help in this Crisis.
> Be cheerful. . . .
> Write encouragingly to friends at the front. . . .
> Don't repeat foolish gossip.
> Don't listen to idle rumors.
> Don't think you know better than Haig.

Into this pit of death and deception came the United States, in the spring of 1917. Mutinies were beginning to occur in the French army. Soon, out of 112 divisions, 68 would have mutinies; 629 men would be tried and condemned, 50 shot by firing squads. American troops were badly needed.

President Woodrow Wilson had promised that the United States would stay neutral in the war: "There is such a thing as a nation being too proud to fight." But in April of 1917, the Germans had announced they would have their submarines sink any ship bringing supplies to their enemies; and they had sunk a number of merchant vessels. Wilson now said he must stand by the right of Americans to travel on merchant ships in the war zone. "I cannot consent to any abridgement of the rights of American citizens in any respect. . . ."

As Richard Hofstadter points out *(The American Political Tradition)*: "This was rationalization of the flimsiest sort. . . ." The British had also been intruding on the rights of American citizens on the high seas, but Wilson was not suggesting we go to war with them. Hofstadter says Wilson "was forced to find legal reasons for policies that were based not upon law but upon the balance of power and economic necessities."

It was unrealistic to expect that the Germans should treat the United States as neutral in the war when the U.S. had been shipping great amounts of war materials to Germany's enemies. In early 1915, the British liner *Lusitania* was torpedoed and sunk by a German submarine. She sank in eighteen minutes, and 1,198 people died, including 124 Americans. The United States claimed the *Lusitania* carried an innocent cargo, and therefore the torpedoing was a monstrous German atrocity. Actually, the *Lusitania* was heavily armed: it carried 1,248 cases of 3-inch shells, 4,927 boxes of cartridges (1,000 rounds in each box), and 2,000 more cases of small-arms ammunition. Her manifests were falsified to hide this fact, and the British and American governments lied about the cargo.

Hofstadter wrote of "economic necessities" behind Wilson's war policy. In 1914 a serious recession had begun in the United States. J. P. Morgan later testified: "The war opened during a period of hard times. . . . Business throughout the country was depressed, farm prices were deflated, unemployment was serious, the heavy industries were working far below capacity and bank clearings were off." But by 1915, war orders for the Allies (mostly England) had stimulated the economy, and by April 1917 more than $2 billion worth of goods had been sold to the Allies. As Hofstadter says: "America became bound up with the Allies in a fateful union of war and prosperity."

Prosperity depended much on foreign markets, it was believed by the leaders of the country. In 1897, the private foreign investments of the United States amounted to $700 million dollars. By 1914 they were $3½ billion. Wilson's Secretary of State, William Jennings Bryan, while a believer in neutrality in the war, also believed that the United States needed overseas markets; in May of 1914 he praised the President as one who had "opened the doors of all the weaker countries to an invasion of American capital and American enterprise."

Back in 1907, Woodrow Wilson had said in a lecture at Columbia University: "Concessions obtained by financiers must be safeguarded by ministers of state, even if the sovereignty of unwilling nations be outraged in the process. . . . the doors of the nations which are closed must be battered down." In his 1912 campaign he said: "Our domestic markets no longer suffice, we need foreign markets." In a memo to Bryan he described his aim as "an open door to the world," and in 1914 he said he supported "the righteous conquest of foreign markets."

With World War I, England became more and more a market for American goods and for loans at interest. J. P. Morgan and Company acted as agents for the Allies, and when, in 1915, Wilson lifted the ban on private bank loans to the Allies, Morgan could now begin lending money in such great amounts as to both make great profit and tie American finance closely to the interest of a British victory in the war against Germany.

The industrialists and the political leaders talked of prosperity as if it were classless, as if everyone gained from Morgan's loans. True, the war meant more production, more employment, but did the workers in the steel plants gain as much as U.S. Steel, which made $348 million in profit in 1916 alone? When the United States entered the war, it was the rich who took even more direct charge of the economy. Financier Bernard Baruch headed the War Industries Board, the most powerful of the wartime government agencies. Bankers, railroad men, and industrialists dominated these agencies.

A remarkably perceptive article on the nature of the First World War appeared in May 1915 in the *Atlantic Monthly*. Written by W. E. B. Du Bois, it was titled "The African Roots of War." It was a war for empire, of which the struggle between Germany and the Allies over Africa was both symbol and reality: ". . . in a very real sense Africa is a prime cause of this terrible overturning of civilization which we have lived to see." Africa, Du Bois said, is "the Land of the Twentieth Century," because of the gold and diamonds of South Africa, the cocoa of Angola and Nigeria, the rubber and ivory of the Congo, the palm oil of the West Coast.

Du Bois saw more than that. He was writing several years before Lenin's *Imperialism*, which noted the new possibility of giving the working class of the imperial country a share of the loot. He pointed to the paradox of greater "democracy" in America alongside "increased aristocracy and hatred toward darker races." He explained the paradox by the fact that "the white workingman has been asked to share the spoil of exploiting 'chinks and niggers.'" Yes, the average citizen of England, France, Germany, the United States, had a higher standard of living than before. But: "Whence comes this new wealth? . . . It comes primarily from the darker nations of the world—Asia and Africa, South and Central America, the West Indies, and the islands of the South Seas."

Du Bois saw the ingenuity of capitalism in uniting exploiter and exploited—creating a safety valve for explosive class conflict. "It is no longer simply the merchant prince, or the aristocratic monopoly, or even the employing class, that is exploiting the world: it is the nation, a new democratic nation composed of united capital and labor."

The United States fitted that idea of Du Bois. American capitalism needed international rivalry—and periodic war—to create an artificial community of interest between rich and poor, supplanting the genuine community of interest among the poor that showed itself in sporadic movements. How conscious of this were individual entrepreneurs and statesmen? That is hard to know. But their actions, even if half-conscious, instinctive drives to survive, matched such a scheme. And in 1917 this demanded a national consensus for war.

The government quickly succeeded in creating such a consensus, according to the traditional histories. Woodrow Wilson's biographer Arthur Link wrote: "In the final analysis American policy was determined by the President and public opinion." In fact, there is no way of measuring public opinion at that time, and there is no persuasive evidence that the public wanted war. The government had to work hard to create its consensus. That there was no spontaneous urge to fight is suggested by the strong measures taken: a draft of young men, an elaborate propaganda campaign throughout the country, and harsh punishment for those who refused to get in line.

Despite the rousing words of Wilson about a war "to end all wars" and "to make the world safe for democracy," Americans did not rush to enlist. A million men were needed, but in the first six weeks after the declaration of war only 73,000 volunteered. Congress voted overwhelmingly for a draft.

George Creel, a veteran newspaperman, became the government's official propagandist for the war; he set up a Committee on Public Information to persuade Americans the war was right. It sponsored 75,000 speakers, who gave 750,000 four-minute speeches in five thousand American cities and towns. It was a massive effort to excite a reluctant public. At the beginning of 1917, a member of the National Civic Federation had complained that "neither workingmen nor farmers" were taking "any part or interest in the efforts of the security or defense leagues or other movements for national preparedness."

The day after Congress declared war, the Socialist party met in emergency convention in St. Louis and called the declaration "a crime against the people of the United States." In the summer of 1917, Socialist antiwar meetings in Minnesota drew large crowds—five thousand, ten thousand, twenty thousand farmers—protesting the war, the draft, profiteering. A local newspaper in Wisconsin, the Plymouth *Review*, said that probably no party ever gained more rapidly in strength than the Socialist party just at the present time." It reported that "thousands assemble to hear Socialist speakers in places where ordinarily a few hundred are considered large assemblages." The Akron *Beacon-Journal*, a conservative newspaper in Ohio, said there was "scarcely a political observer . . . but what will admit that were an election to come now a mighty tide of socialism would inundate the Middle West." It said the country had "never embarked upon a more unpopular war."

In the municipal elections of 1917, against the tide of propaganda and patriotism, the Socialists made remarkable gains. Their candidate for mayor of New York, Morris Hillquit, got 22 percent of the vote, five times the normal Socialist vote there. Ten Socialists were elected to the New York State legislature. In Chicago, the party vote went from 3.6 percent in 1915 to 34.7 percent in 1917. In Buffalo, it went from 2.6 percent to 30.2 percent.

George Creel and the government were behind the formation of an American Alliance for Labor and Democracy, whose president was Samuel Gompers and whose aim was to "unify sentiment in the nation" for the war. There were branches in 164 cities; many labor leaders went along. According to James Weinstein, however, the Alliance did not work: "Rank-and-file working class support for the war remained lukewarm...." And although some prominent Socialists—Jack London, Upton Sinclair, Clarence Darrow—became prowar after the U.S. entered, most Socialists continued their opposition.

Congress passed, and Wilson signed, in June of 1917, the Espionage Act. From its title one would suppose it was an act against spying. However, it had a clause that provided penalties up to twenty years in prison for "Whoever, when the United States is at war, shall wilfully cause or attempt to cause insubordination, disloyalty, mutiny, or refusal of duty in the military or naval forces of the United States, or shall wilfully obstruct the recruiting or enlistment service of the U.S...." Unless one had a theory about the nature of governments, it was not clear how the Espionage Act would be used. It even had a clause that said "nothing in this section shall be construed to limit or restrict ... any discussion, comment, or criticism of the acts or policies of the Government...." But its double-talk concealed a singleness of purpose. The Espionage Act was used to imprison Americans who spoke or wrote against the war.

Two months after the law passed, a Socialist named Charles Schenck was arrested in Philadelphia for printing and distributing fifteen thousand leaflets that denounced the draft law and the war. The leaflet recited the Thirteenth Amendment provision against "involuntary servitude" and said the Conscription Act violated this. Conscription, it said, was "a monstrous deed against humanity in the interests of the financiers of Wall Street." And: "Do not submit to intimidation."

Schenck was indicted, tried, found guilty, and sentenced to six months in jail for violating the Espionage Act. (It turned out to be one of the shortest sentences given in such cases.) Schenck appealed, arguing that the Act, by prosecuting speech and writing, violated the First Amendment: "Congress shall make no law . . . abridging the freedom of speech, or of the press. . . ."

The Supreme Court's decision was unanimous and was written by its most famous liberal, Oliver Wendell Holmes. He summarized the contents of the leaflet and said it was undoubtedly intended to "obstruct" the carrying out of the draft law. Was Schenck protected by the First Amendment? Holmes said:

> The most stringent protection of free speech would not protect a man in falsely shouting fire in a theatre and causing a panic. . . . The question in every case is whether the words used are used in such circumstances and are of such a nature as to create a clear and present danger that they will bring about the substantive evils that Congress has a right to prevent.

Holmes's analogy was clever and attractive. Few people would think free speech should be conferred on someone shouting fire in a theater and causing a panic. But did that example fit criticism of the war? Zechariah Chafee, a Harvard law school professor, wrote later (*Free Speech in the United States*) that a more apt analogy for Schenck was someone getting up between the acts at a theater and declaring that there were not enough fire exits. To play further with the example: was not Schenck's act more like someone shouting, not falsely, but truly, to people about to buy tickets and enter a theater, that there was a fire raging inside?

Perhaps free speech could not be tolerated by any reasonable person if it constituted a "clear and present danger" to life and liberty; after all, free speech must compete with other vital rights. But was not the war itself a "clear and present danger," indeed, more clear and more present and more dangerous to life than any argument against it? Did citizens not have a right to object to war, a right to be a danger to dangerous policies?

(The Espionage Act, thus approved by the Supreme Court, has remained on the books all these years since World War I, and although it is supposed to apply only in wartime, it has been constantly in force since 1950, because the United States has legally been in a "state of emergency" since the Korean war. In 1963, the Kennedy administration pushed a bill [unsuccessfully] to apply the Espionage Act to statements uttered by Americans abroad; it was concerned, in the words of a cable from Secretary of State Rusk to Ambassador Lodge in Vietnam, about journalists in Vietnam writing "critical articles . . . on Diem and his government" that were "likely to impede the war effort.")

The case of Eugene Debs soon came before the Supreme Court. In June of 1918, Debs visited three Socialists who were in prison for opposing the draft, and then spoke, across the street from the jail, to an audience he kept enthralled for two hours. He was one of the country's great orators, and was interrupted again and again by laughter and applause. "Why, the other day, by a vote of five-to-four—a kind of craps game, come seven, come eleven—they declared the child labor law unconstitutional." He spoke of his comrades in jail. He dealt with the charges that Socialists were pro-German. "I hate, I loathe, I despise Junkers and Junkerdom. I have no earthly use for the Junkers of Germany, and not one particle more use for the Junkers in the United States." (Thunderous applause and cheers.)

> They tell us that we live in a great free republic; that our institutions are democratic; that we are a free and self-governing people. That is too much, even for a joke. . . .
> Wars throughout history have been waged for conquest and plunder. . . . And that is war in a nutshell. The master class has always declared the wars; the subject class has always fought the battles. . . .

Debs was arrested for violating the Espionage Act. There were draft-age youths in his audience, and his words would "obstruct the recruiting or enlistment service."

His words were intended to do much more than that:

> Yes, in good time we are going to sweep into power in this nation and throughout the world. We are going to destroy all enslaving and degrading capitalist institutions and re-create them as free and humanizing institutions. The world is daily changing before our eyes. The sun of capitalism is setting; the sun of Socialism is rising. . . . In due time the hour will strike and this great cause triumphant . . . will proclaim the emancipation of the working class and the brotherhood of all mankind. (Thunderous and prolonged applause.)

Debs refused at his trial to take the stand in his defense, or to call a witness on his behalf. He denied nothing about what he said. But before the jury began its deliberations, he spoke to them:

> I have been accused of obstructing the war. I admit it. Gentlemen, I abhor war. I would oppose war if I stood alone. . . . I have sympathy with the suf-

fering, struggling people everywhere. It does not make any difference under what flag they were born, or where they live. . . .

The jury found him guilty of violating the Espionage Act. Debs addressed the judge before sentencing:

> Your honor, years ago I recognized my kinship with all living beings, and I made up my mind that I was not one bit better than the meanest on earth. I said then, and I say now, that while there is a lower class, I am in it; while there is a criminal element, I am of it; while there is a soul in prison, I am not free.

The judge denounced those "who would strike the sword from the hand of this nation while she is engaged in defending herself against a foreign and brutal power." He sentenced Debs to ten years in prison.

Debs's appeal was not heard by the Supreme Court until 1919. The war was over. Oliver Wendell Holmes, for a unanimous court, affirmed Debs's guilt. Holmes discussed Debs's speech: "He then expressed opposition to Prussian militarism in a way that naturally might have been thought to be intended to include the mode of proceeding in the United States." Holmes said Debs made "the usual contrasts between capitalists and laboring men . . . with the implication running through it all that the working men are not concerned in the war." Thus, Holmes said, the "natural and intended effect" of Debs's speech would be to obstruct recruiting.

Debs was locked up in the West Virginia state penitentiary, and then in the Atlanta federal penitentiary, where he spent thirty-two months until, at the age of sixty-six, he was released by President Harding in 1921.

About nine hundred people went to prison under the Espionage Act. This substantial opposition was put out of sight, while the visible national mood was represented by military bands, flag waving, the mass buying of war bonds, the majority's acquiescence to the draft and the war. This acquiescence was achieved by shrewd public relations and by intimidation—an effort organized with all the power of the federal government and the money of big business behind it. The magnitude of that campaign to discourage opposition says something about the spontaneous feelings of the population toward the war.

The newspapers helped create an atmosphere of fear for possible opponents of the war. In April of 1917, the *New York Times* quoted Elihu Root (former Secretary of War, a corporation lawyer) as saying: "We must have no criticism now." A few months later it quoted him again that "there are men walking about the streets of this city tonight who ought to be taken out at sunrise tomorrow and shot for treason." At the same time, Theodore Roosevelt was talking to the Harvard Club about Socialists, IWWs, and others who wanted peace as "a whole raft of sexless creatures."

In the summer of 1917, the American Defense Society was formed. The New York *Herald* reported: "More than one hundred men enrolled yesterday in the American Vigilante Patrol at the offices of the American Defense Society. . . . The Patrol was formed to put an end to seditious street oratory."

The Department of Justice sponsored an American Protective League, which by June of 1917 had units in six hundred cities and towns, a membership of nearly 100,000. The press reported that their members were "the leading men in their communities . . . bankers . . . railroad men . . . hotel men." One study of the League describes their methods:

> The mails are supposed to be sacred. . . . But let us call the American Protective League sometimes almost clairvoyant as to letters done by suspects. . . . It is supposed that breaking and entering a man's home or office place without warrant is burglary. Granted. But the League has done that thousands of times and has never been detected!

The League claimed to have found 3 million cases of disloyalty. Even if these figures are exaggerated, the very size and scope of the League gives a clue to the amount of "disloyalty."

The states organized vigilante groups. The Minnesota Commission of Public Safety, set up by state law, closed saloons and moving picture theaters, took count of land owned by aliens, boosted Liberty bonds, tested people for loyalty. The Minneapolis *Journal* carried an appeal by the Commission "for all patriots to join in the suppression of antidraft and seditious acts and sentiment."

The national press cooperated with the government. The *New York Times* in the summer of 1917 carried an editorial: "It is the duty of every good citizen to communicate to proper authorities any evidence of sedition that comes to his notice." And the *Literary Digest* asked its readers "to clip and send to us any editorial utterances they encounter which seem to them seditious or treasonable." Creel's Committee on Public Information advertised that people should "report the man who spreads pessimistic stories. Report him to the Department of Justice." In 1918, the Attorney General said: "It is safe to say that never in its history has this country been so thoroughly policed."

Why these huge efforts? On August 1, 1917, the New York *Herald* reported that in New York City ninety of the first hundred draftees claimed exemption. In Minnesota, headlines in the Minneapolis *Journal* of August 6 and 7 read: "DRAFT OPPOSITION FAST SPREADING IN STATE," and "CONSCRIPTS GIVE FALSE ADDRESSES." In Florida, two Negro farm hands went into the woods with a shotgun and mutilated themselves to avoid the draft: one blew off four fingers of his hand; the other shot off his arm below the elbow. Senator Thomas Hardwick of Georgia said "there was undoubtedly general and widespread opposition on the part of many thousands . . . to the enactment of the draft law. Numerous and largely attended mass meetings held in every part of the State protested against it. . . ." Ultimately, over 330,000 men were classified as draft evaders.

In Oklahoma, the Socialist party and the IWW had been active among tenant farmers and sharecroppers who formed a "Working Class Union." At a mass meeting of the Union, plans were made to destroy a railroad bridge and cut telegraph wires in order to block military enlistments. A march on Washington was planned for draft objectors throughout the country. (This was called the Green Corn Rebellion because they planned to eat green corn on their march.) Before the Union could carry out its plans, its members were rounded up and arrested, and soon 450 individuals accused of rebellion were in the state penitentiary. Leaders were given three to ten years in jail, others sixty days to two years.

On July 1, 1917, radicals organized a parade in Boston against the war, with banners:

IS THIS A POPULAR WAR, WHY CONSCRIPTION?

WHO STOLE PANAMA? WHO CRUSHED HAITI?

WE DEMAND PEACE.

The New York *Call* said eight thousand people marched, including "4000 members of the Central Labor Union, 2000 members of the Lettish Socialist Organizations, 1500 Lithuanians, Jewish members of cloak trades, and other branches of the party." The parade was attacked by soldiers and sailors, on orders from their officers.

The Post Office Department began taking away the mailing privileges of newspapers and magazines that printed antiwar articles. *The Masses*, a socialist magazine of politics, literature, and art, was banned from the mails. It had carried an editorial by Max Eastman in the summer of 1917, saying, among other things: "For what specific purposes are you shipping our bodies, and the bodies of our sons, to Europe? For my part, I do not recognize the right of a government to draft me to a war whose purposes I do not believe in."

In Los Angeles, a film was shown that dealt with the American Revolution and depicted British atrocities against the colonists. It was called *The Spirit of '76*. The man who made the film was prosecuted under the Espionage Act because, the judge said, the film tended "to question the good faith of our ally, Great Britain." He was sentenced to ten years in prison. The case was officially listed as *U.S. v. Spirit of '76*.

In a small town in South Dakota, a farmer and socialist named Fred Fairchild, during an argument about the war, said, according to his accusers: "If I were of conscription age and had no dependents and were drafted, I would refuse to serve. They could shoot me, but they could not make me fight." He was tried under the Espionage Act, sentenced to a year and a day at Leavenworth penitentiary. And so it went, multiplied two thousand times (the number of prosecutions under the Espionage Act).

About 65,000 men declared themselves conscientious objectors and asked for noncombatant service. At the army bases where they worked, they were often treated with sadistic brutality. Three men who were jailed at Fort Riley, Kansas, for refusing to perform any military duties, combatant or noncombatant, were taken one by one into the corridor and:

> . . . a hemp rope slung over the railing of the upper tier was put about their necks, hoisting them off their feet until they were at the point of collapse. Meanwhile the officers punched them on their ankles and shins. They were then lowered and the rope was tied to their arms, and again they were hoisted off their feet. This time a garden hose was played on their faces with a nozzle about six inches from them, until they collapsed completely. . . .

Schools and universities discouraged opposition to the war. At Columbia University, J. McKeen Cattell, a psychologist, a long-time critic of the Board of Trustees' control of the university, and an opponent of the war, was fired. A week later, in protest, the famous historian Charles Beard resigned from the Columbia faculty, charging the trustees with being "reactionary and visionless in politics, narrow and medieval in religion. . . ."

In Congress, a few voices spoke out against the war. The first woman in the House of Representatives, Jeannette Rankin, did not respond when her name was called in the roll call on the declaration of war. One of the veteran politicians of the House, a supporter of the war, went to her and whispered, "Little woman, you cannot afford not to vote. You represent the womanhood of the country. . . ." On the next roll call she stood up: "I want to stand by my country, but I cannot vote for war. I vote No." A popular song of the time was: "I Didn't Raise My Boy to Be a Soldier." It was overwhelmed, however, by songs like "Over There," "It's a Grand Old Flag," and "Johnny Get Your Gun."

Socialist Kate Richards O'Hare, speaking in North Dakota in July of 1917, said, it was reported, that "the women of the United States were nothing more nor less than brood sows, to raise children to get into the army and be made into fertilizer." She was arrested, tried, found guilty, and sentenced to five years in the Missouri state penitentiary. In prison she continued to fight. When she and fellow prisoners protested the lack of air, because the window above the cell block was kept shut, she was pulled out in the corridor by guards for punishment. In her hand she was carrying a book of poems, and as she was dragged out she flung the book up at the window and broke it, the fresh air streaming in, her fellow prisoners cheering.

Emma Goldman and her fellow anarchist, Alexander Berkman (he had already been locked up fourteen years in Pennsylvania; she had served a year on Blackwell's Island), were sentenced to prison for opposing the draft. She spoke to the jury:

> Verily, poor as we are in democracy how can we give of it to the world? . . . a democracy conceived in the military servitude of the masses, in their economic enslavement, and nurtured in their tears and blood, is not democracy at all. It is despotism—the cumulative result of a chain of abuses which, according to that dangerous document, the Declaration of Independence, the people have the right to overthrow. . . .

The war gave the government its opportunity to destroy the IWW. The IWW newspaper, the *Industrial Worker*, just before the declaration of war, wrote: "Capitalists of America, we will fight against you, not for you! Conscription! There is not a power in the world that can make the working class fight if they refuse." Philip Foner, in his history of the IWW, says that the Wobblies were not as active against the war as the Socialists, perhaps because they were fatalistic, saw the war as inevitable, and thought that only victory in class struggle, only revolutionary change, could end war.

In early September 1917, Department of Justice agents made simultaneous raids on forty-eight IWW meeting halls across the country, seizing correspondence and literature that would become courtroom evidence. Later that month, 165 IWW leaders were arrested for conspiring to hinder the draft, encourage desertion, and intimidate others in connection with labor disputes. One hundred and one went on trial in April 1918; it lasted five months, the longest criminal trial in American history up to that time. John Reed, the Socialist writer just back from reporting on the Bolshevik Revolution in Russia *(Ten Days That Shook the World)*, covered the IWW trial for *The Masses* magazine and described the defendants:

> I doubt if ever in history there has been a sight just like them. One hundred and one lumberjacks, harvest hands, miners, editors ... who believe the wealth of the world belongs to him who creates it ... the outdoor men, hard-rock blasters, tree-fellers, wheat-binders, longshoremen, the boys who do the strongwork of the world. ...

The IWW people used the trial to tell about their activities, their ideas. Sixty-one of them took the stand, including Big Bill Haywood, who testified for three days. One IWW man told the court:

> You ask me why the I.W.W. is not patriotic to the United States. If you were a bum without a blanket; if you had left your wife and kids when you went west for a job, and had never located them since; if your job had never kept you long enough in a place to qualify you to vote; if you slept in a lousy, sour bunkhouse, and ate food just as rotten as they could give you and get by with it; if deputy sheriffs shot your cooking cans full of holes and spilled your grub on the ground; if your wages were lowered on you when the bosses thought they had you down; if there was one law for Ford, Suhr, and Mooney, and another for Harry Thaw; if every person who represented law and order and the nation beat you up, railroaded you to jail, and the good Christian people cheered and told them to go to it, how in hell do you expect a man to be patriotic? This war is a business man's war and we don't see why we should go out and get shot in order to save the lovely state of affairs that we now enjoy.

The jury found them all guilty. The judge sentenced Haywood and fourteen others to twenty years in prison; thirty-three were given ten years, the rest shorter sentences. They were fined a total of $2,500,000. The IWW was shattered. Haywood jumped bail and fled to revolutionary Russia, where he remained until his death ten years later.

The war ended in November 1918. Fifty thousand American soldiers had died, and it did not take long, even in the case of patriots, for bitterness and disillusionment to spread through the country. This was reflected in the literature of the postwar decade. John Dos Passos, in his novel *1919*, wrote of the death of John Doe:

> In the tarpaper morgue at Chalons-sur-Marne in the reek of chloride of lime and the dead, they picked out the pine box that held all that was left of ... John Doe. . . .
> ... the scraps of dried viscera and skin bundled in khaki
> they took to Chalons-sur-Marne
> and laid it out neat in a pine coffin
> and took it home to God's Country on a battleship
> and buried it in a sarcophagus in the Memorial Amphitheatre in the Arlington National Cemetery
> and draped the Old Glory over it
> and the bugler played taps
> and Mr. Harding prayed to God and the diplomats and the generals and the admirals and the brass hats and the politicians and the handsomely dressed ladies out of the society column of the Washington Post stood up solemn
> and thought how beautiful sad Old Glory God's Country it was to have the bugler play taps and the three volleys made their ears ring.
> Where his chest ought to have been they pinned the Congressional Medal. . . .

Ernest Hemingway would write *A Farewell to Arms*. Years later a college student named Irwin Shaw would write a play, *Bury the Dead*. And a Hollywood screenwriter named Dalton Trumbo would write a powerful and chilling antiwar novel about a torso and brain left alive on the battlefield of World War I, *Johnny Got His Gun*. Ford Madox Ford wrote *No More Parades*.

With all the wartime jailings, the intimidation, the drive for national unity, when the war was over, the Establishment still feared socialism. There seemed to be a need again for the twin tactics of control in the face of revolutionary challenge: reform and repression.

The first was suggested by George L. Record, one of Wilson's friends, who wrote to him in early 1919 that something would have to be done for economic democracy, "to meet this menace of socialism." He said: "You should become the real leader of the radical forces in America, and present to the country a constructive program of fundamental reform, which shall be an alternative to the program presented by the socialists, and the Bolsheviki. . . ."

That summer of 1919, Wilson's adviser Joseph Tumulty reminded him that the conflict between the Republicans and Democrats was unimportant compared with that which threatened them both:

> What happened in Washington last night in the attempt upon the Attorney General's life is but a symptom of the terrible unrest that is stalking about the country.... As a Democrat I would be disappointed to see the Republican Party regain power. That is not what depresses one so much as to see growing steadily from day to day, under our very eyes, a movement that, if it is not checked, is bound to express itself in attack upon everything we hold dear. In this era of industrial and social unrest both parties are in disrepute with the average man....

"What happened in Washington last night" was the explosion of a bomb in front of the home of Wilson's Attorney General A. Mitchell Palmer. Six months after that bomb exploded, Palmer carried out the first of his mass raids on aliens—immigrants who were not citizens. A law passed by Congress near the end of the war provided for the deportation of aliens who opposed organized government or advocated the destruction of property. Palmer's men, on December 21, 1919, picked up 249 aliens of Russian birth (including Emma Goldman and Alexander Berkman), put them on a transport, and deported them to what had become Soviet Russia. The Constitution gave no right to Congress to deport aliens, but the Supreme Court had said, back in 1892, in affirming the right of Congress to exclude Chinese, that as a matter of self-preservation, this was a natural right of the government.

In January 1920, four thousand persons were rounded up all over the country, held in seclusion for long periods of time, brought into secret hearings, and ordered deported. In Boston, Department of Justice agents, aided by local police, arrested six hundred people by raiding meeting halls or by invading their homes in the early morning. A troubled federal judge described the process:

> Pains were taken to give spectacular publicity to the raid, and to make it appear that there was great and imminent public danger.... The arrested aliens, in most instances perfectly quiet and harmless working people, many of them not long ago Russian peasants, were handcuffed in pairs, and then, for the purposes of transfer on trains and through the streets of Boston, chained together....

In the spring of 1920, a typesetter and anarchist named Andrea Salsedo was arrested in New York by FBI agents and held for eight weeks in the FBI offices on the fourteenth floor of the Park Row Building, not allowed to contact family or friends or lawyers. Then his crushed body was found on the pavement below the building and the FBI said he had committed suicide by jumping from the fourteenth floor window.

Two friends of Salsedo, anarchists and workingmen in the Boston area, having just learned of his death, began carrying guns. They were arrested on a streetcar in Brockton, Massachusetts, and charged with a holdup and murder that had taken place two weeks before at a shoe factory. These were Nicola Sacco and Bartolomeo Vanzetti. They went on trial, were found guilty, and spent seven years in jail while appeals went on, and while all over the country and the world, people became involved in their case. The trial record and the surrounding circumstances suggested that Sacco and Vanzetti were sentenced to death because they were anarchists and foreigners. In August 1927, as police broke up marches and picket lines with arrests and beatings, and troops surrounded the prison, they were electrocuted.

Sacco's last message to his son Dante, in his painfully learned English, was a message to millions of others in the years to come:

> So, Son, instead of crying, be strong, so as to be able to comfort your mother . . . take her for a long walk in the quiet country, gathering wild flowers here and there. . . . But remember always, Dante, in the play of happiness, don't you use all for yourself only. . . . help the persecuted and the victim because they are your better friends. . . . In this struggle of life you will find more and love and you will be loved.

There had been reforms. The patriotic fervor of war had been invoked. The courts and jails had been used to reinforce the idea that certain ideas, certain kinds of resistance, could not be tolerated. And still, even from the cells of the condemned, the message was going out: the class war was still on in that supposedly classless society, the United States. Through the twenties and the thirties, it was still on.

15

SELF-HELP IN
HARD TIMES

The war was hardly over, it was February 1919, the IWW leadership was in jail, but the IWW idea of the general strike became reality for five days in Seattle, Washington, when a walkout of 100,000 working people brought the city to a halt.

It began with 35,000 shipyard workers striking for a wage increase. They appealed for support to the Seattle Central Labor Council, which recommended a city-wide strike, and in two weeks 110 locals—mostly American Federation of Labor, only a few IWW—voted to strike. The rank and file of each striking local elected three members to a General Strike Committee, and on February 6, 1919, at 10:00 A.M., the strike began.

Unity was not easy to achieve. The IWW locals were in tension with the AFL locals. Japanese locals were admitted to the General Strike Committee but were not given a vote. Still, sixty thousand union members were out, and forty thousand other workers joined in sympathy.

Seattle workers had a radical tradition. During the war, the president of the Seattle AFL, a socialist, was imprisoned for opposing the draft, was tortured, and there were great labor rallies in the streets to protest.

The city now stopped functioning, except for activities organized by the strikers to provide essential needs. Firemen agreed to stay on the job. Laundry workers handled only hospital laundry. Vehicles authorized to move carried signs "Exempted by the General Strike Committee." Thirty-five neighborhood milk stations were set up. Every day thirty thousand meals were prepared in large kitchens, then transported to halls all over the city and served cafeteria style, with strikers paying twenty-five cents a meal, the general public thirty-five cents. People were allowed to eat as much as they wanted of the beef stew, spaghetti, bread, and coffee.

A Labor War Veteran's Guard was organized to keep the peace. On the blackboard at one of its headquarters was written: "The purpose of this organization is to preserve law and order without the use of force. No volunteer will have any police power or be allowed to carry weapons of any sort, but to use persuasion only." During the strike, crime in the city decreased. The commander of the U.S. army detachment sent into the area told the strikers' committee that in forty years of military experience he hadn't seen so quiet and orderly a city. A poem printed in the Seattle *Union Record* (a daily newspaper put out by labor people) by someone named Anise:

What scares them most is
That NOTHING HAPPENS!
They are ready
For DISTURBANCES.
They have machine guns
And soldiers,
But this SMILING SILENCE
   Is uncanny.
The business men
Don't understand
That sort of weapon . . .
It is your SMILE
That is UPSETTING
Their reliance
   On Artillery, brother!
It is the garbage wagons
That go along the street
Marked "EXEMPT
by STRIKE COMMITTEE."
It is the milk stations
That are getting better daily,
And the three hundred
WAR Veterans of Labor
Handling the crowds
WITHOUT GUNS,
For these things speak
Of a NEW POWER
And a NEW WORLD
That they do not feel
At HOME in.

The mayor swore in 2,400 special deputies, many of them students at the University of Washington. Almost a thousand sailors and marines were brought into the city by the U.S. government. The general strike ended after five days, according to the General Strike Committee because of pressure from the international officers of the various unions, as well as the difficulties of living in a shut-down city.

The strike had been peaceful. But when it was over, there were raids and arrests: on the Socialist party headquarters, on a printing plant. Thirty-nine members of the IWW were jailed as "ring-leaders of anarchy."

In Centralia, Washington, where the IWW had been organizing lumber workers, the lumber interests made plans to get rid of the IWW. On November 11, 1919, Armistice Day, the Legion paraded through town with rubber hoses and gas pipes, and the IWW prepared for an attack. When the Legion passed the IWW hall, shots were fired—it is unclear who fired first. They stormed the hall, there was more firing, and three Legion men were killed.

Inside the headquarters was an IWW member, a lumberjack named Frank Everett, who had been in France as a soldier while the IWW national leaders were on trial for obstructing the war effort. Everett was in army uniform and carrying a rifle. He emptied it into the crowd, dropped it, and ran for the woods, followed by a mob. He started to wade across the river, found the current too strong, turned, shot the leading man dead, threw his gun into the river, and fought the mob with his fists. They dragged him back to town behind an automobile, suspended him from a telegraph pole, took him down, locked him in jail. That night, his jailhouse door was broken down, he was dragged out, put on the floor of a car, his genitals were cut off, and then he was taken to a bridge, hanged, and his body riddled with bullets.

No one was ever arrested for Everett's murder, but eleven Wobblies were put on trial for killing an American Legion leader during the parade, and six of them spent fifteen years in prison.

Why such a reaction to the general strike, to the organizing of the Wobblies? A statement by the mayor of Seattle suggests that the Establishment feared not just the strike itself but what it symbolized. He said:

> The so-called sympathetic Seattle strike was an attempted revolution. That there was no violence does not alter the fact. . . . The intent, openly and covertly announced, was for the overthrow of the industrial system; here first, then everywhere. . . . True, there were no flashing guns, no bombs, no

killings. Revolution, I repeat, doesn't need violence. The general strike, as practiced in Seattle, is of itself the weapon of revolution, all the more dangerous because quiet. To succeed, it must suspend everything; stop the entire life stream of a community. . . . That is to say, it puts the government out of operation. And that is all there is to revolt—no matter how achieved.

Furthermore, the Seattle general strike took place in the midst of a wave of postwar rebellions all over the world. A writer in *The Nation* commented that year:

> The most extraordinary phenomenon of the present time . . . is the unprecedented revolt of the rank and file. . . .
>
> In Russia it has dethroned the Czar. . . . In Korea and India and Egypt and Ireland it keeps up an unyielding resistance to political tyranny. In England it brought about the railway strike, against the judgement of the men's own executives. In Seattle and San Francisco it has resulted in the stevedores' recent refusal to handle arms or supplies destined for the overthrow of the Soviet Government. In one district of Illinois it manifested itself in a resolution of striking miners, unanimously requesting their state executive "to go to Hell". In Pittsburgh, according to Mr. Gompers, it compelled the reluctant American Federation officers to call the steel strike, lest the control pass into the hands of the I.W.W.'s and other "radicals". In New York, it brought about the longshoremen's strike and kept the men out in defiance of union officials, and caused the upheaval in the printing trade, which the international officers, even though the employers worked hand in glove with them, were completely unable to control.
>
> The common man . . . losing faith in the old leadership, has experienced a new access of self-confidence, or at least a new recklessness, a readiness to take chances on his own account . . . authority cannot any longer be imposed from above; it comes automatically from below.

In the steel mills of western Pennsylvania later in 1919, where men worked twelve hours a day, six days a week, doing exhausting work under intense heat, 100,000 steelworkers were signed up in twenty different AFL craft unions. A National Committee attempting to tie them together in their organizing drive found in the summer of 1919 "the men are letting it be known that if we do not do something for them they will take the matter into their own hands."

The National Council was getting telegrams like the one from the Johnstown Steel Workers Council: "Unless the National Committee authorizes a national strike vote to be taken this week we will be compelled to go on strike here alone." William Z. Foster (later a Communist leader, at this time secretary-treasurer to the National Committee in charge of organizing) received a telegram from organizers in the Youngstown district: "We cannot be expected to meet the enraged workers, who will consider us traitors if strike is postponed."

There was pressure from President Woodrow Wilson and Samuel Gompers, AFL president, to postpone the strike. But the steelworkers were too insistent, and in September 1919, not only the 100,000 union men but 250,000 others went out on strike.

The sheriff of Allegheny County swore in as deputies five thousand employees of U.S. Steel who had not gone on strike, and announced that outdoor meetings would be forbidden. A report of the Interchurch World Movement made at the time said:

> In Monessen . . . the policy of the State Police was simply to club men off the streets and drive them into their homes. . . . In Braddock . . . when a striker was clubbed in the street he would be taken to jail, kept there over night. . . . Many of those arrested in Newcastle . . . were ordered not to be released until the strike was over.

The Department of Justice moved in, carrying out raids on workers who were aliens, holding them for deportation. At Gary, Indiana, federal troops were sent in.

Other factors operated against the strikers. Most were recent immigrants, of many nationalities, many languages. Sherman Service, Inc., hired by the steel corporations to break the strike, instructed its men in South Chicago: "We want you to stir up as much bad feeling as you possibly can between the Serbians and the Italians. Spread data among the Serbians that the Italians are going back to work. . . . Urge them to go back to work or the Italians will get their jobs." More than thirty thousand black workers were brought into the area as strikebreakers—they had been excluded from AFL unions and so felt no loyalty to unionism.

As the strike dragged on, the mood of defeat spread, and workers began to drift back to work. After ten weeks, the number of strikers was down to 110,000, and then the National Committee called the strike off.

In the year following the war, 120,000 textile workers struck in New England and New Jersey, and 30,000 silk workers struck in Paterson, New Jersey. In Boston the police went out on strike, and in New York City cigarmakers, shirtmakers, carpenters, bakers, teamsters, and barbers were out on strike. In Chicago, the press reported, "More strikes and lockouts accompany the mid-summer heat than ever known before at any one time." Five thousand workers at International Harvester and five thousand city workers were in the streets.

When the twenties began, however, the situation seemed under control. The IWW was destroyed, the Socialist party falling apart. The strikes were beaten down by force, and the economy was doing just well enough for just enough people to prevent mass rebellion.

Congress, in the twenties, put an end to the dangerous, turbulent flood of immigrants (14 million between 1900 and 1920) by passing laws setting immigration quotas: the quotas favored Anglo-Saxons, kept out black and yellow people, limited severely the coming of Latins, Slavs, Jews. No African country could send more than 100 people; 100 was the limit for China, for Bulgaria, for Palestine; 34,007 could come from England or Northern Ireland, but only 3,845 from Italy; 51,227 from Germany, but only 124 from Lithuania; 28,567 from the Irish Free State, but only 2,248 from Russia.

The Ku Klux Klan was revived in the 1920s, and it spread into the North. By 1924 it had 4½ million members. The NAACP seemed helpless in the face of mob violence and race hatred everywhere. The impossibility of the black person's ever being considered equal in white America was the theme of the nationalist movement led in the 1920s by Marcus Garvey. He preached black pride, racial separation, and a return to Africa, which to him held the only hope for black unity and survival. But Garvey's movement, inspiring as it was to some blacks, could not make much headway against the powerful white supremacy currents of the postwar decade.

There was some truth to the standard picture of the twenties as a time of prosperity and fun—the Jazz Age, the Roaring Twenties. Unemployment was down, from 4,270,000 in 1921 to a little over 2 million in 1927. The general level of wages for workers rose. Some farmers made a lot of money. The 40 percent of all families who made over $2,000 a year could buy new gadgets: autos, radios, refrigerators. Millions of people were not doing badly—and they could shut out of the picture the others—the tenant farmers, black and white, the immigrant families in the big cities either without work or not making enough to get the basic necessities.

But prosperity was concentrated at the top. While from 1922 to 1929 real wages in manufacturing went up per capita 1.4 percent a year, the holders of common stocks gained 16.4 percent a year. Six million families (42 percent of the total) made less than $1,000 a year. One-tenth of 1 percent of the families at the top received as much income as 42 percent of the families at the bottom, according to a report of the Brookings Institution. Every year in the 1920s, about 25,000 workers were killed on the job and 100,000 permanently disabled. Two million people in New York City lived in tenements condemned as firetraps.

The country was full of little industrial towns like Muncie, Indiana, where, according to Robert and Helen Lynd *(Middletown)*, the class system was revealed by the time people got up in the morning: for two-thirds of the city's families, "the father gets up in the dark in winter, eats hastily in the kitchen in the gray dawn, and is at work from an hour to two and a quarter hours before his children have to be at school."

There were enough well-off people to push the others into the background. And with the rich controlling the means of dispensing information, who would tell? Historian Merle Curti observed about the twenties:

> It was, in fact, only the upper ten percent of the population that enjoyed a marked increase in real income. But the protests which such facts normally have evoked could not make themselves widely or effectively felt. This was in part the result of the grand strategy of the major political parties. In part it was the result of the fact that almost all the chief avenues to mass opinion were now controlled by large-scale publishing industries.

Some writers tried to break through: Theodore Dreiser, Sinclair Lewis, Lewis Mumford. F. Scott Fitzgerald, in an article, "Echoes of the Jazz Age," said: "It was borrowed time anyway—the whole upper tenth of a nation living with the insouciance of a grand duc and the casualness of chorus girls." He saw ominous signs amid that prosperity: drunkenness, unhappiness, violence:

> A classmate killed his wife and himself on Long Island, another tumbled "accidentally" from a skyscraper in Philadelphia, another purposely from a skyscraper in New York. One was killed in a speak-easy in Chicago; another was beaten to death in a speak-easy in New York and crawled home to the Princeton Club to die; still another had his skull crushed by a maniac's axe in an insane asylum where he was confined.

Sinclair Lewis captured the false sense of prosperity, the shallow pleasure of the new gadgets for the middle classes, in his novel *Babbitt*:

> It was the best of nationally advertised and quantitatively produced alarm-clocks, with all modern attachments, including cathedral chime, intermittent alarm, and a phosphorescent dial. Babbitt was proud of being awakened by such a rich device. Socially it was almost as creditable as buying expensive cord tires.

He sulkily admitted now that there was no more escape, but he lay and detested the grind of the real-estate business, and disliked his family, and disliked himself for disliking them.

Women had finally, after long agitation, won the right to vote in 1920 with the passage of the Nineteenth Amendment, but voting was still a middle-class and upper-class activity. Eleanor Flexner, recounting the history of the movement, says the effect of female suffrage was that "women have shown the same tendency to divide along orthodox party lines as male voters."

Few political figures spoke out for the poor of the twenties. One was Fiorello La Guardia, a Congressman from a district of poor immigrants in East Harlem (who ran, oddly, on both Socialist and Republican tickets). In the mid-twenties he was made aware by people in his district of the high price of meat. When La Guardia asked Secretary of Agriculture William Jardine to investigate the high price of meat, the Secretary sent him a pamphlet on how to use meat economically. La Guardia wrote back:

> I asked for help and you send me a bulletin. The people of New York City cannot feed their children on Department bulletins. . . . Your bulletins . . . are of no use to the tenement dwellers of this great city. The housewives of New York have been trained by hard experience on the economical use of meat. What we want is the help of your department on the meat profiteers who are keeping the hard-working people of this city from obtaining proper nourishment.

During the presidencies of Harding and Coolidge in the twenties, the Secretary of the Treasury was Andrew Mellon, one of the richest men in America. In 1923, Congress was presented with the "Mellon Plan," calling for what looked like a general reduction of income taxes, except that the top income brackets would have their tax rates lowered from 50 percent to 25 percent, while the lowest-income group would have theirs lowered from 4 percent to 3 percent. A few Congressmen from working-class districts spoke against the bill, like William P. Connery of Massachusetts:

> I am not going to have my people who work in the shoe factories of Lynn and in the mills in Lawrence and the leather industry of Peabody, in these days of so-called Republican prosperity when they are working but three days in the week think that I am in accord with the provisions of this bill. . . .

When I see a provision in this Mellon tax bill which is going to save Mr. Mellon himself $800,000 on his income tax and his brother $600,000 on his, I cannot give it my support.

The Mellon Plan passed. In 1928, La Guardia toured the poorer districts of New York and said: "I confess I was not prepared for what I actually saw. It seemed almost incredible that such conditions of poverty could really exist."

Buried in the general news of prosperity in the twenties were, from time to time, stories of bitter labor struggles. In 1922, coal miners and railroad men went on strike, and Senator Burton Wheeler of Montana, a Progressive elected with labor votes, visited the strike area and reported:

All day long I have listened to heartrending stories of women evicted from their homes by the coal companies. I heard pitiful pleas of little children crying for bread. I stood aghast as I heard most amazing stories from men brutally beaten by private policemen. It has been a shocking and nerve-racking experience.

A textile strike in Rhode Island in 1922 among Italian and Portuguese workers failed, but class feelings were awakened and some of the strikers joined radical movements. Luigi Nardella recalled:

... my oldest brother, Guido, he started the strike. Guido pulled the handles on the looms in the Royal Mills, going from one section to the next shouting, "Strike! Strike!" ... When the strike started we didn't have any union organizers. ... We got together a group of girls and went from mill to mill, and that morning we got five mills out. We'd motion to the girls in the mills, "Come out! Come out!" Then we'd go on to the next. ...

Somebody from the Young Workers' League came out to bring a check, and invited me to a meeting, and I went. Then I joined, and in a few years I was in the Risorgimento Club in Providence. We were anti-Fascists. I spoke on street corners, bring a stand, jump up and talk to good crowds. And we led the support for Sacco and Vanzetti. ...

After the war, with the Socialist party weakened, a Communist party was organized, and Communists were involved in the organization of the Trade Union Education League, which tried to build a militant spirit inside the AFL. When a Communist named Ben Gold, of the furriers' section of the TUEL, challenged the AFL union leadership at a meeting, he was knifed and beaten. But in 1926, he and other

Communists organized a strike of furriers who formed mass picket lines, battled the police to hold their lines, were arrested and beaten, but kept striking, until they won a forty-hour week and a wage increase.

Communists again played a leading part in the great textile strike that spread through the Carolinas and Tennessee in the spring of 1929. The mill owners had moved to the South to escape unions, to find more subservient workers among the poor whites. But these workers rebelled against the long hours, the low pay. They particularly resented the "stretch-out"—an intensification of work. For instance, a weaver who had operated twenty-four looms and got $18.91 a week would be raised to $23, but he would be "stretched out" to a hundred looms and had to work at a punishing pace.

The first of the textile strikes was in Tennessee, where five hundred women in one mill walked out in protest against wages of $9 to $10 a week. Then at Gastonia, North Carolina, workers joined a new union, the National Textile Workers Union, led by Communists, which admitted both blacks and whites to membership. When some of them were fired, half of the two thousand workers went out on strike. An atmosphere of anti-Communism and racism built up and violence began. Textile strikes began to spread across South Carolina.

One by one the various strikes were settled, with some gains, but not at Gastonia. There, with the textile workers living in a tent colony, and refusing to renounce the Communists in their leadership, the strike went on. But strikebreakers were brought in and the mills kept operating. Desperation grew; there were violent clashes with the police. One dark night, the chief of police was killed in a gun battle and sixteen strikers and sympathizers were indicted for murder, including Fred Beal, a Communist party organizer. Ultimately seven were tried and given sentences of from five to twenty years. They were released on bail, and left the state; the Communists escaped to Soviet Russia. Through all the defeats, the beatings, the murders, however, it was the beginning of textile mill unionism in the South.

The stock market crash of 1929, which marked the beginning of the Great Depression of the United States, came directly from wild speculation which collapsed and brought the whole economy down with it. But, as John Galbraith says in his study of that event (The Great Crash), behind that speculation was the fact that "the economy was fundamentally unsound." He points to very unhealthy corporate and banking structures, an unsound foreign trade, much economic misinformation, and the "bad distribution of income" (the highest 5 percent of the population received about one-third of all personal income).

A socialist critic would go further and say that the capitalist system was by its nature unsound: a system driven by the one overriding motive of corporate profit and therefore unstable, unpredictable, and blind to human needs. The result of all that: permanent depression for many of its people, and periodic crises for almost everybody. Capitalism, despite its attempts at self-reform, its organization for better control, was still in 1929 a sick and undependable system.

After the crash, the economy was stunned, barely moving. Over five thousand banks closed and huge numbers of businesses, unable to get money, closed too. Those that continued laid off employees and cut the wages of those who remained, again and again. Industrial production fell by 50 percent, and by 1933 perhaps 15 million (no one knew exactly)—one-fourth or one-third of the labor force—were out of work. The Ford Motor Company, which in the spring of 1929 had employed 128,000 workers, was down to 37,000 by August of 1931. By the end of 1930, almost half the 280,000 textile mill workers in New England were out of work. Former President Calvin Coolidge commented with his customary wisdom: "When more and more people are thrown out of work, unemployment results." He spoke again in early 1931, "This country is not in good condition."

Clearly, those responsible for organizing the economy did not know what had happened, were baffled by it, refused to recognize it, and found reasons other than the failure of the system. Herbert Hoover had said, not long before the crash: "We in America today are nearer to the final triumph over poverty than ever before in the history of any land." Henry Ford, in March 1931, said the crisis was here because "the average man won't really do a day's work unless he is caught and cannot get out of it. There is plenty of work to do if people would do it." A few weeks later he laid off 75,000 workers.

There were millions of tons of food around, but it was not profitable to transport it, to sell it. Warehouses were full of clothing, but people could not afford it. There were lots of houses, but they stayed empty because people couldn't pay the rent, had been evicted, and now lived in shacks in quickly formed "Hoovervilles" built on garbage dumps.

Brief glimpses of reality in the newspapers could have been multiplied by the millions: A *New York Times* story in early 1932:

> After vainly trying to get a stay of dispossession until January 15 from his apartment at 46 Hancock Street in Brooklyn, yesterday, Peter J. Cornell, 48 years old, a former roofing contractor out of work and penniless, fell dead in the arms of his wife.

A doctor gave the cause of his death as heart disease, and the police said it had at least partly been caused by the bitter disappointment of a long day's fruitless attempt to prevent himself and his family being put out on the street. . . .

Cornell owed $5 in rent in arrears and $39 for January which his landlord required in advance. Failure to produce the money resulted in a dispossess order being served on the family yesterday and to take effect at the end of the week.

After vainly seeking assistance elsewhere, he was told during the day by the Home Relief Bureau that it would have no funds with which to help him until January 15.

A dispatch from Wisconsin to *The Nation*, in late 1932:

Throughout the middle west the tension between the farmers and authorities has been growing . . . as a result of tax and foreclosure sales. In many cases evictions have been prevented only by mass action on the part of the farmers. However, until the Cichon homestead near Elkhorn, Wisconsin, was besieged on December 6 by a host of deputy sheriffs armed with machine-guns, rifles, shotguns, and tear-gas bombs, there had been no actual violence. Max Cichon's property was auctioned off at a foreclosure sale last August, but he refused to allow either the buyer or the authorities to approach his home. He held off unwelcome visitors with a shotgun. The sheriff called upon Cichon to submit peacefully. When he refused to do so, the sheriff ordered deputies to lay down a barrage of machine-gun and rifle fire . . . Cichon is now in jail in Elkhorn, and his wife and two children, who were with him in the house, are being cared for in the county hospital. Cichon is not a trouble-maker. He enjoys the confidence of his neighbors, who only recently elected him justice of the peace of the town of Sugar Creek. That a man of his standing and disposition should go to such lengths in defying the authorities is a clear warning that we may expect further trouble in the agricultural districts unless the farmers are soon helped.

A tenement dweller on 113th Street in East Harlem wrote to Congressman Fiorello La Guardia in Washington:

You know my condition is bad. I used to get pension from the government and they stopped. It is now nearly seven months I am out of work. I hope you will try to do something for me. . . . I have four children who are in need of clothes and food. . . . My daughter who is eight is very ill and not recovering. My rent is due two months and I am afraid of being put out.

In Oklahoma, the farmers found their farms sold under the auctioneer's hammer, their farms turning to dust, the tractors coming in and taking over. John Steinbeck, in his novel of the depression, *The Grapes of Wrath*, describes what happened:

> And the dispossessed, the migrants, flowed into California, two hundred and fifty thousand, and three hundred thousand. Behind them new tractors were going on the land and the tenants were being forced off. And new waves were on the way, new waves of the dispossessed and the homeless, hard, intent, and dangerous. . . .
>
> And a homeless hungry man, driving the road with his wife beside him and his thin children in the back seat, could look at the fallow fields which might produce food but not profit, and that man could know how a fallow field is a sin and the unused land a crime against the thin children. . . .
>
> And in the south he saw the golden oranges hanging on the trees, the little golden oranges on the dark green trees; and guards with shotguns patrolling the lines so a man might not pick an orange for a thin child, oranges to be dumped if the price was low. . . .

These people were becoming "dangerous," as Steinbeck said. The spirit of rebellion was growing. Mauritz Hallgren, in a 1933 book, *Seeds of Revolt*, compiled newspaper reports of things happening around the country:

> England, Arkansas, January 3, 1931. The long drought that ruined hundreds of Arkansas farms last summer had a dramatic sequel late today when some 500 farmers, most of them white men and many of them armed, marched on the business section of this town. . . . Shouting that they must have food for themselves and their families, the invaders announced their intention to take it from the stores unless it were provided from some other source without cost.

> Detroit, July 9, 1931. An incipient riot by 500 unemployed men turned out of the city lodging house for lack of funds was quelled by police reserves in Cadillac Square tonight. . . .

> Indiana Harbor, Indiana, August 5, 1931. Fifteen hundred jobless men stormed the plant of the Fruit Growers Express Company here, demanding that they be given jobs to keep from starving. The company's answer was to call the city police, who routed the jobless with menacing clubs.

Boston, November 10, 1931. Twenty persons were treated for injuries, three were hurt so seriously that they may die, and dozens of others were nursing wounds from flying bottles, lead pipe, and stones after clashes between striking longshoremen and Negro strikebreakers along the Charlestown-East Boston waterfront.

Detroit, November 28, 1931. A mounted patrolman was hit on the head with a stone and unhorsed and one demonstrator was arrested during a disturbance in Grand Circus Park this morning when 2000 men and women met there in defiance of police orders.

Chicago, April 1, 1932. Five hundred school children, most with haggard faces and in tattered clothes, paraded through Chicago's downtown section to the Board of Education offices to demand that the school system provide them with food.

Boston, June 3, 1932. Twenty-five hungry children raided a buffet lunch set up for Spanish War veterans during a Boston parade. Two automobile-loads of police were called to drive them away.

New York, January 21, 1933. Several hundred jobless surrounded a restaurant just off Union Square today demanding they be fed without charge. . . .

Seattle, February 16, 1933. A two-day siege of the County-City Building, occupied by an army of about 5,000 unemployed, was ended early tonight, deputy sheriffs and police evicting the demonstrators after nearly two hours of efforts.

Yip Harburg, the songwriter, told Studs Terkel about the year 1932: "I was walking along the street at that time, and you'd see the bread lines. The biggest one in New York City was owned by William Randolph Hearst. He had a big truck with several people on it, and big cauldrons of hot soup, bread. Fellows with burlap on their feet were lined up all around Columbus Circle, and went for blocks and blocks around the park, waiting." Harburg had to write a song for the show *Americana*. He wrote "Brother, Can You Spare a Dime?"

Once in khaki suits,
Gee, we looked swell,
Full of that Yankee Doodle-de-dum.
Half a million boots went sloggin' through Hell,
I was the kid with the drum.

Say, don't you remember, they called me Al—
It was Al all the time.
Say, don't you remember I'm your pal—
Brother, can you spare a dime?

It was not just a song of despair. As Yip Harburg told Terkel:

In the song the man is really saying: I made an investment in this country. Where the hell are my dividends? . . . It's more than just a bit of pathos. It doesn't reduce him to a beggar. It makes him a dignified human, asking questions—and a bit outraged, too, as he should be.

The anger of the veteran of the First World War, now without work, his family hungry, led to the march of the Bonus Army to Washington in the spring and summer of 1932. War veterans, holding government bonus certificates which were due years in the future, demanded that Congress pay off on them now, when the money was desperately needed. And so they began to move to Washington from all over the country, with wives and children or alone. They came in broken-down old autos, stealing rides on freight trains, or hitchhiking. They were miners from West Virginia, sheet metal workers from Columbus, Georgia, and unemployed Polish veterans from Chicago. One family—husband, wife, three-year-old boy—spent three months on freight trains coming from California. Chief Running Wolf, a jobless Mescalero Indian from New Mexico, showed up in full Indian dress, with bow and arrow.

More than twenty thousand came. Most camped across the Potomac River from the Capitol on Anacostia Flats where, as John Dos Passos wrote, "the men are sleeping in little lean-tos built out of old newspapers, cardboard boxes, packing crates, bits of tin or tarpaper roofing, every kind of cockeyed makeshift shelter from the rain scraped together out of the city dump." The bill to pay off on the bonus passed the House, but was defeated in the Senate, and some veterans, discouraged, left. Most stayed—some encamped in government buildings near the Capitol, the rest on Anacostia Flats, and President Hoover ordered the army to evict them.

Four troops of cavalry, four companies of infantry, a machine gun squadron, and six tanks assembled near the White House. General Douglas MacArthur was in charge of the operation, Major Dwight Eisenhower his aide. George S. Patton was one of the officers. MacArthur led his troops down Pennsylvania Avenue, used tear gas to clear veterans out of the old buildings, and set the buildings on fire. Then the army moved across the bridge to Anacostia. Thousands of veterans, wives, children, began to run as the tear gas spread. The soldiers set fire to some of the huts, and soon the whole encampment was ablaze. When it was all over, two veterans had been shot to death, an eleven-week-old baby had died, an eight-year-old boy was partially blinded by gas, two police had fractured skulls, and a thousand veterans were injured by gas.

The hard, hard times, the inaction of the government in helping, the action of the government in dispersing war veterans—all had their effect on the election of November 1932. Democratic party candidate Franklin D. Roosevelt defeated Herbert Hoover overwhelmingly, took office in the spring of 1933, and began a program of reform legislation which became famous as the "New Deal." When a small veterans' march on Washington took place early in his administration, he greeted them and provided coffee; they met with one of his aides and went home. It was a sign of Roosevelt's approach.

The Roosevelt reforms went far beyond previous legislation. They had to meet two pressing needs: to reorganize capitalism in such a way to overcome the crisis and stabilize the system; also, to head off the alarming growth of spontaneous rebellion in the early years of the Roosevelt administration—organization of tenants and the unemployed, movements of self-help, general strikes in several cities.

That first objective—to stabilize the system for its own protection—was most obvious in the major law of Roosevelt's first months in office, the National Recovery Act (NRA). It was designed to take control of the economy through a series of codes agreed on by management, labor, and the government, fixing prices and wages, limiting competition. From the first, the NRA was dominated by big businesses and served their interests. As Bernard Bellush says (*The Failure of the N.R.A.*), its Title I "turned much of the nation's power over to highly organized, well-financed trade associations and industrial combines. The unorganized public, otherwise known as the consumer, along with the members of the fledgling trade-union movement, had virtually nothing to say about the initial organization of the National Recovery Administration, or the formulation of basic policy."

Where organized labor was strong, Roosevelt moved to make some concessions to working people. But: "Where organized labor was weak, Roosevelt was unprepared to withstand the pressures of industrial spokesmen to control the . . . NRA codes." Barton Bernstein (*Towards a New Past*) confirms this: "Despite the annoyance of some big business-men with Section 7a, the NRA reaffirmed and consolidated their power. . . ." Bellush sums up his view of the NRA:

The White House permitted the National Association of Manufacturers, the Chamber of Commerce, and allied business and trade associations to assume overriding authority. . . . Indeed, private administration became public administration, and private government became public government, insuring the marriage of capitalism with statism.

When the Supreme Court in 1935 declared the NRA unconstitutional, it claimed it gave too much power to the President, but, according to Bellush, ". . . FDR surrendered an inordinate share of the power of government, through the NRA, to industrial spokesmen throughout the country."

Also passed in the first months of the new administration, the AAA (Agricultural Adjustment Administration) was an attempt to organize agriculture. It favored the larger farmers as the NRA favored big business. The TVA (Tennessee Valley Authority) was an unusual entrance of government into business—a government-owned network of dams and hydroelectric plants to control floods and produce electric power in the Tennessee Valley. It gave jobs to the unemployed, helped the consumer with lower electric rates, and in some respect deserved the accusation that it was "socialistic." But the New Deal's organization of the economy was aimed mainly at stabilizing the economy, and secondly at giving enough help to the lower classes to keep them from turning a rebellion into a real revolution.

That rebellion was real when Roosevelt took office. Desperate people were not waiting for the government to help them; they were helping themselves, acting directly. Aunt Molly Jackson, a woman who later became active in labor struggles in Appalachia, recalled how she walked into the local store, asked for a 24-pound sack of flour, gave it to her little boy to take it outside, then filled a sack of sugar and said to the storekeeper, "Well, I'll see you in ninety days. I have to feed some children . . . I'll pay you, don't worry." And when he objected, she pulled out her pistol (which, as a midwife traveling alone through the hills, she had a permit to carry) and said: "Martin, if you try to take this grub away from me, God knows that if they electrocute me for it tomorrow, I'll shoot you six times in a minute." Then, as she recalls, "I walked out, I got home, and these seven children was so hungry that they was a-grabbin the raw dough off-a their mother's hands and crammin it into their mouths and swallowing it whole."

All over the country, people organized spontaneously to stop evictions. In New York, in Chicago, in other cities—when word spread that someone was being evicted, a crowd would gather; the police would remove the furniture from the house, put it out in the street, and the crowd would bring the furniture back. The Communist party was active in organizing Workers Alliance groups in the cities. Mrs. Willye Jeffries, a black woman, told Studs Terkel about evictions:

> A lot of 'em was put out. They'd call and have the bailiffs come and sit them out, and as soon as they'd leave, we would put 'em back where they came out. All we had to do was call Brother Hilton. . . . Look, such and such a place, there's a family sittin' out there. Everybody passed through the neighborhood, was a member of the Workers Alliance, had one person they would call. When that one person came, he'd have about fifty people with him. . . . Take that stuff right on back up there. The men would connect those lights and go to the hardware and get gas pipe, and connect that stove back. Put the furniture back just like you had it, so it don't look like you been out the door.

Unemployed Councils were formed all over the country. They were described by Charles R. Walker, writing in *The Forum* in 1932:

> I find it is no secret that Communists organize Unemployed Councils in most cities and usually lead them, but the councils are organized democratically and the majority rules. In one I visited at Lincoln Park, Michigan, there were three hundred members of which eleven were Communists. . . . The Council had a right wing, a left wing, and a center. The chairman of the Council . . . was also the local commander of the American Legion. In Chicago there are 45 branches of the Unemployed Council, with a total membership of 22,000.
>
> The Council's weapon is democratic force of numbers, and their function is to prevent evictions of the destitute, or if evicted to bring pressure to bear on the Relief Commission to find a new home; if an unemployed worker has his gas or his water turned off because he can't pay for it, to see the proper authorities; to see that the unemployed who are shoeless and clothesless get both; to eliminate through publicity and pressure discriminations between Negroes and white persons, or against the foreign born, in matters of relief . . . to march people down to relief headquarters and demand they be fed and clothed. Finally to provide legal defense for all unemployed arrested for joining parades, hunger marches, or attending union meetings.

People organized to help themselves, since business and government were not helping them in 1931 and 1932. In Seattle, the fishermen's union caught fish and exchanged them with people who picked fruit and vegetables, and those who cut wood exchanged that. There were twenty-two locals, each with a commissary where food and firewood were exchanged for other goods and services: barbers, seamstresses, and doctors gave of their skills in return for other things. By the end of 1932, there were 330 self-help organizations in thirty-seven states, with over 300,000 members. By early 1933, they seem to have collapsed; they were attempting too big a job in an economy that was more and more a shambles.

Perhaps the most remarkable example of self-help took place in the coal district of Pennsylvania, where teams of unemployed miners dug small mines on company property, mined coal, trucked it to cities, and sold it below the commercial rate. By 1934, 5 million tons of this "bootleg" coal were produced by twenty thousand men using four thousand vehicles. When attempts were made to prosecute, local juries would not convict, local jailers would not imprison.

These were simple actions, taken out of practical need, but they had revolutionary possibilities. Paul Mattick, a Marxist writer, commented:

> All that is really necessary for the workers to do in order to end their miseries is to perform such simple things as to take from where there is, without regard to established property principles or social philosophies, and to start to produce for themselves. Done on a broad social scale, it will lead to lasting results; on a local, isolated plane it will be . . . defeated. . . . The bootleg miners have shown in a rather clear and impressive way, that the so-much bewailed absence of a socialist ideology on the part of the workers really does not prevent workers from acting quite anticapitalistically, quite in accordance with their own needs. Breaking through the confines of private property in order to live up to their own necessities, the miners' action is, at the same time a manifestation of the most important part of class consciousness— namely, that the problems of the workers can be solved only by themselves.

Were the New Dealers—Roosevelt and his advisers, the businessmen who supported him—also class-conscious? Did they understand that measures must be quickly taken, in 1933 and 1934, to give jobs, food baskets, relief, to wipe out the idea "that the problems of the workers can be solved only by themselves"? Perhaps, like the workers' class consciousness, it was a set of actions arising not from held theory, but from instinctive practical necessity.

Perhaps it was such a consciousness that led to the Wagner-Connery Bill, introduced in Congress in early 1934, to regulate labor disputes.

The bill provided elections for union representation, a board to settle problems and handle grievances. Was this not exactly the kind of legislation to do away with the idea that "the problems of the workers can be solved only by themselves"? Big business thought it was too helpful to labor and opposed it. Roosevelt was cool to it. But in the year 1934 a series of labor outbursts suggested the need for legislative action.

A million and a half workers in different industries went on strike in 1934. That spring and summer, longshoremen on the West Coast, in a rank-and-file insurrection against their own union leadership as well as against the shippers, held a convention, demanded the abolition of the shape-up (a kind of early-morning slave market where work gangs were chosen for the day), and went out on strike.

Two thousand miles of Pacific coastline were quickly tied up. The teamsters cooperated, refusing to truck cargo to the piers, and maritime workers joined the strike. When the police moved in to open the piers, the strikers resisted en masse, and two were killed by police gunfire. A mass funeral procession for the strikers brought together tens of thousands of supporters. And then a general strike was called in San Francisco, with 130,000 workers out, the city immobilized.

Five hundred special police were sworn in and 4,500 National Guardsmen assembled, with infantry, machine gun, tank and artillery units. The Los Angeles *Times* wrote:

> The situation in San Francisco is not correctly described by the phrase "general strike." What is actually in progress there is an insurrection, a Communist-inspired and -led revolt against organized government. There is but one thing to be done—put down the revolt with any force necessary.

The pressure became too strong. There were the troops. There was the AFL pushing to end the strike. The longshoremen accepted a compromise settlement. But they had shown the potential of a general strike.

That same summer of 1934, a strike of teamsters in Minneapolis was supported by other working people, and soon nothing was moving in the city except milk, ice, and coal trucks given exemptions by the strikers. Farmers drove their products into town and sold them directly to the people in the city. The police attacked and two strikers were killed. Fifty thousand people attended a mass funeral. There was an enormous protest meeting and a march on City Hall. After a month, the employers gave in to the teamsters' demands.

In the fall of that same year, 1934, came the largest strike of all—325,000 textile workers in the South. They left the mills and set up flying squadrons in trucks and autos to move through the strike areas, picketing, battling guards, entering the mills, unbelting machinery. Here too, as in the other cases, the strike impetus came from the rank and file, against a reluctant union leadership at the top. The *New York Times* said: "The grave danger of the situation is that it will get completely out of the hands of the leaders."

Again, the machinery of the state was set in motion. Deputies and armed strikebreakers in South Carolina fired on pickets, killing seven, wounding twenty others. But the strike was spreading to New England. In Lowell, Massachusetts, 2,500 textile workers rioted; in Saylesville, Rhode Island, a crowd of five thousand people defied state troopers who were armed with machine guns, and shut down the textile mill. In Woonsocket, Rhode Island, two thousand people, aroused because someone had been shot and killed by the National Guard, stormed through the town and closed the mill.

By September 18, 421,000 textile workers were on strike throughout the country. There were mass arrests, organizers were beaten, and the death toll rose to thirteen. Roosevelt now stepped in and set up a board of mediation, and the union called off the strike.

In the rural South, too, organizing took place, often stimulated by Communists, but nourished by the grievances of poor whites and blacks who were tenant farmers or farm laborers, always in economic difficulties but hit even harder by the Depression. The Southern Tenant Farmers Union started in Arkansas, with black and white sharecroppers, and spread to other areas. Roosevelt's AAA was not helping the poorest of farmers; in fact by encouraging farmers to plant less, it forced tenants and sharecroppers to leave the land. By 1935, of 6,800,000 farmers, 2,800,000 were tenants. The average income of a sharecropper was $312 a year. Farm laborers, moving from farm to farm, area to area, no land of their own, in 1933 were earning about $300 a year.

Black farmers were the worst off, and some were attracted to the strangers who began appearing in their area during the Depression, suggesting they organize. Nate Shaw recalls, in Theodore Rosengarten's remarkable interview *(All God's Dangers)*:

> And durin of the pressure years, a union begin to operate in this country, called it the Sharecroppers Union—that was a nice name, I thought . . . and I knowed what was goin on was a turnabout on the southern man, white and colored; it was somethin unusual. And I heard about it bein a organization for the poor class of people—that's just what I wanted to get into, too. I wanted to know the secrets of it enough that I could become in the knowledge of it. . . .

Mac Sloane, white man, said "You stay out of it. These niggers runnin around here carryin on some kind of meetin—you better stay out of it."

I said to myself, "You a fool if you think you can keep me from joinin". I went right on and joined it, just as quick as the next meetin come. . . . And he done just the thing to push me into it—gived me orders not to join.

The teachers of this organization begin to drive through this country—they couldn't let what they was doin be known. One of em was a colored fella; I disremember his name but he did a whole lot of time, holdin meetins with us—that was part of this job. . . .

Had the meetins at our houses or anywhere we could keep a look and a watch-out that nobody was comin in on us. Small meetins, sometimes there'd be a dozen . . . niggers was scared, niggers was scared, that's tellin the truth.

Nate Shaw told of what happened when a black farmer who hadn't paid his debts was about to be dispossessed:

The deputy said, "I'm goin to take all old Virgil Jones got this mornin." . . .

I begged him not to do it, begged him. "You'll dispossess him of bein able to feed his family."

Nate Shaw then told the deputy he was not going to allow it. The deputy came back with more men, and one of them shot and wounded Shaw, who then got his gun and fired back. He was arrested in late 1932, and served twelve years in an Alabama prison. His story is a tiny piece of the great unrecorded drama of the southern poor in those years of the Sharecroppers Union. Years after his release from prison, Nate Shaw spoke his mind on color and class:

O, it's plain as your hand. The poor white man and the poor black man is sittin in the same saddle today—big dudes done branched em off that way. The control of a man, the controllin power, is in the hands of the rich man. . . . That class is standin together and the poor white man is out there on the colored list—I've caught that: ways and actions a heap of times speaks louder than words. . . .

Hosea Hudson, a black man from rural Georgia, at the age of ten a plowhand, later an iron worker in Birmingham, was aroused by the case of the Scottsboro Boys in 1931 (nine black youths accused of raping two white girls and convicted on flimsy evidence by all-white juries). That year he joined the Communist party. In 1932 and 1933, he organized unemployed blacks in Birmingham. He recalls:

Deep in the winter of 1932 we Party members organized a unemployed mass meeting to be held on the old courthouse steps, on 3rd Avenue, North Birmingham. . . . It was about 7000 or more people turned out . . . Negroes and whites. . . .

In 1932 and '33 we began to organize these unemployed block committees in the various communities of Birmingham. . . . If someone get out of food. . . . We wouldn't go around and just say, "That's too bad". We make it our business to go see this person. . . . And if the person was willing . . . we'd work with them. . . .

Block committees would meet every week, had a regular meeting. We talked about the welfare question, what was happening, we read the *Daily Worker* and the *Southern Worker* to see what was going on about unemployed relief, what people doing in Cleveland . . . struggles in Chicago . . . or we talk about the latest developments in the Scottsboro case. We kept up, we was on top, so people always wanted to come cause we had something different to tell them every time.

In 1934 and 1935 hundreds of thousands of workers, left out of the tightly controlled, exclusive unions of the American Federation of Labor, began organizing in the new mass production industries—auto, rubber, packinghouse. The AFL could not ignore them; it set up a Committee for Industrial Organization to organize these workers outside of craft lines, by industry, all workers in a plant belonging to one union. This Committee, headed by John Lewis, then broke away and became the CIO—the Congress of Industrial Organizations.

But it was rank-and-file strikes and insurgencies that pushed the union leadership, AFL and CIO, into action. Jeremy Brecher tells the story in his book *Strike!* A new kind of tactic began among rubber workers in Akron, Ohio, in the early thirties—the sit-down strike. The workers stayed in the plant instead of walking out, and this had clear advantages: they were directly blocking the use of strikebreakers; they did not have to act through union officials but were in direct control of the situation themselves; they did not have to walk outside in the cold and rain, but had shelter; they were not isolated, as in their work, or on the picket line; they were thousands under one roof, free to talk to one another, to form a community of struggle. Louis Adamic, a labor writer, describes one of the early sit-downs:

Sitting by their machines, cauldrons, boilers and work benches, they talked. Some realized for the first time how important they were in the process of rubber production. Twelve men had practically stopped the works! . . .

Superintendents, foremen, and straw bosses were dashing about. . . . In less than an hour the dispute was settled, full victory for the men.

In early 1936, at the Firestone rubber plant in Akron, makers of truck tires, their wages already too low to pay for food and rent, were faced with a wage cut. When several union men were fired, others began to stop work, to sit down on the job. In one day the whole of plant #1 was sitting down. In two days, plant #2 was sitting down, and management gave in. In the next ten days there was a sit-down at Goodyear. A court issued an injunction against mass picketing. It was ignored, and 150 deputies were sworn in. But they soon faced ten thousand workers from all over Akron. In a month the strike was won.

The idea spread through 1936. In December of that year began the longest sit-down strike of all, at Fisher Body plant #1 in Flint, Michigan. It started when two brothers were fired, and it lasted until February 1937. For forty days there was a community of two thousand strikers. "It was like war," one said. "The guys with me became my buddies." Sidney Fine in *Sit-Down* describes what happened. Committees organized recreation, information, classes, a postal service, sanitation. Courts were set up to deal with those who didn't take their turn washing dishes or who threw rubbish or smoked where it was prohibited or brought in liquor. The "punishment" consisted of extra duties; the ultimate punishment was expulsion from the plant. A restaurant owner across the street prepared three meals a day for two thousand strikers. There were classes in parliamentary procedure, public speaking, history of the labor movement. Graduate students at the University of Michigan gave courses in journalism and creative writing.

There were injunctions, but a procession of five thousand armed workers encircled the plant and there was no attempt to enforce the injunction. Police attacked with tear gas and the workers fought back with firehoses. Thirteen strikers were wounded by gunfire, but the police were driven back. The governor called out the National Guard. By this time the strike had spread to other General Motors plants. Finally there was a settlement, a six-month contract, leaving many questions unsettled but recognizing that from now on, the company would have to deal not with individuals but with a union.

In 1936 there were forty-eight sitdown strikes. In 1937 there were 477: electrical workers in St. Louis; shirt workers in Pulaski, Tennessee; broom workers in Pueblo, Colorado; trash collectors in Bridgeport, Connecticut; gravediggers in New Jersey; seventeen blind workers at the New York Guild for the Jewish Blind; prisoners in an Illinois penitentiary; and even thirty members of a National Guard Company who had served in the Fisher Body sit-down, and now sat down themselves because they had not been paid.

The sit-downs were especially dangerous to the system because they were not controlled by the regular union leadership. An AFL business agent for the Hotel and Restaurant Employees said:

> You'd be sitting in the office any March day of 1937, and the phone would ring and the voice at the other end would say: "My name is Mary Jones; I'm a soda clerk at Liggett's; we've thrown the manager out and we've got the keys. What do we do now?" And you'd hurry over to the company to negotiate and over there they'd say, "I think it's the height of irresponsibility to call a strike before you've ever asked for a contract" and all you could answer was, "You're so right."

It was to stabilize the system in the face of labor unrest that the Wagner Act of 1935, setting up a National Labor Relations Board, had been passed. The wave of strikes in 1936, 1937, 1938, made the need even more pressing. In Chicago, on Memorial Day, 1937, a strike at Republic Steel brought the police out, firing at a mass picket line of strikers, killing ten of them. Autopsies showed the bullets had hit the workers in the back as they were running away: this was the Memorial Day Massacre. But Republic Steel was organized, and so was Ford Motor Company, and the other huge plants in steel, auto, rubber, meatpacking, the electrical industry.

The Wagner Act was challenged by a steel corporation in the courts, but the Supreme Court found it constitutional—that the government could regulate interstate commerce, and that strikes hurt interstate commerce. From the trade unions' point of view, the new law was an aid to union organizing. From the government's point of view it was an aid to the stability of commerce.

Unions were not wanted by employers, but they were more controllable—more stabilizing for the system than the wildcat strikes, the factory occupations of the rank and file. In the spring of 1937, a *New York Times* article carried the headline "Unauthorized Sit-Downs Fought by CIO Unions." The story read: "Strict orders have been issued to all organizers and representatives that they will be dismissed if they authorize any stoppages of work without the consent of the international officers. . . ." The *Times* quoted John L. Lewis, dynamic leader of the CIO: "A CIO contract is adequate protection against sit-downs, lie-downs, or any other kind of strike."

The Communist party, some of whose members played critical roles in organizing CIO unions, seemed to take the same position. One Communist leader in Akron was reported to have said at a party strategy meeting after the sit-downs: "Now we must work for regular relations between the union and the employers—and strict observance of union procedure on the part of the workers."

Thus, two sophisticated ways of controlling direct labor action developed in the mid-thirties. First, the National Labor Relations Board would give unions legal status, listen to them, settling certain of their grievances. Thus it could moderate labor rebellion by channeling energy into elections—just as the constitutional system channeled possibly troublesome energy into voting. The NLRB would set limits in economic conflict as voting did in political conflict. And second, the workers' organization itself, the union, even a militant and aggressive union like the CIO, would channel the workers' insurrectionary energy into contracts, negotiations, union meetings, and try to minimize strikes, in order to build large, influential, even respectable organizations.

The history of those years seems to support the argument of Richard Cloward and Frances Piven, in their book *Poor People's Movements*, that labor won most during its spontaneous uprisings, before the unions were recognized or well organized: "Factory workers had their greatest influence, and were able to exact their most substantial concessions from government, during the Great Depression, in the years before they were organized into unions. Their power during the Depression was not rooted in organization, but in disruption."

Piven and Cloward point out that union membership rose enormously in the forties, during the Second World War (the CIO and AFL had over 6 million members each by 1945), but its power was less than before—its gains from the use of strikes kept getting whittled down. The members appointed to the NLRB were less sympathetic to labor, the Supreme Court declared sit-downs to be illegal, and state governments were passing laws to hamper strikes, picketing, boycotts.

The coming of World War II weakened the old labor militancy of the thirties because the war economy created millions of new jobs at higher wages. The New Deal had succeeded only in reducing unemployment from 13 million to 9 million. It was the war that put almost everyone to work, and the war did something else: patriotism, the push for unity of all classes against enemies overseas, made it harder to mobilize anger against the corporations. During the war, the CIO and AFL pledged to call no strikes.

Still, the grievances of workers were such—wartime "controls" meant their wages were being controlled better than prices—that they felt impelled to engage in many wildcat strikes: there were more strikes in 1944 than in any previous year in American history, says Jeremy Brecher.

The thirties and forties showed more clearly than before the dilemma of working people in the United States. The system responded to workers' rebellions by finding new forms of control—internal control by their own organizations as well as outside control by law and force. But along with the new controls came new concessions. These concessions didn't solve basic problems; for many people they solved nothing. But they helped enough people to create an atmosphere of progress and improvement, to restore some faith in the system.

The minimum wage of 1938, which established the forty-hour week and outlawed child labor, left many people out of its provisions and set very low minimum wages (twenty-five cents an hour the first year). But it was enough to dull the edge of resentment. Housing was built for only a small percentage of the people who needed it. "A modest, even parsimonious, beginning," Paul Conkin says (*F.D.R. and the Origins of the Welfare State*), but the sight of federally subsidized housing projects, playgrounds, vermin-free apartments, replacing dilapidated tenements, was refreshing. The TVA suggested exciting possibilities for regional planning to give jobs, improve areas, and provide cheap power, with local instead of national control. The Social Security Act gave retirement benefits and unemployment insurance, and matched state funds for mothers and dependent children—but it excluded farmers, domestic workers, and old people, and offered no health insurance. As Conkin says: "The meager benefits of Social Security were insignificant in comparison to the building of security for large, established businesses."

The New Deal gave federal money to put thousands of writers, artists, actors, and musicians to work—in a Federal Theatre Project, a Federal Writers Project, a Federal Art Project: murals were painted on public buildings; plays were put on for working-class audiences who had never seen a play; hundreds of books and pamphlets were written and published. People heard a symphony for the first time. It was an exciting flowering of arts for the people, such as had never happened before in American history, and which has not been duplicated since. But in 1939, with the country more stable and the New Deal reform impulse weakened, programs to subsidize the arts were eliminated.

When the New Deal was over, capitalism remained intact. The rich still controlled the nation's wealth, as well as its laws, courts, police, newspapers, churches, colleges. Enough help had been given to enough people to make Roosevelt a hero to millions, but the same system that had brought depression and crisis—the system of waste, of inequality, of concern for profit over human need—remained.

For black people, the New Deal was psychologically encouraging (Mrs. Roosevelt was sympathetic; some blacks got posts in the administration), but most blacks were ignored by the New Deal programs. As tenant farmers, as farm laborers, as migrants, as domestic workers, they didn't qualify for unemployment insurance, minimum wages, social security, or farm subsidies. Roosevelt, careful not to offend southern white politicians whose political support he needed, did not push a bill against lynching. Blacks and whites were segregated in the armed forces. And black workers were discriminated against in getting jobs. They were the last hired, the first fired. Only when A. Philip Randolph, head of the Sleeping-Car Porters Union, threatened a massive march on Washington in 1941 would Roosevelt agree to sign an executive order establishing a Fair Employment Practices Committee. But the FEPC had no enforcement powers and changed little.

Black Harlem, with all the New Deal reforms, remained as it was. There 350,000 people lived, 233 persons per acre compared with 133 for the rest of Manhattan. In twenty-five years, its population had multiplied six times. Ten thousand families lived in rat-infested cellars and basements. Tuberculosis was common. Perhaps half of the married women worked as domestics. They traveled to the Bronx and gathered on street corners—"slave markets," they were called—to be hired. Prostitution crept in. Two young black women, Ella Baker and Marvel Cooke, wrote about this in *The Crisis* in 1935:

> Not only is human labor bartered and sold for the slave wage, but human love is also a marketable commodity. Whether it is labor or love, the women arrive as early as eight a.m. and remain as late as one p.m. or until they are hired. In rain or shine, hot or cold, they wait to work for ten, fifteen, and twenty cents per hour.

In Harlem Hospital in 1932, proportionately twice as many people died as in Bellevue Hospital, which was in the white area downtown. Harlem was a place that bred crime—"the bitter blossom of poverty," as Roi Ottley and William Weatherby say in their essay "The Negro in New York."

On March 19, 1935, even as the New Deal reforms were being passed, Harlem exploded. Ten thousand Negroes swept through the streets, destroying the property of white merchants. Seven hundred policemen moved in and brought order. Two blacks were killed.

In the mid-thirties, a young black poet named Langston Hughes wrote a poem, "Let America Be America Again":

. . . I am the poor white, fooled and pushed apart,
I am the Negro bearing slavery's scars.
I am the red man driven from the land,
I am the immigrant clutching the hope I seek—
And finding only the same old stupid plan.
Of dog eat dog, of mighty crush the weak. . . .

O, let America be America again—
The land that never has been yet—
And yet must be—the land where every man is free.
The land that's mine—the poor man's, Indian's, Negro's
        ME—
Who made America,
Whose sweat and blood, whose faith and pain,
Whose hand at the foundry, whose plow in the rain,
Must bring back our mighty dream again.

Sure, call me any ugly name you choose—
The steel of freedom does not stain.
From those who live like leeches on the people's lives,
We must take back our land again,
America! . . .

To white Americans of the thirties, however, North and South, blacks were invisible. Only the radicals made an attempt to break the racial barriers: Socialists, Trotskyists, Communists most of all. The CIO, influenced by the Communists, was organizing blacks in the mass production industries. Blacks were still being used as strikebreakers, but now there were also attempts to bring blacks and whites together against their common enemy. A woman named Mollie Lewis, writing in *The Crisis*, in 1938, told of her experience in a steel strike in Gary, Indiana:

> While the municipal government of Gary continues to keep the children apart in a system of separate schools, their parents are getting together in the union and in the auxiliary. . . . The only public eating place in Gary where both races may be freely served is a cooperative restaurant largely patronized by members of the union and auxiliary. . . .
>
> When the black and white workers and members of their families are convinced that their basic economic interests are the same, they may be expected to make common cause for the advancement of these interests. . . .

There was no great feminist movement in the thirties. But many women became involved in the labor organizing of those years. A Minnesota poet, Meridel LeSeuer, was thirty-four when the great teamsters' strike tied up Minneapolis in 1934. She became active in it, and later described her experiences:

> I have never been in a strike before. . . . The truth is I was afraid. . . . "Do you need any help?" I said eagerly. . . . We kept on pouring thousands of cups of coffee, feeding thousands of men. . . . The cars were coming back. The announcer cried, "This is murder." . . . I saw them taking men out of cars and putting them on the hospital cots, on the floor. . . . The picket cars keep coming in. Some men have walked back from the market, holding their own blood in. . . . Men, women and children are massing outside, a living circle close packed for protection. . . . We have living blood on our skirts. . . .
>
> Tuesday, the day of the funeral, one thousand more militia were massed downtown.
>
> It was over ninety in the shade. I went to the funeral parlors and thousands of men and women were massed there waiting in the terrific sun. One block of women and children were standing two hours waiting. I went over and stood near them. I didn't know whether I could march. I didn't like marching in parades. . . . Three women drew me in. "We want all to march," they said gently. "Come with us.". . .

Sylvia Woods spoke to Alice and Staughton Lynd years later about her experiences in the thirties as a laundry worker and union organizer:

> You have to tell people things they can see. Then they'll say, "Oh, I never thought of that" or "I have never seen it like that." . . . Like Tennessee. He hated black people. A poor sharecropper. . . . He danced with a black woman. . . . So I have seen people change. This is the faith you've got to have in people.

Many Americans began to change their thinking in those days of crisis and rebellion. In Europe, Hitler was on the march. Across the Pacific, Japan was invading China. The Western empires were being threatened by new ones. For the United States, war was not far off.

16

A PEOPLE'S WAR?

"We, the governments of Great Britain and the United States, in the name of India, Burma, Malaya, Australia, British East Africa, British Guiana, Hongkong, Siam, Singapore, Egypt, Palestine, Canada, New Zealand, Northern Ireland, Scotland, Wales, as well as Puerto Rico, Guam, the Philippines, Hawaii, Alaska, and the Virgin Islands, hereby declare most emphatically, that this is not an imperialist war." Thus went a skit put on in the United States in the year 1939 by the Communist party.

Two years later, Germany invaded Soviet Russia, and the American Communist party, which had repeatedly described the war between the Axis Powers and the Allied Powers as an imperialist war, now called it a "people's war" against Fascism. Indeed almost all Americans were now in agreement—capitalists, Communists, Democrats, Republicans, poor, rich, and middle class—that this was indeed a people's war.

Was it?

By certain evidence, it was the most popular war the United States had ever fought. Never had a greater proportion of the country participated in a war: 18 million served in the armed forces, 10 million overseas; 25 million workers gave of their pay envelope regularly for war bonds. But could this be considered a manufactured support, since all the power of the nation—not only of the government, but the press, the church, and even the chief radical organizations—was behind the calls for all-out war? Was there an undercurrent of reluctance; were there unpublicized signs of resistance?

It was a war against an enemy of unspeakable evil. Hitler's Germany was extending totalitarianism, racism, militarism, and overt aggressive warfare beyond what an already cynical world had experienced. And yet, did the governments conducting this war—England, the United States, the Soviet Union—represent something significantly different, so that their victory would be a blow to imperialism, racism, totalitarianism, militarism, in the world?

Would the behavior of the United States during the war—in military action abroad, in treatment of minorities at home—be in keeping with a "people's war"? Would the country's wartime policies respect the rights of ordinary people everywhere to life, liberty, and the pursuit of happiness? And would postwar America, in its policies at home and overseas, exemplify the values for which the war was supposed to have been fought?

These questions deserve thought. At the time of World War II, the atmosphere was too dense with war fervor to permit them to be aired.

For the United States to step forward as a defender of helpless countries matched its image in American high school history textbooks, but not its record in world affairs. It had opposed the Hatian revolution for independence from France at the start of the nineteenth century. It had instigated a war with Mexico and taken half of that country. It had pretended to help Cuba win freedom from Spain, and then planted itself in Cuba with a military base, investments, and rights of intervention. It had seized Hawaii, Puerto Rico, Guam, and fought a brutal war to subjugate the Filipinos. It had "opened" Japan to its trade with gunboats and threats. It had declared an Open Door Policy in China as a means of assuring that the United States would have opportunities equal to other imperial powers in exploiting China. It had sent troops to Peking with other nations, to assert Western supremacy in China, and kept them there for over thirty years.

While demanding an Open Door in China, it had insisted (with the Monroe Doctrine and many military interventions) on a Closed Door in Latin America—that is, closed to everyone but the United States. It had engineered a revolution against Colombia and created the "independent" state of Panama in order to build and control the Canal. It sent five thousand marines to Nicaragua in 1926 to counter a revolution, and kept a force there for seven years. It intervened in the Dominican Republic for the fourth time in 1916 and kept troops there for eight years. It intervened for the second time in Haiti in 1915 and kept troops there for nineteen years. Between 1900 and 1933, the United States intervened in Cuba four times, in Nicaragua twice, in Panama six times, in Guatemala once, in Honduras seven times. By 1924 the finances of half of the twenty Latin American states were being directed to some extent by the United States. By 1935, over half of U.S. steel and cotton exports were being sold in Latin America.

Just before World War I ended, in 1918, an American force of seven thousand landed at Vladivostok as part of an Allied intervention in Russia, and remained until early 1920. Five thousand more troops were landed at Archangel, another Russian port, also as part of an Allied expeditionary force, and stayed for almost a year. The State Department told Congress: "All these operations were to offset effects of the Bolshevik revolution in Russia."

In short, if the entrance of the United States into World War II was (as so many Americans believed at the time, observing the Nazi invasions) to defend the principle of nonintervention in the affairs of other countries, the nation's record cast doubt on its ability to uphold that principle.

What seemed clear at the time was that the United States was a democracy with certain liberties, while Germany was a dictatorship persecuting its Jewish minority, imprisoning dissidents, whatever their religion, while proclaiming the supremacy of the Nordic "race." However, blacks, looking at anti-Semitism in Germany, might not see their own situation in the U.S. as much different. And the United States had done little about Hitler's policies of persecution. Indeed, it had joined England and France in appeasing Hitler throughout the thirties. Roosevelt and his Secretary of State, Cordell Hull, were hesitant to criticize publicly Hitler's anti-Semitic policies; when a resolution was introduced in the Senate in January 1934 asking the Senate and the President to express "surprise and pain" at what the Germans were doing to the Jews, and to ask restoration of Jewish rights, the State Department "caused this resolution to be buried in committee," according to Arnold Offner (*American Appeasement*).

When Mussolini's Italy invaded Ethiopia in 1935, the U.S. declared an embargo on munitions but let American businesses send oil to Italy in huge quantities, which was essential to Italy's carrying on the war. When a Fascist rebellion took place in Spain in 1936 against the elected social-ist-liberal government, the Roosevelt administration sponsored a neutrality act that had the effect of shutting off help to the Spanish government while Hitler and Mussolini gave critical aid to Franco. Offner says:

> ... the United States went beyond even the legal requirements of its neutrality legislation. Had aid been forthcoming from the United States and from England and France, considering that Hitler's position on aid to Franco was not firm at least until November 1936, the Spanish Republicans could well have triumphed. Instead, Germany gained every advantage from the Spanish civil war.

Was this simply poor judgment, an unfortunate error? Or was it the logical policy of a government whose main interest was not stopping Fascism but advancing the imperial interests of the United States? For those interests, in the thirties, an anti-Soviet policy seemed best. Later, when Japan and Germany threatened U.S. world interests, a pro-Soviet, anti-Nazi policy became preferable. Roosevelt was as much concerned to end the oppression of Jews as Lincoln was to end slavery during the Civil War; their priority in policy (whatever their personal compassion for victims of persecution) was not minority rights, but national power.

It was not Hitler's attacks on the Jews that brought the United States into World War II, any more than the enslavement of 4 million blacks brought Civil War in 1861. Italy's attack on Ethiopia, Hitler's invasion of Austria, his takeover of Czechoslovakia, his attack on Poland—none of those events caused the United States to enter the war, although Roosevelt did begin to give important aid to England. What brought the United States fully into the war was the Japanese attack on the American naval base at Pearl Harbor, Hawaii, on December 7, 1941. Surely it was not the humane concern for Japan's bombing of civilians that led to Roosevelt's outraged call for war—Japan's attack on China in 1937, her bombing of civilians at Nanking, had not provoked the United States to war. It was the Japanese attack on a link in the American Pacific Empire that did it.

So long as Japan remained a well-behaved member of that imperial club of Great Powers who—in keeping with the Open Door Policy—were sharing the exploitation of China, the United States did not object. It had exchanged notes with Japan in 1917 saying "the Government of the United States recognizes that Japan has special interests in China." In 1928, according to Akira Iriye (*After Imperialism*), American consuls in China supported the coming of Japanese troops. It was when Japan threatened potential U.S. markets by its attempted takeover of China, but especially as it moved toward the tin, rubber, and oil of Southeast Asia, that the United States became alarmed and took those measures which led to the Japanese attack: a total embargo on scrap iron, a total embargo on oil in the summer of 1941.

As Bruce Russett says (*No Clear and Present Danger*): "Throughout the 1930s the United States government had done little to resist the Japanese advance on the Asian continent." But: "The Southwest Pacific area was of undeniable economic importance to the United States—at the time most of America's tin and rubber came from there, as did substantial quantities of other raw materials."

Pearl Harbor was presented to the American public as a sudden, shocking, immoral act. Immoral it was, like any bombing—but not really sudden or shocking to the American government. Russett says: "Japan's strike against the American naval base climaxed a long series of mutually antagonistic acts. In initiating economic sanctions against Japan the United States undertook actions that were widely recognized in Washington as carrying grave risks of war."

Putting aside the wild accusations against Roosevelt (that he knew about Pearl Harbor and didn't tell, or that he deliberately provoked the Pearl Harbor raid—these are without evidence), it does seem clear that he did as James Polk had done before him in the Mexican war and Lyndon Johnson after him in the Vietnam war—he lied to the public for what he thought was a right cause. In September and October 1941, he misstated the facts in two incidents involving German submarines and American destroyers. A historian sympathetic to Roosevelt, Thomas A. Bailey, has written:

> Franklin Roosevelt repeatedly deceived the American people during the period before Pearl Harbor. . . . He was like the physician who must tell the patient lies for the patient's own good . . . because the masses are notoriously shortsighted and generally cannot see danger until it is at their throats. . . .

One of the judges in the Tokyo War Crimes Trial after World War II, Radhabinod Pal, dissented from the general verdicts against Japanese officials and argued that the United States had clearly provoked the war with Japan and expected Japan to act. Richard Minear *(Victors' Justice)* sums up Pal's view of the embargoes on scrap iron and oil, that "these measures were a clear and potent threat to Japan's very existence." The records show that a White House conference two weeks before Pearl Harbor anticipated a war and discussed how it should be justified.

A State Department memorandum on Japanese expansion, a year before Pearl Harbor, did not talk of the independence of China or the principle of self-determination. It said:

> . . . our general diplomatic and strategic position would be considerably weakened—by our loss of Chinese, Indian and South Seas markets (and by our loss of much of the Japanese market for our goods, as Japan would become more and more self-sufficient) as well as by insurmountable restrictions upon our access to the rubber, tin, jute, and other vital materials of the Asian and Oceanic regions.

Once joined with England and Russia in the war (Germany and Italy declared war on the United States right after Pearl Harbor), did the behavior of the United States show that her war aims were humanitarian, or centered on power and profit? Was she fighting the war to end the control by some nations over others or to make sure the controlling nations were friends of the United States? In August 1941, Roosevelt and Churchill met off the coast of Newfoundland and released to the world the Atlantic Charter, setting forth noble goals for the postwar world, saying their countries "seek no aggrandizement, territorial or other," and that they respected "the right of all peoples to choose the form of government under which they will live." The Charter was celebrated as declaring the right of nations to self-determination.

Two weeks before the Atlantic Charter, however, the U.S. Acting Secretary of State, Sumner Welles, had assured the French government that they could keep their empire intact after the end of the war: "This Government, mindful of its traditional friendship for France, has deeply sympathized with the desire of the French people to maintain their territories and to preserve them intact." The Department of Defense history of Vietnam *(The Pentagon Papers)* itself pointed to what it called an "ambivalent" policy toward Indochina, noting that "in the Atlantic Charter and other pronouncements, the U.S. proclaimed support for national self-determination and independence" but also "early in the war repeatedly expressed or implied to the French an intention to restore to France its overseas empire after the war."

In late 1942, Roosevelt's personal representative assured French General Henri Giraud: "It is thoroughly understood that French sovereignty will be re-established as soon as possible throughout all the territory, metropolitan or colonial, over which flew the French flag in 1939." (These pages, like the others in the *Pentagon Papers*, are marked "TOP SECRET—Sensitive.") By 1945 the "ambivalent" attitude was gone. In May, Truman assured the French he did not question her "sovereignty over Indochina." That fall, the United States urged Nationalist China, put temporarily in charge of the northern part of Indochina by the Potsdam Conference, to turn it over to the French, despite the obvious desire of the Vietnamese for independence.

That was a favor for the French government. But what about the United States' own imperial ambitions during the war? What about the "aggrandizement, territorial or other" that Roosevelt had renounced in the Atlantic Charter?

In the headlines were the battles and troop movements: the invasion of North Africa in 1942, Italy in 1943, the massive, dramatic cross-Channel invasion of German-occupied France in 1944, the bitter battles as Germany was pushed back toward and over her frontiers, the increasing bombardment by the British and American air forces. And, at the same time, the Russian victories over the Nazi armies (the Russians, by the time of the cross-Channel invasion, had driven the Germans out of Russia, and were engaging 80 percent of the German troops). In the Pacific, in 1943 and 1944, there was the island-by-island move of American forces toward Japan, finding closer and closer bases for the thunderous bombardment of Japanese cities.

Quietly, behind the headlines in battles and bombings, American diplomats and businessmen worked hard to make sure that when the war ended, American economic power would be second to none in the world. United States business would penetrate areas that up to this time had been dominated by England. The Open Door Policy of equal access would be extended from Asia to Europe, meaning that the United States intended to push England aside and move in.

That is what happened to the Middle East and its oil. In August 1945 a State Department officer said that "a review of the diplomatic history of the past 35 years will show that petroleum has historically played a larger part in the external relations of the United States than any other commodity." Saudi Arabia was the largest oil pool in the Middle East. The ARAMCO oil corporation, through Secretary of the Interior Harold Ickes, got Roosevelt to agree to Lend Lease aid to Saudi Arabia, which would involve the U.S. government there and create a shield for the interests of ARAMCO. In 1944 Britain and the U.S. signed a pact on oil agreeing on "the principle of equal opportunity," and Lloyd Gardner concludes (*Economic Aspects of New Deal Diplomacy*) that "the Open Door Policy was triumphant throughout the Middle East."

Historian Gabriel Kolko, after a close study of American wartime policy (*The Politics of War*), concludes that "the American economic war aim was to save capitalism at home and abroad." In April 1944 a State Department official said: "As you know, we've got to plan on enormously increased production in this country after the war, and the American domestic market can't absorb all that production indefinitely. There won't be any question about our needing greatly increased foreign markets."

Anthony Sampson, in his study of the international oil business (*The Seven Sisters*), says:

> By the end of the war the dominant influence in Saudi Arabia was unquestionably the United States. King Ibn Saud was regarded no longer as a wild desert warrior, but as a key piece in the power-game, to be wooed by the West. Roosevelt, on his way back from Yalta in February 1945, entertained

the King on the cruiser *Quincy,* together with his entourage of fifty, including two sons, a prime minister, an astrologer and flocks of sheep for slaughter.

Roosevelt then wrote to Ibn Saud, promising the United States would not change its Palestine policy without consulting the Arabs. In later years, the concern for oil would constantly compete with political concern for the Jewish state in the Middle East, but at this point, oil seemed more important.

With British imperial power collapsing during World War II, the United States was ready to move in. Hull said early in the war:

> Leadership toward a new system of international relationships in trade and other economic affairs will devolve very largely upon the United States because of our great economic strength. We should assume this leadership, and the responsibility that goes with it, primarily for reasons of pure national self-interest.

Before the war was over, the administration was planning the outlines of the new international economic order, based on partnership between government and big business. Lloyd Gardner says of Roosevelt's chief adviser, Harry Hopkins, who had organized the relief programs of the New Deal: "No conservative outdid Hopkins in championing foreign investment, and its protection."

The poet Archibald MacLeish, then an Assistant Secretary of State, spoke critically of what he saw in the postwar world: "As things are now going, the peace we will make, the peace we seem to be making, will be a peace of oil, a peace of gold, a peace of shipping, a peace, in brief . . . without moral purpose or human interest. . . ."

During the war, England and the United States set up the International Monetary Fund to regulate international exchanges of currency; voting would be proportional to capital contributed, so American dominance would be assured. The International Bank for Reconstruction and Development was set up, supposedly to help reconstruct war-destroyed areas, but one of its first objectives was, in its own words, "to promote foreign investment."

The economic aid countries would need after the war was already seen in political terms: Averell Harriman, ambassador to Russia, said in early 1944: "Economic assistance is one of the most effective weapons at our disposal to influence European political events in the direction we desire. . . ."

The creation of the United Nations during the war was presented to the world as international cooperation to prevent future wars. But the U.N. was dominated by the Western imperial countries—the United States, England, and France—and a new imperial power, with military bases and powerful influence in Eastern Europe—the Soviet Union. An important conservative Republican Senator, Arthur Vandenburg, wrote in his diary about the United Nations Charter:

> The striking thing about it is that it is so conservative from a nationalist standpoint. It is based virtually on a four-power alliance. . . . This is anything but a wild-eyed internationalist dream of a world State. . . . I am deeply impressed (and surprised) to find Hull so carefully guarding our American veto in his scheme of things.

The plight of Jews in German-occupied Europe, which many people thought was at the heart of the war against the Axis, was not a chief concern of Roosevelt. Henry Feingold's research (*The Politics of Rescue*) shows that, while the Jews were being put in camps and the process of annihilation was beginning that would end in the horrifying extermination of 6 million Jews and millions of non-Jews, Roosevelt failed to take steps that might have saved thousands of lives. He did not see it as a high priority; he left it to the State Department, and in the State Department anti-Semitism and a cold bureaucracy became obstacles to action.

Was the war being fought to establish that Hitler was wrong in his ideas of white Nordic supremacy over "inferior" races? The United States' armed forces were segregated by race. When troops were jammed onto the *Queen Mary* in early 1945 to go to combat duty in the European theater, the blacks were stowed down in the depths of the ship near the engine room, as far as possible from the fresh air of the deck, in a bizarre reminder of the slave voyages of old.

The Red Cross, with government approval, separated the blood donations of black and white. It was, ironically, a black physician named Charles Drew who developed the blood bank system. He was put in charge of the wartime donations, and then fired when he tried to end blood segregation. Despite the urgent need for wartime labor, blacks were still being discriminated against for jobs. A spokesman for a West Coast aviation plant said: "The Negro will be considered only as janitors and in other similar capacities. . . . Regardless of their training as aircraft workers, we will not employ them." Roosevelt never did anything to enforce the orders of the Fair Employment Practices Commission he had set up.

The Fascist nations were notorious in their insistence that the woman's place was in the home. Yet, the war against Fascism, although it utilized women in defense industries where they were desperately needed, took no special steps to change the subordinate role of women. The War Manpower Commission, despite the large numbers of women in war work, kept women off its policymaking bodies. A report of the Women's Bureau of the Department of Labor, by its director, Mary Anderson, said the War Manpower Commission had "doubts and uneasiness" about "what was then regarded as a developing attitude of militancy or a crusading spirit on the part of women leaders. . . ."

In one of its policies, the United States came close to direct duplication of Fascism. This was in its treatment of the Japanese-Americans living on the West Coast. After the Pearl Harbor attack, anti-Japanese hysteria spread in the government. One Congressman said: "I'm for catching every Japanese in America, Alaska and Hawaii now and putting them in concentration camps. . . . Damn them! Let's get rid of them!"

Franklin D. Roosevelt did not share this frenzy, but he calmly signed Executive Order 9066, in February 1942, giving the army the power, without warrants or indictments or hearings, to arrest every Japanese-American on the West Coast—110,000 men, women, and children—to take them from their homes, transport them to camps far into the interior, and keep them there under prison conditions. Three-fourths of these were Nisei—children born in the United States of Japanese parents and therefore American citizens. The other fourth—the Issei, born in Japan—were barred by law from becoming citizens. In 1944 the Supreme Court upheld the forced evacuation on the grounds of military necessity. The Japanese remained in those camps for over three years.

Michi Weglyn was a young girl when her family experienced evacuation and detention. She tells *(Years of Infamy)* of bungling in the evacuation, of misery, confusion, anger, but also of Japanese-American dignity and fighting back. There were strikes, petitions, mass meetings, refusal to sign loyalty oaths, riots against the camp authorities. The Japanese resisted to the end.

Not until after the war did the story of the Japanese-Americans begin to be known to the general public. The month the war ended in Asia, September 1945, an article appeared in *Harper's Magazine* by Yale Law Professor Eugene V. Rostow, calling the Japanese evacuation "our worst wartime mistake." Was it a "mistake"—or was it an action to be expected from a nation with a long history of racism and which was fighting a war, not to end racism, but to retain the fundamental elements of the American system?

It was a war waged by a government whose chief beneficiary—despite volumes of reforms—was a wealthy elite. The alliance between big business and the government went back to the very first proposals of Alexander Hamilton to Congress after the Revolutionary War. By World War II that partnership had developed and intensified. During the Depression, Roosevelt had once denounced the "economic royalists," but he always had the support of certain important business leaders. During the war, as Bruce Catton saw it from his post in the War Production Board: "The economic royalists, denounced and derided . . . had a part to play now. . . ."

Catton (*The War Lords of Washington*) described the process of industrial mobilization to carry on the war, and how in this process wealth became more and more concentrated in fewer and fewer large corporations. In 1940 the United States had begun sending large amounts of war supplies to England and France. By 1941 three-fourths of the value of military contracts were handled by fifty-six large corporations. A Senate report, "Economic Concentration and World War II," noted that the government contracted for scientific research in industry during the war, and although two thousand corporations were involved, of $1 billion spent, $400 million went to ten large corporations.

Management remained firmly in charge of decision making during the war, and although 12 million workers were organized in the CIO and AFL, labor was in a subordinate position. Labor-management committees were set up in five thousand factories, as a gesture toward industrial democracy, but they acted mostly as disciplinary groups for absentee workers, and devices for increasing production. Catton writes: "The big operators who made the working decisions had decided that nothing very substantial was going to be changed."

Despite the overwhelming atmosphere of patriotism and total dedication to winning the war, despite the no-strike pledges of the AFL and CIO, many of the nation's workers, frustrated by the freezing of wages while business profits rocketed skyward, went on strike. During the war, there were fourteen thousand strikes, involving 6,770,000 workers, more than in any comparable period in American history. In 1944 alone, a million workers were on strike, in the mines, in the steel mills, in the auto and transportation equipment industries.

When the war ended, the strikes continued in record numbers—3 million on strike in the first half of 1946. According to Jeremy Brecher (*Strike!*), if not for the disciplinary hand of the unions there might have been "a general confrontation between the workers of a great many industries, and the government, supporting the employers."

In Lowell, Massachusetts, for example, according to an unpublished manuscript by Marc Miller ("The Irony of Victory: Lowell During World War II"), there were as many strikes in 1943 and 1944 as in 1937. It may have been a "people's war," but here was dissatisfaction at the fact that the textile mill profits grew 600 percent from 1940 to 1946, while wage increases in cotton goods industries went up 36 percent. How little the war changed the difficult condition of women workers is shown by the fact that in Lowell, among women war workers with children, only 5 percent could have their children taken care of by nursery schools; the others had to make their own arrangements.

Beneath the noise of enthusiastic patriotism, there were many people who thought war was wrong, even in the circumstances of Fascist aggression. Out of 10 million drafted for the armed forces during World War II, only 43,000 refused to fight. But this was three times the proportion of C.O.'s (conscientious objectors) in World War I. Of these 43,000, about 6,000 went to prison, which was, proportionately, four times the number of C.O.'s who went to prison during World War I. Of every six men in federal prison, one was there as a C.O.

Many more than 43,000 refusers did not show up for the draft at all. The government lists about 350,000 cases of draft evasion, including technical violations as well as actual desertion, so it is hard to tell the true number, but it may be that the number of men who either did not show up or claimed C.O. status was in the hundreds of thousands—not a small number. And this in the face of an American community almost unanimously for the war.

Among those soldiers who were not conscientious objectors, who seemed willing fighters, it is hard to know how much resentment there was against authority, against having to fight in a war whose aims were unclear, inside a military machine whose lack of democracy was very clear. No one recorded the bitterness of enlisted men against the special privileges of officers in the army of a country known as a democracy. To give just one instance: combat crews in the air force in the European theater, going to the base movies between bombing missions, found two lines—an officers' line (short), and an enlisted men's line (very long). There were two mess halls, even as they prepared to go into combat: the enlisted men's food was different—worse—than the officers'.

The literature that followed World War II, James Jones's *From Here to Eternity*, Joseph Heller's *Catch-22*, and Norman Mailer's *The Naked and the Dead*, captured this GI anger against the army "brass." In *The Naked and the Dead*, the soldiers talk in battle, and one of them says: "The only thing wrong with this Army is it never lost a war."

Toglio was shocked. "You think we ought to lose this one?"

Red found himself carried away. "What have I against the goddam Japs? You think I care if they keep this fuggin jungle? What's it to me if Cummings gets another star?"

"General Cummings, he's a good man," Martinez said.

"There ain't a good officer in the world," Red stated.

There seemed to be widespread indifference, even hostility, on the part of the Negro community to the war despite the attempts of Negro newspapers and Negro leaders to mobilize black sentiment. Lawrence Wittner (*Rebels Against War*) quotes a black journalist: "The Negro . . . is angry, resentful, and utterly apathetic about the war. 'Fight for what?' he is asking. 'This war doesn't mean a thing to me. If we win I lose, so what?'" A black army officer, home on furlough, told friends in Harlem he had been in hundreds of bull sessions with Negro soldiers and found no interest in the war.

A student at a Negro college told his teacher: "The Army jim-crows us. The Navy lets us serve only as messmen. The Red Cross refuses our blood. Employers and labor unions shut us out. Lynchings continue. We are disenfranchised, jim-crowed, spat upon. What more could Hitler do than that?" NAACP leader Walter White repeated this to a black audience of several thousand people in the Midwest, thinking they would disapprove, but instead, as he recalled: "To my surprise and dismay the audience burst into such applause that it took me some thirty or forty seconds to quiet it."

In January 1943, there appeared in a Negro newspaper this "Draftee's Prayer":

Dear Lord, today
I go to war:
To fight, to die,
Tell me what for?
Dear Lord, I'll fight,
I do not fear,
Germans or Japs;
My fears are here.
America!

But there was no organized Negro opposition to the war. In fact, there was little organized opposition from any source. The Communist party was enthusiastically in support. The Socialist party was divided, unable to make a clear statement one way or the other.

A few small anarchist and pacifist groups refused to back the war. The Women's International League for Peace and Freedom said: ". . . war between nations or classes or races cannot permanently settle conflicts or heal the wounds that brought them into being." The *Catholic Worker* wrote: "We are still pacifists. . . ."

The difficulty of merely calling for "peace" in a world of capitalism, Fascism, Communism—dynamic ideologies, aggressive actions—troubled some pacifists. They began to speak of "revolutionary nonviolence." A. J. Muste of the Fellowship of Reconciliation said in later years: "I was not impressed with the sentimental, easygoing pacifism of the earlier part of the century. People then felt that if they sat and talked pleasantly of peace and love, they would solve the problems of the world." The world was in the midst of a revolution, Muste realized, and those against violence must take revolutionary action, but without violence. A movement of revolutionary pacifism would have to "make effective contacts with oppressed and minority groups such as Negroes, share-croppers, industrial workers."

Only one organized socialist group opposed the war unequivocally. This was the Socialist Workers Party. The Espionage Act of 1917, still on the books, applied to wartime statements. But in 1940, with the United States not yet at war, Congress passed the Smith Act. This took Espionage Act prohibitions against talk or writing that would lead to refusal of duty in the armed forces and applied them to peacetime. The Smith Act also made it a crime to advocate the overthrow of the government by force and violence, or to join any group that advocated this, or to publish anything with such ideas. In Minneapolis in 1943, eighteen members of the Socialist Workers party were convicted for belonging to a party whose ideas, expressed in its Declaration of Principles, and in the *Communist Manifesto*, were said to violate the Smith Act. They were sentenced to prison terms, and the Supreme Court refused to review their case.

A few voices continued to insist that the real war was inside each nation: Dwight Macdonald's wartime magazine *Politics* presented, in early 1945, an article by the French worker-philosopher Simone Weil:

Whether the mask is labelled Fascism, Democracy, or Dictatorship of the Proletariat, our great adversary remains the Apparatus—the bureaucracy, the police, the military. Not the one facing us across the frontier or the battlelines, which is not so much our enemy as our brothers' enemy, but the one that calls itself our protector and makes us its slaves. No matter what the circumstances, the worst betrayal will always be to subordinate ourselves to this Apparatus, and to trample underfoot, in its service, all human values in ourselves and in others.

Still, the vast bulk of the American population was mobilized, in the army, and in civilian life, to fight the war, and the atmosphere of war enveloped more and more Americans. Public opinion polls show large majorities of soldiers favoring the draft for the postwar period. Hatred against the enemy, against the Japanese particularly, became widespread. Racism was clearly at work. *Time* magazine, reporting the battle of Iwo Jima, said: "The ordinary unreasoning Jap is ignorant. Perhaps he is human. Nothing . . . indicates it."

So, there was a mass base of support for what became the heaviest bombardment of civilians ever undertaken in any war: the aerial attacks on German and Japanese cities. One might argue that this popular support made it a "people's war." But if "people's war" means a war of people against attack, a defensive war—if it means a war fought for humane reasons instead of for the privileges of an elite, a war against the few, not the many—then the tactics of all-out aerial assault against the populations of Germany and Japan destroy that notion.

Italy had bombed cities in the Ethiopian war; Italy and Germany had bombed civilians in the Spanish Civil War; at the start of World War II German planes dropped bombs on Rotterdam in Holland, Coventry in England, and elsewhere. Roosevelt had described these as "inhuman barbarism that has profoundly shocked the conscience of humanity."

These German bombings were very small compared with the British and American bombings of German cities. In January 1943 the Allies met at Casablanca and agreed on large-scale air attacks to achieve "the destruction and dislocation of the German military, industrial and economic system and the undermining of the morale of the German people to the point where their capacity for armed resistance is fatally weakened." And so, the saturation bombing of German cities began—with thousand-plane raids on Cologne, Essen, Frankfurt, Hamburg. The English flew at night with no pretense of aiming at "military" targets; the Americans flew in the daytime and pretended precision, but bombing from high altitudes made that impossible. The climax of this terror bombing was the bombing of Dresden in early 1945, in which the tremendous heat generated by the bombs created a vacuum into which fire leaped swiftly in a great firestorm through the city. More than 100,000 died in Dresden. (Winston Churchill, in his wartime memoirs, confined himself to this account of the incident: "We made a heavy raid in the latter month on Dresden, then a centre of communication of Germany's Eastern Front.")

The bombing of Japanese cities continued the strategy of saturation bombing to destroy civilian morale; one nighttime fire-bombing of

Tokyo took 80,000 lives. And then, on August 6, 1945, came the lone American plane in the sky over Hiroshima, dropping the first atomic bomb, leaving perhaps 100,000 Japanese dead, and tens of thousands more slowly dying from radiation poisoning. Twelve U.S. navy fliers in the Hiroshima city jail were killed in the bombing, a fact that the U.S. government has never officially acknowledged, according to historian Martin Sherwin (*A World Destroyed*). Three days later, a second atomic bomb was dropped on the city of Nagasaki, with perhaps 50,000 killed.

The justification for these atrocities was that this would end the war quickly, making unnecessary an invasion of Japan. Such an invasion would cost a huge number of lives, the government said—a million, according to Secretary of State Byrnes; half a million, Truman claimed was the figure given him by General George Marshall. (When the papers of the Manhattan Project—the project to build the atom bomb—were released years later, they showed that Marshall urged a warning to the Japanese about the bomb, so people could be removed and only military targets hit.) These estimates of invasion losses were not realistic, and seem to have been pulled out of the air to justify bombings which, as their effects became known, horrified more and more people. Japan, by August 1945, was in desperate shape and ready to surrender. *New York Times* military analyst Hanson Baldwin wrote, shortly after the war:

> The enemy, in a military sense, was in a hopeless strategic position by the time the Potsdam demand for unconditional surrender was made on July 26.
>
> Such then, was the situation when we wiped out Hiroshima and Nagasaki.
>
> Need we have done it? No one can, of course, be positive, but the answer is almost certainly negative.

The United States Strategic Bombing Survey, set up by the War Department in 1944 to study the results of aerial attacks in the war, interviewed hundreds of Japanese civilian and military leaders after Japan surrendered, and reported just after the war:

> Based on a detailed investigation of all the facts and supported by the testimony of the surviving Japanese leaders involved, it is the Survey's opinion that certainly prior to 31 December 1945, and in all probability prior to 1 November 1945, Japan would have surrendered even if the atomic bombs had not been dropped, even if Russia had not entered the war, and even if no invasion had been planned or contemplated.

But could American leaders have known this in August 1945? The answer is, clearly, yes. The Japanese code had been broken, and Japan's messages were being intercepted. It was known the Japanese had instructed their ambassador in Moscow to work on peace negotiations with the Allies. Japanese leaders had begun talking of surrender a year before this, and the Emperor himself had begun to suggest, in June 1945, that alternatives to fighting to the end be considered. On July 13, Foreign Minister Shigenori Togo wired his ambassador in Moscow: "Unconditional surrender is the only obstacle to peace. . . ." Martin Sherwin, after an exhaustive study of the relevant historical documents, concludes: "Having broken the Japanese code before the war, American Intelligence was able to—and did—relay this message to the President, but it had no effect whatever on efforts to bring the war to a conclusion."

If only the Americans had not insisted on unconditional surrender— that is, if they were willing to accept one condition to the surrender, that the Emperor, a holy figure to the Japanese, remain in place—the Japanese would have agreed to stop the war.

Why did the United States not take that small step to save both American and Japanese lives? Was it because too much money and effort had been invested in the atomic bomb not to drop it? General Leslie Groves, head of the Manhattan Project, described Truman as a man on a toboggan, the momentum too great to stop it. Or was it, as British scientist P. M. S. Blackett suggested *(Fear, War, and the Bomb)*, that the United States was anxious to drop the bomb before the Russians entered the war against Japan?

The Russians had secretly agreed (they were officially not at war with Japan) they would come into the war ninety days after the end of the European war. That turned out to be May 8, and so, on August 8, the Russians were due to declare war on Japan. But by then the big bomb had been dropped, and the next day a second one would be dropped on Nagasaki; the Japanese would surrender to the United States, not the Russians, and the United States would be the occupier of postwar Japan. In other words, Blackett says, the dropping of the bomb was "the first major operation of the cold diplomatic war with Russia. . . ." Blackett is supported by American historian Gar Alperovitz *(Atomic Diplomacy)*, who notes a diary entry for July 28, 1945, by Secretary of the Navy James Forrestal, describing Secretary of State James F. Byrnes as "most anxious to get the Japanese affair over with before the Russians got in."

Truman had said, "The world will note that the first atomic bomb was dropped on Hiroshima, a military base. That was because we wished in this first attack to avoid, insofar as possible, the killing of civilians." It was a preposterous statement. Those 100,000 killed in Hiroshima were almost all civilians. The U.S. Strategic Bombing Survey said in its official report: "Hiroshima and Nagasaki were chosen as targets because of their concentration of activities and population."

The dropping of the second bomb on Nagasaki seems to have been scheduled in advance, and no one has ever been able to explain why it was dropped. Was it because this was a plutonium bomb whereas the Hiroshima bomb was a uranium bomb? Were the dead and irradiated of Nagasaki victims of a scientific experiment? Martin Sherwin says that among the Nagasaki dead were probably American prisoners of war. He notes a message of July 31 from Headquarters, U.S. Army Strategic Air Forces, Guam, to the War Department:

> Reports prisoner of war sources, not verified by photos, give location of Allied prisoner of war camp one mile north of center of city of Nagasaki. Does this influence the choice of this target for initial Centerboard operation? Request immediate reply.

The reply: "Targets previously assigned for Centerboard remain unchanged."

True, the war then ended quickly. Italy had been defeated a year earlier. Germany had recently surrendered, crushed primarily by the armies of the Soviet Union on the Eastern Front, aided by the Allied armies on the West. Now Japan surrendered. The Fascist powers were destroyed.

But what about fascism—as idea, as reality? Were its essential elements—militarism, racism, imperialism—now gone? Or were they absorbed into the already poisoned bones of the victors? A. J. Muste, the revolutionary pacifist, had predicted in 1941: "The problem after a war is with the victor. He thinks he has just proved that war and violence pay. Who will now teach him a lesson?"

The victors were the Soviet Union and the United States (also England, France and Nationalist China, but they were weak). Both these countries now went to work—without swastikas, goose-stepping, or officially declared racism, but under the cover of "socialism" on one side, and "democracy" on the other, to carve out their own empires of influence. They proceeded to share and contest with one another the domination of the world, to build military machines far greater than the Fascist countries had built, to control the destinies of more countries than Hitler, Mussolini, and Japan had been able to do. They also acted to control their own populations, each country with its own techniques—crude in the Soviet Union, sophisticated in the United States—to make their rule secure.

The war not only put the United States in a position to dominate much of the world; it created conditions for effective control at home. The unemployment, the economic distress, and the consequent turmoil that had marked the thirties, only partly relieved by New Deal measures, had been pacified, overcome by the greater turmoil of the war. The war brought higher prices for farmers, higher wages, enough prosperity for enough of the population to assume against the rebellions that so threatened the thirties. As Lawrence Wittner writes, "The war rejuvenated American capitalism." The biggest gains were in corporate profits, which rose from $6.4 billion in 1940 to $10.8 billion in 1944. But enough went to workers and farmers to make them feel the system was doing well for them.

It was an old lesson learned by governments: that war solves problems of control. Charles E. Wilson, the president of General Motors, was so happy about the wartime situation that he suggested a continuing alliance between business and the military for "a permanent war economy."

That is what happened. When, right after the war, the American public, war-weary, seemed to favor demobilization and disarmament, the Truman administration (Roosevelt had died in April 1945) worked to create an atmosphere of crisis and cold war. True, the rivalry with the Soviet Union was real—that country had come out of the war with its economy wrecked and 20 million people dead, but was making an astounding comeback, rebuilding its industry, regaining military strength. The Truman administration, however, presented the Soviet Union as not just a rival but an immediate threat.

In a series of moves abroad and at home, it established a climate of fear—a hysteria about Communism—which would steeply escalate the military budget and stimulate the economy with war-related orders. This combination of policies would permit more aggressive actions abroad, more repressive actions at home.

Revolutionary movements in Europe and Asia were described to the American public as examples of Soviet expansionism—thus recalling the indignation against Hitler's aggressions.

In Greece, which had been a right-wing monarchy and dictatorship before the war, a popular left-wing National Liberation Front (the EAM) was put down by a British army of intervention immediately after the war. A right-wing dictatorship was restored. When opponents of the regime were jailed, and trade union leaders removed, a left-wing guerrilla movement began to grow against the regime, soon consisting of 17,000 fighters, 50,000 active supporters, and perhaps 250,000 sympathizers, in a country of 7 million. Great Britain said it could not handle the rebellion, and asked the United States to come in. As a State Department officer said later: "Great Britain had within the hour handed the job of world leadership . . . to the United States."

The United States responded with the Truman Doctrine, the name given to a speech Truman gave to Congress in the spring of 1947, in which he asked for $400 million in military and economic aid to Greece and Turkey. Truman said the U.S. must help "free peoples who are resisting attempted subjugation by armed minorities or by outside pressures."

In fact, the biggest outside pressure was the United States. The Greek rebels were getting some aid from Yugoslavia, but no aid from the Soviet Union, which during the war had promised Churchill a free hand in Greece if he would give the Soviet Union its way in Rumania, Poland, Bulgaria. The Soviet Union, like the United States, did not seem to be willing to help revolutions it could not control.

Truman said the world "must choose between alternative ways of life." One was based on "the will of the majority . . . distinguished by free institutions"; the other was based on "the will of a minority . . . terror and oppression . . . the suppression of personal freedoms." Truman's adviser Clark Clifford had suggested that in his message Truman connect the intervention in Greece to something less rhetorical, more practical—"the great natural resources of the Middle East" (Clifford meant oil), but Truman didn't mention that.

The United States moved into the Greek civil war, not with soldiers, but with weapons and military advisers. In the last five months of 1947, 74,000 tons of military equipment were sent by the United States to the right-wing government in Athens, including artillery, dive bombers, and stocks of napalm. Two hundred and fifty army officers, headed by General James Van Fleet, advised the Greek army in the field. Van Fleet started a policy—standard in dealing with popular insurrections—of forcibly removing thousands of Greeks from their homes in the countryside, to try to isolate the guerrillas, to remove the source of their support.

With that aid, the rebellion was defeated by 1949. United States economic and military aid continued to the Greek government. Investment capital from Esso, Dow Chemical, Chrysler, and other U.S. corporations flowed into Greece. But illiteracy, poverty, and starvation remained widespread there, with the country in the hands of what

Richard Barnet *(Intervention and Revolution)* called "a particularly brutal and backward military dictatorship."

In China, a revolution was already under way when World War II ended, led by a Communist movement with enormous mass support. A Red Army, which had fought against the Japanese, now fought to oust the corrupt dictatorship of Chiang Kai-shek, which was supported by the United States. The United States, by 1949, had given $2 billion in aid to Chiang Kai-shek's forces, but, according to the State Department's own White Paper on China, Chiang Kai-shek's government had lost the confidence of its own troops and its own people. In January 1949, Chinese Communist forces moved into Peking, the civil war was over, and China was in the hands of a revolutionary movement, the closest thing, in the long history of that ancient country, to a people's government, independent of outside control.

The United States was trying, in the postwar decade, to create a national consensus—excluding the radicals, who could not support a foreign policy aimed at suppressing revolution—of conservatives and liberals, Republicans and Democrats, around the policies of cold war and anti-Communism. Such a coalition could best be created by a liberal Democratic President, whose aggressive policy abroad would be supported by conservatives, and whose welfare programs at home (Truman's "Fair Deal") would be attractive to liberals. If, in addition, liberals and traditional Democrats could—the memory of the war was still fresh—support a foreign policy against "aggression," the radical-liberal bloc created by World War II would be broken up. And perhaps, if the anti-Communist mood became strong enough, liberals could support repressive moves at home which in ordinary times would be seen as violating the liberal tradition of tolerance. In 1950, there came an event that speeded the formation of the liberal-conservative consensus—Truman's undeclared war in Korea.

Korea, occupied by Japan for thirty-five years, was liberated from Japan after World War II and divided into North Korea, a socialist dictatorship, part of the Soviet sphere of influence, and South Korea, a right-wing dictatorship, in the American sphere. There had been threats back and forth between the two Koreas, and when on June 25, 1950, North Korean armies moved southward across the 38th parallel in an invasion of South Korea, the United Nations, dominated by the United States, asked its members to help "repel the armed attack." Truman ordered the American armed forces to help South Korea, and the American army became the U.N. army. Truman said: "A return to the rule of force in international affairs would have far-reaching effects. The United States will continue to uphold the rule of law."

The United States' response to "the rule of force" was to reduce Korea, North and South, to a shambles, in three years of bombing and shelling. Napalm was dropped, and a BBC journalist described the result:

> In front of us a curious figure was standing, a little crouched, legs straddled, arms held out from his sides. He had no eyes, and the whole of his body, nearly all of which was visible through tatters of burnt rags, was covered with a hard black crust speckled with yellow pus. . . . He had to stand because he was no longer covered with a skin, but with a crust-like crackling which broke easily. . . . I thought of the hundreds of villages reduced to ash which I personally had seen and realized the sort of casualty list which must be mounting up along the Korean front.

Perhaps 2 million Koreans, North and South, were killed in the Korean war, all in the name of opposing "the rule of force."

As for the rule of law Truman spoke about, the American military moves seemed to go beyond that. The U.N. resolution had called for action "to repel the armed attack and to restore peace and security in the area." But the American armies, after pushing the North Koreans back across the 38th parallel, advanced all the way up through North Korea to the Yalu River, on the border of China—which provoked the Chinese into entering the war. The Chinese then swept southward and the war was stalemated at the 38th parallel until peace negotiations restored, in 1953, the old boundary between North and South.

The Korean war mobilized liberal opinion behind the war and the President. It created the kind of coalition that was needed to sustain a policy of intervention abroad, militarization of the economy at home. This meant trouble for those who stayed outside the coalition as radical critics. Alonzo Hamby noted (*Beyond the New Deal*) that the Korean war was supported by *The New Republic*, by *The Nation*, and by Henry Wallace (who in 1948 had run against Truman on a left coalition Progressive party ticket). The liberals didn't like Senator Joseph McCarthy (who hunted for Communists everywhere, even among liberals), but the Korean war, as Hamby says, "had given McCarthyism a new lease on life."

The left had become very influential in the hard times of the thirties, and during the war against Fascism. The actual membership of the Communist party was not large—fewer than 100,000 probably—but it was a potent force in trade unions numbering millions of members, in the arts, and among countless Americans who may have been led by the failure of the capitalist system in the thirties to look favorably on

Communism and Socialism. Thus, if the Establishment, after World War II, was to make capitalism more secure in the country, and to build a consensus of support for the American Empire, it had to weaken and isolate the left.

Two weeks after presenting to the country the Truman Doctrine for Greece and Turkey, Truman issued, on March 22, 1947, Executive Order 9835, initiating a program to search out any "infiltration of disloyal persons" in the U.S. government. In their book *The Fifties*, Douglas Miller and Marion Nowack comment:

> Though Truman would later complain of the "great wave of hysteria" sweeping the nation, his commitment to victory over communism, to completely safeguarding the United States from external and internal threats, was in large measure responsible for creating that very hysteria. Between the launching of his security program in March 1947 and December 1952, some 6.6 million persons were investigated. Not a single case of espionage was uncovered, though about 500 persons were dismissed in dubious cases of "questionable loyalty." All of this was conducted with secret evidence, secret and often paid informers, and neither judge nor jury. Despite the failure to find subversion, the broad scope of the official Red hunt gave popular credence to the notion that the government was riddled with spies. A conservative and fearful reaction coursed the country. Americans became convinced of the need for absolute security and the preservation of the established order.

World events right after the war made it easier to build up public support for the anti-Communist crusade at home. In 1948, the Communist party in Czechoslovakia ousted non-Communists from the government and established their own rule. The Soviet Union that year blockaded Berlin, which was a jointly occupied city isolated inside the Soviet sphere of East Germany, forcing the United States to airlift supplies into Berlin. In 1949, there was the Communist victory in China, and in that year also, the Soviet Union exploded its first atomic bomb. In 1950 the Korean war began. These were all portrayed to the public as signs of a world Communist conspiracy.

Not as publicized as the Communist victories, but just as disturbing to the American government, was the upsurge all over the world of colonial peoples demanding independence. Revolutionary movements were growing—in Indochina against the French; in Indonesia against the Dutch; in the Philippines, armed rebellion against the United States.

In Africa there were rumblings of discontent in the form of strikes. Basil Davidson (*Let Freedom Come*) tells of the longest recorded strike

(160 days) in African history, of 19,000 railwaymen in French West Africa in 1947, whose message to the governor general showed the new mood of militancy: "Open your prisons, make ready your machine guns and cannon. Nevertheless, at midnight on 10 October, if our demands are not met, we declare the general strike." The year before in South Africa, 100,000 gold mine workers stopped work, demanding ten shillings (about $2.50) a day in wages, the greatest strike in the history of South Africa, and it took a military attack to get them back to work. In 1950, in Kenya, there was a general strike against starvation wages.

So it was not just Soviet expansion that was threatening to the United States government and to American business interests. In fact, China, Korea, Indochina, the Philippines, represented local Communist movements, not Russian fomentation. It was a general wave of anti-imperialist insurrection in the world, which would require gigantic American effort to defeat: national unity for militarization of the budget, for the suppression of domestic opposition to such a foreign policy. Truman and the liberals in Congress proceeded to try to create a new national unity for the postwar years—with the executive order on loyalty oaths, Justice Department prosecutions, and anti-Communist legislation.

In this atmosphere, Senator Joseph McCarthy of Wisconsin could go even further than Truman. Speaking to a Women's Republican Club in Wheeling, West Virginia, in early 1950, he held up some papers and shouted: "I have here in my hand a list of 205—a list of names that were made known to the Secretary of State as being members of the Communist Party and who nevertheless are still working and shaping policy in the State Department." The next day, speaking in Salt Lake City, McCarthy claimed he had a list of fifty-seven (the number kept changing) such Communists in the State Department. Shortly afterward, he appeared on the floor of the Senate with photostatic copies of about a hundred dossiers from State Department loyalty files. The dossiers were three years old, and most of the people were no longer with the State Department, but McCarthy read from them anyway, inventing, adding, and changing as he read. In one case, he changed the dossier's description of "liberal" to "communistically inclined," in another form "active fellow traveler" to "active Communist," and so on.

McCarthy kept on like this for the next few years. As chairman of the Permanent Investigations Sub-Committee of a Senate Committee on Government Operations, he investigated the State Department's information program, its Voice of America, and its overseas libraries, which included books by people McCarthy considered Communists. The State Department reacted in panic, issuing a stream of directives to its library centers across the world. Forty books were removed, including *The Selected Works of Thomas Jefferson*, edited by Philip Foner, and *The Children's Hour* by Lillian Hellman. Some books were burned.

McCarthy became bolder. In the spring of 1954 he began hearings to investigate supposed subversives in the military. When he began attacking generals for not being hard enough on suspected Communists, he antagonized Republicans as well as Democrats, and in December 1954, the Senate voted overwhelmingly to censure him for "conduct . . . unbecoming a Member of the United States Senate." The censure resolution avoided criticizing McCarthy's anti-Communist lies and exaggerations; it concentrated on minor matters—on his refusal to appear before a Senate Subcommittee on Privileges and Elections, and his abuse of an army general at his hearings.

At the very time the Senate was censuring McCarthy, Congress was putting through a whole series of anti-Communist bills. Liberal Hubert Humphrey introduced an amendment to one of them to make the Communist party illegal, saying: "I do not intend to be a half patriot. . . . Either Senators are for recognizing the Communist Party for what it is, or they will continue to trip over the niceties of legal technicalities and details."

The liberals in the government were themselves acting to exclude, persecute, fire, and even imprison Communists. It was just that McCarthy had gone too far, attacking not only Communists but liberals, endangering that broad liberal-conservative coalition which was considered essential. For instance, Lyndon Johnson, as Senate minority leader, worked not only to pass the censure resolution on McCarthy but also to keep it within the narrow bounds of "conduct . . . unbecoming a Member of the United States Senate" rather than questioning McCarthy's anti-Communism.

John F. Kennedy was cautious on the issue, didn't speak out against McCarthy (he was absent when the censure vote was taken and never said how he would have voted). McCarthy's insistence that Communism had won in China because of softness on Communism in the American government was close to Kennedy's own view, expressed in the House of Representatives, January 1949, when the Chinese Communists took over Peking. Kennedy said:

> Mr. Speaker, over this weekend we have learned the extent of the disaster that has befallen China and the United States. The responsibility for the failure of our foreign policy in the Far East rests squarely with the White House and the Department of State.

The continued insistence that aid would not be forthcoming unless a coalition government with the Communists was formed, was a crippling blow to the National Government.

So concerned were our diplomats and their advisers, the Lattimores and the Fairbanks [both scholars in the field of Chinese history, Owen Lattimore a favorite target of McCarthy, John Fairbank, a Harvard professor], with the imperfection of the democratic system in China after 20 years of war and the tales of corruption in high places that they lost sight of our tremendous stake in a non-Communist China. . . .

This House must now assume the responsibility of preventing the onrushing tide of Communism from engulfing all of Asia.

When, in 1950, Republicans sponsored an Internal Security Act for the registration of organizations found to be "Communist-action" or "Communist-front," liberal Senators did not fight that head-on. Instead, some of them, including Hubert Humphrey and Herbert Lehman, proposed a substitute measure, the setting up of detention centers (really, concentration camps) for suspected subversives, who, when the President declared an "internal security emergency," would be held without trial. The detention-camp bill became not a substitute for, but an addition to, the Internal Security Act, and the proposed camps were set up, ready for use. (In 1968, a time of general disillusionment with anti-Communism, this law was repealed.)

Truman's executive order on loyalty in 1947 required the Department of Justice to draw up a list of organizations it decided were "totalitarian, fascist, communist or subversive . . . or as seeking to alter the form of government of the United States by unconstitutional means." Not only membership in, but also "sympathetic association" with, any organization on the Attorney General's list would be considered in determining disloyalty. By 1954, there were hundreds of groups on this list, including, besides the Communist party and the Ku Klux Klan, the Chopin Cultural Center, the Cervantes Fraternal Society, the Committee for the Negro in the Arts, the Committee for the Protection of the Bill of Rights, the League of American Writers, the Nature Friends of America, People's Drama, the Washington Bookshop Association, and the Yugoslav Seaman's Club.

It was not McCarthy and the Republicans, but the liberal Democratic Truman administration, whose Justice Department initiated a series of prosecutions that intensified the nation's anti-Communist mood. The most important of these was the prosecution of Julius and Ethel Rosenberg in the summer of 1950.

The Rosenbergs were charged with espionage. The major evidence was supplied by a few people who had already confessed to being spies, and were either in prison or under indictment. David Greenglass, the brother of Ethel Rosenberg, was the key witness. He had been a machinist at the Manhattan Project laboratory at Los Alamos, New Mexico, in 1944–1945 when the atomic bomb was being made there and testified that Julius Rosenberg had asked him to get information for the Russians. Greenglass said he had made sketches from memory for his brother-in-law of experiments with lenses to be used to detonate atomic bombs. He said Rosenberg had given him half of the cardboard top to a box of Jell-O, and told him a man would show up in New Mexico with the other half, and that, in June 1945, Harry Gold appeared with the other half of the box top, and Greenglass gave him information he had memorized.

Gold, already serving a thirty-year sentence in another espionage case, came out of jail to corroborate Greenglass's testimony. He had never met the Rosenbergs, but said a Soviet embassy official gave him half of a Jell-O box top and told him to contact Greenglass, saying, "I come from Julius." Gold said he took the sketches Greenglass had drawn from memory and gave them to the Russian official.

There were troubling aspects to all this. Did Gold cooperate in return for early release from prison? After serving fifteen years of his thirty-year sentence, he was paroled. Did Greenglass—under indictment at the time he testified—also know that his life depended on his cooperation? He was given fifteen years, served half of it, and was released. How reliable a memorizer of atomic information was David Greenglass, an ordinary-level machinist, not a scientist, who had taken six courses at Brooklyn Polytechnical Institute and flunked five of them? Gold's and Greenglass's stories had first not been in accord. But they were both placed on the same floor of the Tombs prison in New York before the trial, giving them a chance to coordinate their testimony.

How reliable was Gold's testimony? It turned out that he had been prepared for the Rosenberg case by four hundred hours of interviews with the FBI. It also turned out that Gold was a frequent and highly imaginative liar. He was a witness in a later trial where defense counsel asked Gold about his invention of a fictional wife and fictional children. The attorney asked: ". . . you lied for a period of six years?" Gold responded: "I lied for a period of sixteen years, not alone six years." Gold was the only witness at the trial to connect Julius Rosenberg and David Greenglass to the Russians. The FBI agent who had questioned

Gold was interviewed twenty years after the case by a journalist. He was asked about the password Gold was supposed to have used—"Julius sent me." The FBI man said:

> Gold couldn't remember the name he had given. He thought he had said: I come from—or something like that. I suggested, "Might it have been Julius?" That refreshed his memory.

When the Rosenbergs were found guilty, and Judge Irving Kaufman pronounced sentence, he said:

> I believe your conduct in putting into the hands of the Russians the A-bomb years before our best scientists predicted Russia would perfect the bomb has already caused the Communist aggression in Korea with the resultant casualties exceeding 50,000 Americans and who knows but that millions more of innocent people may pay the price of your treason. . . .

He sentenced them both to die in the electric chair.

Morton Sobell was also on trial as a co-conspirator with the Rosenbergs. The chief witness against him was an old friend, the best man at his wedding, a man who was facing possible perjury charges by the federal government for lying about his political past. This was Max Elitcher, who testified that he had once driven Sobell to a Manhattan housing project where the Rosenbergs lived, and that Sobell got out of the car, took from the glove compartment what appeared to be a film can, went off, and then returned without the can. There was no evidence about what was in the film can. The case against Sobell seemed so weak that Sobell's lawyer decided there was no need to present a defense. But the jury found Sobell guilty, and Kaufman sentenced him to thirty years in prison. He was sent to Alcatraz, parole was repeatedly denied, and he spent nineteen years in various prisons before he was released.

FBI documents subpoenaed in the 1970s showed that Judge Kaufman had conferred with the prosecutors secretly about the sentences he would give in the case. Another document shows that after three years of appeal a meeting took place between Attorney General Herbert Brownell and Chief Justice Fred Vinson of the Supreme Court, and the chief justice assured the Attorney General that if any Supreme Court justice gave a stay of execution, he would immediately call a full court session and override it.

There had been a worldwide campaign of protest. Albert Einstein, whose letter to Roosevelt early in the war had initiated work on the atomic bomb, appealed for the Rosenbergs, as did Jean-Paul Sartre, Pablo Picasso, and the sister of Bartolomeo Vanzetti. There was an appeal to President Truman, just before he left office in the spring of 1953. It was turned down. Then, another appeal to the new President, Dwight Eisenhower, was also turned down.

At the last moment, Justice William O. Douglas granted a stay of execution. Chief Justice Vinson sent out special jets to bring the vacationing justices back to Washington from various parts of the country. They canceled Douglas's stay in time for the Rosenbergs to be executed June 19, 1953. It was a demonstration to the people of the country, though very few could identify with the Rosenbergs, of what lay at the end of the line for those the government decided were traitors.

In that same period of the early fifties, the House Un-American Activities Committee was at its heyday, interrogating Americans about their Communist connections, holding them in contempt if they refused to answer, distributing millions of pamphlets to the American public: "One Hundred Things You Should Know About Communism" ("Where can Communists be found? Everywhere"). Liberals often criticized the Committee, but in Congress, liberals and conservatives alike voted to fund it year after year. By 1958, only one member of the House of Representatives (James Roosevelt) voted against giving it money. Although Truman criticized the Committee, his own Attorney General had expressed, in 1950, the same idea that motivated its investigations: "There are today many Communists in America. They are everywhere—in factories, offices, butcher shops, on street corners, in private business—and each carries in himself the germs of death for society."

Liberal intellectuals rode the anti-Communist bandwagon. *Commentary* magazine denounced the Rosenbergs and their supporters. One of *Commentary's* writers, Irving Kristol, asked in March 1952: "Do we defend our rights by protecting Communists?" His answer: "No."

It was Truman's Justice Department that prosecuted the leaders of the Communist party under the Smith Act, charging them with conspiring to teach and advocate the overthrow of the government by force and violence. The evidence consisted mostly of the fact that the Communists were distributing Marxist-Leninist literature, which the prosecution contended called for violent revolution. There was certainly not evidence of any immediate danger of violent revolution by the Communist party. The Supreme Court decision was given by Truman's appointee, Chief Justice Vinson. He stretched the old doctrine of the "clear and present danger" by saying there was a clear and present conspiracy to make a revolution at some convenient time. And so, the top leadership of the Communist party was put in prison, and soon after, most of its organizers went underground.

Undoubtedly, there was success in the attempt to make the general public fearful of Communists and ready to take drastic actions against them—imprisonment at home, military action abroad. The whole culture was permeated with anti-Communism. The large-circulation magazines had articles like "How Communists Get That Way" and "Communists Are After Your Child." The *New York Times* in 1956 ran an editorial: "We would not knowingly employ a Communist party member in the news or editorial departments . . . because we would not trust his ability to report the news objectively or to comment on it honestly. . . ." An FBI informer's story about his exploits as a Communist who became an FBI agent—"I Led Three Lives"—was serialized in five hundred newspapers and put on television. Hollywood movies had titles like *I Married a Communist* and *I Was a Communist for the FBI*. Between 1948 and 1954, more than forty anti-Communist films came out of Hollywood.

Even the American Civil Liberties Union, set up specifically to defend the liberties of Communists and all other political groups, began to wilt in the cold war atmosphere. It had already started in this direction back in 1940 when it expelled one of its charter members, Elizabeth Gurley Flynn, because she was a member of the Communist party. In the fifties, the ACLU was hesitant to defend Corliss Lamont, its own board member, and Owen Lattimore, when both were under attack. It was reluctant to defend publicly the Communist leaders during the first Smith Act trial, and kept completely out of the Rosenberg case, saying no civil liberties issues were involved.

Young and old were taught that anti-Communism was heroic. Three million copies were sold of the book by Mickey Spillane published in 1951, *One Lonely Night*, in which the hero, Mike Hammer, says: "I killed more people tonight than I have fingers on my hands. I shot them in cold blood and enjoyed every minute of it. . . . They were Commies . . . red sons-of-bitches who should have died long ago. . . ." A comic strip hero, Captain America, said: "Beware, commies, spies, traitors, and foreign agents! Captain America, with all loyal, free men behind him, is looking for you. . . ." And in the fifties, schoolchildren all over the country participated in air raid drills in which a Soviet attack on America was signaled by sirens: the children had to crouch under their desks until it was "all clear."

It was an atmosphere in which the government could get mass support for a policy of rearmament. The system, so shaken in the thirties, had learned that war production could bring stability and high profits. Truman's anti-Communism was attractive. The business publication *Steel* had said in November 1946—even before the Truman Doctrine—that Truman's policies gave "the firm assurance that maintaining and building our preparations for war will be big business in the United States for at least a considerable period ahead."

That prediction turned out to be accurate. At the start of 1950, the total U.S. budget was about $40 billion, and the military part of it was about $12 billion. But by 1955, the military part alone was $40 billion out of a total of $62 billion. A small but courageous movement against the military buildup, led by the War Resister's League and other groups, failed to stop it.

In 1960, the military budget was $45.8 billion—49.7 percent of the budget. That year John F. Kennedy was elected President, and he immediately moved to increase military spending. In fourteen months, the Kennedy administration added $9 billion to defense funds, according to Edgar Bottome *(The Balance of Terror)*.

By 1962, based on a series of invented scares about Soviet military build-ups, a false "bomber gap" and a false "missile gap," the United States had overwhelming nuclear superiority. It had the equivalent, in nuclear weapons, of 1,500 Hiroshima-size atomic bombs, far more than enough to destroy every major city in the world—the equivalent, in fact, of 10 tons of TNT for every man, woman, and child on earth. To deliver these bombs, the United States had more than 50 intercontinental ballistic missiles, 80 missiles on nuclear submarines, 90 missiles on stations overseas, 1,700 bombers capable of reaching the Soviet Union, 300 fighter-bombers on aircraft carriers, able to carry atomic weapons, and 1,000 land-based supersonic fighters able to carry atomic bombs.

The Soviet Union was obviously behind—it had between fifty and a hundred intercontinental ballistic missiles and fewer than two hundred long-range bombers. But the U.S. budget kept mounting, the hysteria kept growing, the profits of corporations getting defense contracts multiplied, and employment and wages moved ahead just enough to keep a substantial number of Americans dependent on war industries for their living.

By 1970, the U.S. military budget was $80 billion and the corporations involved in military production were making fortunes. Two-thirds of the 40 billion spent on weapons systems was going to twelve or fifteen giant industrial corporations, whose main reason for existence was to fulfill government military contracts. Senator Paul Douglass, an economist and chairman of the Joint Economic Committee of the

Senate, noted that "six-sevenths of these contracts are not competitive. . . . In the alleged interest of secrecy, the government picks a company and draws up a contract in more or less secret negotiations."

C. Wright Mills, in his book of the fifties, *The Power Elite*, counted the military as part of the top elite, along with politicians and corporations. These elements were more and more intertwined. A Senate report showed that the one hundred largest defense contractors, who held 67.4 percent of the military contracts, employed more than two thousand former high-ranking officers of the military.

Meanwhile, the United States, giving economic aid to certain countries, was creating a network of American corporate control over the globe, and building its political influence over the countries it aided. The Marshall Plan of 1948, which gave $16 billion in economic aid to Western European countries in four years, had an economic aim: to build up markets for American exports. George Marshall (a general, then Secretary of State) was quoted in an early 1948 State Department bulletin: "It is idle to think that a Europe left to its own efforts . . . would remain open to American business in the same way that we have known it in the past."

The Marshall Plan also had a political motive. The Communist parties of Italy and France were strong, and the United States decided to use pressure and money to keep Communists out of the cabinets of those countries. When the Plan was beginning, Truman's Secretary of State Dean Acheson said: "These measures of relief and reconstruction have been only in part suggested by humanitarianism. Your Congress has authorized and your Government is carrying out, a policy of relief and reconstruction today chiefly as a matter of national self-interest."

From 1952 on, foreign aid was more and more obviously designed to build up military power in non-Communist countries. In the next ten years, of the $50 billion in aid granted by the United States to ninety countries, only $5 billion was for nonmilitary economic development.

When John F. Kennedy took office, he launched the Alliance for Progress, a program of help for Latin America, emphasizing social reform to better the lives of people. But it turned out to be mostly military aid to keep in power right-wing dictatorships and enable them to stave off revolutions.

From military aid, it was a short step to military intervention. What Truman had said at the start of the Korean war about "the rule of force" and the "rule of law" was again and again, under Truman and his successors, contradicted by American action. In Iran, in 1953, the Central Intelligence Agency succeeded in overthrowing a government which nationalized the oil industry. In Guatemala, in 1954, a legally elected government was overthrown by an invasion force of mercenaries trained by the CIA at military bases in Honduras and Nicaragua and supported by four American fighter planes flown by American pilots. The invasion put into power Colonel Carlos Castillo Armas, who had at one time received military training at Fort Leavenworth, Kansas.

The government that the United States overthrew was the most democratic Guatemala had ever had. The President, Jacobo Arbenz, was a left-of-center Socialist; four of the fifty-six seats in the Congress were held by Communists. What was most unsettling to American business interests was that Arbenz had expropriated 234,000 acres of land owned by United Fruit, offering compensation that United Fruit called "unacceptable." Armas, in power, gave the land back to United Fruit, abolished the tax on interest and dividends to foreign investors, eliminated the secret ballot, and jailed thousands of political critics.

In 1958, the Eisenhower government sent thousands of marines to Lebanon to make sure the pro-American government there was not toppled by a revolution, and to keep an armed presence in that oil-rich area.

The Democrat-Republican, liberal-conservative agreement to prevent or overthrow revolutionary governments whenever possible—whether Communist, Socialist, or anti–United Fruit—became most evident in 1961 in Cuba. That little island 90 miles from Florida had gone through a revolution in 1959 by a rebel force led by Fidel Castro, in which the American-backed dictator, Fulgencio Batista, was overthrown. The revolution was a direct threat to American business interests. Franklin D. Roosevelt's Good Neighbor Policy had repealed the Platt Amendment (which permitted American intervention in Cuba), but the United States still kept a naval base in Cuba at Guantanamo, and U.S. business interests still dominated the Cuban economy. American companies controlled 80 to 100 percent of Cuba's utilities, mines, cattle ranches, and oil refineries, 40 percent of the sugar industry, and 50 percent of the public railways.

Fidel Castro had spent time in prison after he led an unsuccessful attack in 1953 on an army barracks in Santiago. Out of prison, he went to Mexico, met Argentine revolutionary Che Guevara, and returned in 1956 to Cuba. His tiny force fought guerrilla warfare from the jungles and mountains against Batista's army, drawing more and more popular support, then came out of the mountains and marched across the country to Havana. The Batista government fell apart on New Year's Day 1959.

In power, Castro moved to set up a nationwide system of education, of housing, of land distribution to landless peasants. The government confiscated over a million acres of land from three American companies, including United Fruit.

Cuba needed money to finance its programs, and the United States was not eager to lend it. The International Monetary Fund, dominated by the United States, would not loan money to Cuba because Cuba would not accept its "stabilization" conditions, which seemed to undermine the revolutionary program that had begun. When Cuba now signed a trade agreement with the Soviet Union, American-owned oil companies in Cuba refused to refine crude oil that came from the Soviet Union. Castro seized these companies. The United States cut down on its sugar buying from Cuba, on which Cuba's economy depended, and the Soviet Union immediately agreed to buy all the 700,000 tons of sugar that the United States would not buy.

Cuba had changed. The Good Neighbor Policy did not apply. In the spring of 1960, President Eisenhower secretly authorized the Central Intelligence Agency to arm and train anti-Castro Cuban exiles in Guatemala for a future invasion of Cuba. When Kennedy took office in the spring of 1961 the CIA had 1,400 exiles, armed and trained. He moved ahead with the plans, and on April 17, 1961, the CIA-trained force, with some Americans participating, landed at the Bay of Pigs on the south shore of Cuba, 90 miles from Havana. They expected to stimulate a general rising against Castro. But it was a popular regime. There was no rising. In three days, the CIA forces were crushed by Castro's army.

The whole Bay of Pigs affair was accompanied by hypocrisy and lying. The invasion was a violation—recalling Truman's "rule of law"— of a treaty the U.S. had signed, the Charter of the Organization of American States, which reads: "No state or group of states has the right to intervene, directly or indirectly, for any reason whatever, in the internal or external affairs of any other state."

Four days before the invasion—because there had been press reports of secret bases and CIA training for invaders—President Kennedy told a press conference: ". . . there will not be, under any conditions, any intervention in Cuba by United States armed forces." True, the landing force was Cuban, but it was all organized by the United States, and American war planes, including American pilots, were involved; Kennedy had approved the use of unmarked navy jets in the invasion. Four American pilots of those planes were killed, and their families were not told the truth about how those men died.

The success of the liberal-conservative coalition in creating a national anti-Communist consensus was shown by how certain important news publications cooperated with the Kennedy administration in deceiving the American public on the Cuban invasion. *The New Republic* was about to print an article on the CIA training of Cuban exiles, a few weeks before the invasion. Historian Arthur Schlesinger was given copies of the article in advance. He showed them to Kennedy, who asked that the article not be printed, and *The New Republic* went along.

James Reston and Turner Catledge of the *New York Times*, on the government's request, did not run a story about the imminent invasion. Arthur Schlesinger said of the *New York Times* action: "This was another patriotic act, but in retrospect I have wondered whether, if the press had behaved irresponsibly, it would not have spared the country a disaster." What seemed to bother him, and other liberals in the cold war consensus, was not that the United States was interfering in revolutionary movements in other countries, but that it was doing so unsuccessfully.

Around 1960, the fifteen-year effort since the end of World War II to break up the Communist-radical upsurge of the New Deal and wartime years seemed successful. The Communist party was in disarray—its leaders in jail, its membership shrunken, its influence in the trade union movement very small. The trade union movement itself had become more controlled, more conservative. The military budget was taking half of the national budget, but the public was accepting this.

The radiation from the testing of nuclear weapons had dangerous possibilities for human health, but the public was not aware of that. The Atomic Energy Commission insisted that the deadly effects of atomic tests were exaggerated, and an article in 1955 in the *Reader's Digest* (the largest-circulation magazine in the United States) said: "The scare stories about this country's atomic tests are simply not justified."

In the mid-fifties, there was a flurry of enthusiasm for air-raid shelters; the public was being told these would keep them safe from atomic blasts. A government consultant and scientist, Herman Kahn, wrote a book, *On Thermonuclear War*, in which he explained that it was possible to have a nuclear war without total destruction of the world, that people should not be so frightened of it. A political scientist named Henry Kissinger wrote a book published in 1957 in which he said: "With proper tactics, nuclear war need not be as destructive as it appears. . . ."

The country was on a permanent war economy which had big pockets of poverty, but there were enough people at work, making enough money, to keep things quiet. The distribution of wealth was still unequal. From 1944 to 1961, it had not changed much: the lowest fifth of the families received 5 percent of all the income; the highest fifth received 45 percent of all the income. In 1953, 1.6 percent of the adult population owned more than 80 percent of the corporate stock and nearly 90 percent of the corporate bonds. About 200 giant corporations out of 200,000 corporations—one-tenth of 1 percent of all corporations—controlled about 60 percent of the manufacturing wealth of the nation.

When John F. Kennedy presented his budget to the nation after his first year in office, it was clear that, liberal Democrat or not, there would be no major change in the distribution of income or wealth or tax advantages. *New York Times* columnist James Reston summed up Kennedy's budget messages as avoiding any "sudden transformation of the home front" as well as "a more ambitious frontal attack on the unemployment problem." Reston said:

> He agreed to a tax break for business investment in plant expansion and modernization. He is not spoiling for a fight with the Southern conservatives over civil rights. He has been urging the unions to keep wage demands down so that prices can be competitive in the world markets and jobs increased. And he has been trying to reassure the business community that he does not want any cold war with them on the home front.
>
> . . . this week in his news conference he refused to carry out his promise to bar discrimination in Government-insured housing, but talked instead of postponing this until there was a "national consensus" in its favor. . . .
>
> During these twelve months the President has moved over into the decisive middle ground of American politics. . . .

On this middle ground, all seemed secure. Nothing had to be done for blacks. Nothing had to be done to change the economic structure. An aggressive foreign policy could continue. The country seemed under control. And then, in the 1960s, came a series of explosive rebellions in every area of American life, which showed that all the system's estimates of security and success were wrong.

17

"OR DOES IT EXPLODE?"

The black revolt of the 1950s and 1960s—North and South—came as a surprise. But perhaps it should not have. The memory of oppressed people is one thing that cannot be taken away, and for such people, with such memories, revolt is always an inch below the surface. For blacks in the United States, there was the memory of slavery, and after that of segregation, lynching, humiliation. And it was not just a memory but a living presence—part of the daily lives of blacks in generation after generation.

In the 1930s, Langston Hughes wrote a poem, "Lenox Avenue Mural":

> What happens to a dream deferred?
>   Does it dry up
>   like a raisin in the sun?
>   Or fester like a sore—
>   And then run?
> Does it stink like rotten meat?
> Or crust and sugar over—
> like a syrupy sweet?
>
> Maybe it just sags like a heavy load.
>
> Or does it explode?

In a society of complex controls, both crude and refined, secret thoughts can often be found in the arts, and so it was in black society. Perhaps the blues, however pathetic, concealed anger; and the jazz, however joyful, portended rebellion. And then the poetry, the thoughts no longer so secret. In the 1920s, Claude McKay, one of the figures of what came to be called the "Harlem Renaissance," wrote a poem that Henry Cabot Lodge put in the *Congressional Record* as an example of dangerous currents among young blacks:

> If we must die, let it not be like hogs
> Hunted and penned in an inglorious spot. . . .
> Like men we'll face the murderous cowardly pack,
> Pressed to the wall, dying, but fighting back!

Countee Cullen's poem "Incident" evoked memories—all different, all the same—out of every black American's childhood:

> Once riding in old Baltimore,
> Heart-filled, head-filled with glee,
> I saw a Baltimorean
> Keep looking straight at me.
>
> Now I was eight and very small,
> And he was no whit bigger,
> And so I smiled, but he poked out
> His tongue, and called me, "Nigger."
>
> I saw the whole of Baltimore
> From May until December;
> Of all the things that happened there
> That's all that I remember.

At the time of the Scottsboro Boys incident, Cullen wrote a bitter poem noting that white poets had used their pens to protest in other cases of injustice, but now that blacks were involved, most were silent. His last stanza was:

> Surely, I said,
>   Now will the poets sing.
> But they have raised no cry.
>   I wonder why.

Even outward subservience—Uncle Tom behavior in real situations, the comic or fawning Negro on the stage, the self-ridicule, the caution—concealed resentment, anger, energy. The black poet Paul Laurence Dunbar, in the era of the black minstrel, around the turn of the century, wrote "We Wear the Mask":

> We wear the mask that grins and lies,
> It hides our cheeks and shades our eyes,—
>
> ... We sing, but oh, the clay is vile
> Beneath our feet, and long the mile;
> But let the world dream otherwise,
> We wear the mask.

Two black performers of that time played the minstrel and satirized it at the same time. When Bert Williams and George Walker billed themselves as "Two Real Coons," they were, Nathan Huggins says, "intending to give style and comic dignity to a fiction that white men had created. . . ."

By the 1930s the mask was off for many black poets. Langston Hughes wrote "I, Too."

> I, too, sing America
>
> I am the darker brother.
> They send me to eat in the kitchen
> When company comes,
> But I laugh,
> And eat well,
> And grow strong.
>
> Tomorrow,
> I'll be at the table
> When company comes. . . .

Gwendolyn Bennett wrote:

> I want to see lithe Negro girls,
> Etched dark against the sky
> While sunset lingers. . . .
>
> I want to hear the chanting
> Around a heathen fire
> Of a strange black race. . . .

I want to feel the surging
Of my sad people's soul
Hidden by a minstrel-smile.

There was Margaret Walker's prose-poem "For My People":

> . . . Let a new earth rise. Let another world be born. Let a bloody peace be written in the sky. Let a second generation full of courage issue forth, let a people loving freedom come to growth, let a beauty full of healing and a strength of final clenching be the pulsing in our spirits and our blood. Let the martial songs be written, let the dirges disappear. Let a race of men now rise and take control!

By the 1940s there was Richard Wright, a gifted novelist, a black man. His autobiography of 1937, *Black Boy*, gave endless insights: for instance, how blacks were set against one another, when he told how he was prodded to fight another black boy for the amusement of white men. *Black Boy* expressed unashamedly every humiliation and then:

> The white South said that it knew "niggers," and I was what the white South called a "nigger." Well, the white South had never known me—never known what I thought, what I felt. The white South said that I had a "place" in life. Well, I had never felt my "place"; or, rather, my deepest instincts had always made me reject the "place" to which the white South had assigned me. It had never occurred to me that I was in any way an inferior being. And no word that I had ever heard fall from the lips of southern white men had ever made me really doubt the worth of my own humanity.

It was all there in the poetry, the prose, the music, sometimes masked, sometimes unmistakably clear—the signs of a people unbeaten, waiting, hot, coiled.

In *Black Boy*, Wright told about the training of black children in America to keep them silent. But also:

> How do Negroes feel about the way they have to live? How do they discuss it when alone among themselves? I think this question can be answered in a single sentence. A friend of mine who ran an elevator once told me:
> "Lawd, man! Ef it wuzn't fer them polices 'n' them ol' lynch mobs, there wouldn't be nothin' but uproar down here!"

Richard Wright, for a time, joined the Communist party (he tells of this period of his life, and his disillusionment with the party, in *The God That Failed*). The Communist party was known to pay special attention to the problem of race equality. When the Scottsboro case unfolded in the 1930s in Alabama, it was the Communist party that had become associated with the defense of these young black men imprisoned, in the early years of the Depression, by southern injustice.

The party was accused by liberals and the NAACP of exploiting the issue for its own purposes, and there was a half-truth in it, but black people were realistic about the difficulty of having white allies who were pure in motive. The other half of the truth was that black Communists in the South had earned the admiration of blacks by their organizing work against enormous obstacles. There was Hosea Hudson, the black organizer of the unemployed in Birmingham, for instance. And in Georgia, in 1932, a nineteen-year-old black youth named Angelo Herndon, whose father died of miner's pneumonia, who had worked in mines as a boy in Kentucky, joined an Unemployment Council in Birmingham organized by the Communist party, and then joined the party. He wrote later:

> All my life I'd been sweated and stepped-on and Jim-Crowed. I lay on my belly in the mines for a few dollars a week, and saw my pay stolen and slashed, and my buddies killed. I lived in the worst section of town, and rode behind the "Colored" signs on streetcars, as though there was something disgusting about me. I heard myself called "nigger" and "darky" and I had to say "Yes, sir" to every white man, whether he had my respect or not.
>
> I had always detested it, but I had never known that anything could be done about it. And here, all of a sudden, I had found organizations in which Negroes and whites sat together, and worked together, and knew no difference of race or color. . . .

Herndon became a Communist party organizer in Atlanta. He and his fellow Communists organized block committees of Unemployment Councils in 1932 which got rent relief for needy people. They organized a demonstration to which a thousand people came, six hundred of them white, and the next day the city voted $6,000 in relief to the jobless. But soon after that Herndon was arrested, held incommunicado, and charged with violating a Georgia statute against insurrection. He recalled his trial:

> The state of Georgia displayed the literature that had been taken from my room, and read passages of it to the jury. They questioned me in great detail.

Did I believe that the bosses and government ought to pay insurance to unemployed workers? That Negroes should have complete equality with white people? Did I believe in the demand for the self-determination of the Black Belt—that the Negro people should be allowed to rule the Black Belt territory, kicking out the white landlords and government officials? Did I feel that the working-class could run the mills and mines and government? That it wasn't necessary to have bosses at all?

I told them I believed all of that—and more. . . .

Herndon was convicted and spent five years in prison until in 1937 the Supreme Court ruled unconstitutional the Georgia statute under which he was found guilty. It was men like him who represented to the Establishment a dangerous militancy among blacks, made more dangerous when linked with the Communist party.

There were others who made that same connection, magnifying the danger: Benjamin Davis, the black lawyer who defended Herndon at his trial; nationally renowned men like singer and actor Paul Robeson, and writer and scholar W. E. B. Du Bois, who did not hide their support and sympathy for the Communist party. The Negro was not as anti-Communist as the white population. He could not afford to be, his friends were so few—so that Herndon, Davis, Robeson, Du Bois, however their political views might be maligned by the country as a whole, found admiration for their fighting spirit in the black community.

The black militant mood, flashing here and there in the thirties, was reduced to a subsurface simmering during World War II, when the nation on the one hand denounced racism, and on the other hand maintained segregation in the armed forces and kept blacks in low-paying jobs. When the war ended, a new element entered the racial balance in the United States—the enormous, unprecedented upsurge of black and yellow people in Africa and Asia.

President Harry Truman had to reckon with this, especially as the cold war rivalry with the Soviet Union began, and the dark-skinned revolt of former colonies all over the world threatened to take Marxist form. Action on the race question was needed, not just to calm a black population at home emboldened by war promises, frustrated by the basic sameness of their condition. It was needed to present to the world a United States that could counter the continuous Communist thrust at the most flagrant failure of American society—the race question. What Du Bois had said long ago, unnoticed, now loomed large in 1945: "The problem of the 20th century is the problem of the color line."

President Harry Truman, in late 1946, appointed a Committee on

Civil Rights, which recommended that the civil rights section of the Department of Justice be expanded, that there be a permanent Commission on Civil Rights, that Congress pass laws against lynching and to stop voting discrimination, and suggested new laws to end racial discrimination in jobs.

Truman's Committee was blunt about its motivation in making these recommendations. Yes, it said, there was "moral reason": a matter of conscience. But there was also an "economic reason"—discrimination was costly to the country, wasteful of its talent. And, perhaps most important, there was an international reason:

> Our position in the post-war world is so vital to the future that our smallest actions have far-reaching effects. . . . We cannot escape the fact that our civil rights record has been an issue in world politics. The world's press and radio are full of it. . . . Those with competing philosophies have stressed—and are shamelessly distorting—our shortcomings. . . . They have tried to prove our democracy an empty fraud, and our nation a consistent oppressor of under-privileged people. This may seem ludicrous to Americans, but it is sufficiently important to worry our friends. The United States is not so strong, the final triumph of the democratic ideal is not so inevitable that we can ignore what the world thinks of us or our record.

The United States was out in the world now in a way it had never been. The stakes were large—world supremacy. And, as Truman's Committee said: ". . . our smallest actions have far-reaching effects."

And so the United States went ahead to take small actions, hoping they would have large effects. Congress did not move to enact the legislation asked for by the Committee on Civil Rights. But Truman—four months before the presidential election of 1948, and challenged from the left in that election by Progressive party candidate Henry Wallace— issued an executive order asking that the armed forces, segregated in World War II, institute policies of racial equality "as rapidly as possible." The order may have been prompted not only by the election but by the need to maintain black morale in the armed forces, as the possibility of war grew. It took over a decade to complete the desegregation in the military.

Truman could have issued executive orders in other areas, but did not. The Fourteenth and Fifteenth Amendments, plus the set of laws passed in the late 1860s and early 1870s, gave the President enough authority to wipe out racial discrimination. The Constitution demanded that the President execute the laws, but no President had used that power. Neither did Truman. For instance, he asked Congress for legislation "prohibiting discrimination in interstate transportation facilities"; but specific legislation in 1887 already barred discrimination in interstate transportation and had never been enforced by executive action.

Meanwhile, the Supreme Court was taking steps—ninety years after the Constitution had been amended to establish racial equality—to move toward that end. During the war it ruled that the "white primary" used to exclude blacks from voting in the Democratic party primaries—which in the South were really the elections—was unconstitutional.

In 1954, the Court finally struck down the "separate but equal" doctrine that it had defended since the 1890s. The NAACP brought a series of cases before the Court to challenge segregation in the public schools, and now in *Brown* v. *Board of Education* the Court said the separation of schoolchildren "generates a feeling of inferiority . . . that may affect their hearts and minds in a way unlikely ever to be undone." In the field of public education, it said, "the doctrine of 'separate but equal' has no place." The Court did not insist on immediate change: a year later it said that segregated facilities should be integrated "with all deliberate speed." By 1965, ten years after the "all deliberate speed" guideline, more than 75 percent of the school districts in the South remained segregated.

Still, it was a dramatic decision—and the message went around the world in 1954 that the American government had outlawed segregation. In the United States too, for those not thinking about the customary gap between word and fact, it was an exhilarating sign of change.

What to others seemed rapid progress to blacks was apparently not enough. In the early 1960s black people rose in rebellion all over the South. And in the late 1960s they were engaging in wild insurrection in a hundred northern cities. It was all a surprise to those without that deep memory of slavery, that everyday presence of humiliation, registered in the poetry, the music, the occasional outbursts of anger, the more frequent sullen silences. Part of that memory was of words uttered, laws passed, decisions made, which turned out to be meaningless.

For such a people, with such a memory, and such daily recapitulation of history, revolt was always minutes away, in a timing mechanism which no one had set, but which might go off with some unpredictable set of events. Those events came, at the end of 1955, in the capital city of Alabama—Montgomery.

Three months after her arrest, Mrs. Rosa Parks, a forty-three-year-old seamstress, explained why she refused to obey the Montgomery law providing for segregation on city buses, why she decided to sit down in the "white" section of the bus:

Well, in the first place, I had been working all day on the job. I was quite tired after spending a full day working. I handle and work on clothing that white people wear. That didn't come in my mind but this is what I wanted to know: when and how would we ever determine our rights as human beings? . . . It just happened that the driver made a demand and I just didn't feel like obeying his demand. He called a policeman and I was arrested and placed in jail. . . .

Montgomery blacks called a mass meeting. A powerful force in the community was E. D. Nixon, a veteran trade unionist and experienced organizer. There was a vote to boycott all city buses. Car pools were organized to take Negroes to work; most people walked. The city retaliated by indicting one hundred leaders of the boycott, and sent many to jail. White segregationists turned to violence. Bombs exploded in four Negro churches. A shotgun blast was fired through the front door of the home of Dr. Martin Luther King, Jr., the twenty-seven-year-old Altanta-born minister who was one of the leaders of the boycott. King's home was bombed. But the black people of Montgomery persisted, and in November 1956, the Supreme Court outlawed segregation on local bus lines.

Montgomery was the beginning. It forecast the style and mood of the vast protest movement that would sweep the South in the next ten years: emotional church meetings, Christian hymns adapted to current battles, references to lost American ideals, the commitment to nonviolence, the willingness to struggle and sacrifice. A *New York Times* reporter described a mass meeting in Montgomery during the boycott:

> One after the other, indicted Negro leaders took the rostrum in a crowded Baptist church tonight to urge their followers to shun the city's buses and "walk with God."
>
> More than two thousand Negroes filled the church from basement to balcony and overflowed into the street. They chanted and sang; they shouted and prayed; they collapsed in the aisles and they sweltered in an eighty-five degree heat. They pledged themselves again and again to "passive resistance." Under this banner they have carried on for eighty days a stubborn boycott of the city's buses.

Martin Luther King at that meeting gave a preview of the oratory that would soon inspire millions of people to demand racial justice. He said the protest was not merely over buses but over things that "go deep down into the archives of history." He said:

> We have known humiliation, we have known abusive language, we have been plunged into the abyss of oppression. And we decided to raise up only

with the weapon of protest. It is one of the greatest glories of America that we have the right of protest.

If we are arrested every day, if we are exploited every day, if we are trampled over every day, don't ever let anyone pull you so low as to hate them. We must use the weapon of love. We must have compassion and understanding for those who hate us. We must realize so many people are taught to hate us that they are not totally responsible for their hate. But we stand in life at midnight, we are always on the threshold of a new dawn.

King's stress on love and nonviolence was powerfully effective in building a sympathetic following throughout the nation, among whites as well as blacks. But there were blacks who thought the message naïve, that while there were misguided people who might be won over by love, there were others who would have to be bitterly fought, and not always with nonviolence. Two years after the Montgomery boycott, in Monroe, North Carolina, an ex-marine named Robert Williams, the president of the local NAACP, became known for his view that blacks should defend themselves against violence, with guns if necessary. When local Klansmen attacked the home of one of the leaders of the Monroe NAACP, Williams and other blacks, armed with rifles, fired back. The Klan left. (The Klan was being challenged now with its own tactic of violence; a Klan raid on an Indian community in North Carolina was repelled by Indians firing rifles.)

Still, in the years that followed, southern blacks stressed nonviolence. On February 1, 1960, four freshmen at a Negro college in Greensboro, North Carolina, decided to sit down at the Woolworth's lunch counter downtown, where only whites ate. They were refused service, and when they would not leave, the lunch counter was closed for the day. The next day they returned, and then, day after day, other Negroes came to sit silently.

In the next two weeks, sit-ins spread to fifteen cities in five southern states. A seventeen-year-old sophomore at Spelman College in Atlanta, Ruby Doris Smith, heard about Greensboro:

When the student committee was formed . . . I told my older sister . . . to put me on the list. And when two hundred students were selected for the first demonstration I was among them. I went through the food line in the restaurant at the State Capitol with six other students, but when we got to the cashier she wouldn't take our money. . . . The Lieutenant-Governor came down and told us to leave. We didn't and went to the county jail.

In his Harlem apartment in New York, a young Negro teacher of mathematics named Bob Moses saw a photo in the newspapers of the Greensboro sit-inners. "The students in that picture had a certain look on their faces, sort of sullen, angry, determined. Before, the Negro in the South had always looked on the defensive, cringing. This time they were taking the initiative. They were kids my age, and I knew this had something to do with my own life."

There was violence against the sit-inners. But the idea of taking the initiative against segregation took hold. In the next twelve months, more than fifty thousand people, mostly black, some white, participated in demonstrations of one kind or another in a hundred cities, and over 3,600 people were put in jail. But by the end of 1960, lunch counters were open to blacks in Greensboro and many other places.

A year after the Greensboro incident, a northern-based group dedicated to racial equality—CORE (Congress of Racial Equality)—organized "Freedom Rides" in which blacks and whites traveled together on buses going through the South, to try to break the segregation pattern in interstate travel. Such segregation had long been illegal, but the federal government never enforced the law in the South; the President now was John F. Kennedy, but he too seemed cautious about the race question, concerned about the support of southern white leaders of the Democratic party.

The two buses that left Washington, D.C., on May 4, 1961, headed for New Orleans, never got there. In South Carolina, riders were beaten. In Alabama, a bus was set afire. Freedom Riders were attacked with fists and iron bars. The southern police did not interfere with any of this violence, nor did the federal government. FBI agents watched, took notes, did nothing.

At this point, veterans of the sit-ins, who had recently formed the Student Nonviolent Coordinating Committee (SNCC), dedicated to nonviolent but militant action for equal rights, organized another Freedom Ride, from Nashville to Birmingham. Before they started out, they called the Department of Justice in Washington, D.C., to ask for protection. As Ruby Doris Smith reported: ". . . the Justice Department said no, they couldn't protect anyone, but if something happened, they would investigate. You know how they do. . . ."

The racially mixed SNCC Freedom Riders were arrested in Birmingham, Alabama, spent a night in jail, were taken to the Tennessee border by police, made their way back to Birmingham, took a bus to Montgomery, and there were attacked by whites with fists and clubs, in a bloody scene. They resumed their trip, to Jackson, Mississippi.

By this time the Freedom Riders were in the news all over the world, and the government was anxious to prevent further violence. Attorney General Robert Kennedy, instead of insisting on their right to travel without being arrested, agreed to the Freedom Riders' being arrested in Jackson, in return for Mississippi police protection against possible mob violence. As Victor Navasky comments in *Kennedy Justice*, about Robert Kennedy: "He didn't hesitate to trade the freedom riders' constitutional right to interstate travel for Senator Eastland's guarantee of their right to live."

The Freedom Riders did not become subdued in jail. They resisted, protested, sang, demanded their rights. Stokely Carmichael recalled later how he and his fellow inmates were singing in the Parchman jail in Mississippi and the sheriff threatened to take away their mattresses:

> I hung on to the mattress and said, "I think we have a right to them and I think you're unjust." And he said, "I don't want to hear all that shit, nigger," and started to put on the wristbreakers. I wouldn't move and started to sing "I'm Gonna Tell God How You Treat Me" and everybody started to sing it, and by this time Tyson was really to pieces. He called to the trusties, "Get him in there!" and he went out the door and slammed it, and left everybody else with their mattresses.

In Albany, Georgia, a small deep-South town where the atmosphere of slavery still lingered, mass demonstrations took place in the winter of 1961 and again in 1962. Of 22,000 black people in Albany, over a thousand went to jail for marching, assembling, to protest segregation and discrimination. Here, as in all the demonstrations that would sweep over the South, little black children participated—a new generation was learning to act. The Albany police chief, after one of the mass arrests, was taking the names of prisoners lined up before his desk. He looked up and saw a Negro boy about nine years old. "What's your name?" The boy looked straight at him and said: "Freedom, Freedom."

There is no way of measuring the effect of that southern movement on the sensibilities of a whole generation of young black people, or of tracing the process by which some of them became activists and leaders. In Lee County, Georgia, after the events of 1961–1962, a black teenager named James Crawford joined SNCC and began taking black people to the county courthouse to vote. One day, bringing a woman there, he was approached by the deputy registrar. Another SNCC worker took notes on the conversation:

REGISTRAR: What do you want?

CRAWFORD: I brought this lady down to register.

REGISTRAR: (after giving the woman a card to fill out and sending her outside in the hall) Why did you bring this lady down here?

CRAWFORD: Because she wants to be a first class citizen like y'all.

REGISTRAR: Who are you to bring people down to register?

CRAWFORD: It's my job.

REGISTRAR: Suppose you get two bullets in your head right now?

CRAWFORD: I got to die anyhow.

REGISTRAR: If I don't do it, I can get somebody else to do it. (No reply)

REGISTRAR: Are you scared?

CRAWFORD: No.

REGISTRAR: Suppose somebody came in that door and shoot you in the back
of the head right now. What would you do?

CRAWFORD: I couldn't do nothing. If they shoot me in the back of the head
there are people coming from all over the world.

REGISTRAR: What people?

CRAWFORD: The people I work for.

In Birmingham in 1963, thousands of blacks went into the streets, facing police clubs, tear gas, dogs, high-powered water hoses. And meanwhile, all over the deep South, the young people of SNCC, mostly black, a few white, were moving into communities in Georgia, Alabama, Mississippi, Arkansas. Joined by local black people, they were organiz-ing, to register people to vote, to protest against racism, to build up courage against violence. The Department of Justice recorded 1412 demonstrations in three months of 1963. Imprisonment became com-monplace, beatings became frequent. Many local people were afraid. Others came forward. A nineteen-year-old black student from Illinois named Carver Neblett, working for SNCC in Terrell County, Georgia, reported:

I talked with a blind man who is extremely interested in the civil rights movement. He has been keeping up with the movement from the begin-ning. Even though this man is blind he wants to learn all the questions on the literacy test. Imagine, while many are afraid that white men will burn our houses, shoot into them, or put us off their property, a blind man, sev-enty years old, wants to come to our meetings.

As the summer of 1964 approached, SNCC and other civil rights groups working together in Mississippi, and facing increasing violence, decided to call upon young people from other parts of the country for help. They hoped that would bring attention to the situation in Mississippi. Again and again in Mississippi and elsewhere, the FBI had stood by, lawyers for the Justice Department had stood by, while civil rights workers were beaten and jailed, while federal laws were violated.

On the eve of the Mississippi Summer, in early June 1964, the civil rights movement rented a theater near the White House, and a busload of black Mississippians traveled to Washington to testify publicly about the daily violence, the dangers facing the volunteers coming into Mississippi. Constitutional lawyers testified that the national government had the legal power to give protection against such violence. The transcript of this testimony was given to President Johnson and Attorney General Kennedy, accompanied by a request for a protective federal presence during the Mississippi Summer. There was no response.

Twelve days after the public hearing, three civil rights workers, James Chaney, a young black Mississippian, and two white volunteers, Andrew Goodman and Michael Schwerner, were arrested in Philadelphia, Mississippi, released from jail late at night, then seized, beaten with chains, and shot to death. Ultimately, an informer's testimony led to jail sentences for the sheriff and deputy sheriff and others. That came too late. The Mississippi murders had taken place after the repeated refusal of the national government, under Kennedy or Johnson, or any other President, to defend blacks against violence.

Dissatisfaction with the national government intensified. Later that summer, during the Democratic National Convention in Washington, Mississippi, blacks asked to be seated as part of the state delegation to represent the 40 percent of the state's population who were black. They were turned down by the liberal Democratic leadership, including vice-presidential candidate Hubert Humphrey.

Congress began reacting to the black revolt, the turmoil, the world publicity. Civil rights laws were passed in 1957, 1960, and 1964. They promised much, on voting equality, on employment equality, but were enforced poorly or ignored. In 1965, President Johnson sponsored and Congress passed an even stronger Voting Rights Law, this time ensuring on-the-spot federal protection of the right to register and vote. The effect on Negro voting in the South was dramatic. In 1952, a million southern blacks (20 percent of those eligible) registered to vote. In 1964 the number was 2 million—40 percent. By 1968, it was 3 million, 60 percent—the same percentage as white voters.

The federal government was trying—without making fundamental changes—to control an explosive situation, to channel anger into the traditional cooling mechanism of the ballot box, the polite petition, the officially endorsed quiet gathering. When black civil rights leaders planned a huge march on Washington in the summer of 1963 to protest the failure of the nation to solve the race problem, it was quickly embraced by President Kennedy and other national leaders, and turned into a friendly assemblage.

Martin Luther King's speech there thrilled 200,000 black and white Americans—"I have a dream. . . ." It was magnificent oratory, but without the anger that many blacks felt. When John Lewis, a young Alabama-born SNCC leader, much arrested, much beaten, tried to introduce a stronger note of outrage at the meeting, he was censored by the leaders of the march, who insisted he omit certain sentences critical of the national government and urging militant action.

Eighteen days after the Washington gathering, almost as if in deliberate contempt for its moderation, a bomb exploded in the basement of a black church in Birmingham and four girls attending a Sunday school class were killed. President Kennedy had praised the "deep fervor and quiet dignity" of the march, but the black militant Malcolm X was probably closer to the mood of the black community. Speaking in Detroit two months after the march on Washington and the Birmingham bombing, Malcolm X said, in his powerful, icy-clear, rhythmic style:

The Negroes were out there in the streets. They were talking about how they were going to march on Washington. . . . That they were going to march on Washington, march on the Senate, march on the White House, march on the Congress, and tie it up, bring it to a halt, not let the government proceed. They even said they were going out to the airport and lay down on the runway and not let any airplanes land. I'm telling you what they said. That was revolution. That was revolution. That was the black revolution.

It was the grass roots out there in the street. It scared the white man to death, scared the white power structure in Washington, D.C. to death; I was there. When they found out that this black steamroller was going to come down on the capital, they called in . . . these national Negro leaders that you respect and told them, "Call it off," Kennedy said. "Look you all are letting this thing go too far." And Old Tom said, "Boss, I can't stop it because I didn't start it." I'm telling you what they said. They said, "I'm not even in it, much less at the head of it." They said, "These Negroes are doing things on their own. They're running ahead of us." And that old shrewd fox, he said, "If you all aren't in it, I'll put you in it. I'll put you at the head of it. I'll endorse it. I'll welcome it. I'll help it. I'll join it."

This is what they did with the march on Washington. They joined it . . . became part of it, took it over. And as they took it over, it lost its militancy. It ceased to be angry, it ceased to be hot, it ceased to be uncompromising. Why, it even ceased to be a march. It became a picnic, a circus. Nothing but a circus, with clowns and all. . . .

No, it was a sellout. It was a takeover. . . . They controlled it so tight, they told those Negroes what time to hit town, where to stop, what signs to carry, what song to sing, what speech they could make, and what speech they couldn't make, and then told them to get out of town by sundown. . . .

The accuracy of Malcolm X's caustic description of the march on Washington is corroborated in the description from the other side— from the Establishment, by White House adviser Arthur Schlesinger, in his book *A Thousand Days*. He tells how Kennedy met with the civil rights leaders and said the march would "create an atmosphere of intimidation" just when Congress was considering civil rights bills. A. Philip Randolph replied: "The Negroes are already in the streets. It is very likely impossible to get them off. . . ." Schlesinger says: "The conference with the President did persuade the civil rights leaders that they should not lay siege to Capitol Hill." Schlesinger describes the Washington march admiringly and then concludes: "So in 1963 Kennedy moved to incorporate the Negro revolution into the democratic coalition. . . ."

But it did not work. The blacks could not be easily brought into "the democratic coalition" when bombs kept exploding in churches, when new "civil rights" laws did not change the root condition of black people. In the spring of 1963, the rate of unemployment for whites was 4.8 percent. For nonwhites it was 12.1 percent. According to government estimates, one-fifth of the white population was below the poverty line, and one-half of the black population was below that line. The civil rights bills emphasized voting, but voting was not a fundamental solution to racism or poverty. In Harlem, blacks who had voted for years still lived in rat-infested slums.

In precisely those years when civil rights legislation coming out of Congress reached its peak, 1964 and 1965, there were black outbreaks in every part of the country: in Florida, set off by the killing of a Negro woman and a bomb threat against a Negro high school; in Cleveland, set off by the killing of a white minister who sat in the path of a bulldozer to protest discrimination against blacks in construction work; in New York, set off by the fatal shooting of a fifteen-year-old Negro boy during a fight with an off-duty policeman. There were riots also in Rochester, Jersey City, Chicago, Philadelphia.

In August 1965, just as Lyndon Johnson was signing into law the strong Voting Rights Act, providing for federal registration of black voters to ensure their protection, the black ghetto in Watts, Los Angeles, erupted in the most violent urban outbreak since World War II. It was provoked by the forcible arrest of a young Negro driver, the clubbing of a bystander by police, the seizure of a young black woman falsely accused of spitting on the police. There was rioting in the streets, looting and firebombing of stores. Police and National Guardsmen were called in; they used their guns. Thirty-four people were killed, most of them black, hundreds injured, four thousand arrested. Robert Conot, a West Coast journalist, wrote of the riot *(Rivers of Blood, Years of Darkness)*: "In Los Angeles the Negro was going on record that he would no longer turn the other cheek. That, frustrated and goaded, he would strike back, whether the response of violence was an appropriate one or no."

In the summer of 1966, there were more outbreaks, with rock throwing, looting, and fire bombing by Chicago blacks and wild shootings by the National Guard; three blacks were killed, one a thirteen-year-old boy, another a fourteen-year-old pregnant girl. In Cleveland, the National Guard was summoned to stop a commotion in the black community; four Negroes were shot to death, two by troopers, two by white civilians.

It seemed clear by now that the nonviolence of the southern movement, perhaps tactically necessary in the southern atmosphere, and effective because it could be used to appeal to national opinion against the segregationist South, was not enough to deal with the entrenched problems of poverty in the black ghetto. In 1910, 90 percent of Negroes lived in the South. But by 1965, mechanical cotton pickers harvested 81 percent of Mississippi Delta cotton. Between 1940 and 1970, 4 million blacks left the country for the city. By 1965, 80 percent of blacks lived in cities and 50 percent of the black people lived in the North.

There was a new mood in SNCC and among many militant blacks. Their disillusionment was expressed by a young black writer, Julius Lester:

Now it is over. America has had chance after chance to show that it really meant "that all men are endowed with certain inalienable rights." . . . Now it is over. The days of singing freedom songs and the days of combating bullets and billy clubs with love. . . . Love is fragile and gentle and seeks a like response. They used to sing "I Love Everybody" as they ducked bricks and bottles. Now they sing:

Too much love,
Too much love,
Nothing kills a nigger like
Too much love.

In 1967, in the black ghettos of the country, came the greatest urban riots of American history. According to the report of the National Advisory Committee on Urban Disorders, they "involved Negroes acting against local symbols of white American society," symbols of authority and property in the black neighborhoods—rather than purely against white persons. The Commission reported eight major uprisings, thirty-three "serious but not major" outbreaks, and 123 "minor" disorders. Eighty-three died of gunfire, mostly in Newark and Detroit. "The overwhelming majority of the persons killed or injured in all the disorders were Negro civilians."

The "typical rioter," according to the Commission, was a young, high school dropout but "nevertheless, somewhat better educated than his non-rioting Negro neighbor" and "usually underemployed or employed in a menial job." He was "proud of his race, extremely hostile to both whites and middle-class Negroes and, although informed about politics, highly distrustful of the political system."

The report blamed "white racism" for the disorders, and identified the ingredients of the "explosive mixture which has been accumulating in our cities since the end of World War II":

Pervasive discrimination and segregation in employment, education, and housing . . . growing concentrations of impoverished Negroes in our major cities, creating a growing crisis of deteriorating facilities and services and unmet human needs. . . .

A new mood has sprung up among Negroes, particularly the young, in which self-esteem and enhanced racial pride are replacing apathy and submission to the "system."

But the Commission Report itself was a standard device of the system when facing rebellion: set up an investigating committee, issue a report; the words of the report, however strong, will have a soothing effect.

That didn't completely work either. "Black Power" was the new slogan—an expression of distrust of any "progress" given or conceded by whites, a rejection of paternalism. Few blacks (or whites) knew the statement of the white writer Aldous Huxley: "Liberties are not given, they are taken." But the idea was there, in Black Power. Also, a pride in race, an insistence on black independence, and often, on black separation to achieve this independence. Malcolm X was the most eloquent spokesman for this. After he was assassinated as he spoke on a public platform in February 1965, in a plan whose origins are still obscure, he became the martyr of this movement. Hundreds of thousands read his *Autobiography*. He was more influential in death than during his lifetime.

Martin Luther King, though still respected, was being replaced now by new heroes: Huey Newton of the Black Panthers, for instance. The Panthers had guns; they said blacks should defend themselves.

Malcolm X in late 1964 had spoken to black students from Mississippi visiting Harlem:

> You'll get freedom by letting your enemy know that you'll do anything to get your freedom; then you'll get it. It's the only way you'll get it. When you get that kind of attitude, they'll label you as a "crazy Negro," or they'll call you a "crazy nigger"—they don't say Negro. Or they'll call you an extremist or a subversive, or seditious, or a red or a radical. But when you stay radical long enough and get enough people to be like you, you'll get your freedom.

Congress responded to the riots of 1967 by passing the Civil Rights Act of 1968. Presumably it would make stronger the laws prohibiting violence against blacks; it increased the penalties against those depriving people of their civil rights. However, it said: "The provisions of this section shall not apply to acts or omissions on the part of law enforcement officers, members of the National Guard . . . or members of the Armed Forces of the United States, who are engaged in suppressing a riot or civil disturbance. . . ."

Furthermore, it added a section—agreed to by liberal members of Congress in order to get the whole bill passed—that provided up to five years in prison for anyone traveling interstate or using interstate facilities (including mail and telephone) "to organize, promote, encourage, participate in, or carry on a riot." It defined a riot as an action by three or more people involving threats of violence. The first person prosecuted under the Civil Rights Act of 1968 was a young black leader of SNCC, H. Rap Brown, who had made a militant, angry speech in Maryland, just before a racial disturbance there. (Later the Act would be used against antiwar demonstrators in Chicago—the Chicago Eight.)

Martin Luther King himself became more and more concerned about problems untouched by civil rights laws—problems coming out of poverty. In the spring of 1968, he began speaking out, against the advice of some Negro leaders who feared losing friends in Washington, against the war in Vietnam. He connected war and poverty:

. . . it's inevitable that we've got to bring out the question of the tragic mixup in priorities. We are spending all of this money for death and destruction, and not nearly enough money for life and constructive development . . . when the guns of war become a national obsession, social needs inevitably suffer.

King now became a chief target of the FBI, which tapped his private phone conversations, sent him fake letters, threatened him, blackmailed him, and even suggested once in an anonymous letter that he commit suicide. FBI internal memos discussed finding a black leader to replace King. As a Senate report on the FBI said in 1976, the FBI tried "to destroy Dr. Martin Luther King."

King was turning his attention to troublesome questions. He still insisted on nonviolence. Riots were self-defeating, he thought. But they did express a deep feeling that could not be ignored. And so, nonviolence, he said, "must be militant, massive non-violence." He planned a "Poor People's Encampment" in Washington, this time not with the paternal approval of the President. And he went to Memphis, Tennessee, to support a strike of garbage workers in that city. There, standing on a balcony outside his hotel room, he was shot to death by an unseen marksman. The Poor People's Encampment went on, and then it was broken up by police action, just as the World War I veterans' Bonus Army of 1932 was dispersed.

The killing of King brought new urban outbreaks all over the country, in which thirty-nine people were killed, thirty-five of them black. Evidence was piling up that even with all of the civil rights laws now on the books, the courts would not protect blacks against violence and injustice:

1. In the 1967 riots in Detroit, three black teen-agers were killed in the Algiers Motel. Three Detroit policemen and a black private guard were tried for this triple murder. The defense conceded, a UPI dispatch said, that the four men had shot two of the blacks. A jury exonerated them.
2. In Jackson, Mississippi, in the spring of 1970, on the campus of Jackson State College, a Negro college, police laid down a 28-second barrage of gunfire, using shotguns, rifles, and a submachine gun. Four hundred bullets or pieces of buckshot struck the girls' dormitory and two black students were killed. A local grand jury found the attack "justified" and U.S. District Court Judge Harold Cox (a Kennedy appointee) declared that students who engage in civil disorders "must expect to be injured or killed."

3. In Boston in April 1970, a policeman shot and killed an unarmed black man, a patient in a ward in the Boston City Hospital, firing five shots after the black man snapped a towel at him. The chief judge of the municipal court of Boston exonerated the policeman.

4. In Augusta, Georgia, in May 1970, six Negroes were shot to death during looting and disorder in the city. The *New York Times* reported:

> A confidential police report indicates that at least five of the victims were killed by the police. . . .
>
> An eyewitness to one of the deaths said he had watched a Negro policeman and his white partner fire nine shots into the back of a man suspected of looting. They did not fire warning shots or ask him to stop running, said Charles A. Reid, a 38-year-old businessman. . . .

5. In April 1970, a federal jury in Boston found a policeman had used "excessive force" against two black soldiers from Fort Devens, and one of them required twelve stitches in his scalp; the judge awarded the servicemen $3 in damages.

These were "normal" cases, endlessly repeated in the history of the country, coming randomly but persistently out of a racism deep in the institutions, the mind of the country. But there was something else—a planned pattern of violence against militant black organizers, carried on by the police and the Federal Bureau of Investigation. On December 4, 1969, a little before five in the morning, a squad of Chicago police, armed with a submachine gun and shotguns, raided an apartment where Black Panthers lived. They fired at least eighty-two and perhaps two hundred rounds into the apartment, killing twenty-one-year-old Black Panther leader Fred Hampton as he lay in his bed, and another Black Panther, Mark Clark. Years later, it was discovered in a court proceeding that the FBI had an informer among the Panthers, and that they had given the police a floor plan of the apartment, including a sketch of where Fred Hampton slept.

Was the government turning to murder and terror because the concessions—the legislation, the speeches, the intonation of the civil rights hymn "We Shall Overcome" by President Lyndon Johnson—were not working? It was discovered later that the government in all the years of the civil rights movement, while making concessions through Congress, was acting through the FBI to harass and break up black militant groups. Between 1956 and 1971 the FBI concluded a massive Counterintelligence Program (known as COINTELPRO) that took 295 actions against black groups. Black militancy seemed stubbornly resistant to destruction. A secret FBI report to President Nixon in 1970 said "a recent poll indicates that approximately 25% of the black population has a great respect for the Black Panther Party, including 43% of blacks under 21 years of age." Was there fear that blacks would turn their attention from the controllable field of voting to the more dangerous arena of wealth and poverty—of class conflict? In 1966, seventy poor black people in Greenville, Mississippi, occupied an unused air force barracks, until they were evicted by the military. A local woman, Mrs. Unita Blackwell, said:

> I feel that the federal government have proven that it don't care about poor people. Everything that we have asked for through these years had been handed down on paper. It's never been a reality. We the poor people of Mississippi is tired. We're tired of it so we're going to build for ourselves, because we don't have a government that represents us.

Out of the 1967 riots in Detroit came an organization devoted to organizing black workers for revolutionary change. This was the League of Revolutionary Black Workers, which lasted until 1971 and influenced thousands of black workers in Detroit during its period of activity.

The new emphasis was more dangerous than civil rights, because it created the possibility of blacks and whites uniting on the issue of class exploitation. Back in November 1963, A. Philip Randolph had spoken to an AFL-CIO convention about the civil rights movement, and foreseen its direction: "The Negro's protest today is but the first rumbling of the 'under-class.' As the Negro has taken to the streets, so will the unemployed of all races take to the streets."

Attempts began to do with blacks what had been done historically with whites—to lure a small number into the system with economic enticements. There was talk of "black capitalism." Leaders of the NAACP and CORE were invited to the White House. James Farmer of CORE, a former Freedom Rider and militant, was given a job in President Nixon's administration. Floyd McKissick of CORE received a $14 million government loan to build a housing development in North Carolina. Lyndon Johnson had given jobs to some blacks through the Office of Economic Opportunity; Nixon set up an Office of Minority Business Enterprise.

Chase Manhattan Bank and the Rockefeller family (controllers of Chase) took a special interest in developing "black capitalism." The Rockefellers had always been financial patrons of the Urban League, and a strong influence in black education through their support of

Negro colleges in the South. David Rockefeller tried to persuade his fellow capitalists that while helping black businessmen with money might not be fruitful in the short run, it was necessary "to shape an environment in which the business can continue earning a profit four or five or ten years from now." With all of this, black business remained infinitesimally small. The largest black corporation (Motown Industries) had sales in 1974 of $45 million, while Exxon Corporation had sales of $42 billion. The total receipts of black-owned firms accounted for 0.3 percent of all business income.

There was a small amount of change and a lot of publicity. There were more black faces in the newspapers and on television, creating an impression of change—and siphoning off into the mainstream a small but significant number of black leaders.

Some new black voices spoke against this. Robert Allen *(Black Awakening in Capitalist America)* wrote:

> If the community as a whole is to benefit, then the community as a whole must be organized to manage collectively its internal economy and its business relations with white America. Black business firms must be treated and operated as social property, belonging to the general black community, not as the private property of individual or limited groups of individuals. This necessitates the dismantling of capitalist property relations in the black community and their replacement with a planned communal economy.

A black woman, Patricia Robinson, in a pamphlet distributed in Boston in 1970 *(Poor Black Woman)*, tied male supremacy to capitalism and said the black woman "allies herself with the have-nots in the wider world and their revolutionary struggles." She said the poor black woman did not in the past "question the social and economic system" but now she must, and in fact, "she has begun to question aggressive male domination and the class society which enforces it, capitalism."

Another black woman, Margaret Wright, said she was not fighting for equality with men if it meant equality in the world of killing, the world of competition. "I don't want to compete on no damned exploitative level. I don't want to exploit nobody. . . . I want the right to be black and me. . . ."

The system was working hard, by the late sixties and early seventies, to contain the frightening explosiveness of the black upsurge. Blacks were voting in large numbers in the South, and in the 1968 Democratic Convention three blacks were admitted into the Mississippi delegation. By 1977, more than two thousand blacks held office in eleven southern states (in 1965 the number was seventy-two). There were two Congressmen, eleven state senators, ninety-five state representatives, 267 county commissioners, seventy-six mayors, 824 city council members, eighteen sheriffs or chiefs of police, 508 school board members. It was a dramatic advance. But blacks, with 20 percent of the South's population, still held less than 3 percent of the elective offices. A *New York Times* reporter, analyzing the new situation in 1977, pointed out that even where blacks held important city offices: "Whites almost always retain economic power." After Maynard Jackson, a black, became mayor of Atlanta, "the white business establishment continued to exert its influence."

Those blacks in the South who could afford to go to downtown restaurants and hotels were no longer barred because of their race. More blacks could go to colleges and universities, to law schools and medical schools. Northern cities were busing children back and forth in an attempt to create racially mixed schools, despite the racial segregation in housing. None of this, however, was halting what Frances Piven and Richard Cloward (*Poor People's Movements*) called "the destruction of the black lower class"—the unemployment, the deterioration of the ghetto, the rising crime, drug addiction, violence.

In the summer of 1977, the Department of Labor reported that the rate of unemployment among black youths was 34.8 percent. A small new black middle class of blacks had been created, and it raised the overall statistics for black income—but there was a great disparity between the newly risen middle-class black and the poor left behind. Despite the new opportunities for a small number of blacks, the median black family income of 1977 was only about 60 percent that of whites; blacks were twice as likely to die of diabetes; seven times as likely to be victims of homicidal violence rising out of the poverty and despair of the ghetto.

A *New York Times* report in early 1978 said: ". . . the places that experienced urban riots in the 1960's have, with a few exceptions, changed little, and the conditions of poverty have spread in most cities."

Statistics did not tell the whole story. Racism, always a national fact, not just a southern one, emerged in northern cities, as the federal government made concessions to poor blacks in a way that pitted them against poor whites for resources made scarce by the system. Blacks, freed from slavery to take their place under capitalism, had long been forced into conflict with whites for scarce jobs. Now, with desegregation in housing, blacks tried to move into neighborhoods where whites, themselves poor, crowded, troubled, could find in them a target for their anger. In the Boston *Globe*, November 1977:

A Hispanic family of six fled their apartment in the Savin Hill section of Dorchester yesterday after a week of repeated stonings and window-smashings by a group of white youths, in what appears to have been racially motivated attacks, police said.

In Boston, the busing of black children to white schools, and whites to black schools, set off a wave of white neighborhood violence. The use of busing to integrate schools—sponsored by the government and the courts in response to the black movement—was an ingenious concession to protest. It had the effect of pushing poor whites and poor blacks into competition for the miserable inadequate schools which the system provided for all the poor.

Was the black population—hemmed into the ghetto, divided by the growth of a middle class, decimated by poverty, attacked by the government, driven into conflict with whites—under control? Surely, in the mid-seventies, there was no great black movement under way. Yet, a new black consciousness had been born and was still alive. Also, whites and blacks were crossing racial lines in the South to unite as a class against employers. In 1971, two thousand woodworkers in Mississippi, black and white, joined together to protest a new method of measuring wood that led to lower wages. In the textile mills of J. P. Stevens, where 44,000 workers were employed in eighty-five plants, mostly in the South, blacks and whites were working together in union activity. In Tifton, Georgia, and Milledgeville, Georgia, in 1977, blacks and whites served together on the union committees of their plants.

Would a new black movement go beyond the limits of the civil rights actions of the sixties, beyond the spontaneous urban riots of the seventies, beyond separatism to a coalition of white and black in a historic new alliance? There was no way of knowing this in 1978. In 1978, 6 million black people were unemployed. As Langston Hughes said, what happens to a dream deferred? Does it dry up, or does it explode? If it did explode, as it had in the past, it would come with a certain inevitability—out of the conditions of black life in America—and yet, because no one knew when, it would come as a surprise.

18

THE IMPOSSIBLE VICTORY: VIETNAM

From 1964 to 1972, the wealthiest and most powerful nation in the history of the world made a maximum military effort, with everything short of atomic bombs, to defeat a nationalist revolutionary movement in a tiny, peasant country—and failed. When the United States fought in Vietnam, it was organized modern technology versus organized human beings, and the human beings won.

In the course of that war, there developed in the United States the greatest antiwar movement the nation had ever experienced, a movement that played a critical part in bringing the war to an end.

It was another startling fact of the sixties.

In the fall of 1945 Japan, defeated, was forced to leave Indochina, the former French colony it had occupied at the start of the war. In the meantime, a revolutionary movement had grown there, determined to end colonial control and to achieve a new life for the peasants of Indochina. Led by a Communist named Ho Chi Minh, the revolutionists fought against the Japanese, and when they were gone held a spectacular celebration in Hanoi in late 1945, with a million people in the streets, and issued a Declaration of Independence. It borrowed from the Declaration of the Rights of Man and the Citizen, in the French Revolution, and from the American Declaration of Independence, and began: "All men are created equal. They are endowed by their Creator with certain inalienable rights; among these are Life, Liberty, and the pursuit of Happiness." Just as the Americans in 1776 had listed their grievances against the English King, the Vietnamese listed their complaints against French rule:

They have enforced inhuman laws. . . . They have built more prisons than schools. They have mercilessly slain our patriots, they have drowned uprisings in rivers of blood. They have fettered public opinion. . . . They have robbed us of our rice fields, our mines, our forests, and our raw materials. . . .

They have invented numerous unjustifiable taxes and reduced our people, especially our peasantry, to a state of extreme poverty. . . .

. . . from the end of last year, to the beginning of this year . . . more than two million of our fellow-citizens died of starvation. . . .

The whole Vietnamese people, animated by a common purpose, are determined to fight to the bitter end against any attempt by the French colonialists to reconquer their country.

The U.S. Defense Department study of the Vietnam war, intended to be "top secret" but released to the public by Daniel Ellsberg and Anthony Russo in the famous *Pentagon Papers* case, described Ho Chi Minh's work:

> . . . Ho had built the Viet Minh into the only Vietnam-wide political organization capable of effective resistance to either the Japanese or the French. He was the only Vietnamese wartime leader with a national following, and he assured himself wider fealty among the Vietnamese people when in August-September, 1945, he overthrew the Japanese . . . established the Democratic Republic of Vietnam, and staged receptions for in-coming allied occupation forces. . . . For a few weeks in September, 1945, Vietnam was—for the first and only time in its modern history—free of foreign domination, and united from north to south under Ho Chi Minh. . . .

The Western powers were already at work to change this. England occupied the southern part of Indochina and then turned it back to the French. Nationalist China (this was under Chiang Kai-shek, before the Communist revolution) occupied the northern part of Indochina, and the United States persuaded it to turn that back to the French. As Ho Chi Minh told an American journalist: "We apparently stand quite alone. . . . We shall have to depend on ourselves."

Between October 1945 and February 1946, Ho Chi Minh wrote eight letters to President Truman, reminding him of the self-determination promises of the Atlantic Charter. One of the letters was sent both to Truman and to the United Nations:

> I wish to invite attention of your Excellency for strictly humanitarian reasons to following matter. Two million Vietnamese died of starvation during

winter of 1944 and spring 1945 because of starvation policy of French who seized and stored until it rotted all available rice. . . . Three-fourths of cultivated land was flooded in summer 1945, which was followed by a severe drought; of normal harvest five-sixths was lost. . . . Many people are starving. . . . Unless great world powers and international relief organizations bring us immediate assistance we face imminent catastrophe. . . .

Truman never replied.

In October of 1946, the French bombarded Haiphong, a port in northern Vietnam, and there began the eight-year war between the Vietminh movement and the French over who would rule Vietnam. After the Communist victory in China in 1949 and the Korean war the following year, the United States began giving large amounts of military aid to the French. By 1954, the United States had given 300,000 small arms and machine guns, enough to equip the entire French army in Indochina, and $1 billion; all together, the U.S. was financing 80 percent of the French war effort.

Why was the United States doing this? To the public, the word was that the United States was helping to stop Communism in Asia, but there was not much public discussion. In the secret memoranda of the National Security Council (which advised the President on foreign policy) there was talk in 1950 of what came to be known as the "domino theory"—that, like a row of dominoes, if one country fell to Communism, the next one would do the same and so on. It was important therefore to keep the first one from falling.

A secret memo of the National Security Council in June 1952 also pointed to the chain of U.S. military bases along the coast of China, the Philippines, Taiwan, Japan, South Korea:

Communist control of all of Southeast Asia would render the U.S. position in the Pacific offshore island chain precarious and would seriously jeopardize fundamental U.S. security interests in the Far East.

And:

Southeast Asia, especially Malaya and Indonesia, is the principal world source of natural rubber and tin, and a producer of petroleum and other strategically important commodities. . . .

It was also noted that Japan depended on the rice of Southeast Asia, and Communist victory there would "make it extremely difficult to prevent Japan's eventual accommodation to communism."

In 1953, a congressional study mission reported: "The area of Indochina is immensely wealthy in rice, rubber, coal and iron ore. Its position makes it a strategic key to the rest of Southeast Asia." That year, a State Department memorandum said that the French were losing the war in Indochina, had failed "to win a sufficient native support," feared that a negotiated settlement "would mean the eventual loss to Communism not only of Indo-China but of the whole of Southeast Asia," and concluded: "If the French actually decided to withdraw, the U.S. would have to consider most seriously whether to take over in this area."

In 1954, the French, having been unable to win Vietnamese popular support, which was overwhelmingly behind Ho Chi Minh and the revolutionary movement, had to withdraw.

An international assemblage at Geneva presided over the peace agreement between the French and the Vietminh. It was agreed that the French would temporarily withdraw into the southern part of Vietnam, that the Vietminh would remain in the north, and that an election would take place in two years in a unified Vietnam to enable the Vietnamese to choose their own government.

The United States moved quickly to prevent the unification and to establish South Vietnam as an American sphere. It set up in Saigon as head of the government a former Vietnamese official named Ngo Dinh Diem, who had recently been living in New Jersey, and encouraged him not to hold the scheduled elections for unification. A memo in early 1954 of the Joint Chiefs of Staff said that intelligence estimates showed "a settlement based on free elections would be attended by almost certain loss of the Associated States [Laos, Cambodia, and Vietnam—the three parts of Indochina created by the Geneva Conference] to Communist control." Diem again and again blocked the elections requested by the Vietminh, and with American money and arms his government became more and more firmly established. As the *Pentagon Papers* put it: "South Viet Nam was essentially the creation of the United States."

The Diem regime became increasingly unpopular. Diem was a Catholic, and most Vietnamese were Buddhists; Diem was close to the landlords, and this was a country of peasants. His pretenses at land reform left things basically as they were. He replaced locally selected provincial chiefs with his own men, appointed in Saigon; by 1962, 88 percent of these provincial chiefs were military men. Diem imprisoned more and more Vietnamese who criticized the regime for corruption, for lack of reform.

Opposition grew quickly in the countryside, where Diem's apparatus could not reach well, and around 1958 guerrilla activities began
against the regime. The Communist regime in Hanoi gave aid, encouragement, and sent people south—most of them southerners who had
gone north after the Geneva accords—to support the guerrilla movement. In 1960, the National Liberation Front was formed in the South.
It united the various strands of opposition to the regime; its strength
came from South Vietnamese peasants, who saw it as a way of changing
their daily lives. A U.S. government analyst named Douglas Pike, in his
book *Viet Cong*, based on interviews with rebels and captured documents, tried to give a realistic assessment of what the United States faced:

> In the 2561 villages of South Vietnam, the National Liberation Front cre-
> ated a host of nation-wide socio-political organizations in a country where
> mass organizations . . . were virtually nonexistent. . . . Aside from the NLF
> there had never been a truly mass-based political party in South Vietnam.

Pike wrote: "The Communists have brought to the villages of South
Vietnam significant social change and have done so largely by means of
the communication process." That is, they were organizers much more
than they were warriors. "What struck me most forcibly about the NLF
was its totality as a social revolution first and as a war second." Pike was
impressed with the mass involvement of the peasants in the movement.
"The rural Vietnamese was not regarded simply as a pawn in a power
struggle but as the active element in the thrust. He was the thrust." Pike
wrote:

> The purpose of this vast organizational effort was . . . to restructure the
> social order of the village and train the villages to control themselves. This
> was the NLF's one undeviating thrust from the start. Not the killing of
> ARVN (Saigon) soldiers, not the occupation of real estate, not the prepara-
> tion for some great pitched battle . . . but organization in depth of the rural
> population through the instrument of self-control.

Pike estimated that the NLF membership by early 1962 stood at
around 300,000. The *Pentagon Papers* said of this period: "Only the Viet
Cong had any real support and influence on a broad base in the countryside."

When Kennedy took office in early 1961 he continued the policies of
Truman and Eisenhower in Southeast Asia. Almost immediately, he
approved a secret plan for various military actions in Vietnam and Laos,

including the "dispatch of agents to North Vietnam" to engage in "sabotage and light harassment," according to the *Pentagon Papers*. Back in 1956, he had spoken of "the amazing success of President Diem" and said of Diem's Vietnam: "Her political liberty is an inspiration."

One day in June 1963, a Buddhist monk sat down in the public square in Saigon and set himself afire. More Buddhist monks began committing suicide by fire to dramatize their opposition to the Diem regime. Diem's police raided the Buddhist pagodas and temples, wounded thirty monks, arrested 1,400 people, and closed down the pagodas. There were demonstrations in the city. The police fired, killing nine people. Then, in Hué, the ancient capital, ten thousand demonstrated in protest.

Under the Geneva Accords, the United States was permitted to have 685 military advisers in southern Vietnam. Eisenhower secretly sent several thousand. Under Kennedy, the figure rose to sixteen thousand, and some of them began to take part in combat operations. Diem was losing. Most of the South Vietnam countryside was now controlled by local villagers organized by the NLF.

Diem was becoming an embarrassment, an obstacle to effective control over Vietnam. Some Vietnamese generals began plotting to overthrow his regime, staying in touch with a CIA man named Lucien Conein. Conein met secretly with American Ambassador Henry Cabot Lodge, who was enthusiastically for the coup. Lodge reported to Kennedy's assistant, McGeorge Bundy, on October 25 *(Pentagon Papers)*: "I have personally approved each meeting between General Tran Van Don and Conein who has carried out my orders in each instance explicitly." Kennedy seemed hesitant, but no move was made to warn Diem. Indeed, just before the coup, and just after he had been in touch through Conein with the plotters, Lodge spent a weekend with Diem at a seaside resort. When, on November 1, 1963, the generals attacked the presidential palace, Diem phoned Ambassador Lodge, and the conversation went as follows:

> Diem: Some units have made a rebellion and I want to know what is the attitude of the United States?
>
> Lodge: I do not feel well enough informed to be able to tell you. I have heard the shooting, but am not acquainted with all of the facts. Also it is 4:30 A.M. in Washington and the U.S. Government cannot possibly have a view.
>
> Diem: But you must have some general ideas. . . .

Lodge told Diem to phone him if he could do anything for his physical safety.

That was the last conversation any American had with Diem. He fled the palace, but he and his brother were apprehended by the plotters, taken out in a truck, and executed.

Earlier in 1963, Kennedy's Undersecretary of State, U. Alexis Johnson, was speaking before the Economic Club of Detroit:

> What is the attraction that Southeast Asia has exerted for centuries on the great powers flanking it on all sides? Why is it desirable, and why is it important? First, it provides a lush climate, fertile soil, rich natural resources, a relatively sparse population in most areas, and room to expand. The countries of Southeast Asia produce rich exportable surpluses such as rice, rubber, teak, corn, tin, spices, oil, and many others. . . .

This is not the language that was used by President Kennedy in his explanations to the American public. He talked of Communism and freedom. In a news conference February 14, 1962, he said: "Yes, as you know, the U.S. for more than a decade has been assisting the government, the people of Vietnam, to maintain their independence."

Three weeks after the execution of Diem, Kennedy himself was assassinated, and his Vice-President, Lyndon Johnson, took office.

The generals who succeeded Diem could not suppress the National Liberation Front. Again and again, American leaders expressed their bewilderment at the popularity of the NLF, at the high morale of its soldiers. The Pentagon historians wrote that when Eisenhower met with President-elect Kennedy in January 1961, he "wondered aloud why, in interventions of this kind, we always seemed to find that the morale of the Communist forces was better than that of the democratic forces." And General Maxwell Taylor reported in late 1964:

> The ability of the Viet-Cong continuously to rebuild their units and to make good their losses is one of the mysteries of the guerrilla war. . . . Not only do the Viet-Cong units have the recuperative powers of the phoenix, but they have an amazing ability to maintain morale. Only in rare cases have we found evidences of bad morale among Viet-Cong prisoners or recorded in captured Viet-Cong documents.

In early August 1964, President Johnson used a murky set of events in the Gulf of Tonkin, off the coast of North Vietnam, to launch full-scale war on Vietnam. Johnson and Secretary of Defense Robert

McNamara told the American public there was an attack by North Vietnamese torpedo boats on American destroyers. "While on routine patrol in international waters," McNamara said, "the U.S. destroyer *Maddox* underwent an unprovoked attack." It later turned out that the Gulf of Tonkin episode was a fake, that the highest American officials had lied to the public—just as they had in the invasion of Cuba under Kennedy. In fact, the CIA had engaged in a secret operation attacking North Vietnamese coastal installations—so if there had been an attack it would not have been "unprovoked." It was not a "routine patrol," because the *Maddox* was on a special electronic spying mission. And it was not in international waters but in Vietnamese territorial waters. It turned out that no torpedoes were fired at the *Maddox*, as McNamara said. Another reported attack on another destroyer, two nights later, which Johnson called "open aggression on the high seas," seems also to have been an invention.

At the time of the incident, Secretary of State Rusk was questioned on NBC television:

> REPORTER: What explanation, then, can you come up with for this unpro-
> voked attack?
> RUSK: Well, I haven't been able, quite frankly, to come to a fully satisfactory
> explanation. There is a great gulf of understanding, between that world
> and our world, ideological in character. They see what we think of as the
> real world in wholly different terms. Their very processes of logic are
> different. So that it's very difficult to enter into each other's minds across
> that great ideological gulf.

The Tonkin "attack" brought a congressional resolution, passed unanimously in the House, and with only two dissenting votes in the Senate, giving Johnson the power to take military action as he saw fit in Southeast Asia.

Two months before the Gulf of Tonkin incident, U.S. government leaders met in Honolulu and discussed such a resolution. Rusk said, in this meeting, according to the *Pentagon Papers*, that "public opinion on our Southeast Asia policy was badly divided in the United States at the moment and that, therefore, the President needed an affirmation of support."

The Tonkin Resolution gave the President the power to initiate hostilities without the declaration of war by Congress that the Constitution required. The Supreme Court, supposed to be the watchdog of the Constitution, was asked by a number of petitioners in the course of the

Vietnam war to declare the war unconstitutional. Again and again, it refused even to consider the issue.

Immediately after the Tonkin affair, American warplanes began bombarding North Vietnam. During 1965, over 200,000 American soldiers were sent to South Vietnam, and in 1966, 200,000 more. By early 1968, there were more than 500,000 American troops there, and the U.S. Air Force was dropping bombs at a rate unequaled in history. Tiny glimmerings of the massive human suffering under this bombardment came to the outside world. On June 5, 1965, the *New York Times* carried a dispatch from Saigon:

> As the Communists withdrew from Quangngai last Monday, United States jet bombers pounded the hills into which they were headed. Many Vietnamese—one estimate is as high as 500—were killed by the strikes. The American contention is that they were Vietcong soldiers. But three out of four patients seeking treatment in a Vietnamese hospital afterward for burns from napalm, or jellied gasoline, were village women.

On September 6, another press dispatch from Saigon:

> In Bien Hoa province south of Saigon on August 15 United States aircraft accidentally bombed a Buddhist pagoda and a Catholic church . . . it was the third time their pagoda had been bombed in 1965. A temple of the Cao Dai religious sect in the same area had been bombed twice this year.
>
> In another delta province there is a woman who has both arms burned off by napalm and her eyelids so badly burned that she cannot close them. When it is time for her to sleep her family puts a blanket over her head. The woman had two of her children killed in the air strike that maimed her.
>
> Few Americans appreciate what their nation is doing to South Vietnam with airpower . . . innocent civilians are dying every day in South Vietnam.

Large areas of South Vietnam were declared "free fire zones," which meant that all persons remaining within them—civilians, old people, children—were considered an enemy, and bombs were dropped at will. Villages suspected of harboring Viet Cong were subject to "search and destroy" missions—men of military age in the villages were killed, the homes were burned, the women, children, and old people were sent off to refugee camps. Jonathan Schell, in his book *The Village of Ben Suc*, describes such an operation: a village surrounded, attacked, a man riding on a bicycle shot down, three people picnicking by the river shot to death, the houses destroyed, the women, children, old people herded together, taken away from their ancestral homes.

The CIA in Vietnam, in a program called "Operation Phoenix," secretly, without trial, executed at least twenty thousand civilians in South Vietnam who were suspected of being members of the Communist underground. A pro-administration analyst wrote in the journal *Foreign Affairs* in January 1975: "Although the Phoenix program did undoubtedly kill or incarcerate many innocent civilians, it did also eliminate many members of the Communist infrastructure."

After the war, the release of records of the International Red Cross showed that in South Vietnamese prison camps, where at the height of the war 65,000 to 70,000 people were held and often beaten and tortured, American advisers observed and sometimes participated. The Red Cross observers found continuing, systematic brutality at the two principal Vietnamese POW camps—at Phu Quoc and Qui Nhon, where American advisers were stationed.

By the end of the Vietnam war, 7 million tons of bombs had been dropped on Vietnam, more than twice the total bombs dropped on Europe and Asia in World War II—almost one 500-pound bomb for every human being in Vietnam. It was estimated that there were 20 million bomb craters in the country. In addition, poisonous sprays were dropped by planes to destroy trees and any kind of growth—an area the size of the state of Massachusetts was covered with such poison. Vietnamese mothers reported birth defects in their children. Yale biologists, using the same poison (2,4,5,T) on mice, reported defective mice born and said they had no reason to believe the effect on humans was different.

On March 16, 1968, a company of American soldiers went into the hamlet of My Lai 4, in Quang Ngai province. They rounded up the inhabitants, including old people and women with infants in their arms. These people were ordered into a ditch, where they were methodically shot to death by American soldiers. The testimony of James Dursi, a rifleman, at the later trial of Lieutenant William Calley, was reported in the *New York Times*:

Lieutenant Calley and a weeping rifleman named Paul D. Meadlo—the same soldier who had fed candy to the children before shooting them—pushed the prisoners into the ditch. . . .

"There was an order to shoot by Lieutenant Calley, I can't remember the exact words—it was something like 'Start firing.'

"Meadlo turned to me and said: 'Shoot, why don't you shoot?'

"He was crying.

"I said, 'I can't. I won't.'

"Then Lieutenant Calley and Meadlo pointed their rifles into the ditch and fired.

"People were diving on top of each other; mothers were trying to protect their children. . . ."

Journalist Seymour Hersh, in his book *My Lai 4*, writes:

When Army investigators reached the barren area in November, 1969, in connection with the My Lai probe in the United States, they found mass graves at three sites, as well as a ditch full of bodies. It was estimated that between 450 and 500 people—most of them women, children and old men—had been slain and buried there.

The army tried to cover up what happened. But a letter began circulating from a GI named Ron Ridenhour, who had heard about the massacre. There were photos taken of the killing by an army photographer, Ronald Haeberle. Seymour Hersh, then working for an antiwar news agency in Southeast Asia called Dispatch News Service, wrote about it. The story of the massacre had appeared in May 1968 in two French publications, one called *Sud Vietnam en Lutte*, and another published by the North Vietnamese delegation to the peace talks in Paris—but the American press did not pay any attention.

Several of the officers in the My Lai massacre were put on trial, but only Lieutenant William Calley was found guilty. He was sentenced to life imprisonment, but his sentence was reduced twice; he served three years—Nixon ordered that he be under house arrest rather than a regular prison—and then was paroled. Thousands of Americans came to his defense. Part of it was in patriotic justification of his action as necessary against the "Communists." Part of it seems to have been a feeling that he was unjustly singled out in a war with many similar atrocities. Colonel Oran Henderson, who had been charged with covering up the My Lai killings, told reporters in early 1971: "Every unit of brigade size has its My Lai hidden someplace."

Indeed, My Lai was unique only in its details. Hersh reported a letter sent by a GI to his family, and published in a local newspaper:

Dear Mom and Dad:

Today we went on a mission and I am not very proud of myself, my friends, or my country. We burned every hut in sight!

It was a small rural network of villages and the people were incredibly poor. My unit burned and plundered their meager possessions. Let me try to explain the situation to you.

The huts here are thatched palm leaves. Each one has a dried mud bunker inside. These bunkers are to protect the families. Kind of like air raid shelters.

My unit commanders, however, chose to think that these bunkers are offensive. So every hut we find that has a bunker we are ordered to burn to the ground.

When the ten helicopters landed this morning, in the midst of these huts, and six men jumped out of each "chopper", we were firing the moment we hit the ground. We fired into all the huts we could. . . .

It is then that we burned these huts. . . . Everyone is crying, begging and praying that we don't separate them and take their husbands and fathers, sons and grandfathers. The women wail and moan.

Then they watch in terror as we burn their homes, personal possessions and food. Yes, we burn all rice and shoot all livestock.

The more unpopular became the Saigon government, the more desperate the military effort became to make up for this. A secret congressional report of late 1967 said the Viet Cong were distributing about five times more land to the peasants than the South Vietnamese government, whose land distribution program had come "to a virtual standstill." The report said: "The Viet Cong have eliminated landlord domination and reallocated lands owned by absentee landlords and the G.V.N. [Government of Viet Nam] to the landless and others who cooperate with Viet Cong authorities."

The unpopularity of the Saigon government explains the success of the National Liberation Front in infiltrating Saigon and other government-held towns in early 1968, without the people there warning the government. The NLF thus launched a surprise offensive (it was the time of "Tet," their New Year holiday) that carried them into the heart of Saigon, immobilized Tan San Nhut airfield, even occupied the American Embassy briefly. The offensive was beaten back, but it demonstrated that all the enormous firepower delivered on Vietnam by the United States had not destroyed the NLF, its morale, its popular support, its will to fight. It caused a reassessment in the American government, more doubts among the American people.

The massacre at My Lai by a company of ordinary soldiers was a small event compared with the plans of high-level military and civilian leaders to visit massive destruction on the civilian population of

Vietnam. Assistant Secretary of Defense John McNaughton in early 1966, seeing that large-scale bombing of North Vietnam villages was not producing the desired result, suggested a different strategy. The air strikes on villages, he said, would "create a counterproductive wave of revulsion abroad and at home." He suggested instead:

> Destruction of locks and dams, however—if handled right—might . . . offer promise. It should be studied. Such destruction doesn't kill or drown people. By shallow-flooding the rice, it leads after a time to widespread starvation (more than a million?) unless food is provided—which we could offer to do "at the conference table." . . .

The heavy bombings were intended to destroy the will of ordinary Vietnamese to resist, as in the bombings of German and Japanese population centers in World War II—despite President Johnson's public insistence that only "military targets" were being bombed. The government was using language like "one more turn of the screw" to describe bombing. The CIA at one point in 1966 recommended a "bombing program of greater intensity," according to the *Pentagon Papers*, directed against, in the CIA's words, "the will of the regime as a target system."

Meanwhile, just across the border of Vietnam, in a neighboring country, Laos, where a right-wing government installed by the CIA faced a rebellion, one of the most beautiful areas in the world, the Plain of Jars, was being destroyed by bombing. This was not reported by the government or the press, but an American who lived in Laos, Fred Branfman, told the story in his book *Voices from the Plain of Jars*:

> Over 25,000 attack sorties were flown against the Plain of Jars from May, 1964, through September, 1969; over 75,000 tons of bombs were dropped on it; on the ground, thousands were killed and wounded, tens of thousands driven underground, and the entire aboveground society leveled.

Branfman, who spoke the Laotian language and lived in a village with a Laotian family, interviewed hundreds of refugees from the bombing who poured into the capital city of Vientiane. He recorded their statements and preserved their drawings. A twenty-six-year-old nurse from Xieng Khouang told of her life in her village:

> I was at one with the earth, the air, the upland fields, the paddy and the seedbeds of my village. Each day and night in the light of the moon I and my friends from the village would wander, calling out and singing, through

forest and field, amidst the cries of the birds. During the harvesting and planting season, we would sweat and labor together, under the sun and the rain, contending with poverty and miserable conditions, continuing the farmer's life which has been the profession of our ancestors.

But in 1964 and 1965 I could feel the trembling of the earth and the shock from the sounds of arms exploding around my village. I began to hear the noise of airplanes, circling about in the heavens. One of them would stick its head down and, plunging earthward, loose a loud roar, shocking the heart as light and smoke covered everything so that one could not see anything at all. Each day we would exchange news with the neighboring villagers of the bombings that had occurred: the damaged houses, the injured and the dead. . . .

The holes! The holes! During that time we needed holes to save our lives. We who were young took our sweat and our strength, which should have been spent raising food in the ricefields and forests to sustain our lives, and squandered it digging holes to protect ourselves. . . .

One young woman explained why the revolutionary movement in Laos, the Neo Lao, attracted her and so many of her friends:

As a young girl, I had found that the past had not been very good, for men had mistreated and made fun of women as the weaker sex. But after the Neo Lao party began to administer the region . . . it became very different . . . under the Neo Lao things changed psychologically, such as their teaching that women should be as brave as men. For example: although I had gone to school before, my elders advised me not to. They had said that it would not be useful for me as I could not hope to be a high ranking official after graduation, that only the children of the elite or rich could expect that.

But the Neo Lao said that women should have the same education as men, and they gave us equal privileges and did not allow anyone to make fun of us. . . .

And the old associations were changed into new ones. For example, most of the new teachers and doctors trained were women. And they changed the lives of the very poor. . . . For they shared the land of those who had many rice fields with those who had none.

A seventeen-year-old boy told about the Pathet Lao revolutionary army coming to his village:

Some people were afraid, mostly those with money. They offered cows to the Pathet Lao soldiers to eat, but the soldiers refused to take them. If they did take them, they paid a suitable price. The truth is that they led the people not to be afraid of anything.

Then they organized the election of village and canton chief, and the people were the ones who chose them. . . .

Desperation led the CIA to enlist the Hmong tribesmen in military campaigns, which led to the deaths of thousands of Hmong. This was accompanied by secrecy and lying, as was so much of what happened in Laos. In September 1973, a former government official in Laos, Jerome Doolittle, wrote in the *New York Times*:

The Pentagon's most recent lies about bombing Cambodia bring back a question that often occurred to me when I was press attache at the American Embassy in Vientiane, Laos.

Why did we bother to lie?

When I first arrived in Laos, I was instructed to answer all press questions about our massive and merciless bombing campaign in that tiny country with: "At the request of the Royal Laotian Government, the United States is conducting unarmed reconnaissance flights accompanied by armed escorts who have the right to return if fired upon."

This was a lie. Every reporter to whom I told it knew it was a lie. Hanoi knew it was a lie. The International Control Commission knew it was a lie. Every interested Congressman and newspaper reader knew it was a lie. . . .

After all, the lies did serve to keep something from somebody, and the somebody was us.

By early 1968, the cruelty of the war began touching the conscience of many Americans. For many others, the problem was that the United States was unable to win the war, while 40,000 American soldiers were dead by this time, 250,000 wounded, with no end in sight. (The Vietnam casualties were many times this number.)

Lyndon Johnson had escalated a brutal war and failed to win it. His popularity was at an all-time low; he could not appear publicly without a demonstration against him and the war. The chant "LBJ, LBJ, how many kids did you kill today?" was heard in demonstrations throughout the country. In the spring of 1968 Johnson announced he would not run again for President, and that negotiations for peace would begin with the Vietnamese in Paris.

In the fall of 1968, Richard Nixon, pledging that he would get the United States out of Vietnam, was elected President. He began to withdraw troops; by February 1972, less than 150,000 were left. But the bombing continued. Nixon's policy was "Vietnamization"—the Saigon government, with Vietnamese ground troops, using American money and air power, would carry on the war. Nixon was not ending the war; he was ending the most unpopular aspect of it, the involvement of American soldiers on the soil of a faraway country.

In the spring of 1970, Nixon and Secretary of State Henry Kissinger launched an invasion of Cambodia, after a long bombardment that the government never disclosed to the public. The invasion not only led to an outcry of protest in the United States, it was a military failure, and Congress resolved that Nixon could not use American troops in extending the war without congressional approval. The following year, without American troops, the United States supported a South Vietnamese invasion of Laos. This too failed. In 1971, 800,000 tons of bombs were dropped by the United States on Laos, Cambodia, Vietnam. Meantime, the Saigon military regime, headed by President Nguyen Van Thieu, the last of a long succession of Saigon chiefs of state, was keeping thousands of opponents in jail.

Some of the first signs of opposition in the United States to the Vietnam war came out of the civil rights movement—perhaps because the experience of black people with the government led them to distrust any claim that it was fighting for freedom. On the very day that Lyndon Johnson was telling the nation in early August 1964 about the Gulf of Tonkin incident, and announcing the bombing of North Vietnam, black and white activists were gathering near Philadelphia, Mississippi, at a memorial service for the three civil rights workers killed there that summer. One of the speakers pointed bitterly to Johnson's use of force in Asia, comparing it with the violence used against blacks in Mississippi.

In mid-1965, in McComb, Mississippi, young blacks who had just learned that a classmate of theirs was killed in Vietnam distributed a leaflet:

> No Mississippi Negroes should be fighting in Viet Nam for the White man's freedom, until all the Negro People are free in Mississippi.
>
> Negro boys should not honor the draft here in Mississippi. Mothers should encourage their sons not to go. . . .
>
> No one has a right to ask us to risk our lives and kill other Colored People in Santo Domingo and Viet Nam, so that the White American can get richer.

When Secretary of Defense Robert McNamara visited Mississippi and praised Senator John Stennis, a prominent racist, as a "man of very genuine greatness," white and black students marched in protest, with placards saying "In Memory of the Burned Children of Vietnam."

The Student Nonviolent Coordinating Committee declared in early 1966 that "the United States is pursuing an aggressive policy in violation of international law" and called for withdrawal from Vietnam. That summer, six members of SNCC were arrested for an invasion of an induction center in Atlanta. They were convicted and sentenced to several years in prison. Around the same time, Julian Bond, a SNCC activist who had just been elected to the Georgia House of Representatives, spoke out against the war and the draft, and the House voted that he not be seated because his statements violated the Selective Service Act and "tend to bring discredit to the House." The Supreme Court restored Bond to his seat, saying he had the right to free expression under the First Amendment.

One of the great sports figures of the nation, Muhammad Ali, the black boxer and heavyweight champion, refused to serve in what he called a "white man's war"; boxing authorities took away his title as champion. Martin Luther King, Jr., spoke out in 1967 at Riverside Church in New York:

> Somehow this madness must cease. We must stop now. I speak as a child of God and brother to the suffering poor of Vietnam. I speak for those whose land is being laid waste, whose homes are being destroyed, whose culture is being subverted. I speak for the poor of America who are paying the double price of smashed hopes at home and death and corruption in Vietnam. I speak as a citizen of the world, for the world as it stands aghast at the path we have taken. I speak as an American to the leaders of my own nation. The great initiative in this war is ours. The initiative to stop it must be ours.

Young men began to refuse to register for the draft, refused to be inducted if called. As early as May 1964 the slogan "We Won't Go" was widely publicized. Some who had registered began publicly burning their draft cards to protest the war. One, David O'Brien, burned his draft card in South Boston; he was convicted, and the Supreme Court overruled his argument that this was a protected form of free expression. In October of 1967 there were organized draft-card "turn-ins" all over the country; in San Francisco alone, three hundred draft cards were returned to the government. Just before a huge demonstration at the Pentagon that month, a sack of collected draft cards was presented to the Justice Department.

By mid-1965, 380 prosecutions were begun against men refusing to be inducted; by mid-1968 that figure was up to 3,305. At the end of 1969, there were 33,960 delinquents nationwide.

In May 1969 the Oakland induction center, where draftees reported from all of northern California, reported that of 4,400 men ordered to report for induction, 2,400 did not show up. In the first quarter of 1970 the Selective Service system, for the first time, could not meet its quota.

A Boston University graduate student in history, Philip Supina, wrote on May 1, 1968, to his draft board in Tucson, Arizona:

> I am enclosing the order for me to report for my pre-induction physical exam for the armed forces. I have absolutely no intention to report for that exam, or for induction, or to aid in any way the American war effort against the people of Vietnam. . . .

He ended his letter by quoting the Spanish philosopher Miguel Unamuno, who during the Spanish Civil War said: "Sometimes to be Silent is to Lie." Supina was convicted and sentenced to four years in prison.

Early in the war, there had been two separate incidents, barely noticed by most Americans. On November 2, 1965, in front of the Pentagon in Washington, as thousands of employees were streaming out of the building in the late afternoon, Norman Morrison, a thirty-two-year-old pacifist, father of three, stood below the third-floor windows of Secretary of Defense Robert McNamara, doused himself with kerosene, and set himself afire, giving up his life in protest against the war. Also that year, in Detroit, an eighty-two-year-old woman named Alice Herz burned herself to death to make a statement against the horror of Indochina.

A remarkable change in sentiment took place. In early 1965, when the bombing of North Vietnam began, a hundred people gathered on the Boston Common to voice their indignation. On October 15, 1969, the number of people assembled on the Boston Common to protest the war was 100,000. Perhaps 2 million people across the nation gathered that day in towns and villages that had never seen an antiwar meeting.

In the summer of 1965, a few hundred people had gathered in Washington to march in protest against the war: the first in line, historian Staughton Lynd, SNCC organizer Bob Moses, and long-time pacifist David Dellinger, were splattered with red paint by hecklers. But by 1970, the Washington peace rallies were drawing hundreds of thousands of people. In 1971, twenty thousand came to Washington to commit civil disobedience, trying to tie up Washington traffic to express their revulsion against the killing still going on in Vietnam. Fourteen thousand of them were arrested, the largest mass arrest in American history.

Hundreds of volunteers in the Peace Corps spoke out against the war. In Chile, ninety-two volunteers defied the Peace Corps director and issued a circular denouncing the war. Eight hundred former members of the Corps issued a statement of protest against what was happening in Vietnam.

The poet Robert Lowell, invited to a White House function, refused to come. Arthur Miller, also invited, sent a telegram to the White House: "When the guns boom, the arts die." Singer Eartha Kitt was invited to a luncheon on the White House lawn and shocked all those present by speaking out, in the presence of the President's wife, against the war. A teenager, called to the White House to accept a prize, came and criticized the war. In Hollywood, local artists erected a 60-foot Tower of Protest on Sunset Boulevard. At the National Book Award ceremonies in New York, fifty authors and publishers walked out on a speech by Vice-President Humphrey in a display of anger at his role in the war.

In London, two young Americans gate-crashed the American ambassador's elegant Fourth of July reception and called out a toast: "To all the dead and dying in Vietnam." They were carried out by guards. In the Pacific Ocean, two young American seamen hijacked an American munitions ship to divert its load of bombs from airbases in Thailand. For four days they took command of the ship and its crew, taking amphetamine pills to stay awake until the ship reached Cambodian waters. The Associated Press reported in late 1972, from York, Pennsylvania: "Five antiwar activists were arrested by the state police today for allegedly sabotaging railroad equipment near a factory that makes bomb casings used in the Vietnam war."

Middle-class and professional people unaccustomed to activism began to speak up. In May 1970, the *New York Times* reported from Washington: "1000 'ESTABLISHMENT' LAWYERS JOIN WAR PROTEST." Corporations began to wonder whether the war was going to hurt their long-range business interests; the *Wall Street Journal* began criticizing the continuation of the war.

As the war became more and more unpopular, people in or close to the government began to break out of the circle of assent. The most dramatic instance was the case of Daniel Ellsberg.

Ellsberg was a Harvard-trained economist, a former marine officer, employed by the RAND Corporation, which did special, often secret research for the U.S. government. Ellsberg helped write the Department of Defense history of the war in Vietnam, and then decided to make the top-secret document public, with the aid of his friend, Anthony Russo, a former RAND Corporation man. The two had met in Saigon, where both had been affected, in different experiences, by direct sight of the war, and had become powerfully indignant at what the United States was doing to the people of Vietnam.

Ellsberg and Russo spent night after night, after hours, at a friend's advertising agency, duplicating the 7,000-page document. Then Ellsberg gave copies to various Congressmen and to the *New York Times*. In June 1971 the *Times* began printing selections from what came to be known as the *Pentagon Papers*. It created a national sensation.

The Nixon administration tried to get the Supreme Court to stop further publication, but the Court said this was "prior restraint" of the freedom of the press and thus unconstitutional. The government then indicted Ellsberg and Russo for violating the Espionage Act by releasing classified documents to unauthorized people; they faced long terms in prison if convicted. The judge, however, called off the trial during the jury deliberations, because the Watergate events unfolding at the time revealed unfair practices by the prosecution.

Ellsberg, by his bold act, had broken with the usual tactic of dissidents inside the government who bided their time and kept their opinions to themselves, hoping for small changes in policy. A colleague urged him not to leave the government because there he had "access," saying, "Don't cut yourself off. Don't cut your throat." Ellsberg replied: "Life exists outside the Executive Branch."

The antiwar movement, early in its growth, found a strange, new constituency: priests and nuns of the Catholic Church. Some of them had been aroused by the civil rights movement, others by their experiences in Latin America, where they saw poverty and injustice under governments supported by the United States. In the fall of 1967, Father Philip Berrigan (a Josephite priest who was a veteran of World War II), joined by artist Tom Lewis and friends David Eberhardt and James Mengel, went to the office of a draft board in Baltimore, Maryland, drenched the draft records with blood, and waited to be arrested. They were put on trial and sentenced to prison terms of two to six years.

The following May, Philip Berrigan—out on bail in the Baltimore case—was joined in a second action by his brother Daniel, a Jesuit priest who had visited North Vietnam and seen the effects of U.S. bombing. They and seven other people went into a draft board office in Catonsville, Maryland, removed records, and set them afire outside in the presence of reporters and onlookers. They were convicted and sentenced to prison, and became famous as the "Catonsville Nine." Dan Berrigan wrote a "Meditation" at the time of the Catonsville incident:

> Our apologies, good friends, for the fracture of good order, the burning of paper instead of children, the angering of the orderlies in the front parlor of the charnel house. We could not, so help us God, do otherwise. . . . We say: killing is dis-

order, life and gentleness and community and unselfishness is the only order we recognize. For the sake of that order, we risk our liberty, our good name. The time is past when good men can remain silent, when obedience can segregate men from public risk, when the poor can die without defense.

When his appeals had been exhausted, and he was supposed to go to prison, Daniel Berrigan disappeared. While the FBI searched for him, he showed up at an Easter festival at Cornell University, where he had been teaching. With dozens of FBI men looking for him in the crowd, he suddenly appeared on stage. Then the lights went out, he hid inside a giant figure of the Bread and Puppet Theatre which was on stage, was carried out to a truck, and escaped to a nearby farmhouse. He stayed underground for four months, writing poems, issuing statements, giving secret interviews, appearing suddenly in a Philadelphia church to give a sermon and then disappearing again, baffling the FBI, until an informer's interception of a letter disclosed his whereabouts and he was captured and imprisoned.

The one woman among the Catonsville Nine, Mary Moylan, a former nun, also refused to surrender to the FBI. She was never found. Writing from underground, she reflected on her experience and how she came to it:

. . . We had all known we were going to jail, so we all had our toothbrushes. I was just exhausted. I took my little box of clothes and stuck it under the cot and climbed into bed. Now all the women in the Baltimore County jail were black—I think there was only one white. The women were waking me up and saying, "Aren't you going to cry?" I said, "What about?" They said, "You're in jail." And I said, "Yeah, I knew I'd be here." . . .

I was sleeping between two of these women, and every morning I'd wake up and they'd be leaning on their elbows watching me. They'd say, "You slept all night." And they couldn't believe it. They were good. We had good times. . . .

I suppose the political turning point in my life came while I was in Uganda. I was there when American planes were bombing the Congo, and we were very close to the Congo border. The planes came over and bombed two villages in Uganda. . . . Where the hell did the American planes come in?

Later I was in Dar Es Salaam and Chou En-lai came to town. The American Embassy sent out letters saying that no Americans were to be on the street, because this was a dirty Communist leader; but I decided this was a man who was making history and I wanted to see him. . . .

When I came home from Africa I moved to Washington, and had to deal with the scene there and the insanity and brutality of the cops and the type of life that was led by most of the citizens of that city—70 percent black. . . .

And then Vietnam, and the napalm and the defoliants, and the bombings. . . .

I got involved with the women's movement about a year ago. . . .

At the time of Catonsville, going to jail made sense to me, partially because of the black scene—so many blacks forever filling the jails. . . . I don't think it's a valid tactic anymore. . . . I don't want to see people marching off to jail with smiles on their faces. I just don't want them going. The Seventies are going to be very difficult, and I don't want to waste the sisters and brothers we have by marching them off to jail and having mystical experiences or whatever they're going to have. . . .

The effect of the war and of the bold action of some priests and nuns was to crack the traditional conservatism of the Catholic community. On Moratorium Day 1969, at the Newton College of the Sacred Heart near Boston, a sanctuary of bucolic quiet and political silence, the great front door of the college displayed a huge painted red fist. At Boston College, a Catholic institution, six thousand people gathered that evening in the gymnasium to denounce the war.

Students were heavily involved in the early protests against the war. A survey by the Urban Research Corporation, for the first six months of 1969 only, and for only 232 of the nation's two thousand institutions of higher education, showed that at least 215,000 students had participated in campus protests, that 3,652 had been arrested, that 956 had been suspended or expelled. Even in the high schools, in the late sixties, there were five hundred underground newspapers. At the Brown University commencement in 1969, two-thirds of the graduating class turned their backs when Henry Kissinger stood up to address them.

The climax of protest came in the spring of 1970 when President Nixon ordered the invasion of Cambodia. At Kent State University in Ohio, on May 4, when students gathered to demonstrate against the war, National Guardsmen fired into the crowd. Four students were killed. One was paralyzed for life. Students at four hundred colleges and universities went on strike in protest. It was the first general student strike in the history of the United States. During that school year of 1969–1970, the FBI listed 1,785 student demonstrations, including the occupation of 313 buildings.

The commencement day ceremonies after the Kent State killings were unlike any the nation had ever seen. From Amherst, Massachusetts, came this newspaper report:

The 100th Commencement of the University of Massachusetts yesterday was a protest, a call for peace.

The roll of the funeral drum set the beat for 2600 young men and women marching "in fear, in despair and in frustration."

Red fists of protest, white peace symbols, and blue doves were stenciled on black academic gowns, and nearly every other senior wore an armband representing a plea for peace.

Student protests against the ROTC (Reserve Officers Training Program) resulted in the canceling of those programs in over forty colleges and universities. In 1966, 191,749 college students enrolled in ROTC. By 1973, the number was 72,459. The ROTC was depended on to supply half the officers in Vietnam. In September 1973, for the sixth straight month, the ROTC could not fulfill its quota. One army official said: "I just hope we don't get into another war, because if we do, I doubt we could fight it."

The publicity given to the student protests created the impression that the opposition to the war came mostly from middle-class intellectuals. When some construction workers in New York attacked student demonstrators, the news was played up in the national media. However, a number of elections in American cities, including those where mostly blue-collar workers lived, showed that antiwar sentiment was strong in the working classes. For instance, in Dearborn, Michigan, an automobile manufacturing town, a poll as early as 1967 showed 41 percent of the population favored withdrawal from the Vietnam war. In 1970, in two counties in California where petitioners placed the issue on the ballot—San Francisco County and Marin County—referenda asking withdrawal of the U.S. forces from Vietnam received a majority vote.

In late 1970, when a Gallup poll presented the statement: "The United States should withdraw all troops from Vietnam by the end of next year," 65 percent of those questioned said, "Yes." In Madison, Wisconsin, in the spring of 1971, a resolution calling for an immediate withdrawal of U.S. forces from Southeast Asia won by 31,000 to 16,000 (in 1968 such a resolution had lost).

But the most surprising data were in a survey made by the University of Michigan. This showed that, throughout the Vietnam war, Americans with only a grade school education were much stronger for withdrawal from the war than Americans with a college education. In June 1966, of people with a college education, 27 percent were for immediate withdrawal from Vietnam; of people with only a grade school education, 41 percent were for immediate withdrawal. By September 1970, both groups were more antiwar: 47 percent of the college-educated were for withdrawal, and 61 percent of grade school graduates.

There is more evidence of the same kind. In an article in the *American Sociological Review* (June 1968), Richard F. Hamilton found in his survey of public opinion: "Preferences for 'tough' policy alternatives are most frequent among the following groups, the highly educated, high status occupations, those with high incomes, younger persons, and those paying much attention to newspapers and magazines." And a political scientist, Harlan Hahn, doing a study of various city referenda on Vietnam, found support for withdrawal from Vietnam highest in groups of lower socioeconomic status. He also found that the regular polls, based on samplings, underestimated the opposition to the war among lower-class people.

All this was part of a general change in the entire population of the country. In August of 1965, 61 percent of the population thought the American involvement in Vietnam was not wrong. By May 1971 it was exactly reversed; 61 percent thought our involvement *was* wrong. Bruce Andrews, a Harvard student of public opinion, found that the people most opposed to the war were people over fifty, blacks, and women. He also noted that a study in the spring of 1964, when Vietnam was a minor issue in the newspapers, showed that 53 percent of college-educated people were willing to send troops to Vietnam, but only 33 percent of grade school-educated people were so willing.

It seems that the media, themselves controlled by higher-education, higher-income people who were more aggressive in foreign policy, tended to give the erroneous impression that working-class people were superpatriots for the war. Lewis Lipsitz, in a mid-1968 survey of poor blacks and whites in the South, paraphrased an attitude he found typical: "The only way to help the poor man is to get out of that war in Vietnam. . . . These taxes—high taxes—it's going over yonder to kill people with and I don't see no cause in it."

The capacity for independent judgement among ordinary Americans is probably best shown by the swift development of antiwar feeling among American GIs—volunteers and draftees who came mostly from lower-income groups. There had been, earlier in American history, instances of soldiers' disaffection from the war: isolated mutinies in the Revolutionary War, refusal of reenlistment in the midst of hostilities in the Mexican war, desertion and conscientious objection in World War I and World War II. But Vietnam produced opposition by soldiers and veterans on a scale, and with a fervor, never seen before.

It began with isolated protests. As early as June 1965, Richard

Steinke, a West Point graduate in Vietnam, refused to board an aircraft taking him to a remote Vietnamese village. "The Vietnamese war," he said, "is not worth a single American life." Steinke was court-martialed and dismissed from the service. The following year, three army privates, one black, one Puerto Rican, one Lithuanian-Italian—all poor—refused to embark for Vietnam, denouncing the war as "immoral, illegal, and unjust." They were court-martialed and imprisoned.

In early 1967, Captain Howard Levy, an army doctor at Fort Jackson, South Carolina, refused to teach Green Berets, a Special Forces elite in the military. He said they were "murderers of women and children" and "killers of peasants." He was court-martialed on the grounds that he was trying to promote disaffection among enlisted men by his statements. The colonel who presided at the trial said: "The truth of the statements is not an issue in this case." Levy was convicted and sentenced to prison.

The individual acts multiplied: A black private in Oakland refused to board a troop plane to Vietnam, although he faced eleven years at hard labor. A navy nurse, Lieutenant Susan Schnall, was court-martialed for marching in a peace demonstration while in uniform, and for dropping antiwar leaflets from a plane on navy installations. In Norfolk, Virginia, a sailor refused to train fighter pilots because he said the war was immoral. An army lieutenant was arrested in Washington, D.C., in early 1968 for picketing the White House with a sign that said: "120,000 American Casualties—Why?" Two black marines, George Daniels and William Harvey, were given long prison sentences (Daniels, six years, Harvey, ten years, both later reduced) for talking to other black marines against the war.

As the war went on, desertions from the armed forces mounted. Thousands went to Western Europe—France, Sweden, Holland. Most deserters crossed into Canada; some estimates were 50,000, others 100,000. Some stayed in the United States. A few openly defied the military authorities by taking "sanctuary" in churches, where, surrounded by antiwar friends and sympathizers, they waited for capture and court-martial. At Boston University, a thousand students kept vigil for five days and nights in the chapel, supporting an eighteen-year-old deserter, Ray Kroll.

Kroll's story was a common one. He had been inveigled into joining the army; he came from a poor family, was brought into court, charged with drunkenness, and given the choice of prison or enlistment. He enlisted. And then he began to think about the nature of the war.

On a Sunday morning, federal agents showed up at the Boston University chapel, stomped their way through aisles clogged with students, smashed down doors, and took Kroll away. From the stockade, he wrote back to friends: "I ain't gonna kill; it's against my will. . . ." A friend he had made at the chapel brought him books, and he noted a saying he had found in one of them: "What we have done will not be lost to all Eternity. Everything ripens at its time and becomes fruit at its hour."

The GI antiwar movement became more organized. Near Fort Jackson, South Carolina, the first "GI coffeehouse" was set up, a place where soldiers could get coffee and doughnuts, find antiwar literature, and talk freely with others. It was called the UFO, and lasted for several years before it was declared a "public nuisance" and closed by court action. But other GI coffeehouses sprang up in half a dozen other places across the country. An antiwar "bookstore" was opened near Fort Devens, Massachusetts, and another one at the Newport, Rhode Island, naval base.

Underground newspapers sprang up at military bases across the country; by 1970 more than fifty were circulating. Among them: *About Face* in Los Angeles; *Fed Up!* in Tacoma, Washington; *Short Times* at Fort Jackson; *Vietnam GI* in Chicago; *Graffiti* in Heidelberg, Germany; *Bragg Briefs* in North Carolina; *Last Harass* at Fort Gordon, Georgia; *Helping Hand* at Mountain Home Air Base, Idaho. These newspapers printed antiwar articles, gave news about the harassment of GIs and practical advice on the legal rights of servicemen, told how to resist military domination.

Mixed with feeling against the war was resentment at the cruelty, the dehumanization, of military life. In the army prisons, the stockades, this was especially true. In 1968, at the Presidio stockade in California, a guard shot to death an emotionally disturbed prisoner for walking away from a work detail. Twenty-seven prisoners then sat down and refused to work, singing "We Shall Overcome." They were court-martialed, found guilty of mutiny, and sentenced to terms of up to fourteen years, later reduced after much public attention and protest.

The dissidence spread to the war front itself. When the great Moratorium Day demonstrations were taking place in October 1969 in the United States, some GIs in Vietnam wore black armbands to show their support. A news photographer reported that in a platoon on patrol near Da Nang, about half of the men were wearing black armbands. One soldier stationed at Cu Chi wrote to a friend on October 26, 1970, that separate companies had been set up for men refusing to go into the field to fight. "It's no big thing here anymore to refuse to go." The French newspaper *Le Monde* reported that in four months, 109 soldiers of the first air cavalry division were charged with refusal to fight. "A common sight," the correspondent for *Le Monde* wrote, "is the black soldier, with his left fist clenched in defiance of a war he has never considered his own."

Wallace Terry, a black American reporter for *Time* magazine, taped conversations with hundreds of black soldiers; he found bitterness against army racism, disgust with the war, generally low morale. More and more cases of "fragging" were reported in Vietnam—incidents where servicemen rolled fragmentation bombs under the tents of officers who were ordering them into combat, or against whom they had other grievances. The Pentagon reported 209 fraggings in Vietnam in 1970 alone.

Veterans back from Vietnam formed a group called Vietnam Veterans Against the War. In December 1970, hundreds of them went to Detroit to what was called the "Winter Soldier" investigations, to testify publicly about atrocities they had participated in or seen in Vietnam, committed by Americans against Vietnamese. In April 1971 more than a thousand of them went to Washington, D.C., to demonstrate against the war. One by one, they went up to a wire fence around the Capitol, threw over the fence the medals they had won in Vietnam, and made brief statements about the war, sometimes emotionally, sometimes in icy, bitter calm.

In the summer of 1970, twenty-eight commissioned officers of the military, including some veterans of Vietnam, saying they represented about 250 other officers, announced formation of the Concerned Officers Movement against the war. During the fierce bombings of Hanoi and Haiphong, around Christmas 1972, came the first defiance of B-52 pilots who refused to fly those missions.

On June 3, 1973, the *New York Times* reported dropouts among West Point cadets. Officials there, the reporter wrote, "linked the rate to an affluent, less disciplined, skeptical, and questioning generation and to the anti-military mood that a small radical minority and the Vietnam war had created."

But most of the antiwar action came from ordinary GIs, and most of these came from lower-income groups—white, black, Native American, Chinese, and Chicano. (Chicanos back home were demonstrating by the thousands against the war.)

A twenty-year-old New York City Chinese-American named Sam Choy enlisted at seventeen in the army, was sent to Vietnam, was made a cook, and found himself the target of abuse by fellow GIs, who called him "Chink" and "gook" (the term for the Vietnamese) and said he looked like the enemy. One day he took a rifle and fired warning shots at his tormenters. "By this time I was near the perimeter of the base and was thinking of joining the Viet Cong; at least they would trust me."

Choy was taken by military police, beaten, court-martialed, sentenced to eighteen months of hard labor at Fort Leavenworth. "They beat me up every day, like a time clock." He ended his interview with a New York Chinatown newspaper saying: "One thing: I want to tell all the Chinese kids that the army made me sick. They made me so sick that I can't stand it."

A dispatch from Phu Bai in April 1972 said that fifty GIs out of 142 men in the company refused to go on patrol, crying: "This isn't our war!" The *New York Times* on July 14, 1973, reported that American prisoners of war in Vietnam, ordered by officers in the POW camp to stop cooperating with the enemy, shouted back: "Who's the enemy?" They formed a peace committee in the camp, and a sergeant on the committee later recalled his march from capture to the POW camp:

> Until we got to the first camp, we didn't see a village intact; they were all destroyed. I sat down and put myself in the middle and asked myself: Is this right or wrong? Is it right to destroy villages? Is it right to kill people en masse? After a while it just got to me.

Pentagon officials in Washington and navy spokesmen in San Diego announced, after the United States withdrew its troops from Vietnam in 1973, that the navy was going to purge itself of "undesirables"—and that these included as many as six thousand men in the Pacific fleet, "a substantial proportion of them black." All together, about 700,000 GIs had received less than honorable discharges. In the year 1973, one of every five discharges was "less than honorable," indicating something less than dutiful obedience to the military. By 1971, 177 of every 1,000 American soldiers were listed as "absent without leave," some of them three or four times. Deserters doubled from 47,000 in 1967 to 89,000 in 1971.

One of those who stayed, fought, but then turned against the war was Ron Kovic. His father worked in a supermarket on Long Island. In 1963, at the age of seventeen, he enlisted in the marines. Two years later, in Vietnam, at the age of nineteen, his spine was shattered by shellfire. Paralyzed from the waist down, he was put in a wheelchair. Back in the States, he observed the brutal treatment of wounded veterans in the veterans' hospitals, thought more and more about the war, and joined the Vietnam Veterans Against the War. He went to demonstrations to speak against the war. One evening he heard actor Donald Sutherland read from the post–World War I novel by Dalton Trumbo, *Johnny Got His*

Gun, about a soldier whose limbs and face were shot away by gunfire, a thinking torso who invented a way of communicating with the outside world and then beat out a message so powerful it could not be heard without trembling.

> Sutherland began to read the passage and something I will never forget swept over me. It was as if someone was speaking for everything I ever went through in the hospital. . . . I began to shake and I remember there were tears in my eyes.

Kovic demonstrated against the war, and was arrested. He tells his story in *Born on the Fourth of July*:

> They help me back into the chair and take me to another part of the prison building to be booked.
> "What's your name?" the officer behind the desk says.
> "Ron Kovic," I say. "Occupation, Vietnam veteran against the war."
> "What?" he says sarcastically, looking down at me.
> "I'm a Vietnam veteran against the war," I almost shout back.
> "You should have died over there," he says. He turns to his assistant. "I'd like to take this guy and throw him off the roof."
> They fingerprint me and take my picture and put me in a cell. I have begun to wet my pants like a little baby. The tube has slipped out during my examination by the doctor. I try to fall asleep but even though I am exhausted, the anger is alive in me like a huge hot stone in my chest. I lean my head up against the wall and listen to the toilets flush again and again.

Kovic and the other veterans drove to Miami to the Republican National Convention in 1972, went into the Convention Hall, wheeled themselves down the aisles, and as Nixon began his acceptance speech shouted, "Stop the bombing! Stop the war!" Delegates cursed them: "Traitor!" and Secret Service men hustled them out of the hall.

In the fall of 1973, with no victory in sight and North Vietnamese troops entrenched in various parts of the South, the United States agreed to accept a settlement that would withdraw American troops and leave the revolutionary troops where they were, until a new elected government would be set up including Communist and non-Communist elements. But the Saigon government refused to agree, and the United States decided to make one final attempt to bludgeon the North Vietnamese into submission. It sent waves of B-52s over Hanoi and Haiphong, destroying homes and hospitals, killing unknown numbers of civilians. The attack did not work. Many of the B-52s were shot down, there was angry protest all over the world—and Kissinger went back to Paris and signed very much the same peace agreement that had been agreed on before.

The United States withdrew its forces, continuing to give aid to the Saigon government, but when the North Vietnamese launched attacks in early 1975 against the major cities in South Vietnam, the government collapsed. In late April 1975, North Vietnamese troops entered Saigon. The American embassy staff fled, along with many Vietnamese who feared Communist rule, and the long war in Vietnam was over. Saigon was renamed Ho Chi Minh City, and both parts of Vietnam were unified as the Democratic Republic of Vietnam.

Traditional history portrays the end of wars as coming from the initiatives of leaders—negotiations in Paris or Brussels or Geneva or Versailles—just as it often finds the coming of war a response to the demand of "the people." The Vietnam war gave clear evidence that at least for that war (making one wonder about the others) the political leaders were the last to take steps to end the war—"the people" were far ahead. The President was always far behind. The Supreme Court silently turned away from cases challenging the Constitutionality of the war. Congress was years behind public opinion.

In the spring of 1971, syndicated columnists Rowland Evans and Robert Novak, two firm supporters of the war, wrote regretfully of a "sudden outbreak of anti-war emotionalism" in the House of Representatives, and said: "The anti-war animosities now suddenly so pervasive among House Democrats are viewed by Administration backers as less anti-Nixon than as a response to constituent pressures."

It was only after the intervention in Cambodia ended, and only after the nationwide campus uproar over that invasion, that Congress passed a resolution declaring that American troops should not be sent into Cambodia without its approval. And it was not until late 1973, when American troops had finally been removed from Vietnam, that Congress passed a bill limiting the power of the President to make war without congressional consent; even there, in that "War Powers Resolution," the President could make war for sixty days on his own without a congressional declaration.

The administration tried to persuade the American people that the war was ending because of its decision to negotiate a peace—not because it was losing the war, not because of the powerful antiwar movement in the United States. But the government's own secret memoranda all through the war testify to its sensitivity at each stage about "public opinion" in the United States and abroad. The data is in the *Pentagon Papers*.

In June of 1964, top American military and State Department officials, including Ambassador Henry Cabot Lodge, met in Honolulu. "Rusk stated that public opinion on our SEA policy was badly divided and that, therefore, the President needed an affirmation of support." Diem had been replaced by a general named Khanh. The Pentagon historians write: "Upon his return to Saigon on June 5 Ambassador Lodge went straight from the airport to call on General Khanh . . . the main thrust of his talk with Khanh was to hint that the United States Government would in the immediate future be preparing U.S. public opinion for actions against North Vietnam." Two months later came the Gulf of Tonkin affair.

On April 2, 1965, a memo from CIA director John McCone suggested that the bombing of North Vietnam be increased because it was "not sufficiently severe" to change North Vietnam's policy. "On the other hand . . . we can expect increasing pressure to stop the bombing . . . from various elements of the American public, from the press, the United Nations and world opinion." The U.S. should try for a fast knockout before this opinion could build up, McCone said.

Assistant Secretary of Defense John McNaughton's memo of early 1966 suggested destruction of locks and dams to create mass starvation, because "strikes at population targets" would "create a counterproductive wave of revulsion abroad and at home." In May 1967, the Pentagon historians write: "McNaughton was also very deeply concerned about the breadth and intensity of public unrest and dissatisfaction with the war . . . especially with young people, the underprivileged, the intelligentsia and the women." McNaughton worried: "Will the move to call up 20,000 Reserves . . . polarize opinion to the extent that the 'doves' in the United States will get out of hand—massive refusals to serve, or to fight, or to cooperate, or worse?" He warned:

There may be a limit beyond which many Americans and much of the world will not permit the United States to go. The picture of the world's greatest superpower killing or seriously injuring 1000 non-combatants a week, while trying to pound a tiny backward nation into submission, on an issue whose merits are hotly disputed, is not a pretty one. It could conceivably produce a costly distortion in the American national consciousness.

That "costly distortion" seems to have taken place by the spring of 1968, when, with the sudden and scary Tet offensive of the National

Liberation Front, Westmoreland asked President Johnson to send him 200,000 more troops on top of the 525,000 already there. Johnson asked a small group of "action officers" in the Pentagon to advise him on this. They studied the situation and concluded that 200,000 troops would totally Americanize the war and would not strengthen the Saigon government because: "The Saigon leadership shows no signs of a willingness—let alone an ability—to attract the necessary loyalty or support of the people." Furthermore, the report said, sending troops would mean mobilizing reserves, increasing the military budget. There would be more U.S. casualties, more taxes. And:

> This growing disaffection accompanied as it certainly will be, by increased defiance of the draft and growing unrest in the cities because of the belief that we are neglecting domestic problems, runs great risks of provoking a domestic crisis of unprecedented proportions.

The "growing unrest in the cities" must have been a reference to the black uprisings that had taken place in 1967—and showed the link, whether blacks deliberately made it or not—between the war abroad and poverty at home.

The evidence from the *Pentagon Papers* is clear—that Johnson's decision in the spring of 1968 to turn down Westmoreland's request, to slow down for the first time the escalation of the war, to diminish the bombing, to go to the conference table, was influenced to a great extent by the actions Americans had taken in demonstrating their opposition to the war.

When Nixon took office, he too tried to persuade the public that protest would not affect him. But he almost went berserk when one lone pacifist picketed the White House. The frenzy of Nixon's actions against dissidents—plans for burglaries, wiretapping, mail openings—suggests the importance of the antiwar movement in the minds of national leaders.

One sign that the ideas of the antiwar movement had taken hold in the American public was that juries became more reluctant to convict antiwar protesters, and local judges too were treating them differently. In Washington, by 1971, judges were dismissing charges against demonstrators in cases where two years before they almost certainly would have been sent to jail. The antiwar groups who had raided draft boards—the Baltimore Four, the Catonsville Nine, the Milwaukee Fourteen, the Boston Five, and more—were receiving lighter sentences for the same crimes.

The last group of draft board raiders, the "Camden 28," were priests, nuns, and laypeople who raided a draft board in Camden, New Jersey, in August 1971. It was essentially what the Baltimore Four had done four years earlier, when all were convicted and Phil Berrigan got six years in prison. But in this instance, the Camden defendants were acquitted by the jury on all counts. When the verdict was in, one of the jurors, a fifty-three-year-old black taxi driver from Atlantic City named Samuel Braithwaite, who had spent eleven years in the army, left a letter for the defendants:

> To you, the clerical physicians with your God-given talents, I say, well done. Well done for trying to heal the sick irresponsible men, men who were chosen by the people to govern and lead them. These men, who failed the people, by raining death and destruction on a hapless country. . . . You went out to do your part while your brothers remained in their ivory towers watching . . . and hopefully some day in the near future, peace and harmony may reign to people of all nations.

That was in May of 1973. The American troops were leaving Vietnam. C. L. Sulzberger, the *New York Times* correspondent (a man close to the government), wrote: "The U.S. emerges as the big loser and history books must admit this. . . . We lost the war in the Mississippi valley, not the Mekong valley. Successive American governments were never able to muster the necessary mass support at home."

In fact, the United States had lost the war in both the Mekong Valley and the Mississippi Valley. It was the first clear defeat to the global American empire formed after World War II. It was administered by revolutionary peasants abroad, and by an astonishing movement of protest at home.

Back on September 26, 1969, President Richard Nixon, noting the growing antiwar activity all over the country, announced that "under no circumstance will I be affected whatever by it." But nine years later, in his *Memoirs*, he admitted that the antiwar movement caused him to drop plans for an intensification of the war: "Although publicly I continued to ignore the raging antiwar controversy. . . . I knew, however, that after all the protests and the Moratorium, American public opinion would be seriously divided by any military escalation of the war." It was a rare presidential admission of the power of public protest.

From a long-range viewpoint, something perhaps even more important had happened. The rebellion at home was spreading beyond the issue of war in Vietnam.

19

SURPRISES

Helen Keller had said in 1911: "We vote? What does that mean?" And Emma Goldman around the same time: "Our modern fetish is universal suffrage." After 1920, women were voting, as men did, and their subordinate condition had hardly changed.

Right after women got the vote, the measure of their social progress can be seen in an advice column written by Dorothy Dix that appeared in newspapers all over the country. The woman should not merely be a domestic drudge, she said:

> . . . a man's wife is the show window where he exhibits the measure of his achievement. . . . The biggest deals are put across over luncheon tables; . . . we meet at dinner the people who can push our fortunes. . . . The woman who cultivates a circle of worthwhile people, who belongs to clubs, who makes herself interesting and agreeable . . . is a help to her husband.

Robert and Helen Lynd, studying Muncie, Indiana (*Middletown*), in the late twenties, noted the importance of good looks and dress in the assessment of women. Also, they found that when men spoke frankly among themselves they were "likely to speak of women as creatures purer and morally better than men but as relatively impractical, emotional, unstable, given to prejudice, easily hurt, and largely incapable of facing facts or doing hard thinking."

A writer in early 1930, boosting the beauty business, started off a magazine article with the sentence: "The average American woman has sixteen square feet of skin." He went on to say that there were forty thousand beauty shops in the country, and that $2 billion was spent each year on cosmetics for women—but this was insufficient: "American women are not yet spending even one-fifth of the amount necessary to improve their appearance." He then gave an itemized list of the "annual beauty needs of every woman": twelve hot-oil treatments, fifty-two facials, twenty-six eyebrow plucks, etc.

It seems that women have best been able to make their first escape from the prison of wifeliness, motherhood, femininity, housework, beautification, isolation, when their services have been desperately needed—whether in industry, or in war, or in social movements. Each time practicality pulled the woman out of her prison—in a kind of work-parole program—the attempt was made to push her back once the need was over, and this led to women's struggle for change.

World War II had brought more women than ever before out of the home into work. By 1960, 36 percent of all women sixteen and older—23 million women—worked for paid wages. But although 43 percent of women with school-age children worked, there were nursery schools for only 2 percent—the rest had to work things out themselves. Women were 50 percent of the voters—but (even by 1967) they held 4 percent of the state legislative seats, and 2 percent of the judgeships. The median income of the working woman was about one-third that of the man. And attitudes toward women did not seem to have changed much since the twenties.

"There is no overt anti-feminism in our society in 1964," wrote feminist and sociologist Alice Rossi, "not because sex equality has been achieved, but because there is practically no feminist spark left among American women."

In the civil rights movement of the sixties, the signs of a collective stirring began to appear. Women took the place they customarily took in social movements, in the front lines—as privates, not generals. In the office of the Student Nonviolent Coordinating Committee in Atlanta, a Spelman College student named Ruby Doris Smith, who had been jailed during the sit-ins, expressed her anger at the way women were relegated to the routine office work, and she was joined in her protest by two white women in SNCC, Sandra Hayden and Mary King. The men in SNCC listened to them respectfully, read the position paper they had put together asserting their rights, but did not do very much. Ella Baker, a veteran fighter from Harlem, now organizing in the South, knew the pattern: "I knew from the beginning that as a woman, an older woman in a group of ministers who are accustomed to having women largely as supporters, there was no place for me to have come into a leadership role."

Nevertheless, women played a crucial role in those early dangerous years of organizing in the South, and were looked on with admiration. Many of these were older women like Ella Baker, and Amelia Boynton in Selma, Alabama, and "Mama Dolly" in Albany, Georgia. Younger women—Gloria Richardson in Maryland, Annelle Ponder in Mississippi—were not only active, but leaders. Women of all ages demonstrated, went to jail. Mrs. Fannie Lou Hamer, a sharecropper in Ruleville, Mississippi, became legendary as organizer and speaker. She sang hymns; she walked picket lines with her familiar limp (as a child she contracted polio). She roused people to excitement at mass meetings: "I'm sick an' tired o' bein' sick an' tired!"

Around the same time, white, middle-class, professional women were beginning to speak up. A pioneering, early book, strong and influential, was Betty Friedan's *The Feminine Mystique*.

> Just what was the problem that has no name? What were the words women used when they tried to express it? Sometimes a woman would say "I feel empty somehow . . . incomplete." Or she would say, "I feel as if I don't exist." Sometimes. . . . "A tired feeling . . . I get so angry with the children it scares me. . . . I feel like crying without any reason."

Friedan wrote out of her experience as a middle-class housewife, but what she spoke about touched something inside all women:

> The problem lay buried, unspoken for many years in the minds of American women. It was a strange stirring, a sense of dissatisfaction, a yearning that women suffered in the middle of the twentieth century in the United States. Each suburban wife struggled with it alone. As she made the beds, shopped for groceries, matched slip-cover material, ate peanut butter sandwiches with her children, chauffeured Cub Scouts and Brownies, lay beside her husband at night—she was afraid to ask even of herself the silent question—"Is this all?". . .
>
> But on an April morning in 1959, I heard a mother of four, having coffee with four other mothers in a suburban development fifteen miles from New York, say in a tone of quiet desperation, "the problem." And the others knew, without words, that she was not talking about a problem with her husband, or her children, or her home. Suddenly they realized they all shared the same problem, the problem that has no name. They began, hesitantly, to talk about it. Later, after they had picked up their children at nursery school and taken them home to nap, two of the women cried, in sheer relief, just to know they were not alone.

The "mystique" that Friedan spoke of was the image of the woman as mother, as wife, living through her husband, through her children, giving up her own dreams for that. She concluded: "The only way for a woman, as for a man, to find herself, to know herself as a person, is by creative work of her own."

In the summer of 1964, in McComb, Mississippi, at a Freedom House (a civil rights headquarters where people worked and lived together) the women went on strike against the men who wanted them to cook and make beds while the men went around in cars organizing. The stirring that Friedan spoke of was true of women everywhere, it seemed.

By 1969, women were 40 percent of the entire labor force of the United States, but a substantial number of these were secretaries, cleaning women, elementary school teachers, saleswomen, waitresses, and nurses. One out of every three working women had a husband earning less than $5,000 a year.

What of the women who didn't have jobs? They worked very hard, at home, but this wasn't looked on as work, because in a capitalist society (or perhaps in any modern society where things and people are bought and sold for money), if work is not paid for, not given a money value, it is considered valueless. Women began to think more about this fact in the 1960s, and Margaret Benston wrote about it ("The Political Economy of Women's Liberation"). Women doing housework were people outside the modern economic system, therefore they were like serfs or peasants, she said.

The women who worked in the typical "woman's job"—secretary, receptionist, typist, salesperson, cleaning woman, nurse—were treated to the full range of humiliations that men in subordinate positions faced at work, plus another set of humiliations stemming from being a woman: gibes at their mental processes, sexual jokes and aggression, invisibility except as sexual objects, cold demands for more efficiency. A commercial "Guide to Clerical Times Standards" printed a question-and-answer column:

Q. I'm a businessman, and my secretary seems to move entirely too slowly. How many times a minute should she be able to open and close a file drawer?
A. Exactly 25 times. Times for other "open and close operations" . . . are .04 minutes for opening or closing a folder, and .026 minutes for opening a standard center desk drawer. If you're worried about her "chair activity," clock her against these standards: "Got up from chair," .033 minutes; "turn in swivel chair," .009 minutes.

A woman factory worker in New Bedford, Massachusetts, in the early seventies, in a medium-sized corporation whose president's dividends from the corporation in 1970 amounted to $325,000, wrote in an organizing newspaper that 90 percent of the workers in her department were women, but all the supervisors were men.

> A few years ago I was suspended for three days from work because my children were still young and I had to take time off when they were sick. . . . They want people who keep quiet, squeal on one another, and are very good little robots. The fact that many have to take nerve pills before starting their day, and a week doesn't go by that there aren't two or three people who break down and cry, doesn't mean a thing to them.

She added: "But times are changing, and from now on, more people will speak out and demand from their so-called bosses that they be treated the way the bosses themselves would like to be treated."

Times indeed were changing. Around 1967, women in the various movements—civil rights, Students for a Democratic Society, antiwar groups—began meeting as women, and in early 1968, at a women's antiwar meeting in Washington, hundreds of women carrying torches paraded to the Arlington National Cemetery and staged "The Burial of Traditional Womanhood." At this point, and later too, there was some disagreement among women, and even more among men, on whether women should battle on specifically women's issues, or just take part in general movements against racism, war, capitalism. But the idea of a feminist focus grew.

In the fall of 1968, a group called Radical Women attracted national attention when they protested the selection of Miss America, which they called "an image that oppresses women." They all threw bras, girdles, curlers, false eyelashes, wigs, and other things they called "women's garbage" into a Freedom Trash Can. A sheep was crowned Miss America. More important, people were beginning to speak of "Women's Liberation."

Some of the New York Radical Women shortly afterward formed WITCH (Women's International Terrorist Conspiracy from Hell), and its members, dressed as witches, appeared suddenly on the floor of the New York Stock Exchange. A leaflet put out by WITCH in New York said:

> WITCH lives and laughs in every woman. She is the free part of each of us, beneath the shy smiles, the acquiescence to absurd male domination, the

make-up or flesh-suffocating clothes our sick society demands. There is no "joining" WITCH. If you are a woman and dare to look within yourself, you are a WITCH. You make your own rules.

WITCH in Washington, D.C., protested at the United Fruit Company for the corporation's activities in the Third World and its treatment of its women office workers. In Chicago it protested the firing of a radical feminist teacher named Marlene Dixon.

Poor women, black women, expressed the universal problem of women in their own way. In 1964 Robert Coles *(Children of Crisis)* interviewed a black woman from the South recently moved to Boston, who spoke of the desperation of her life, the difficulty of finding happiness: "To me, having a baby inside me is the only time I'm really alive."

Without talking specifically about their problems as women, many women, among the poor, did as they had always done, quietly organized neighborhood people to right injustices, to get needed services. In the mid-1960s, ten thousand black people in a community in Atlanta called Vine City joined together to help one another: they set up a thrift shop, a nursery, a medical clinic, monthly family suppers, a newspaper, a family counseling service. One of the organizers, Helen Howard, told Gerda Lerner *(Black Women in White America)* about it:

I organized this neighborhood organization, two men and six ladies started it. That was a hard pull. A lot of people joined in later. For about five months we had meetings pretty near every night. We learned how to work with other people. . . . A lot of people were afraid to really do anything. You were afraid to go to the city hall or ask for anything. You didn't even ask the landlord for anything, you were afraid of him. Then we had meetings and then we weren't afraid so much anymore. . . .

The way we got this playground: we blocked off the street, wouldn't let anything come through. We wouldn't let the trolley bus come through. The whole neighborhood was in it. Took record players and danced; it went on for a week. We didn't get arrested, they was too many of us. So then the city put up this playground for the kids. . . .

A woman named Patricia Robinson wrote a pamphlet called *Poor Black Woman*, in which she connected the problems of women with the need for basic social change:

Rebellion by poor black women, the bottom of a class hierarchy heretofore not discussed, places the question of what kind of society will the poor black woman demand and struggle for. Already she demands the right to have birth control, like middle class black and white women. She is aware that it takes two to oppress and that she and other poor people no longer are submitting to oppression, in this case genocide. She allies herself with the have-nots in the wider world and their revolutionary struggles. She had been forced by historical conditions to withdraw the children from male dominance and to educate and support them herself. In this very process, male authority and exploitation are seriously weakened. Further, she realizes that the children will be used as all poor children have been used through history—as poorly paid mercenaries fighting to keep or put an elite group in power. Through these steps . . . she has begun to question aggressive male domination and the class society which enforces it, capitalism.

In 1970, Dorothy Bolden, a laundry worker in Atlanta and mother of six, told why in 1968 she began organizing women doing housework, into the National Domestic Workers Union. She said: "I think women should have a voice in making decisions in their community for betterment. Because this woman in the slum is scuffling hard, and she's got a very good intelligent mind to do things, and she's been overlooked for so many years. I think she should have a voice."

Women tennis players organized. A woman fought to be a jockey, won her case, became the first woman jockey. Women artists picketed the Whitney Museum, charging sex discrimination in a sculptors' show. Women journalists picketed the Gridiron Club in Washington, which excluded women. By the start of 1974, women's studies programs existed at seventy-eight institutions, and about two thousand courses on women were being offered at about five hundred campuses.

Women's magazines and newspapers began appearing, locally and nationally, and books on women's history and the movement came out in such numbers that some bookstores had special sections for them. The very jokes on television, some sympathetic, some caustic, showed how national was the effect of the movement. Certain television commercials, which women felt humiliated them, were eliminated after protest.

In 1967, after lobbying by women's groups, President Johnson signed an executive order banning sex discrimination in federally connected employment, and in the years that followed, women's groups demanded that this be enforced. Over a thousand suits were initiated by NOW (National Organization for Women, formed in 1966) against U.S. corporations charging sex discrimination.

The right to abortion became a major issue. Before 1970, about a million abortions were done every year, of which only about ten thousand were legal. Perhaps a third of the women having illegal abortions—mostly poor people—had to be hospitalized for complications. How many thousands died as a result of these illegal abortions no one really knows. But the illegalization of abortion clearly worked against the poor, for the rich could manage either to have their baby or to have their abortion under safe conditions.

Court actions to do away with the laws against abortions were begun in over twenty states between 1968 and 1970, and public opinion grew stronger for the right of women to decide for themselves without government interference. In the book *Sisterhood Is Powerful*, an important collection of women's writing around 1970, an article by Lucinda Cisler, "Unfinished Business: Birth Control," said that "abortion is a woman's right . . . no one can veto her decision and compel her to bear a child against her will. . . ." In the spring of 1969 a Harris poll showed that 64 percent of those polled thought the decision on abortion was a private matter.

Finally, in early 1973, the Supreme Court decided (*Roe* v. *Wade, Doe* v. *Bolton*) that the state could prohibit abortions only in the last three months of pregnancy, that it could regulate abortion for health purposes during the second three months of pregnancy, and during the first three months, a woman and her doctor had the right to decide.

There was a push for child care centers, and although women did not succeed in getting much help from government, thousands of cooperative child care centers were set up.

Women also began to speak openly, for the first time, about the problem of rape. Each year, fifty thousand rapes were reported and many more were unreported. Women began taking self-defense courses. There were protests against the way police treated women, interrogated them, insulted them, when women filed rape charges. A book by Susan Brownmiller, *Against Our Will*, was widely read—it is a powerful, indignant history and analysis of rape, suggesting self-defense, individual or collective:

> Fighting back. On a multiplicity of levels, that is the activity we must engage in, together, if we—women—are to redress the imbalance and rid ourselves and men of the ideology of rape. Rape can be eradicated, not merely controlled or avoided on an individual basis, but the approach must be long-range and cooperative, and must have the understanding and good will of many men as well as women. . . .

Many women were active in trying to get a Constitutional amendment, ERA (Equal Rights Amendment), passed by enough states. But it seemed clear that even if it became law, it would not be enough, that what women had accomplished had come through organization, action, protest. Even where the law was helpful it was helpful only if backed by action. Shirley Chisholm, a black Congresswoman, said:

> The law cannot do it for us. We must do it for ourselves. Women in this country must become revolutionaries. We must refuse to accept the old, the traditional roles and stereotypes. . . . We must replace the old, negative thoughts about our femininity with positive thoughts and positive action. . . .

Perhaps the most profound effect of the women's movement of the sixties—beyond the actual victories on abortion, in job equality—was called "consciousness raising," often done in "women's groups," which met in homes all across the country. This meant the rethinking of roles, the rejection of inferiority, the confidence in self, a bond of sisterhood, a new solidarity of mother and daughter. The Atlanta poet Esta Seaton wrote "Her Life":

> This is the picture that keeps forming in my mind:
> my young mother, barely seventeen,
> cooking their Kosher dinner on the coal stove,
> that first winter in Vermont,
> and my father, mute in his feelings
> except when he shouted,
> eating to show his love.
>
> Fifty years later her blue eyes would grow cold
> with the shock of that grey house
> and the babies one after another
> and the doctor who said
> "If you don't want any more children
> move out of the house."

For the first time, the sheer biological uniqueness of women was openly discussed. Some theorists (Shulamith Firestone, in *The Dialectics of Sex*, for instance) thought this was more fundamental to their oppression than any particular economic system. It was liberating to talk frankly about what had for so long been secret, hidden, cause for shame and embarrassment: menstruation, masturbation, menopause, abortion, lesbianism.

One of the most influential books to appear in the early seventies was a book assembled by eleven women in the Boston Women's Health

Book Collective called *Our Bodies, Ourselves*. It contained an enormous amount of practical information, on women's anatomy, on sexuality and sexual relationships, on lesbianism, on nutrition and health, on rape, self-defense, venereal disease, birth control, abortion, pregnancy, child-birth, and menopause. More important even than the information, the charts, the photos, the candid exploration of the previously unmentioned, was the mood of exuberance throughout the book, the enjoyment of the body, the happiness with the new-found understanding, the new sisterhood with young women, middle-aged women, older women. They quoted the English suffragette Christabel Pankhurst:

> Remember the dignity
> of your womanhood.
> Do not appeal,
> do not beg,
> do not grovel.
> Take courage
> join hands,
> stand beside us.
> Fight with us. . . .

The fight began, many women were saying, with the body, which seemed to be the beginning of the exploitation of women—as sex plaything (weak and incompetent), as pregnant woman (helpless), as middle-aged woman (no longer considered beautiful), as older woman (to be ignored, set aside). A biological prison had been created by men and society. As Adrienne Rich said *(Of Woman Born)*: "Women are controlled by lashing us to our bodies." She wrote:

> I have a very clear, keen memory of myself the day after I was married: I was sweeping a floor. Probably the floor did not really need to be swept; probably I simply did not know what else to do with myself. But as I swept that floor I thought: "Now I am a woman. This is an age-old action, this is what women have always done." I felt I was bending to some ancient form, too ancient to question. *This is what women have always done.*
>
> As soon as I was visibly and clearly pregnant, I felt, for the first time in my adolescent and adult life, not-guilty. The atmosphere of approval in which I was bathed—even by strangers on the street, it seemed—was like an aura I carried with me, in which doubts, fears, misgivings met with absolute denial. *This is what women have always done.. . .*

Rich said women could use the body "as a resource, rather than a destiny." Patriarchal systems, she said, whether under capitalism or "socialism," limited women's bodies to their own needs. She discussed the training of passivity in women. Generations of schoolgirls were raised on *Little Women*, where Jo is told by her mother: "I am angry nearly every day of my life, Jo; but I have learned not to show it; and I still hope to learn not to feel it, though it may take me another forty years to do so."

Male doctors used instruments to bring out children, replacing the sensitive hands of midwives, in the era of "anesthetized, technologized childbirth." Rich disagreed with her fellow feminist Firestone, who wanted to change the biological inevitability of childbirth, because it is painful and a source of subordination; she wanted, under different social conditions, to make childbirth a source of physical and emotional joy.

One could not talk of Freud's ignorance of women, Rich said, as his one "blind spot," which implied that in other matters his vision was clear; such ignorance distorts all. There is a dilemma of the body:

> I know no woman—virgin, mother, lesbian, married, celibate—whether she earns her keep as a housewife, a cocktail waitress, or a scanner of brain waves—for whom her body is not a fundamental problem: its clouded meaning, its fertility, its desire, its so-called frigidity, its bloody speech, its silences, its changes and mutilations, its rapes and ripenings.

Her reply to this: the "repossession of our bodies . . . a world in which every woman is the presiding genius of her own body" as a basis for bringing forth not just children but new visions, new meanings, a new world.

For most women who were not intellectuals, the question was even more immediate: how to eliminate hunger, suffering, subordination, humiliation, in the here and now. A woman named Johnnie Tillmon wrote in 1972:

> I'm a woman. I'm a black woman. I'm a poor woman. I'm a fat woman. I'm a middle-aged woman. And I'm on welfare. . . . I have raised six children. . . . I grew up in Arkansas . . . worked there for fifteen years in a laundry . . . moved to California. . . . In 1963 I got too sick to work anymore. Friends helped me to go on welfare. . . .
>
> Welfare's like a traffic accident. It can happen to anybody, but especially it happens to women.
>
> And that is why welfare is a women's issue. For a lot of middle-class women in this country, Women's Liberation is a matter of concern. For women on welfare it's a matter of survival.

Welfare, she said, was like "a supersexist marriage. You trade in *a* man for *the* man. . . . *The* man runs everything . . . controls your money. . . ." She and other welfare mothers organized a National Welfare Rights Organization. They urged that women be paid for their work—housekeeping, child rearing. ". . . No woman can be liberated, until all women get off their knees."

In the problem of women was the germ of a solution, not only for their oppression, but for everybody's. The control of women in society was ingeniously effective. It was not done directly by the state. Instead, the family was used—men to control women, women to control children, all to be preoccupied with one another, to turn to one another for help, to blame one another for trouble, to do violence to one another when things weren't going right. Why could this not be turned around? Could women liberating themselves, children freeing themselves, men and women beginning to understand one another, find the source of their common oppression outside rather than in one another? Perhaps then they could create nuggets of strength in their own relationships, millions of pockets of insurrection. They could revolutionize thought and behavior in exactly that seclusion of family privacy which the system had counted on to do its work of control and indoctrination. And together, instead of at odds—male, female, parents, children—they could undertake the changing of society itself.

It was a time of uprisings. If there could be rebellion inside that most subtle and complex of prisons—the family—it was reasonable that there be rebellions in the most brutal and obvious of prisons: the penitentiary system itself. In the sixties and early seventies, those rebellions multiplied. They also took on an unprecedented political character and the ferocity of class war, coming to a climax at Attica, New York, in September of 1971.

The prison had arisen in the United States as an attempt at Quaker reform, to replace mutilation, hanging, exile—the traditional punishments during colonial times. The prison was intended, through isolation, to produce repentance and salvation, but prisoners went insane and died in that isolation. By mid-nineteenth century, the prison was based on hard labor, along with various punishments: sweat boxes, iron yokes, solitary. The approach was summed up by the warden at the Ossining, New York, penitentiary: "In order to reform a criminal you must first break his spirit." That approach persisted.

Prison officials would convene annually to congratulate themselves on the progress being made. The president of the American Correctional

Association, delivering the annual address in 1966, described the new edition of the *Manual of Correctional Standards*: "It permits us to linger, if we will, at the gates of correctional Valhalla—with an abiding pride in the sense of a job superbly done! We may be proud, we may be satisfied, we may be content." He said this just after, in the midst of, and just before the most intense series of prison uprisings the country had ever seen.

There had always been prison riots. A wave of them in the 1920s ended with a riot at Clinton, New York, a prison of 1,600 inmates, which was suppressed with three prisoners killed. Between 1950 and 1953 more than fifty major riots occurred in American prisons. In the early 1960s, prisoners on a work gang in Georgia smashing rocks used the same sledgehammers to break their legs, to call attention to their situation of daily brutality.

At San Quentin prison in California, which housed four thousand prisoners, there was a series of revolts in the late sixties: a race riot in 1967, a united black-white general strike in early 1968 that shut down almost all the prison industries, and then a second strike that summer.

At the Queens House of Detention on Long Island in New York in the fall of 1970, prisoners took over the jail, took hostages, issued demands. The prisoners' negotiating committee included four blacks, one Puerto Rican, one white; they demanded immediate bail hearings on forty-seven cases that they said were examples of racism in the granting of bail. Judges came inside the prison, granted some paroles and reductions, and the hostages were released. But when the prisoners continued to hold out, police stormed the jail with tear gas and clubs and the revolt was over.

Around the same time, in November 1970, in Folsom prison in California, a work stoppage began which became the longest prison strike in the history of the United States. Most of the 2,400 prisoners held out in their cells for nineteen days, without food, in the face of threats and intimidation. The strike was broken with a combination of force and deception, and four of the prisoners were sent on a fourteen-hour ride to another prison, shackled and naked on the floor of a van. One of the rebels wrote: ". . . the spirit of awareness has grown. . . . The seed has been planted. . . ."

The prisons in the United States had long been an extreme reflection of the American system itself: the stark life differences between rich and poor, the racism, the use of victims against one another, the lack of resources of the underclass to speak out, the endless "reforms" that changed little. Dostoevski once said: "The degree of civilization in a society can be judged by entering its prisons."

It had long been true, and prisoners knew this better than anyone, that the poorer you were the more likely you were to end up in jail. This was not just because the poor committed more crimes. In fact, they did. The rich did not have to commit crimes to get what they wanted; the laws were on their side. But when the rich did commit crimes, they often were not prosecuted, and if they were they could get out on bail, hire clever lawyers, get better treatment from judges. Somehow, the jails ended up full of poor black people.

In 1969, there were 502 convictions for tax fraud. Such cases, called "white-collar crimes," usually involve people with a good deal of money. Of those convicted, 20 percent ended up in jail. The fraud averaged $190,000 per case; their sentences averaged seven months. That same year, for burglary and auto theft (crimes of the poor) 60 percent ended up in prison. The auto thefts averaged $992; the sentences averaged eighteen months. The burglaries averaged $321; the sentences averaged thirty-three months.

Willard Gaylin, a psychiatrist, relates (*Partial Justice*) a case which, with changes in details, could be multiplied thousands of times. He had just interviewed seventeen Jehovah's Witnesses who refused to register for the draft during the Vietnam war, and all had received two-year sentences. He came to a young black man who had notified his draft board he could not in conscience cooperate with the draft because he was repelled by the violence of the Vietnam war. He received a five-year sentence. Gaylin writes: "Hank's was the first five-year sentence I had encountered. He was also the first black man." There were additional factors:

"How was your hair then?" I asked.

"Afro."

"And what were you wearing?"

"A dashiki."

"Don't you think that might have affected your sentence?"

"Of course."

"Was it worth a year or two of your life?" I asked.

"That's all of my life," he said, looking at me with a combination of dismay and confusion. "Man, don't you know! That's what it's all about! Am I free to have my style, am I free to have my hair, am I free to have my skin?"

"Of course," I said. "You're right."

Gaylin found enormous discretion given to judges in the handing out of sentences. In Oregon, of thirty-three men convicted of violating the draft law, eighteen were put on probation. In southern Texas, of sixteen men violating the same law, none was put on probation, and in southern Mississippi, every defendant was convicted and given the maximum of five years. In one part of the country (New England), the average sentence for all crimes was eleven months; in another part (the South), it was seventy-eight months. But it wasn't simply a matter of North and South. In New York City, one judge handling 673 persons brought before him for public drunkenness (all poor; the rich get drunk behind closed doors) discharged 531 of them. Another judge, handling 566 persons on the same charge, discharged one person.

With such power in the hands of the courts, the poor, the black, the odd, the homosexual, the hippie, the radical are not likely to get equal treatment before judges who are almost uniformly white, upper middle class, orthodox.

While in any one year (1972, for instance) perhaps 375,000 people will be in jail (county or city) or in prisons (state or federal), and 54,000 in juvenile detention, there will also be 900,000 under probation and 300,000 on parole—a total of 1,600,000 people affected by the criminal justice system. Considering turnover, in any one year, several million people will come in and go out of this system. It is a population largely invisible to middle-class America, but if 20 million blacks could be invisible for so long, why not four or five million "criminals"? A study by the Children's Defense Fund (Thomas Cottle, *Children in Jail*) in the mid-seventies revealed that more than 900,000 young people under eighteen are jailed in the course of a year.

Anyone trying to describe the reality of prison falters. A man in Walpole prison in Massachusetts wrote:

> Every program that we get is used as a weapon against us. The right to go to school, to go to church, to have visitors, to write, to go to the movies. They all end up being weapons of punishment. None of the programs are *ours*. Everything is treated as a privilege that can be taken away from us. The result is insecurity—a frustration that keeps eating away at you.

Another Walpole prisoner:

> I haven't eaten in the mess hall for four years. I just couldn't take it any more. You'd go into the serving line in the morning and 100 or 200 cockroaches would go running away from the trays. The trays were grimy and the food was raw or had dirt or maggots in it.
>
> Many a night I'd go hungry, living on peanut butter and sandwiches, getting a loaf of bread here or a hunk of bologna there. Other guys

couldn't do that because they didn't have my connections or they didn't have money for the canteen.

Communication with the outside world was difficult. Guards would tear up letters. Others would be intercepted and read. Jerry Sousa, a prisoner at Walpole in 1970, sent two letters—one to a judge, the other to the parole board—to tell about a beating by guards. They went unanswered. Eight years later, at a court hearing, he discovered the prison authorities had intercepted them, never sent them out.

The families suffered with the prisoner: "During the last lock-up my four-year-old son sneaked off into the yard and picked me a flower. A guard in the tower called the warden's office and a deputy came in with the State Police at his side. He announced that if any child went into the yard and picked another flower, all visits would be terminated."

The prison rebellions of the late sixties and early seventies had a distinctly different character than the earlier ones. The prisoners in the Queens House of Detention referred to themselves as "revolutionaries." All over the country, prisoners were obviously affected by the turmoil in the country, the black revolt, the youth upsurge, the antiwar movement.

The events of those years underlined what prisoners already sensed—that whatever crimes they had committed, the greatest crimes were being committed by the authorities who maintained the prisons, by the government of the United States. The law was being broken daily by the President, sending bombers to kill, sending men to be killed, outside the Constitution, outside the "highest law of the land." State and local officials were violating the civil rights of black people, which was against the law, and were not being prosecuted for it.

Literature about the black movement, books on the war, began to seep into the prisons. The example set in the streets by blacks, by antiwar demonstrators, was exhilarating—against a lawless system, defiance was the only answer.

It was a system which sentenced Martin Sostre, a fifty-two-year-old black man running an Afro-Asian bookstore in Buffalo, New York, to twenty-five to thirty years in prison for allegedly selling $15 worth of heroin to an informer who later recanted his testimony. The recantation did not free Sostre—he could find no court, including the Supreme Court of the United States, to revoke the judgment. He spent eight years in prison, was beaten ten times by guards, spent three years in solitary confinement, battling and defying the authorities all the way until his release. Such injustice deserved only rebellion.

There had always been political prisoners—people sent to jail for belonging to radical movements, for opposing war. But now a new kind of political prisoner appeared—the man, or woman, convicted of an ordinary crime, who, in prison, became awakened politically. Some prisoners began making connections between their personal ordeal and the social system. They then turned not to individual rebellion but to collective action. They became concerned—amid an environment whose brutality demanded concentration on one's own safety, an atmosphere of cruel rivalry—for the rights, the safety of others.

George Jackson was one of these new political prisoners. In Soledad prison, California, on an indeterminate sentence for a $70 robbery, having already served ten years of it, Jackson became a revolutionary. He spoke with a fury that matched his condition:

> This monster—the monster they've engendered in me will return to torment its maker, from the grave, the pit, the profoundest pit. Hurl me into the next existence, the descent into hell won't turn me. . . . I'm going to charge them reparations in blood. I'm going to charge them like a maddened, wounded, rogue male elephant, ears flared, trunk raised, trumpet blaring. . . . War without terms.

A prisoner like this would not last. And when his book *Soledad Brother* became one of the most widely read books of black militancy in the United States—by prisoners, by black people, by white people—perhaps this ensured he would not last.

> All my life I've done exactly what I wanted to do just when I wanted, no more, perhaps less sometimes, but never any more, which explains why I had to be jailed. . . . I never adjusted. I haven't adjusted even yet, with half of my life already in prison.

He knew what might happen:

> Born to a premature death, a menial, subsistence-wage worker, odd-job man, the cleaner, the caught, the man under hatches, without bail—that's me, the colonial victim. Anyone who can pass the civil service examination today can kill me tomorrow . . . with complete immunity.

In August 1971 he was shot in the back by guards at San Quentin prison while he was allegedly trying to escape. The state's story (analyzed by Eric Mann in *Comrade George*) was full of holes. Prisoners in jails and state prisons all over the country knew, even before the final autopsy was in, even before later disclosures suggested a government plot to kill Jackson, that he had been murdered for daring to be a revolutionary in prison. Shortly after Jackson's death, there was a chain of rebellions around the country, in San Jose Civic Center jail, in Dallas county jail, in Suffolk county jail in Boston, in Cumberland county jail in Bridgeton, New Jersey, in Bexar county jail in San Antonio, Texas.

The most direct effect of the George Jackson murder was the rebellion at Attica prison in September 1971—a rebellion that came from long, deep grievances, but that was raised to boiling point by the news about George Jackson. Attica was surrounded by a 30-foot wall, 2 feet thick, with fourteen gun towers. Fifty-four percent of the inmates were black; 100 percent of the guards were white. Prisoners spent fourteen to sixteen hours a day in their cells, their mail was read, their reading material restricted, their visits from families conducted through a mesh screen, their medical care disgraceful, their parole system inequitable, racism everywhere. How perceptive the prison administration was about these conditions can be measured by the comment of the superintendent of Attica, Vincent Mancusi, when the uprising began: "Why are they destroying their home?"

Most of the Attica prisoners were there as a result of plea bargaining. Of 32,000 felony indictments a year in New York State, 4,000 to 5,000 were tried. The rest (about 75 percent) were disposed of by deals made under duress, called "plea bargaining," described as follows in the Report of the Joint Legislative Committee on Crime in New York:

> The final climactic act in the plea bargaining procedure is a charade which in itself has aspects of dishonesty which rival the original crime in many instances. The accused is made to assert publicly his guilt on a specific crime, which in many cases he has not committed; in some cases he pleads guilty to a non-existing crime. He must further indicate that he is entering his plea freely . . . and that he is not doing so because of any promises . . . made to him.
>
> In plea bargaining, the accused pleads guilty, whether he is or not, and saves the state the trouble of a trial in return for the promise of a less severe punishment.

When Attica prisoners were up for parole, the average time of their hearing, including the reading of the file and deliberation among the three members, was 5.9 minutes. Then the decision was handed out, with no explanation.

The official report on the Attica uprising tells how an inmate-instructed sociology class there became a forum for ideas about change. Then there was a series of organized protest efforts, and in July an inmate manifesto setting forth a series of moderate demands, after which "tensions at Attica had continued to mount," culminating in a day of protest over the killing of George Jackson at San Quentin, during which few inmates ate at lunch and dinner and many wore black armbands.

On September 9, 1971, a series of conflicts between prisoners and guards ended with a group of inmates breaking through a gate with a defective weld and taking over one of the four prison yards, with forty guards as hostages. Then followed five days in which the prisoners set up a remarkable community in the yard. A group of citizen-observers, invited by the prisoners, included *New York Times* columnist Tom Wicker, who wrote *(A Time to Die)*: "The racial harmony that prevailed among the prisoners—it was absolutely astonishing. . . . That prison yard was the first place I have ever seen where there was no racism." One black prisoner later said: "I never thought whites could really get it on. . . . But I can't tell you what the yard was like, I actually cried it was so close, everyone so together. . . ."

After five days, the state lost patience. Governor Nelson Rockefeller approved a military attack on the prison (see Cinda Firestone's stunning film *Attica*). National Guardsmen, prison guards, and local police went in with automatic rifles, carbines, and submachine guns in a full-scale assault on the prisoners, who had no firearms. Thirty-one prisoners were killed. The first stories given the press by prison authorities said that nine guards held hostage had their throats slashed by the prisoners during the attack. The official autopsies almost immediately showed this to be false: the nine guards died in the same hail of bullets that killed the prisoners.

The effects of Attica are hard to measure. Two months after the revolt at Attica, men at Norfolk prison in Massachusetts began to organize. On November 8, 1971, armed guards and state troopers, in a surprise raid, moved into the cells at Norfolk, pulled out sixteen men, and shipped them out. A prisoner described the scene:

> Between one and two last night I was awakened (I've been a light sleeper since Vietnam) and I looked out my window. There were troopers. And screws. Lots. Armed with sidearms, and big clubs. They were going into dorms and taking people, all kinds of people. . . .
>
> They took a friend of mine. . . . Being pulled outside in our underwear, at 1:30, in bare feet by two troopers and a housescrew. Looking at those troops, with guns, and masks and clubs, with the moon shining off the hel-

mets and the hate that you could see in their faces. Thinking that this is where these guys live, with the guns and the hate, and the helmets and masks, and you, you're trying to wake up, flashing on Kent State and Jackson, and Chicago. And Attica. Most of all, Attica. . . .

That same week at Concord prison in Massachusetts, another raid. It was as if everywhere, in the weeks and months after Attica, the authorities were taking preventive action to break up organizing efforts among the prisoners. Jerry Sousa, a young leader of the prison reform movement at Concord, was taken away, dumped into Walpole in the middle of the night, and immediately put into Nine Block, the dreaded segregation unit. He had been there only a short time when he managed to get a report out to friends. The content of this report tells much about what was happening before and after Attica to the thinking of prisoners:

> We are writing a somber report regarding the circumstances and events leading up to and surrounding the death of prisoner Joseph Chesnulavich which occurred here an hour ago in Nine Block.
> Since Christmas eve, vicious prison guards here in Nine Block have created a reign of terror directed toward us prisoners. Four of us have been beaten, one who was prisoner Donald King.
> In an attempt to escape constant harassment and inhuman treatment, prisoner George Hayes ate razor blades and prisoner Fred Ahern swallowed a needle . . . they both were rushed to Mass General Hospital.
> This evening at 6 P.M. prison guards Baptist, Sainsbury, and Montiega turned a fire extinguisher containing a chemical foam on Joe then slammed the solid steel door sealing him in his cell and walked away, voicing threats of, "We'll get that punk."
> At 9:25 P.M. Joe was found dead. . . . Prison authorities as well as news media will label little Joe's death a suicide, but the men here in Block Nine who witnessed this murder know. But are we next?

What was happening was the organization of prisoners—the caring of prisoners for one another, the attempt to take the hatred and anger of individual rebellion and turn it into collective effort for change. On the outside, something new was also happening, the development of prison support groups all over the country, the building of a body of literature about prisons. There were more studies of crime and punishment, a growing movement for the abolition of prisons on the grounds that they did not prevent crime or cure it, but expanded it. Alternatives were discussed: community houses in the short run (except for the incorrigibly violent); guaranteed minimum economic security, in the long run.

The prisoners were thinking about issues beyond prison, victims other than themselves and their friends. In Walpole prison a statement asking for American withdrawal from Vietnam was circulated; it was signed by every single prisoner—an amazing organizing feat by a handful of inmates. One Thanksgiving day there, most of the prisoners, not only in Walpole but in three other prisons, refused to eat the special holiday meal, saying they wanted to bring attention to the hungry all over the United States.

Prisoners worked laboriously on lawsuits, and some victories were won in the courts. The publicity around Attica, the community of support, had its effect. Although the Attica rebels were indicted on heavy charges and faced double and triple life terms, the charges were finally dropped. But in general, the courts declared their unwillingness to enter the closed, controlled world of the prison, and so the prisoners remained as they had been so long, on their own.

Even where an occasional "victory" came in the courts it turned out, on close reading, to leave things not much different. In 1973 (*Procunier* v. *Martinez*) the U.S. Supreme Court declared unconstitutional certain mail censorship regulations of the California Department of Corrections. But when one looked closely, the decision, with all its proud language about "First Amendment liberties," said: ". . . we hold that censorship of prison mail is justified if the following criteria are met. . . ." When the censorship could be said to "further an important or substantial government interest" or where it was in the "substantial governmental interests of security, order, and rehabilitation," censorship would be allowed.

In 1978 the Supreme Court ruled that the news media do not have guaranteed rights of access to jails and prisons. It ruled also that prison authorities could forbid inmates to speak to one another, assemble, or spread literature about the formation of a prisoners' union.

It became clear—and prisoners seemed to know this from the start—that their condition would not be changed by law, but by protest, organization, resistance, the creation of their own culture, their own literature, the building of links with people on the outside. There were more outsiders now who knew about prisons. Tens of thousands of Americans had spent time behind bars in the civil rights and antiwar movements. They had learned about the prison system and could hardly forget their experiences. There was a basis now for breaking through the long isolation of the prisoners from the community and finding support there. In the mid-seventies, this was beginning to happen.

It was a time of upsurge. Women, guarded in their very homes, rebelled. Prisoners, put out of sight and behind bars, rebelled. The greatest surprise was still to come.

It was thought that the Indians, once the only occupants of the continent, then pushed back and annihilated by the white invaders, would not be heard from again. In the last days of the year 1890, shortly after Christmas, the last massacre of Indians took place at Pine Ridge, South Dakota, near Wounded Knee Creek. Sitting Bull, the great Sioux leader, had just been assassinated by Indian police in the pay of the United States, and the remaining Sioux sought refuge at Pine Ridge, 120 men and 230 women and children, surrounded by U.S. cavalry, with two Hotchkiss guns—capable of hurling shells over 2 miles—on a rise overlooking the camp. When the troopers ordered the Indians to turn over their weapons, one of them fired his rifle. The soldiers then let loose with their carbines, and the big guns on the hill shelled the tepees. When it was over between 200 and 300 of the original 350 men, women, and children were dead. The twenty-five soldiers who died were mostly hit by their own shrapnel or bullets, since the Indians had only a few guns.

The Indian tribes, attacked, subdued, starved out, had been divided up by putting them on reservations where they lived in poverty. In 1887, an Allotment Act tried to break up the reservations into small plots of land owned by individual Indians, to turn them into American-type small farmers—but much of this land was taken by white speculators, and the reservations remained.

Then, during the New Deal, with a friend of the Indians, John Collier, in charge of the Bureau of Indian Affairs, there was an attempt to restore tribal life. But in the decades that followed, no fundamental change took place. Many Indians stayed on the impoverished reservations. The younger ones often left. An Indian anthropologist said: "An Indian reservation is the most complete colonial system in the world that I know about."

For a time, the disappearance or amalgamation of the Indians seemed inevitable—only 300,000 were left at the turn of the century, from the original million or more in the area of the United States. But then the population began to grow again, as if a plant left to die refused to do so, began to flourish. By 1960 there were 800,000 Indians, half on reservations, half in towns all over the country.

The autobiographies of Indians show their refusal to be absorbed by the white man's culture. One wrote:

Oh, yes, I went to the white man's schools. I learned to read from school books, newspapers, and the Bible. But in time I found that these were not enough. Civilized people depend too much on man-made printed pages. I turn to the Great Spirit's book which is the whole of his creation. . . .

A Hopi Indian named Sun Chief said:

I had learned many English words and could recite part of the Ten Commandments. I knew how to sleep on a bed, pray to Jesus, comb my hair, eat with a knife and fork, and use a toilet. . . . I had also learned that a person thinks with his head instead of his heart.

Chief Luther Standing Bear, in his 1933 autobiography, *From the Land of the Spotted Eagle*, wrote:

True, the white man brought great change. But the varied fruits of his civilization, though highly colored and inviting, are sickening and deadening. And if it be the part of civilization to maim, rob, and thwart, then what is progress?

I am going to venture that the man who sat on the ground in his tipi meditating on life and its meaning, accepting the kinship of all creatures, and acknowledging unity with the universe of things, was infusing into his being the true essence of civilization. . . .

As the civil rights and antiwar movements developed in the 1960s, Indians were already gathering their energy for resistance, thinking about how to change their situation, beginning to organize. In 1961, five hundred tribal and urban Indian leaders met in Chicago. Out of this came another gathering of university-educated young Indians who formed the National Indian Youth Council. Mel Thom, a Paiute Indian, their first president, wrote:

There is increased activity over on the Indian side. There are disagreements, laughing, singing, outbursts of anger, and occasionally some planning. . . . Indians are gaining confidence and courage that their cause is right.

The struggle goes on. . . . Indians are gathering together to deliberate their destiny. . . .

Around this time, Indians began to approach the United States government on an embarrassing topic: treaties. In his widely read 1969 book, *Custer Died for Your Sins*, Vine Deloria, Jr., noted that President

Lyndon Johnson talked about America's "commitments," and President Nixon talked about Russia's failure to respect treaties. He said: "Indian people laugh themselves sick when they hear these statements."

The United States government had signed more than four hundred treaties with Indians and violated every single one. For instance, back in George Washington's administration, a treaty was signed with the Iroquois of New York: "The United States acknowledge all the land within the aforementioned boundaries to be the property of the Seneka nation. . . ." But in the early sixties, under President Kennedy, the United States ignored the treaty and built a dam on this land, flooding most of the Seneca reservation.

Resistance was already taking shape in various parts of the country. In the state of Washington, there was an old treaty taking land from the Indians but leaving them fishing rights. This became unpopular as the white population grew and wanted the fishing areas exclusively for themselves. When state courts closed river areas to Indian fishermen, in 1964, Indians had "fish-ins" on the Nisqually River, in defiance of the court orders, and went to jail, hoping to publicize their protest.

A local judge the following year ruled that the Puyallup tribe did not exist, and its members could not fish on the river named for them, the Puyallup River. Policemen raided Indian fishing groups, destroyed boats, slashed nets, manhandled people, arrested seven Indians. A Supreme Court ruling in 1968 confirmed Indian rights under the treaty but said a state could "regulate all fishing" if it did not discriminate against Indians. The state continued to get injunctions and to arrest Indians fishing. They were doing to the Supreme Court ruling what whites in the South had done with the Fourteenth Amendment for many years—ignoring it. Protests, raids, arrests, continued into the early seventies.

Some of the Indians involved in the fish-ins were veterans of the Vietnam war. One was Sid Mills, who was arrested in a fish-in at Frank's Landing on the Nisqually River in Washington on October 13, 1968. He made a statement:

> I am a Yakima and Cherokee Indian, and a man. For two years and four months, I've been a soldier in the United States Army. I served in combat in Vietnam—until critically wounded. . . . I hereby renounce further obligation in service or duty to the United States Army.
>
> My first obligation now lies with the Indian People fighting for the lawful Treaty to fish in usual and accustomed water of the Nisqually, Columbia and other rivers of the Pacific Northwest, and in serving them in this fight in any way possible. . . .

My decision is influenced by the fact that we have already buried Indian fishermen returned dead from Vietnam, while Indian fishermen live here without protection and under steady attack. . . .

Just three years ago today, on October 13, 1965, 19 women and children were brutalized by more than 45 armed agents of the State of Washington at Frank's Landing on the Nisqually river in a vicious, unwarranted attack. . . .

Interestingly, the oldest human skeletal remains ever found in the Western Hemisphere were recently uncovered on the banks of the Columbia River—the remains of Indian fishermen. What kind of government or society would spend millions of dollars to pick upon our bones, restore our ancestral life patterns, and protect our ancient remains from damage—while at the same time eating upon the flesh of our living People . . . ?

We will fight for our rights.

Indians fought back not only with physical resistance, but also with the artifacts of white culture—books, words, newspapers. In 1968, members of the Mohawk Nation at Akwesasne, on the St. Lawrence River between the United States and Canada, began a remarkable newspaper, *Akwesasne Notes*, with news, editorials, poetry, all flaming with the spirit of defiance. Mixed in with all that was an irrepressible humor. Vine Deloria, Jr., wrote:

Every now and then I am impressed with the thinking of the non-Indian. I was in Cleveland last year and got to talking with a non-Indian about American history. He said that he was really sorry about what had happened to Indians, but that there was a good reason for it. The continent had to be developed and he felt that Indians had stood in the way, and thus had had to be removed. "After all," he remarked, "what did you do with the land when you had it?" I didn't understand him until later when I discovered that the Cuyahoga River running through Cleveland is inflammable. So many combustible pollutants are dumped into the river that the inhabitants have to take special precautions during the summer to avoid setting it on fire. After reviewing the argument of my non-Indian friend I decided that he was probably correct. Whites had made better use of the land. How many Indians could have thought of creating an inflammable river?

In 1969, November 9, there took place a dramatic event which focused attention on Indian grievances as nothing else had. It burst through the invisibility of previous local Indian protests and declared to the entire world that the Indians still lived and would fight for their rights. On that day, before dawn, seventy-eight Indians landed on Alcatraz Island in San Francisco Bay and occupied the island. Alcatraz was an abandoned federal prison, a hated and terrible place nicknamed "The Rock." In 1964 some young Indians had occupied it to establish an Indian university, but they were driven off and there was no publicity.

This time, it was different. The group was led by Richard Oakes, a Mohawk who directed Indian Studies at San Francisco State College, and Grace Thorpe, a Sac and Fox Indian, daughter of Jim Thorpe, the famous Indian college football star and Olympic runner, jumper, hurdler. More Indians landed, and by the end of November nearly six hundred of them, representing more than fifty tribes, were living on Alcatraz. They called themselves "Indians of All Tribes" and issued a proclamation, "We Hold the Rock." In it they offered to buy Alcatraz in glass beads and red cloth, the price paid Indians for Manhattan Island over three hundred years earlier. They said:

> We feel that this so-called Alcatraz Island is more than suitable for an Indian reservation, as determined by the white man's own standards. By this we mean that this place resembles most Indian reservations in that:
> 1. It is isolated from modern facilities, and without adequate means of transportation.
> 2. It has no fresh running water.
> 3. It has inadequate sanitation facilities.
> 4. There are no oil or mineral rights.
> 5. There is no industry and so unemployment is very great.
> 6. There are no health care facilities.
> 7. The soil is rocky and non-productive; and the land does not support game.
> 8. There are no educational facilities.
> 9. The population has always exceeded the land base.
> 10. The population has always been held as prisoners and dependent upon others.

They announced they would make the island a center for Native American Studies for Ecology: "We will work to de-pollute the air and waters of the Bay Area . . . restore fish and animal life. . . ."

In the months that followed, the government cut off telephones, electricity, and water to Alcatraz Island. Many of the Indians had to leave, but others insisted on staying. A year later they were still there, and they sent out a message to "our brothers and sisters of all races and tongues upon our Earth Mother":

We are still holding the Island of Alcatraz in the true names of Freedom, Justice and Equality, because you, our brothers and sisters of this earth, have lent support to our just cause. We reach out our hands and hearts and send spirit messages to each and every one of you—WE HOLD THE ROCK. . . .

We have learned that violence breeds only more violence and we therefore have carried on our occupation of Alcatraz in a peaceful manner, hoping that the government of these United States will also act accordingly. . . .

We are a proud people! We are Indians! We have observed and rejected much of what so-called civilization offers. We are Indians! We will preserve our traditions and ways of life by educating our own children. We are Indians! We will join hands in a unity never before put into practice. We are Indians! Our Earth Mother awaits our voices.

We are Indians Of All Tribes! WE HOLD THE ROCK!

Six months later, federal forces invaded the island and physically removed the Indians living there.

It had been thought that the Navajo Indians would not be heard from again. In the mid-1800s, United States troops under "Kit" Carson burned Navajo villages, destroyed their crops and orchards, forced them from their lands. But in the Black Mesa of New Mexico they never surrendered. In the late 1960s, the Peabody Coal Company began strip mining on their land—a ruthless excavation of the topsoil. The company pointed to a "contract" signed with some Navajos. It was reminiscent of the "treaties" signed with some Indians in the past that took away all Indian land.

One hundred and fifty Navajos met in the spring of 1969 to declare that the strip mining would pollute the water and the air, destroy the grazing land for livestock, use up their scarce water resources. A young woman pointed to a public relations pamphlet put out by the Peabody Coal Company, showing fishing lakes, grassland, trees, and said: "We're not going to have anything like those you see in the pictures. . . . What is the future going to be like for our children, our children's children?" An elderly Navajo woman, one of the organizers of the meeting, said, "Peabody's monsters are digging up the heart of our mother earth, our sacred mountain, and we also feel the pains. . . . I have lived here for years and I'm not about to move."

The Hopi Indians were also affected by the Peabody operations. They wrote to President Nixon in protest:

Today the sacred lands where the Hopi live are being desecrated by men who seek coal and water from our soil that they may create more power for the whiteman's cities. . . . The Great Spirit said not to allow this to happen. . . . The Great Spirit said not to take from the Earth—not to destroy living things. . . .

It is said by the Great Spirit that if a gourd of ashes is dropped upon the Earth, that many men will die and that the end of this way of life is near at hand. We interpret this as the dropping of atomic bombs on Hiroshima and Nagasaki. We do not want to see this happen to any place or any nation again, but instead we should turn all this energy for peaceful uses, not for war. . . .

In the fall of 1970, a magazine called *La Raza*, one of the countless local publications coming out of the movements of those years to supply information ignored in the regular media, told about the Pit River Indians of northern California. Sixty Pit Indians occupied land they said belonged to them; they defied the Forest Services when ordered to leave. One of them, Darryl B. Wilson, later recalled: "As the flames danced orange making the trees come to life, and the cold creeped out of the darkness to challenge the speaking fire, and our breath came in small clouds, we spoke." They asked the government by what treaty it claimed the land. It could point to none. They cited a federal statute *(25 USCA 194)* that where there was a land dispute between Indian and white "the burden of proof falls on the white man."

They had built a quonset hut, and the marshals told them it was ugly and ruined the landscape. Wilson wrote later:

The whole world is rotting. The water is poisoned, the air polluted, the politics deformed, the land gutted, the forest pillaged, the shores ruined, the towns burned, the lives of the people destroyed . . . and the federals spent the best part of October trying to tell us the quonset hut was "ugly"!

To us it was beautiful. It was the beginning of our school. The meeting place. Home for our homeless. A sanctuary for those needing rest. Our church. Our headquarters. Our business office. Our symbol of approaching freedom. And it still stands.

It was also the center for the reviving of our stricken, diluted and separated culture. Our beginning. It was our sun rising on a clear spring day when the sky holds no clouds. It was a good and pure thing for the heart to look upon. That small place on earth. Our place.

But 150 marshals came, with machine guns, shotguns, rifles, pistols, riot sticks, Mace, dogs, chains, manacles. "The old people were frightened. The young questioned bravery. The small children were like a deer that has been shot by the thunder stick. Hearts beat fast as though a

race was just run in the heat of summer." The marshals began swinging
their riot sticks, and blood started flowing. Wilson grabbed one marshal's club, was thrown down, manacled, and while lying face down on
the ground was struck behind the head several times. A sixty-six-year-
old man was beaten into unconsciousness. A white reporter was arrested,
his wife beaten. They were all thrown into trucks and taken away,
charged with assaulting state and federal officers and cutting trees—but
not with trespassing, which might have brought into question the ownership of the land. When the episode was all over, they were still defiant.

Indians who had been in the Vietnam war made connections. At the
"Winter Soldier Investigations" in Detroit, where Vietnam veterans
testified about their experiences, an Oklahoma Indian named Evan
Haney told about his:

> The same massacres happened to the Indians 100 years ago. Germ warfare
> was used then. They put smallpox in the Indians' blankets. . . .
>
> I got to know the Vietnamese people and I learned they were just like
> us. . . . What we are doing is destroying ourselves and the world.
>
> I have grown up with racism all my life. When I was a child, watching
> cowboys and Indians on TV, I would root for the cavalry, not the Indians. It
> was that bad. I was that far toward my own destruction. . . .
>
> Though 50 percent of the children at the country school I attended in
> Oklahoma were Indians, nothing in school, on television, or on the radio
> taught anything about Indian culture. There were no books on Indian history,
> not even in the library. . . .
>
> But I knew something was wrong. I started reading and learning my own
> culture. . . .
>
> I saw the Indian people at their happiest when they went to Alcatraz or
> to Washington to defend their fishing rights. They at last felt like human
> beings.

Indians began to do something about their "own destruction"—the
annihilation of their culture. In 1969, at the First Convocation of
American Indian Scholars, Indians spoke indignantly of either the
ignoring or the insulting of Indians in textbooks given to little children
all over the United States. That year the Indian Historian Press was
founded. It evaluated four hundred textbooks in elementary and secondary schools and found that not one of them gave an accurate depic-
tion of the Indian.

A counterattack began in the schools. In early 1971, forty-five Indian
students at Copper Valley School, in Glennalen, Alaska, wrote a letter to

their Congressman opposing the Alaska oil pipeline as ruinous to the ecology, a threat to the "peace, quiet and security of our Alaska."

Other Americans were beginning to pay attention, to rethink their own learning. The first motion pictures attempting to redress the history of the Indian appeared: one was *Little Big Man*, based on a novel by Thomas Berger. More and more books appeared on Indian history, until a whole new literature came into existence. Teachers became sensitive to the old stereotypes, threw away the old textbooks, started using new material. In the spring of 1977 a teacher named Jane Califf, in the New York City elementary schools, told of her experiences with fourth and fifth grade students. She brought into class the traditional textbooks and asked the students to locate the stereotypes in them. She read aloud from Native American writers and articles from *Akwesasne Notes*, and put protest posters around the room. The children then wrote letters to the editors of the books they had read:

> Dear Editor,
>   I don't like your book called *The Cruise of Christopher Columbus*. I didn't like it because you said some things about Indians that weren't true. . . . Another thing I didn't like was on page 69, it says that Christopher Columbus invited the Indians to Spain, but what really happened was that he stole them!
>
>   censearly, Raymond Miranda

On Thanksgiving Day 1970, at the annual celebration of the landing of the Pilgrims, the authorities decided to do something different: invite an Indian to make the celebratory speech. They found a Wampanoag Indian named Frank James and asked him to speak. But when they saw the speech he was about to deliver, they decided they did not want it. His speech, not heard at Plymouth, Massachusetts, on that occasion, said, in part (the whole speech is in *Chronicles of American Indian Protest*):

> I speak to you as a Man—a Wampanoag Man. . . . It is with mixed emotions that I stand here to share my thoughts. . . . The Pilgrims had hardly explored the shores of Cape Cod four days before they had robbed the graves of my ancestors, and stolen their corn, wheat, and beans. . . .
>   Our spirit refuses to die. Yesterday we walked the woodland paths and sandy trails. Today we must walk the macadam highways and roads. We are uniting. We're standing not in our wigwams but in your concrete tent. We stand tall and proud and before too many moons pass we'll right the wrongs we have allowed to happen to us. . . .

For Indians there has never been a clear line between prose and poetry. When an Indian studying in New Mexico was praised for his poetry he said, "In my tribe we have no poets. Everyone talks in poetry." There are, however, "poems," collected in William Brandon's *The Last Americans* and in *The Way* by Shirley Hill Witt and Stan Steiner.

An Ashinabe "spring poem" translated by Gerald Vizenor:

> as my eyes
> look across the prairie
> i feel the summer
> in the spring

"Snow the Last" by Joseph Concha:

> Snow comes last
> for it quiets down everything

This from a fifth-year group in a Special Navajo Program in the year 1940, called "It is Not!"

> The Navajo Reservation a lonesome place?
> It is Not!
> The skies are sunny,
> Clear blue,
> Or grey with rain.
> Each day is gay—
> in Nature's way.
> It is not a lonesome place at all.
> A Navajo house shabby and small?
> It is Not!
> Inside there's love,
> Good laughter,
> And Big Talk.
> But best—
> it's home
> With an open door
> And room for all
> A Castle could have no more.

In March of 1973 came a powerful affirmation that the Indians of North America were still alive. On the site of the 1890 massacre, on

Pine Ridge reservation, several hundred Oglala Sioux and friends returned to the village of Wounded Knee to occupy it as a symbol of the demand for Indian land, Indian rights. The history of that event, in the words of the participants, has been captured in a rare book published by *Akwesasne Notes* (*Voices from Wounded Knee*, 1973).

In the 1970s, 54 percent of the adult males on the Pine Ridge reservation were unemployed, one-third of the families were on welfare or pensions, alcoholism was widespread, and suicide rates were high. The life expectancy of an Oglala Sioux was forty-six years. Just before the Wounded Knee occupation, there was violence at the town of Custer. An Indian named Wesley Bad Heart Bull was killed by a white gas station attendant. The man was let out on $5,000 bond and indicted for manslaughter, facing a possible ten-year term. A gathering of Indians to protest this led to a clash with police. The murder victim's mother, Mrs. Sarah Bad Heart Bull, was arrested, on charges that called for a maximum sentence of thirty years.

On February 27, 1973, about three hundred Oglala Sioux, many of them members of the new militant organization called the American Indian Movement (AIM), entered the village of Wounded Knee and declared it liberated territory. Ellen Moves Camp later said: "We decided that we did need the American Indian Movement in here because our men were scared, they hung to the back. It was mostly the women that went forward and spoke out."

Within hours, more than two hundred FBI agents, federal marshals, and police of the Bureau of Indian Affairs surrounded and blockaded the town. They had armored vehicles, automatic rifles, machine guns, grenade launchers, and gas shells, and soon began firing. Gladys Bissonette said three weeks later: "Since we are here, in Wounded Knee, we've been shot at, over and over, always after dark. But last night we were hit the hardest. I guess the Great Spirit is with us, and no bullets find their way into our bodies. We ran through a hail of bullets one night. . . . We're going to hold our stand until we are completely an independent sovereign nation, Oglala Sioux Nation."

After the siege began, food supplies became short. Indians in Michigan sent food via a plane that landed inside the encampment. The next day FBI agents arrested the pilot and a doctor from Michigan who had hired the plane. In Nevada, eleven Indians were arrested for taking food, clothing, and medical supplies to South Dakota. In mid-April three more planes dropped 1,200 pounds of food, but as people scrambled to gather it up, a government helicopter appeared overhead and fired down on them while groundfire came from all sides. Frank

Clearwater, an Indian man lying on a cot inside a church, was hit by a bullet. When his wife accompanied him to a hospital, she was arrested and jailed. Clearwater died.

There were more gun battles, another death. Finally, a negotiated peace was signed, in which both sides agreed to disarm (the Indians had refused to disarm while surrounded by armed men, recalling the 1890 massacre). The United States government promised to investigate Indian affairs, and a presidential commission would reexamine the 1868 treaty. The siege ended and 120 occupiers were arrested. The U.S. government then said that it had reexamined the 1868 treaty, found it valid, but that it was superseded by the U.S. power of "eminent domain"—the government's power to take land.

The Indians had held out for seventy-one days, creating a marvelous community inside the besieged territory. Communal kitchens were set up, a health clinic, and hospital. A Navajo Vietnam veteran:

> There's a tremendous amount of coolness considering that we're outgunned. . . . But people stay because they believe; they have a cause. That's why we lost in Viet Nam, cause there was no cause. We were fighting a rich man's war, for the rich man. . . . In Wounded Knee, we're doing pretty damn good, morale-wise. Because we can still laugh.

Messages of support had come to Wounded Knee from Australia, Finland, Germany, Italy, Japan, England. One message came from some of the Attica brothers, two of whom were Indians: "You fight for our Earth Mother and Her Children. Our spirits fight with you!" Wallace Black Elk replied: "Little Wounded Knee is turned into a giant world."

After Wounded Knee, in spite of the deaths, the trials, the use of the police and courts to try to break the movement, the Native American movement continued.

In the Akwesasne community itself, which put out *Akwesasne Notes*, the Indians had always insisted their territory was separate, not to be invaded by the white man's law. One day New York State police gave three traffic tickets to a Mohawk Indian truck driver, and a council of Indians met with a police lieutenant. At first, he insisted that he had to follow orders and give out tickets, even in Akwesasne territory, although he obviously was trying to be reasonable. He finally agreed that they would not arrest an Indian in the territory or even outside of it without first having a meeting with the Mohawk council. The lieutenant then sat down and lit a cigar. Indian Chief Joahquisoh, a distinguished-looking man with long hair, rose and addressed the lieutenant with a serious voice. "There is one more thing before you go," he said looking straight at the lieutenant. "I want to know," he said slowly, "if you've got an extra cigar." The meeting ended in laughter.

Akwesasne Notes continued to publish. On its poetry page, late autumn, 1976, appeared poems reflecting the spirit of the times. Ila Abernathy wrote:

> I am grass growing and the shearer of grass,
> I am the willow and the splitter of laths,
> weaver and the thing woven, marriage of willow and grass.
> I am frost on the land and the land's life,
> breath and beast and the sharp rock underfoot;
> in me the mountain lives, and the owl strikes,
> and I in them. I am the sun's twin,
> mover of blood and the blood lost,
> I am the deer and the deer's death;
> I am the burr in your conscience:
> acknowledge me.

And Buffy Sainte-Marie:

> You think I have visions
> because I am an Indian.
>
> I have visions because
> there are visions to be seen.

In the sixties and seventies, it was not just a women's movement, a prisoner's movement, an Indian movement. There was general revolt against oppressive, artificial, previously unquestioned ways of living. It touched every aspect of personal life: childbirth, childhood, love, sex, marriage, dress, music, art, sports, language, food, housing, religion, literature, death, schools.

The new temper, the new behavior, shocked many Americans. It created tensions. Sometimes it was seen as a "generation gap"—the younger generation moving far away from the older one in its way of life. But it seemed after a while to be not so much a matter of age—some young people remained "straight" while some middle-aged people were changing their ways and old people were beginning to behave in ways that astounded others.

Sexual behavior went through startling changes. Premarital sex was no longer a matter for silence. Men and women lived together outside of marriage, and struggled for words to describe the other person when introduced: "I want you to meet my . . . friend." Married couples candidly spoke of their affairs, and books appeared discussing "open marriage." Masturbation could be talked about openly, even approvingly. Homosexuality was no longer concealed. "Gay" men and "gay" women—lesbians—organized to combat discrimination against them, to give themselves a sense of community, to overcome shame and isolation.

All this was reflected in the literature and in the mass media. Court decisions overruled the local banning of books that were erotic or even pornographic. A new literature appeared (*The Joy of Sex* and others) to teach men and women how sexual fulfillment could be attained. The movies now did not hesitate to show nudity, although the motion picture industry, wanting to preserve principle as well as profit, set up a classification system (R for Restricted, X for prohibited to children). The language of sex became more common both in literature and in ordinary conversation.

All this was connected with new living arrangements. Especially among young people, communal living arrangements flourished. A few were truly communes—that is, based on the sharing of money and decisions, creating a community of intimacy, affection, trust. Most were practical arrangements for sharing the rent, with varying degrees of friendship and intimate association among the participants. It was no longer unusual for men and women to be "roommates"—in groups of two or three or larger, and without sexual relations—as practical, unselfconscious arrangements.

The most important thing about dress in the cultural change of the sixties was the greater informality. For women it was a continuation of the historic feminist movement's insistence on discarding of "feminine," hampering clothes. Many women stopped wearing bras. The restrictive "girdle"—almost a uniform of the forties and fifties—became rare. Young men and women dressed more nearly alike, in jeans, in discarded army uniforms. Men stopped wearing neckties, women of all ages wore pants more often—unspoken homage to Amelia Bloomer.

There was a new popular music of protest. Pete Seeger had been singing protest songs since the forties, but now he came into his own, his audiences much larger. Bob Dylan and Joan Baez, singing not only protest songs, but songs reflecting the new abandon, the new culture, became popular idols. A middle-aged woman on the West Coast, Malvina Reynolds, wrote and sang songs that fit her socialist thinking and her libertarian spirit, as well as her critique of the modern commercial culture. Everybody now, she sang, lived in "little boxes" and they "all came out just the same."

Bob Dylan was a phenomenon unto himself: powerful songs of protest, personal songs of freedom and self-expression. In an angry song, "Masters of War," he hopes that one day they will die and he will follow their casket "in the pale afternoon." "A Hard Rain's A-Gonna Fall" recounts the terrible stories of the last decades, of starvation and war, and tears, and dead ponies, and poisoned waters, and damp, dirty prisons—"It's a hard rain's a-gonna fall." Dylan sang a bitter antiwar song, "With God on Our Side," and one about the killer of the black activist Medgar Evers, "Only a Pawn in Their Game." He offered a challenge to the old, hope to the new, for "The Times They Are A-Changin'."

The Catholic upsurge against the war was part of a general revolt inside the Catholic Church, which had for so long been a bulwark of conservatism, tied to racism, jingoism, war. Priests and nuns resigned from the church, opened their lives to sex, got married and had children—sometimes without bothering to leave the church officially. True, there was still enormous popularity for the old-time religious revivalists, and Billy Graham commanded the obedience of millions, but now there were small swift currents against the mainstream.

There was a new suspicion of big business, of profiteering as the motive for ruining the environment. There was a reexamination of the "death industry," of moneymaking funerals and profitable tombstones, as in Jessica Mitford's *The American Way of Death*.

With the loss of faith in big powers—business, government, religion—there arose a stronger belief in self, whether individual or collective. The experts in all fields were now looked at skeptically: the belief grew that people could figure out for themselves what to eat, how to live their lives, how to be healthy. There was suspicion of the medical industry and campaigns against chemical preservatives, valueless foods, advertising. By now the scientific evidence of the evils of smoking—cancer, heart disease—was so powerful that the government barred advertising of cigarettes on television and in newspapers.

Traditional education began to be reexamined. The schools had taught whole generations the values of patriotism, of obeying authority, and had perpetuated ignorance, even contempt for people of other nations, races, Native Americans, women. Not just the content of education was challenged, but the style—the formality, the bureaucracy, the insistence on subordination to authority. This made only a small dent in the formidable national system of orthodox education, but it was reflected in a new generation of teachers all over the country, and a new literature to sustain them: Jonathan Kozol, *Death at an Early Age*; George Denison, *The Lives of Children*; Ivan Illich, *De-schooling Society*.

Never in American history had more movements for change been concentrated in so short a span of years. But the system in the course of two centuries had learned a good deal about the control of people. In the mid-seventies, it went to work.

20

THE SEVENTIES:
UNDER CONTROL?

In the early seventies, the system seemed out of control—it could not hold the loyalty of the public. As early as 1970, according to the University of Michigan's Survey Research Center, "trust in government" was low in every section of the population. And there was a significant difference by class. Of professional people, 40 percent had "low" political trust in the government; of unskilled blue-collar workers, 66 percent had "low" trust.

Public opinion surveys in 1971—after seven years of intervention in Vietnam—showed an unwillingness to come to the aid of other countries, assuming they were attacked by Communist-backed forces. Even for countries allied to the United States in the North Atlantic Treaty Organization, or Mexico, right on our southern border, there was no majority opinion for intervening with American troops. As for Thailand, if it were under Communist attack, only 12 percent of whites interrogated would send troops, 4 percent of nonwhites would do so.

In the summer of 1972, antiwar people in the Boston area were picketing Honeywell Corporation. The literature they distributed pointed out that Honeywell was producing antipersonnel weapons used in Vietnam, like the deadly cluster bomb that had riddled thousands of Vietnamese civilians with painful, hard-to-extricate pellets. About six hundred ballots were given to the Honeywell employees, asking if they thought that Honeywell should discontinue making these weapons. Of the 231 persons who returned the ballots, 131 said that Honeywell should stop, 88 said it should not. They were invited to make comments. A typical "no" comment: "Honeywell is not responsible for what the Department of Defense does with the goods it buys. . . ." A typical "yes" comment: "How may we have pride in our work when the entire basis for this work is immoral?"

The Survey Research Center of the University of Michigan had been posing the question: "Is the government run by a few big interests looking out for themselves?" The answer in 1964 had been "yes" from 26 percent of those polled; by 1972 the answer was "yes" from 53 percent of those polled. An article in the *American Political Science Review* by Arthur H. Miller, reporting on the extensive polling done by the Survey Research Center, said that the polls showed "widespread, basic discontent and political alienation." He added (political scientists often took on the worries of the Establishment): "What is startling and somewhat alarming is the rapid degree of change in this basic attitude over a period of only six years."

More voters than ever before refused to identify themselves as either Democrats or Republicans. Back in 1940, 20 percent of those polled called themselves "independents." In 1974, 34 percent called themselves "independents."

The courts, the juries, and even judges were not behaving as usual. Juries were acquitting radicals: Angela Davis, an acknowledged Communist, was acquitted by an all-white jury on the West Coast. Black Panthers, whom the government had tried in every way to malign and destroy, were freed by juries in several trials. A judge in western Massachusetts threw out a case against a young activist, Sam Lovejoy, who had toppled a 500-foot tower erected by a utility company trying to set up a nuclear plant. In Washington, D.C., in August 1973, a Superior Court judge refused to sentence six men charged with unlawful entry who had stepped from a White House tour line to protest the bombing of Cambodia.

Undoubtedly, much of this national mood of hostility to government and business came out of the Vietnam war, its 55,000 casualties, its moral shame, its exposure of government lies and atrocities. On top of this came the political disgrace of the Nixon administration in the scandals that came to be known by the one-word label "Watergate," and which led to the historic resignation from the presidency—the first in American history—of Richard Nixon in August 1974.

It began during the presidential campaign in June of 1972, when five burglars, carrying wiretapping and photo equipment, were caught in the act of breaking into the offices of the Democratic National Committee, in the Watergate apartment complex of Washington, D.C. One of the five, James McCord, Jr., worked for the Nixon campaign; he was "security" officer for the Committee to Re-elect the President (CREEP).

Another of the five had an address book in which was listed the name of E. Howard Hunt, and Hunt's address was listed as the White House. He was assistant to Charles Colson, who was special counsel to President Nixon.

Both McCord and Hunt had worked for many years for the CIA. Hunt had been the CIA man in charge of the invasion of Cuba in 1961, and three of the Watergate burglars were veterans of the invasion. McCord, as CREEP security man, worked for the chief of CREEP, John Mitchell, the Attorney General of the United States.

Thus, due to an unforeseen arrest by police unaware of the high-level connections of the burglars, information was out to the public before anyone could stop it, linking the burglars to important officials in Nixon's campaign committee, to the CIA, and to Nixon's Attorney General. Mitchell denied any connection with the burglary, and Nixon, in a press conference five days after the event, said "the White House has had no involvement whatever in this particular incident."

What followed the next year, after a grand jury in September indicted the Watergate burglars—plus Howard Hunt and G. Gordon Liddy—was that, one after another, lesser officials of the Nixon administration, fearing prosecution, began to talk. They gave information in judicial proceedings, to a Senate investigating committee, to the press. They implicated not only John Mitchell, but Robert Haldeman and John Ehrlichman, Nixon's highest White House aides, and finally Richard Nixon himself—in not only the Watergate burglaries, but a whole series of illegal actions against political opponents and antiwar activists. Nixon and his aides lied again and again as they tried to cover up their involvement.

These facts came out in the various testimonies:

1. Attorney General John Mitchell controlled a secret fund of $350,000 to $700,000—to be used against the Democratic party—for forging letters, leaking false news items to the press, stealing campaign files.
2. Gulf Oil Corporation, ITT (International Telephone and Telegraph), American Airlines, and other huge American corporations had made illegal contributions, running into millions of dollars, to the Nixon campaign.
3. In September of 1971, shortly after the *New York Times* printed Daniel Ellsberg's copies of the top-secret *Pentagon Papers*, the administration planned and carried out—Howard Hunt and Gordon Liddy themselves doing it—the burglary of the office of Ellsberg's psychiatrist, looking for Ellsberg's records.

4. After the Watergate burglars were caught, Nixon secretly pledged to give them executive clemency if they were imprisoned, and suggested that up to a million dollars be given them to keep them quiet. In fact, $450,000 was given to them, on Erlichman's orders.

5. Nixon's nominee for head of the FBI (J. Edgar Hoover had recently died), L. Patrick Gray, revealed that he had turned over the FBI records on its investigation of the Watergate burglary to Nixon's legal assistant, John Dean, and that Attorney General Richard Kleindienst (Mitchell had just resigned, saying he wanted to pursue his private life) had ordered him not to discuss Watergate with the Senate Judiciary Committee.

6. Two former members of Nixon's cabinet—John Mitchell and Maurice Stans—were charged with taking $250,000 from a financier named Robert Vesco in return for their help with a Securities and Exchange Commission investigation of Vesco's activities.

7. It turned out that certain material had disappeared from FBI files— material from a series of illegal wiretaps ordered by Henry Kissinger, placed on the telephones of four journalists and thirteen government officials—and was in the White House safe of Nixon's adviser John Erlichman.

8. One of the Watergate burglars, Bernard Barker, told the Senate committee that he had also been involved in a plan to physically attack Daniel Ellsberg while Ellsberg spoke at an antiwar rally in Washington.

9. A deputy director of the CIA testified that Haldeman and Ehrlichman told him it was Nixon's wish that the CIA tell the FBI not to pursue its investigation beyond the Watergate burglary.

10. Almost by accident, a witness told the Senate committee that President Nixon had tapes of all personal conversations and phone conversations at the White House. Nixon at first refused to turn over the tapes, and when he finally did, they had been tampered with: eighteen and a half minutes of one tape had been erased.

11. In the midst of all this, Nixon's Vice-President, Spiro Agnew, was indicted in Maryland for receiving bribes from Maryland contractors in return for political favors, and resigned from the vice-presidency in October 1973. Nixon appointed Congressman Gerald Ford to take Agnew's place.

12. Over $10 million in government money had been used by Nixon on his private homes in San Clemente and Key Biscayne on grounds of "security," and he had illegally taken—with the aid of a bit of forgery—a $576,000 tax deduction for some of his papers.

13. It was disclosed that for over a year in 1969–1970 the U.S. had engaged in a secret, massive bombing of Cambodia, which it kept from the American public and even from Congress.

It was a swift and sudden fall. In the November 1972 presidential election, Nixon and Agnew had won 60 percent of the popular vote and carried every state except Massachusetts, defeating an antiwar candidate, Senator George McGovern. By June of 1973 a Gallup poll showed 67 percent of those polled thought Nixon was involved in the Watergate break-in or lied to cover up.

By the fall of 1973 eight different resolutions had been introduced in the House of Representatives for the impeachment of President Nixon. The following year a House committee drew up a bill of impeachment to present it to a full House. Nixon's advisers told him it would pass the House by the required majority and then the Senate would vote the necessary two-thirds majority to remove him from office. On August 8, 1974, Nixon resigned.

Six months before Nixon resigned, the business magazine *Dun's Review* reported a poll of three hundred corporation executives. Almost all had voted for Nixon in 1972, but now a majority said he should resign. "Right now, 90% of Wall Street would cheer if Nixon resigns," said a vice-president of Merrill Lynch Government Securities. When he did, there was relief in all sectors of the Establishment.

Gerald Ford, taking Nixon's office, said: "Our long national nightmare is over." Newspapers, whether they had been for or against Nixon, liberal or conservative, celebrated the successful, peaceful culmination of the Watergate crisis. "The system is working," said a long-time strong critic of the Vietnam war, *New York Times* columnist Anthony Lewis. The two journalists who had much to do with investigating and exposing Nixon, Carl Bernstein and Bob Woodward of the Washington *Post*, wrote that with Nixon's departure, there might be "restoration." All of this was in a mood of relief, of gratitude.

No respectable American newspaper said what was said by Claude Julien, editor of *Le Monde Diplomatique* in September 1974. "The elimination of Mr. Richard Nixon leaves intact all the mechanisms and all the false values which permitted the Watergate scandal." Julien noted that Nixon's Secretary of State, Henry Kissinger, would remain at his post— in other words, that Nixon's foreign policy would continue. "That is to say," Julien wrote, "that Washington will continue to support General Pinochet in Chile, General Geisel in Brazil, General Stroessner in Paraguay, etc. . . ."

Months after Julien wrote this, it was disclosed that top Democratic and Republican leaders in the House of Representatives had given secret assurance to Nixon that if he resigned they would not support criminal proceedings against him. One of them, the ranking Republican of the Judiciary Committee, said: "We had all been shuddering about what two weeks of televised floor debates on impeachment would do, how it would tear the country apart and affect foreign policy." The *New York Times's* articles that reported on Wall Street's hope for Nixon's resignation quoted one Wall Street financier as saying that if Nixon resigned: "What we will have is the same play with different players."

When Gerald Ford, a conservative Republican who had supported all of Nixon's policies, was nominated for President, a liberal Senator from California, Alan Cranston, spoke for him on the floor, saying he had polled many people, Republicans and Democrats, and found "an almost startling consensus of conciliation that is developing around him." When Nixon resigned and Ford became President, the *New York Times* said: "Out of the despair of Watergate has come an inspiring new demonstration of the uniqueness and strength of the American democracy." A few days later the *Times* wrote happily that the "peaceful transfer of power" brought "a cleansing sense of relief to the American people."

In the charges brought by the House Committee on Impeachment against Nixon, it seemed clear that the committee did not want to emphasize those elements in his behavior which were found in other Presidents and which might be repeated in the future. It stayed clear of Nixon's dealings with powerful corporations; it did not mention the bombing of Cambodia. It concentrated on things peculiar to Nixon, not on fundamental policies continuous among American Presidents, at home and abroad.

The word was out: get rid of Nixon, but keep the system. Theodore Sorensen, who had been an adviser to President Kennedy, wrote at the time of Watergate: "The underlying causes of the gross misconduct in our law-enforcement system now being revealed are largely personal, not institutional. Some structural changes are needed. All the rotten apples should be thrown out. But save the barrel."

Indeed, the barrel was saved. Nixon's foreign policy remained. The government's connections to corporate interests remained. Ford's closest friends in Washington were corporate lobbyists. Alexander Haig, who had been one of Nixon's closest advisers, who had helped in "processing" the tapes before turning them over to the public, and who gave the public misinformation about the tapes, was appointed by President

Ford to be head of the armed forces of the North Atlantic Treaty Organization. One of Ford's first acts was to pardon Nixon, thus saving him from possible criminal proceedings and allowing him to retire with a huge pension in California.

The Establishment had cleansed itself of members of the club who had broken the rules—but it took some pains not to treat them too harshly. Those few who received jail sentences got short terms, were sent to the most easygoing federal institutions available, and were given special privileges not given to ordinary prisoners. Richard Kleindienst pleaded guilty; he got a $100 fine and one month in jail, which was suspended.

That Nixon would go, but that the power of the President to do anything he wanted in the name of "national security" would stay—this was underscored by a Supreme Court decision in July 1974. The Court said Nixon had to turn over his White House tapes to the special Watergate prosecutor. But at the same time it affirmed "the confidentiality of Presidential communications," which it could not uphold in Nixon's case, but which remained as a general principle when the President made a "claim of need to protect military, diplomatic or sensitive national security secrets."

The televised Senate Committee hearings on Watergate stopped suddenly before the subject of corporate connections was reached. It was typical of the selective coverage of important events by the television industry: bizarre shenanigans like the Watergate burglary were given full treatment, while instances of ongoing practice—the My Lai massacre, the secret bombing of Cambodia, the work of the FBI and CIA— were given the most fleeting attention. Dirty tricks against the Socialist Workers party, the Black Panthers, other radical groups, had to be searched for in a few newspapers. The whole nation heard the details of the quick break-in at the Watergate apartment; there was never a similar television hearing on the long-term break-in in Vietnam.

In the trial of John Mitchell and Maurice Stans for obstruction of justice in impeding a Securities and Exchange Commission investigation of Robert Vesco (a contributor to Nixon), George Bradford Cook, former general counsel of the SEC, testified that on November 13, 1972, he crouched in a Texas rice field while on a goose hunt with Maurice Stans, and told him he wanted to be chairman of the SEC. For this, he would cut out a critical paragraph in the SEC charges against Vesco that referred to Vesco's $200,000 secret contribution to the Nixon campaign.

Corporate influence on the White House is a permanent fact of the American system. Most of it is wise enough to stay within the law; under

Nixon they took chances. An executive in the meatpacking industry said during the Watergate events that he had been approached by a Nixon campaign official and told that while a $25,000 contribution would be appreciated, "for $50,000 you get to talk to the President."

Many of these corporations gave money to both sides, so that whichever won they would have friends in the administration. Chrysler Corporation urged its executives to "support the party and candidate of their choice," and then collected the checks from them and delivered the checks to Republican or Democratic campaign committees.

International Telephone and Telegraph was an old hand at giving money on both sides. In 1960 it had made illegal contributions to Bobby Baker, who worked with Democratic Senators, including Lyndon Johnson. A senior vice-president of ITT was quoted by one of his assistants as saying the board of directors "have it set up to 'butter' both sides so we'll be in good position whoever wins." And in 1970, an ITT director, John McCone, who also had been head of the CIA, told Henry Kissinger, Secretary of State, and Richard Helms, CIA director, that ITT was willing to give $1 million to help the U.S. government in its plans to overthrow the Allende government in Chile.

In 1971 ITT planned to take over the $1½ billion Hartford Fire Insurance Company—the largest merger in corporate history. The antitrust division of the Justice Department moved to prosecute ITT for violating the antitrust laws. However, the prosecution did not take place and ITT was allowed to merge with Hartford. It was all settled out of court, in a secret arrangement in which ITT agreed to donate $400,000 to the Republican party. It seemed that Richard Kleindienst, deputy Attorney General, had six meetings with an ITT director named Felix Rohatyn, and then brought in the head of the antitrust division, Richard McLaren, who was persuaded by Rohatyn that to stop the merger would cause a "hardship" for ITT stockholders. McLaren agreed. He was later appointed a federal judge.

One of the items not mentioned in the impeachment charges and never televised in the Senate hearings was the way the government cooperated with the milk industry. In early 1971 the Secretary of Agriculture announced the government would not increase its price supports for milk—the regular subsidy to the big milk producers. Then the Associated Milk Producers began giving money to the Nixon campaign, met in the White House with Nixon and the Secretary of Agriculture, gave more money, and the secretary announced that "new analysis" made it necessary to raise milk price supports from $4.66 to $4.93 a hundredweight. More contributions were made, until the total exceeded

$400,000. The price increases added $500 million to the profits of dairy farmers (mostly big corporations) at the expense of consumers.

Whether Nixon or Ford or any Republican or Democrat was President, the system would work pretty much the same way. A Senate subcommittee investigating multinational corporations revealed a document (given passing mention in a few newspapers) in which oil company economists discussed holding back production of oil to keep prices up. ARAMCO—the Arabian-American Oil Corporation, 75 percent of whose stock was held by American oil companies and 25 percent by Saudi Arabia—had made $1 profit on a barrel of oil in 1973. In 1974 it was making $4.50. None of this would be affected by who was President.

Even in the most diligent of investigations in the Watergate affair, that of Archibald Cox, a special prosecutor later fired by Nixon, the corporations got off easy. American Airlines, which admitted making illegal contributions to the Nixon campaign, was fined $5,000; Goodyear was fined $5,000; 3M Corporation was fined $3,000. A Goodyear official was fined $1,000; a 3M official was fined $500. The *New York Times* (October 20, 1973) reported:

> Mr. Cox charged them only with the misdemeanor of making illegal contributions. The misdemeanor, under the law, involved "nonwillful" contributions. The felony count, involving willful contributions, is punishable by a fine of $10,000 and/or a two-year jail term; the misdemeanor by a $1000 fine and/or a one-year jail term.
>
> Asked at the courthouse here how the two executives—who had admitted making the payments—could be charged with making non-willing contributions, Mr. McBride [Cox's staff] replied: "That's a legal question which frankly baffles me as well."

With Gerald Ford in office, the long continuity in American policy was maintained. He continued Nixon's policy of aid to the Saigon regime, apparently still hoping that the Thieu government would remain stable. The head of a congressional committee, John Calkins, visiting South Vietnam just around the time of Nixon's fall from office, reported:

> The South Vietnamese Army shows every sign of being an effective and spirited security force. . . .
> Oil exploration will begin very soon. Tourism can be encouraged by continued security of scenic and historic areas and by the erection of a new Hyatt Hotel. . . .

South Vietnam needs foreign investment to finance these and other developments. . . . She has a large labor pool of talented, industrious people whose cost of labor is far less than Hong Kong, Singapore, or even Korea or Taiwan. . . .

I also feel there is much profit to be made there. The combination of serving both God and Mammon had proved attractive to Americans and others in the past. . . . Vietnam can be the next "take off" capitalistic show-place in Asia.

In the spring of 1975, everything that radical critics of American policy in Vietnam had been saying—that without American troops, the Saigon government's lack of popular support would be revealed—came true. An offensive by North Vietnamese troops, left in the South by terms of the 1973 truce, swept through town after town.

Ford continued to be optimistic. He was the last of a long line of government officials and journalists who promised victory. (Secretary of Defense Robert McNamara, February 19, 1963: "Victory is in sight." General William Westmoreland, November 15, 1967: "I have never been more encouraged in my four years in Vietnam." Columnist Joseph Alsop, November 1, 1972: "Hanoi has accepted near-total defeat.") On April 16, 1975, Ford said: "I am absolutely convinced if Congress made available $722 million in military assistance by the time I asked—or sometime shortly thereafter—the South Vietnamese could stabilize the military situation in Vietnam today."

Two weeks later, April 29, 1975, the North Vietnamese moved into Saigon, and the war was over.

Most of the Establishment had already—despite Ford and a few stalwarts—given up on Vietnam. What they worried about was the readiness of the American public now to support other military actions overseas. There were trouble signs in the months before the defeat in Vietnam.

In early 1975 Senator John C. Culver of Iowa was unhappy that Americans would not fight for Korea: "He said that Vietnam had taken a mighty toll on the national will of the American people." Shortly before that, Secretary of Defense James Schlesinger, speaking to the Georgetown Center for Strategic and International Studies, was reported as being "generally gloomy," saying that "the world no longer regarded American military power as awesome."

In March 1975 a Catholic organization, making a survey of American attitudes on abortion, learned other things. To the statement: "The people running this country (government, political, church and civic leaders) don't tell us the truth," more than 83 percent agreed.

New York Times international correspondent C. L. Sulzberger, a consistent supporter of government cold-war foreign policy, wrote in a troubled mood in early 1975 from Ankara, Turkey, that "the glow has worn off from the era of the Truman Doctrine" (when military aid was given to Greece and Turkey). He added: "And one cannot say that the bleak outlook here is balanced by any brilliant United States successes in Greece, where a vast mob recently battered the United States Embassy." He concluded, "There must be something seriously wrong with the way we present ourselves these days." The problem, according to Sulzberger, was not the United States' behavior, but the way this behavior was presented to the world.

It was a few months after these reports, in April of 1975, that Secretary of State Kissinger, invited to be commencement speaker at the University of Michigan, was faced with petitions protesting the invitation, because of Kissinger's role in the Vietnam war. Also a counter-commencement program was planned. He withdrew. It was a low time for the administration. Vietnam was "lost" (the very word supposed it was ours to lose). Kissinger was quoted that April (by Washington *Post* columnist Tom Braden): "The U.S. must carry out some act somewhere in the world which shows its determination to continue to be a world power."

The following month came the *Mayaguez* affair.

The *Mayaguez* was an American cargo ship sailing from South Vietnam to Thailand in mid-May 1975, just three weeks after the victory of the revolutionary forces in Vietnam. When it came close to an island in Cambodia, where a revolutionary regime had just taken power, the ship was stopped by the Cambodians, taken to a port at a nearby island, and the crew removed to the mainland. The crew later described their treatment as courteous: "A man who spoke English greeted us with a handshake and welcomed us to Cambodia." The press reported: "Captain Miller and his men all say they were never abused by their captors. There were even accounts of kind treatment—of Cambodian soldiers feeding them first and eating what the Americans left, of the soldiers giving the seamen the mattresses off their beds." But the Cambodians did ask the crew about spying and the CIA.

President Ford sent a message to the Cambodian government to release the ship and crew, and when thirty-six hours had elapsed and there was no response (the message had been given to the Chinese liaison mission in Washington, but was returned the next day, "ostensibly undelivered," one press account said), he began military operations—U.S. planes bombed Cambodian ships. They strafed the very boat that was taking the American sailors to the mainland.

The men had been detained on a Monday morning. On Wednesday evening the Cambodians released them—putting them on a fishing boat headed for the American fleet. That afternoon, knowing the seamen had been taken off Tang Island, Ford nevertheless ordered a marine assault on Tang Island. That assault began about 7:15 Wednesday evening, but an hour earlier the crewmen were already headed back to the American fleet. About 7:00 P.M. the release had been announced on the radio in Bangkok. Indeed, the boat carrying the returned crewmen was spotted by a U.S. reconnaissance plane that signaled them.

Not mentioned in any press account at the time or in any government statement was a fact that emerged in October 1976 when the General Accounting Office made a report on the *Mayaguez* affair: the U.S. had received a message from a Chinese diplomat saying China was using its influence with Cambodia on the ship "and expected it to be released soon." This message was received fourteen hours before the marine assault began.

No American soldier was hurt by the Cambodians. The marines invading Tang Island, however, met unexpectedly tough resistance, and of two hundred invaders, one-third were soon dead or wounded (this exceeded the casualty rate in the World War II invasion of Iwo Jima). Five of eleven helicopters in the invasion force were blown up or disabled. Also, twenty-three Americans were killed in a helicopter crash over Thailand on their way to participate in the action, a fact the government tried to keep secret. All together, forty-one Americans were killed in the military actions ordered by Ford. There were thirty-nine sailors on the *Mayaguez*. Why the rush to bomb, strafe, attack? Why, even after the ship and crew were recovered, did Ford order American planes to bomb the Cambodian mainland, with untold Cambodian casualties? What could justify such a combination of moral blindness and military bungling?

The answer to this came soon: It was necessary to show the world that giant America, defeated by tiny Vietnam, was still powerful and resolute. The *New York Times* reported on May 16, 1975:

> Administration officials, including Secretary of State Henry Kissinger and Secretary of Defense James Schlesinger, were said to have been eager to find some dramatic means of underscoring President Ford's stated intention to "maintain our leadership on a world-wide basis." The occasion came with the capture of the vessel. . . . Administration officials . . . made it clear that they welcomed the opportunity. . . .

Another press dispatch from Washington, in the midst of the *Mayaguez* events, said: "High-ranking sources familiar with military strategy and planning said privately that the seizure of the vessel might provide the test of American determination in Southeast Asia that, they asserted, the U.S. had been seeking since the collapse of allied governments in South Vietnam and Cambodia."

Columnist James Reston wrote: "In fact, the Administration almost seems grateful for the opportunity to demonstrate that the President can act quickly. . . . Officials here have been bridling over a host of silly taunts about the American 'paper tiger' and hope the Marines have answered the charge."

It was not surprising that Secretary of Defense Schlesinger called it a "very successful operation," done "for purposes that were necessary for the well-being of this society." But why would the prestigious *Times* columnist James Reston, a strong critic of Nixon and Watergate, call the *Mayaguez* operation "melodramatic and successful"? And why would the *New York Times*, which had criticized the Vietnam war, talk about the "admirable efficiency" of the operation?

What seemed to be happening was that the Establishment—Republicans, Democrats, newspapers, television—was closing ranks behind Ford and Kissinger, and behind the idea that American authority must be asserted everywhere in the world.

Congress at this time behaved much as it had done in the early years of the Vietnam war, like a flock of sheep. Back in 1973, in a mood of fatigue and disgust with the Vietnam war, Congress had passed a War Powers Act that required the President, before taking military action, to consult with Congress. In the *Mayaguez* affair, Ford ignored this—he had several aides make phone calls to eighteen Congressmen to inform them that military action was under way. But, as I. F. Stone said (he was the maverick journalist who published the anti-Establishment *I. F. Stone's Weekly*), "Congress raped as easily as it did in the Tonkin Gulf affair." Congressman Robert Drinan of Massachusetts was an exception. Senator McGovern, Nixon's presidential opponent in 1972 and long-time antiwar critic, opposed the action. So did Senator Gaylord Nelson of Wisconsin. Senator Edward Brooke raised questions. Senator Edward Kennedy did not speak out, nor did other Senators who during the Vietnam war had influenced Congress to ban further military action in Indochina but now said their own legislation did not apply.

Secretary of State Kissinger would say: "We are forced into this." When Kissinger was asked why the U.S. was risking the lives of the *Mayaguez* seamen by firing on ships in the area without knowing where they were, he called it a "necessary risk."

Kissinger also said the incident "ought to make clear that there are limits beyond which the United States cannot be pushed, that the

United States is prepared to defend those interests, and that it can get public support and congressional support for these actions."

Indeed, Congressmen, Democrats as well as Republicans, who had been critical of the Vietnam war now seemed anxious to pull things together in a unified show of strength to the rest of the world. A week before the *Mayaguez* affair (two weeks before Saigon fell), fifty-six Congressmen had signed a statement saying: "Let no nation read the events in Indochina as the failure of the American will." One of them was a black Congressman from Georgia, Andrew Young.

It was a complex process of consolidation that the system undertook in 1975. It included old-type military actions, like the *Mayaguez* affair, to assert authority in the world and at home. There was also a need to satisfy a disillusioned public that the system was criticizing and correcting itself. The standard way was to conduct publicized investigations that found specific culprits but left the system intact. Watergate had made both the FBI and the CIA look bad—breaking the laws they were sworn to uphold, cooperating with Nixon in his burglary jobs and illegal wiretapping. In 1975, congressional committees in the House and Senate began investigations of the FBI and CIA.

The CIA inquiry disclosed that the CIA had gone beyond its original mission of gathering intelligence and was conducting secret operations of all kinds. For instance, back in the 1950s, it had administered the drug LSD to unsuspecting Americans to test its effects: one American scientist, given such a dose by a CIA agent, leaped from a New York hotel window to his death.

The CIA had also been involved in assassination plots against Castro of Cuba and other heads of state. It had introduced African swine fever virus into Cuba in 1971, bringing disease and then slaughter to 500,000 pigs. A CIA operative told a reporter he delivered the virus from an army base in the Canal Zone to anti-Castro Cubans.

It was also learned from the investigation that the CIA—with the collusion of a secret Committee of Forty headed by Henry Kissinger—had worked to "destabilize" the Chilean government headed by Salvadore Allende, a Marxist who had been elected president in one of the rare free elections in Latin America. ITT, with large interests in Chile, played a part in this operation. When in 1974 the American ambassador to Chile, David Popper, suggested to the Chilean junta (which, with U.S. aid, had overthrown Allende) that they were violating human rights, he was rebuked by Kissinger, who sent word: "Tell Popper to cut out the political science lectures."

The investigation of the FBI disclosed many years of illegal actions to disrupt and destroy radical groups and left-wing groups of all kinds. The FBI had sent forged letters, engaged in burglaries (it admitted to ninety-two between 1960 and 1966), opened mail illegally, and, in the case of Black Panther leader Fred Hampton, seems to have conspired in murder.

Valuable information came out of the investigations, but it was just enough, and in just the right way—moderate press coverage, little television coverage, thick books of reports with limited readership—to give the impression of an honest society correcting itself.

The investigations themselves revealed the limits of government willingness to probe into such activities. The Church Committee, set up by the Senate, conducted its investigations with the cooperation of the agencies being investigated and, indeed, submitted its findings on the CIA to the CIA to see if there was material that the Agency wanted omitted. Thus, while there was much valuable material in the report, there is no way of knowing how much more there was—the final report was a compromise between committee diligence and CIA caution.

The Pike Committee, set up in the House of Representatives, made no such agreement with the CIA or FBI, and when it issued its final report, the same House that had authorized its investigation voted to keep the report secret. When the report was leaked via a CBS newscaster, Daniel Schorr, to the *Village Voice* in New York, it was never printed by the important newspapers in the country—the *Times*, the Washington *Post*, or others. Schorr was suspended by CBS. It was another instance of cooperation between the mass media and the government in instances of "national security."

The Church Committee, in its report of CIA attempts to assassinate Fidel Castro and other foreign leaders, revealed an interesting point of view. The committee seemed to look on the killing of a head of state as an unpardonable violation of some gentlemen's agreement among statesmen, much more deplorable than military interventions that killed ordinary people. The Committee wrote, in the introduction to its assassination report:

> Once methods of coercion and violence are chosen, the probability of loss of life is always present. There is, however, a significant difference between a cold-blooded, targeted, intentional killing of an individual foreign leader and other forms of intervening in the affairs of foreign nations.

The Church Committee uncovered CIA operations to secretly influence the minds of Americans:

The CIA is now using several hundred American academics (administrators, faculty members, graduate students engaged in teaching) who, in addition to providing leads and, on occasion, making introductions for intelligence purposes, write books and other material to be used for propaganda purposes abroad. . . . These academics are located in over 100 American colleges, universities and related institutions. At the majority of institutions, no one other than the individual concerned is aware of the CIA link. At the others, at least one university official is aware of the operational use of academics on his campus. . . . The CIA considers these operational relationships within the U.S. academic community as perhaps its most sensitive domestic area and has strict controls governing these operations. . . .

In 1961 the chief of the CIA's Covert Action Staff wrote that books were "the most important weapon of strategic propaganda." The Church Committee found that more than a thousand books were produced, subsidized, or sponsored by the CIA before the end of 1967.

When Kissinger testified before the Church Committee about the bombing of Laos, orchestrated by the CIA as a secret activity, he said: "I do not believe in retrospect that it was a good national policy to have the CIA conduct the war in Laos. I think we should have found some other way of doing it." There was no indication that anyone on the Committee challenged this idea—that what was done should have been done, but by another method.

Thus, in 1974–1975, the system was acting to purge the country of its rascals and restore it to a healthy, or at least to an acceptable, state. The resignation of Nixon, the succession of Ford, the exposure of bad deeds by the FBI and CIA—all aimed to regain the badly damaged confidence of the American people. However, even with these strenuous efforts, there were still many signs in the American public of suspicion, even hostility, to the leaders of government, military, big business.

Two months after the end of the Vietnam war, only 20 percent of Americans polled thought the collapse of the Saigon government was a threat to United States security.

June 14, 1975, was Flag Day, and President Gerald Ford spoke at Fort Benning, Georgia, where the army staged a march symbolizing its involvement in thirteen wars. Ford commented that he was glad to see so many flags, but a reporter covering the event wrote: "Actually, there were few American flags to be seen near the President's reviewing stand. One, held aloft by demonstrators, bore an inked-in inscription saying, 'No more genocide in our name.' It was torn down by spectators as their neighbors applauded."

That July the Lou Harris poll, looking at the public's confidence in the government from 1966 to 1975, reported that confidence in the military during that period had dropped from 62 percent to 29 percent, in business from 55 percent to 18 percent, in both President and Congress from 42 percent to 13 percent. Shortly after that, another Harris poll reported "65% of Americans oppose military aid abroad because they feel it allows dictatorships to maintain control over their population."

Perhaps much of the general dissatisfaction was due to the economic state of most Americans. Inflation and unemployment had been rising steadily since 1973, which was the year when, according to a Harris poll, the number of Americans feeling "alienated" and "disaffected" with the general state of the country climbed (from 29 percent in 1966) to over 50 percent. After Ford succeeded Nixon, the percentage of "alienated" was 55 percent. The survey showed that people were troubled most of all by inflation.

In the fall of 1975 a *New York Times* survey of 1,559 persons, and interviews with sixty families in twelve cities, showed "a substantial decline in optimism about the future." The *Times* reported:

> Inflation, the apparent inability of the country to solve its economic problems, and a foreboding that the energy crisis will mean a permanent step backward for the nation's standard of living have made inroads into Americans' confidence, expectations, and aspirations. . . .
>
> Pessimism about the future is particularly acute among those who earn less than $7000 annually, but it is also high within families whose annual incomes range from $10,000 to $15,000. . . .
>
> There is also concern that . . . no longer will hard work and a conscientious effort to save money bring them a nice home in the suburbs. . . .

Even higher-income people, the survey found, "are not as optimistic now as they were in past years, indicating that discontent is moving up from the lower middle-income to higher economic levels."

Around the same time, that fall of 1975, public opinion analysts testifying before a congressional committee reported, according to the *New York Times,* "that public confidence in the Government and in the country's economic future is probably lower than it has ever been since they began to measure such things scientifically."

Government statistics suggested the reasons. The Census Bureau reported that from 1974 to 1975 the number of Americans "legally" poor (that is, below an income of $5,500) had risen 10 percent and was now 25.9 million people. Also, the unemployment rate, which had been

5.6 percent in 1974, had risen to 8.3 percent in 1975, and the number of people who exhausted their unemployment benefits increased from 2 million in 1974 to 4.3 million in 1975.

Government figures, however, generally underestimated the amount of poverty, set the "legally" poor level too low, and underestimated the amount of unemployment. For instance, if 16.6 percent of the population averaged six months of unemployment during 1975, or 33.2 percent averaged three months of unemployment, the "average annual figure" given by the government was 8.3 percent, which sounded better.

In the year 1976, with a presidential election approaching, there was worry in the Establishment about the public's faith in the system. William Simon, Secretary of the Treasury under both Nixon and Ford (before then an investment banker earning over $2 million a year), spoke in the fall of 1976 to a Business Council meeting in Hot Springs, Virginia. He said that when "so much of the world is lurching towards socialism or totalitarianism" it was urgent to make the American business system understood, because "private enterprise is losing by default—in many of our schools, in much of the communications media, and in a growing portion of the public consciousness." His speech could well be taken to represent the thinking of the American corporate elite:

> Vietnam, Watergate, student unrest, shifting moral codes, the worst recession in a generation, and a number of other jarring cultural shocks have all combined to create a new climate of questions and doubt. . . . It all adds up to a general malaise, a society-wide crisis of institutional confidence. . . .

Too often, Simon said, Americans "have been taught to distrust the very word profit and the profit motive that makes our prosperity possible, to somehow feel this system, that has done more to alleviate human suffering and privation than any other, is somehow cynical, selfish, and amoral." We must, Simon said, "get across the human side of capitalism."

As the United States prepared in 1976 to celebrate the bicentennial of the Declaration of Independence, a group of intellectuals and political leaders from Japan, the United States, and Western Europe, organized into "The Trilateral Commission," issued a report. It was entitled "The Governability of Democracies." Samuel Huntington, a political science professor at Harvard University and long-time consultant to the White House on the war in Vietnam, wrote the part of the report that dealt with the United States. He called it "The Democratic Distemper" and identified the problem he was about to discuss: "The 1960's witnessed a dramatic upsurge of democratic fervor in America." In the sixties, Huntington wrote, there was a huge growth of citizen participation "in the forms of marches, demonstrations, protest movements, and 'cause' organizations." There were also "markedly higher levels of self-consciousness on the part of blacks, Indians, Chicanos, white ethnic groups, students and women, all of whom became mobilized and organized in new ways. . . ." There was a "marked expansion of white-collar unionism," and all this added up to "a reassertion of equality as a goal in social, economic and political life."

Huntington pointed to the signs of decreasing government authority: The great demands in the sixties for equality had transformed the federal budget. In 1960 foreign affairs spending was 53.7 percent of the budget, and social spending was 22.3 percent. By 1974 foreign affairs took 33 percent and social spending 31 percent. This seemed to reflect a change in public mood: In 1960 only 18 percent of the public said the government was spending too much on defense, but in 1969 this jumped to 52 percent.

Huntington was troubled by what he saw:

> The essence of the democratic surge of the 1960's was a general challenge to existing systems of authority, public and private. In one form or another, this challenge manifested itself in the family, the university, business, public and private associations, politics, the governmental bureaucracy, and the military services. People no longer felt the same obligation to obey those whom they had previously considered superior to themselves in age, rank, status, expertise, character, or talents.

All this, he said, "produced problems for the governability of democracy in the 1970's. . . ."

Critical in all this was the decline in the authority of the President. And:

> To the extent that the United States was governed by anyone during the decades after World War II, it was governed by the President acting with the support and cooperation of key individuals and groups in the executive office, the federal bureaucracy, Congress, and the more important businesses, banks, law firms, foundations, and media, which constitute the private sector's "Establishment."

This was probably the frankest statement ever made by an Establishment adviser.

Huntington further said that the President, to win the election, needed the support of a broad coalition of people. However: "The day after his election, the size of his majority is almost—if not entirely—irrelevant to his ability to govern the country. What counts then is his ability to mobilize support from the leaders of key institutions in a society and government. . . . This coalition must include key people in Congress, the executive branch, and the private-sector 'Establishment.'" He gave examples:

> Truman made a point of bringing a substantial number of non-partisan soldiers, Republican bankers, and Wall Street lawyers into his Administration. He went to the existing sources of power in the country to get help he needed in ruling the country. Eisenhower in part inherited this coalition and was in part almost its creation. . . . Kennedy attempted to re-create a somewhat similar structure of alliances.

What worried Huntington was the loss in governmental authority. For instance, the opposition to Vietnam had brought the abolition of the draft. "The question necessarily arises, however, whether if a new threat to security should materialize in the future (as it inevitably will at some point), the government will possess the authority to command the resources, as well as the sacrifices, which are necessary to meet that threat."

Huntington saw the possible end of that quarter century when "the United States was the hegemonic power in a system of world order." His conclusion was that there had developed "an excess of democracy," and he suggested "desirable limits to the extension of political democracy."

Huntington was reporting all this to an organization that was very important to the future of the United States. The Trilateral Commission was organized in early 1973 by David Rockefeller and Zbigniew Brzezinski. Rockefeller was an official of the Chase Manhattan Bank and a powerful financial figure in the United States and the world; Brzezinski, a Columbia University professor, specialized in international relations and was a consultant to the State Department. As reported in the *Far Eastern Economic Review* (March 25, 1977) by Robert Manning:

> The initiative for the Commission came entirely from Rockefeller. According to George Franklin, the Commission's executive secretary, Rockefeller "was getting worried about the deteriorating relations between the United States, Europe and Japan." Franklin explained that Rockefeller

began to present his ideas to another elite fraternity: ". . . at the Bilderberg Group—a very distinguished Anglo-American group which has been meeting for a long time—Mike Blumenthal said he thought things were in a very serious condition in the world and couldn't some kind of private group do more about it? . . . So then David again made his proposal. . . ." Then Brzezinski, a close friend of Rockefeller's, carried the Rockefeller-funded ball and organized the Commission.

It seems probable that the "very serious condition" mentioned as the reason for the Trilateral Commission was the need for greater unity among Japan, Western Europe, and the United States in the face of a much more complicated threat to tri-continental capitalism than a monolithic Communism: revolutionary movements in the Third World. These movements had directions of their own.

The Trilateral Commission wanted also to deal with another situation. Back in 1967, George Ball, who had been Undersecretary of State for economic affairs in the Kennedy administration and who was director of Lehman Brothers, a large investment banking firm, told members of the International Chamber of Commerce:

> In these twenty postwar years, we have come to recognize in action, though not always in words, that the political boundaries of nation-states are too narrow and constricted to define the scope and activities of modern business.

To show the growth of international economics for United States corporations, one would only have to note the situation in banking. In 1960 there were eight United States banks with foreign branches; in 1974 there were 129. The assets of these overseas branches amounted to $3.5 billion in 1960, $155 billion in 1974.

The Trilateral Commission apparently saw itself as helping to create the necessary international links for the new multinational economy. Its members came from the highest circles of politics, business, and the media in Western Europe, Japan, and the United States. They were from Chase Manhattan, Lehman Brothers, Bank of America, Banque de Paris, Lloyd's of London, Bank of Tokyo, etc. Oil, steel, auto, aeronautic, and electric industries were represented. Other members were from *Time* magazine, the Washington *Post*, the Columbia Broadcasting System, *Die Zeit*, the *Japan Times*, *The Economist* of London, and more.

1976 was not only a presidential election year—it was the much-anticipated year of the bicentennial celebration, and it was filled with much-publicized events all over the country. The great effort that went into the celebration suggests that it was seen as a way of restoring American patriotism, invoking the symbols of history to unite people and government and put aside the protest mood of the recent past.

But there did not seem to be great enthusiasm for it. When the 200th anniversary of the Boston Tea Party was celebrated in Boston, an enormous crowd turned out, not for the official celebration, but for the "People's Bi-Centennial" countercelebration, where packages marked "Gulf Oil" and "Exxon" were dumped into the Boston Harbor, to symbolize opposition to corporate power in America.

21

CARTER-REAGAN-BUSH: THE BIPARTISAN CONSENSUS

Halfway through the twentieth century, the historian Richard Hofstadter, in his book *The American Political Tradition*, examined our important national leaders, from Jefferson and Jackson to Herbert Hoover and the two Roosevelts—Republicans and Democrats, liberals and conservatives. Hofstadter concluded that "the range of vision embraced by the primary contestants in the major parties has always been bounded by the horizons of property and enterprise. . . . They have accepted the economic virtues of capitalist culture as necessary qualities of man. . . . That culture has been intensely nationalistic. . . ."

Coming to the end of the century, observing its last twenty-five years, we have seen exactly that limited vision Hofstadter talked about— a capitalistic encouragement of enormous fortunes alongside desperate poverty, a nationalistic acceptance of war and preparations for war. Governmental power swung from Republicans to Democrats and back again, but neither party showed itself capable of going beyond that vision.

After the disastrous war in Vietnam came the scandals of Watergate. There was a deepening economic insecurity for much of the population, along with environmental deterioration, and a growing culture of violence and family disarray. Clearly, such fundamental problems could not be solved without bold changes in the social and economic structure. But no major party candidates proposed such changes. The "American political tradition" held fast.

In recognition of this, perhaps only vaguely conscious of this, voters stayed away from the polls in large numbers, or voted without enthusiasm. More and more they declared, if only by nonparticipation, their alienation from the political system. In 1960, 63 percent of those eligible to vote voted in the presidential election. By 1976, this figure had dropped to 53 percent. In a CBS News and *New York Times* survey, over half of the respondents said that public officials didn't care about people like them. A typical response came from a plumber: "The President of the United States isn't going to solve our problems. The problems are too big."

There was a troubling incongruity in the society. Electoral politics dominated the press and television screens, and the doings of presidents, members of Congress, Supreme Court justices, and other officials were treated as if they constituted the history of the country. Yet there was something artificial in all this, something pumped up, a straining to persuade a skeptical public that this was all, that they must rest their hopes for the future in Washington politicians, none of whom were inspiring because it seemed that behind the bombast, the rhetoric, the promises, their major concern was their own political power.

The distance between politics and the people was reflected clearly in the culture. In what was supposed to be the best of the media, uncontrolled by corporate interest—that is, in *public* television, the public was largely invisible. On the leading political forum on public television, the nightly "MacNeil-Lehrer Report," the public was uninvited, except as viewer of an endless parade of Congressmen, Senators, government bureaucrats, experts of various kinds.

On commercial radio, the usual narrow band of consensus, excluding fundamental criticism, was especially apparent. In the mid-1980s, with Ronald Reagan as President, the "fairness doctrine" of the Federal Communications Commission, requiring air time for dissenting views, was eliminated. By the 1990s, "talk radio" had perhaps 20 million listeners, treated to daily tirades from right-wing talk-show "hosts," with left-wing guests uninvited.

A citizenry disillusioned with politics and with what pretended to be intelligent discussions of politics turned its attention (or had its attention turned) to entertainment, to gossip, to ten thousand schemes for self-help. Those at its margins became violent, finding scapegoats within one's group (as with poor-black on poor-black violence), or against other races, immigrants, demonized foreigners, welfare mothers, minor criminals (standing in for untouchable major criminals).

There were other citizens, those who tried to hold on to ideas and ideals still remembered from the sixties and early seventies, not just by recollecting but by acting. Indeed, all across the country there was a part of the public unmentioned in the media, ignored by political leaders— energetically active in thousands of local groups around the country. These organized groups were campaigning for environmental protection or women's rights or decent health care (including anguished concern about the horrors of AIDS) or housing for the homeless, or against military spending.

This activism was unlike that of the sixties, when the surge of protest against race segregation and war became an overwhelming national force. It struggled uphill, against callous political leaders, trying to reach fellow Americans most of whom saw little hope in either the politics of voting or the politics of protest.

The presidency of Jimmy Carter, covering the years 1977 to 1980, seemed an attempt by one part of the Establishment, that represented in the Democratic party, to recapture a disillusioned citizenry. But Carter, despite a few gestures toward black people and the poor, despite talk of "human rights" abroad, remained within the historic political boundaries of the American system, protecting corporate wealth and power, maintaining a huge military machine that drained the national wealth, allying the United States with right-wing tyrannies abroad.

Carter seemed to be the choice of that international group of powerful influence-wielders—the Trilateral Commission. Two founding members of the commission, according to the *Far Eastern Economic Review*— David Rockefeller and Zbigniew Brzezinski—thought Carter was the right person for the presidential election of 1976 given that "the Watergate-plagued Republican Party was a sure loser. . . ."

Carter's job as President, from the point of view of the Establishment, was to halt the rushing disappointment of the American people with the government, with the economic system, with disastrous military ventures abroad. In his campaign, he tried to speak to the disillusioned and angry. His strongest appeal was to blacks, whose rebellion in the late sixties was the most frightening challenge to authority since the labor and unemployed upsurges in the thirties.

His appeal was "populist"—that is, he appealed to various elements of American society who saw themselves beleaguered by the powerful and wealthy. Although he himself was a millionaire peanut grower, he presented himself as an ordinary American farmer. Although he had been a supporter of the Vietnam war until its end, he presented himself as a sympathizer with those who had been against the war, and he appealed to many of the young rebels of the sixties by his promise to cut the military budget.

In a much-publicized speech to lawyers, Carter spoke out against the use of the law to protect the rich. He appointed a black woman, Patricia Harris, as Secretary of Housing and Urban Development, and a black civil rights veteran, Andrew Young, as ambassador to the United Nations. He gave the job of heading the domestic youth service corps to a young former antiwar activist, Sam Brown.

His most crucial appointments, however, were in keeping with the Trilateral Commission report of Harvard political scientist Samuel Huntington, which said that, whatever groups voted for a president, once elected "what counts then is his ability to mobilize support from the leaders of key institutions." Brzezinski, a traditional cold war intellectual, became Carter's National Security Adviser. His Secretary of Defense, Harold Brown, had, during the Vietnam war, according to the *Pentagon Papers*, "envisaged the elimination of virtually all the constraints under which the bombing then operated." His Secretary of Energy, James Schlesinger, as Secretary of Defense under Nixon, was described by a member of the Washington press corps as showing "an almost missionary drive in seeking to reverse a downward trend in the defense budget." Schlesinger was also a strong proponent of nuclear energy.

His other cabinet appointees had strong corporate connections. A financial writer wrote, not long after Carter's election: "So far, Mr. Carter's actions, commentary, and particularly his Cabinet appointments, have been highly reassuring to the business community." Veteran Washington correspondent Tom Wicker wrote: "The available evidence is that Mr. Carter so far is opting for Wall Street's confidence."

Carter did initiate more sophisticated policies toward governments that oppressed their own people. He used United Nations Ambassador Andrew Young to build up good will for the United States among the black African nations, and urged that South Africa liberalize its policies toward blacks. A peaceful settlement in South Africa was necessary for strategic reasons; South Africa was used for radar tracking systems. Also, it had important U.S. corporate investments and was a critical source of needed raw materials (diamonds, especially). Therefore, what the United States needed was a stable government in South Africa; the continued oppression of blacks might create civil war.

The same approach was used in other countries—combining practical strategic needs with the advancement of civil rights. But because the chief motivation was practicality, not humanity, there was a tendency toward token changes—as in Chile's release of a few political prisoners. When Congressman Herman Badillo introduced in Congress a proposal that required the U.S. representatives to the World Bank and other international financial institutions to vote against loans to countries that systematically violated essential rights, by the use of torture or imprisonment without trial, Carter sent a personal letter to every Congressman urging the defeat of this amendment. It won a voice vote in the House, but lost in the Senate.

Under Carter, the United States continued to support, all over the world, regimes that engaged in imprisonment of dissenters, torture, and mass murder: in the Philippines, in Iran, in Nicaragua, and in Indonesia, where the inhabitants of East Timor were being annihilated in a campaign bordering on genocide.

The *New Republic* magazine, presumably on the liberal side of the Establishment, commented approvingly on the Carter policies: ". . . American foreign policy in the next four years will essentially extend the philosophies developed . . . in the Nixon-Ford years. This is not at all a negative prospect. . . . There should be continuity. It is part of history. . . ."

Carter had presented himself as a friend of the movement against the war, but when Nixon mined Haiphong harbor and resumed bombing of North Vietnam in the spring of 1973, Carter urged that "we give President Nixon our backing and support—whether or not we agree with specific decisions." Once elected, Carter declined to give aid to Vietnam for reconstruction, despite the fact that the land had been devastated by American bombing. Asked about this at a press conference, Carter replied that there was no special obligation on the United States to do this because "the destruction was mutual."

Considering that the United States had crossed half the globe with an enormous fleet of bombers and 2 million soldiers, and after eight years left a tiny nation with over a million dead and its land in ruins, this was an astounding statement.

One Establishment intention, perhaps, was that future generations see the war not as it appeared in the Defense Department's own *Pentagon Papers*—as a ruthless attack on civilian populations for strategic military and economic interests—but as an unfortunate error. Noam Chomsky, one of the leading antiwar intellectuals during the Vietnam period, looked in mid-1978 at how the history of the war was being presented in the major media and wrote that they were "destroying the historical record and supplanting it with a more comfortable story . . . reducing 'lessons' of the war to the socially neutral categories of error, ignorance, and cost."

The Carter administration clearly was trying to end the disillusionment of the American people after the Vietnam war by following foreign policies more palatable, less obviously aggressive. Hence, the emphasis on "human rights," the pressure on South Africa and Chile to liberalize their policies. But on close examination, these more liberal policies were designed to leave intact the power and influence of the American military and American business in the world.

The renegotiation of the Panama Canal treaty with the tiny Central American republic of Panama was an example. The canal saved American companies $1.5 billion a year in delivery costs, and the United States collected $150 million a year in tolls, out of which it paid the Panama government $2.3 million dollars, while maintaining fourteen military bases in the area.

Back in 1903 the United States had engineered a revolution against Colombia, set up the new tiny republic of Panama in Central America, and dictated a treaty giving the United States military bases, control of the Panama Canal, and sovereignty "in perpetuity." The Carter administration in 1977, responding to anti-American protests in Panama, decided to renegotiate the treaty. The *New York Times* was candid about the Canal: "We stole it, and removed the incriminating evidence from our history books."

By 1977 the canal had lost military importance. It could not accommodate large tankers or aircraft carriers. That, plus the anti-American riots in Panama, led the Carter administration, over conservative opposition, to negotiate a new treaty which called for a gradual removal of U.S. bases (which could easily be relocated elsewhere in the area). The canal's legal ownership would be turned over to Panama after a period. The treaty also contained vague language which could be the basis for American military intervention under certain conditions.

Whatever Carter's sophistication in foreign policy, certain fundamentals operated in the late sixties and the seventies. American corporations were active all over the world on a scale never seen before. There were, by the early seventies, about three hundred U.S. corporations, including the seven largest banks, which earned 40 percent of their net profits outside the United States. They were called "multinationals," but actually 98 percent of their top executives were Americans. As a group, they now constituted the third-largest economy in the world, next to the United States and the Soviet Union.

The relationship of these global corporations with the poorer countries had long been an exploiting one, it was clear from U.S. Department of Commerce figures. Whereas U.S. corporations in Europe between 1950 and 1965 invested $8.1 billion and made $5.5 billion in profits, in Latin America they invested $3.8 billion and made

$11.2 billion in profits, and in Africa they invested $5.2 billion and made $14.3 billion in profits.

It was the classical imperial situation, where the places with natural wealth became victims of more powerful nations whose power came from that seized wealth. American corporations depended on the poorer countries for 100 percent of their diamonds, coffee, platinum, mercury, natural rubber, and cobalt. They got 98 percent of their manganese from abroad, 90 percent of their chrome and aluminum. And 20 to 40 percent of certain imports (platinum, mercury, cobalt, chrome, manganese) came from Africa.

Another fundamental of foreign policy, whether Democrats or Republicans were in the White House, was the training of foreign military officers. The Army had a "School of the Americas" in the Canal Zone, from which thousands of military leaders in Latin America had graduated. Six of the graduates, for instance, were in the Chilean military junta that overthrew the democratically elected Allende government in 1973. The American commandant of the school told a reporter: "We keep in touch with our graduates and they keep in touch with us."

And yet the United States cultivated a reputation for being generous with its riches. Indeed, it had frequently given aid to disaster victims. This aid, however, often depended on political loyalty. In one six-year drought in West Africa, 100,000 Africans died of starvation. A report by the Carnegie Endowment said the Agency for International Development (AID) of the United States had been inefficient and neglectful in giving aid to nomads in the Sahel area of West Africa, an area covering six countries. The response of AID was that those countries had "no close historical, economic, or political ties to the United States."

In early 1975 the press carried a dispatch from Washington: "Secretary of State Henry A. Kissinger has formally initiated a policy of selecting for cutbacks in American aid those nations that have sided against the U.S. in votes in the United Nations. In some cases the cutbacks involve food and humanitarian relief."

Most aid was openly military, and by 1975, the United States exported $9.5 billion in arms. The Carter administration promised to end the sale of arms to repressive regimes, but when it took office the bulk of the sales continued.

And the military continued to take a huge share of the national budget. When Carter was running for election, he told the Democratic Platform Committee: "Without endangering the defense of our nation or commitments to our allies, we can reduce present defense expenditures by about 5 to 7 billion dollars annually." But his first budget proposed not a decrease but an increase of $10 billion for the military. Indeed, he proposed that the U.S. spend a thousand billion dollars (a trillion dollars) in the next five years on its military forces. And the administration had just announced that the Department of Agriculture would save $25 million a year by no longer giving free second helpings of milk to 1.4 million needy schoolchildren who got free meals in school.

If Carter's job was to restore faith in the system, here was his greatest failure—solving the economic problems of the people. The price of food and the necessities of life continued to rise faster than wages were rising. Unemployment remained officially at 6 or 8 percent; unofficially, the rates were higher. For certain key groups in the population—young people, and especially young black people—the unemployment rate was 20 or 30 percent.

It soon became clear that blacks in the United States, the group most in support of Carter for President, were bitterly disappointed with his policies. He opposed federal aid to poor people who needed abortions, and when it was pointed out to him that this was unfair, because rich women could get abortions with ease, he replied: "Well, as you know, there are many things in life that are not fair, that wealthy people can afford and poor people cannot."

Carter's "populism" was not visible in his administration's relationship to the oil and gas interests. It was part of Carter's "energy plan" to end price regulation of natural gas for the consumer. The largest producer of natural gas was Exxon Corporation, and the largest blocs of private stock in Exxon were owned by the Rockefeller family.

Early in Carter's administration, the Federal Energy Administration found that Gulf Oil Corporation had overstated by $79.1 million its costs for crude oil obtained from foreign affiliates. It then passed on these false costs to consumers. In the summer of 1978 the administration announced that "a compromise" had been made with Gulf Oil in which Gulf agreed to pay back $42.2 million. Gulf informed its stockholders that "the payments will not affect earnings since adequate provision was made in prior years."

The lawyer for the Energy Department who worked out the compromise with Gulf said it had been done to avoid a lengthy and costly lawsuit. Would the lawsuit have cost the $36.9 million dropped in the compromise? Would the government have considered letting off a bank robber without a jail term in return for half the loot? The settlement was a perfect example of what Carter had told a meeting of lawyers during his presidential campaign—that the law was on the side of the rich.

The fundamental facts of maldistribution of wealth in America were clearly not going to be affected by Carter's policies, any more than by previous administrations, whether conservative or liberal. According to Andrew Zimbalist, an American economist writing in *Le Monde Diplomatique* in 1977, the top 10 percent of the American population had an income thirty times that of the bottom tenth; the top 1 percent of the nation owned 33 percent of the wealth. The richest 5 percent owned 83 percent of the personally owned corporate stock. The one hundred largest corporations (despite the graduated income tax that misled people into thinking the very rich paid at least 50 percent in taxes) paid an average of 26.9 percent in taxes, and the leading oil companies paid 5.8 percent in taxes (Internal Revenue Service figures for 1974). Indeed, 244 individuals who earned over $200,000 paid no taxes.

In 1979, as Carter weakly proposed benefits for the poor, and Congress strongly turned them down, a black woman, Marian Wright Edelman, director of the Children's Defense Fund in Washington, pointed to some facts. One of every seven American children (10 million altogether) had no known regular source of primary health care. One of every three children under seventeen (18 million altogether) had never seen a dentist. In an article on the *New York Times* op-ed page, she wrote:

> The Senate Budget Committee recently . . . knocked off $88 million from a modest $288 million Administration request to improve the program that screens and treats children's health problems. At the same time the Senate found $725 million to bail out Litton Industries and to hand to the Navy at least two destroyers ordered by the Shah of Iran.

Carter approved tax "reforms" which benefited mainly the corporations. Economist Robert Lekachman, writing in *The Nation*, noted the sharp increase in corporate profits (44 percent) in the last quarter of 1978 over the previous year's last quarter. He wrote: "Perhaps the President's most outrageous act occurred last November when he signed into law an $18 billion tax reduction, the bulk of whose benefits accrue to affluent individuals and corporations."

In 1979, while the poor were taking cuts, the salary of the chairman of Exxon Oil was being raised to $830,000 a year and that of the chairman of Mobil Oil to over a million dollars a year. That year, while Exxon's net income rose 56 percent to more than $4 billion, three thousand small independent gasoline stations went out of business.

Carter made some efforts to hold onto social programs, but this was undermined by his very large military budgets. Presumably, this was to guard against the Soviet Union, but when the Soviet Union invaded Afghanistan in 1979, Carter could take only symbolic actions, like reinstituting the draft, or calling for a boycott of the 1980 Moscow Olympics.

On the other hand, American weaponry was used to support dictatorial regimes battling left-wing rebels abroad. A report by the Carter administration to Congress in 1977 was blunt, saying that "a number of countries with deplorable records of human rights observance are also countries where we have important security and foreign policy interests."

Thus, Carter asked Congress in the spring of 1980 for $5.7 million in credits for the military junta fighting off a peasant rebellion in El Salvador. In the Philippines, after the 1978 National Assembly elections, President Ferdinand Marcos imprisoned ten of the twenty-one losing opposition candidates; many prisoners were tortured, many civilians were killed. Still, Carter urged Congress to give Marcos $300 million in military aid for the next five years.

In Nicaragua, the United States had helped maintain the Somoza dictatorship for decades. Misreading the basic weakness of that regime, and the popularity of the revolution against it, the Carter administration continued its support for Somoza until close to the regime's fall in 1979.

In Iran, toward the end of 1978, the long years of resentment against the Shah's dictatorship culminated in mass demonstrations. On September 8, 1978, hundreds of demonstrators were massacred by the Shah's troops. The next day, according to a UPI dispatch from Teheran, Carter affirmed his support for the Shah:

> Troops opened fire on demonstrators against the Shah for the third straight day yesterday and President Jimmy Carter telephoned the royal palace to express support for Shah Mohammad Reza Pahlevi, who faced the worst crisis of his 37-year reign. Nine members of parliament walked out on a speech by Iran's new premier, shouting that his hands were "stained with blood" in the crackdown on conservative Moslems and other protesters.

On December 13, 1978, Nicholas Gage reported for the *New York Times*:

> The staff of the United States Embassy here has been bolstered by dozens of specialists flown in to back an effort to help the Shah against a growing challenge to his rule according to embassy sources. . . . The new arrivals, according to the embassy sources, include a number of Central Intelligence Agency specialists on Iran, in addition to diplomats and military personnel.

In early 1979, as the crisis in Iran was intensifying, the former chief analyst on Iran for the CIA told *New York Times* reporter Seymour Hersh that "he and his colleagues knew of the tortures of Iranian dissenters by Savak, the Iranian secret police set up during the late 1950s by the Shah with help from the CIA." Furthermore, he told Hersh that a senior CIA official was involved in instructing officials in Savak on torture techniques.

It was a popular, massive revolution, and the Shah fled. The Carter administration later accepted him into the country, presumably for medical treatment, and the anti-American feelings of the revolutionaries reached a high point. On November 4, 1979, the U.S. embassy in Teheran was taken over by student militants who, demanding that the Shah be returned to Iran for punishment, held fifty-two embassy employees hostage.

For the next fourteen months, with the hostages still held in the embassy compound, that issue took the forefront of foreign news in the United States and aroused powerful nationalist feelings. When Carter ordered the Immigration and Naturalization Service to start deportation proceedings against Iranian students who lacked valid visas, the *New York Times* gave cautious but clear approval. Politicians and the press played into a general hysteria. An Iranian-American girl who was slated to give a high school commencement address was removed from the program. The bumper sticker "Bomb Iran" appeared on autos all over the country.

It was a rare journalist bold enough to point out, as Alan Richman of the Boston *Globe* did when the fifty-two hostages were released alive and apparently well, that there was a certain lack of proportion in American reactions to this and other violations of human rights: "There were 52 of them, a number easy to comprehend. It wasn't like 15,000 innocent people permanently disappearing in Argentina. . . . They [the American hostages] spoke our language. There were 3000 people summarily shot in Guatemala last year who did not."

The hostages were still in captivity when Jimmy Carter faced Ronald Reagan in the election of 1980. That fact, and the economic distress felt by many, were largely responsible for Carter's defeat.

Reagan's victory, followed eight years later by the election of George Bush, meant that another part of the Establishment, lacking even the faint liberalism of the Carter presidency, would be in charge. The policies would be more crass—cutting benefits to poor people, lowering taxes for the wealthy, increasing the military budget, filling the federal court system with conservative judges, actively working to destroy revolutionary movements in the Caribbean.

The dozen years of the Reagan-Bush presidency transformed the federal judiciary, never more than moderately liberal, into a predominantly conservative institution. By the fall of 1991, Reagan and Bush had filled more than half of the 837 federal judgeships, and appointed enough right-wing justices to transform the Supreme Court.

In the seventies, with liberal justices William Brennan and Thurgood Marshall in the lead, the Court had declared death penalties unconstitutional, had supported (in *Roe* v. *Wade*) the right of women to choose abortions, and had interpreted the civil rights law as permitting special attention to blacks and women to make up for past discrimination (affirmative action).

William Rehnquist, first named to the Supreme Court by Richard Nixon, was made Chief Justice by Ronald Reagan. In the Reagan-Bush years, the Rehnquist Court made a series of decisions that weakened *Roe* v. *Wade*, brought back the death penalty, reduced the rights of detainees against police powers, prevented doctors in federally supported family planning clinics from giving women information on abortions, and said that poor people could be forced to pay for public education (education was not "a fundamental right").

Justices William Brennan and Thurgood Marshall were the last of the Court's liberals. Old and ill, though reluctant to give up the fight, they retired. The final act to create a conservative Supreme Court was President Bush's nomination to replace Marshall. He chose a black conservative, Clarence Thomas. Despite dramatic testimony from a former colleague, a young black law professor named Anita Hill, that Thomas had sexually harassed her, Thomas was approved by the Senate and now the Supreme Court moved even more decisively to the right.

With conservative federal judges, with pro-business appointments to the National Labor Relations Board, judicial decisions and board findings weakened a labor movement already troubled by a decline in manufacturing. Workers who went out on strike found themselves with no legal protection. One of the first acts of the Reagan administration was to dismiss from their jobs, en masse, striking air traffic controllers. It was a warning to future strikers, and a sign of the weakness of a labor movement which in the thirties and forties had been a powerful force.

Corporate America became the greatest beneficiary of the Reagan-Bush years. In the sixties and seventies an important environmental movement had grown in the nation, horrified at the poisoning of the air, the seas and rivers, and the deaths of thousands each year as a result of work conditions. After a mine explosion in West Virginia killed seventy-eight miners in November 1968 there had been angry protest in the mine district, and Congress passed the Coal Mine Health and Safety Act of 1969. Nixon's Secretary of Labor spoke of "a new national passion, passion for environmental improvement."

The following year, yielding to strong demands from the labor movement and consumer groups, but also seeing it as an opportunity to win the support of working-class voters, President Nixon had signed the Occupational Safety and Health Act of 1970. This was an important piece of legislation, establishing a universal right to a safe and healthy workplace, and creating an enforcement machinery. Reflecting on this years later, Herbert Stein, who had been the chairman of Nixon's Council of Economic Advisers, lamented that "the juggernaut of environmental regulation proved not to be controllable by the Nixon administration."

While President Jimmy Carter came into office praising the OSHA program, he was also eager to please the business community. The woman he appointed to head OSHA, Eula Bingham, fought for strong enforcement of the act, and was occasionally successful. But as the American economy showed signs of trouble, with oil prices, inflation, and unemployment rising, Carter seemed more and more concerned about the difficulties the act created for business. He became an advocate of removing regulations on corporations and giving them more leeway, even if this was hurtful to labor and to consumers. Environmental regulation became more and more a victim of "cost-benefit" analysis, in which regulations protecting the health and safety of the public became secondary to how costly this would be for business.

Under Reagan and Bush this concern for "the economy," which was a short-hand term for corporate profit, dominated any concern for workers or consumers. President Reagan proposed to replace tough enforcement of environmental laws by a "voluntary" approach, leaving it to businesses to decide for themselves what they would do. He appointed as head of OSHA a businessman who was hostile to OSHA's aims. One of his first acts was to order the destruction of 100,000 government booklets pointing out the dangers of cotton dust to textile workers.

Political scientist William Grover (*The President as Prisoner*), evaluating environmental policy under Carter and Reagan as part of his penetrating "structural critique" of both presidents, concluded:

> OSHA appears caught in a cycle of liberal presidents—who want to retain some health and safety regulatory programs, but who also need economic growth for political survival—and conservative presidents, who focus almost

exclusively on the growth side of the equation. Such a cycle will always tend to subordinate the need for safe and healthful workplaces to . . . ensuring that commitment to OSHA will only be as strong as the priorities of business will allow.

George Bush presented himself as the "environmental president," and pointed with pride to his signing of the Clean Air Act of 1990. But two years after that act was passed, it was seriously weakened by a new rule of the Environmental Protection Agency that allowed manufacturers to increase by 245 tons a year hazardous pollutants in the atmosphere.

Furthermore, little money was allocated for enforcement. Contaminated drinking water had caused over 100,000 illnesses between 1971 and 1985, according to an EPA report. But in Bush's first year in office, while the EPA received 80,000 complaints of contaminated drinking water, only one in a hundred was investigated. And in 1991 and 1992, according to a private environmental group, the Natural Resources Defense Council, there were some 250,000 violations of the Safe Water Drinking Act (which had been passed during the Nixon administration).

Shortly after Bush took office, a government scientist prepared testimony for a Congressional committee on the dangerous effects of industrial uses of coal and other fossil fuels in contributing to "global warming," a depletion of the earth's protective ozone layer. The White House changed the testimony, over the scientist's objections, to minimize the danger (Boston *Globe*, October 29, 1990). Again, business worries about regulation seemed to override the safety of the public.

The ecological crisis in the world had become so obviously serious that Pope John Paul II felt the need to rebuke the wealthy classes of the industrialized nations for creating that crisis: "Today, the dramatic threat of ecological breakdown is teaching us the extent to which greed and selfishness, both individual and collective, are contrary to the order of creation."

At international conferences to deal with the perils of global warming, the European Community and Japan proposed specific levels and timetables for carbon dioxide emissions, in which the United States was the leading culprit. But, as the *New York Times* reported in the summer of 1991, "the Bush Administration fears that . . . it would hurt the nation's economy in the short term for no demonstrable long-term climatic benefit." Scientific opinion was quite clear on the long-term benefit, but this was not as important as "the economy"—that is, the needs of corporations.

Evidence became stronger by the late eighties that renewable energy sources (water, wind, sunlight) could produce more usable energy than nuclear plants, which were dangerous and expensive, and produced radioactive wastes that could not be safely disposed of. Yet the Reagan and Bush administrations made deep cuts (under Reagan, a 90 percent cut) in research into renewable energy possibilities.

In June 1992 more than a hundred countries participated in the Earth Summit environmental conference in Brazil. Statistics showed that the armed forces of the world were responsible for two-thirds of the gases that depleted the ozone layer. But when it was suggested that the Earth Summit consider the effects of the military on environmental degradation, the United States delegation objected and the suggestion was defeated.

Indeed, the preservation of a huge military establishment and the retention of profit levels of oil corporations appeared to be twin objectives of the Reagan-Bush administrations. Shortly after Ronald Reagan took office, twenty-three oil industry executives contributed $270,000 to redecorate the White House living quarters. According to the Associated Press:

> The solicitation drive . . . came four weeks after the President decontrolled oil prices, a decision worth $2 billion to the oil industry . . . Jack Hodges of Oklahoma City, owner of Core Oil and Gas Company, said: "The top man of this country ought to live in one of the top places. Mr. Reagan has helped the energy business."

While he built up the military (allocations of over a trillion dollars in his first four years in office), Reagan tried to pay for this with cuts in benefits for the poor. There would be $140 billion of cuts in social programs through 1984 and an increase of $181 billion for "defense" in the same period. He also proposed tax cuts of $190 billion (most of this going to the wealthy).

Despite the tax cuts and the military appropriations, Reagan insisted he would still balance the budget because the tax cuts would so stimulate the economy as to generate new revenue. Nobel Prize–winning economist Wassily Leontief remarked dryly: "This is not likely to happen. In fact, I personally guarantee that it will not happen."

Indeed, Department of Commerce figures showed that periods of lowered corporate taxes (1973–1975, 1979–1982) did not at all show higher capital investment, but a steep drop. The sharpest rise of capital investment (1975–1979) took place when corporate taxes were slightly higher than they had been the preceding five years.

The human consequences of Reagan's budget cuts went deep. For instance, Social Security disability benefits were terminated for 350,000 people. A man injured in an oil field accident was forced to go back to work, the federal government overruling both the company doctor and a state supervisor who testified that he was too disabled to work. The man died, and federal officials said, "We have a P.R. problem." A war hero of Vietnam, Roy Benavidez, who had been presented with the Congressional Medal of Honor by Reagan, was told by Social Security officials that the shrapnel pieces in his heart, arms, and leg did not prevent him from working. Appearing before a Congressional committee, he denounced Reagan.

Unemployment grew in the Reagan years. In the year 1982, 30 million people were unemployed all or part of the year. One result was that over 16 million Americans lost medical insurance, which was often tied to holding a job. In Michigan, where the unemployment rate was the highest in the country, the infant death rate began to rise in 1981.

New requirements eliminated free school lunches for more than one million poor children, who depended on the meal for as much as half of their daily nutrition. Millions of children entered the ranks of the officially declared "poor" and soon a quarter of the nation's children— twelve million—were living in poverty. In parts of Detroit, one-third of the children were dying before their first birthday, and the *New York Times* commented: "Given what's happening to the hungry in America, this Administration has cause only for shame."

Welfare became an object of attack: aid to single mothers with children through the AFDC (Aid to Families with Dependent Children) program, food stamps, health care for the poor through Medicaid. For most people on welfare (the benefits differed from state to state) this meant $500 to $700 a month in aid, leaving them well below the poverty level of about $900 a month. Black children were four times as likely as white children to grow up on welfare.

Early in the Reagan administration, responding to the argument that government aid was not needed, that private enterprise would take care of poverty, a mother wrote to her local newspaper:

> I am on Aid to Families with Dependent Children, and both my children are in school. . . . I have graduated from college with distinction, 128th in a class of over 1000, with a B.A. in English and sociology. I have experience in library work, child care, social work and counseling.
>
> I have been to the CETA office. They have nothing for me. . . . I also go every week to the library to scour the newspaper Help Wanted ads. I have

kept a copy of every cover letter that I have sent out with my resume; the stack is inches thick. I have applied for jobs paying as little as $8000 a year. I work part-time in a library for $3.50 an hour, welfare reduces my allotment to compensate. . . .

It appears we have employment offices that can't employ, governments that can't govern and an economic system that can't produce jobs for people ready to work. . . .

Last week I sold my bed to pay for the insurance on my car, which, in the absence of mass transportation, I need to go job hunting. I sleep on a piece of rubber foam somebody gave me.

So this is the great American dream my parents came to this country for: Work hard, get a good education, follow the rules, and you will be rich. I don't want to be rich. I just want to be able to feed my children and live with some semblance of dignity. . . ."

Democrats often joined Republicans in denouncing welfare programs. Presumably, this was done to gain political support from a middle-class public that believed they were paying taxes to support teenage mothers and people they thought too lazy to work. Much of the public did not know, and were not informed by either political leaders or the media, that welfare took a tiny part of the taxes, and military spending took a huge chunk of it. Yet, the public's attitude on welfare was different from that of the two major parties. It seemed that the constant attacks on welfare by politicians, reported endlessly in the press and on television, did not succeed in eradicating a fundamental generosity felt by most Americans.

A *New York Times*/CBS News poll conducted in early 1992 showed that public opinion on welfare changed depending on how the question was worded. If the word "welfare" was used, 44 percent of those questioned said too much was being spent on welfare (while 50 percent said either that the right amount was being spent, or that too little was being spent. But when the question was about "assistance to the poor," only 13 percent thought too much was being spent, and 64 percent thought too little was being spent.

This suggested that both parties were trying to manufacture an anti-human-needs mood by constant derogatory use of the word "welfare," and then to claim they were acting in response to public opinion. The Democrats as well as the Republicans had strong connections to wealthy corporations. Kevin Phillips, a Republican analyst of national politics, wrote in 1990 that the Democratic Party was "history's second-most enthusiastic capitalist party."

Phillips pointed out that the greatest beneficiaries of government policy during the Republican presidencies of Ronald Reagan and George Bush were the superrich: "It was the truly wealthy, more than anyone else, who flourished under Reagan. . . . The 1980s were the triumph of upper America . . . the political ascendancy of the rich, and a glorification of capitalism, free markets, and finance."

When government policy enriched the already rich, it was not called welfare. This was not as obvious as the monthly checks to the poor; it most often took the form of generous changes in the tax system.

In *America: Who Really Pays The Taxes?*, two investigative reporters with the *Philadelphia Inquirer*, Donald Barlett and James Steele, traced the path by which tax rates for the very rich got lower and lower. It was not the Republicans but the Democrats—the Kennedy-Johnson administrations—who, under the guise of "tax reform," first lowered the World War II–era rate of 91 percent on incomes over $400,000 a year to 70 percent. During the Carter Administration (though over his objections) Democrats and Republicans in Congress joined to give even more tax breaks to the rich.

The Reagan administration, with the help of Democrats in Congress, lowered the tax rate on the very rich to 50 percent and in 1986 a coalition of Republicans and Democrats sponsored another "tax reform" bill that lowered the top rate to 28 percent. Barlett and Steele noted that a schoolteacher, a factory worker, and a billionaire could all pay 28 percent. The idea of a "progressive" income in which the rich paid at higher rates than everyone else was now almost dead.

As a result of all the tax bills from 1978 to 1990, the net worth of the "Forbes 400," chosen as the richest in the country by *Forbes Magazine* (advertising itself as "capitalist tool"), was tripled. About $70 billion a year was lost in government revenue, so that in those thirteen years the wealthiest 1 percent of the country gained a trillion dollars.

As William Greider pointed out, in his remarkable book *Who Will Tell The People? The Betrayal of American Democracy*:

> For those who blame Republicans for what has happened and believe that equitable taxation will be restored if only the Democrats can win back the White House, there is this disquieting fact: The turning point on tax politics, when the monied elites first began to win big, occurred in 1978 with the Democratic party fully in power and well before Ronald Reagan came to Washington. Democratic majorities have supported this great shift in tax burden every step of the way.

Not only did the income tax become less progressive during the last decades of the century, but the Social Security tax became more *regressive*. That is, more and more was deducted from the salary checks of the poor and middle classes, but when salaries reached $42,000 no more was deducted, By the early 1990s, a middle-income family earning $37,800 a year paid 7.65 percent of its income in Social Security taxes. A family earning ten times as much, $378,000 paid 1.46 percent of its income in Social Security taxes.

The result of these higher payroll taxes was that three-fourths of all wage earners paid more each year through the Social Security tax than through the income tax. Embarrassingly for the Democratic party, which was supposed to be the party of the working class, those higher payroll taxes had been put in motion under the administration of Jimmy Carter.

In a two-party system, if *both* parties ignore public opinion, there is no place voters can turn. And in the matter of taxation, it has been clear that American citizens have wanted taxes that are truly progressive. William Greider informs us that shortly after World War II, when rates on the very rich were up to 90 percent, a Gallup poll showed that 85 percent of the public thought the federal tax code was "fair." But by 1984, when all those tax "reforms" had been put into effect by Democrats and Republicans, a public opinion survey by the Internal Revenue Service found that 80 percent of those polled agreed with the statement: "The present tax system benefits the rich and is unfair to the ordinary working man and woman."

By the end of the Reagan years, the gap between rich and poor in the United States had grown dramatically. Where in 1980, the chief executive officers (CEOs) of corporations made forty times as much in salary as the average factory worker, by 1989 they were making ninety-three times as much. In the dozen years from 1977 to 1989, the before-tax income of the richest 1 percent rose 77 percent; meanwhile, for the poorest two-fifths of the population, there was no gain at all, indeed a small decline.

And because of favorable changes for the rich in the tax structure, the richest 1 percent, in the decade ending in 1990, saw their after-tax income increase 87 percent. In the same period, the after-tax income of the lower four-fifths of the population either went down 5 percent (at the poorest level) or went up no more than 8.6 percent.

While everybody at the lower levels was doing worse, there were especially heavy losses for blacks, Hispanics, women, and the young. The general impoverishment of the lowest-income groups that took place in the Reagan-Bush years hit black families hardest, with their lack of resources to start with and with racial discrimination facing them in jobs. The victories of the civil rights movement had opened up spaces for some African-Americans, but left others far behind.

At the end of the eighties, at least a third of African-American families fell below the official poverty level, and black unemployment seemed fixed at two and a half times that of whites, with young blacks out of work at the rate of 30 to 40 percent. The life expectancy of blacks remained at least ten years lower than that of whites. In Detroit, Washington, and Baltimore, the mortality rate for black babies was higher than in Jamaica or Costa Rica.

Along with poverty came broken homes, family violence, street crime, drugs. In Washington, D.C., with a concentrated population of black poor within walking distance of the marbled buildings of the national government, 42 percent of young black men between the ages of eighteen and thirty-five were either in jail, or out on probation or parole. The crime rate among blacks, instead of being seen as a crying demand for the elimination of poverty, was used by politicians to call for the building of more prisons.

The 1954 Supreme Court decision in *Brown* v. *Board of Education* had begun the process of desegregating schools. But poverty kept black children in ghettos and many schools around the country remained segregated by race and class. Supreme Court decisions in the seventies determined that there need be no equalization of funds for poor school districts and rich school districts (*San Antonio Independent School District* v. *Rodriguez*) and that the busing of children need not take place between wealthy suburbs and inner cities (*Milliken* v. *Bradley*).

To admirers of free enterprise and laissez-faire, those people were poor who did not work and produce, and so had themselves to blame for their poverty. They ignored the fact that women taking care of children on their own were working very hard indeed. They did not ask why babies who were not old enough to show their work skills should be penalized—to the point of death—for growing up in a poor family.

Ironically, it was Republican Kevin Phillips who, analyzing the Reagan years, wrote: "Less and less wealth was going to people who produced something . . . disproportionate rewards to society's economic, legal and cultural manipulators—from lawyers to financial advisers."

In the mid-eighties, a major scandal began to emerge in Washington. The deregulation of the savings and loan banks begun in the Carter administration had continued under Reagan, leading to risky investments which drained the assets of the banks, leaving them owing billions of dollars to depositors, which the government had insured.

As the years went by and the problem was kept behind a screen, it was going to take more and more money to pay depositors and bail out these banks. The figure began to reach $200 billion. During the 1988 presidential campaign, the Democratic candidate Michael Dukakis was restrained from pointing the finger at the Republican administration because the Democrats in Congress were heavily involved in bringing about and then covering up the situation. So the voters were kept in the dark.

The enormous drain of money from the treasury for defense had once been declared by President Eisenhower to be a "theft" from human needs. But it was accepted by both parties, as Democrats competed with Republicans to show the electorate how "tough" they were.

Jimmy Carter as president had proposed a $10 billion increase in the military budget, an enactment of exactly what Eisenhower had described. All of the huge military budgets of the post–World War II period, from Truman to Reagan and Bush, were approved overwhelmingly by both Democrats and Republicans.

The spending of trillions of dollars to build up nuclear and nonnuclear forces was justified by fears that the Soviet Union, also building up its military forces, would invade Western Europe. But George Kennan, the former ambassador to the Soviet Union and one of the theoreticians of the cold war, said this fear had no basis in reality. And Harry Rositzke, who worked for the CIA for twenty-five years and was at one time CIA director of espionage operations against the Soviet Union, wrote in the 1980s: "In all of my years in government and since I have never seen an intelligence estimate that shows how it would be profitable to Soviet interests to invade Western Europe or to attack the United States."

However, the creation of such a fear in the public mind was useful in arguing for the building of frightful and superfluous weapons. For instance, the *Trident* submarine, which was capable of firing hundreds of nuclear warheads, cost $1.5 billion. It was totally useless except in a nuclear war, in which case it would only add several hundred warheads to the tens of thousands already available. That $1.5 billion was enough to finance a five-year program of child immunization around the world against deadly diseases, and prevent five million deaths (Ruth Sivard, *World Military and Social Expenditures 1987–1988*).

In the mid-1980s, an analyst with the Rand Corporation, which did research for the Defense Department, told an interviewer in an unusually candid statement, that the enormous number of weapons was unnecessary from a military point of view, but were useful to convey a certain *image* at home and abroad:

If you had a strong president, a strong secretary of defense they could temporarily go to Congress and say, "We're only going to build what we need. . . . And if the Russians build twice as many, tough." But it would be unstable politically. . . . And it is therefore better for our own domestic stability as well as international perceptions to insist that we remain good competitors even though the objective significance of the competition is . . . dubious.

In 1984, the CIA admitted that it had exaggerated Soviet military expenditures, that since 1975 it had claimed Soviet military spending was growing by 4 to 5 percent each year when the actual figure was 2 percent. Thus, by misinformation, even deception, the result was to inflate military expenditures.

One of the favorite military programs of the Reagan administration was the Star Wars program, in which billions were spent, supposedly to build a shield in space to stop enemy nuclear missiles in midair. But the first three tests of the technology failed. A fourth test was undertaken, with government funding for the program at stake. There was another failure, but Reagan's Secretary of Defense, Caspar Weinberger, approved the faking of results to show that the test had succeeded.

When the Soviet Union began to disintegrate in 1989, and there was no longer the familiar "Soviet threat," the military budget was reduced somewhat, but still remained huge, with support from both Democrats and Republicans. In 1992, the head of the House Armed Services Committee, Les Aspin, a Democrat, proposed, in view of the new international situation, that the military budget be cut by 2%, from $281 billion to $275 billion.

That same year, as Democrats and Republicans both supported minor cuts in the military budget, a public opinion survey done for the National Press Club showed that 59 percent of American voters wanted a 50 percent cut in defense spending over the next five years.

It seemed that both parties had failed in persuading the citizenry that the military budget should continue at its high level. But they continued to ignore the public they were supposed to represent. In the summer of 1992, Congressional Democrats and Republicans joined to vote against a transfer of funds from the military budget to human needs, and voted to spend $120 billion to "defend" Europe, which everyone acknowledged was no longer in danger—if it ever had been—from Soviet attack.

Democrats and Republicans had long been joined in a "bipartisan foreign policy," but in the Reagan-Bush years the United States government showed a special aggressiveness in the use of military force abroad.

This was done either directly in invasions, or through both overt and covert support of right-wing tyrannies that cooperated with the United States.

Reagan came into office just after a revolution had taken place in Nicaragua, in which a popular Sandinista movement (named after the 1920s revolutionary hero Augusto Sandino) overthrew the corrupt Somoza dynasty (long supported by the United States). The Sandinistas, a coalition of Marxists, left-wing priests, and assorted nationalists, set about to give more land to the peasants and to spread education and health care among the poor.

The Reagan administration, seeing in this a "Communist" threat, but even more important, a challenge to the long U.S. control over governments in Central America, began immediately to work to overthrow the Sandinista government. It waged a secret war by having the CIA organize a counterrevolutionary force (the "contras"), many of whose leaders were former leaders of the hated National Guard under Somoza.

The contras seemed to have no popular support inside Nicaragua and so were based next door in Honduras, a very poor country dominated by the United States. From Honduras they moved across the border, raiding farms and villages, killing men, women and children, committing atrocities. A former colonel with the contras, Edgar Chamorro, testified before the World Court:

> We were told that the only way to defeat the Sandinistas was to use the tactics the agency [the CIA] attributed to Communist insurgencies elsewhere: kill, kidnap, rob, and torture. . . . Many civilians were killed in cold blood. Many others were tortured, mutilated, raped, robbed, or otherwise abused. . . . When I agreed to join . . . I had hoped that it would be an organization of Nicaraguans. . . . [It] turned out to be an instrument of the U.S. government. . . .

There was a reason for the secrecy of the U.S. actions in Nicaragua; public opinion surveys showed that the American public was opposed to military involvement there. In 1984, the CIA, using Latin American agents to conceal its involvement, put mines in the harbors of Nicaragua to blow up ships. When information leaked out, Secretary of Defense Weinberger told ABC news: "The United States is not mining the harbors of Nicaragua."

Later that year Congress, responding perhaps to public opinion and the memory of Vietnam, made it illegal for the United States to support "directly or indirectly, military or paramilitary operations in

Nicaragua." The Reagan administration decided to ignore this law and to find ways to fund the contras secretly, looking for "third-party support." Reagan himself solicited funds from Saudi Arabia, at least $32 million. The friendly dictatorship in Guatemala was used to get arms surreptitiously to the contras. Israel, dependent on U.S. aid and always dependable for support, was also used.

In 1986, a story appearing in a Beirut magazine created a sensation: that weapons had been sold by the United States to Iran (supposedly an enemy), that in return Iran had promised to release hostages being held by extremist Moslems in Lebanon, and that profits from the sale were being given to the contras to buy arms.

When asked about this at a press conference in November 1986, President Reagan told four lies: that the shipment to Iran consisted of a few token antitank missiles (in fact, 2,000), that the United States didn't condone shipments by third parties, that weapons had not been traded for hostages, and that the purpose of the operation was to promote a dialogue with Iranian moderates. In reality, the purpose was a double one: to free hostages and get credit for that, and to help the contras.

The previous month, when a transport plane that had carried arms to the contras was downed by Nicaraguan gunfire and the American pilot captured, the lies had multiplied. Assistant Secretary of State Elliot Abrams lied. Secretary of State Shultz lied ("no connection with the U.S. government at all"). Evidence mounted that the captured pilot was working for the CIA.

The whole Iran-contra affair became a perfect example of the double line of defense of the American Establishment. The first defense is to deny the truth. If exposed, the second defense is to investigate, but not too much; the press will publicize, but they will not get to the heart of the matter.

Once the scandal was out in the open, neither the Congressional investigating committees nor the press nor the trial of Colonel Oliver North, who oversaw the contra aid operation, got to the critical questions: What is U.S. foreign policy all about? How are the president and his staff permitted to support a terrorist group in Central America to overthrow a government that, whatever its faults, is welcomed by its own people as a great improvement over the terrible governments the U.S. has supported there for years? What does the scandal tell us about democracy, about freedom of expression, about an open society?

Out of the much-publicized "contragate" scandal came no powerful critique of secrecy in government or of the erosion of democracy by actions taken in secret by a small group of men safe from the scrutiny of public opinion. The media, in a country priding itself on its level of education and information, kept the public informed only on the most superficial level.

The limits of Democratic party criticism of the affair were revealed by a leading Democrat, Senator Sam Nunn of Georgia, who, as the investigation was getting under way, said: "We must, all of us, help the President restore his credibility in foreign affairs."

A few Democrats were critical, which was deplored by a Harvard professor, James Q. Wilson, who was a member of Reagan's Foreign Intelligence Advisory Board. Wilson looked back nostalgically to a "bipartisan consensus" (the equivalent of the one-party system in a totalitarian state). He worried most about "a lack of resolve to act like a great power."

It became clear that President Reagan and Vice-President Bush were involved in what became known as the Iran-contra affair. But their underlings scrupulously kept them out of it, illustrating the familiar government device of "plausible denial," in which the top official, shielded by subordinates, can plausibly deny involvement. Although Congressman Henry Gonzalez of Texas introduced a resolution for the impeachment of Reagan, it was quickly suppressed in Congress.

Neither Reagan nor Bush were indicted. Rather, the Congressional committee put the lesser culprits on the witness stand and several of them were indicted. One (Robert McFarlane, a former National Security Adviser to Reagan) tried to commit suicide. Another, Colonel Oliver North, stood trial for lying to Congress, was found guilty, but was not sentenced to prison. Reagan retired in peace and Bush became the next president of the United States.

In an ironic twist, an obscure citizen of the tiny town of Odon, Indiana, became a tangential actor in the Iran-contra controversy. This was a young man named Bill Breeden, a former minister who lived in a tepee in the woods with his wife and two children, teaching the children at home. Breeden's home town of Odon was also the home town of Admiral John Poindexter, McFarlane's successor as Reagan's National Security Adviser, who was heavily involved in the illegal activities of the Iran-contra affair.

One day Bill Breeden noticed that the town, to show its pride in its "home boy," had renamed one of its streets "John Poindexter Street." Breeden, a pacifist and critic of U.S. foreign policy, indignant at what he thought was a celebration of immoral behavior in government, stole the sign. He announced that he was holding it for "ransom"—$30 million, the amount of money that had been given to Iran for transfer to the contras.

He was apprehended, put on trial, and spent a few days in jail. As it turned out, Bill Breeden was the only person to be imprisoned as a result of the Iran-contra affair.

The Iran-contra affair was only one of the many instances in which the government of the United States violated its own laws in pursuit of some desired goal in foreign policy.

Toward the end of the Vietnam war, in 1973, Congress, seeking to limit the presidential power that had been used so ruthlessly in Indochina, passed the War Powers Act, which said:

"The President, in every possible instance, shall consult with Congress before introducing United States Armed Forces into hostilities or into situations where imminent involvement in hostilities is clearly indicated by the circumstances."

Almost immediately, President Gerald Ford violated the act when he ordered the invasion of a Cambodian island and the bombing of a Cambodian town in retaliation for the temporary detention of American merchant seamen on the ship *Mayaguez*. He did not consult Congress before he gave the attack orders.

In the fall of 1982, President Reagan sent American marines into a dangerous situation in Lebanon, where a civil war was raging, again ignoring the requirements of the War Powers Act. The following year, over two hundred of those marines were killed when a bomb was exploded in their barracks by terrorists.

Shortly after that, in October 1983 (with some analysts concluding this was done to take attention away from the Lebanon disaster), Reagan sent U.S. forces to invade the tiny Caribbean island of Grenada. Again, Congress was notified, but not consulted. The reasons given to the American people for this invasion (officially called Operation Urgent Fury) were that a recent coup that had taken place in Grenada put American citizens (students at a medical school on the island) in danger; and that the United States had received an urgent request from the Organization of Eastern Caribbean States to intervene.

An unusually pointed article in the *New York Times* on October 29, 1983, by correspondent Bernard Gwertzman demolished those reasons:

> The formal request that the U.S. and other friendly countries provide military help was made by the Organization of Eastern Caribbean States last Sunday at the request of the United States, which wanted to show proof that it had been requested to act under terms of that group's treaty. The wording of the formal request, however, was drafted in Washington and conveyed to the Caribbean leaders by special American emissaries.

Both Cuba and Grenada, when they saw that American ships were heading for Grenada, sent urgent messages promising that American students
were safe and urging that an invasion not occur. . . . There is no indication
that the Administration made a determined effort to evacuate the Americans
peacefully. . . . Officials have acknowledged that there was no inclination to
try to negotiate with the Grenadian authorities. . . . "We got there just in
time," the President said. . . . A major point in the dispute is whether in fact
the Americans on the island were in such danger as to warrant an invasion.
No official has produced firm evidence that the Americans were being mistreated or that they would not be able to leave if they wanted.

The real reason for the invasion, one high American official told
Gwertzman, was that the United States should show (determined to
overcome the sense of defeat in Vietnam) that it was a truly powerful
nation: "What good are maneuvers and shows of force, if you never
use it?"

The connection between U.S. military intervention and the promotion of capitalist enterprise had always been especially crass in the
Caribbean. As for Grenada, an article in the *Wall Street Journal* eight
years after the military invasion (October 29, 1991) spoke of "an invasion of banks" and noted that St. George's, the capital of Grenada, with
7500 people, had 118 offshore banks, one for every 64 residents. "St.
George's has become the Casablanca of the Caribbean, a fast-growing
haven for money laundering, tax evasion and assorted financial
fraud. . . ."

After a study of various U.S. military interventions, political scientist
Stephen Shalom (*Imperial Alibis*) concluded that people in the invaded
countries died "not to save U.S. nationals, who would have been far
safer without U.S. intervention, but so that Washington might make
clear that it ruled the Caribbean and that it was prepared to engage in a
paroxysm of violence to enforce its will." He continued:

> There have been some cases where American citizens were truly in danger:
> for example, the four churchwomen who were killed by government-
> sponsored death squads in El Salvador in 1980. But there was no U.S. inter-
> vention there, no Marine landings, no protective bombing raids. Instead
> Washington backed the death squad regime with military and economic aid,
> military training, intelligence sharing, and diplomatic support.

The historic role of the United States in El Salvador, where 2 percent of the population owned 60 percent of the land, was to make sure

governments were in power there that would support U.S. business interests, no matter how this impoverished the great majority of people. Popular rebellions that would threaten these business arrangements were to be opposed. When a popular uprising in 1932 threatened the military government, the United States sent a cruiser and two destroyers to stand by while the government massacred thirty thousand Salvadorans.

The administration of Jimmy Carter did nothing to reverse this history. It wanted reform in Latin America, but not revolution that would threaten U.S. corporate interests. In 1980, Richard Cooper, a State Department expert on economic affairs, told Congress that a more equitable distribution of wealth was desirable. "However, we also have an enormous stake in the continuing smooth functioning in the economic system. . . . Major changes in the system can . . . have important implications for our own welfare."

In February 1980 El Salvador Catholic Archbishop Oscar Romero sent a personal letter to President Carter, asking him to stop military aid to El Salvador. Not long before that, the National Guard and National Police had opened fire on a crowd of protesters in front of the Metropolitan Cathedral and killed twenty-four people. But the Carter administration continued the aid. The following month Archbishop Romero was assassinated.

There was mounting evidence that the assassination had been ordered by Roberto D'Aubuisson, a leader of the right wing. But D'Aubuisson had the protection of Nicolas Carranza, a deputy minister of defense, who at the time was receiving $90,000 a year from the CIA. And Elliot Abrams, ironically Assistant Secretary of State for Human Rights, declared that D'Aubuisson "was not involved in murder."

When Reagan became President, military aid to the El Salvador government rose steeply. From 1946 to 1979, total military aid to El Salvador was $16.7 million. In Reagan's first year in office, the figure rose to $82 million.

Congress was sufficiently embarrassed by the killings in El Salvador to require that before any more aid was given the President must certify that progress in human rights was taking place. Reagan did not take this seriously. On January 28, 1982, there were reports of a government massacre of peasants in several villages. The following day, Reagan certified that the Salvadoran government was making progress in human rights. Three days after certification, soldiers stormed the homes of poor people in San Salvador, dragged out twenty people, and killed them.

When, at the end of 1983, Congress passed a law to continue the requirement of certification, Reagan vetoed it.

The press was especially timid and obsequious during the Reagan years, as Mark Hertsgaard documents in his book *On Bended Knee*. When journalist Raymond Bonner continued to report on the atrocities in El Salvador, and on the U.S. role, the *New York Times* removed him from his assignment. Back in 1981 Bonner had reported on the massacre of hundreds of civilians in the town of El Mozote, by a battalion of soldiers trained by the United States. The Reagan administration scoffed at the account, but in 1992, a team of forensic anthropologists began unearthing skeletons from the site of the massacre, most of them children; the following year a UN commission confirmed the story of the massacre at El Mozote.

The Reagan administration, which did not appear at all offended by military juntas governing in Latin America (Guatemala, El Salvador, Chile) if they were "friendly" to the United States, became very upset when a tyranny was hostile, as was the government of Muammar Khadafi in Libya. In 1986, when unknown terrorists bombed a discotheque in West Berlin, killing a U.S. serviceman, the White House immediately decided to retaliate. Khadafi was probably responsible for various acts of terrorism over the years, but there was no real evidence that in this case he was to blame.

Reagan was determined to make a point. Planes were sent over the capital city of Tripoli with specific instructions to aim at Khadafi's house. The bombs fell on a crowded city; perhaps a hundred people were killed, it was estimated by foreign diplomats in Tripoli. Khadafi was not injured, but an adopted daughter of his was killed.

Professor Stephen Shalom, analyzing this incident, writes (*Imperial Alibis*): "If terrorism is defined as politically motivated violence perpetrated against non-combatant targets, then one of the most serious incidents of international terrorism of the year was precisely this U.S. raid on Libya."

Early in the presidency of George Bush, there came the most dramatic developments on the international scene since the end of World War II. In the year 1989, with a dynamic new leader, Mikhail Gorbachev, at the head of the Soviet Union, the long suppressed dissatisfaction with "dictatorships of the proletariat" which had turned out to be dictatorships *over* the proletariat erupted all through the Soviet bloc.

There were mass demonstrations in the Soviet Union and in the countries of Eastern Europe which had been long dominated by the Soviet Union. East Germany agreed to unite with West Germany, and the wall separating East Berlin from West Berlin, long a symbol of the tight control of its citizens by East Germany, was dismantled in the presence of wildly exultant citizens of both Germanies. In

Czechoslovakia, a new non-Communist government came into being, headed by a playwright and former imprisoned dissident named Vaclav Havel. In Poland, Bulgaria, Hungary, a new leadership emerged, promising freedom and democracy. And remarkably, all this took place without civil war, in response to overwhelming popular demand.

In the United States, the Republican party claimed that the hard-line policies of Reagan and the increase in military expenditures had brought down the Soviet Union. But the change had begun much earlier, after the death of Stalin in 1953, and especially with the leadership of Nikita Khrushchev. A remarkably open discussion had been initiated.

But the continued hard line of the United States became an obstacle to further liberalization, according to former ambassador to the Soviet Union George Kennan, who wrote that "the general effect of cold war extremism was to delay rather than hasten the great change that overtook the Soviet Union by the end of the 1980s." While the press and politicians in the United States exulted over the collapse of the Soviet Union, Kennan pointed out that, not only did American policies delay this collapse, but these cold war policies were carried on at a frightful cost to the American people:

> We paid with forty years of enormous and otherwise unnecessary military expenditures. We paid through the cultivation of nuclear weaponry to the point where the vast and useless nuclear arsenal had become (and remains today) a danger to the very environment of the planet. . . .

The sudden collapse of the Soviet Union left the political leadership of the United States unprepared. Military interventions had been undertaken in Korea and Vietnam with enormous loss of life, also in Cuba and the Dominican Republic, and huge amounts of military aid had been given all over the world—in Europe, Africa, Latin America, the Middle East, Asia—on the supposition that this was necessary to deal with a Communist menace emanating from the Soviet Union. Several trillion dollars had been taken from American citizens in the form of taxes to maintain a huge nuclear and nonnuclear arsenal and military bases all over the world—all primarily justified by the "Soviet threat."

Here then was an opportunity for the United States to reconstruct its foreign policy, and to free hundreds of billions of dollars a year from the budget to be used for constructive, healthy projects.

But this did not happen. Along with the exultation "We have won the cold war" came a kind of panic: "What can we do to maintain our military establishment?"

It became clearer now, although it had been suspected, that United States foreign policy was not simply based on the existence of the Soviet Union, but was motivated by fear of revolution in various parts of the world. The radical social critic Noam Chomsky had long maintained that "the appeal to security was largely fraudulent, the Cold War framework having been employed as a device to justify the suppression of independent nationalism—whether in Europe, Japan, or the Third World" (*World Orders Old and New*).

The fear of "independent nationalism" was that this would jeopardize powerful American economic interests. Revolutions in Nicaragua or Cuba or El Salvador or Chile were threats to United Fruit, Anaconda Copper, International Telephone and Telegraph, and others. Thus, foreign interventions presented to the public as "in the national interest" were really undertaken for special interests, for which the American people were asked to sacrifice their sons and their tax dollars.

The CIA now had to prove it was still needed. The *New York Times* (February 4, 1992) declared that "in a world where the postwar enemy has ceased to exist, the C.I.A. and its handful of sister agencies, with their billion-dollar satellites and mountains of classified documents, must somehow remain relevant in the minds of Americans."

The military budget remained huge. The cold war budget of $300 billion was reduced by 7 percent to $280 billion. The Chairman of the Joint Chiefs of Staff, Colin Powell, said: "I want to scare the hell out of the rest of the world. I don't say that in a bellicose way."

As if to prove that the gigantic military establishment was still necessary, the Bush administration, in its four-year term, launched two wars: a "small" one against Panama and a massive one against Iraq.

Coming into office in 1989, George Bush was embarrassed by the new defiant posture of Panama's dictator, General Manuel Noriega. Noriega's regime was corrupt, brutal, authoritarian, but President Reagan and Vice-President Bush had overlooked this because Noriega was useful to the United States. He cooperated with the CIA in many ways, such as offering Panama as a base for contra operations against the Sandinista government of Nicaragua and meeting with Colonel Oliver North to discuss sabotage targets in Nicaragua. When he was director of the CIA in 1976–1977, Bush had protected Noriega.

But by 1987 Noriega's usefulness was over, his activities in the drug trade were in the open, and he became a convenient target for an administration which wanted to prove that the United States, apparently unable to destroy the Castro regime or the Sandinistas or the revolutionary movement in El Salvador, was still a power in the Caribbean.

Claiming that it wanted to bring Noriega to trial as a drug trafficker (he had been indicted in Florida on that charge) and also that it needed to protect U.S. citizens (a military man and his wife had been threatened by Panamanian soldiers), the United States invaded Panama in December 1989, with 26,000 troops.

It was a quick victory. Noriega was captured and brought to Florida to stand trial (where he was subsequently found guilty and sent to prison). But in the invasion, neighborhoods in Panama City were bombarded and hundreds, perhaps thousands of civilians were killed. It was estimated that 14,000 were homeless. Writer Mark Hertsgaard noted that even if the official Pentagon figure of several hundred civilian casualties was correct, this meant that in Panama the U.S. had killed as many people as did the Chinese government in its notorious attack on student demonstrators at Tiananmen Square in Beijing six months earlier. A new president friendly to the United States was installed in Panama, but poverty and unemployment remained, and in 1992 the *New York Times* reported that the invasion and removal of Noriega "failed to stanch the flow of illicit narcotics through Panama."

The United States, however, succeeded in one of its aims, to reestablish its strong influence over Panama. The *Times* reported: "The President [of Panama] and his key aides and the American Ambassador, Deane Hinton, have breakfast together once a week in a meeting that many Panamanians view as the place where important decisions are taken."

Liberal Democrats (John Kerry and Ted Kennedy of Massachusetts, and many others) declared their support of the military action. The Democrats were being true to their historic role as supporters of military intervention, anxious to show that foreign policy was bipartisan. They seemed determined to show they were as tough (or as ruthless) as the Republicans.

But the Panama operation was on too small a scale to accomplish what both the Reagan and Bush administrations badly wanted: to overcome the American public's abhorrence, since Vietnam, of foreign military interventions.

Two years later, the Gulf War against Iraq presented such an opportunity. Iraq, under the brutal dictatorship of Saddam Hussein, had taken over its small but oil-rich neighbor, Kuwait, in August 1990.

George Bush needed something at this point to boost his popularity among American voters. The *Washington Post* (October 16, 1990) had a front-page story headline: "Poll Shows Plunge in Public Confidence: Bush's Rating Plummets." The *Post* reported (October 28): "Some

observers in his own party worry that the president will be forced to initiate combat to prevent further erosion of his support at home."

On October 30, a secret decision was made for war against Iraq. The
United Nations had responded to the invasion of Kuwait by establishing
sanctions against Iraq. Witness after witness testified before
Congressional committees in the fall of 1990 that the sanctions were
having an effect and should continue. Secret CIA testimony to the
Senate affirmed that Iraq's imports and exports had been reduced by
more than 90 percent because of the sanctions.

But after the November elections brought gains for the Democrats
in Congress, Bush doubled American military forces in the Gulf, to
500,000, creating what was now clearly an offensive force rather than a
defensive one. According to Elizabeth Drew, a writer for the *New Yorker*,
Bush's aide John Sununu "was telling people that a short successful war
would be pure political gold for the President and would guarantee his
re-election."

Historian Jon Wiener, analyzing the domestic context of the war
decision shortly afterward, wrote that "Bush abandoned sanctions and
chose war because his time frame was a political one set by the
approaching 1992 presidential elections."

That and the long-time U.S. wish to have a decisive voice in the control of Middle East oil resources were the crucial elements in the decision to go to war against Iraq. Shortly after the war, as representatives of
the thirteen oil-producing nations were about to gather in Geneva, the
business correspondent of the *New York Times* wrote: "By virtue of its
military victory the United States is likely to have more influence in the
Organization of Petroleum Exporting Countries than any industrial
nation has ever exercised."

But those motives were not presented to the American public. It was
told that the United States wanted to liberate Kuwait from Iraqi control.
The major media dwelled on this as a reason for war, without noting
that other countries had been invaded without the United States showing such concern (East Timor by Indonesia, Iran by Iraq, Lebanon by
Israel, Mozambique by South Africa; to say nothing of countries invaded
by the United States itself—Grenada, Panama).

The justification for war that seemed most compelling was that Iraq
was on its way to building a nuclear bomb, but the evidence for this was
very weak. Before the crisis over Kuwait, Western intelligence sources
had estimated it would take Iraq three to ten years to build a nuclear
weapon. Even if Iraq could build a bomb in a year or two, which was the
most pessimistic estimate, it had no delivery system to send it anywhere.

Besides, Israel already had nuclear weapons. And the United States had perhaps 30,000 of them. The Bush administration was trying hard to develop a paranoia in the nation about an Iraqi bomb which did not yet exist.

Bush seemed determined to go to war. There had been several chances to negotiate an Iraqi withdrawal from Kuwait right after the invasion, including an Iraqi proposal reported on August 29 by *Newsday* correspondent Knut Royce. But there was no response from the United States. When Secretary of State James Baker went to Geneva to meet with Iraqi foreign minister Tariq Aziz, the instruction from Bush was "no negotiations."

Despite months of exhortation from Washington about the dangers of Saddam Hussein, surveys showed that less than half of the public favored military action.

In January 1991, Bush, apparently feeling the need for support, asked Congress to give him the authority to make war. This was not a *declaration* of war, as called for by the Constitution; but since Korea and Vietnam, that provision of the Constitution seemed dead, and even the "strict constructionists" on the Supreme Court who prided themselves on taking the words of the Constitution literally and seriously would not intervene.

The debate in Congress was lively. (At one point, a Senate speech was interrupted by protesters in the balcony shouting "No blood for oil!" The protesters were hustled out by guards.) It is likely that Bush was sure of having enough votes, or he would have launched the invasion without Congressional approval; after all, the precedent for ignoring Congress and the Constitution had been set in Korea, Vietnam, Grenada, and Panama.

The Senate voted for military action by only a few votes. The House supported the resolution by a larger majority. However, once Bush ordered the attack on Iraq, both houses, with just a few dissents, Democrats as well as Republicans, voted to "support the war and support the troops."

It was in mid-January 1991, after Saddam Hussein defied an ultimatum to leave Kuwait, that the U.S. launched its air war against Iraq. It was given the name Desert Storm. The government and the media had conjured up a picture of a formidable military power, but Iraq was far from that. The U.S. Air Force had total control of the air, and could bomb at will.

Not only that, U.S. officials had virtual total control of the airwaves. The American public was overwhelmed with television photos of "smart bombs" and confident statements that laser bombs were being guided with perfect precision to military targets. The major networks presented all of these claims without question or criticism.

This confidence in "smart bombs" sparing civilians may have contributed to a shift in public opinion, from being equally divided on going to war, to perhaps 85 percent support for the invasion. Perhaps more important in winning over public support was that once American military were engaged, it seemed to many people who had previously opposed military action that to criticize it now meant betraying the troops who were there. All over the nation yellow ribbons were displayed as a symbol of support for the forces in Iraq.

In fact, the public was being deceived about how "smart" the bombs being dropped on Iraqi towns were. After talking with former intelligence and Air Force officers, a correspondent for the Boston *Globe* reported that perhaps 40 percent of the laser-guided bombs dropped in Operation Desert Storm missed their targets.

John Lehman, Secretary of the Navy under President Reagan, estimated there had been thousands of civilian casualties. The Pentagon officially had no figure on this. A senior Pentagon official told the *Globe*, "To tell you the truth, we're not really focusing on this question."

A Reuters dispatch from Iraq described the destruction of a seventy-three-room hotel in a town south of Baghdad, and quoted an Egyptian witness: "They hit the hotel, full of families, and then they came back to hit it again." Reuters reported that the air raids on Iraq first used laser-guided bombs, but within a few weeks turned to B-52s, which carried conventional bombs, meaning more indiscriminate bombing.

American reporters were kept from seeing the war close-up, and their dispatches were subject to censorship. Apparently recalling how press reports of civilian casualties had affected public opinion during the Vietnam war, the U.S. government was taking no chances this time.

A *Washington Post* reporter complained about the control of information, writing (January 22, 1991):

The bombing has involved . . . dozens of high-flying B-52 bombers equipped with huge, unguided munitions. But the Pentagon has not allowed interviews with B-52 pilots, shown videotapes of their actions or answered any questions about the operations of an aircraft that is the most deadly and least accurate in the armada of more than 2000 U.S. and allied planes in the Persian Gulf region. . . .

In mid-February, U.S. planes dropped bombs on an air raid shelter in Baghdad at four in the morning, killing 400 to 500 people. An Associated Press reporter who was one of few allowed to go to the site said: "Most of the recovered bodies were charred and mutilated beyond recognition. Some clearly were children." The Pentagon claimed it was a military target, but the AP reporter on the scene said: "No evidence of any military presence could be seen inside the wreckage." Other reporters who inspected the site agreed.

After the war, fifteen Washington news bureau chiefs complained in a joint statement that the Pentagon exercised "virtual total control . . . over the American press" during the Gulf War.

But while it was happening, leading television news commentators behaved as if they were working for the United States government. For instance, CBS correspondent Dan Rather, perhaps the most widely seen of the TV newsmen, reported from Saudi Arabia on a film showing a laser bomb (this one dropped by British aircraft in support of the American war) hitting a marketplace and killing civilians. Rather's only comment was: "We can be sure that Saddam Hussein will make propaganda of these casualties."

When the Russian government tried to negotiate an end to the war, bringing Iraq out of Kuwait before the ground war could get under way, top CBS correspondent Lesley Stahl asked another reporter: "Isn't this the nightmare scenario? Aren't the Soviets trying to stop us?" (Ed Siegel, TV reporter for the Boston *Globe*, February 23, 1991).

The final stage of the war, barely six weeks after it had begun, was a ground assault which, like the air war, encountered virtually no resistance. With victory certain and the Iraqi army in full flight, U.S. planes kept bombing the retreating soldiers who clogged the highway out of Kuwait City. A reporter called the scene "a blazing hell . . . a gruesome testament. . . . To the east and west across the sand lay the bodies of those fleeing."

A Yale professor of military history, Michael Howard, writing in the *New York Times* (January 28, 1991), quoted the military strategist Clausewitz approvingly: "The fact that a bloody slaughter is a horrifying act must make us take war more seriously, but not provide an excuse for gradually blunting our swords in the name of humanity." Howard went on to say: "In this conflict of wills, the bottom line remains a readiness to kill and be killed. . . ."

The human consequences of the war became shockingly clear after its end, when it was revealed that the bombings of Iraq had caused starvation, disease, and the deaths of tens of thousands of children. A U.N. team visiting Iraq immediately after the war reported that "the recent conflict has wrought near-apocalyptic results upon the infrastructure. . . . Most means of modern life support have been destroyed or rendered tenuous. . . ."

A Harvard medical team reporting in May said that child mortality had risen steeply, and that 55,000 more children died in the first four months of the year (the war lasted from January 15 to February 28) than in a comparable period the year before.

The director of a pediatric hospital in Baghdad told a *New York Times* reporter that on the first night of the bombing campaign the electricity was knocked out: "Mothers grabbed their children out of incubators, took intravenous tubes out of their arms. Others were removed from oxygen tents and they ran to the basement, where there was no heat. I lost more than 40 prematures in the first 12 hours of the bombing."

Although in the course of the war Saddam Hussein had been depicted by U.S. officials and the press as another Hitler, the war ended short of a march into Baghdad, leaving Hussein in power. It seemed that the United States had wanted to weaken him, but not to eliminate him, in order to keep him as a balance against Iran. In the years before the Gulf War, the United States had sold arms to both Iran and Iraq, at different times favoring one or the other as part of the traditional "balance of power" strategy.

Therefore, as the war ended, the United States did not support Iraqi dissidents who wanted to overthrow the regime of Saddam Hussein. A *New York Times* dispatch from Washington, datelined March 26, 1991, reported: "President Bush has decided to let President Saddam Hussein put down rebellions in his country without American intervention rather than risk the splintering of Iraq, according to official statements and private briefings today."

This left the Kurdish minority, which was rebelling against Saddam Hussein, helpless. And anti-Hussein elements among the Iraqi majority were also left hanging. The *Washington Post* reported (May 3, 1991): "Major defections from the Iraqi military were in the offing in March at the height of the Kurdish rebellion, but never materialized because the officers concluded the U.S. would not back the uprising. . . ."

The man who had been Jimmy Carter's National Security Adviser, Zbigniew Brzezinski, a month after the end of the Gulf War, gave a cold assessment of the pluses and minuses of the event. "The benefits are undeniably impressive. First, a blatant act of aggression was rebuffed and punished. . . . Second, U.S military power is henceforth likely to be taken more seriously. . . . Third, the Middle East and Persian Gulf region is now clearly an American sphere of preponderance."

Brzezinski, however, was concerned about "some negative consequences." One of them was that "the very intensity of the air assault on Iraq gives rise to concern that the conduct of the war may come to be seen as evidence that Americans view Arab lives as worthless. . . . And that raises the moral question of the proportionality of response."

His point about Arab lives being seen as "worthless" was underlined by the fact that the war provoked an ugly wave of anti-Arab racism in the United States, with Arab-Americans insulted or beaten or threatened with death. There were bumper stickers that said "I don't brake for Iraqis." An Arab-American businessman was beaten in Toledo, Ohio.

Brzezinski's measured assessment of the Gulf War could be taken as close to representing the view of the Democratic Party. It went along with the Bush administration. It was pleased with the results. It had some misgivings about civilian casualties. But it did not constitute an opposition.

President George Bush was satisfied. As the war ended, he declared on a radio broadcast: "The specter of Vietnam has been buried forever in the desert sands of the Arabian peninsula."

The Establishment press very much agreed. The two leading news magazines, *Time* and *Newsweek*, had special editions hailing the victory in the war, noting there had been only a few hundred American casualties, without any mention of Iraqi casualties. A *New York Times* editorial (March 30, 1991) said: "America's victory in the Persian Gulf war . . . provided special vindication for the U.S. Army, which brilliantly exploited its firepower and mobility and in the process erased memories of its grievous difficulties in Vietnam."

A black poet in Berkeley, California, June Jordan, had a different view: "I suggest to you it's a hit the same way that crack is, and it doesn't last long."

22

THE UNREPORTED
RESISTANCE

In the early 1990s, a writer for the *New Republic* magazine, reviewing with approval in the *New York Times* a book about the influence of dangerously unpatriotic elements among American intellectuals, warned his readers of the existence of "a permanent adversarial culture" in the United States.

It was an accurate observation. Despite the political consensus of Democrats and Republicans in Washington which set limits on American reform, making sure that capitalism was in place, that national military strength was maintained, that wealth and power remained in the hands of a few, there were millions of Americans, probably tens of millions, who refused, either actively or silently, to go along. Their activities were largely unreported by the media. They constituted this "permanent adversarial culture."

The Democratic party was more responsive to these Americans, on whose votes it depended. But its responsiveness was limited by its own captivity to corporate interests, and its domestic reforms were severely limited by the system's dependency on militarism and war. Thus, President Lyndon Johnson's War on Poverty in the sixties became a victim of the war in Vietnam, and Jimmy Carter could not go far so long as he insisted on a huge outlay of money for the military, much of this to stockpile more nuclear weapons.

As these limits became clear in the Carter years, a small but determined movement against nuclear arms began to grow. The pioneers were a tiny group of Christian pacifists who had been active against the Vietnam war (among them were a former priest, Philip Berrigan, and his wife, Elizabeth McAlister, a former nun). Again and again, members of this group would be arrested for engaging in nonviolent acts of dramatic protest against nuclear war at the Pentagon and the White House—trespassing on forbidden areas, pouring their own blood on symbols of the war machine.

In 1980, small delegations of peace activists from all over the country maintained a series of demonstrations at the Pentagon, in which over a thousand people were arrested for acts of nonviolent civil disobedience.

In September of that year, Philip Berrigan, his brother Daniel (the Jesuit priest and poet), Molly Rush (a mother of six), Anne Montgomery (a nun and counselor to young runaways and prostitutes in Manhattan), and four of their friends made their way past a guard in the General Electric Plant at King of Prussia, Pennsylvania, where nose cones for nuclear missiles were manufactured. They used sledgehammers to smash two of the nose cones and smeared their own blood over missile parts, blueprints, and furniture. Arrested, sentenced to years in prison, they said they were trying to set an example to do as the Bible suggested, to beat swords into plowshares.

They pointed to the huge allocations of taxpayers' money to corporations producing weaponry: "G.E. drains $3 million a day from the public treasury—an enormous larceny against the poor." Before their trial (they came to be known as the Plowshares Eight), Daniel Berrigan had written in the *Catholic Worker*:

> I know of no sure way of predicting where things will go from there, whether others will hear and respond, or how quickly or slowly. Or whether the act will fail to vitalize others, will come to a grinding halt then and there, its actors stigmatized or dismissed as fools. One swallows dry and takes a chance.

In fact, the movement did not come to a halt. Over the next decade, a national movement against nuclear weapons developed, from a small number of men and women willing to go to jail to make others stop and think to millions of Americans frightened at the thought of nuclear holocaust, indignant at the billions of dollars spent on weaponry while people were in need of life's necessities.

Even the very Middle-American Pennsylvania jurors who convicted the Plowshares Eight showed remarkable sympathy with their actions. One juror, Michael DeRosa, told a reporter, "I didn't think they really went to commit a crime. They went to protest." Another, Mary Ann Ingram, said the jury argued about that: "We . . . really didn't want to convict them on anything. But we had to because of the way the judge said the thing you can use is what you get under the law." She added: "These people are not criminals. Here are people who are trying to do some good for the country. But the judge said nuclear power wasn't the issue."

Reagan's huge military budget was to provoke a national movement against nuclear weapons. In the election of 1980 that brought him into the Presidency, local referenda in three districts in western Massachusetts permitted voters to say whether they believed in a mutual Soviet-American halt to testing, production, and deployment of all nuclear weapons, and wanted Congress to devote those funds instead to civilian use. Two peace groups had worked for months on the campaign and all three districts approved the resolution (94,000 to 65,000), even those that voted for Reagan as President. Similar referenda received majority votes between 1978 and 1981 in San Francisco, Berkeley, Oakland, Madison, and Detroit.

Women were in the forefront of the new antinuclear movement. Randall Forsberg, a young specialist in nuclear arms, organized the Council for a Nuclear Weapons Freeze, whose simple program—a mutual Soviet-American freeze on the production of new nuclear weapons—began to catch on throughout the country. Shortly after Reagan's election, two thousand women assembled in Washington, marched on the Pentagon, and surrounded it in a great circle, linking arms or stretching to hold the ends of brightly colored scarves. One hundred forty women were arrested for blocking the Pentagon entrance.

A small group of doctors began to organize meetings around the country to teach citizens the medical consequences of nuclear war. They were the core of the Physicians for Social Responsibility, and Dr. Helen Caldicott, the group's president, became one of the most powerful and eloquent national leaders of the movement. At one of their public symposia, Howard Hiatt, dean of the Harvard School of Public Health, gave a graphic description of the results of one twenty-megaton nuclear bomb falling on Boston. Two million people would die. Survivors would be burned, blinded, crippled. In a nuclear war there would be 25 million severe burn cases in the nation, yet all existing facilities could take care of only 200 cases.

At a national meeting of Catholic bishops early in the Reagan administration, the majority opposed any use of nuclear weapons. In November 1981, there were meetings on 151 college campuses around the country on the issue of nuclear war. And at local elections in Boston that month, a resolution calling for increased federal spending on social programs "by reducing the amount of our tax dollars spent on nuclear weapons and programs of foreign intervention" won a majority in every one of Boston's twenty-two wards, including both white and black working-class districts.

On June 12, 1982, the largest political demonstration in the history of the country took place in Central Park, New York City. Close to a million people gathered to express their determination to bring an end to the arms race.

Scientists who had worked on the atom bomb added their voices to the growing movement. George Kistiakowsky, a Harvard University chemistry professor who had worked on the first atomic bomb, and later was science adviser to President Eisenhower, became a spokesman for the disarmament movement. His last public remarks, before his death from cancer at the age of eighty-two, were in an editorial for the *Bulletin of Atomic Scientists* in December 1982. "I tell you as my parting words: Forget the channels. There simply is not enough time left before the world explodes. Concentrate instead on organizing, with so many others of like mind, a mass movement for peace such as there has not been before."

By the spring of 1983, the nuclear freeze had been endorsed by 368 city and county councils across the country, by 444 town meetings and 17 state legislatures, and by the House of Representatives. A Harris poll at this time indicated that 79 percent of the population wanted a nuclear freeze agreement with the Soviet Union. Even among evangelical Christians—a group of 40 million people presumed to be conservative and pro-Reagan—a Gallup poll sampling showed 60 percent favoring a nuclear freeze.

A year after the great Central Park demonstration, there were over three thousand antiwar groups around the country. And the antinuclear feeling was being reflected in the culture—in books, magazine articles, plays, motion pictures. Jonathan Schell's impassioned book against the arms race, *The Fate of the Earth*, became a national best-seller. A documentary film on the arms race made in Canada was forbidden to enter the country by the Reagan administration, but a federal court ordered it admitted.

In less than three years, there had come about a remarkable change in public opinion. At the time of Reagan's election, nationalist feeling—drummed up by the recent hostage crisis in Iran and by the Russian invasion of Afghanistan—was strong; the University of Chicago's National Opinion Research Center found that only 12 percent of those it polled thought too much was being spent on arms. But when it took another poll in the spring of 1982, that figure rose to 32 percent. And in the spring of 1983, a *New York Times*/CBS News poll found that the figure had risen again, to 48 percent.

Antimilitarist feeling expressed itself also in resistance to the draft. When President Jimmy Carter, responding to the Soviet Union's invasion of Afghanistan, called for the registration of young men for a military draft, more than 800,000 men (10 percent) failed to register. One mother wrote to the *New York Times*:

> To the Editor: Thirty-six years ago I stood in front of the crematorium. The ugliest force in the world had promised itself that I should be removed from the cycle of life—that I should never know the pleasure of giving life. With great guns and great hatred, this force thought itself the equal of the force of life.
>
> I survived the great guns, and with every smile of my son, they grow smaller. It is not for me, sir, to offer my son's blood as lubricant for the next generation of guns. I remove myself and my own from the cycle of death.
>
> Isabella Leitner

Former Nixon aide Alexander Haig warned, in an interview in the French journal *Politique Internationale*, that there might reappear in the U.S. the conditions that forced President Nixon to stop the draft. "There is a Jane Fonda on every doorstep," he said.

One of the young men who refused to register, James Peters, wrote an open letter to President Carter:

> Dear Mr. President: On July 23, 1980, I . . . am expected to report to my local post office for the purpose of registering with the Selective Service System. I hereby inform you, Mr. President, that I will not register on July 23, or at any time thereafter. . . . We have tried militarism, and it has failed the human race in every way imaginable.

Once he was in office, Ronald Reagan hesitated to renew draft registration, because, as his Secretary of Defense, Caspar Weinberger, explained, "President Reagan believes that resuming the draft to meet manpower problems would lead to public unrest comparable to that in the sixties and seventies." William Beecher, a former Pentagon reporter, wrote in November 1981 that Reagan was "obviously concerned, even alarmed, by the mounting voices of discontent and suspicion over emerging U.S. nuclear strategy both in the streets of Europe and more recently on American campuses."

Hoping to intimidate this opposition, the Reagan administration began to prosecute draft resisters. One of those facing prison was Benjamin Sasway, who cited U.S. military intervention in El Salvador as a good reason not to register for the draft.

Aroused by Sasway's civil disobedience, a right-wing columnist (William A. Rusher, of the *National Review*) wrote indignantly that one heritage of the sixties was a new generation of antiwar teachers:

> Almost certainly there was a teacher, or teachers, who taught Benjamin Sasway to look at American society as a hypocritical, exploitative, materialistic roadblock on the path of human progress. The generation of the Vietnam protesters is now in its early thirties, and the academicians among them are already ensconced in the faculties of the country's high schools and colleges. . . . What a pity our jurisprudence doesn't allow us to reach and penalize the real architects of this sort of destruction!

Reagan's policy of giving military aid to the dictatorship of El Salvador was not accepted quietly around the nation. He had barely taken office when the following report appeared in the Boston *Globe*:

> It was a scene reminiscent of the 1960s, a rally of students in Harvard Yard shouting antiwar slogans, a candlelight march through the streets of Cambridge. . . . 2000 persons, mostly students, gathered to protest U.S. involvement in El Salvador. . . . Students from Tufts, MIT, Boston University and Boston College, the University of Massachusetts, Brandeis, Suffolk, Dartmouth, Northeastern, Vassar, Yale and Simmons were represented.

During commencement exercises that spring of 1981 at Syracuse University, when Reagan's Secretary of State, Alexander Haig, was given an honorary doctorate in "public service," two hundred students and faculty turned their backs on the presentation. During Haig's address, the press reported, "Nearly every pause in Mr. Haig's fifteen-minute address was punctuated by chants: 'Human needs, not military greed!' 'Get out of El Salvador!' 'Washington guns killed American nuns!'"

The last slogan was a reference to the execution in the fall of 1980 of four American nuns by Salvadoran soldiers. Thousands of people in El Salvador were being murdered each year by "death squads" sponsored by a government armed by the United States, and the American public was beginning to pay attention to events in this tiny Central American country.

As has been true generally in the making of U.S. foreign policy, there was no pretense at democracy. Public opinion was simply ignored. A *New York Times*/CBS News poll in the spring of 1982 reported that only 16 percent of its sampling favored Reagan's program of sending military and economic aid to El Salvador.

In the spring of 1983, it was disclosed that an American physician named Charles Clement was working with the Salvadoran rebels. As an Air Force pilot in Southeast Asia, he had become disillusioned with U.S. policy there, having seen firsthand that his government was lying, and refused to fly any more missions. The Air Force response was to commit him to a psychiatric hospital, then to discharge him as psychologically unfit. He went to medical school, and then volunteered to be a doctor with the guerrillas in El Salvador.

There was much talk in the American press in the early eighties about the political cautiousness of a new generation of college students concerned mostly with their own careers. But when, at the Harvard commencement of June 1983, Mexican writer Carlos Fuentes criticized American intervention in Latin America, and said, "Because we are your true friends, we will not permit you to conduct yourselves in Latin American affairs as the Soviet Union conducts itself in Central European and Central Asian affairs," he was interrupted twenty times by applause and received a standing ovation when finished.

Among my own students at Boston University, I did not find the pervasive selfishness and unconcern with others that the media kept reporting, in deadening repetition, about the students of the eighties. In the journals they kept, I found the following comments:

A male student: "Do you think anything good that has happened in the world had anything to do with government? I work in Roxbury [a black neighborhood]. I know the government doesn't work. Not for the people of Roxbury, and not for the people anywhere. It works for people with money."

A graduate of a Catholic high school: "America to me is a society, a culture. America is my home; if someone were to rob that *culture* from me, then perhaps there would be reason to resist. I will not die, however, to defend the honor of the *government.*"

A young woman: "As a white middle class person I've never felt discriminated against at all. But I'll say this: If anyone ever tried to make me sit in a different schoolroom, use a different bathroom, or anything like that, I would knock them right on their ass.... The people are the last ones that need their rights stated on paper, for if they're abused or injusticed by government or authority, they can act on the injustice directly.... When you look at the . . . statements of rights and laws, it's really government and authority and institutions and corporations that need laws and rights to insulate them from the physicality, the directness of the people."

Beyond the campuses, out in the country, there was opposition to government policy, not widely known. A report from Tucson, Arizona, early in the Reagan presidency described "demonstrators, mainly middle-aged," protesting at the Federal Building against U.S. involvement in El Salvador. Over a thousand people in Tucson marched in a procession and attended a mass to commemorate the anniversary of the assassination of Archbishop Oscar Romero, who had spoken out against the Salvadoran death squads.

Over 60,000 Americans signed pledges to take action of some sort, including civil disobedience, if Reagan moved to invade Nicaragua. When the President instituted a blockade of the tiny country to try to force its government out of power, there were demonstrations around the country. In Boston alone, 550 people were arrested protesting the blockade.

During Reagan's presidency, there were hundreds of actions throughout the nation against his policies in South Africa. He obviously did not want to see the white ruling minority of South Africa displaced by the radical African National Congress, which represented the black majority. Chester Crocker, Assistant Secretary of State for African Affairs, in his memoirs, called Reagan "insensitive" to the conditions under which blacks lived there. Public opinion was strong enough to cause Congress to legislate economic sanctions against the South African Government in 1986, overriding Reagan's veto.

Reagan's cuts in social services were felt on the local level as vital needs could not be taken care of, and there were angry reactions. In the spring and summer of 1981, residents of East Boston took to the streets; for fifty-five nights they blocked major thoroughfares and the Sumner Tunnel during rush hour, in order to protest cutbacks in funds for fire, police, and teachers. The police superintendent, John Doyle, said: "Maybe these people are starting to take lessons from the protests of the sixties and seventies." The Boston *Globe* reported: "The demonstrators in East Boston were mostly middle-aged, middle- or working-class people who said they had never protested anything before."

The Reagan administration took away federal funds for the arts, suggesting that the performing arts seek help from private donors. In New York, two historic Broadway theaters were razed to make way for a luxury fifty-story hotel, after two hundred theater people demonstrated, picketing, reading plays and singing songs, refusing to disperse when ordered by police. Some of the nation's best-known theater personalities were arrested, including producer Joseph Papp, actresses Tammy Grimes, Estelle Parsons, and Celeste Holm, actors Richard Gere and Michael Moriarty.

The budget cuts spurred strikes across the country, often by groups unaccustomed to striking. In the fall of 1982, United Press International reported:

> Angered by layoffs, salary cuts and uncertainty about job security, more schoolteachers throughout the country have decided to go on strike. Teachers' strikes last week in seven states, from Rhode Island to Washington, have idled more than 300,000 students.

Surveying a series of news events in the first week of January 1983, David Nyhan of the Boston *Globe* wrote: "There is something brewing in the land that bodes ill for those in Washington who ignore it. People have moved from the frightened state to the angry stage and are acting out their frustrations in ways that will test the fabric of civil order." He gave some examples:

> In Little Washington, Pennsylvania, in early 1983, when a 50-year-old computer science teacher who led a teachers' strike was sent to jail, 2000 people demonstrated outside the jailhouse in his support, and the Pittsburgh *Post-Gazette* called it "the largest crowd in Washington County since the 1794 Whiskey Rebellion."
>
> When unemployed or bankrupt home owners in the Pittsburgh area could no longer make mortgage payments, and foreclosure sales were scheduled, 60 pickets jammed the courthouse to protest the auction, and Allegheny sheriff Eugene Coon halted the proceedings.
>
> The foreclosure of a 320-acre wheat farm in Springfield, Colorado, was interrupted by 200 angry farmers, who had to be dispersed by tear gas and Mace.

When Reagan arrived in Pittsburgh in April 1983 to make a speech, 3000 people, many of them unemployed steelworkers, demonstrated against him, standing in the rain outside his hotel. Demonstrations by the unemployed were taking place in Detroit, Flint, Chicago, Cleveland, Los Angeles, Washington—over twenty cities in all.

Just around that time, Miami blacks rioted against police brutality; they were reacting against their general deprivation as well. The unemployment rate among young African-Americans had risen above 50 percent, and the Reagan administration's only response to poverty was to build more jails. Understanding that blacks would not vote for him, Reagan tried, unsuccessfully, to get Congress to eliminate a crucial section of the Voting Rights Act of 1965, which had been very effective in safeguarding the right of blacks to vote in Southern states.

Reagan's policies clearly joined the two issues of disarmament and social welfare. It was guns versus children, and this was expressed dramatically by the head of the Children's Defense Fund, Marian Wright Edelman, in a commencement speech at the Milton Academy in Massachusetts in the summer of 1983:

> You are graduating into a nation and world teetering on the brink of moral and economic bankruptcy. Since 1980, our President and Congress have been turning our national plowshares into swords and been bringing good news to the rich at the expense of the poor. . . . Children are the major victims. Our misguided national and world choices are literally killing children daily. . . . Yet governments throughout the world, led by our own, spend over $600 billion a year on arms, while an estimated 1 billion of our world's people live in poverty and 600 million are under- or unemployed. Where is the human commitment and political will to find the relative pittance of money needed to protect children?

She urged her listeners: "Pick a piece of the problem that you can help solve while trying to see how your piece fits into the broader social change puzzle."

Her words seemed to represent a growing mood that worried the Reagan administration. It withdrew some of its proposed cutbacks, and Congress eliminated others. When, in its second year, the administration proposed $9 billion in cuts in support for children and poor families, Congress accepted only $1 billion. The Washington correspondent of the *New York Times* reported: "Political concerns about the fairness of Mr. Reagan's programs have forced the Administration to curtail its efforts to make further cutbacks in programs for the poor."

The repeated elections of Republican candidates, Reagan in 1980 and 1984, George Bush in 1988, were treated by the press with words like "landslide" and "overwhelming victory." They were ignoring four facts: that roughly half the population, though eligible to vote, did not; that those who did vote were limited severely in their choices to the two parties that monopolized the money and the media; that as a result many of their votes were cast without enthusiasm; and that there was little relationship between voting for a candidate and voting for specific policies.

In 1980 Reagan received 51.6 percent of the popular vote, while Jimmy Carter received 41.7 percent and John Anderson (a liberal Republican running on a third-party ticket) received 6.7 percent. Only 54 percent of the voting-age population voted, so that—of the total eligible to vote—27 percent voted for Reagan.

A survey by the *New York Times* found that only 11 percent of those who voted for Reagan did so because "he's a real conservative." Three times as many said they voted for him because "it is time for a change."

For a second term, running against former Vice-President Walter Mondale, Reagan won 59 percent of the popular vote, but with half the electorate not voting, he had 29 percent of the voting population.

In the 1988 election, with Vice-President George Bush running against Democrat Michael Dukakis, Bush's 54 percent victory added up to 27 percent of the eligible voters.

Because our peculiar voting arrangements allow a small margin of popular votes to become a huge majority of electoral votes, the media can talk about "overwhelming victory," thus deceiving their readers and disheartening those who don't look closely at the statistics. Could one say from these figures that "the American people" wanted Reagan, or Bush, as President? One could certainly say that more voters preferred the Republican candidates to their opponents. But even more seemed to want neither candidate. Nevertheless, on the basis of these slim electoral pluralities, Reagan and Bush would claim that "the people" had spoken.

Indeed, when the people did speak about issues, in surveys of public opinion, they expressed beliefs to which neither the Republican nor Democratic parties paid attention.

For instance, both parties, through the eighties and early nineties, kept strict limits on social programs for the poor, on the grounds that this would require more taxes, and "the people" did not want higher taxes.

This was certainly true as a general proposition, that Americans wanted to pay as little in taxes as possible. But when they were asked if they would be willing to pay higher taxes for specific purposes like health and education, they said yes, they would. For instance, a 1990 poll of Boston area voters showed that 54 percent of them would pay more taxes if that would go toward cleaning up the environment.

And when higher taxes were presented in class terms, rather than as a general proposal, people were quite clear. A *Wall Street Journal*/NBC News poll in December 1990 showed that 84 percent of the respondents favored a surtax on millionaires (this provision was dropped around that time from a Democratic-Republican budget compromise). Even though

51 percent of the respondents were in favor of *raising* the capital gains tax, neither major party favored that.

A Harris/Harvard School of Public Health poll of 1989 showed that most Americans (61 percent) favored a Canadian-type health system, in which the government was the single payer to doctors and hospitals, bypassing the insurance companies, and offering universal medical coverage to everyone. Neither the Democratic nor the Republican party adopted that as its program, although both insisted they wanted to "reform" the health system.

A survey by the Gordon Black Corporation for the National Press Club in 1992 found that 59 percent of all voters wanted a 50 percent cut in defense spending in five years. Neither of the major parties was willing to make major cuts in the military budget.

How the public felt about government aid to the poor seemed to depend on how the question was put. Both parties, and the media, talked incessantly about the "welfare" system, that it was not working, and the word "welfare" became a signal for opposition. When people were asked (a *New York Times*/CBS News poll of 1992) if more money should be allocated to welfare, 23 percent said no. But when the same people were asked, should the government help the poor, 64 percent said yes.

This was a recurring theme. When, at the height of the Reagan presidency, in 1987, people were asked if the government should guarantee food and shelter to needy people, 62 percent answered yes.

Clearly, there was something amiss with a political system, supposed to be democratic, in which the desires of the voters were repeatedly ignored. They could be ignored with impunity so long as the political system was dominated by two parties, both tied to corporate wealth. An electorate forced to choose between Carter and Reagan, or Reagan and Mondale, or Bush and Dukakis could only despair (or decide not to vote) because neither candidate was capable of dealing with a fundamental economic illness whose roots were deeper than any single presidency.

That illness came from a fact which was almost never talked about: that the United States was a class society, in which 1 percent of the population owned 33 percent of the wealth, with an underclass of 30 to 40 million people living in poverty. The social programs of the sixties— Medicare and Medicaid, food stamps, etc.—did not do much more than maintain the historic American maldistribution of resources.

While the Democrats would give more help to the poor than the Republicans, they were not capable (indeed, not really desirous) of seriously tampering with an economic system in which corporate profit comes before human need.

There was no important national movement for radical change, no social democratic (or democratic socialist) party such as existed in countries in Western Europe, Canada, and New Zealand. But there were a thousand signs of alienation, voices of protest, local actions in every part of the country to call attention to deep-felt grievances, to demand that some injustice be remedied.

For instance, the Citizens' Clearinghouse for Hazardous Wastes in Washington, D.C., which had been formed early in the Reagan administration by housewife and activist Lois Gibbs, reported that it was giving help to 8000 local groups around the country. One of these groups, in Oregon, brought a series of successful lawsuits to force the Environmental Protection Agency to do something about unsafe drinking water in the Bull Run reservoir near Portland.

In Seabrook, New Hampshire, there were years of persistent protest against a nuclear power plant which residents considered a danger to themselves and their families. Between 1977 and 1989, over 3500 people were arrested in these protests. Ultimately, the plant, plagued by financial problems and opposition, had to shut down.

Fear of nuclear accidents was intensified by disastrous events at Three Mile Island in Pennsylvania in 1979 and by an especially frightening calamity in Chernobyl in the Soviet Union in 1986. All of this was having an effect on the once-booming nuclear industry. By 1994, the Tennessee Valley Authority had stopped the construction of three nuclear plants, which the *New York Times* called "the symbolic death notice for the current generation of reactors in the United States."

In Minneapolis, Minnesota, thousands of people demonstrated year after year against the Honeywell Corporation's military contracts, and between 1982 and 1988 over 1800 people were arrested.

Furthermore, when those who engaged in such civil disobedience were brought into court, they often found sympathetic support from juries, winning acquittals from ordinary citizens who seemed to understand that even if they had technically broken the law, they had done so in a good cause.

In 1984, a group of Vermont citizens (the "Winooski Forty-four") refused to leave the hallway outside a U.S. Senator's office, protesting his votes to give arms to the Nicaraguan contras. They were arrested, but at their trial they were treated sympathetically by the judge and acquitted by the jury.

At another trial shortly after, a number of people (including activist Abbie Hoffman and Amy Carter, daughter of former President Jimmy Carter) were charged with blocking CIA recruiters at the University of

Massachusetts. They called to the witness stand ex-CIA agents who told the jury that the CIA had engaged in illegal and murderous activities all around the world. The jury acquitted them.

One juror, a woman hospital worker, said later: "I was not familiar with the CIA's activities. . . . I was shocked. . . . I was kind of proud of the students." Another juror said: "It was very educational." The county district attorney, prosecuting the case, concluded: "If there is a message, it was that this jury was composed of middle America. . . . Middle America doesn't want the CIA doing what they are doing."

In the South, while there was no great movement comparable to the civil rights movement of the Sixties, there were hundreds of local groups organizing poor people, white and black. In North Carolina, Linda Stout, the daughter of a mill worker who had died of industrial poisons, coordinated a multiracial network of 500 textile workers, farmers, maids—most of them low-income women of color—in the Piedmont Peace Project.

The historic Highlander Folk School in Tennessee, which had nurtured so many black and white activists throughout the South, was now joined by other folk schools and popular education centers.

Anne Braden, a veteran of racial and labor struggles in the South, was still organizing, leading the Southern Organizing Committee for Economic and Social Justice. The group gave help in local actions: to 300 African-Americans in Tift County, Georgia, who were protesting the existence of a chemical plant which was making them sick; to Native Americans in Cherokee County, North Carolina, who were organizing to stop a polluted landfill.

Back in the sixties, Chicano farm workers, people of Mexican descent who came to work and live mostly in California and the Southwestern states, rebelled against their feudal working conditions. They went out on strike and organized a national boycott of grapes, under the leadership of Cesar Chavez. Soon farmworkers were organizing in other parts of the country.

In the seventies and eighties, their struggles against poverty and discrimination continued. The Reagan years hit them hard, as it did poor people all over the country. By 1984, 42 percent of all Latino children and one-fourth of the families lived below the poverty line.

Copper miners in Arizona, mostly Mexican, went on strike against the Phelps-Dodge company after it cut wages, benefits, and safety measures in 1983. They were attacked by National Guardsmen and state troopers, by tear gas and helicopters, but held out for three years until a combination of governmental and corporate power finally defeated them.

There were victories too. In 1985, 1700 cannery workers, most of them Mexican women, went on strike in Watsonville, California, and won a union contract with medical benefits. In 1990 workers who had been laid off from the Levi Strauss company in San Antonio because the company was moving to Costa Rica called a boycott, organized a hunger strike, and won concessions. In Los Angeles, Latino janitors went on strike in 1990 and despite police attacks, won recognition of their union, a pay raise, and sick benefits.

Latino and Latina activists (not necessarily Chicano, which refers to those of Mexican ancestry), through the eighties and early nineties, campaigned for better labor conditions, for representation in local government, for tenants' rights, for bilingual education in the schools. Kept out of the media, they organized a bilingual radio movement, and by 1991 had fourteen Latino stations in the country, twelve of them bilingual.

In New Mexico, Latinos fought for land and water rights against real estate developers who tried to throw them off land they had lived on for decades. In 1988 there was a confrontation, and the people organized an armed occupation, built bunkers for protection against attack, and won support from other communities in the Southwest; finally, a court ruled in their favor.

Abnormal rates of cancer for farmworkers in California aroused the Chicano community. Cesar Chavez of the United Farm Workers fasted for thirty-five days in 1988 to call attention to these conditions. There were now United Farm Workers unions in Texas, Arizona, and other states.

The importation of Mexican workers for low wages, under terrible conditions, spread from the Southwest to other parts of the country. By 1991, 80,000 Latinos lived in North Carolina, 30,000 in north Georgia. The Farm Labor Organizing Committee, which had won a difficult strike in the Ohio tomato fields in 1979, the largest agricultural strike ever in the Midwest, brought thousands of farmworkers together in several Midwest states.

As the Latino population of the country kept growing, it soon matched the 12 percent of the population that was African-American and began to have a distinct effect on American culture. Much of its music, art, and drama was much more consciously political and satirical than mainstream culture.

The Border Arts workshop was formed in 1984 by artists and writers in San Diego and Tijuana, and its work dealt powerfully with issues of racism and injustice. In Northern California, Teatro Campesino and Teatro de la Esperanza performed for working people all over the country, turning schoolhouses, churches, and fields into theaters.

Latinos were especially conscious of the imperial role the United States had played in Mexico and the Caribbean, and many of them became militant critics of U.S. policy toward Nicaragua, El Salvador, and Cuba. In 1970 a great march in Los Angeles against the Vietnam war, which had been attacked by police, left three Chicanos dead.

When the Bush administration was preparing for war against Iraq in the summer of 1990, thousands of people in Los Angeles marched along the same route they had taken twenty years before, when they were protesting the Vietnam war. As Elizabeth Martinez wrote (*500 Years of Chicano History in Pictures*):

> Before and during President Bush's war in the Persian Gulf many people—including Raza [literally "race"; a term adopted by Latino activists]—had doubts about it or were opposed. We had learned some lessons about wars started in the name of democracy that turned out to benefit only the rich and powerful. Raza mobilized to protest this war of mass murder, even faster than the U.S. war in Vietnam, though we could not stop it.

In 1992, a fund-raising group which came out of the Vietnam war called Resist made donations to 168 organizations around the country—community groups, peace groups, Native American groups, prisoners' rights organizations, health and environmental groups.

A new generation of lawyers, schooled in the sixties, constituted a small but socially conscious minority within the legal profession. They were in court defending the poor and the helpless, or bringing suit against powerful corporations. One law firm used its talent and energy to defend whistleblowers—men and women who were fired because they "blew the whistle" on corporate corruption that victimized the public.

The women's movement, which had managed to raise the consciousness of the whole nation on the issue of sexual equality, faced a powerful backlash in the eighties. The Supreme Court's defense of abortion rights in its 1973 *Roe* v. *Wade* decision aroused a pro-life movement that had strong supporters in Washington. Congress passed, and the Supreme Court later let stand, a law that eliminated federal medical benefits to help poor women pay for abortions. But the National Organization of Women and other groups remained strong; in 1989, a Washington rally for what had come to be known as the right to choose drew over 300,000 people. When, in 1994 and 1995, abortion clinics were attacked and several supporters murdered, the conflict became grimly intense.

The rights of gay and lesbian Americans had come vividly to the forefront in the Seventies with radical changes in ideas about sexuality and freedom. The gay movement then became a visible presence in the nation, with parades, demonstrations, campaigns for the elimination of state statutes discriminating against homosexuals. One result was a growing literature about the hidden history of gay life in the United States and in Europe.

In 1994, there was a Stonewall 25 march in Manhattan, which commemorated an event homosexuals regarded as a turning point: twenty-five years earlier, gay men fought back vigorously against a police raid on the Stonewall bar in Greenwich Village. In the early nineties, gay and lesbian groups campaigned more openly, more determinedly, against discrimination, and for more attention to the scourge of AIDS, which they claimed was being given only marginal attention by the national government.

In Rochester, New York, a local campaign achieved an unprecedented decision barring military recruiters from a school district because of the Defense Department discrimination against gay soldiers.

The labor movement in the eighties and nineties was considerably weakened by the decline of manufacturing, by the flight of factories to other countries, by the hostility of the Reagan administration and its appointees on the National Labor Relations Board. Yet organizing continued, especially among white collar workers and low-income people of color. The AFL-CIO put on hundreds of new organizers to work among Latinos, African-Americans, and Asian-Americans.

Rank-and-file workers in old, stagnant unions began to rebel. In 1991, the notoriously corrupt leadership of the powerful Teamsters Union was voted out of office by a reform slate. The new leadership immediately became a force in Washington, and took the lead in working for independent political coalitions outside the two major parties. But the labor movement as a whole, much diminished, was struggling for survival.

Against the overwhelming power of corporate wealth and governmental authority, the spirit of resistance was kept alive in the early nineties, often by small-scale acts of courage and defiance. On the West Coast, a young activist named Keith McHenry and hundreds of others were arrested again and again for distributing free food to poor people without a license. They were part of a program called Food Not Bombs. More Food Not Bombs groups sprang up in communities around the country.

In 1992, a New York group interested in revising traditional ideas about American history received approval from the New York City Council to put up thirty metal plaques high on lampposts around the city. One of them, placed opposite the Morgan corporate headquarters, identified the famous banker J.P. Morgan as a Civil War "draft dodger." In fact, Morgan had avoided the draft and profited in business deals with the government during the war. Another plaque, placed near the Stock Exchange, portrayed a suicide and carried the label "Advantage of an Unregulated Free Market."

The general disillusionment with government during the Vietnam years and the Watergate scandals, the exposure of anti-democratic actions by the FBI and the CIA, led to resignations from government and open criticism by former employees.

A number of former CIA officials left the agency, and wrote books critical of its activities. John Stockwell, who had headed the CIA operation in Angola, resigned, wrote a book exposing the CIA's activities, and lectured all over the country about his experiences. David MacMichael, a historian and former CIA specialist, testified at trials on behalf of people who had protested government policy in Central America.

FBI Agent Jack Ryan, a twenty-one-year veteran of the bureau, was fired when he refused to investigate peace groups. He was deprived of his pension and for some time had to live in a shelter for homeless people.

Sometimes the war in Vietnam, which had ended in 1975, came back to public attention in the eighties and nineties through people who had been involved in the conflicts of that day. Some of them had since made dramatic turnabouts in their thinking. John Wall, who prosecuted Dr. Benjamin Spock and four others in Boston for "conspiring" to obstruct the draft, showed up at a dinner honoring the defendants in 1994, saying the trial had changed his ideas.

Even more striking was the statement by Charles Hutto, a U.S. soldier who had participated in the atrocity known as the My Lai massacre, in which a company of American soldiers shot to death women and children by the hundreds in a tiny Vietnamese village. Interviewed in the eighties, Hutto told a reporter:

> I was nineteen years old, and I'd always been told to do what the grown-ups told me to do. . . . But now I'll tell my sons, if the government calls, to go, to serve their country, but to use their own judgment at times . . . to forget about authority . . . to use their own conscience. I wish somebody had told me that before I went to Vietnam. I didn't know. Now I don't think there should be even a thing called war . . . cause it messes up a person's mind.

It was this legacy of the Vietnam war—the feeling among a great majority of Americans that it was a terrible tragedy, a war that should not have been fought—that plagued the Reagan and Bush administrations, which still hoped to extend American power around the world.

In 1985, when George Bush was Vice-President, former Defense Secretary James Schlesinger had warned the Senate Foreign Relations Committee: "Vietnam brought a sea change in domestic attitudes . . . a breakdown in the political consensus behind foreign policy. . . ."

When Bush became President, he was determined to overcome what came to be called the Vietnam syndrome—the resistance of the American people to a war desired by the Establishment. And so, he launched the air war against Iraq in mid-January 1991 with overwhelming force, so the war could be over quickly, before there was time for a national antiwar movement to develop.

The signs of a possible movement were there in the months of the prewar buildup. On Halloween, 600 students marched through downtown Missoula, Montana, shouting "Hell no, we won't go!" In Shreveport, Louisiana, despite the *Shreveport Journal*'s front-page headline: "Poll Favors Military Action," the story was that 42 percent of the respondents thought the U.S. should "initiate force" and 41 percent said "wait and see."

The November 11, 1990, Veterans Parade in Boston was joined by a group called Veterans for Peace, carrying signs: "No More Vietnams. Bring 'Em Home Now" and "Oil and Blood Do Not Mix, Wage Peace." The Boston *Globe* reported that "the protesters were greeted with respectful applause and, at some places, strong demonstrations of support by onlookers." One of those onlookers, a woman named Mary Belle Dressler, said: "Personally, parades that honor the military are somewhat troublesome to me because the military is about war, and war is troublesome to me."

Most Vietnam veterans were supporting military action, but there was a strong dissident minority. In one survey that showed 53 percent of the veterans polled saying they would gladly serve in the Gulf War, 37 percent said they would not.

Perhaps the most famous Vietnam veteran, Ron Kovic, author of *Born on the Fourth of July*, made a thirty-second television speech as Bush moved toward war. In the appeal, broadcast on 200 television stations in 120 cities across the country, he asked all citizens to "stand up and speak out" against war. "How many more Americans coming home in wheelchairs—like me—will it take before we learn?"

That November of 1990, several months into the Kuwait crisis, college students in St. Paul, Minnesota, demonstrated against war. The local press reported:

It was a full-blown antiwar demonstration with mothers pushing kids in strollers, college professors and grade school teachers carrying signs, peace activists bedecked in peace symbols, and hundreds of students from a dozen schools singing, beating drums and chanting, "Hey, hey, ho ho, we won't fight for Amoco."

Ten days before the bombing began, at a town meeting in Boulder, Colorado, with 800 people present, the question was put: "Do you support Bush's policy for war?" Only four people raised their hands. A few days before the war began, 4000 people in Santa Fe, New Mexico, blocked a four-lane highway for an hour, asking that there be no war. Residents said this was larger than any demonstration in the Vietnam era.

On the eve of war, 6000 people marched through Ann Arbor, Michigan, to ask for peace. On the night the war began, 5000 people gathered in San Francisco to denounce the war and formed a human chain around the Federal Building. Police broke the chain by swinging their clubs at the hands of the protesters. But the San Francisco Board of Supervisors passed a resolution declaring the city and county a sanctuary for those who for "moral, ethical or religious reasons cannot participate in war."

The night before Bush gave the order to launch the bombing, a seven-year-old girl in Lexington, Massachusetts, told her mother she wanted to write a letter to the President. Her mother suggested it was late and she should write the next day. "No, tonight," the girl said. She was still learning to write, so she dictated a letter:

> Dear President Bush. I don't like the way you are behaving. If you would make up your mind there won't be a war we won't have to have peace vigils. If you were in a war you wouldn't want to get hurt. What I'm saying is: I don't want any fighting to happen. Sincerely yours. Serena Kabat.

After the bombing of Iraq began along with the bombardment of public opinion, the polls showed overwhelming support for Bush's action, and this continued through the six weeks of the war. But was it an accurate reflection of the citizenry's long-term feelings about war? The split vote in the polls just before the war reflected a public still thinking its opinion might have an effect. Once the war was on, and clearly irreversible, in an atmosphere charged with patriotic fervor (the president of the United Church of Christ spoke of "the steady drumbeat of war messages"), it was not surprising that a great majority of the country would declare its support.

Nevertheless, even with little time to organize, and with the war over very fast, there was an opposition—a minority for sure, but a determined one, and with the potential to grow. Compared to the first months of the military escalation in Vietnam, the movement against the Gulf War expanded with extraordinary speed and vigor.

That first week of the war, while it was clear most Americans were supporting Bush's action, tens of thousands of people took to the streets in protest, in towns and cities all over the country. In Athens, Ohio, over 100 people were arrested, as they clashed with a prowar group. In Portland, Maine, 500 marched wearing white arm bands or carrying white paper crosses with one word, "Why?," written in red.

At the University of Georgia, 70 students opposed to the war held an all-night vigil, and in the Georgia Legislature, Representative Cynthia McKinnon made a speech attacking the bombing of Iraq, leading many of the other legislators to walk off the floor. She held her ground, and it seemed that there had been at least some change in thinking since Representative Julian Bond was expelled from the very same legislature for criticizing the war in Vietnam during the 1960s. At a junior high school in Newton, Massachusetts, 350 students marched to city hall to present a petition to the mayor declaring their opposition to the war in the Gulf. Clearly, many were trying to reconcile their feelings about war with their sympathy for soldiers sent to the Middle East. A student leader, Carly Baker, said: "We don't think bloodshed is the right way. We are supporting the troops and are proud of them, but we don't want war."

In Ada, Oklahoma, while East Central Oklahoma State University was "adopting" two National Guard units, two young women sat quietly on top of the concrete entrance gate with signs that read "Teach Peace ... Not War." One of them, Patricia Biggs, said: "I don't think we should be over there. I don't think it's about justice and liberty, I think it's about economics. The big oil corporations have a lot to do with what is going on over there. . . . We are risking people's lives for money."

Four days after the United States launched its air attack, 75,000 people (the estimate of the Capitol Police) marched in Washington, rallying near the White House to denounce the war. In Southern California, Ron Kovic addressed 6000 people who chanted "Peace Now!" In Fayetteville, Arkansas, a group supporting military policy was confronted by the Northwest Arkansas Citizens Against War, who marched carrying a flag-draped coffin and a banner that read "Bring Them Home Alive."

Another disabled Vietnam veteran, a professor of history and political science at York College in Pennsylvania named Philip Avillo, wrote in a local newspaper: "Yes, we need to support our men and women under arms. But let's support them by bringing them home; not by condoning this barbarous, violent policy." In Salt Lake City, hundreds of demonstrators, many with children, marched through the city's main streets chanting antiwar slogans.

In Vermont, which had just elected Socialist Bernie Sanders to Congress, over 2000 demonstrators disrupted a speech by the governor at the state house, and in Burlington, Vermont's largest city, 300 protesters walked through the downtown area, asking shop owners to close their doors in solidarity.

On January 26, nine days after the beginning of the war, over 150,000 people marched through the streets of Washington, D.C., and listened to speakers denounce the war, including the movie stars Susan Sarandon and Tim Robbins. A woman from Oakland, California, held up the folded American flag that was given to her when her husband was killed in Vietnam, saying, "I learned the hard way there is no glory in a folded flag."

Labor unions had supported the war in Vietnam for the most part, but after the bombing started in the Gulf, eleven affiliates of the AFL-CIO, including some of its more powerful unions—like steel, auto, communications, chemical workers—spoke out against the war.

The black community was far less enthusiastic than the rest of the country about what the U.S. Air Force was doing to Iraq. An ABC News/*Washington Post* poll in early February, 1991, found that support for the war was 84 percent among whites, but only 48 percent among African-Americans.

When the war had been going on for a month, with Iraq devastated by the incessant bombing, there were feelers from Saddam Hussein that Iraq would withdraw from Kuwait if the United States would stop its attacks. Bush rejected the idea, and a meeting of black leaders in New York sharply criticized him, calling the war "an immoral and unspiritual diversion . . . a blatant evasion of our domestic responsibilities."

In Selma, Alabama, which had been the scene of bloody police violence against civil rights marchers twenty-six years before, a meeting to observe the anniversary of that "bloody Sunday" demanded that "our troops be brought home alive to fight for justice at home."

The father of a twenty-one-year-old Marine in the Persian Gulf, Alex Molnar, wrote an angry open letter, published in the *New York Times*, to President Bush:

> Where were you, Mr. President, when Iraq was killing its own people with poison gas? Why, until the recent crisis, was it business as usual with Saddam

Hussein, the man you now call a Hitler? Is the American "way of life" that you say my son is risking his life for the continued "right" of Americans to consume 25 to 30 percent of the world's oil? . . . I intend to support my son and his fellow soldiers by doing everything I can to oppose any offensive American military action in the Persian Gulf.

There were courageous individual acts by citizens, speaking out in spite of threats.

Peg Mullen, of Brownsville, Texas, whose son had been killed by "friendly fire" in Vietnam, organized a busload of mothers to protest in Washington, in spite of a warning that her house would be burned down if she persisted.

The actress Margot Kidder ("Lois Lane" in the *Superman* films), despite the risk to her career, spoke out eloquently against the war.

A basketball player for Seton Hall University in New Jersey refused to wear the American flag on his uniform, and when he became the object of derision for this, he left the team and the university, and returned to his native Italy.

More tragically, a Vietnam veteran in Los Angeles set fire to himself and died, to protest the war.

In Amherst, Massachusetts, a young man carrying a cardboard peace sign knelt on the town common, poured two cans of flammable fluid on himself, struck two matches, and died in the flames. Two hours later, students from nearby universities gathered on the common for a candle-light vigil, and placed peace signs at the site of death. One of the signs read, "Stop this crazy war."

There was no time, as there had been during the Vietnam conflict, for a large antiwar movement to develop in the military. But there were men and women who defied their commanders and refused to partici-pate in the war.

When the first contingents of U.S. troops were being sent to Saudi Arabia, in August of 1990, Corporal Jeff Paterson, a twenty-two-year-old Marine stationed in Hawaii, sat down on the runway of the airfield and refused to board a plane bound for Saudi Arabia. He asked to be dis-charged from the Marine Corps:

I have come to believe that there are no justified wars. . . . I began to ques-tion exactly what I was doing in the Marine Corps about the time I began to read about history. I began to read up on America's support for the murder-ous regimes of Guatemala, Iran under the Shah, and El Salvador. . . . I object to the military use of force against any people, anywhere, any time.

Fourteen Marine Corps reservists at Camp Lejeune, North Carolina, filed for conscientious objector status, despite the prospect of a court-martial for desertion. A lance corporal in the Marines, Erik Larsen, issued a statement:

> I declare myself a conscientious objector. Here is my sea bag full of personal gear. Here is my gas mask. I no longer need them. I am no longer a Marine. . . . It, to me, is embarrassing to fight for a way of life in which basic human needs, like a place to sleep, one hot meal a day and some medical attention, cannot even be met in our nation's capital.

Yolanda Huet-Vaughn, a physician who was a captain in the Army Reserve Medical Corps, a mother of three young children, and a member of the Physicians for Social Responsibility, was called to active duty in December 1990, a month before the start of the war. She replied: "I am refusing orders to be an accomplice in what I consider an immoral, inhumane and unconstitutional act, namely an offensive military mobilization in the Middle East." She was court-martialed, convicted of desertion, and sentenced to 2½ years in prison.

Another soldier, Stephanie Atkinson of Murphysboro, Illinois, refused to report for active duty, saying she thought the U.S. military was in the Persian Gulf solely for economic reasons. She was first placed under house arrest, then given a discharge under "other than honorable conditions."

An Army physician named Harlow Ballard, stationed at Fort Devens in Massachusetts, refused to follow an order to go to Saudi Arabia. "I would rather go to jail than support this war," he said. "I don't believe there is any such thing as a just war."

Over a thousand reservists declared themselves conscientious objectors. A twenty-three-year-old Marine Corps reservist named Rob Calabro was one of them. "My father tells me that he's ashamed of me, he screams at me that he's embarrassed by me. But I believe that killing people is morally wrong. I believe I'm serving my country more by being true to my conscience than by living a lie."

An information network sprang up during the Gulf War to tell what was not being told in the major media. There were alternative newspapers in many cities. There were over a hundred community radio stations, able to reach only a fraction of those tuned in to the major networks but the only sources, during the Gulf War, of critical analyses of the war. An ingenious radio person in Boulder, Colorado, named David Barsamian recorded a speech by Noam Chomsky made at Harvard—a devastating critique of the war. He then sent the cassette out to his net-work of community stations, which were eager for a point of view differ-ent from the official one. Two young men in New Jersey then tran-scribed the talk, put it in pamphlet form, in a shape easily photocopied, and placed the pamphlets in bookstores all over the country.

After "victorious" wars there is almost always a sobering effect, as the war fervor wears off, and citizens assess the costs and wonder what was gained. War fever was at its height in February 1991. In that month, when people being polled were reminded of the huge costs of the war, only 17 percent said the war was not worth it. Four months later, in June, the figure was 30 percent. In the months that followed, Bush's sup-port in the nation dropped steeply, as economic conditions deteriorated. (And in 1992, with the war spirit evaporated, Bush went down to defeat.)

After the disintegration of the Soviet bloc began in 1989, there had been talk in the United States of a "peace dividend," the opportunity to take billions of dollars from the military budget and use it for human needs. The war in the Gulf became a convenient excuse for the govern-ment determined to stop such talk. A member of the Bush administra-tion said: "We owe Saddam a favor. He saved us from the peace divi-dend" (*New York Times*, March 2, 1991).

But the idea of a peace dividend could not be stifled so long as Americans were in need. Shortly after the war, historian Marilyn Young warned:

> The U.S. can destroy Iraq's highways, but not build its own; create the con-ditions for epidemic in Iraq, but not offer health care to millions of Americans. It can excoriate Iraqi treatment of the Kurdish minority, but not deal with domestic race relations; create homelessness abroad but not solve it here; keep a half million troops drug free as part of a war, but refuse to fund the treatment of millions of drug addicts at home. . . . We shall lose the war after we have won it.

In 1992, the limits of military victory became apparent during the quincentennial celebrations of Columbus's arrival in the Western Hemisphere. Five hundred years ago Columbus and his fellow con-querors had wiped out the native population of Hispaniola. This was fol-lowed during the next four centuries by the methodical destruction of Indian tribes by the United States government as it marched across the continent. But now, there was a dramatic reaction.

The Indians—the Native Americans—had become a visible force since the sixties and seventies, and in 1992 were joined by other

Americans to denounce the quincentennial celebrations. For the first time in all the years that the country had celebrated Columbus Day, there were nationwide protests against honoring a man who had kidnapped, enslaved, mutilated, murdered the natives who greeted his arrival with gifts and friendship.

Preparations for the quincentennial began on both sides of the controversy. Official commissions, nationally and in the states, were set up long before the year of the quincentennial.

This spurred action by Native Americans. In the summer of 1990 350 Indians, representatives from all over the hemisphere, met in Quito, Ecuador, at the first intercontinental gathering of indigenous people in the Americas, to mobilize against the glorification of the Columbus conquest.

The following summer, in Davis, California, over a hundred Native Americans gathered for a follow-up meeting to the Quito conference. They declared October 12, 1992, International Day of Solidarity with Indigenous People, and resolved to inform the king of Spain that the replicas of Columbus's three ships, the *Niña, Pinta,* and *Santa Maria,* "will not receive permission from the Native Nations to land in the western hemisphere unless he apologizes for the original incursion 500 years ago. . . ."

The movement grew. The largest ecumenical body in the United States, the National Council of Churches, called on Christians to refrain from celebrating the Columbus quincentennial, saying, "What represented newness of freedom, hope and opportunity for some was the occasion for oppression, degradation and genocide for others."

The National Endowment for the Humanities funded a traveling exhibition called "First Encounter," which romanticized the Columbus conquest. When the exhibition opened at the Florida Museum of National History, Michelle Diamond, a freshman at the University of Florida, climbed aboard a replica of one of Columbus's ships with a sign reading "Exhibit Teaches Racism." She said: "It's a human issue—not just a Red [Indian] issue." She was arrested and charged with trespassing, but demonstrations continued for sixteen days against the exhibit.

A newspaper called *Indigenous Thought* began publication in early 1991 to create a link among all the counter-Columbus quincentenary activities. It carried articles by Native Americans about current struggles over land stolen by treaty.

In Corpus Christi, Texas, Indians and Chicanos joined to protest the city's celebrations of the quincentennial. A woman named Angelina Mendez spoke for the Chicanos: "The Chicano nation, in solidarity with our Indian brothers and sisters to the north, come together with them on this day to denounce the atrocity the U.S. government proposes in reenacting the arrival of the Spanish, more specifically the arrival of Cristóbal Colón, to the shores of this land."

The Columbus controversy brought an extraordinary burst of educational and cultural activity. A professor at the University of California at San Diego, Deborah Small, put together an exhibit of over 200 paintings on wood panels called "1492." She juxtaposed words from Columbus's diary with blown-up fragments from sixteenth-century engravings to dramatize the horrors that accompanied Columbus's arrival in the hemisphere. A reviewer wrote that "it does remind us, in the most vivid way, of how the coming of Western-style civilization to the New World doesn't provide us with a sunny tale."

When President Bush attacked Iraq in 1991, claiming that he was acting to end the Iraqi occupation of Kuwait, a group of Native Americans in Oregon distributed a biting and ironic "open letter":

Dear President Bush. Please send your assistance in freeing our small nation from occupation. This foreign force occupied our lands to steal our rich resources. They used biological warfare and deceit, killing thousands of elders, children and women in the process. As they overwhelmed our land, they deposed our leaders and people of our own government, and in its place, they installed their own government systems that yet today control our daily lives in many ways. As in your own words, the occupation and overthrow of one small nation . . . is one too many. Sincerely, An American Indian.

The publication *Rethinking Schools*, which represented socially conscious schoolteachers all over the country, printed a 100-page book called *Rethinking Columbus*, featuring articles by Native Americans and others, a critical review of children's books on Columbus, a listing of resources for people wanting more information on Columbus, and more reading material on counter-quincentenary activities. In a few months, 200,000 copies of the book were sold.

A Portland, Oregon, teacher named Bill Bigelow, who helped put together *Rethinking Schools*, took a year off from his regular job to tour the country in 1992, giving workshops to other teachers, so that they could begin to tell those truths about the Columbus experience that were omitted from the traditional books and class curricula.

One of Bigelow's own students wrote to the publisher Allyn and Bacon with a critique of their history text *The American Spirit*:

I'll just pick one topic to keep it simple. How about Columbus. No, you didn't lie, but saying, "Though they had a keen interest in the peoples of the Caribbean, Columbus and his crews were never able to live peacefully among them," makes it seem as if Columbus did no wrong. The reason for not being able to live peacefully is that he and crew took slaves and killed thousands of Indians for not bringing enough gold.

Another student wrote: "It seemed to me as if the publishers had just printed up some 'glory story' that was supposed to make us feel more patriotic about our country. . . . They want us to look at our country as great and powerful and forever right. . . ."

A student named Rebecca wrote: "Of course, the writers of the books probably think it's harmless enough—what does it matter who discovered America, really. . . . But the thought that I have been lied to all my life about this, and who knows what else, really makes me angry."

A group was formed on the West Coast called Italian-Americans Against Christopher Columbus, saying: "When Italian-Americans identify with Native people . . . we are bringing ourselves, each of us, closer to possible change in the world."

In Los Angeles, a high school student named Blake Lindsey went before the city council to argue against celebrating the quincentennial. She spoke to the council about the genocide of the Arawaks, but she got no official response. However, when she told her story on a talk show, a woman phoned in who said she was from Haiti: "The girl is right. We have no Indians left. At our last uprising in Haiti people destroyed the statue of Columbus. Let's have statues for the aborigines."

There were counter-Columbus activities all over the country, unmentioned in the press or on television. In Minnesota alone, a listing of such activities for 1992 reported dozens of workshops, meetings, films, art shows. At Lincoln Center in New York City, on October 12, there was a performance of Leonard Lehrmann's *New World: An Opera About What Columbus Did to the Indians*. In Baltimore, there was a multimedia show about Columbus. In Boston and then in a national tour, the Underground Railway Theater performed *The Christopher Columbus Follies* to packed audiences.

The protests, the dozens of new books that were appearing about Indian history, the discussions taking place all over the country, were bringing about an extraordinary transformation in the educational world. For generations, exactly the same story had been told all American schoolchildren about Columbus, a romantic, admiring story. Now, thousands of teachers around the country were beginning to tell that story differently.

This aroused anger among defenders of the old history, who derided what they called a movement for "political correctness" and "multiculturalism." They resented the critical treatment of Western expansion and imperialism, which they considered an attack on Western civilization. Ronald Reagan's Secretary of Education, William Bennett, had called Western civilization "our common culture . . . its highest ideas and aspirations."

A much-publicized book by a philosopher named Allan Bloom, *The Closing of the American Mind,* expressed horror at what the social movements of the sixties had done to change the educational atmosphere of American universities. To him Western civilization was the high point of human progress, and the United States its best representative: "America tells one story: the unbroken, ineluctable progress of freedom and equality. From its first settlers and its political foundings on, there has been no dispute that freedom and equality are the essence of justice for us."

In the seventies and eighties, disabled people organized and created a movement powerful enough to bring about the passage by Congress of the Americans with Disabilities Act. It was an unprecedented piece of legislation, setting standards which would enable persons with disabilities to contest discrimination against them, and ensuring they would have access to places where their disabilities would otherwise bar them.

In the civil rights movement, black people disputed that claim of America's standing for "freedom and equality." The women's movement had disputed that claim, too. And now, in 1992, Native Americans were pointing to the crimes of Western civilization against their ancestors. They were recalling the communitarian spirit of the Indians Columbus met and conquered, trying to tell the history of those millions of people who were here before Columbus, giving the lie to what a Harvard historian (Perry Miller) had called "the movement of European culture into the vacant wilderness of America."

As the United States entered the nineties, the political system, whether Democrats or Republicans were in power, remained in the control of those who had great wealth. The main instruments of information were also dominated by corporate wealth. The country was divided, though no mainstream political leader would speak of it, into classes of extreme wealth and extreme poverty, separated by an insecure and jeopardized middle class.

Yet, there was, unquestionably, though largely unreported, what a worried mainstream journalist had called "a permanent adversarial culture" which refused to surrender the possibility of a more equal, more humane society. If there was hope for the future of America, it lay in the promise of that refusal.

23

THE COMING REVOLT
OF THE GUARDS

The title of this chapter is not a prediction, but a hope, which I will soon explain.

As for the subtitle of this book, it is not quite accurate; a "people's history" promises more than any one person can fulfill, and it is the most difficult kind of history to recapture. I call it that anyway because, with all its limitations, it is a history disrespectful of governments and respectful of people's movements of resistance.

That makes it a biased account, one that leans in a certain direction. I am not troubled by that, because the mountain of history books under which we all stand leans so heavily in the other direction—so tremblingly respectful of states and statesmen and so disrespectful, by inattention, to people's movements—that we need some counterforce to avoid being crushed into submission.

All those histories of this country centered on the Founding Fathers and the Presidents weigh oppressively on the capacity of the ordinary citizen to act. They suggest that in times of crisis we must look to someone to save us: in the Revolutionary crisis, the Founding Fathers; in the slavery crisis, Lincoln; in the Depression, Roosevelt; in the Vietnam-Watergate crisis, Carter. And that between occasional crises everything is all right, and it is sufficient for us to be restored to that normal state. They teach us that the supreme act of citizenship is to choose among saviors, by going into a voting booth every four years to choose between two white and well-off Anglo-Saxon males of inoffensive personality and orthodox opinions.

The idea of saviors has been built into the entire culture, beyond politics. We have learned to look to stars, leaders, experts in every field, thus surrendering our own strength, demeaning our own ability, obliterating our own selves. But from time to time, Americans reject that idea and rebel.

These rebellions, so far, have been contained. The American system is the most ingenious system of control in world history. With a country so rich in natural resources, talent, and labor power the system can afford to distribute just enough wealth to just enough people to limit discontent to a troublesome minority. It is a country so powerful, so big, so pleasing to so many of its citizens that it can afford to give freedom of dissent to the small number who are not pleased.

There is no system of control with more openings, apertures, leeways, flexibilities, rewards for the chosen, winning tickets in lotteries. There is none that disperses its controls more complexly through the voting system, the work situation, the church, the family, the school, the mass media—none more successful in mollifying opposition with reforms, isolating people from one another, creating patriotic loyalty.

One percent of the nation owns a third of the wealth. The rest of the wealth is distributed in such a way as to turn those in the 99 percent against one another: small property owners against the propertyless, black against white, native-born against foreign-born, intellectuals and professionals against the uneducated and unskilled. These groups have resented one another and warred against one another with such vehemence and violence as to obscure their common position as sharers of leftovers in a very wealthy country.

Against the reality of that desperate, bitter battle for resources made scarce by elite control, I am taking the liberty of uniting those 99 percent as "the people." I have been writing a history that attempts to represent their submerged, deflected, common interest. To emphasize the commonality of the 99 percent, to declare deep enmity of interest with the 1 percent, is to do exactly what the governments of the United States, and the wealthy elite allied to them—from the Founding Fathers to now—have tried their best to prevent. Madison feared a "majority faction" and hoped the new Constitution would control it. He and his colleagues began the Preamble to the Constitution with the words "We the people . . . ," pretending that the new government stood for everyone, and hoping that this myth, accepted as fact, would ensure "domestic tranquillity."

The pretense continued over the generations, helped by all-embracing symbols, physical or verbal: the flag, patriotism, democracy, national interest, national defense, national security. The slogans were dug into the earth of American culture like a circle of covered wagons on the western plain, from inside of which the white, slightly privileged American could shoot to kill the enemy outside—Indians or blacks or foreigners or other whites too wretched to be allowed inside the circle. The managers of the caravan watched at a safe distance, and when the battle was over and the field strewn with dead on both sides, they would take over the land, and prepare another expedition, for another territory.

The scheme never worked perfectly. The Revolution and the Constitution, trying to bring stability by containing the class angers of the colonial period—while enslaving blacks, annihilating or displacing Indians—did not quite succeed, judging by the tenant uprisings, the slave revolts, the abolitionist agitation, the feminist upsurge, the Indian guerrilla warfare of the pre–Civil War years. After the Civil War, a new coalition of southern and northern elites developed, with southern whites and blacks of the lower classes occupied in racial conflict, native workers and immigrant workers clashing in the North, and the farmers dispersed over a big country, while the system of capitalism consolidated itself in industry and government. But there came rebellion among industrial workers and a great opposition movement among farmers.

At the turn of the century, the violent pacification of blacks and Indians and the use of elections and war to absorb and divert white rebels were not enough, in the conditions of modern industry, to prevent the great upsurge of socialism, the massive labor struggles, before the First World War. Neither that war nor the partial prosperity of the twenties, nor the apparent destruction of the socialist movement, could prevent, in the situation of economic crisis, another radical awakening, another labor upsurge in the thirties.

World War II created a new unity, followed by an apparently successful attempt, in the atmosphere of the cold war, to extinguish the strong radical temper of the war years. But then, surprisingly, came the surge of the sixties, from people thought long subdued or put out of sight—blacks, women, Native Americans, prisoners, soldiers—and a new radicalism, which threatened to spread widely in a population disillusioned by the Vietnam war and the politics of Watergate.

The exile of Nixon, the celebration of the Bicentennial, the presidency of Carter, all aimed at restoration. But restoration to the old order was no solution to the uncertainty, the alienation, which was intensified in the Reagan-Bush years. The election of Clinton in 1992, carrying with it a vague promise of change, did not fulfill the expectations of the hopeful.

With such continuing malaise, it is very important for the Establishment—that uneasy club of business executives, generals, and politicos—to maintain the historic pretension of national unity, in which the government represents all the people, and the common enemy is overseas, not at home, where disasters of economics or war are unfortunate errors or tragic accidents, to be corrected by the members of the same club that brought the disasters. It is important for them also to make sure this artificial unity of highly privileged and slightly privileged is the only unity—that the 99 percent remain split in countless ways, and turn against one another to vent their angers.

How skillful to tax the middle class to pay for the relief of the poor, building resentment on top of humiliation! How adroit to bus poor black youngsters into poor white neighborhoods, in a violent exchange of impoverished schools, while the schools of the rich remain untouched and the wealth of the nation, doled out carefully where children need free milk, is drained for billion-dollar aircraft carriers. How ingenious to meet the demands of blacks and women for equality by giving them small special benefits, and setting them in competition with everyone else for jobs made scarce by an irrational, wasteful system. How wise to turn the fear and anger of the majority toward a class of criminals bred—by economic inequity—faster than they can be put away, deflecting attention from the huge thefts of national resources carried out within the law by men in executive offices.

But with all the controls of power and punishment, enticements and concessions, diversions and decoys, operating throughout the history of the country, the Establishment has been unable to keep itself secure from revolt. Every time it looked as if it had succeeded, the very people it thought seduced or subdued, stirred and rose. Blacks, cajoled by Supreme Court decisions and congressional statutes, rebelled. Women, wooed and ignored, romanticized and mistreated, rebelled. Indians, thought dead, reappeared, defiant. Young people, despite lures of career and comfort, defected. Working people, thought soothed by reforms, regulated by law, kept within bounds by their own unions, went on strike. Government intellectuals, pledged to secrecy, began giving away secrets. Priests turned from piety to protest.

To recall this is to remind people of what the Establishment would like them to forget—the enormous capacity of apparently helpless people to resist, of apparently contented people to demand change. To uncover such history is to find a powerful human impulse to assert one's humanity. It is to hold out, even in times of deep pessimism, the possibility of surprise.

True, to overestimate class consciousness, to exaggerate rebellion and its successes, would be misleading. It would not account for the fact that the world—not just the United States, but everywhere else—is still in the hands of the elites, that people's movements, although they show an infinite capacity for recurrence, have so far been either defeated or absorbed or perverted, that "socialist" revolutionists have betrayed socialism, that nationalist revolutions have led to new dictatorships.

But most histories understate revolt, overemphasize statesmanship, and thus encourage impotency among citizens. When we look closely at resistance movements, or even at isolated forms of rebellion, we discover that class consciousness, or any other awareness of injustice, has multiple levels. It has many ways of expression, many ways of revealing itself—open, subtle, direct, distorted. In a system of intimidation and control, people do not show how much they know, how deeply they feel, until their practical sense informs them they can do so without being destroyed.

History which keeps alive the memory of people's resistance suggests new definitions of power. By traditional definitions, whoever possesses military strength, wealth, command of official ideology, cultural control, has power. Measured by these standards, popular rebellion never looks strong enough to survive.

However, the unexpected victories—even temporary ones—of insurgents show the vulnerability of the supposedly powerful. In a highly developed society, the Establishment cannot survive without the obedience and loyalty of millions of people who are given small rewards to keep the system going: the soldiers and police, teachers and ministers, administrators and social workers, technicians and production workers, doctors, lawyers, nurses, transport and communications workers, garbagemen and firemen. These people—the employed, the somewhat privileged—are drawn into alliance with the elite. They become the guards of the system, buffers between the upper and lower classes. If they stop obeying, the system falls.

That will happen, I think, only when all of us who are slightly privileged and slightly uneasy begin to see that we are like the guards in the prison uprising at Attica—expendable; that the Establishment, whatever rewards it gives us, will also, if necessary to maintain its control, kill us.

Certain new facts may, in our time, emerge so clearly as to lead to general withdrawal of loyalty from the system. The new conditions of technology, economics, and war, in the atomic age, make it less and less possible for the guards of the system—the intellectuals, the home owners, the taxpayers, the skilled workers, the professionals, the servants of government—to remain immune from the violence (physical and psychic) inflicted on the black, the poor, the criminal, the enemy overseas. The internationalization of the economy, the movement of refugees and illegal immigrants across borders, both make it more difficult for the people of the industrial countries to be oblivious to hunger and disease in the poor countries of the world.

All of us have become hostages in the new conditions of doomsday technology, runaway economics, global poisoning, uncontainable war. The atomic weapons, the invisible radiations, the economic anarchy, do not distinguish prisoners from guards, and those in charge will not be scrupulous in making distinctions. There is the unforgettable response of the U.S. high command to the news that American prisoners of war might be near Nagasaki: "Targets previously assigned for Centerboard remain unchanged."

There is evidence of growing dissatisfaction among the guards. We have known for some time that the poor and ignored were the nonvoters, alienated from a political system they felt didn't care about them, and about which they could do little. Now alienation has spread upward into families above the poverty line. These are white workers, neither rich nor poor, but angry over economic insecurity, unhappy with their work, worried about their neighborhoods, hostile to government—combining elements of racism with elements of class consciousness, contempt for the lower classes along with distrust for the elite, and thus open to solutions from any direction, right or left.

In the twenties there was a similar estrangement in the middle classes, which could have gone in various directions—the Ku Klux Klan had millions of members at that time—but in the thirties the work of an organized left wing mobilized much of this feeling into trade unions, farmers' unions, socialist movements. We may, in the coming years, be in a race for the mobilization of middle-class discontent.

The fact of that discontent is clear. The surveys since the early seventies show 70 to 80 percent of Americans distrustful of government, business, the military. This means the distrust goes beyond blacks, the poor, the radicals. It has spread among skilled workers, white-collar workers, professionals; for the first time in the nation's history, perhaps, both the lower classes and the middle classes, the prisoners and the guards, were disillusioned with the system.

There are other signs: the high rate of alcoholism, the high rate of divorce (from one of three marriages ending in divorce, the figure was climbing to one of two), of drug use and abuse, of nervous breakdowns and mental illness. Millions of people have been looking desperately for solutions to their sense of impotency, their loneliness, their frustration, their estrangement from other people, from the world, from their work, from themselves. They have been adopting new religions, joining self-help groups of all kinds. It is as if a whole nation were going through a critical point in its middle age, a life crisis of self-doubt, self-examination.

All this, at a time when the middle class is increasingly insecure economically. The system, in its irrationality, has been driven by profit to build steel skyscrapers for insurance companies while the cities decay, to spend billions for weapons of destruction and virtually nothing for children's playgrounds, to give huge incomes to men who make dangerous or useless things, and very little to artists, musicians, writers, actors. Capitalism has always been a failure for the lower classes. It is now beginning to fail for the middle classes.

The threat of unemployment, always inside the homes of the poor, has spread to white-collar workers, professionals. A college education is no longer a guarantee against joblessness, and a system that cannot offer a future to the young coming out of school is in deep trouble. If it happens only to the children of the poor, the problem is manageable; there are the jails. If it happens to the children of the middle class, things may get out of hand. The poor are accustomed to being squeezed and always short of money, but in recent years the middle classes, too, have begun to feel the press of high prices, high taxes.

In the seventies, eighties, and early nineties there was a dramatic, frightening increase in the number of crimes. It was not hard to understand, when one walked through any big city. There were the contrasts of wealth and poverty, the culture of possession, the frantic advertising. There was the fierce economic competition, in which the legal violence of the state and the legal robbery by the corporations were accompanied by the illegal crimes of the poor. Most crimes by far involved theft. A disproportionate number of prisoners in American jails were poor and non-white, with little education. Half were unemployed in the month prior to their arrest.

The most common and most publicized crimes have been the violent crimes of the young, the poor—a virtual terrorization in the big cities—in which the desperate or drug-addicted attack and rob the middle class, or even their fellow poor. A society so stratified by wealth and education lends itself naturally to envy and class anger.

The critical question in our time is whether the middle classes, so long led to believe that the solution for such crimes is more jails and more jail terms, may begin to see, by the sheer uncontrollability of crime, that the only prospect is an endless cycle of crime and punishment. They might then conclude that physical security for a working person in the city can come only when everyone in the city is working. And that would require a transformation of national priorities, a change in the system.

In recent decades, the fear of criminal assault has been joined by an even greater fear. Deaths from cancer began to multiply, and medical researchers seemed helpless to find the cause. It began to be evident that more and more of these deaths were coming from an environment poisoned by military experimentation and industrial greed. The water people drank, the air they breathed, the particles of dust from the buildings in which they worked, had been quietly contaminated over the years by a system so frantic for growth and profit that the safety and health of human beings had been ignored. A new and deadly scourge appeared, the AIDS virus, which spread with special rapidity among homosexuals and drug addicts.

In the early nineties, the false socialism of the Soviet system had failed. And the American system seemed out of control—a runaway capitalism, a runaway technology, a runaway militarism, a running away of government from the people it claimed to represent. Crime was out of control, cancer and AIDS were out of control. Prices and taxes and unemployment were out of control. The decay of cities and the breakdown of families were out of control. And people seemed to sense all this.

Perhaps much of the general distrust of government reported in recent years comes from a growing recognition of the truth of what the U.S. Air Force bombardier Yossarian said in the novel *Catch-22* to a friend who had just accused him of giving aid and comfort to the enemy: "The enemy is anybody who's going to get you killed, no matter which side he's on. And don't you forget that, because the longer you remember it the longer you might live." The next line in the novel is: "But Clevinger did forget, and now he was dead."

Let us imagine the prospect—for the first time in the nation's history—of a population united for fundamental change. Would the elite turn as so often before, to its ultimate weapon—foreign intervention—to unite the people with the Establishment, in war? It tried to do that in 1991, with the war against Iraq. But, as June Jordan said, it was "a hit the same way that crack is, and it doesn't last long."

With the Establishment's inability either to solve severe economic problems at home or to manufacture abroad a safety valve for domestic discontent, Americans might be ready to demand not just more tinkering, more reform laws, another reshuffling of the same deck, another New Deal, but radical change. Let us be utopian for a moment so that when we get realistic again it is not that "realism" so useful to the Establishment in its discouragement of action, that "realism" anchored to a certain kind of history empty of surprise. Let us imagine what radical change would require of us all.

The society's levers of powers would have to be taken away from those whose drives have led to the present state—the giant corporations, the military, and their politician collaborators. We would need—by a coordinated effort of local groups all over the country—to reconstruct the economy for both efficiency and justice, producing in a cooperative way what people need most. We would start on our neighborhoods, our cities, our workplaces. Work of some kind would be needed by everyone, including people now kept out of the work force—children, old people, "handicapped" people. Society could use the enormous energy now idle, the skills and talents now unused. Everyone could share the routine but necessary jobs for a few hours a day, and leave most of the time free for enjoyment, creativity, labors of love, and yet produce enough for an equal and ample distribution of goods. Certain basic things would be abundant enough to be taken out of the money system and be available—free—to everyone: food, housing, health care, education, transportation.

The great problem would be to work out a way of accomplishing this without a centralized bureaucracy, using not the incentives of prison and punishment, but those incentives of cooperation which spring from natural human desires, which in the past have been used by the state in times of war, but also by social movements that gave hints of how people might behave in different conditions. Decisions would be made by small groups of people in their workplaces, their neighborhoods—a network of cooperatives, in communication with one another, a neighborly socialism avoiding the class hierarchies of capitalism and the harsh dictatorships that have taken the name "socialist."

People in time, in friendly communities, might create a new, diversified, nonviolent culture, in which all forms of personal and group expression would be possible. Men and women, black and white, old and young, could then cherish their differences as positive attributes, not as reasons for domination. New values of cooperation and freedom might then show up in the relations of people, the upbringing of children.

To do all that, in the complex conditions of control in the United States, would require combining the energy of all previous movements in American history—of labor insurgents, black rebels, Native Americans, women, young people—along with the new energy of an angry middle class. People would need to begin to transform their immediate environments—the workplace, the family, the school, the community—by a series of struggles against absentee authority, to give control of these places to the people who live and work there.

These struggles would involve all the tactics used at various times in the past by people's movements: demonstrations, marches, civil disobedience; strikes and boycotts and general strikes; direct action to redistribute wealth, to reconstruct institutions, to revamp relationships; creating—in music, literature, drama, all the arts, and all the areas of work and play in everyday life—a new culture of sharing, of respect, a new joy in the collaboration of people to help themselves and one another.

There would be many defeats. But when such a movement took hold in hundreds of thousands of places all over the country it would be impossible to suppress, because the very guards the system depends on to crush such a movement would be among the rebels. It would be a new kind of revolution, the only kind that could happen, I believe, in a country like the United States. It would take enormous energy, sacrifice, commitment, patience. But because it would be a process over time, starting without delay, there would be the immediate satisfactions that people have always found in the affectionate ties of groups striving together for a common goal.

All this takes us far from American history, into the realm of imagination. But not totally removed from history. There are at least glimpses in the past of such a possibility. In the sixties and seventies, for the first time, the Establishment failed to produce national unity and patriotic fervor in a war. There was a flood of cultural changes such as the country had never seen—in sex, family, personal relations—exactly those situations most difficult to control from the ordinary centers of power. And never before was there such a general withdrawal of confidence from so many elements of the political and economic system. In every period of history, people have found ways to help one another—even in the midst of a culture of competition and violence—if only for brief periods, to find joy in work, struggle, companionship, nature.

The prospect is for times of turmoil, struggle, but also inspiration. There is a chance that such a movement could succeed in doing what the system itself has never done—bring about great change with little violence. This is possible because the more of the 99 percent that begin to see themselves as sharing needs, the more the guards and the prisoners see their common interest, the more the Establishment becomes isolated, ineffectual. The elite's weapons, money, control of information would be useless in the face of a determined population. The servants of the system would refuse to work to continue the old, deadly order, and would begin using their time, their space—the very things given them by the system to keep them quiet—to dismantle that system while creating a new one.

The prisoners of the system will continue to rebel, as before, in ways that cannot be foreseen, at times that cannot be predicted. The new fact of our era is the chance that they may be joined by the guards. We readers and writers of books have been, for the most part, among the guards. If we understand that, and act on it, not only will life be more satisfying, right off, but our grandchildren, or our great grandchildren, might possibly see a different and marvelous world.

24

THE CLINTON
PRESIDENCY

The eight-year presidential term of Bill Clinton, a personable, articulate graduate of Yale Law School, a Rhodes Scholar, and former governor of Arkansas, began with a hope that a bright, young person would bring to the country what he promised: "change." But Clinton's presidency ended with no chance that it would, as he had wished, make his mark in history as one of the nation's great presidents.

His last year in office was marked by sensational scandals surrounding his personal life. More important, he left no legacy of bold innovation in domestic policy or departure from traditional nationalist foreign policy. At home, he surrendered again and again to caution and conservatism, signing legislation that was more pleasing to the Republican Party and big business than to those Democrats who still recalled the bold programs of Franklin Roosevelt. Abroad, there were futile shows of military braggadocio, and a subservience to what President Dwight Eisenhower had once warned against: "the military-industrial complex."

Clinton had barely won election both times. In 1992, with 45 percent of the voting population staying away from the polls, he only received 43 percent of the votes, the senior Bush getting 38 percent, while 19 percent of the voters showed their distaste for both parties by voting for a third-party candidate, Ross Perot. In 1996, with half the population not voting, Clinton won 49 percent of the votes against a lackluster Republican candidate, Robert Dole.

There was a distinct absence of voter enthusiasm. One bumper sticker read: "If God had intended us to vote, he would have given us candidates."

At his second inauguration ceremony, Clinton spoke of the nation at the edge of "a new century, in a new millennium." He said: "We need a new government for a new century." But Clinton's rhetoric was not matched by his performance.

It happened that the inauguration coincided with the nationwide celebration of the birthday of Martin Luther King, Jr., and Clinton invoked King's name several times in his address. The two men, however, represented very different social philosophies.

By the time King was assassinated in 1968, he had come to believe that our economic system was fundamentally unjust and needed radical transformation. He spoke of "the evils of capitalism" and asked for "a radical redistribution of economic and political power."

On the other hand, as major corporations gave money to the Democratic Party on an unprecedented scale, Clinton demonstrated clearly his total confidence in "the market system" and "private enterprise." During his 1992 campaign, the chief executive officer of Martin Marietta Corporation (which held huge and lucrative government contracts for military production) noted: "I think the Democrats are moving more toward business and business is moving more toward the Democrats."

Martin Luther King's reaction to the buildup of military power had been the same as his reaction to the Vietnam war: "This madness must cease." And: ". . . the evils of racism, economic exploitation, and militarism are all tied together. . . ."

Clinton was willing to recall King's "dream" of racial equality, but not his dream of a society rejecting violence. Even though the Soviet Union was no longer a military threat, he insisted that the United States must keep its armed forces dispersed around the globe, prepare for "two regional wars," and maintain the military budget at cold war levels.

Despite his lofty rhetoric, Clinton showed, in his eight years in office, that he, like other politicians, was more interested in electoral victory than in social change. To get more votes, he decided he must move the party closer to the center. This meant doing just enough for blacks, women, and working people to keep their support, while trying to win over white conservative voters with a program of toughness on crime, stern measures on welfare, and a strong military.

Clinton in office followed this plan quite scrupulously. He made a few Cabinet appointments that suggested support for labor and for social welfare programs, and appointed a black pro-labor man as head of the National Labor Relations Board. But his key appointments to the Treasury and Commerce Departments were wealthy corporate lawyers, and his foreign policy staff—the Secretary of Defense, the Director of the

CIA, the National Security Adviser—were traditional players on the bipartisan cold war team.

Clinton appointed more people of color to government posts than his Republican predecessors. But if any prospective or actual appointees became too bold, Clinton abandoned them quickly.

His Secretary of Commerce, Ronald Brown (who was killed in a plane crash), was black and a corporate lawyer, and Clinton was clearly pleased with him. On the other hand, Lani Guinier, a black legal scholar who was being considered for a job with the Civil Rights Division of the Justice Department, was abandoned when conservatives objected to her strong ideas on matters of racial equality and voter representation. And when Surgeon General Joycelyn Elders, a black, made the controversial suggestion that masturbation was a proper subject in sex education, Clinton asked her to resign. (This was especially ironic, considering Clinton's later sexual adventures in the White House.)

He showed the same timidity in the two appointments he made to the Supreme Court, making sure that Ruth Bader Ginsburg and Stephen Breyer would be moderate enough to be acceptable to Republicans as well as to Democrats. He was not willing to fight for a strong liberal to follow in the footsteps of Thurgood Marshall or William Brennan, who had recently left the Court. Breyer and Ginsburg both defended the constitutionality of capital punishment, and upheld drastic restrictions on the use of habeas corpus. Both voted with the most conservative judges on the Court to uphold the "constitutional right" of Boston's St. Patrick's Day parade organizers to exclude gay marchers.

In choosing judges for the lower federal courts, Clinton showed himself no more likely to appoint liberals than the Republican Gerald Ford had in the seventies. According to a three-year study published in the *Fordham Law Review* in early 1996, Clinton's appointments made "liberal" decisions in less than half their cases. The *New York Times* noted that while Reagan and Bush had been willing to fight for judges who would reflect their philosophies, "Mr. Clinton, in contrast, has been quick to drop judicial candidates if there is even a hint of controversy."

Clinton was eager to show he was "tough" on matters of "law and order." Running for President in 1992 while still Governor of Arkansas, he flew back to Arkansas to oversee the execution of a mentally retarded man on death row. And early in his administration, in April 1993, he and Attorney General Janet Reno approved an FBI attack on a group of religious zealots who were armed and ensconced in a building complex in Waco, Texas. Instead of waiting for negotiations to bring about a solution, the FBI attacked with rifle fire, tanks, and gas, resulting in a fire that swept through the compound, killing at least 86 men, women, and children.

One of the few survivors of the Waco tragedy was David Thibodeau, who in his book *A Place Called Waco* gives us a rare inside description of the human consequences of the government attack:

> Despite the fact that more than thirty women and children were crowded into the narrow concrete chamber at the base of the residential tower, the tank crashed into the ceiling, shoving chunks of broken concrete onto the people huddled below. Six women and kids were immediately crushed by falling blocks, the rest were suffocated by the dust and gas vapors as the tank injected massive doses of CS directly into their windowless, unventilated shelter.
>
> The charred corpse of six-year-old Star, David's oldest daughter [David Koresh was the leader of the religious sect] was found with her spine bent into a backward bow until her head almost touched her feet. Her muscles were contracted by the combined effect of the fire's heat and the cyanide in her body, a byproduct of CS gas suffocation.

Clinton and Reno gave feeble excuses for what clearly was a reckless decision to launch a military attack on a group of men, women, and children. Reno at one time talked of children being molested, which was totally unsubstantiated, and even if true could hardly justify the massacre that took place.

As so often happens in cases where the government commits murder, the surviving victims were put on trial, with the judge overruling the request of the jury not to levy harsh sentences, and ruling for imprisonment up to forty years. Professor James Fyfe of Temple University, who taught criminal justice, said: "There is no FBI to investigate the FBI. There is no Justice Department to investigate the Justice Department."

One of the people sentenced by the judge was Renos Avraam, who commented: "This nation is supposed to run under laws, not personal feelings. When you ignore the law you sow the seeds of terrorism."

This turned out to be a prophetic statement. Timothy McVeigh, who some years after the Waco tragedy was convicted of bombing the Federal Building in Oklahoma City, which cost 168 lives, had visited the Waco site twice. Later, according to an FBI affidavit, McVeigh was "extremely agitated" about the government's assault on Waco.

Clinton's "law and order" approach led him early in his first term to sign legislation cutting funds for state resource centers that supplied lawyers to indigent prisoners. The result, according to Bob Herbert writing in the *New York Times*, was that a man facing the death penalty in Georgia had to appear at a habeas corpus proceeding without a lawyer.

In 1996, the President signed legislation that made it more difficult for judges to put prison systems under special masters to ensure the improvement of terrible prison conditions. He also approved a new statute withholding federal funds for legal services where lawyers used those funds to handle class action suits (such suits were important for challenging assaults on civil liberties).

The "Crime Bill" of 1996, which both Republicans and Democrats in Congress voted for overwhelmingly, and which Clinton endorsed with enthusiasm, dealt with the problem of crime by emphasizing punishment, not prevention. It extended the death penalty to a whole range of criminal offenses, and provided $8 billion for the building of new prisons.

All this was to persuade voters that politicians were "tough on crime." But, as criminologist Todd Clear wrote in the *New York Times* ("Tougher Is Dumber") about the new crime bill, harsher sentencing had added 1 million people to the prison population, giving the United States the highest rate of incarceration in the world, and yet violent crime continued to increase. "Why," Clear asked, "do harsh penalties seem to have so little to do with crime?" A crucial reason is that "police and prisons have virtually no effect on the sources of criminal behavior." He pointed to those sources: "About 70 percent of prisoners in New York State come from eight neighborhoods in New York City. These neighborhoods suffer profound poverty, exclusion, marginalization, and despair. All these things nourish crime."

Those holding political power—whether Clinton or his Republican predecessors—had something in common. They sought to keep their power by diverting the anger of citizens to groups without the resources to defend themselves. As H. L. Mencken, the acerbic social critic of the 1920s, put it: "The whole aim of practical politics is to keep the populace alarmed by menacing it with an endless series of hobgoblins, all of them imaginary."

Criminals were among these hobgoblins. Also immigrants, people on "welfare," and certain governments—Iraq, North Korea, Cuba. By turning attention to them, by inventing or exaggerating their dangers, the failures of the American system could be concealed.

Immigrants were a convenient object of attack, because as nonvoters their interests could be safely ignored. It was easy for politicians to play upon the xenophobia that has erupted from time to time in American history: the anti-Irish prejudices of the mid-nineteenth century; the continual violence against Chinese who had been brought in to work on the railroads; the hostility toward immigrants from eastern and southern Europe that led to the restrictive immigration laws of the 1920s.

The reform spirit of the sixties had led to an easing of restrictions on immigration, but in the nineties, Democrats and Republicans alike played on the economic fears of working Americans. Jobs were being lost because corporations were firing employees to save money ("downsizing") or moving plants out of the country to more profitable situations. Immigrants, especially the large numbers coming over the southern border from Mexico, were blamed for taking jobs from citizens of the United States, for receiving government benefits, for causing higher taxes on American citizens.

Both major political parties joined to pass legislation, which Clinton then signed, to remove welfare benefits (food stamps, payments to elderly and disabled people) from not only illegal but legal immigrants. By early 1997, letters were going out to close to a million legal immigrants who were poor, old, or disabled, warning them that their food stamps and cash payments would be cut off in a few months unless they became citizens.

For perhaps half a million legal immigrants, passing the tests required for becoming a citizen was quite impossible—they could not read English, were sick or disabled, or were just too old to learn. An immigrant from Portugal living in Massachusetts told a reporter, through an interpreter: "Every day we are afraid the letter will come. What will we do if we lose our checks? We will starve. Oh, my God. It will not be worth living."

Illegal immigrants fleeing poverty in Mexico began to face harsher treatment in the early nineties. Thousands of border guards were added. A Reuters dispatch from Mexico City (April 3, 1997) said about the tougher policy: "Any crackdown against illegal immigration automatically angers Mexicans, millions of whom migrate, legally and illegally, across the 2,000-mile border to the United States in search of jobs each year."

Hundreds of thousands of Central Americans who had fled death squads in Guatemala and El Salvador while the United States was giving military aid to those governments now faced deportation because they had never been deemed "political" refugees. To admit that these cases were political would have given the lie to U.S. claims at the time that those repressive regimes were improving their human rights record and therefore deserved to continue receiving military aid.

In early 1996, Congress and the President joined to pass an "Anti-

Terrorism and Effective Death Penalty Act," allowing deportation of any immigrant ever convicted of a crime, no matter how long ago or how serious. Lawful permanent residents who had married Americans and now had children were not exempt. The *New York Times* reported that July that "hundreds of long-term legal residents have been arrested since the law passed." There was a certain irrationality to this new law, for it was passed in response to the blowing up of the Federal Building in Oklahoma City by Timothy McVeigh, who was native born.

The new government policy toward immigrants, far from fulfilling Clinton's promise of "a new government for a new century," was a throwback to the notorious Alien and Sedition Laws of 1798 and the McCarthy-era McCarran-Walter Act of the 1950s. It was hardly in keeping with the grand claim inscribed on the Statue of Liberty: "Give me your tired, your poor, your huddled masses yearning to breathe free, the wretched refuse of your teeming shore. Send these, the homeless, tempest-tossed to me. I lift my lamp beside the golden door."

In the summer of 1996 (apparently seeking the support of "centrist" voters for the coming election), Clinton signed a law to end the federal government's guarantee, created under the New Deal, of financial help to poor families with dependent children. This was called "welfare reform," and the law itself had the deceptive title of "Personal Responsibility and Work Opportunity Reconciliation Act of 1996."

By this decision, Clinton alienated many of his former liberal supporters. Peter Edelman resigned from his post in the Department of Health, Education, and Welfare, bitterly criticizing what he considered Clinton's surrender to the right and the Republicans. Later, Edelman wrote: "His goal was reelection at all costs. . . . His political approach was not to calculate the risks but to take no risks at all. . . . His penchant for elevating shadow over substance has hurt poor children."

The aim of "welfare reform" was to force poor families receiving federal cash benefits (many of them single mothers with children) to go to work by cutting off their benefits after two years, limiting lifetime benefits to five years, and allowing people without children to get food stamps for only three months in any three-year period.

The *Los Angeles Times* reported: "As legal immigrants lose access to Medicaid, and families battle a new five-year limit on cash benefits . . . health experts anticipate resurgence of tuberculosis and sexually transmitted diseases. . . . " The aim of the welfare cuts was to save $50 billion over a five-year period (less than the cost of a planned new generation of fighter planes). Even the *New York Times*, a supporter of Clinton during the election, said that the provisions of the new law "have nothing to do with creating work but everything to do with balancing the budget by cutting programs for the poor."

There was a simple but overwhelming problem with cutting off benefits to the poor to force them to find jobs. There were not jobs available for all those who would lose their benefits. In New York City in 1990, when 2,000 jobs were advertised in the Sanitation Department at $23,000 a year, 100,000 people applied. Two years later in Chicago, 7,000 people showed up for 550 jobs at Stouffer's, a restaurant chain. In Joliet, Illinois, 200 showed up at Commonwealth Edison at 4:30 A.M. to apply for jobs that did not yet exist. In early 1997, 4,000 people lined up for 700 jobs at the Roosevelt Hotel in Manhattan. It was estimated that at the existing rate of job growth in New York, with 470,000 adults on welfare, it would take twenty-four years to absorb those thrown off the rolls.

What the Clinton administration steadfastly refused to do was to establish government programs to create jobs, as had been done in the New Deal era, when billions were spent to give employment to several million people, from construction workers and engineers to artists and writers. "The era of big government is over," Clinton proclaimed as he ran for President in 1996, seeking votes on the supposition that Americans supported the Republican position that government was spending too much.

Both parties were misreading public opinion, and the press was often complicit in this. When, in the midyear election of 1994, only 37 percent of the electorate went to the polls, and slightly more than half voted Republican, the media reported this as a "revolution." A headline in the *New York Times* read "Public Shows Trust in GOP Congress," suggesting that the American people were supporting the Republican agenda of less government.

But in the story below that headline, a *New York Times*/CBS News public opinion survey found that 65 percent of those polled said that "it is the responsibility of government to take care of people who can't take care of themselves."

Clinton and the Republicans, in joining against "big government," were aiming only at social services. The other manifestations of big government—huge contracts to military contractors and generous subsidies to corporations—continued at exorbitant levels.

"Big government" had, in fact, begun with the Founding Fathers, who deliberately set up a strong central government to protect the interests of the bondholders, the slave owners, the land speculators, the manufacturers. For the next two hundred years, the American government continued to serve the interests of the wealthy and powerful, offering

millions of acres of free land to the railroads, setting high tariffs to protect manufacturers, giving tax breaks to oil corporations, and using its
armed forces to suppress strikes and rebellions.

It was only in the twentieth century, especially in the thirties and sixties, when the government, besieged by protests and fearful of the stability of the system, passed social legislation for the poor, that political
leaders and business executives complained about "big government."

President Clinton reappointed Alan Greenspan as head of the Federal
Reserve system, which regulated interest rates. Greenspan's chief concern
was to avoid "inflation," which bondholders did not want because it would
reduce their profits. His financial constituency saw higher wages for workers as producing inflation and worried that if there was not enough unemployment, wages might rise.

Reduction of the annual deficit in order to achieve a "balanced budget" became an obsession of the Clinton administration. But since
Clinton did not want to raise taxes on the wealthy, or to cut funds for the
military, the only alternative was to sacrifice the poor, the children, the
aged—to spend less for health care, for food stamps, for education, for
single mothers.

Two examples of this appeared early in Clinton's second administration, in the spring of 1997:

- From the *New York Times*, May 8, 1997: "A major element of
  President Clinton's education plan—a proposal to spend $5 billion to
  repair the nation's crumbling schools—was among the items quietly
  killed in last week's agreement to balance the federal budget. . . . "
- From the *Boston Globe*, May 22, 1997: "After White House' intervention, the Senate yesterday . . . rejected a proposal . . . to extend
  health insurance to the nation's 10.5 million uninsured children. . . .
  Seven lawmakers switched their votes . . . after senior White House
  officials . . . called and said the amendment would imperil the delicate
  budget agreement."

The concern about balancing the budget did not extend to military
spending. Immediately after he was elected for the first time, Clinton
had said: "I want to reaffirm the essential continuity in American foreign
policy."

In Clinton's presidency, the government continued to spend at least
$250 billion a year to maintain the military machine. He was accepting
the Republican claim that the nation must be ready to fight "two
regional wars" simultaneously, despite the collapse of the Soviet Union

in 1989. At that time, Bush's Secretary of Defense, Dick Cheney, had said, "The threats have become so remote, so remote that they are difficult to discern." General Colin Powell spoke similarly (reported in *Defense News*, April 8, 1991): "I'm running out of demons. I'm running out of villains. I'm down to Castro and Kim Il Sung."

Clinton had been accused during the election campaign of having evaded military service during the Vietnam war, apparently in opposition to the war, like so many other young Americans. Once in the White House he seemed determined to erase the image of a "draftdodger," and took every opportunity to portray himself as a supporter of the military establishment.

In the fall of 1993, Clinton's Secretary of Defense, Les Aspin, announced the results of a "bottom-up review" of the military budget, envisioning the spending of over $1 trillion for the next five years. It called for virtually no reduction in major weapons systems. A conservative analyst with the Woodrow Wilson International Center (Anthony Cordesman) commented: "There are no radical departures from the Bush Base Force, or even from earlier U.S. strategy."

After being in office two years, and facing a Republican upsurge in the congressional elections of 1994, Clinton proposed even more money for the military than had been envisioned in the bottom-up review. A *New York Times* dispatch from Washington (December 1, 1994) reported:

> Trying to quiet Republican criticism that the military is underfinanced, President Clinton held a Rose Garden ceremony today to announce that he would seek a $25 billion increase in military spending over the next six years.

The examples most often given by the Pentagon of "two simultaneous major regional wars" were Iraq and North Korea. Yet the 1991 war against Iraq had followed repeated U.S. arming of Iraq in the eighties. And it was reasonable to suppose that heavy military aid to South Korea, and a permanent U.S. military force in that country, had provoked increases in the North Korean arms budget, which was still much smaller than that of South Korea.

Despite these facts, the United States under Clinton was continuing to supply arms to nations all over the world. Clinton, coming into office, approved the sale of F-15 combat planes to Saudi Arabia, and F-16s to Taiwan. The *Baltimore Sun* reported (May 30, 1994):

Next year, for the first time, the United States will produce more combat planes for foreign air forces than for the Pentagon, highlighting America's replacement of the Soviet Union as the world's main arms supplier. Encouraged by the Clinton administration, the defense industry last year had its best export year ever, having sold $32 billion worth of weapons overseas, more than twice the 1992 total of $15 billion.

That pattern continued through the Clinton presidency. In the summer of 2000, the *New York Times* reported that in the previous year the United States had sold over $11 billion of arms, one-third of all weapons sold worldwide. Two-thirds of all arms were sold to poor countries. In 1999 the Clinton administration lifted a ban on advanced weapons to Latin America. The *Times* called it "a victory for the big military contractors, like the Lockheed-Martin Corporation and the McDonnell Douglas Corporation."

Clinton seemed anxious to show strength. He had been in office barely six months when he sent the Air Force to drop bombs on Baghdad, presumably in retaliation for an assassination plot against George Bush on the occasion of his visit to Kuwait. The evidence for such a plot was very weak, coming as it did from the notoriously corrupt Kuwaiti police, and Clinton did not wait for the results of the trial supposed to take place in Kuwait of those accused of the plot.

And so, U.S. planes, claiming to have targeted "Intelligence Headquarters" in the Iraqi capital, bombed a suburban neighborhood, killing at least six people, including a prominent Iraqi artist and her husband.

The *Boston Globe* reported: "Since the raid, President Clinton and other officials have boasted of crippling Iraq's intelligence capacity and of sending a powerful message that Iraq leader Saddam Hussein had better behave." It turned out later that there was no significant damage, if any, to Iraqi intelligence facilities and the *New York Times* commented: "Mr. Clinton's sweeping statement was reminiscent of the assertions by President Bush and General Norman Schwartzkopf during the Persian Gulf War that later proved to be untrue."

Democrats rallied behind the bombing, and the *Boston Globe*, referring to the use of Article 51 of the United Nations Charter as legal justification for the bombing, said this was "diplomatically the proper rationale to invoke . . . Clinton's reference to the UN Charter conveyed the American desire to respect international law."

In fact, Article 51 of the UN Charter permits unilateral military action only in defense against an armed attack, and only when there is no opportunity to convene the Security Council. None of these factors were present in the Baghdad bombing.

Columnist Molly Ivins suggested that the bombing of Baghdad for the purpose of "sending a powerful message" fit the definition of terrorism. "The maddening thing about terrorists is that they are indiscriminate in their acts of vengeance, or cries for attention, or whatever. . . . What is true for individuals . . . must also be true of nations."

The bombing of Baghdad was a sign that Clinton, facing several foreign policy crises during his two terms in office, would react to them in traditional ways, usually involving military action, claiming humanitarian motives, and often with disastrous results for people abroad as well as for the United States.

In Somalia, East Africa, in June 1993, with the country in a civil war and people desperate for food, the United States intervened late and badly. As journalist Scott Peterson wrote in *Me Against My Brother: At War in Somalia, Sudan and Rwanda*: "American and other foreign forces in Somalia committed startling acts of savagery, hiding behind the banner of the United Nations."

The Clinton administration made the mistake of intervening in an internal conflict between warlords. It decided to hunt down the most prominent of these, General Mohamed Aidid, in a military operation that ended with the killing of 19 Americans and perhaps 2,000 Somalis in October 1993.

The attention of the American public was concentrated, as usual, on the deaths of Americans (glamorized in the film *Black Hawk Down*). The lives of Somalis seemed much less important. As Peterson wrote: "American and UN officers made clear that numbers of Somali dead did not interest them, and they kept no count."

In fact, the killing of the American Rangers by an angry Somali mob was preceded months before by a critical decision made by the United States to launch a military attack on a house in which tribal elders were meeting. It was a brutal operation. First Cobra attack helicopters launched antitank missiles. "Minutes later," Peterson reports, American ground troops stormed in and began finishing off the survivors—a charge U.S. commanders deny." But a survivor of the raid told Peterson: "If they saw people shouting, they killed them."

U.S. general Thomas Montgomery called the attack "legitimate" because they were "all bad guys." Admiral Jonathan Howe, representing the UN operation (the United States had insisted an American must be in charge), defended the attack by saying the house was a "very key terrorist planning cell" and denied that civilians had died, though it was clear that the dead were tribal elders. The claim was that "tactical radios" were found in the compound later, but Peterson wrote: "I have never heard nor seen any evidence that this attack even remotely met a single criteria of 'direct' military advantage."

Peterson commented: "Though we all had eyes and had witnessed the crime, mission commanders defended the indefensible and stubbornly clung to the illusion that more war could somehow bring peace. They thought that Somalis would forget the carnage, forget the spilled blood of their fathers and brothers. . . . "

The Somalis did not forget, and the killing of the American Rangers in October was one consequence.

The catastrophic policy in Somalia led to another one the following year, in Rwanda, where famine and murderous tribal warfare were ignored. There was a UN force in Rwanda that might have saved tens of thousands of lives, but the United States insisted that it be cut back to a skeleton force. The result was genocide—at least a million Rwandans died. As Richard Heaps, a consultant to the Ford Foundation on Africa wrote to the *New York Times*: "The Clinton administration took the lead in opposing international action."

When, shortly after, the Clinton administration did intervene with military force in Bosnia, journalist Scott Peterson, who had by this time moved to the Balkans, commented on the difference in reactions to genocide in Africa and in Europe. He said that it was "as if a decision had been made, somewhere, that Africa and Africans were not worth justice."

Clinton's foreign policy had very much the traditional bipartisan emphasis on maintaining friendly relations with whatever governments were in power, and promoting profitable trade arrangements with them, whatever their record in protecting human rights. Thus, aid to Indonesia continued, despite that country's record of mass murder (perhaps 200,000 killed out of a population of 700,000) in the invasion and occupation of East Timor.

Democrats and Republicans joined forces as the Senate defeated a proposal to prohibit the sale of lethal weapons to the Suharto regime of Indonesia. The *Boston Globe* wrote (July 11, 1994):

> The arguments presented by senators solicitous of Suharto's regime—and of defense contractors, oil companies and mining concerns doing business with Jakarta—made Americans seem a people willing to overlook genocide for the sake of commerce. Secretary of State Warren Christopher . . . made the all-too-familiar claim that Indonesia's respect for human rights is improving.

This was the Clinton administration's rationale for pursuing business as usual with Suharto and his generals.

In 1996 the Nobel Peace Prize was awarded to Jose Ramos-Horta of East Timor. Speaking at a church in Brooklyn shortly before he won the prize, Ramos-Horta said:

> In the summer of 1977, I was here in New York when I received a message telling me that one of my sisters, Maria, 21 years old, had been killed in an aircraft bombing. The aircraft, named Bronco, was supplied by the United States. . . . Within months, a report about a brother, Guy, 17 years old, killed along with many other people in his village by Bell helicopters, supplied by the United States. Same year, another brother, Nunu, captured and executed with an [American-made] M-16.

Similarly, American-made Sikorski helicopters were used by Turkey to destroy the villages of rebellious Kurds, in what writer John Tirman (*Spoils of War: The Human Cost of the Arms Trade*) called "a campaign of terror against the Kurdish people."

By early 1997, the United States was selling more arms abroad than all other nations combined. Lawrence Korb, a Department of Defense official under Reagan but later a critic of arms sales, wrote: "It has become a money game: an absurd spiral in which we export arms only to have to develop more sophisticated ones to counter those spread out all over the world."

Finally, in the last year of the Clinton administration, when mass resistance in East Timor brought about a referendum for independence, military aid stopped, and the Suharto regime collapsed. At last, East Timor appeared to be winning its freedom.

But military power continued to dominate policy, and the United States often stood alone in refusing to cut back on its weaponry. Though a hundred nations signed an agreement to abolish land mines, which were killing tens of thousands of people each year, the United States refused to go along. Though the Red Cross urged governments to suspend the use of cluster bombs (which spewed out thousands of tiny pellets, killing indiscriminately), the United States, which had used them in Vietnam and in the Gulf War, refused to desist.

At a UN conference in Rome in 1999, the United States opposed the establishment of a permanent international war crimes court. There was fear that American officials and military leaders who, like Henry Kissinger, had been responsible for policies leading to the deaths of large numbers of people might be brought before such a court.

Human rights clearly came second to business profit in U.S. foreign policy. When the international group Human Rights Watch issued its 1996 annual report, the *New York Times* (December 5, 1996) summarized its findings:

> The organization strongly criticized many powerful nations, particularly the United States, accusing them of failing to press governments in China, Indonesia, Mexico, Nigeria, and Saudi Arabia to improve human rights for fear of losing access to lucrative markets.

This criticism was borne out by the Clinton administration's bizarre approach to two nations, China and Cuba, both of which considered themselves "communist." China had massacred protesting students in Beijing in 1991 and put dissenters in prison. Yet the United States continued to give China economic aid and certain trade privileges ("most favored nation" status) for the sake of U.S. business interests.

Cuba had imprisoned critics of the regime, but had no bloody record of suppression as did communist China or other governments in the world that received U.S. aid. But the Clinton administration continued, and even extended, a blockade of Cuba that was depriving its population of food and medicine.

In its relations with Russia, a concern for "stability" over morality seemed to motivate the Clinton administration. It insisted on firm support for the regime of Boris Yeltsin, even after Russia initiated a brutal invasion and bombardment of the outlying region of Chechnya, which wanted independence.

Both Clinton and Yeltsin, on the occasion of the death of Richard Nixon, expressed admiration for the man who had continued the war in Vietnam, who had violated his oath of office, and who had escaped criminal charges only because he was pardoned by his own Vice President. Yeltsin called Nixon "one of the greatest politicians in the world," and Clinton said that Nixon, throughout his career, "remained a fierce advocate for freedom and democracy around the world."

Clinton's foreign economic policy was in keeping with the nation's history, in which both major parties were more concerned for corporate interests than for the rights of working people, here or abroad, and saw foreign aid as a political and economic tool more than as a humanitarian act.

In November 1993, an Associated Press dispatch reported the phasing out of economic aid to thirty-five countries. The administrator for the Agency for International Development, J. Brian Atwood, explained: "We no longer need an AID program to purchase influence."

A humanitarian organization, Bread for the World, said that most of the cuts would harm very poor countries and added, with some bitterness, that hunger, poverty, and environmental degradation were not priorities for the Clinton administration.

The World Bank and the International Monetary Fund, both dominated by the United States, adopted a hard-nosed banker's approach to debt-ridden Third World countries. They insisted that these poor nations allocate a good part of their meager resources to repaying their loans to the rich countries, at the cost of cutting social services to their already-desperate populations.

The emphasis in foreign economic policy was on "the market economy" and "privatization." This forced the people of former Soviet-bloc countries to fend for themselves in a supposedly "free" economy, without the social benefits that they had received under the admittedly inefficient and oppressive former regimes. Unregulated market capitalism turned out to be disastrous for people in the Soviet Union, who saw huge fortunes accumulated by a few and deprivation for the masses.

The slogan of "free trade" became an important objective for the Clinton administration, and, with the support of Republicans as well as Democrats, Congress enacted the North American Free Trade Agreement (NAFTA) with Mexico. This removed obstacles for corporate capital and goods to move freely back and forth across the Mexican-United States border.

There was vigorous disagreement over the effects of NAFTA. Some economists claimed it would benefit the United States economy by opening up a larger Mexican market for United States goods. Opponents, including the major trade unions, said there would be a loss of jobs for American workers as corporations moved their operations across the border to hire Mexicans at low pay.

Two economists for the Institute for Policy Studies, examining NAFTA in early 1995, after a year of its operation, found that it had caused a net loss of 10,000 U.S. jobs. While more workers in Mexico were now hired by U.S. corporations that moved there, they were working at low wages, with "lax enforcement of workers' rights and environmental standards."

The claim of the United States to support "free trade" was hardly to be believed, since the government interfered with trade when this did not serve the "national interest," which was a euphemism for corporate interest. Thus, it went to lengths to prevent tomato growers in Mexico from entering the U.S. market.

In an even more flagrant violation of the principle of free trade, the United States would not allow shipments of food or medicine to Iraq or to Cuba. In 1996, on the television program *60 Minutes*, U.S. Ambassador to the United Nations Madeleine Albright was asked about the report that "a half million children have died as a result of sanctions against Iraq. . . . That is more children than died in Hiroshima. . . . Is the price worth it?" Albright replied: "I think this is a very hard choice, but the price, we think the price is worth it."

The U.S. government did not seem to recognize that its punitive foreign policies, its military installations in countries all over the globe, might arouse anger in foreign countries, and that anger might turn to violence. When it did, the only response that the United States could think of was to react with more violence.

Thus, when U.S. embassies in Kenya and Tanzania were bombed in 1998, the Clinton administration responded by bombing targets in Afghanistan and the Sudan. The claim was that the Afghanistan target was a base for terrorist activity, though there was no proof of this. As for the Sudan, the United States insisted it had bombed a plant manufacturing chemical weapons, but it turned out to be a factory that produced medicines for half the population of the country. The human consequences of that loss of medicine could not be calculated.

In that same year, Clinton faced the greatest crisis of his presidency. The nation learned that a young government worker, Monica Lewinsky, had been making secret visits to the White House for sexual liaisons with the President. This became a sensational story, occupying the front pages of newspapers for months. An Independent Counsel was appointed to investigate, who took lurid, detailed testimony from Monica Lewinsky (who had been exposed by a friend who had taped their conversations) about sexual contact with Clinton.

Clinton lied about his relationship with Lewinsky, and the House of Representatives voted to impeach him on the ground that he had lied in denying "sexual relations" with the young woman, and that he had obstructed justice by trying to conceal information about their relationship. This was only the second time in American history that a president had been impeached, and here too, as in the case of Andrew Johnson after the Civil War, the impeachment did not lead to the end of Clinton's presidency because the Senate did not vote for removal.

What the incident showed was that a matter of personal behavior could crowd out of the public's attention far more serious matters, indeed, matters of life and death. The House of Representatives would impeach the president on matters of sexual behavior, but it would not impeach him for endangering the lives of children by welfare reform, or for violating international law in bombing other countries (Iran, Afghanistan, Sudan), or for allowing hundreds of thousands of children to die as a result of economic sanctions (Iraq).

In 1999, Clinton's last year in office, a crisis erupted in the Balkans that once again showed the U.S. government as disposed to use force rather than diplomacy in solving matters of international concern. The problem that arose came out of the breakup ten years earlier of the Republic of Yugoslavia, and the ensuing conflicts among the separated elements of a once united country.

One of the parts of the former Yugoslavia was Bosnia-Herzegovina, with Croats massacring Serbs, and Serbs massacring Croats and Moslems. After a vicious Serb attack on the city of Srebrenica, the United States bombed Serb positions, and then negotiations in Dayton, Ohio, in 1995 stopped the fighting, dividing Bosnia-Herzegovina into Croat and Serbian entities.

But the Dayton accord had failed to deal with the problem of another part of the old Yugoslavia, the province of Kosovo, which, with a majority of its population Albanian and a minority being Serbian, was demanding independence from Serbia. The Serbian president Slobodan Milosevic had shown his ruthlessness earlier in Bosnia, and now, facing armed attack from Kosovo nationalists, attacked Kosovo, killing perhaps 2,000 people and causing several hundred thousand to become refugees.

An international gathering in Rambouillet, France, was supposed to try to solve the problem diplomatically. But it presented terms to Yugoslavia that seemed certain to be rejected: NATO control of all of Kosovo, and NATO military occupation of the rest of Yugoslavia. On March 23, 1999, the Serbian National Assembly responded with a counterproposal, rejecting NATO occupation and calling for negotiations leading "toward the reaching of a political agreement on a wide-ranging autonomy for Kosovo. . . . "

The Serbian proposal was ignored, and was not reported in the major newspapers of the United States. The following day, NATO forces (meaning mostly U.S. forces) began the bombing of Yugoslavia. Presumably, the bombing was to stop the "ethnic cleansing" of Kosovo, that is, the forcing of Albanians out of the province by death or intimidation. But after two weeks of bombing, the *New York Times* reported (April 5, 1999) that "more than 350,000 have left Kosovo since March 24." Two months later, with the bombing still going on, the figure had risen to over 800,000.

The bombing of Yugoslavia, including the capital city of Belgrade, apparently intended to unseat Milosevic, led to an untold number of civilian casualties. An e-mail message came to the United States from a professor at the University of Nis:

> The little town of Aleksinac, 20 miles away from my home town, was hit last night with full force. The local hospital was hit, and a whole street was simply wiped out. What I know for certain is 6 dead civilians and more than 50 badly hurt. There was no military target around whatsoever.

A *New York Times* reporter, Steven Erlanger, described "the mounded rubble across narrow Zmaj Jovina Street, where Aleksandar Milic, 37, died on Tuesday. Mr. Milic's wife, Vesna, 35, also died. So did his mother and his two children, Miljana, 15, and Vladimir, 11—all of them killed about noon when an errant NATO bomb obliterated their new house and the cellar in which they were sheltering."

When a peace agreement was finally signed on June 3, 1999, it was a compromise between the Rambouillet accord, which Yugoslavia had rejected, and the Serbian National Assembly proposal, which had never been seriously considered. Noam Chomsky, in his book *The New Military Humanism*, examined in detail the events of that spring, and concluded: "The outcome as of June 3 suggests that diplomatic initiatives could have been pursued on March 23, averting a terrible human tragedy. . . . "

But it seemed that the Clinton administration, like so many before it (Truman in Korea, Johnson in Vietnam, Bush in the Gulf War) chose military solutions when diplomatic ones were possible.

The militarization of the nation—the huge military budgets, the maintenance of armed forces all over the world, the repeated use of weapons against other countries—meant that the resources available for human needs were not available. In one of his finer moments, President Dwight Eisenhower had said: "Every gun that is made, every warship launched, every rocket fired, signifies in a final sense a theft from those who are hungry and are not fed, those who are cold and not clothed."

Clinton's economic program, at first announced as a job-creation program, was soon to change direction and concentrate on reduction of the deficit, which under Reagan and Bush had left a national debt of $4 trillion. But this emphasis meant that there would be no bold program of expenditures for universal health care, education, child care, housing, the environment, the arts, or job creation.

Clinton's small gestures would not come close to what was needed in a nation where one-fourth of the children lived in poverty; where homeless people lived on the streets in every major city; where women could not look for work for lack of child care; where the air, the water, were deteriorating dangerously.

The United States was the richest country in the world, with 5 percent of the earth's population yet consuming 30 percent of what was produced worldwide. But only a tiny portion of the American population benefited; this richest 1 percent of the population saw its wealth increase enormously starting in the late 1970s. As a result of changes in the tax structure, by 1995 that richest 1 percent had gained over $1 trillion and now owned over 40 percent of the nation's wealth.

According to the business magazine *Forbes*, the 400 richest families owned $92 billion in 1982, but thirteen years later this had jumped to $480 billion. In the nineties, the wealth of the 500 corporations of the Standard and Poor's Index had increased by 335 percent. The Dow Jones average of stock prices had gone up 400 percent between 1980 and 1995, while the average wage of workers had declined in purchasing power by 15 percent.

It was therefore possible to say that the U.S. economy was "healthy"— but only if you considered the richest part of the population. Meanwhile, 40 million people were without health insurance (the number having risen by 33 percent in the nineties), and infants died of sickness and malnutrition at a rate higher than that of any other industrialized country. There seemed to be unlimited funds for the military, but people who performed vital human services, in health and education, had to struggle to barely survive.

A 27-year-old woman named Kim Lee Jacobson, interviewed in the *Boston Globe*, epitomized the distorted national priorities. She had been named "U.S. Toddler Teacher of 1999" but, as she said: "I'm hitting $20,000 this year, after five years in the field. It all works out. I didn't come for a lot of money, so I don't expect to have a lot."

According to the Bureau of Labor Statistics of the U.S. Census Bureau, in 1998, one of every three working people in the United States had jobs paying at or below the federal poverty level. The writer Barbara Ehrenreich spent a year working at various jobs—house cleaner, waitress, factory worker—and reported (in her book *Nickeled and Dimed*) that jobs such as those left workers unable to afford housing or medical care, or even adequate food.

For people of color, the statistics were especially troubling. Black infants died at twice the rate of white children, and the life expectancy of a black man in Harlem, according to a United Nations report, was 46 years, less than that in Cambodia or the Sudan.

This racial discrepancy was explained by some people as racial inferiority, as "genetic" deficiency. But what was clear was that growing up in a terrible environment, whatever one's natural abilities, became an insurmountable handicap for millions of Americans, whether white or black.

A Carnegie Endowment study showed that two young people of equal standing on intelligence tests (even accepting the dubious worth of intelligence tests for children brought up under different circumstances) had very different futures depending on whom their parents were. The child of a lawyer, though rating no higher on mental tests than the child of a janitor, was four times as likely to go to college, 12 times as likely to finish college, and 27 times as likely to end up in the top 10 percent of American incomes.

To change that situation, to bring about even a rough equality of opportunity, would require a drastic redistribution of wealth, a huge expenditure of money for job creation, health, education, and the environment.

The United States, instead, was consigning its people to the mercy of the "free market," forgetting, or choosing to forget, the disastrous consequence of such a policy in the twenties. The "market" did not care about the environment or the arts. And it left many Americans without the basic means of subsistence, including adequate housing. Under Reagan, the government had reduced the number of housing units getting subsidies from 400,000 to 40,000; in the Clinton administration, the program ended altogether.

Despite Clinton's 1997 Inauguration Day promise of a "new government," his presidency offered no bold program to take care of these needs. For instance, although public-opinion polls through the eighties and nineties indicated that the American people would support a program of free universal medical care supported by the general treasury, Clinton was reluctant to advocate this. Instead, he put his wife, Hillary, in charge of a commission whose final report was over a thousand pages long, impossibly dense and complicated, and yet offering no answer to the problem: how to assure every American medical care, free of the intervention of profiteering insurance companies.

Aside from creating an even larger deficit (and there were economists who did not believe that reducing the deficit was necessary, when crucial needs were not being met), there were two possible sources to pay for a bold program of social reconstruction, and the Clinton administration was not inclined to tap either one.

One source was the military budget. Randall Forsberg, an expert on military expenditures, had suggested during the presidential campaign of 1992 that "a military budget of $60 billion, to be achieved over a number of years, would support a demilitarized U.S. foreign policy, appropriate to the needs and opportunities of the post–Cold War world." However, the military budget kept increasing, even after the fall of the supposed target of the military buildup, and by the end of Clinton's term was about $300 billion a year.

A radical reduction of the military budget would require a renunciation of war, a withdrawal of military bases from around the world, an acceptance, finally, of the principle enunciated in the UN Charter that the world should renounce "the scourge of war." It would speak to the fundamental human desire (overwhelmed too often by barrages of superpatriotic slogans) to live at peace with others.

The public appeal for such a dramatic policy change would be based on a simple but powerful moral argument: that given the nature of modern warfare, the victims would be mostly civilians. To put it another way, war in our time is always a war against children. And if the children of other countries are to be granted an equal right to life with our own children, then we must use our extraordinary human ingenuity to find nonmilitary solutions for world problems.

The other possible source to pay for social reform was the wealth of the superrich. The richest 1 percent of the country had gained over $1 trillion in the eighties and nineties as a result of tax breaks. A "wealth tax"—something not yet done as national policy, but perfectly feasible—could retrieve that trillion dollars, for instance, at $100 billion dollars a year for ten years, and still leave that 1 percent very, very rich.

In addition, a truly progressive income tax—going back to the post–World War II levels of 70–90 percent on very high incomes—could yield another $100 billion a year. Clinton did raise taxes on the super-rich, by a few percentage points, changing the top rate from 31 percent to 37 percent, and corporate taxes from 34 percent to 35 percent. But this was a pitifully small step in view of the need.

With the four or five hundred billion dollars gained each year by progressive taxation and demilitarization, there would be funds available to pay for a universal health-care system funded by the government as Medicare is administered, as the health-care system in Canada is handled, without the profit-taking by insurance companies. Those funds could pay for a full-employment program, for the first time implementing the 1946 Full Employment Act, which committed the national government to creating "useful employment opportunities" for all people able and willing to work. (One of Marge Piercy's poems ends with "The pitcher cries for water to carry/And a person for work that is real.")

Instead of giving out contracts for jet bombers and nuclear sub-marines, contracts could be offered to nonprofit corporations to hire people to build homes, construct public transport systems, clean up the rivers and lakes, turn our cities into decent places to live.

The alternative to such a bold program was to continue as before, allowing the cities to fester, forcing rural people to face debt and fore-closures, offering no useful work for the young, creating a marginal population of idle, desperate people, many of them young, many of them people of color, who turn to drugs and crime, constituting a threat to the physical security of the rest of the population.

The response of the government to such signs of desperation, anger, and alienation has been, historically, quite predictable: Build more jails, lock up more people, execute more prisoners. And continue with the same policies that produced the desperation. And so, by the end of the Clinton administration, the United States had more of its population in prison per capita—a total of two million people—than any other country in the world, with the possible exception of China.

Clinton claimed to be moderating his policies to match public opin-ion. But opinion surveys in the eighties and early nineties indicated that Americans favored bold policies that neither Democrats nor Republicans were willing to put forward: universal free health care, guaranteed employment, government help for the poor and homeless, with taxes on the rich and cuts in the military budget to pay for social programs.

The gap between national policy and the feelings of the American public suggested that another scenario was possible, one that envisioned, in the new millennium, citizens organizing to demand what the Declaration of Independence promised: a government that protected the equal right of everyone to life, liberty, and the pursuit of happiness. This meant economic arrangements that distributed the national wealth rationally and humanely. This meant a culture where the young no longer were taught to strive for "success" as a mask for greed.

Throughout the nineties, while conservative Republicans and mod-erate Democrats were running the government, there were large num-bers of American citizens, unrepresented in Washington, unreported in the press, who were protesting government policy in various ways, and demanding a more just and peaceful society.

The signs of citizen energy outside the circles of power in Washington were not given much attention in the national media, except when a phenomenon was too big to ignore. Even a gathering of a half million adults and children, of all colors, arriving in the nation's capital to "Stand for Children" was paid little or no attention by television and newspapers. The signs of defiance and resistance were many and varied.

In Minneapolis, there was a continuing campaign against a corporation that manufactured land mines. An ex-GI who had been mutilated by an American land mine came to Minneapolis to join the campaign, joined by a young woman who was traveling all over the world to tell people of the children dying on all continents as a result of millions of land mines planted by the United States and other nations. Four nuns, the "McDonald sisters," who were indeed sisters, participated in the protest, and were arrested.

In 1994 in Los Angeles, in opposition to a new California law that took away basic health and educational rights from the children of illegal immigrants, a quarter of a million people took to the streets in protest.

When the United States made clear its intention to drop bombs on Iraq, presumably because Iraq was not allowing inspection of what American officials called "weapons of mass destruction," Secretary of State Madeleine Albright and other officials spoke to a town meeting in Columbus, Ohio, to build up public support for the bombing. But the planned scenario was interrupted by a young man who, despite plans to control all questions, managed to get the floor and ask Madeleine Albright about all the other nations, allies of the United States, that possessed "weapons of mass destruction."

The Secretary of State was obviously taken by surprise and stumbled through an answer, which a national TV audience could plainly see. Plans for the bombing were quickly postponed, though some time later the regular bombing of Iraq, of which the press took no notice, resumed.

When Madeleine Albright was given an honorary degree by the University of California at Berkeley in the year 2000, there were protests in the audience and a huge banner: "Madeleine Albright Is a War Criminal." Protesters and the banner were removed from the theater.

It happened that the student selected to receive the university's prestigious University Medal and to give the student address at commencement was a young Palestinian woman named Fadia Rafeedie. She was moved to the end of the program so that Albright could speak and leave, but she was determined to speak to Albright's defense of the U.S. sanctions against Iraq. She spoke of the medical supplies not allowed into Iraq, about the hundreds of thousands of deaths of children as a result of the sanctions. She agreed that Saddam Hussein was a brutal dictator. But, she said:

When he was gassing the Kurds, he was gassing them using chemical weapons that were manufactured in Rochester, New York. And when he was fighting a long and protracted war with Iran, where one million people died, it was the CIA that was funding him. It was U.S. policy that built this dictator. When they didn't need him, they started imposing sanctions on his people. Sanctions should be directed at people's governments, not at the people.

In 1998, 7,000 people from all over the country traveled to Fort Benning, Georgia, to protest the existence of the School of the Americas, whose graduates, trained by the United States, had participated in atrocities in various Latin American countries. They carried eight caskets representing the six priests, a cook, and a young girl who had been assassinated by military men invading their home. Ironically, the Georgia federal judge who sentenced them to prison terms, Robert J. Elliot, was the same judge who had pardoned Lieutenant William Calley, found guilty of the My Lai massacre of villagers in Vietnam.

On the anniversary of the bombing of Nagasaki in August 1999, eight pacifists decided to block four lanes of traffic leading to a nuclear submarine base in Bangor, Maine. At that base, eight Trident submarines were housed, carrying over a thousand nuclear warheads. The protesters were arrested. They managed to explain to the jury, however, the reason for their opposition to nuclear weapons, and they were acquitted. The woman who headed the jury said later: "I am proud to sit with these people."

The culture had been affected by the movements of the sixties in a way that could not be obliterated. There was an unmistakable, stubborn new consciousness—manifested from time to time in the cinema, on television, in the world of music—an awareness that women deserved equal rights, that the sexual preferences of men and women were their own affair, that the growing gap between rich and poor gave the lie to the word "democracy."

Racism was still deeply embedded in American society—the evidence was in continued police brutality against people of color, in the higher rates of infant mortality in the black population, the lack of jobs for young blacks, and the corresponding growth of crime and imprisonment. But the country was becoming more diverse—more Latino people, more Asians, more interracial marriages. It was projected that by the year 2050 people of color would be equal in number to whites in the United States. There were sporadic attempts to organize the discontent among the nations' African Americans. In the late eighties, there had been a hint of a future possibility as the black leader Jesse Jackson, speaking for the poor and dispossessed of all colors, a "Rainbow Coalition," won millions of votes in the presidential primary and gave the nation a brief, rare surge of political excitement.

In 1995 a million men traveled from all over the country to Washington, D.C.—the "Million Man March"—to declare to the nation's leaders that they intended to become a force for change. The march did not have a clear agenda, but it was an expression of solidarity. In the summer of 1998, 2,000 African American men met in Chicago to found the Black Radical Congress.

The following year, the West Coast Longshoremen's Union carried out an eight-hour work stoppage in protest against the incarceration and death sentence of Mumia Abu-Jamal. Jamal was a respected black journalist who had been tried and sentenced under circumstances that suggested his race and his radicalism, as well as his persistent criticism of the Philadelphia police, were the reasons he now sat on death row.

The labor movement, in the nineties, was showing signs of a new energy. This despite the gradual decline in union membership as manufacturing plants moved out of the country, and industrial workers were being outnumbered by service and white collar workers, who were more difficult to organize.

There was an impetus for a new militancy as it became clear that the wealth of the nation was going mostly to the very rich, and the gap between rich and poor was growing. In the nineties, the income of the richest 5 percent of the population grew by 20 percent while the income of the poor and middle class, taking into consideration the rise in cost of living, either fell or remained the same. In 1990 the average pay of the chief executive officers of the 500 largest corporations was 84 times that of the average worker. By 1999, it was 475 times the average worker's pay.

A new president of the AFL-CIO, John Sweeney, coming out of the Service Employees International Union—a sign of the change in the labor force—appeared to depart sharply from the conservatism of his predecessors. He encouraged the idea of a "Union Summer" (inspired by the Freedom Summer in Mississippi in 1964), tapping the idealism of young people by inviting them to help in the organizing of the new service workers, white-collar workers, farm workers, immigrant workers.

The unions were losing some strikes, as in the long, bitter struggles in the nineties in Decatur, Illinois, against three corporate giants: Caterpillar, Firestone, and Staley. But there were also victories: United Parcel Service workers went on strike for 15 days, a strike that brought great national attention and won their demand that part-time jobs, without health and other benefits, be converted to 10,000 full-time jobs with benefits. The machinists' union won strikes at the Boeing Company and McDonnell Douglas.

Hotel workers won strikes in Minneapolis and San Francisco. Cleaning women, mostly immigrants, were victorious in Los Angeles, striking against owners of skyscrapers, where the poorly paid workers cleaned the offices of the city's most prosperous businesspeople. In the year 2000, the biggest white-collar strike in the nation's history was won for 19,000 engineers and professional workers of Boeing, who succeeded in having their salaries match those of workers in other Boeing plants.

One of the greatest union victories in decades took place in Los Angeles County in 1999, where, after an 11-year campaign, the Service Employees International Union won the right to represent 74,000 home health-care workers. That same year, the newly merged unions of garment workers and textile workers called UNITE (Union of Needletrades, Industrial and Textile Employees) workers, which had been trying for 25 years to organize Cannon Mills in North Carolina, won their union election at two mills in Kannapolis.

Women were taking a leading role in the new leadership of the AFL-CIO. Karen Nussbaum, who had been president of the 9 to 5 National Association of Working Women, became director of the Working Women's Department of the AFL-CIO, and by 1998, 10 of the 21 departments of the union were headed by women.

An alliance between students and the labor movement was being forged by the campaign for a "living wage" for campus workers, which soon spread to 150 college campuses. For instance, at Harvard University, students organized to demand that the Harvard administration, sitting on a treasury of $20 billion, pay their janitors and other service employees a wage sufficient to support their families. Many of these workers had to work two jobs—as much as 80 hours a week—to pay for rent and food and medical care.

The Harvard students staged colorful rallies in which janitors and other campus workers spoke about their needs. Members of the Cambridge City Council, and trade union leaders including John Sweeney and other high officers of the AFL-CIO, took the microphone to declare their support. The arrival of two young movie stars, Matt Damon and Ben Affleck, to support the campaign attracted a huge crowd. Both had lived and gone to school in Cambridge. Matt Damon had spent a few years at Harvard before dropping out to go to Hollywood. Ben Affleck spoke movingly about his father working, poorly paid, at a menial job at Harvard.

When the Harvard administration continued to refuse to negotiate, forty students took over one of the Harvard administrative buildings and remained there day and night for several weeks, supported by hundreds of people outside, with tents spread out on the campus grass. Support for the sit-in came from all over the country, and finally Harvard agreed to negotiate. The upshot was a victory for the campus workers, with Harvard agreeing to raise the pay of janitors to $14 an hour and to give health benefits, and to insist that outside contractors match those conditions.

In the spring of 2000, students at Wesleyan University in Connecticut occupied the admissions office, insisting that the university president guarantee a living wage, health and retirement benefits, and job security to janitors and other service workers. After several days of the sit-in, the university agreed to comply with the demands.

Students around the country organized a Workers Rights Consortium. At Yale University, the University of Arizona, Syracuse University, the University of Kentucky, and on many other campuses, students carried on campaigns to support the demands of working people.

The living-wage campaign took a powerful hold on popular sympathies at a time when the rich were becoming richer. In Duluth, Minnesota, 56 organizations joined forces to demand that the city give contracts only to businesses that gave a living wage—this meant several dollars above the official minimum wage—to employees.

The five-year limit on federal aid to families with dependent children, set in the 1996 "welfare reform" legislation, meant that millions of people would face deprivation when their benefits expired.

Activists began organizing seriously in the year 2000 for that eventuality, bringing people from all over the country into a campaign to end poverty. A veteran of the welfare rights movement in Boston, Diane Dujon, declared: "In the richest country in the year 2000, no one should be living hungry, homeless, and under stress of not knowing how to feed their children and still pay their rent."

The Poor People's Economic Human Rights Campaign in 1998 organized a bus tour of 35 cities to pull together the stories of people who could not feed their families, whose electricity had been cut off, who had been evicted from their homes because they could not afford to pay their bills. The following year, some of the PPEHRC traveled to Geneva, Switzerland, to testify before the UN Commission on Human Rights. They pointed to the UN Universal Declaration of Human Rights, which Eleanor Roosevelt had helped to draw up, and which declared that decent wages, food, housing, health care, and education was a right of all people.

Religious leaders, who had been quiet since their involvement in the movements for civil rights and against the Vietnam war, began to speak out on economic inequality. In the summer of 1996, the *New York Times* reported:

> More than at any other time in decades, religious leaders are making common cause with trade unions, lending their moral authority to denounce sweatshops, back a higher minimum wage and help organize janitors and poultry workers. The clergy has not lined up with labor to such an extent since the heyday of Cesar Chavez, the charismatic farm workers' leader, in the 1970s, and perhaps the Depression. . . .

All of these groups, and the people they represented—the homeless, the struggling mothers, the families unable to pay their bills, the 40 million without health insurance and the many more with inadequate insurance—were facing an enormous barrier of silence in the national culture. Their lives, their plight was not being reported in the major media, and so the myth of a prosperous America, proclaimed by powerful people in Washington and Wall Street, persisted.

There were valiant attempts to break through the control of information, especially after the Telecommunications Act of 1996, which enabled the handful of corporations dominating the airwaves to expand their power further. Mergers enabled tighter control of information. Two gigantic media corporations, CBS and Viacom, joined in a $37 billion deal. The Latin American writer Eduardo Galeano commented: "Never have so many been held incommunicado by so few."

Alternative media made desperate attempts to break through this control. There were several hundred community radio stations around the country—the Pacifica network was the most successful of these—bringing alternative information and ideas to their listeners. A one-man operation by David Barsamian, "Alternative Radio," distributed dissident views—interviews and lectures—via satellite to radio stations around the country.

Community newspapers in towns and cities around the country, though their circulation was small, tried to tell the stories of ordinary people. In Boston, homeless people joined to publish the newspaper *Spare Change*, to tell their stories, print their poems, and then to sell the newspaper on the streets of Boston and Cambridge as a way of making some money. They declared their aims, to be "a voice for the voiceless" and to be "an organizing tool for the homeless community." By the turn of the century they had been turning out the newspaper for eight years.

This idea spread to other parts of the country, and soon there were street newspapers in 40 different cities, which formed the North American Street Newspaper Association. The National Coalition for the Homeless, set up in the nation's capital, distributed a monthly newsletter.

Probably the most dramatic attempt to bring to the American people and to the world the facts of corporate domination over the lives of ordinary people was the great gathering of demonstrators in Seattle, Washington, in the last months of 1999. Seattle had been chosen as the meeting place of the World Trade Organization, and representatives of the most wealthy and powerful institutions on the globe were there to make plans to maintain their wealth and power, to bring the principles of capitalism to work across national boundaries, over all the earth.

Tens of thousands of people converged on Seattle to protest the plans of the World Trade Organization to expand "free trade" agreements. This, the protesters argued, meant the freedom of corporations to roam the globe in search of cheap labor and no restrictions on industrial policies that poisoned the environment.

The issues around "free trade" were complex, but a simple idea seemed to unite those who showed up in Seattle to oppose the WTO: that the health and freedom of ordinary people all over the world should not be sacrificed on behalf of corporate profit.

More than a thousand organizations from 90 countries—representing labor unions, environmental groups, consumers, religious groups, farmers, indigenous people, women's groups, and more—had signed a statement asking governments to stop the expansion of the World Trade Organization. In Seattle, there was a remarkable set of alliances—steelworkers rallied with environmentalists, and machinists joined animal rights activists. Farmers joined a huge labor march of 40,000 on November 30, and then union people attended a family farm rally a few days later.

The press gave disproportionate attention to a small number of demonstrators who broke windows and created a ruckus, but the overwhelming majority in Seattle were nonviolent, and it was these that the police chose to attack with tear gas and then arrest. Hundreds were jailed, but the demonstrations continued. News of the events in Seattle went to the nation and all over the world.

The official WTO meeting was clearly disturbed by the crowds of protesters, and there were signs of division between the industrial countries and Third World countries. As John Nichols reported in the *Progressive*:

> While the official WTO sessions were characterized by deep divides between delegations from the Northern and Southern hemispheres, there was an unprecedented level of North-South unity on the streets. Farmers from around the world came together. . . . The huge AFL-CIO rally cheered speakers from close to a dozen countries. And after events organized to highlight the devastating impact that globalization was having on women in the Third World, throngs of women from Africa, Latin America, India, Europe, and the United States marched together in human chains through the streets of downtown Seattle.

The summit meeting of the World Trade Organization was shaken by all this, and at a certain point the talks collapsed. It was a remarkable illustration of the ability of organized citizens to challenge the most powerful corporations in the world. Mike Brannan, writing in the newspaper of the insurgent Teamsters, caught the mood of exultation:

> The kind of solidarity that all of us dream of was in the air as people sang, chanted, played music, and stood up to the cops and the WTO. The people owned the streets that day and it was as much a lesson for us as it was for corporate America.

The Seattle demonstrations coincided with a growing movement throughout the nation, on college campuses and in communities against sweatshop conditions endured by Third World men, women, even children working for American corporations.

The *New York Times* reported, a month after Seattle:

> Pressure from college students and other opponents of sweatshops has led some factories that make goods for industry giants like Nike and the Gap to cut back on child labor, to use less dangerous chemicals, and to require fewer employees to work 80-hour weeks, according to groups that monitor such factories.
>
> At last month's protests in Seattle conditions in such factories were a major focus, with many demonstrators demanding that trade treaties punish countries that permit violations of minimum labor standards. Many corporate executives acknowledge that the anti-sweatshop movement's efforts are paying off.

Seattle was the first of a series of international gatherings of trade union people, students, environmentalists, in opposition to the increasing control of the world economy by giant corporations. In the year following the Seattle demonstrations, protesters showed up wherever a summit of wealthy entrepreneurs was taking place: Washington, D.C.; Philadelphia; Davos, Switzerland; Los Angeles; and Prague.

Officials of the World Bank and the International Monetary Fund could not ignore such a protest movement. They began to declare their concern for the environment and the conditions of their workers. Whether this would result in real changes was unclear, but undoubtedly the corporate leaders of the world could no longer ignore their critics.

Would the various strands of protest and resistance, in politics, in the workplace, in the culture, come together in the next century, the next millennium, to fulfill the promise of the Declaration of Independence, of equal rights to life, liberty, and the pursuit of happiness? No one could predict. All one could do was to act on the possibility, knowing that inaction would make any prediction a gloomy one.

If democracy were to be given any meaning, if it were to go beyond the limits of capitalism and nationalism, this would not come—if history were any guide—from the top. It would come through citizens' movements, educating, organizing, agitating, striking, boycotting, demonstrating, threatening those in power with disruption of the stability they needed.

25

THE 2000 ELECTION
AND THE
"WAR ON TERRORISM"

It was clear as Clinton ended his two-term presidency (the Twenty-second Amendment to the Constitution set two terms as a limit) that the Democratic candidate for president would now be the man who served him faithfully as Vice President, Albert Gore. The Republican Party chose as its candidate for President the Governor of Texas, George W. Bush, Jr. known for his connection to oil interests and the record number of executions of prisoners during his term in office.

Although Bush, during the campaign, accused Gore of appealing to "class warfare," the candidacy of Gore and his Vice President, Senator Joseph Lieberman, posed no threat to the superrich. A front-page story in the *New York Times* was headlined "As a Senator, Lieberman Is Proudly Pro-Business" and went on to give the details: he was loved by the Silicon Valley high-tech industry, and the military-industrial complex of Connecticut was grateful to him for their $7.5 billion in contracts for the Seawolf submarine.

The degree of difference in the corporate support of the two presidential candidates can be measured by the $220 million raised by the Bush campaign and the $170 million raised by the Gore campaign. Neither Gore nor Bush had a plan for free national health care, for extensive low-cost housing, for dramatic changes in environmental controls. Both supported the death penalty and the growth of prisons. Both favored a large military establishment, the continued use of land mines, and the use of sanctions against the people of Cuba and Iraq.

There was a third-party candidate, Ralph Nader, whose national reputation came from decades of persistent criticism of corporate control of the economy. His program was sharply different from the two major candidates, emphasizing health care, education, and the environment. But he was shut out of the nationally televised debates during the campaign, and, without the support of big business, he had to raise money from the small contributions of people who believed in his program.

It was predictable, given the unity of both major parties around class issues, and the barriers put up against any third-party candidate, that half the country, mostly at lower-income levels, and unenthusiastic about either major party, would not even vote.

A journalist spoke to a cashier at a filling station, wife of a construction worker, who told him: "I don't think they think about people like us. . . . Maybe if they lived in a two-bedroom trailer, it would be different." An African American woman, a manager at McDonald's, who made slightly more than the minimum wage of $5.15 an hour, said about Bush and Gore: "I don't even pay attention to those two, and all my friends say the same. My life won't change."

It turned out to be the most bizarre election in the nation's history. Al Gore received hundreds of thousands of votes more than Bush, but the Constitution required that the victor be determined by the electors of each state. The electoral vote was so close that the outcome was going to be determined by the electors of the state of Florida. This difference between popular vote and electoral vote had happened twice before, in 1876 and 1888.

The candidate with the most votes in Florida would get all that state's electors, and win the presidency. But there was a raging dispute over whether Bush or Gore had received more votes in Florida. It seemed that many votes had not been counted, especially in districts where many black people lived; that ballots had been disqualified on technical grounds; that the marks made on the ballots by the voting machines were not clear.

Bush had this advantage: his brother Jeb Bush was governor of Florida, and the secretary of state in Florida, Katherine Harris, a Republican, had the power to certify who had more votes and had won the election. Facing claims of tainted ballots, Harris rushed through a partial recounting that left Bush ahead.

An appeal to the Florida Supreme Court, dominated by Democrats, resulted in the Court ordering Harris not to certify a winner and for recounting to continue. Harris set a deadline for recounting, and while there were still thousands of disputed ballots, she went ahead and certified that Bush was the winner by 537 votes. This was certainly the closest call in the history of presidential elections. With Gore ready to challenge the certification, and ask that recounting continue, as the Florida Supreme Court had ruled, the Republican Party took the case to the U.S. Supreme Court.

The Supreme Court split along ideological lines. The five conservative judges (Rehnquist, Scalia, Thomas, Kennedy, O'Connor), despite the usual conservative position of noninterference with state powers, overruled the Florida Supreme Court and prohibited any more counting of ballots. They said the recounting violated the constitutional requirement for "equal protection of the laws" because there were different standards in different counties of Florida for counting ballots.

The four liberal judges (Stevens, Ginsburg, Breyer, Souter) argued that the Court did not have the right to interfere with the Florida Supreme Court's interpretation of state law. Breyer and Souter argued even if there was a failure to have a uniform standard in counting, the remedy was to let there be a new election in Florida with a uniform standard.

The fact that the Supreme Court refused to allow any reconsideration of the election meant that it was determined to see that its favorite candidate, Bush, would be President. Justice Stevens pointed this out, with some bitterness, in his minority report: "Although we may never know with complete certainty the identity of the winner of this year's presidential election, the identity of the loser is perfectly clear. It is the nation's confidence in the judge as an impartial guardian of the rule of law."

Bush, taking office, proceeded to pursue his pro-big-business agenda with total confidence, as if he had the overwhelming approval of the nation. And the Democratic Party, its fundamental philosophy not too different, became a timid opposition, going along completely with Bush on his foreign policy, and differing from him only mildly on his domestic policy.

Bush's program became immediately clear. He pushed tax cuts for the wealthy, opposed strict environmental regulations that would cost money for the business interests, and planned to "privatize" Social Security by having the retirement funds of citizens depend on the stock market. He moved to increase the military budget, and to pursue the "Star Wars" program though the consensus of scientific opinion was that antiballistic missiles in space could not work, and that even if the plan worked, it would only trigger a more furious arms race throughout the world.

Nine months into his presidency, on September 11, 2001, a cataclysmic event pushed all other issues into the background. Hijackers on three different planes flew the huge jets, loaded with fuel, into the twin towers of the World Trade Center in downtown New York, and into one side of the Pentagon in Washington, D.C. As Americans all over the country watched, horrified, they saw on their television screens the towers collapse in an inferno of concrete and metal, burying thousands of workers and hundreds of firemen and policemen who had gone to their rescue.

It was an unprecedented assault against enormous symbols of American wealth and power, undertaken by 19 men from the Middle East, most of them from Saudi Arabia. They were willing to die in order to deliver a deadly blow against what they clearly saw as their enemy, a superpower that had thought itself invulnerable.

President Bush immediately declared a "war on terrorism" and proclaimed: "We shall make no distinction between terrorists and countries that harbor terrorists." Congress rushed to pass resolutions giving Bush the power to proceed with military action, without the declaration of war that the Constitution required. The resolution passed unanimously in the Senate, and in the House of Representatives only one member dissented—Barbara Lee, an African American from California.

On the supposition that the Islamic militant Osama bin Laden was responsible for the September 11 attacks, and that he was somewhere in Afghanistan, Bush ordered the bombing of Afghanistan.

Bush had declared as his objective the apprehension ("dead or alive") of Osama bin Laden, and the destruction of the Islamic militant organization Al Qaeda. But after five months of bombing Afghanistan, when Bush delivered his State of the Union address to both houses of Congress, he had to admit, while saying "we are winning the war on terror," that "tens of thousands of trained terrorists are still at large" and that "dozens of countries" were harboring terrorists.

It should have been obvious to Bush and his advisers that terrorism could not be defeated by force. The historical evidence was easily available. The British had reacted to terrorist acts by the Irish Republican Army with military action again and again, only to face even more terrorism. The Israelis, for decades, had responded to Palestinian terrorism with military strikes, which only resulted in more Palestinian bombings. Bill Clinton, after the attack on U.S. embassies in Tanzania and Kenya in 1998, had bombed Afghanistan and the Sudan. Clearly, looking at September 11, this had not stopped terrorism.

Furthermore, the months of bombings had been devastating to a country that had gone through decades of civil war and destruction. The

Pentagon claimed that it was only bombing "military targets," that the killing of civilians was "unfortunate . . . an accident . . . regrettable." However, according to human rights groups and accumulated stories in the American and West European press, at least 1,000 and perhaps 4,000 Afghan civilians were killed by American bombs.

It seemed that the United States was reacting to the horrors perpetrated by terrorists against innocent people in New York by killing other innocent people in Afghanistan. Every day the *New York Times* ran heartrending vignettes of the victims of the World Trade Center tragedy, with accompanying portraits and descriptions of their work, their interests, their families.

There was no way of getting similar information on the Afghan victims, but there were moving accounts by reporters writing from hospitals and villages about the effects of American bombing. A journalist with the *Boston Globe*, writing from a hospital in Jalalabad, wrote: "In one bed lay Noor Mohammad, 10, who was a bundle of bandages. He lost his eyes and hands to the bomb that hit his house after Sunday dinner. Hospital director Guloja Shimwari shook his head at the boy's wounds. 'The United States must be thinking he is Osama,' Shimwari said. 'If he is not Osama, then why would they do this?'"

The report continued: "The hospital's morgue received 17 bodies last weekend, and officials here estimate at least 89 civilians were killed in several villages. In the hospital yesterday, a bomb's damage could be chronicled in the life of one family. A bomb had killed the father, Faisal Karim. In one bed his wife, Mustafa Jama, who had severe head injuries. . . . Around her, six of her children were in bandages. . . . One of them, Zahidullah, 8, lay in a coma."

The American public, ever since the calamity of September 11, was overwhelmingly supportive of Bush's policy of a "war on terrorism." The Democratic Party went along, vying with the Republicans on who could speak tougher language against terrorism. The *New York Times*, which had opposed Bush in the election, editorialized in December 2001: "Mr. Bush . . . has proved himself a strong wartime leader who gives the nation a sense of security during a period of crisis."

But the full extent of the human catastrophe caused by the bombing of Afghanistan was not being conveyed to Americans by the mainstream press and the major television networks, which seemed determined to show their "patriotism."

The head of the television network CNN, Walter Isaacson, sent a memo to his staff saying that images of civilian casualties should be accompanied with an explanation that this was retaliation for the harboring of terrorists. "It seems perverse to focus too much on the casualties or hardships in Afghanistan," he said. The television anchorman Dan Rather declared: "George Bush is the President. . . . Wherever he wants me to line up, just tell me where."

The United States government went to great lengths to control the flow of information from Afghanistan. It bombed the building housing the largest television station in the Middle East, Al-Jazeera, and bought up a satellite organization that was taking photos showing the results, on the ground, of the bombing.

Mass circulation magazines fostered an atmosphere of revenge. In *Time* magazine, one of its writers, under the headline "The Case for Rage and Retribution," called for a policy of "focused brutality." A popular television commentator, Bill O'Reilly, called on the United States to "bomb the Afghan infrastructure to rubble—the airport, the power plants, their water facilities, and the roads."

The display of the American flag in the windows of homes, on automobiles, on shop windows, became widespread, and in the atmosphere of wartime jingoism, it became difficult for citizens to criticize government policy. A retired telephone worker in California who, working out in his health club, made a remark critical of President Bush, was visited by the FBI and questioned. A young woman found at her door two FBI men who said they had reports of posters on her wall criticizing the President.

Congress passed the "USA Patriot Act," which gave the Department of Justice the power to detain noncitizens simply on suspicion, without charges, without the procedural rights provided in the Constitution. It said the Secretary of State could designate any group as "terrorist," and any person who was a member of or raised funds for such an organization could be arrested and held until deported.

President Bush cautioned the nation not to react with hostility to Arab Americans, but in fact the government began to round up people for questioning, almost all Moslems, holding a thousand or more in detention, without charges. *New York Times* columnist Anthony Lewis told of one man arrested on secret evidence, and when a federal judge found there was no reason to conclude that the man was a threat to national security, the man was released. However, after September 11 the Department of Justice, ignoring the judge's finding, imprisoned him again, holding him in solitary confinement 23 hours a day, not allowing his family to see him.

There were minority voices criticizing the war. Teach-ins, peace rallies took place all over the country. Typical signs at these gatherings read "Justice, Not War" and "Our Grief Is Not a Cry for Revenge." In Arizona, not a place known for antiestablishment activism, 600 citizens signed a newspaper ad that pointed to the Universal Declaration of Human Rights. They called on the United States and the international community "to shift resources away from the destruction of Afghanistan and toward removing the obstacles that prevent sufficient food from reaching those who need it."

Some family members of those who had died in the World Trade Center or the Pentagon wrote to President Bush, urging that he not match violence with violence, that he not proceed to bomb the people of Afghanistan. Amber Amundson, whose husband, an army pilot, was killed in the attack on the Pentagon, said:

> I have heard angry rhetoric by some Americans, including many of our nation's leaders, who advise a heavy dose of revenge and punishment. To those leaders, I would like to make clear that my family and I take no comfort in your words of rage. If you choose to respond to this incomprehensible brutality by perpetuating violence against other innocent human beings, you may not do so in the name of justice for my husband.

Some of the families of victims traveled to Afghanistan in January 2002, to meet with Afghan families who had lost loved ones in the American bombing. They met with Abdul and Shakila Amin, whose five-year-old daughter, Nazila, was killed by an American bomb. One of the Americans was Rita Lasar, whose brother had been cited as a hero by President Bush (he had stayed with a paraplegic friend on a top floor of the collapsing building rather than escaping himself) and who said she would devote the rest of her life to the cause of peace.

Critics of the bombing campaign argued that terrorism was rooted in deep grievances against the United States, and that to stop terrorism, these must be addressed. The grievances were not hard to identify: the stationing of U.S. troops in Saudi Arabia, site of the most holy of Moslem shrines; the ten years of sanctions against Iraq which, according to the United Nations, had resulted in the deaths of hundreds of thousands of children; the continued U.S. support of Israel's occupation of Palestinian land, including billions in military aid.

However, these issues could not be addressed without fundamental changes in American foreign policy. Such changes could not be accepted by the military-industrial complex that dominated both major parties, because they would require withdrawing military forces from around the world, giving up political and economic domination of other countries—in short, relinquishing the cherished role of the United States as a superpower.

Such fundamental changes would require a radical change in priorities, from spending $300 to $400 billion a year for the military, to using this wealth to improve the living conditions of Americans and people in other parts of the world. For instance, it was estimated by the World Health Organization that a small portion of the American military budget, if given to the treatment of tuberculosis in the world, could save millions of lives.

The United States, by such a drastic change in its policies, would no longer be a military superpower, but it could be a humanitarian superpower, using its wealth to help people in need.

Three years before the terrible events of September 11, 2001, a former lieutenant colonel in the U.S. Air Force, Robert Bowman, who had flown 101 combat missions in Vietnam, and then had become a Catholic bishop, commented on the terrorist bombings of the U.S. embassies in Kenya and Tanzania. In an article in the *National Catholic Reporter* he wrote about the roots of terrorism:

> We are not hated because we practice democracy, value freedom, or uphold human rights. We are hated because our government denies these things to people in Third World countries whose resources are coveted by our multinational corporations. That hatred we have sown has come back to haunt us in the form of terrorism. . . . Instead of sending our sons and daughters around the world to kill Arabs so we can have the oil under their sand, we should send them to rebuild their infrastructure, supply clean water, and feed starving children. . . .
>
> In short, we should do good instead of evil. Who would try to stop us? Who would hate us? Who would want to bomb us? That is the truth the American people need to hear.

Voices like that were mostly shut out of the major American media after the September 11 attacks. But it was a prophetic voice, and there was at least a possibility that its powerful moral message might spread among the American people, once the futility of meeting violence with violence became clear. Certainly, if historical experience had any meaning, the future of peace and justice in America could not depend on the good will of government.

The democratic principle, enunciated in the words of the Declaration of Independence, declared that government was secondary, that the people who established it were primary. Thus, the future of democracy depended on the people, and their growing consciousness of what was the decent way to relate to their fellow human beings all over the world.

AFTERWORD

I am often asked how I came to write this book. One answer is that my wife Roslyn urged me to write it, and continued to urge me at those times when, daunted by the magnitude of the project, I wanted to abandon it. Another is that the circumstances of my own life (which, as I now write, has spanned a fourth of the nation's history—a startling thought) demanded of me that I try to fashion a new kind of history. By that I mean a history different from what I had learned in college and in graduate school and from what I saw in the history texts given to students all over the country.

When I set out to write the book, I had been teaching history and what is grandiosely called "political science" for twenty years. Half of that time I was involved in the civil rights movement in the South (mostly while teaching at Spelman College in Atlanta, Georgia). And then there were ten years of activity against the war in Vietnam. These experiences were hardly a recipe for neutrality in the teaching and writing of history.

But my partisanship was undoubtedly shaped even earlier, by my upbringing in a family of working-class immigrants in New York, by my three years as a shipyard worker, and by my Air Force duty as a bombardier in the European theater (a strange word for that—"theater") in the second World War. That was all before I went to college under the GI Bill of Rights and began to study history.

By the time I began teaching and writing, I had no illusions about "objectivity," if that meant avoiding a point of view. I knew that a historian (or a journalist, or anyone telling a story) was forced to choose, out of an infinite number of facts, what to present, what to omit. And that decision inevitably would reflect, whether consciously or not, the interests of the historian.

There is a certain drumbeat of scolding one hears these days, about the need for students to learn facts. "Our young people are not being taught facts," said presidential candidate Robert Dole (and candidates are always so scrupulous about facts) to a gathering of American Legionnaires. I was reminded of the character in Dickens' *Hard Times*, the pedant Gradgrind, who admonished a younger teacher: "Teach nothing but facts, facts, facts."

But there is no such thing as a pure fact, innocent of interpretation. Behind every fact presented to the world—by a teacher, a writer, anyone—is a judgment. The judgment that has been made is that this fact is important, and that other facts, omitted, are not important.

There were themes of profound importance to me which I found missing in the orthodox histories that dominated American culture. The consequence of those omissions has been not simply to give a distorted view of the past but, more important, to mislead us all about the present.

For instance, there is the issue of class. It is pretended that, as in the Preamble to the Constitution, it is "we the people" who wrote that document, rather than fifty-five privileged white males whose class interest required a strong central government. That use of government for class purposes, to serve the needs of the wealthy and powerful, has continued throughout American history, down to the present day. It is disguised by language that suggests all of us—rich and poor and middle class—have a common interest.

Thus, the state of the nation is described in universal terms. The novelist Kurt Vonnegut invented the term "granfalloon" to describe a great bubble that must be punctured to see the complexity inside. When the president declares happily that "our economy is sound," he will not acknowledge that it is not at all sound for 40 or 50 million people who are struggling to survive, although it may be moderately sound for many in the middle class, and extremely sound for the richest 1 percent of the nation who own 40 percent of the nation's wealth.

Labels are given to periods in our history which reflect the well-being of one class and ignore the rest. When I was going through the files of Fiorello LaGuardia, who as a Congressman in the twenties represented East Harlem, I read the letters of desperate housewives, their husbands out of work, their children hungry, unable to pay their rent—all this in that period known as "the Jazz Age," the "Roaring Twenties."

What we learn about the past does not give us absolute truth about the present, but it may cause us to look deeper than the glib statements made by political leaders and the "experts" quoted in the press.

Class interest has always been obscured behind an all-encompassing veil called "the national interest." My own war experience, and the history of all those military interventions in which the United States was engaged, made me skeptical when I heard people in high political office invoke "the national interest" or "national security" to justify their policies. It was with such justifications that Truman initiated a "police action" in Korea that killed several million people, that Johnson and Nixon carried out a war in Indochina in which perhaps 3 million people died, that Reagan invaded Grenada, Bush attacked Panama and then Iraq, and Clinton bombed Iraq again and again.

Is there a "national interest" when a few people decide on war, and huge numbers of others—here and abroad—are killed or crippled as a result of such a decision? Should citizens not ask in whose interest are we doing what we are doing? Then why not, I came to think, tell the story of wars not through the eyes of the generals and diplomats but from the viewpoints of the GIs, of the parents who received the black-bordered telegrams, even of "the enemy."

What struck me as I began to study history was how nationalist fervor—inculcated from childhood on by pledges of allegiance, national anthems, flags waving and rhetoric blowing—permeated the educational systems of all countries, including our own. I wonder now how the foreign policies of the United States would look if we wiped out the national boundaries of the world, at least in our minds, and thought of all children everywhere as our own. Then we could never drop an atomic bomb on Hiroshima, or napalm on Vietnam, or wage war anywhere, because wars, especially in our time, are always wars against children, indeed our children.

And then there is, much as we would want to erase it, the ineradicable issue of race. It did not occur to me, when I first began to immerse myself in history, how badly twisted was the teaching and writing of history by its submersion of nonwhite people. Yes, Indians were there, and then gone. Black people were visible when slaves, then free and invisible. It was a white man's history.

From first grade to graduate school, I was given no inkling that the landing of Christopher Columbus in the New World initiated a genocide, in which the indigenous population of Hispaniola was annihilated. Or that this was just the first stage of what was presented as a benign expansion of the new nation (Louisiana "Purchase," Florida "Purchase," Mexican "Cession"), but which involved the violent expulsion of Indians, accompanied by unspeakable atrocities, from every square mile of the continent, until there was nothing to do with them but herd them into reservations.

I was invited, sometime in 1998, to speak at a symposium in Boston's historic Faneuil Hall, on the Boston Massacre. I said I would be glad to do that, so long as I did not have to deal with the Boston Massacre. And so my talk was not about the killing of five colonists by British troops in 1770. I thought that had been given an inordinate amount of attention for over two hundred years, because it served a certain patriotic function. Instead, I wanted to talk about the many massacres of nonwhite people in our history, which would not reinforce patriotic pride but remind us of the long legacy of racism in our country, still smoldering and needing attention.

Every American schoolchild learns about the Boston Massacre. But who learns about the massacre of 600 men, women, and children of the Pequot tribe in New England in 1637? Or the massacre—in the midst of the Civil War—of hundreds of Indian families at Sand Creek, Colorado, by U.S. soldiers? Or the military attack by 200 U.S. cavalrymen in 1870 which wiped out a sleeping camp of Piegan Indians in Montana?

It was not until I joined the faculty of Spelman College, a college for black women in Atlanta, Georgia, that I began to read the African-American historians who never appeared on my reading lists in graduate school (W. E. B. Du Bois, Rayford Logan, Lawrence Reddick, Horace Mann Bond, John Hope Franklin). Nowhere in my history education had I learned about the massacres of black people that took place again and again, amid the silence of a national government pledged, by the Constitution, to protect equal rights for all.

For instance, in East St. Louis in 1917 there occurred one of the many "race riots" that took place in what our white-oriented history books called the "Progressive Era." There, white workers, angered by the influx of black workers, killed perhaps 200 people, provoking an angry article by W. E. B. Du Bois called "The Massacre of East St. Louis," and causing the performing artist Josephine Baker to say: "The very idea of America makes me shake and tremble and gives me nightmares."

I wanted, in writing this book, to awaken a greater consciousness of class conflict, racial injustice, sexual inequality, and national arrogance. But even as I tried to make up for what I saw as serious omissions, I nevertheless neglected groups in American society that had always been missing from orthodox histories. I became aware of this, and embarrassed by it, when people wrote to me after reading *A People's History*, praising the book but pointing gently (sometimes not so gently) to its shortcomings.

It was perhaps my stronger connection to the East Coast of the United States that caused me to ignore the large numbers of Latino and Latina people who lived in California and the Southwest, and their struggles for justice. Readers who want to learn more about that might look into these extraordinary books: *De Colores Means All of Us* by Elizabeth Martinez; *Zapata's Disciple: Essays* by Martin Espada; *Aztlan and Viet Nam: Chicano and Chicana Experiences of the War*, edited by George Mariscal.

And I suppose, it was my own sexual orientation that accounted for my minimal treatment of the issue of gay and lesbian rights. I tried, when a new edition appeared in 1995, to make up for this. But readers will have to look further to get a more substantial account of the remarkable change in the national culture that took place when men and women who were "queer" (a pejorative term for some people; an honorable one for others) asserted their humanity boldly, courageously, to the larger society.

As we pass from one century to another, one millennium to another, we would like to think that history itself is transformed as dramatically as the calendar. However, it rushes on, as it always did, with two forces racing toward the future, one splendidly uniformed, the other ragged but inspired.

There is the past and its continuing horrors: violence, war, prejudices against those who are different, outrageous monopolization of the good earth's wealth by a few, political power in the hands of liars and murderers, the building of prisons instead of schools, the poisoning of the press and the entire culture by money. It is easy to become discouraged observing this, especially since this is what the press and television insist that we look at, and nothing more.

But there is also (though much of this is kept from us, to keep us intimidated and without hope) the bubbling of change under the surface of obedience: the growing revulsion against the endless wars (I think of the Russian women in the nineties, demanding their country end its military intervention in Chechnya, as did Americans during the Vietnam war); the insistence of women all over the world that they will no longer tolerate abuse and subordination—we see, for instance, the new international movement against female genital mutilation, and the militancy of welfare mothers against punitive laws. There is civil disobedience against the military machine, protest against police brutality directed especially at people of color.

In the United States, we see the educational system, a burgeoning new literature, alternative radio stations, a wealth of documentary films outside the mainstream, even Hollywood itself and sometimes television—compelled to recognize the growing multiracial character of the nation. Yes, we have in this country, dominated by corporate wealth and military power and two antiquated political parties, what a fearful conservative characterized as "a permanent adversarial culture" challenging the present, demanding a new future.

It is a race in which we can all choose to participate, or just to watch. But we should know that our choice will help determine the outcome.

I think of the words of the poet Shelley, recited by women garment workers in New York to one another at the start of the twentieth century.

> Rise like lions after slumber
> In unvanquishable number!
> Shake your chains to earth, like dew
> Which in sleep had fallen on you—
> Ye are many; they are few!

BIBLIOGRAPHY

This book, written in a few years, is based on twenty years of teaching and research in American history, and as many years of involvement in social movements. But it could not have been written without the work of several generations of scholars, and especially the current generation of historians who have done immense work in the history of blacks, Indians, women, and working people of all kinds. It also could not have been written without the work of many people, not professional historians, who were stimulated by the social struggles around them to put together material about the lives and activities of ordinary people trying to make a better world, or just trying to survive.

To indicate every source of information in the text would have meant a book impossibly cluttered with footnotes, and yet I know the curiosity of the reader about where a startling fact or pungent quote comes from. Therefore, as often as I can, I mention in the text authors and titles of books for which the full information is in this bibliography. Where you cannot tell the source of a quotation right from the text, you can probably figure it out by looking at the asterisked books for that chapter. The asterisked books are those I found especially useful and often indispensable.

I have gone through the following standard scholarly periodicals: *American Historical Review, Mississippi Valley Historical Review, Journal of American History, Journal of Southern History, Journal of Negro History, Labor History, William and Mary Quarterly, Phylon, The Crisis, American Political Science Review, Journal of Social History.*

Also, some less orthodox but important periodicals for a work like this: *Monthly Review, Science and Society, Radical America, Akwesasne Notes, Signs: Journal of Women in Culture and Society, The Black Scholar, Bulletin of Concerned Asian Scholars, The Review of Radical Political Economics, Socialist Revolution, Radical History Review.*

1. COLUMBUS, THE INDIANS, AND HUMAN PROGRESS

Brandon, William. *The Last Americans: The Indian in American Culture.* New York: McGraw-Hill, 1974.

*Collier, John. *Indians of the Americas.* New York: W. W. Norton, 1947.

*de las Casas, Bartolomé. *History of the Indies.* New York: Harper & Row, 1971.

*Jennings, Francis. *The Invasion of America: Indians, Colonialism, and the Cant of Conquest.* Chapel Hill: University of North Carolina Press, 1975.

*Koning, Hans. *Columbus: His Enterprise*. New York: Monthly Review Press, 1976.
*Morgan, Edmund S. *American Slavery, American Freedom: The Ordeal of Colonial Virginia*. New York: W. W. Norton, 1975.
Morison, Samuel Eliot. *Admiral of the Ocean Sea*. Boston: Little, Brown, 1942.
————. *Christopher Columbus, Mariner*. Boston: Little, Brown, 1955.
*Nash, Gary B. *Red, White, and Black: The Peoples of Early America*. Englewood Cliffs: Prentice-Hall, 1970.
Vogel, Virgil, ed. *This Country Was Ours*. New York: Harper & Row, 1972.

2. DRAWING THE COLOR LINE

*Aptheker, Herbert, ed. *A Documentary History of the Negro People in the United States*. Secaucus, N.J.: Citadel, 1974.
Boskin, Joseph. *Into Slavery: Radical Decisions in the Virginia Colony*. Philadelphia, Lippincott, 1966.
Catterall, Helen. *Judicial Cases Concerning American Slavery and the Negro*. 5 vols. Washington, Negro University Press, 1937.
Davidson, Basil. *The African Slave Trade*. Boston: Little, Brown, 1961.
Donnan, Elizabeth, ed. *Documents Illustrative of the History of the Slave Trade to America*. 4 vols. New York: Octagon, 1965.
Elkins, Stanley. *Slavery: A Problem in American Institutional and Intellectual Life*. Chicago: University of Chicago Press, 1976.
Federal Writers Project. *The Negro in Virginia*. New York: Arno, 1969.
Franklin, John Hope. *From Slavery to Freedom: A History of American Negroes*. New York: Knopf, 1974.
*Jordan, Winthrop. *White Over Black: American Attitudes Toward the Negro, 1550–1812*. Chapel Hill: University of North Carolina Press, 1968.
*Morgan, Edmund S. *American Slavery, American Freedom: The Ordeal of Colonial Virginia*. New York: W. W. Norton, 1975.
Mullin, Gerald. *Flight and Rebellion: Slave Resistance in Eighteenth-Century Virginia*. New York: Oxford University Press, 1974.
Mullin, Michael, ed. *American Negro Slavery: A Documentary History*. New York: Harper & Row, 1975.
Phillips, Ulrich B. *American Negro Slavery: A Survey of the Supply, Employment and Control of Negro Labor as Determined by the Plantation Regime*. Baton Rouge: Louisiana State University Press, 1966.
Redding, J. Saunders. *They Came in Chains*. Philadelphia: Lippincott, 1973.
Stampp, Kenneth M. *The Peculiar Institution*. New York: Knopf, 1956.
Tannenbaum, Frank. *Slave and Citizen: The Negro in the Americas*. New York: Random House, 1963.

3. PERSONS OF MEAN AND VILE CONDITION

Andrews, Charles, ed. *Narratives of the Insurrections 1675–1690*. New York: Barnes & Noble, 1915.
*Bridenbaugh, Carl. *Cities in the Wilderness: The First Century of Urban Life in America*. New York: Oxford University Press, 1971.

Henretta, James. "Economic Development and Social Structure in Colonial Boston." *William and Mary Quarterly*, 3rd Series, Vol. 22, January 1965.

Herrick, Cheesman. *White Servitude in Pennsylvania: Indentured and Redemption Labor in Colony and Commonwealth*. Washington: Negro University Press, 1926.

Hofstadter, Richard. *America at 1750: A Social History*. New York: Knopf, 1971.

Hofstadter, Richard, and Wallace, Michael, eds. *American Violence: A Documentary History*. New York: Knopf, 1970.

Mohl, Raymond. *Poverty in New York, 1783–1825*. New York: Oxford University Press, 1971.

*Morgan, Edward S. *American Slavery, American Freedom: The Ordeal of Colonial Virginia*. New York: W. W. Norton, 1975.

*Morris, Richard B. *Government and Labor in Early America*. New York: Harper & Row, 1965.

*Nash, Gary B., ed. *Class and Society in Early America*. Englewood Cliffs: Prentice-Hall, 1970.

*———. *Red, White, and Black: The Peoples of Early America*. Englewood Cliffs: Prentice-Hall, 1974.

*———. "Social Change and the Growth of Prerevolutionary Urban Radicalism," *The American Revolution*, ed. Alfred Young. DeKalb: Northern Illinois University Press, 1976.

*Smith, Abbot E. *Colonists in Bondage: White Servitude and Convict Labor in America*. New York: W. W. Norton, 1971.

*Washburn, Wilcomb E. *The Governor and the Rebel: A History of Bacon's Rebellion in Virginia*. New York: W. W. Norton, 1972.

4. TYRANNY IS TYRANNY

Bailyn, Bernard, and Garrett, N., eds. *Pamphlets of the American Revolution*. Cambridge: Harvard University Press, 1965.

Becker, Carl. *The Declaration of Independence: A Study in the History of Political Ideas*. New York: Random House, 1958.

Brown, Richard Maxwell. "Violence and the American Revolution," *Essays on the American Revolution*, ed. Stephen G. Kurtz and James H. Hutson. Chapel Hill: University of North Carolina Press, 1973.

Countryman, Edward, " 'Out of the Bounds of the Law': Northern Land Rioters in the Eighteenth Century," *The American Revolution: Explorations in the History of American Radicalism*, ed. Alfred F. Young. DeKalb: Northern Illinois University Press, 1976.

Ernst, Joseph. " 'Ideology' and an Economic Interpretation of the Revolution," *The American Revolution: Explorations in the History of American Radicalism*, ed. Alfred F. Young. DeKalb: Northern Illinois University Press, 1976.

Foner, Eric. "Tom Paine's Republic: Radical Ideology and Social Change," *The American Revolution: Explorations in the History of American Radicalism*, ed. Alfred F. Young. DeKalb: Northern Illinois University Press, 1976.

Fox-Bourne, H. R. *The Life of John Locke*, 2 vols. New York: King, 1876.

Greene, Jack P. "An Uneasy Connection: An Analysis of the Preconditions of the American Revolution," *Essays on the American Revolution*, ed. Stephen G. Kurtz and James H. Hutson. Chapel Hill: University of North Carolina Press, 1973.

Hill, Christopher. *Puritanism and Revolution*. New York: Schocken, 1964.

*Hoerder, Dirk. "Boston Leaders and Boston Crowds, 1765–1776," *The American Revolution: Explorations in the History of American Radicalism*, ed. Alfred F. Young. DeKalb: Northern Illinois University Press, 1976.

Lemisch, Jesse. "Jack Tar in the Streets: Merchant Seamen in the Politics of Revolutionary America," *William and Mary Quarterly*, July 1968.

Maier, Pauline. *From Resistance to Revolution: Colonial Radicals and the Development of American Opposition to Britain, 1765–1776*. New York: Knopf, 1972.

5. A KIND OF REVOLUTION

Aptheker, Herbert, ed. *A Documentary History of the Negro People in the United States*. Secaucus, N.J.: Citadel Press, 1974.

Bailyn, Bernard. "Central Themes of the Revolution," *Essays on the American Revolution*, ed. Stephen G. Kurtz and James H. Hutson. Chapel Hill: University of North Carolina Press, 1973.

———. *The Ideological Origins of the American Revolution*. Cambridge, Mass.: Harvard University Press, 1967.

*Beard, Charles. *An Economic Interpretation of the Constitution of the United States*. New York: Macmillan, 1935.

Berlin, Ira. "The Negro in the American Revolution," *The American Revolution: Explorations in the History of American Radicalism*, ed. Alfred F. Young. DeKalb: Northern Illinois University Press, 1976.

Berthoff, Rowland, and Murrin, John. "Feudalism, Communalism, and the Yeoman Freeholder, *Essays on the American Revolution*, ed. Stephen G. Kurtz and James H. Hutson. Chapel Hill: University of North Carolina Press, 1973.

Brown, Robert E. *Charles Beard and the Constitution*. New York: W. W. Norton, 1965.

Degler, Carl. *Out of Our Past*. Harper & Row, 1970.

Henderson, H. James. "The Structure of Politics in the Continental Congress," *Essays on the American Revolution*, ed. Stephen G. Kurtz and James H. Hutson. Chapel Hill: University of North Carolina Press, 1973.

*Hoffman, Ronald. "The 'Disaffected' in the Revolutionary South," *The American Revolution: Explorations in the History of American Radicalism*, ed. Alfred F. Young. DeKalb: Northern Illinois University Press, 1976.

Jennings, Francis. "The Indians' Revolution," *The American Revolution: Explorations in the History of American Radicalism*, ed. Alfred F. Young. DeKalb: Northern Illinois University Press, 1976.

Levy, Leonard W. *Freedom of Speech and Press in Early American History*. New York: Harper & Row, 1963.

*Lynd, Staughton. *Anti-Federalism in Dutchess County, New York*. Chicago: Loyola University Press, 1962.

————. *Class Conflict, Slavery, and the Constitution.* Indianapolis: Bobbs-Merrill, 1967.

————. "Freedom Now: The Intellectual Origins of American Radicalism," *The American Revolution: Explorations in the History of American Radicalism,* ed. Alfred F. Young. DeKalb: Northern Illinois University Press, 1976.

McLoughlin, William G. "The Role of Religion in the Revolution," *Essays on the American Revolution,* ed. Stephen G. Kurtz and James H. Hutson. Chapel Hill: University of North Carolina Press, 1973.

Morgan, Edmund S. "Conflict and Consensus in Revolution," *Essays on the American Revolution,* ed. Stephen G. Kurtz and James H. Hutson. Chapel Hill: University of North Carolina Press, 1973.

Morris, Richard B. "We the People of the United States." Presidential address, American Historical Association, 1976.

*Shy, John. *A People Numerous and Armed: Reflections on the Military Struggle for American Independence.* New York: Oxford University Press, 1976.

Smith, Page. *A New Age Now Begins: A People's History of the American Revolution.* New York: McGraw-Hill, 1976.

Starkey, Marion. *A Little Rebellion.* New York: Knopf, 1949.

Van Doren, Carl. *Mutiny in January.* New York: Viking, 1943.

*Young, Alfred, ed. *The American Revolution: Explorations in the History of American Radicalism.* DeKalb: Northern Illinois University Press, 1976.

6. THE INTIMATELY OPPRESSED

Barker-Benfield, G. J. *The Horrors of the Half-Known Life.* New York: Harper & Row, 1976.

*Baxandall, Rosalyn, Gordon, Linda, and Reverby, Susan, eds. *America's Working Women.* New York: Random House, 1976.

*Cott, Nancy. *The Bonds of Womanhood.* New Haven: Yale University Press, 1977.

*————, ed. *Root of Bitterness.* New York: Dutton, 1972.

Farb, Peter. "The Pueblos of the Southwest," *Women in American Life,* ed. Anne Scott. Boston: Houghton Mifflin, 1970.

*Flexner, Eleanor. *A Century of Struggle.* Cambridge, Mass.: Harvard University Press, 1975.

Gordon, Ann, and Buhle, Mary Jo. "Sex and Class in Colonial and Nineteenth-Century America," *Liberating Women's History,* ed. Berenice Carroll. Urbana: University of Illinois Press, 1975.

*Lerner, Gerda, ed. *The Female Experience: An American Documentary.* Indianapolis: Bobbs-Merrill, 1977.

Sandoz, Mari. "These Were the Sioux," *Women in American Life,* ed. Anne Scott. Boston: Houghton Mifflin, 1970.

Spruill, Julia Cherry. *Women's Life and Work in the Southern Colonies.* Chapel Hill: University of North Carolina, 1938.

Tyler, Alice Felt. *Freedom's Ferment.* Minneapolis: University of Minnesota Press, 1944.

Vogel, Lise. "Factory Tracts," *Signs: Journal of Women in Culture and Society,* Spring 1976.

Welter, Barbara. *Dimity Convictions: The American Woman in the Nineteenth Century.* Athens, Ohio: Ohio University Press, 1976.

Wilson, Joan Hoff. "The Illusion of Change: Women in the American Revolution," *The American Revolution: Explorations in the History of American Radicalism,* ed. Alfred F. Young. DeKalb: Northern Illinois University Press, 1976.

7. As Long as Grass Grows or Water Runs

Drinnon, Richard. *Violence in the American Experience: Winning the West.* New York: New American Library, 1979.

Filler, Louis E., and Guttmann, Allen, eds. *The Removal of the Cherokee Nation.* Huntington, N.Y.: R. E. Krieger, 1977.

Foreman, Grant. *Indian Removal.* Norman: University of Oklahoma Press, 1972.

*McLuhan, T. C., ed. *Touch the Earth: A Self-Portrait of Indian Existence.* New York: Simon & Schuster, 1976.

*Rogin, Michael. *Fathers and Children: Andrew Jackson and the Subjugation of the American Indian.* New York: Knopf, 1975.

*Van Every, Dale. *The Disinherited: The Lost Birthright of the American Indian.* New York: Morrow, 1976.

Vogel, Virgil, ed. *This Country Was Ours.* New York: Harper & Row, 1972.

8. We Take Nothing by Conquest, Thank God

*Foner, Philip. *A History of the Labor Movement in the United States.* 4 vols. New York: International Publishers, 1947–1965.

Graebner, Norman A. "Empire in the Pacific: A Study in American Continental Expansion," *The Mexican War: Crisis for American Democracy,* ed. Archie P. McDonald.

———, ed. *Manifest Destiny.* Indianapolis: Bobbs-Merrill, 1968.

Jay, William. *A Review of the Causes and Consequences of the Mexican War.* Boston: B. B. Mussey & Co., 1849.

McDonald, Archie P., ed. *The Mexican War: Crisis for American Democracy.* Lexington, Mass: D. C. Heath, 1969.

Morison, Samuel Eliot, Merk, Frederick, and Friedel, Frank. *Dissent in Three American Wars.* Cambridge, Mass.: Harvard University Press, 1970.

O'Sullivan, John, and Meckler, Alan. *The Draft and Its Enemies: A Documentary History.* Urbana: University of Illinois Press, 1974.

Perry, Bliss, ed. *Lincoln: Speeches and Letters.* Garden City, N.Y.: Doubleday, 1923.

*Schroeder, John H. *Mr. Polk's War: American Opposition and Dissent 1846–1848.* Madison: University of Wisconsin Press, 1973.

*Smith, George Winston, and Judah, Charles, eds. *Chronicles of the Gringos: The U.S. Army in the Mexican War 1846–1848.* Albuquerque: University of New Mexico Press, 1966.

*Smith, Justin. *The War with Mexico.* 2 vols. New York: Macmillan, 1919.

*Weems, John Edward. *To Conquer a Peace.* New York: Doubleday, 1974.

Weinberg, Albert K. *Manifest Destiny: A Study of Nationalist Expansion in American History.* Baltimore: Johns Hopkins Press, 1935.

9. SLAVERY WITHOUT SUBMISSION, EMANCIPATION WITHOUT FREEDOM

Allen, Robert. *The Reluctant Reformers.* New York: Anchor, 1975.

*Aptheker, Herbert. *American Negro Slave Revolts.* New York: International Publishers, 1969.

*———, ed. *A Documentary History of the Negro People in the United States.* New York: Citadel, 1974.

———. *Nat Turner's Slave Rebellion.* New York: Grove Press, 1968.

Bond, Horace Mann. "Social and Economic Forces in Alabama Reconstruction," *Journal of Negro History,* July 1938.

Conrad, Earl. *Harriet Tubman.* Middlebury, Vt.: Eriksson, 1970.

Cox, LaWanda and John, eds. *Reconstruction, the Negro, and the Old South.* New York: Harper & Row, 1973.

Douglass, Frederick. *Narrative of the Life of Frederick Douglass,* ed. Benjamin Quarles. Cambridge, Mass.: Harvard University Press, 1960.

Du Bois, W. E. B. *John Brown.* New York: International Publishers, 1962.

Fogel, Robert, and Engerman, Stanley. *Time on the Cross: The Economics of American Negro Slavery.* Boston: Little, Brown, 1974.

Foner, Philip, ed. *The Life and Writings of Frederick Douglass.* 5 vols. New York: International Publishers, 1975.

*Franklin, John Hope. *From Slavery to Freedom.* New York: Knopf, 1974.

*Genovese, Eugene. *Roll, Jordan, Roll: The World the Slaves Made.* New York: Pantheon, 1974.

*Gutman, Herbert. *The Black Family in Slavery and Freedom, 1750–1925.* New York: Pantheon, 1976.

*———. *Slavery and the Numbers Game: A Critique of "Time on the Cross."* Urbana: University of Illinois Press, 1975.

Herschfield, Marilyn. "Women in the Civil War." Unpublished paper, 1977.

*Hofstadter, Richard. *The American Political Tradition.* New York: Knopf, 1973.

Killens, John O., ed. *The Trial Record of Denmark Vesey.* Boston: Beacon Press, 1970.

Kolchin, Peter. *First Freedom: The Response of Alabama's Blacks to Emancipation and Reconstruction.* New York: Greenwood, 1972.

*Lerner, Gerda, ed. *Black Women in White America: A Documentary History.* New York: Random House, 1973.

Lester, Julius, ed. *To Be a Slave.* New York: Dial Press, 1968.

*Levine, Lawrence J. *Black Culture and Black Consciousness: Afro-American Folk Thought from Slavery to Freedom.* New York: Oxford University Press, 1977.

*Logan, Rayford. *The Betrayal of the Negro: From Rutherford B. Hayes to Woodrow Wilson.* New York: Macmillan, 1965.

*MacPherson, James. *The Negro's Civil War.* New York: Pantheon, 1965.

*———. *The Struggle for Equality.* Princeton: Princeton University Press, 1964.

*Meltzer, Milton, ed. *In Their Own Words: A History of the American Negro.* New York: T. Y. Crowell, 1964–1967.

Mullin, Michael, ed. *American Negro Slavery: A Documentary History*. New York: Harper & Row, 1975.

Osofsky, Gilbert. *Puttin' on Ole Massa*. New York: Harper & Row, 1969.

Painter, Nell Irvin. *Exodusters: Black Migration to Kansas After Reconstruction*. New York: Knopf, 1977.

Phillips, Ulrich B. *American Negro Slavery: A Survey of the Supply. Employment and Control of Negro Labor as Determined by the Plantation Regime*. Baton Rouge: Louisiana State University Press, 1966.

Rawick, George P. *From Sundown to Sunup: The Making of the Black Community*. Westport, Conn.: Greenwood Press, 1972.

*Rosengarten, Theodore. *All God's Dangers: The Life of Nate Shaw*. New York: Knopf, 1974.

Starobin, Robert S., ed. *Blacks in Bondage: Letters of American Slaves*. New York: Franklin Watts, 1974.

Tragle, Henry I. *The Southampton Slave Revolt of 1831*. Amherst, Mass.: University of Massachusetts Press, 1971.

Wiltse, Charles M., ed. *David Walker's Appeal*. New York: Hill & Wang, 1965.

*Woodward, C. Vann. *Reunion and Reaction: The Compromise of 1877 and the End of Reconstruction*. Boston: Little, Brown, 1966.

Works Progress Administration. *The Negro in Virginia*. New York: Arno Press, 1969.

10. THE OTHER CIVIL WAR

Bimba, Anthony. *The Molly Maguires*. New York: International Publishers, 1970.

Brecher, Jeremy. *Strike!* Boston: South End Press, 1979.

*Bruce, Robert V. *1877: Year of Violence*. New York: Franklin Watts, 1959.

Burbank, David. *Reign of Rabble: The St. Louis General Strike of 1877*. Fairfield, N.J.: Augustus Kelley, 1966.

*Christman, Henry. *Tin Horns and Calico*. New York: Holt, 1945.

*Cochran, Thomas, and Miller, William. *The Age of Enterprise*. New York: Macmillan, 1942.

Coulter, E. Merton, *The Confederate States of America 1861–1865*. Baton Rouge: Louisiana State University Press, 1950.

Dacus, Joseph A. "Annals of the Great Strikes of the United States," *Except to Walk Free: Documents and Notes in the History of American Labor*, ed. Albert Fried. New York: Anchor, 1974.

*Dawley, Alan. *Class and Community: The Industrial Revolution in Lynn*. Cambridge, Mass.: Harvard University Press, 1976.

*Feldstein, Stanley, and Costello, Lawrence, eds. *The Ordeal of Assimilation: A Documentary History of the White Working Class, 1830's to the 1970's*. New York: Anchor, 1974.

Fite, Emerson. *Social and Industrial Conditions in the North During the Civil War*. New York: Macmillan, 1910.

*Foner, Philip. *A History of the Labor Movement in the United States*. 4 vols. New York: International Publishers, 1947–1964.

*———, ed. *We, the Other People.* Urbana: University of Illinois Press, 1976.

Fried, Albert, ed. *Except to Walk Free: Documents and Notes in the History of American Labor.* New York: Anchor, 1974.

*Gettleman, Marvin. *The Dorr Rebellion.* New York: Random House, 1973.

Gutman, Herbert. "The Buena Vista Affair, 1874–1875," *Workers in the Industrial Revolution: Recent Studies of Labor in the United States and Europe,* ed. Peter N. Stearns and Daniel Walkowitz. New Brunswick, N.J.: Transaction, 1974.

———. *Work, Culture and Society in Industrializing America.* New York: Random House, 1977.

———. "Work, Culture and Society in Industrialising America, 1815–1919," *American Historical Review,* June 1973.

Headley, Joel Tyler. *The Great Riots of New York, 1712–1873.* Indianapolis: Bobbs-Merrill, 1970.

*Hofstadter, Richard, and Wallace, Michael, eds. *American Violence: A Documentary History.* New York: Knopf, 1970.

*Horwitz, Morton. *The Transformation of American Law, 1780–1860.* Cambridge, Mass.: Harvard University Press, 1977.

Knights, Peter R. *The Plain People of Boston 1830–1860: A Study in City Growth.* New York: Oxford University Press, 1973.

Meyer, Marvin. *The Jacksonian Persuasion.* New York: Vintage, 1960.

Miller, Douglas T. *The Birth of Modern America.* Indianapolis: Bobbs-Merrill, 1970.

Montgomery, David. "The Shuttle and the Cross: Weavers and Artisans in the Kensington Riots of 1844," *Journal of Social History,* Summer 1972.

*Myers, Gustavus. *History of the Great American Fortunes.* New York: Modern Library, 1936.

Pessen, Edward. *Jacksonian America.* Homewood, Ill.: Dorsey, 1969.

———. *Most Uncommon Jacksonians.* Albany: State University of New York Press, 1967.

Remini, Robert V. *The Age of Jackson.* New York: Harper & Row, 1972.

Schlesinger, Arthur M., Jr. *The Age of Jackson.* Boston: Little, Brown, 1945.

Stearns, Peter N., and Walkowitz, Daniel, eds. *Workers in the Industrial Revolution: Recent Studies of Labor in the United States and Europe.* New Brunswick, N.J.: Transaction, 1974.

Tatum, Georgia Lee. *Disloyalty in the Confederacy.* New York: A.M.S. Press, 1970.

*Wertheimer, Barbara. *We Were There: The Story of Working Women in America.* New York: Pantheon, 1977.

Wilson, Edmund. *Patriotic Gore: Studies in the Literature of the American Civil War.* New York: Oxford University Press, 1962.

Yellen, Samuel. *American Labor Struggles.* New York: Pathfinder, 1974.

Zinn, Howard. "The Conspiracy of Law," *The Rule of Law,* ed. Robert Paul Wolff. New York: Simon & Schuster, 1971.

11. ROBBER BARONS AND REBELS

Allen, Robert. *Reluctant Reformers: Racism and Social Reform Movements in the United States.* New York: Anchor, 1975.

Bellamy, Edward. *Looking Backward.* Cambridge: Harvard University Press, 1967.

Bowles, Samuel, and Gintis, Herbert. *Schooling in Capitalist America.* New York: Basic Books, 1976.

Brandeis, Louis. *Other People's Money.* New York: Frederick Stokes, 1914.

Brecher, Jeremy. *Strike!* Boston: South End Press, 1979.

Carwardine, William. *The Pullman Strike.* Chicago: Charles Kerr, 1973.

*Cochran, Thomas, and Miller, William. *The Age of Enterprise.* New York: Macmillan, 1942.

Conwell, Russell H. *Acres of Diamonds.* New York: Harper & Row, 1915.

Crowe, Charles. "Tom Watson, Populists, and Blacks Reconsidered," *Journal of Negro History,* April 1970.

David, Henry. *A History of the Haymarket Affair.* New York: Collier, 1963.

Feldstein, Stanley, and Costello, Lawrence, eds. *The Ordeal of Assimilation: A Documentary History of the White Working Class, 1830's to the 1970's.* Garden City, N.Y.: Anchor, 1974.

*Foner, Philip. *A History of the Labor Movement in the United States.* 4 vols. New York: International Publishers, 1947–1964.

———. *Organized Labor and the Black Worker 1619–1973.* New York: International Publishers, 1974.

George, Henry. *Progress and Poverty.* New York: Robert Scholkenbach Foundation, 1937.

Ginger, Ray. *The Age of Excess: The U.S. from 1877 to 1914.* New York: Macmillan, 1975.

*———. *The Bending Cross: A Biography of Eugene Victor Debs.* New Brunswick: Rutgers University Press, 1949.

*Goodwyn, Lawrence. *Democratic Promise: The Populist Movement in America.* New York: Oxford University Press, 1976.

Hair, William Ivy. *Bourbonism and Agrarian Protest: Louisiana Politics, 1877–1900.* Baton Rouge: Louisiana State University Press, 1969.

Heilbroner, Robert, and Singer, Aaron. *The Economic Transformation of America.* New York: Harcourt Brace Jovanovich, 1977.

Hofstadter, Richard, and Wallace, Michael, eds. *American Violence: A Documentary History.* New York: Knopf, 1970.

*Josephson, Matthew. *The Politicos.* New York: Harcourt Brace Jovanovich, 1963.

*———. *The Robber Barons.* New York: Harcourt Brace Jovanovich, 1962.

Mason, Alpheus T., and Beaney, William M. *American Constitutional Law.* Englewood Cliffs, N.J.: Prentice-Hall, 1972.

*Myers, Gustavus. *History of the Great American Fortunes.* New York: Modern Library, 1936.

Pierce, Bessie L. *Public Opinion and the Teaching of History in the United States.* New York: DaCapo, 1970.

Pollack, Norman. *The Populist Response to Industrial America.* Cambridge, Mass.: Harvard University Press, 1976.

Smith, Henry Nash. *Virgin Land.* Cambridge, Mass.: Harvard University Press, 1970.

Spring, Joel H. *Education and the Rise of the Corporate State.* Boston: Beacon Press, 1973.

Wasserman, Harvey. *Harvey Wasserman's History of the United States.* New York: Harper & Row, 1972.

*Wertheimer, Barbara. *We Were There: The Story of Working Women in America.* New York: Pantheon, 1977.

*Woodward, C. Vann. *Origins of the New South.* Baton Rouge: Louisiana State University Press, 1972.

*———. *Tom Watson, Agrarian Rebel.* New York: Oxford University Press, 1963.

*Yellen, Samuel. *American Labor Struggles.* New York: Pathfinder, 1974.

12. THE EMPIRE AND THE PEOPLE

Aptheker, Herbert, ed. *A Documentary History of the Negro People in the United States.* New York: Citadel, 1973.

Beale, Howard K. *Theodore Roosevelt and the Rise of America to World Power.* New York: Macmillan, 1962.

Beisner, Robert. *Twelve Against Empire: The Anti-Imperialists, 1898–1902.* New York: McGraw-Hill, 1968.

*Foner, Philip. *A History of the Labor Movement in the United States.* 4 vols. New York: International Publishers, 1947–1964.

*———. *The Spanish-Cuban-American War and the Birth of American Imperialism.* 2 vols. New York: Monthly Review Press, 1972.

Francisco, Luzviminda. "The First Vietnam: The Philippine-American War, 1899–1902," *Bulletin of Concerned Asian Scholars*, 1973.

*Gatewood, Willard B. *"Smoked Yankees" and the Struggle for Empire: Letters from Negro Soldiers, 1898–1902.* Urbana: University of Illinois Press, 1971.

Lafeber, Walter. *The New Empire: An Interpretation of American Expansion.* Ithaca, N.Y.: Cornell University Press, 1963.

Pratt, Julius. "American Business and the Spanish-American War," *Hispanic-American Historical Review*, 1934.

Schirmer, Daniel Boone. *Republic or Empire: American Resistance to the Philippine War.* Cambridge, Mass.: Schenkman, 1972.

Williams, William Appleman. *The Roots of the Modern American Empire.* New York: Random House, 1969.

———. *The Tragedy of American Diplomacy.* New York: Dell, 1972.

Wolff, Leon. *Little Brown Brother.* Garden City, N.Y.: Doubleday, 1961.

Young, Marilyn. *The Rhetoric of Empire.* Cambridge, Mass.: Harvard University Press, 1968.

13. THE SOCIALIST CHALLENGE

*Aptheker, Herbert. *A Documentary History of the Negro People in the United States*. New York: Citadel, 1974.

*Baxandall, Rosalyn, Gordon, Linda, and Reverby, Susan, eds. *America's Working Women*. New York: Random House, 1976.

Braverman, Harry. *Labor and Monopoly Capital: The Degradation of Work in the Twentieth Century*. New York: Monthly Review, 1975.

Brody, David. *Steelworkers in America: The Non-Union Era*. Cambridge, Mass.: Harvard University Press, 1960.

Chafe, William. *Women and Equality: Changing Patterns in American Culture*. New York: Oxford University Press, 1977.

Cochran, Thomas, and Miller, William. *The Age of Enterprise*. New York: Macmillan, 1942.

Dancis, Bruce. "Socialism and Women," *Socialist Revolution*, January-March 1976.

Dubofsky, Melvyn. *We Shall Be All: A History of the Industrial Workers of the World*. New York: Quadrangle, 1974.

Du Bois, W. E. B. *The Souls of Black Folk*. New York: Fawcett, 1961.

Faulkner, Harold. *The Decline of Laissez Faire 1897–1917*. White Plains, N.Y.: M. E. Sharpe, 1977.

*Flexner, Eleanor. *A Century of Struggle*. Cambridge, Mass.: Harvard University Press, 1975.

Flynn, Elizabeth Gurley. *The Rebel Girl*. New York: International Publishers, 1973.

Foner, Philip, ed. *Helen Keller: Her Socialist Years*. New York: International Publishers, 1967.

*———. *A History of the Labor Movement in the United States*. 4 vols. New York: International Publishers, 1947–1964.

Gilman, Charlotte Perkins. *Women and Economics*. New York: Harper & Row, 1966.

*Ginger, Ray. *The Bending Cross: A Biography of Eugene Victor Debs*. New Brunswick: Rutgers University Press, 1969.

Goldman, Emma. *Anarchism and Other Essays*. New York: Dover, 1970.

Green, James. *Grass-Roots Socialism: Radical Movements in the Southwest, 1895–1943*. Baton Rouge: Louisiana State University Press, 1978.

Hays, Samuel. "The Politics of Reform in Municipal Government in the Progressive Era," *Pacific Northwest Quarterly*, October 1964. (Reprinted by New England Free Press.)

Haywood, Bill. *The Autobiography of Big Bill Haywood*. New York: International Publishers, 1929.

Hofstadter, Richard. *The American Political Tradition*. New York: Random House, 1954.

James, Henry. *The American Scene*. Bloomington: Indiana University Press, 1968.

Jones, Mary. *The Autobiography of Mother Jones*. Chicago: Charles Kerr, 1925.

Kaplan, Justin. *Mr. Clemens and Mark Twain: A Biography*. New York: Simon & Schuster, 1966.

*Kolko, Gabriel. *The Triumph of Conservatism*. New York: Free Press, 1977.

*Kornbluh, Joyce, ed. *Rebel Voices: An I.W.W. Anthology*. Ann Arbor: University of Michigan Press, 1964.

*Lerner, Gerda, ed. *Black Women in White America*. New York: Random House, 1973.

*———. *The Female Experience: An American Documentary*. Indianapolis: Bobbs-Merrill, 1977.

London, Jack. *The Iron Heel*. New York: Bantam, 1971.

Naden, Corinne J. *The Triangle Shirtwaist Fire, March 25, 1911*. New York: Franklin Watts, 1971.

Sanger, Margaret. *Woman and the New Race*. New York: Brentano's, 1920.

Schoener, Allon, ed. *Portal to America: The Lower East Side, 1870–1925*. New York: Holt, Rinehart and Winston, 1967.

Sinclair, Upton. *The Jungle*. New York: Harper & Row, 1951.

Sochen, June. *Movers and Shakers: American Women Thinkers and Activists, 1900–1970*. New York: Quadrangle, 1974.

Stein, Leon. *The Triangle Fire*. Philadelphia: Lippincott, 1965.

Wasserman, Harvey. *Harvey Wasserman's History of the United States*. New York: Harper & Row, 1972.

*Weinstein, James. *The Corporate Ideal in the Liberal State, 1900–1918*. Boston: Beacon Press, 1968.

*Wertheimer, Barbara. *We Were There: The Story of Working Women in America*. New York: Pantheon, 1977.

Wiebe, Robert H. *The Search for Order, 1877–1920*. New York: Hill & Wang, 1966.

*Yellen, Samuel. *American Labor Struggles*. New York: Pathfinder, 1974.

Zinn, Howard. *The Politics of History*. Boston: Beacon Press, 1970.

14. WAR IS THE HEALTH OF THE STATE

Baritz, Loren, ed. *The American Left*. New York: Basic Books, 1971.

*Chafee, Zechariah, Jr. *Free Speech in the United States*. New York: Atheneum, 1969.

Dos Passos, John. *1919*. New York: Signet, 1969.

Du Bois, W. E. B. "The African Roots of War," *Atlantic Monthly*, May 1915.

Fleming, D. F. *The Origins and Legacies of World War I*. Garden City, N.Y.: Doubleday, 1968.

*Fussell, Paul. *The Great War and Modern Memory*. New York: Oxford University Press, 1975.

*Ginger, Ray. *The Bending Cross: A Biography of Eugene Victor Debs*. New Brunswick: Rutgers University Press, 1969.

Goldman, Eric. *Rendezvous with Destiny*. New York: Random House, 1956.

Gruber, Carol S. *Mars and Minerva: World War I and the Uses of Higher Learning in America*. Baton Rouge: Louisiana State University Press, 1975.

Joughin, Louis, and Morgan, Edmund. *The Legacy of Sacco and Vanzetti*. New York: Quadrangle, 1964.

Knightley, Philip. *The First Casualty: The War Correspondent as Hero, Propagandist, and Myth Maker.* New York: Harcourt Brace Jovanovich, 1975.

Kornbluh, Joyce, ed. *Rebel Voices: An I.W.W. Anthology.* Ann Arbor: University of Michigan Press, 1964.

Levin, Murray. *Political Hysteria in America.* New York: Basic Books, 1971.

Mayer, Arno J. *The Politics and Diplomacy of Peace-Making 1918–1919.* New York: Knopf, 1967.

*Peterson, H. C., and Fite, Gilbert C. *Opponents of War, 1917–1918.* Seattle: University of Washington Press, 1968.

Simpson, Colin. *Lusitania.* Boston: Little, Brown, 1973.

Sinclair, Upton. *Boston.* Cambridge, Mass.: Robert Bentley, 1978.

Weinstein, James. *The Corporate Ideal in the United States 1900–1918.* Boston: Beacon Press, 1969.

15. Self-help in Hard Times

Adamic, Louis. *My America, 1928–1938.* New York: Harper & Row, 1938.

*Baxandall, Rosalyn, Gordon, Linda, and Reverby, Susan, eds. *America's Working Women.* New York: Random House, 1976.

Bellush, Bernard. *The Failure of the N.R.A.* New York: W. W. Norton, 1976.

Bernstein, Barton, J., ed. *Towards a New Past: Dissenting Essays in American History.* New York: Pantheon, 1968.

Bernstein, Irving. *The Lean Years: A History of the American Worker, 1920–1933.* Boston: Houghton Mifflin, 1960.

———. *The Turbulent Years: A History of the American Worker, 1933–1941.* Boston: Houghton Mifflin, 1969.

Borden, Morton, ed. *Voices of the American Past: Readings in American History.* Lexington, Mass.: D. C. Heath, 1972.

Boyer, Richard, and Morais, Herbert. *Labor's Untold Story.* United Front, 1955.

*Brecher, Jeremy. *Strike!* Boston, Mass.: South End Press, 1979.

Buhle, Paul. "An Interview with Luigi Nardella," *Radical History Review*, Spring 1978.

*Cloward, Richard A., and Piven, Frances F. *Poor People's Movements.* New York: Pantheon, 1977.

Conkin, Paul. *F.D.R. and the Origins of the Welfare State.* New York: Crowell, 1967.

Cook, Blanche Wiesen. *Eleanor Roosevelt.* Vol. 1. New York: Penguin Books, 1992.

Cook, Blanche Wiesen. *Eleanor Roosevelt.* Vol. 2. New York: Viking Penguin, 1999.

Curti, Merle. *The Growth of American Thought.* New York: Harper & Row, 1943.

*Fine, Sidney. *Sit-Down: The General Motors Strike of 1936–1937.* Ann Arbor: University of Michigan Press, 1969.

Galbraith, John Kenneth. *The Great Crash: 1929.* Boston: Houghton Mifflin, 1972.

General Strike Committee. *The Seattle General Strike.* Charlestown, Mass.: gum press, 1972.

*Hallgren, Mauritz. *Seeds of Revolt.* New York: Knopf, 1934.

*Lerner, Gerda, ed. *Black Women in White America: A Documentary History*. New York: Random House, 1977.

Lewis, Sinclair. *Babbitt*. New York: Harcourt Brace Jovanovich, 1949.

Lynd, Alice and Staughton, eds. *Rank and File: Personal Histories by Working-Class Organizers*. Boston: Beacon Press, 1974.

Lynd, Robert and Helen. *Middletown*. New York: Harcourt Brace Jovanovich, 1959.

Mangione. Jerre. *The Dream and the Deal: The Federal Writers Project, 1935–1943*. Boston: Little, Brown, 1972.

Mills, Frederick C. *Economic Tendencies in the United States: Aspects of Pre-War and Post-War Changes*. New York: National Bureau of Economic Research, 1932.

Ottley, Roi, and Weatherby, William J. "The Negro in New York: An Informal History," *Justice Denied: The Black Man in White America*, ed. William Chace and Peter Collier. New York: Harcourt Brace Jovanovich, 1970.

Painter, Nell, and Hudson, Hosea. "A Negro Communist in the Deep South," *Radical America*. July-August 1977.

Renshaw, Patrick. *The Wobblies*. New York: Anchor, 1968.

*Rosengarten, Theodore. *All God's Dangers: The Life of Nate Shaw*. New York: Knopf, 1974.

Steinbeck, John. *The Grapes of Wrath*. New York: Viking, 1939.

Swados, Harvey, ed. *The American Writer and the Great Depression*. Indianapolis: Bobbs-Merrill, 1966.

*Terkel, Studs. *Hard Times: An Oral History of the Great Depression in America*. New York: Pantheon, 1970.

Wright, Richard. *Black Boy*. New York: Harper & Row, 1937.

Zinn, Howard. *La Guardia in Congress*. Ithaca, N.Y.: Cornell University Press, 1959.

16. A PEOPLE'S WAR?

Alperovitz, Gar. *Atomic Diplomacy*. New York: Vintage, 1967.

Aronson, James. *The Press and the Cold War*. Indianapolis: Bobbs-Merrill, 1970.

Barnet, Richard J. *Intervention and Revolution: The U.S. and the Third World*. New York: New American Library, 1969.

Blackett, P. M. S. *Fear, War and the Bomb: Military and Political Consequences of Atomic Energy*. New York: McGraw-Hill, 1948.

Bottome, Edgar. *The Balance of Terror: A Guide to the Arms Race*. Boston: Beacon Press, 1972.

Butow, Robert. *Japan's Decision to Surrender*. Stanford: Stanford University Press, 1954.

Catton, Bruce. *The War Lords of Washington*. New York: Harcourt Brace, 1948.

Chomsky, Noam. *American Power and the New Mandarins*. New York: Pantheon, 1969.

Cook, Blanche Wiesen. *The Declassified Eisenhower*. New York: Doubleday, 1981.

Davidson, Basil. *Let Freedom Come: Africa in Modern History.* Boston: Little, Brown, 1978.

Feingold, Henry L. *The Politics of Rescue: The Roosevelt Administration and the Holocaust.* New Brunswick, N.J.: Rutgers University Press, 1970.

Freeland, Richard M. *The Truman Doctrine and the Origins of McCarthyism.* New York: Knopf, 1971.

Gardner, Lloyd. *Economic Aspects of New Deal Diplomacy.* Madison: University of Wisconsin Press, 1964.

Griffith, Robert W. *The Politics of Fear: Joseph R. McCarthy and the Senate.* Rochelle Park, N.J.: Hayden, 1971.

Hamby, Alonzo L. *Beyond the New Deal: Harry S. Truman and American Liberalism.* New York: Columbia University Press, 1953.

Irving, David. *The Destruction of Dresden.* New York: Ballantine, 1965.

Kahn, Herman. *On Thermonuclear War.* New York: Free Press, 1969.

*Kolko, Gabriel. *The Politics of War: The World and United States Foreign Policy, 1943–1945.* New York: Random House, 1968.

Lemisch, Jesse. *On Active Service in War and Peace: Politics and Ideology in the American Historical Profession.* Toronto: New Hogtown Press, 1975.

Mailer, Norman. *The Naked and the Dead.* New York: Holt, Rinehart and Winston, 1948.

Miller, Douglas, and Nowak, Marion. *The Fifties: The Way We Really Were.* New York: Doubleday, 1977.

Miller, Marc. "The Irony of Victory: Lowell During World War II." Unpublished doctoral dissertation. Boston University, 1977.

Mills, C. Wright. *The Power Elite.* New York: Oxford University Press, 1970.

Minear, Richard H. *Victor's Justice: The Tokyo War Crimes Trial.* Princeton, N.J.: Princeton University Press, 1973.

Offner, Arnold. *American Appeasement: U.S. Foreign Policy and Germany, 1933–1938.* New York: W. W. Norton, 1976.

Rostow, Eugene V. "Our Worst Wartime Mistake," *Harper's,* September 1945.

Russett, Bruce. *No Clear and Present Danger.* New York: Harper & Row, 1972.

Sampson, Anthony. *The Seven Sisters: The Great Oil Companies and the World They Shaped.* New York: Viking, 1975.

Schneir, Walter and Miriam. *Invitation to an Inquest.* New York: Doubleday, 1965.

*Sherwin, Martin. *A World Destroyed: The Atom Bomb and the Grand Alliance.* New York: Knopf, 1975.

Stone, I. F. *The Hidden History of the Korean War.* New York: Monthly Review Press, 1969.

United States Strategic Bombing Survey. *Japan's Struggle to End the War.* Washington: Government Printing Office, 1946.

Weglyn, Michi. *Years of Infamy: The Untold Story of America's Concentration Camps.* New York: William Morrow, 1976.

Wittner, Lawrence S. *Rebels Against War: The American Peace Movement, 1941–1960.* New York: Columbia University Press, 1969.

*Zinn, Howard. *Postwar America: 1945–1971*. Indianapolis: Bobbs-Merrill, 1973.

17. "OR DOES IT EXPLODE?"

Allen, Robert. *Black Awakening in Capitalist America*. Garden City, N.Y.: Doubleday, 1969.

Bontemps, Arna, ed. *American Negro Poetry*. New York: Hill & Wang, 1974.

Broderick, Francis, and Meier, August. *Black Protest Thought in the Twentieth Century*. Indianapolis: Bobbs-Merrill, 1971.

Cloward, Richard A., and Piven, Frances F. *Poor People's Movements*. New York: Pantheon, 1977.

Conot, Robert. *Rivers of Blood, Years of Darkness*. New York: Morrow, 1968.

Cullen, Countee. *On These I Stand*. New York: Harper & Row, 1947.

Herndon, Angelo. "You Cannot Kill the Working Class," *Black Protest*, ed. Joanne Grant. New York: Fawcett, 1975.

Huggins, Nathan I. *Harlem Renaissance*. New York: Oxford University Press, 1971.

Hughes, Langston. *Selected Poems of Langston Hughes*. New York: Knopf, 1959.

Lerner, Gerda, ed. *Black Women in White America: A Documentary History*. New York: Random House, 1977.

Malcolm X. *Malcolm X Speaks*. New York: Meret, 1965.

Navasky, Victor. *Kennedy Justice*. New York: Atheneum, 1977.

Perkus, Cathy, ed. *Cointelpro: The FBI's Secret War on Political Freedom*. New York: Monad Press, 1976.

Wright, Richard. *Black Boy*. New York: Harper & Row, 1937.

Zinn, Howard. *Postwar America: 1945–1971*. Indianapolis: Bobbs-Merrill, 1973.

———. *SNCC: The New Abolitionists*. Boston: Beacon Press, 1964.

18. THE IMPOSSIBLE VICTORY: VIETNAM

*Branfman, Fred. *Voices from the Plain of Jars*. New York: Harper & Row, 1972.

Green, Philip, and Levinson, Sanford. *Power and Community: Dissenting Essays in Political Science*. New York: Pantheon, 1970.

Hersch, Seymour. *My Lai 4: A Report on the Massacre and Its Aftermath*. New York: Random House, 1970.

Kovic, Ron. *Born on the Fourth of July*. New York: McGraw-Hill, 1976.

Lipsitz, Lewis. "On Political Belief: The Grievances of the Poor," *Power and Community: Dissenting Essays in Political Science*, ed. Philip Green and Sanford Levinson. New York: Pantheon, 1970.

Modigliani, Andrew. "Hawks and Doves, Isolationism and Political Distrust: An Analysis of Public Opinion on Military Policy," *American Political Science Review*, September 1972.

Pentagon Papers. 4 vols. Boston: Beacon Press, 1971.

Pike, Douglas. *Viet Cong*. Cambridge, Mass.: MIT Press, 1966.

Schell, Jonathan. *The Village of Ben Suc*. New York: Knopf, 1967.

Zinn, Howard. *Vietnam: The Logic of Withdrawal*. Boston: Beacon Press, 1967.

19. SURPRISES

Akwesasne Notes. *Voices from Wounded Knee, 1973.* Mohawk Nation, Rooseveltown, N.Y.: Akwesasne Notes, 1974.

Baxandall, Rosalyn, Gordon, Linda, and Reverby, Susan, eds. *America's Working Women.* New York: Random House, 1976.

Benston, Margaret. "The Political Economy of Women's Liberation," *Monthly Review,* Fall 1969.

Boston Women's Health Book Collective. *Our Bodies, Ourselves.* New York: Simon & Schuster, 1976.

Brandon, William. *The Last Americans.* McGraw-Hill, 1974.

*Brown, Dee. *Bury My Heart at Wounded Knee.* New York: Holt, Rinehart and Winston, 1971.

Brownmiller, Susan. *Against Our Will: Men, Women and Rape.* New York: Simon & Schuster, 1975.

Coles, Robert. *Children of Crisis.* Boston: Little, Brown, 1967.

Cottle, Thomas J. *Children in Jail.* Boston: Beacon Press, 1977.

The Council on Interracial Books for Children, ed. *Chronicles of American Indian Protest.* New York: Fawcett, 1971.

Deloria, Vine, Jr. *Custer Died for Your Sins.* New York: Macmillan, 1969.

————. *We Talk, You Listen.* New York: Macmillan, 1970.

Firestone, Shulamith. *The Dialectics of Sex.* New York: Bantam, 1970.

20. THE SEVENTIES: UNDER CONTROL?

Blair, John M. *The Control of Oil.* New York: Pantheon, 1977.

Dommergues, Pierre. "L'Essor Du conservatisme Americain," *Le Monde Diplomatique,* May 1978.

*Evans, Les, and Myers, Allen. *Watergate and the Myth of American Democracy.* New York: Pathfinder Press, 1974.

Frieden, Jess. "The Trilateral Commission," *Monthly Review,* December 1977.

Gardner, Richard. *Alternative America: A Directory of 5000 Alternative Lifestyle Groups and Organizations.* Cambridge: Richard Gardner, 1976.

Glazer, Nathan, and Kristol, Irving. *The American Commonwealth 1976.* New York: Basic Books, 1976.

New York Times. *The Watergate Hearings.* Bantam, 1973.

*U.S., Congress, Senate Committee to Study Governmental Operations with Respect to Intelligence Activities. *Hearings.* 94th Congress. 1976.

21. CARTER-REAGAN-BUSH: THE BIPARTISAN CONSENSUS

Barlett, Donald, and Steele, James. *America: What Went Wrong?* Kansas City: Andrews & McMeel, 1992.

Barlett, Donald, and Steele, James. *America: Who Really Pays the Taxes?* New York: Simon & Schuster, 1994.

Chomsky, Noam. *World Orders Old and New.* New York: Columbia University Press, 1994.

Croteau, David, and Hoynes, William. *By Invitation Only: How the Media Limit the Political Debate.* Monroe, Maine: Common Courage Press, 1994.

Danaher, Kevin, ed. *50 Years Is Enough: The Case Against the World Bank.* Boston: South End Press, 1994.

Derber, Charles. *Money, Murder and the American Dream.* Boston: Faber & Faber, 1992.

Edsall, Thomas and Mary. *Chain Reaction.* New York: W. W. Norton, 1992.

Ehrenreich, Barbara. *The Worst Years of Our Lives.* New York: HarperCollins, 1990.

Greider, William. *Who Will Tell the People?* New York: Simon & Schuster, 1992.

Grover, William F. *The President as Prisoner.* Albany: State University of New York, 1989.

Hellinger, Daniel, and Judd, Dennis. *The Democratic Facade.* Pacific Grove, California: Brooks/Cole Publishing Company, 1991.

Hofstadter, Richard. *The American Political Tradition.* New York: Vintage, 1974.

Kozol, Jonathan. *Savage Inequalities: Children in America's Schools.* New York: Crown Publishers, 1991.

Piven, Frances Fox, and Cloward, Richard. *Regulating the Poor.* New York: Vintage Books, 1993.

Rosenberg, Gerald N. *The Hollow Hope.* Chicago: University of Chicago Press, 1992.

Savage, David. *Turning Right: The Making of the Rehnquist Supreme Court.* New York: John Wiley & Sons, 1992.

Sexton, Patricia Cayo. *The War on Labor and the Left.* Boulder: Westview Press, 1991.

Shalom, Stephen. *Imperial Alibis.* Boston: South End Press, 1993.

22. THE UNREPORTED RESISTANCE

Ewen, Alexander, ed. *Voice of Indigenous Peoples.* Santa Fe, New Mexico: Clear Light Publishers, 1994.

Grover, William, and Peschek, Joseph, ed. *Voices of Dissent.* New York: HarperCollins, 1993.

Loeb, Paul. *Generations at the Crossroads.* New Brunswick: Rutgers University Press, 1994.

Lofland, John. *Polite Protesters: The American Peace Movement of the 1980s.* Syracuse: Syracuse University Press, 1993.

Lynd, Staughton and Alice. *Nonviolence in America: A Documentary History.* Maryknoll, New York: Orbis Books, 1995.

Martinez, Elizabeth, ed. *500 Years of Chicano History.* Albuquerque: Southwest Organizing Project, 1991.

Piven, Frances, and Cloward, Richard. *Why Americans Don't Vote.* New York: Pantheon Books, 1988.

Vanneman, Reeve, and Cannon, Lynn. *The American Perception of Class.* Philadelphia: Temple University Press, 1987.

NOTE: Much of the material in this chapter comes from my own files of social action by organizations around the country, from my collection of news clippings, and from publications outside the mainstream, including: *The Nation. In These Times, The Nuclear Resister, Peacework, The Resist Newsletter, Rethinking Schools, Indigenous Thought.*

23. THE COMING REVOLT OF THE GUARDS

Bryan, C. D. B. *Friendly Fire.* New York: Putnam, 1976.

Levin, Murray B. *The Alienated Voter.* New York: Irvington, 1971.

Warren, Donald I. *The Radical Center: Middle America and the Politics of Alienation.* Notre Dame, Ind.: University of Notre Dame Press, 1976.

Weizenbaum, Joseph. *Computer Power and Human Reason.* San Francisco: Freeman, 1976.

24. THE CLINTON PRESIDENCY

Bagdikian, Ben. *The Media Monopoly.* Boston: Beacon Press, 1992.

Chomsky, Noam. *World Orders, Old and New.* New York: Columbia University Press, 1994.

Dowd, Doug. *Blues for America.* New York: Monthly Review Press, 1997.

Garrow, David. *Bearing the Cross.* New York: Morrow, 1986.

Greider, William. *One World or Not.* New York: Simon & Schuster, 1997.

Kuttner, Robert. *Everything for Sale.* New York: Knopf, 1997.

Smith, Sam. *Shadows of Hope: A Freethinker's Guide to Politics in the Time of Clinton.* Bloomington: Indiana University Press, 1994.

Solomon, Norman. *False Hope: The Politics of Illusion in the Clinton Era.* Monroe, Maine: Common Courage Press, 1994.

The State of America's Children. Washington, D.C.: Children's Defense Fund, 1994.

Tirman, John. *Spoils of War: The Human Cost of the Arms Trade.* New York: Free Press, 1997.

25. THE 2000 ELECTION AND THE "WAR ON TERRORISM"

Ahmad, Eqbal. *Terrorism, Theirs and Ours.* (Interviews with David Barsamian). New York: Seven Stories Press, 2001.

Brecher, Jeremy, Costello, Tim, and Smith, Brendan. *Globalization from Below.* Boston: South End Press, 2002.

Chomsky, Noam. *9-11.* New York: Seven Stories Press, 2002.

Ehrenreich, Barbara. *Nickeled and Dimed.* New York: Henry Holt, 2001.

Kaplan, Daniel. *The Accidental President.* New York: HarperCollins, 2000.

Lapham, Lewis. *Theater of War.* New York: The New Press, 2002.

Nader, Ralph. *Crashing the Party.* New York: St. Martin's Press, 2001.

Zinn, Howard. *Terrorism and War.* (Interviews with Anthony Arnove). New York: Seven Stories Press, 2002.

INDEX